*The Selected Correspondence of
Karl A. Menninger, 1919-1945*

The Selected

Correspondence of

Karl A. Menninger, 1919-1945

EDITED AND WITH AN INTRODUCTION BY

HOWARD J. FAULKNER AND VIRGINIA D. PRUITT

Yale University Press
New Haven and London

Designed by Nancy Ovedovitz and set in Palatino type by Vail-Ballou Press. Printed in the United States of America by Vail-Ballou Press, Binghamton, New York.

Library of Congress Cataloging-in-Publication Data

Menninger, Karl A. (Karl Augustus), 1893–
   [Correspondence.   Selections.   1988]
   The selected correspondence of Karl A. Menninger, 1919–1945 / edited and with an introduction by Howard Faulkner and Virginia Pruitt.
   p.   cm.
   ISBN 0-300-03978-6 (alk. paper)
   1. Menninger, Karl A. (Karl Augustus), 1893–   —Correspondence.
2. Psychiatrists—United States—Correspondence. I. Faulkner,
Howard, 1945– . II. Pruitt, Virginia, 1943– . III. Title.
   [DNLM: 1. Psychiatry—correspondence. WZ 100 M5475c]
RC438.6.M46A4 1988
616.89′0092′4—dc19
DNLM/DLC   88–5502
for Library of Congress   CIP

The paper in this book meets the guidelines for permanence and durability of the Committee on Production Guidelines for Book Longevity of the Council on Library Resources.

10   9   8   7   6   5   4   3   2   1

for the memory
of Ruth and Howard Faulkner,
of Lillian Rasmussen Pruitt,
and for Raymond Pruitt, M.D.,
with love and appreciation
for all they have given us

Contents

Acknowledgments

$\mathcal{W}$e would like to thank the following individuals and institutions for granting us permission to publish letters written to Karl Menninger: Francesca Alexander-Levine for Franz Alexander; Mrs. Edgar V. Allen for Edgar V. Allen; Mary Bartemeier Hurley for Leo Bartemeier; Ira Blitzsten for Lionel Blitzsten; Matilda B. Stewart for Ruth Mack Brunswick; Norman Cousins; Joan G. Dollard for John Dollard; K. R. Eissler; Malcolm W. Finlayson for Alan D. Finlayson; Bertha C. Flom for Charles Flom; Walter Freeman III, for Walter Freeman; Sigmund Freud Copyrights Ltd. for Sigmund Freud; Martha H. Rusnak and Jane H. Rumsey for Ives Hendrick; Carel Goldschmidt for Smith Ely Jelliffe and Belinda Jelliffe; Mervyn Jones for Ernest Jones; Lawson G. Lowrey, Jr., for Lawson G. Lowrey; Joseph Mankiewicz; Enoch Pratt Free Library in accordance with the terms of the will of H. L. Mencken; Catherine W. Menninger for William C. Menninger; the Alan Mason Chesney Medical Archives of the Johns Hopkins University School of Medicine for Adolf Meyer; Adam Moore for Merrill Moore; Paul Graves Myerson for Abraham Myerson; Peter T. Rado for Sandor Rado; Dorothy Colodny for May Romm; Daniel Mayer Selznick for David Selznick; Michael Hunter and Edward C. Simmel for Ernst Simmel; the Countway Medical Library for E. E. Southard; Robert Stragnell for Gregory Stragnell; the National Archives, RG 418, Records of St. Elizabeths Hospital for William A. White; and Margaret S. Zilboorg for Gregory Zilboorg.

Photographs are courtesy of the Menninger Foundation Archives.

We owe thanks to many people for their support and for their willingness to aid us in our research and editing. Particularly helpful have been Rebecca Breden, Alice Brand, Susan Hulme, Nancy Bower, Lynda Jones, and Lois Bogia of the Menninger Foundation Library; Wilma Rife, Margo Murphy, Steve Thomas, and David Winchester of the Mabee Library at Washburn University; Kay Galbraith of the Topeka Public Library; Ellen Gilbert, archivist of the New York Psychoanalytic Institute; Glenn Miller, archivist of the Chicago Psychoanalytic Institute; and Bea Horne, Mark West, and Kelly Elizabeth Burket, the unfailingly patient and resourceful Menninger archivists. Carol Vogel and William Langdon of Washburn University translated letters from German into English. Special appreciation is owed to our chairman at Washburn University, Robert Stein, and to the Dean Emeritus of the College of Arts and Sciences, Paul Sanford Salter, for granting us released time for the completion of this project and for their enthusiastic support. The research committees at Washburn University have aided us with financial support. Susan Barnes diligently typed the manuscript. Paul Pruyser, late Henry March Pfeiffer Professor at the Menninger Foundation, and Larry Friedman, Professor of History at Bowling Green University, have given thoughtful advice and editing assistance. Special appreciation is also due to Laura Miller Fisher, Dr. Karl's executive secretary, who assisted and sustained us, and to Virginia Eicholz, former Director of the Division of Scientific Publications and former Managing Editor of the *Bulletin of the Menninger Clinic*. Further thanks go to Dorothy Rabe, secretary to Dr. Karl; to Ann Minihan, secretary to Dr. Robert Menninger; to Pete North, editor of the *Menninger Perspective*; to Judy Craig, Assistant Director of Communications at the Menninger Foundation; and to Peter Herdic for his inspired idea. Our editor at Yale, Gladys Topkis, has been unflagging in her patience and invaluable in her advice, and Carl Rosen, manuscript editor, performed an extraordinary task with grace and good humor.

Of course our final thanks must go to Dr. Karl himself both for writing such superb letters and for his dedicated assistance during our work.

Editing, annotating, and writing were all truly mutual efforts; we shared equally in the pains and pleasures of preparing this book, and the ordering of the names reflects nothing more than the exigencies of printing.

Chronology of Karl Menninger's life

1931   Starts a monthly column in *Ladies Home Journal* that continues
       until 1932
1932   Completes analysis with Alexander in Boston
1934   Visits Sigmund Freud in Vienna
1937   Certified by the American Board of Psychiatry and Neurology in
       both specialties
1938   Publishes *Man Against Himself*
1939   Visits New York for a year and a half of psychoanalysis with
       Ruth Mack Brunswick
       Organizes and becomes first president of the Topeka Psychoan-
       alytic Society
1941   Becomes president of the newly incorporated, nonprofit Men-
       ninger Foundation
       Divorces Grace Gaines Menninger
       Marries Jeanetta Lyle
1942   Publishes (with Jeanetta Menninger) *Love Against Hate*
       Becomes president of the newly established Topeka Institute for
       Psychoanalysis
1945   Publishes revised edition of *The Human Mind*
       As scientific consultant, tours the European Theater of Opera-
       tions, assessing the need for psychiatric care of military per-
       sonnel
1946   Establishes the Menninger School of Psychiatry
       Becomes manager of Winter Veterans Administration Hospital
1948   Resigns as manager of Winter Veterans Administration Hospital
       Appointed to the Kansas Committee for State Mental Hospitals
       to investigate conditions in the state hospital system
       Adopts a daughter, Rosemary
1950   Publishes (with George Devereaux) *A Guide to Psychiatric Books*
1952   Publishes (with Martin Mayman) *Manual for Psychiatric Case Study*
       Appointed chief of staff, the Menninger Foundation
1954   Elected chairman of the Board of Trustees, the Menninger Foun-
       dation
1958   Publishes (with Philip Holzman) *Theory of Psychoanalytic Tech-
       nique*
1959   Publishes *A Psychiatrist's World*, edited by Bernard Hall
1963   Publishes (with Martin Mayman and Paul Pruyser) *The Vital Bal-
       ance*
       Receives the Isaac Ray Award from the American Psychiatric As-
       sociation for contributions in legal psychiatry
1965   Receives the Distinguished Service Award from the American
       Psychiatric Association
       Becomes senior consultant at the Stone-Brandel Center, Chicago

1966   Founds The Villages, Inc., a nonprofit organization providing homes for homeless children

1968   Publishes *The Crime of Punishment*, based on the Isaac Ray Award lectures

1973   Publishes *Sparks* (edited by Lucy Freeman), a collection of excerpts from his writings

Publishes *Whatever Became of Sin?*

1976   Undergoes the removal of a benign brain tumor at the Mayo Clinic

1978   Receives the first American Psychiatric Association Founders Award

Serves as co-project director with the U.S. Departments of Housing and Urban Development and Health, Education, and Welfare to develop specialized programs and housing for five Southwest Indian tribes

1981   Receives the Medal of Freedom from President Jimmy Carter

Introduction

Do the British write as many letters as we do?" Karl Menninger inquired in a 1939 letter to his friend Harley Williams, a British psychiatrist. "If so I should think it would take half the population of London to examine the letters of the other half. . . . I would estimate that I write about eighty letters a week." The multitude of letters in the Menninger Archives, where virtually all of Menninger's correspondence from 1919 to the present has been preserved, suggests that his 1939 calculation was accurate.

Beyond its social and professional functions, the epistolary medium often served as an important clarifier in the development of Menninger's thought. Although the three books he published between 1930 and 1945[1] provide a more systematic presentation of his psychological tenets than his letters offer, Menninger works through certain ideas in the letters, both preliminary formulations and, later, revisions, modifications, and defenses in response to suggestions or attacks by correspondents.

Menninger's books were successful with both a general and a professional audience. What made his books so popular was in part his ability to translate abstract principle into paradigmatic case, effecting smooth transitions between intellectual levels. The combination of the concrete and the specific gave immediate vitality to Menninger's works, whether treatises or letters. Although this approach made him vulnerable to the charge of being a mere popularizer, Erik Erikson said, "Menninger translates Freud into American literature. He is not a popularizer, but an enlightener."[2]

When he received the Medal of Freedom from President Jimmy Carter in 1981—the only psychiatrist to be so honored—Karl Menninger was acknowledged as probably the single psychiatrist ever to attain full acceptance

1 *The Human Mind* (New York: Knopf, 1930), *Man Against Himself* (New York: Harcourt, Brace, 1938), and *Love Against Hate,* with Jeanetta Lyle Menninger (New York: Harcourt, Brace, 1942).

2 Karl Menninger, "The Middle of the Journey: Dragons and Grails," filmed speech, The National Portrait Gallery Series of the Smithsonian Institution, Washington, D.C., April 1978.

by professional colleagues as well as recognition by the general public. Writer of both specialized psychiatric texts and more popular books on psychiatry, founder of the most famous psychiatric hospital in the United States, and active for nearly seventy years in American psychiatry, Menninger occupies a central place in the evolution of American psychology and psychiatry.

Menninger began preserving his correspondence in 1919, an especially eventful year for the young doctor: he commenced medical practice in Topeka, planned and taught a course in mental hygiene at Washburn College, and became a father for the first time. During the next two and a half decades, Karl Menninger's name became firmly identified with mental health and psychiatry in America. His books defined and discussed mental illness and its treatment with a clarity and precision that appealed to an eclectic audience and exhibited a sophistication and rigor that made them standards in the medical community. Two columns in national magazines—*Household* and *Ladies Home Journal*—disseminated his opinions even more widely, while his scholarly articles appeared regularly in professional journals. He was equally tireless in his organizational work, not only joining and rising to prominence in major psychiatric and medical groups (he was, for example, chairman of the American Psychiatric Association's Committee on Legal Aspects of Psychiatry in 1926 and served twice as president of the American Psychoanalytic Association) but also founding important organizations, such as the American Orthopsychiatric Association.

Perhaps his most enduring achievement, however, was the establishment of the Menninger Clinic, the Menninger Sanitarium, and the Southard School for children. The clinic was formed in 1919 on Menninger's return to Topeka to join his father's medical practice. Six years later, eight investors, including Menninger and his father, received a charter from the Kansas Charter Board for the Menninger Sanitarium Corporation and Psychopathic Hospital. They purchased twenty acres of land and opened the sanitarium on May 6, 1925. In the first year, forty-six patients stayed at the sanitarium, paying from forty-five dollars (for a bed in a four-occupant room) to one hundred dollars a week. The number reached 158 in 1930, when the average daily count (twenty-eight patients) was twice what it had been in the first year of operation. (The records for 1926 also list an inventory of two cows, 186 large chickens, 125 small chickens, fifteen setting hens, and six ducks.) In 1926, the Menningers extended their enterprise by establishing a school for disturbed children. Originally called the Pearson School after its first director, Stella Pearson, in 1927 it was renamed the Southard School, after Menninger's mentor at Harvard. Expansion marked the course for the following years of development: two new buildings were constructed in the late 1920s, more than doubling the number of patients the sanitarium could handle. In 1926, William C. Menninger, the youngest of the three Menninger brothers, joined Karl and their father at the clinic.[3] In 1931, the first psychiatric resident, Ralph Fellows, arrived, and the sanitarium was approved for psychiatric nurses' training.

It was during these years that Menninger left Topeka to be psychoanalyzed by Franz Alexander in Chicago. When Alexander went to Boston, Menninger followed and spent four months there. In both cities Menninger treated patients of his own. Meanwhile, the Menninger Clinic, Sanitarium, and the Southard School in Topeka continued to grow. By middecade, Dwight Macdonald, who was a contributing editor at *Fortune* magazine, brought the sanitarium to national attention;[4] despite the depression, the patient population remained at 158, and there was talk of converting the sanitarium into a nonprofit organization.

In 1941, the various enterprises were incorporated as the Menninger Foundation, with Karl Menninger as the first president. Up to that time, a total of 1,950 patients had been admitted to the sanitarium; 20 percent of the foundation's resources were allocated to research and education. The following year, the Topeka Institute for Psychoanalysis was established and recognized by the American Psychoanalytic Association, and by 1945, plans were in place for the Menninger Foundation School of Psychiatry.

When Menninger began his career as a neuropsychiatrist in 1919, American psychiatry had already been established: the National Committee for Mental Health, which Clifford Beers had founded in 1909, had experienced ten years of growth. It had helped change Americans' perception of the appropriate treatment of mental illness from custodial care to active intervention by psychiatrists and social workers. In addition, Freud's visit to Clark University in 1909 and his subsequent work had challenged American intellectuals with new ideas that tantalized them even when they contravened indigenous suppositions. His assumption of fixed psychosexual stages and his emphasis on the potency of the hypothesized death instinct went against the American pragmatic and progressive grain. Although Menninger would not fully integrate psychoanalytic concepts into his thinking and clinical practice until the end of the decade, he was attracted to them early in the 1920s.

Several of Menninger's eminent American colleagues had already established their reputations, and two of them in particular conspicuously fostered Menninger's nascent philosophy of medical care. Although Mennin-

3 To avoid confusion, the Menninger doctors came to be referred to as Dr. C. F., Dr. Karl, and Dr. Will. Our notes in this volume refer to Karl Menninger as KAM, C. F. Menninger as CFM, and William C. Menninger as WCM. Another son, Edwin, who was born in 1896, has spent much of his adult life in Stuart, Florida, where he published a newspaper and wrote numerous books on horticulture.

4 Dwight Macdonald, "Sanitariums," *Fortune* 11, 4 (April 1935): 167–204.

ger criticized the dominating influence of Adolf Meyer in Baltimore, Meyer's view of mental illness as the organism's faulty adaptation to external and internal stress as well as his emphasis on the organism as a whole and the purposeful, if unhealthy, role of substitutive activity in an ill person were incorporated into Menninger's metapsychological beliefs.[5] Meyer's innovative *life chart*, which treated diagnosis not simply as the establishment of a checklist of malfunctions but rather as a dynamic constellation of life systems, helped shape Menninger's belief that diagnosis was not a static and immutable formulation but a provisional identification of variable, unhealthy emotional and behavioral patterns.

However, Elmer Ernest Southard, professor of neuropathology at Harvard and superintendent of the newly established Boston Psychopathic Hospital (1912), was Menninger's major source of inspiration. In his early letters and papers, Menninger often discussed and defended Southard's nosology, an arrangement of eleven classes of mental illness by syndrome in a descending order of definiteness.[6] As Menninger pointed out, two systems of nomenclature had evolved concurrently in American psychiatry. One system, whose contemporary proponent was Emil Kraepelin, stressed the enumeration of many (ultimately seventeen) specific, discrete entities; such naming became a prerequisite to treatment. The other system stressed a nonspecific, unitary concept of mental illness. Adolf Meyer, who introduced Kraepelin's system in America, later abandoned it in favor of its process-oriented, holistic counterpart, which Southard advocated. During World War II, Menninger and his brother Will would propose a more drastic simplification, reducing diseases to five levels of dysfunction encompassed within a unitary concept of mental disease. Menninger later commented, "It is not that we decry classification as such; we recognize it as a useful tool. But it is dangerous when it leads to reification of terms."[7]

Southard was more than an ideological mentor; he was a personal model. The diversity of Menninger's crusades and social commitments throughout his career, and his insistence on the relation of individual mental health to the social environment, exemplified Southard's conviction that medicine should not exist as an autonomous, isolated discipline but should be responsive to the total human being. In the years following World War I, Menninger became acutely aware of the relationship between physical and mental illness. To Southard, with whom Menninger had worked in the immediate aftermath of the war, shell shock caused the most notable mental disabilities. The illness that most influenced Menninger's concept of neuropsychia-

5 Paul W. Pruyser, "Karl Menninger's Psychiatric Principles and Evolving Theory," *Directions in Psychiatry*, 4:4.

6 Karl Menninger, *A Psychiatrist's World: The Selected Papers of Karl Menninger*, ed. Bernard B. Hall (New York: Viking, 1959), 523.

7 Menninger, *Psychiatrist's World*, 525.

try, however, was the influenza epidemic that raged throughout the country after the war. Later, Menninger would also stress the extent to which the individual's strivings and disappointments contributed to the development of physical ailments.

This book begins with a young doctor, flushed with ideas, committed to neurology, and absorbed in the discourse of the time, returning to his hometown to enter practice with his father. Between 1919 and 1945, Karl Menninger, the clinic and sanitarium in Topeka, and the profession of American psychiatry developed from youth to maturity; the two and a half decades of letters in this book chart that growth.

From his earliest attempt to define the mission of the Menninger Clinic and the formation and nurturing of the Southard School, through a trip to Europe at the end of World War II to study combat exhaustion in preparation for the return of troubled American veterans, Menninger's commitment to family members and surrogate family members, to his profession, his community, and the state of Kansas pervades his letters. As one of "the good old pioneers" (letter of February 7, 1930), he extolled the beauties and advantages of what must have seemed to his largely urban and Eastern audience an extraordinarily dull place for an endeavor like his. He tried unstintingly to persuade others to come (Ernst Simmel was his most interesting failure). And often he succeeded, so that Topeka became the unlikely location of America's fifth psychoanalytic institute and society (after New York, Boston, Washington-Baltimore, and Chicago) and eventually became a colonizer of its own, sending doctors to Pacific Coast cities where additional institutes germinated under the Menninger aegis. Indeed, Menninger and his colleague Robert P. Knight were at one time responsible for all psychoanalytic teaching west of Topeka. In the meantime, physicians trained at the Menninger School of Psychiatry also dispersed across the country, and the Menninger Clinic and Sanitarium became one of the best-known private mental hospitals in the country.

In these efforts, Menninger revealed again and again his ability to take care of details. He was not an ivory tower intellectual; he was a man who could run an institution, make decisions, hire and fire, plan for the future, and, most important, implement his plans. Early in these letters he championed the role of the private institution, a particularly significant cause because state institutions were so often second-rate. But he also worked to improve those state institutions; the Menninger Clinic and Foundation have a history of cooperation with state hospitals in Kansas. And in 1945, the last year represented in this book, Menninger became manager of the Winter Veterans Administration Hospital—a unique amalgamation of federal, state, private, and community funds, buildings, training facilities, and faculties— as well as director of the Menninger School of Psychiatry.

The correspondence not only chronicles these events but displays Menninger's prodigious intellectual energy and delineates the shift in his interest from the broadly conceived and tentatively defined neuropsychiatry that captivated his youthful imagination to the hotly defended Freudianism that characterized his maturity. Menninger's whole-hearted acceptance of Freudian thought began, like most infatuations, with youthful ardor ("head over heels," as he put it in a letter of August 29, 1920, to Gregory Stragnell). His background education before what Menninger himself has called the "conversion"[8] commenced during a stay with Smith Ely Jelliffe, to whom he had been introduced at a psychiatric meeting in New York. Menninger described him as "one of the most vigorous and most gifted of the protagonists of psychoanalysis at that time."[9] While with Jelliffe, Menninger suggested that he would like to "experiment" with an analysis if Jelliffe would take him. Even though there was no commitment to the months or years of daily sessions that psychoanalysis typically entailed, Jelliffe agreed to the unorthodox trial. According to Menninger, Jelliffe told him simply to free-associate while Jelliffe took notes in his own shorthand. The sessions were held daily for only a few weeks, and Jelliffe's fee was a ticket to a psychoanalytic convention. A second analysis, which Menninger now describes as more technically correct but also of short duration, was conducted in New York by Albert Polon. It was not, however, until 1930–31 that Menninger completed his early education in analysis when he underwent an eighteen-month analysis, this time with Franz Alexander of the Chicago Institute for Psychoanalysis, more commonly known as the Chicago Psychoanalytic Institute.

After these experiences, Menninger was a member of the brotherhood, a theoretician initiated into the cult of the believers. As a believer, he was willing to explain and defend the faith against the heresies around him. He reacted especially strongly to the apostasy of his own analyst, Alexander, who advocated "brief therapy,"[10] and to that of his first wife's analyst, Karen Horney, who argued for "self-analysis." Although Menninger's single meeting with Freud in 1934 was unsatisfactory (Freud kept Menninger waiting while talking privately to Alexander and then gave Menninger only a short interview), Menninger's conversion was unequivocal. He wrote to Alexander on March 15, 1940, "Freud did not treat me very nicely, as you know, but nonetheless, I think his ideas, his grasp, his formulations are so infinitely ahead of anything else that has been proposed, that I have nailed my banner on his mast, and I'll defend it against the assault for the rest of my life." And three years later he wrote, to Iago Galdston, "God knows he [Freud] has contributed more to psychiatry than anybody who lived in the past 5,000 years, unless it be Jesus" (letter of March 11, 1943).

8 Menninger, *Psychiatrist's World*, 850.

9 Menninger, *Psychiatrist's World*, 826.

10 "I think now that Alexander was on the right path and might have saved [us from] the decline of psychoanalysis" (KAM, personal communication to the editors, 1985.

What is true of many conversion experiences was also true of Menninger's: his enthusiasm was eventually tempered as he came to believe that divergence from orthodoxy was not necessarily disloyalty. He himself moved away from classical Freudian practice, though he remained faithful to the dual-instinct theory. These letters consistently reflect the tension between Menninger's unswerving allegiance to the two mutually antagonistic drives: his perception of man's penchant for self-destruction, the persistent operation of Freud's death instinct, and his optimistic belief in the potential for improvement, both in individuals and in social structures. The latter conviction was far more common in American psychiatry, which shared during this period the hopeful spirit of progressive-era reformers. In a letter to Dwight Macdonald, Menninger wrote, "I have always liked the idea of modern psychiatry that I set forth in the last two paragraphs of *The Human Mind*—the idea that mental sickness is not hopeless, that most of its victims recover" (February 25, 1935). A prominent theme in the letters of the 1920s, a stubborn belief in the self-regulatory mechanisms of the human being, gives evidence of the melioristic aspect of Menninger's stance.[11]

The crucial regulatory process, Menninger argued, is within the ego; working with both the creative and the destructive drives, it engages in constant adjustment to promote a healthful balance. According to this view, mental illness was an inefficient and maladaptive response, an accommodation of Eros and Thanatos that was not cost-effective for the organism. Although the terms in which the letters discussed balance, efficiency, and adjustment might vary from "mental hygiene" in the 1920s to Freudian parlance in the 1930s and 1940s, the holistic conception of the human being dominated, and the economic metaphor for the drives governing human life reflected Menninger's fascination with the total economy of human existence.

As for his own obligation to promote what he would ultimately call this "vital balance," Menninger often remarked on the special responsibilities to improve the general condition of things that devolved upon those to whom much had been given. This sense of vocation derived not only from the cultural environment of the time but also from the values of the Menninger home. Menninger's parents came from different religious traditions: Flo from an evangelical Protestant background, C. F. from a mixed Lutheran and Catholic heritage. After their marriage, they decided that Presbyterianism best accorded with their diverse beliefs. Flo Menninger developed and taught Bible classes that eventually grew into a four-year program of courses that she taught and supervised for the remainder of her life. A life-long Presby-

---

11 KAM informs us that his first encounter with meliorism was through Walter B. Cannon, professor of physiology at Harvard Medical School, who published a classic study, *Bodily Changes in Pain, Hunger, Fear, and Rage* (New York: Appleton, 1915).

terian and a dedicated member of a student Christian movement during his college years, Menninger had the strong conviction that doing one's duty and assuming responsibility could make a difference not only for oneself but also for others. Yet strict Presbyterians are also children of Calvin, and thus Menninger's religious training reinforced his ambivalent sense of man's nature and of the complexity and magnitude of psychiatry's task.

Reflecting his view of a powerful death instinct, foremost among Menninger's research interests during the first half of the 1930s was the manifestation of Thanatos in suicidal behavior. Although one effect of the Americanization of Freud was often to reduce the role of the death instinct, Menninger refused to deny man's potent aggressive urges. Difficulties of adjustment on the part of the organism, he was convinced, were likely to be disguised and displaced expressions of the organism's intoxication with destruction, including self-destruction. Menninger's *Man Against Himself,* a study of the manifold mechanisms by which Thanatos overpowers the neutralizing force of Eros, embodied both Calvin's depiction of a basic flaw in human nature and Freud's postulation of an aggressive instinct: the will to kill, combined with its internal counterparts, the wish to be killed and the wish to die.

As virulent as he believed the force of Thanatos to be, Menninger stressed throughout his work an equally strong instinctual force: the constructive and reconstructive force of Eros, of love and creativity. Not only did American analysts ignore or minimize Freud's notion of the death instinct, they often desexualized the erotic component of the theory. Menninger did not. In a letter of June 15, 1939 to Chicago psychiatrist Harry Levey, Menninger suggested an idea that would appear three years later in *Love Against Hate,* which focused on Eros; he claimed to be advancing a "major revision of a common psychoanalytic thought." Menninger denied that sublimation could ever be imposed on the erotic instinct; rather, sublimation is the channeling of aggression into higher, more healthful outlets. Since the erotic, he argued, is an innately constructive instinct, sublimation of erotic energy is an impossible contradiction.

The letters supplement Menninger's books and speeches in documenting his evolving ideas and their relation to the intellectual milieu of the American psychoanalytic community. And they provide a privileged personal look at Menninger, his family, and his colleagues and friends in a way that more public documents seldom can. Significantly, Menninger's relationship with his father was remarkably untroubled throughout his father's long life. However, the correspondence reveals a more complicated, if affectionate, relationship with his brother Will, the youngest of the three Menninger sons. In many of the early letters, Menninger, in the role of a wiser, more mature colleague, sought to direct his brother's choices, but during their lifelong association at the clinic a marked division of labor and interests existed. In the 1920s, Dr. Karl organized the Central Neuro-Psychiatric Association and the American Orthopsychiatric Association; in the 1940s, Dr. Will helped found the Group for the Advancement of Psychiatry. Although each brother joined the groups that the other had started, neither participated extensively in them. Dr. Karl twice served as president of the American Psychoanalytic Association but never attained the presidency of the American Psychiatric Association, a position he coveted. Dr. Will headed both groups. Within the clinic, Dr. Karl was the more temperamental individual, the original thinker and innovator; Dr. Will was the outgoing brother who managed the Menninger hospital, raised money for the foundation's educational work and research, and addressed and persuaded state legislatures.

Karl Menninger's first fatherly mentors outside the family were E. E. Southard in Boston, Smith Ely Jelliffe in New York, and William Alanson White in Washington. Menninger saluted both Southard and Jelliffe in his letters as "Chief." However, the personal ideals and magnetism of the two men may have been more important elements of their appeal to Menninger than any specific intellectual credo. Southard is best remembered for his work with Mary Jarrett, a social worker, to broaden the scope of psychiatry beyond the asylum and for his leadership in Massachusetts psychiatry. His untimely death in 1920 at the age of forty-three cut short his relationship with Menninger, but Menninger's relationship with Jelliffe was one of the most enduring of his life. From the ebullience of his initial letters to the "Chief" to his sadness at Jelliffe's death in the last year covered by this book, Menninger's affection and admiration remained constant. Though much of Jelliffe's "paleopsychiatry," an idiosyncratic psychological rendering of the ontological recapitulation of phylogeny, was ignored by his colleagues— it is not even mentioned in these letters—Jelliffe's assimilation of Freudian concepts and his understanding of the death instinct were compatible with Menninger's own predilections. Although the friendship with White was not so intimate as with Southard and Jelliffe, it was to White that Menninger was most likely to turn for professional advice and from him that Menninger was most likely to accept it.

Among Menninger's correspondents, three seem most fraternal, though the terms "brother" and "sister" are frequent forms of greeting among the analysts; indeed, a quasi-religious sense of their profession pervades much of the discourse.[12] Menninger has said that as Jelliffe was to William Alanson White, so he himself was to Lawson Lowrey; by this he seemed to mean

12 John C. Burnham, professor of history and lecturer in psychiatry at Ohio State University, writes that members of analytic groups "acted as apostles who could persuade others to join the ranks, for as in all other major innovations in science, true belief and conversion almost invariably required personal explication before a potential believer made commitment to a new view" ("The Influence of Psychoanalysis upon American Culture," in *American Psychoanalysis: Origins and Development, The Adolf Meyer Seminars*, eds. Jacques M. Quen and Eric T. Carlson [New York: Brunner/Mazel, 1978], 53).

that he and Lowrey shared intellectual kinship to an unusual degree as well as participating in a large number of collaborative projects. It was Lowrey, for instance, who persuaded Menninger to leave Kansas City for Boston Psychopathic Hospital, where he met Southard and learned about psychiatry. Especially in the early letters, Menninger and Lowrey traded research reports, advice, and gossip. Even longer lasting was his friendship with Detroit psychoanalyst Leo Bartemeier; the letters they exchanged were distinguished by a tone of camaraderie, trust, and amicability. Later, the analyst Gregory Zilboorg and Menninger developed a friendship based on their common interest in suicide research and their shared literary sensibilities. Abraham Myerson, a psychiatrist who did not embrace psychoanalysis, and Morris Fishbein, the long-time editor of the *Journal of the American Medical Association*, were also enduring if often disputatious friends, whose letters appear in this book.

The most ambivalent and in many ways the most substantial friendship reflected in the correspondence is that between Menninger and Franz Alexander. Alexander was at first a mentor and father figure: Menninger's psychoanalyst, founder and head of the Chicago Psychoanalytic Institute (where Menninger often taught and attended meetings), and sponsor of the Topeka Psychoanalytic Institute. But perhaps because Alexander was only three years older than Menninger and hence not sufficiently patriarchal, perhaps because he and Menninger were too much alike in their personalities, and certainly because Alexander had been Menninger's analyst, the relationship became strained. Menninger found Alexander disloyal to some of Freud's concepts. He also objected to what he regarded as Alexander's dogmatism and his patronizing attitude. For example, he accused Alexander of dismissing Menninger's views on various issues as "narcissistic claims," of favoring Zilboorg's suicide theories over Menninger's own, and of failing to refer patients to the Menninger Clinic. The tension between the two men produced in their letters a series of stimulating debates, uneasy détentes, and wary reconciliations that aired many of the controversial issues within the American psychoanalytic community of the time and that mirrored the often stormy early history of the psychoanalytic movement. The exalted conception of analysis caused differences to be perceived as heresies and defections as schisms, especially during the exciting but difficult interim between the wars. Writing to Smith Ely Jelliffe near the end of this period, on April 9, 1942, Menninger wondered whether Freud's death had not released even more of the hostility and narcissism that had been steadily simmering in the movement.

The letters also present Menninger in both private and public roles as crusader and evangelist. Early in Menninger's professional life Southard had depicted the world as divided between Saint Georges and Sir Galahads. Saint Georges surveyed the world, saw the kingdom of evil, and set about to slay the dragons, whereas Galahads had visions of the Grail, an ideal of goodness they sought to attain. Though Menninger had his grails—the Menninger Clinic, the Sanitarium, and the Southard School were the most notable of them—it was primarily with St. George that he identified. When, in April 1978, nearing his eighty-fifth birthday, he gave a lecture at the Smithsonian Institution, it was to Southard's metaphor that he returned in an attempt to draw his self-portrait, remarking that the first dragons he had observed were physical: influenza, shell shock, tuberculosis, syphilis. But as he came to realize the psychological causes of physical distress he began to promote mental hygiene, what he called "healthy-mindedness." Later, he would defend psychoanalysis against skeptics in and out of the profession. And in the 1920s he was already arguing for revision of the criminal justice system, for reforms in parole and sentencing, for what he deemed a more "scientific understanding of crime" and its correction. In pursuit of this objective, he attacked abuses within state institutions, especially hospitals and prisons. In a July 10, 1939 letter to the journalist Fred Kelly, Menninger wrote that prisons increase crime rather than diminish it, for they "remove the inner restraints of the individual and give him objective justification for renewing his onslaught on society." And in the late 1930s, when the European analysts who had begun to arrive in America were often badly treated by American colleagues and licensing boards, Menninger defended their rights.

The selected correspondence of Karl Menninger is important for what it reveals about the history of American psychiatric thought and movements and about early psychoanalytic groups. Menninger's views and those expressed by his contemporaries in these personal exchanges constitute a compendium of the ideas circulating among an important segment of the American intellectual community at the time; the letters also shed light on the personalities of the correspondents. Because Menninger, even in his early writings, always regarded the individual in interaction with the larger community, the subject matter of this history encompasses sociology, philosophy, law, education, and religion.

The letters display a variety of rhetorical stances and tactics. Menninger was frequently at odds with his colleagues, and the letters disclose his strategies to disarm their attacks, rhetorical strategies that often parallel psychoanalytic methods: he attempted to uncover hidden motives and challenged his correspondents to franker admissions of their purposes. His declaration of common ends typically mitigated the harshness of his criticism, and his probing for underlying motives made for intriguing character analysis.

The playful and whimsical side of Menninger's personality is more fully revealed in these letters than in any of his previously published writings. The relaxed tone and uninhibited remarks of correspondents like Bartemeier and Zilboorg may have encouraged Menninger not only to share his own delight in psychoanalytic puns and jokes but also to express his mischievous impulses—as conveyed, for example, through his tender and teasing greetings (Chief, Doctor Jelly, Zilly, "Pop" Brill, Glorious).

Finally, Menninger comes across as an acute observer of human behavior and motivation. Whether the subject is the aberrations of patient behavior from the perspective of the physician seeking to impose structure or the sophisticated activities of New York or Los Angeles luminaries as viewed by a Midwestern outsider, Menninger is refreshingly candid about his fellow human beings, illuminating their follies, yet hopeful about their possibilities.

The correspondence begins at the end of one great war with the start of Menninger's career as a psychiatrist, and it closes at the end of a second great war. Nineteen forty-five was the year in which Menninger published the third, and final, edition of *The Human Mind*, was named to the reorganization committee of the American Psychiatric Association, became director of the Menninger School of Psychiatry, and, most important, was appointed manager of the nation's largest veterans administration hospital. We have tried to select letters that illustrate the range of Menninger's talents, interests, and commitments during these years. We have included letters that we believe to be valuable for the history of American psychiatry and psychoanalysis, public and private mental hospitals, and American intellectual thought, and we have chosen letters that indicate and substantiate Menninger's distinctive role in all these fields. We have also selected letters that reveal more personal aspects of Menninger or his correspondents, typical habits of mind or behavior that illuminate their professional lives. The book is divided into three parts, the beginning of each marked by a turn in Menninger's career; for each part we provide an introduction.

We have worked exclusively with the correspondence stored in the Karl Menninger Archives, temporarily deposited at the Menninger Foundation in Topeka, Kansas, and with Menninger's correspondence with William Alanson White and Smith Ely Jelliffe in the National Archives. None of the earlier correspondence from Menninger's years at Harvard has been preserved, and correspondence among members of the family is sparse, as the three Menninger doctors spent most of their adult lives in Topeka. Unless otherwise indicated, all of Menninger's letters were written in Topeka. Menninger's secretaries saved carbon copies of the letters he sent and the originals he received during these years. The version of the letters we have presented is the final draft as sent (Menninger habitually dictated and then revised his first draft). With few exceptions, the correspondence both to and from Menninger was typed. We have silently corrected typographical, spelling, and punctuation errors.

Our access to this material was unrestricted. During our examination of the correspondence, we regularly interviewed Karl Menninger for information about people and events, although we did not discuss the acceptability of individual letters at that time. After we had completed our initial selection, Menninger reviewed our choices. We have complied with his request that a few letters be excluded from the book and that portions of perhaps a dozen others be deleted.

Although we ourselves have chosen to excise occasional nonessential, trivial, or confidential passages, most of the letters are reproduced in entirety. Omissions in the letters are signaled by ellipses, and we have deleted the names of patients, as well as other information that might identify them. Correspondents and individuals referred to in the letters are identified in footnotes at their first mention, except for those individuals who require no explanation because they are well known, because their position is described in the letter, or because neither Menninger nor available reference material could supply information about them.

We have chosen to arrange the letters chronologically rather than by correspondent or topic. Early in the book there are occasional gaps of several months between letters, periods during which the correspondence was less interesting.

Part I
1919–29

In January 1919, at the age of twenty-five, Karl Menninger returned to Topeka after a six-month association with Elmer Ernest Southard and Lawson G. Lowrey at the Boston Psychopathic Hospital. The situation in Topeka was auspicious: C. F. Menninger had built up a robust medical practice and needed assistance; after a visit to the Mayo Clinic in Rochester, Minnesota, he had resolved to start a similar venture of his own, and father and son now became partners. Together they stimulated interest in neuropsychiatry and created the Menninger Clinic and, in 1925, the Menninger Sanitarium. With William Menninger's return to Topeka in 1926, Karl Menninger was able to turn his attention to the establishment of a school for emotionally troubled children. Named after his first mentor, the Southard School became the focus of much pride and extensive discussion in the letters. The decade ends with the involuntary resignation of Stella Pearson, the first director, who had become severely ill with tuberculosis and had entered a sanitarium in Oklahoma for treatment.[1]

The letters of this period reflect Karl Menninger's satisfaction both with the professional opportunities for a gifted psychiatrist in this area of the country where few other psychiatrists practiced and with his personal life. During these years, three children (Julia, Martha, and Robert) were born, and the letters also disclose an affectionate relationship with his younger brother Will, to whom Karl had often been an advisor. The correspondence documents Menninger's continuing friendship with and respect for his two former teachers, Smith Ely Jelliffe and, until his death, E. E. Southard. With his colleague and past classmate Lawson Lowrey, Dr. Karl often played the same advisory role he had played with Dr. Will.

Dr. Karl's assumption of the roles for which he felt a particular affinity—teacher, organizer, and crusader—occurred in these early years. He wanted

---

1 Despite Pearson's departure, the school thrived; in 1946 it became the Children's Division and Hospital of the Menninger Foundation.

to make psychiatry comprehensible both to a broad lay audience and, as he put it, "intraprofessionally." In 1919, at Topeka's Washburn College, he began teaching courses in mental hygiene, abnormal psychology, and criminology. His energies were also expressed in organizational participation and in the expansion and refinement of the Menninger enterprise. He early became a member of many medical, neurological, psychiatric, and mental health groups at the local, regional, and national levels; he spoke at regional medical societies and accepted administrative positions in national mental health organizations. He established an office in Kansas City, Missouri, and hospital connections in Salina and Wellington, Kansas, and in Tulsa, Oklahoma. While broadening the geographic scope of the Menningers' medical practice, he and his father agreed to restrict the function of the clinic and sanitarium to "the study and scientific treatment of conduct disorders" (letter of September 24, 1924).

In all his work, Dr. Karl saw his task as not only to inform colleagues and the public but also to reform attitudes toward mental illness. In a letter to Lawson Lowrey (April 23, 1923), Dr. Karl declared, "My present objective is to get every doctor in Kansas wholly imbued with the idea that neuropsychiatry and myself are for the present synonymous and build up around myself a machine for helping people that no one else pays much attention to or succeeds in helping very much." In addition to his concern for the mentally ill, he was also attentive to the plight of criminals, whose helplessness and hopelessness grieved him. Several letters argued that psychiatrists could treat social deviance "a great deal more expeditiously" than could contemporary penal methods. Indeed, many of the letters of the 1920s mirrored the progressive and expansionist ambitions of psychiatry to enlarge its domain, to psychologize other fields.

In the aftermath of the famous Leopold-Loeb trial of 1924, William Alanson White, president of the American Psychiatric Association (APA), asked Dr. Karl to chair a special APA committee to study the relations of psychiatrists and psychiatry to lawyers and the law, to the control of crime, and to court procedure. During the trial, psychiatrists of differing philosophies had testified for both the prosecution and the defense, and thereby, White feared, created the misperception that psychiatrists either lacked a precise understanding of behavior or were opportunistic. Other members of the Committee on Legal Aspects of Psychiatry were Herman Adler of Chicago; C. Vernon Briggs and William Healy of Boston; Bernard Glueck, Smith Ely Jelliffe, Thomas W. Salmon, and Frankwood E. Williams of New York; and William Alanson White of Washington, D.C., the vice-chairman. The committee's first report was published in 1925. According to Gregory Zilboorg, "It marked a true turning point in the history of the problem, and Karl Menninger's name must rightly occupy an honorable place among the pioneers of an important and difficult task."[2] In 1927, the APA unanimously endorsed the resolution, which contained fundamental recommendations intended to clarify and standardize psychiatrists' assistance of the legal profession in criminal cases. For the next two years, Dr. Karl attended annual gatherings of the American Bar Association (ABA) to advocate the formation of a committee of lawyers to draft a resolution correlative to that of the APA. After consultation with the APA committee, this legal committee presented five parallel recommendations to the ABA, urging psychiatric involvement at every stage of the judicial and penal process.

Despite Dr. Karl's successes, on November 13, 1928 the new president of the APA, Samuel Orton, divested Menninger of his chairmanship. Orton had previously clashed with Menninger's friend Lowrey, who had gone to the University of Iowa, where Orton was chairman of the department of psychiatry at the medical school, to establish a child guidance institute. Orton's and Lowrey's personalities did not mesh, and Orton's hostility to psychoanalysis increased the animosity, so that Lowrey's brief tenure at Iowa, as the letters make clear, was stormy. Now it was Menninger who felt Orton's wrath.

In addition to his work with established organizations, Dr. Karl founded several new groups. In 1922 he organized the Central [States] Neuro-Psychiatric Association to provide a forum at which midwestern psychiatrists could articulate their common concerns. Meanwhile, Menninger's former Harvard professor of psychiatry, Herman Adler, had become director of the Institute of Juvenile Research in Chicago. When Dr. Karl was in Chicago, he and Adler often discussed juvenile delinquents, and Menninger sometimes accompanied Adler on prison visits. Adler thought there should be an association of professionals who shared an interest in applying a psychological approach to crime and criminals. At a 1924 meeting in Hyde Park, Dr. Karl, William Healy, David Levy, and Lawson Lowrey, as well as psychologist Simon Tulchin, agreed to create such an organization, the American Orthopsychiatric Association. The prefix *ortho-* (meaning straightening or correcting) was chosen to suggest, as in orthopedics, the reshaping, in this case of antisocial behavior. Within the new association, not only psychiatrists but psychologists, social workers, and professional child-care workers could trade ideas. In his teaching, too, Menninger filled gaps: at Washburn College he taught one of the nation's first undergraduate courses in mental hygiene, and when he discovered that no appropriate textbook existed, he wrote *The Human Mind.*[3]

2 Gregory Zilboorg, "Legal Aspects of Psychiatry," in *One Hundred Years of American Psychiatry,* ed. J. K. Hall et al. (New York: Columbia University Press, 1944), 579.

3 The title was inspired by Logan Clendening, KAM's friend and Kansas City office partner, whose book *The Human Body* had been published in 1927.

During this decade, Dr. Karl also crusaded to redress what he felt was the neglect of Freud within the profession. Although he worried over the imbalance between his abundant theoretical knowledge and his scant clinical experience, he continued to "frankly espouse Freudianism" (November 25, 1922). In February 1928, after a year of debating where and by whom to be analyzed, he postponed his analysis "indefinitely," but in a letter of November 15, 1929 he again defended psychoanalysis as "one of the great intellectual contributions of the twentieth century."

The correspondence of the 1920s concludes with Dr. Karl's enlightening letter to publicist Frances Whiting of Alfred A. Knopf, his publisher, explaining in detail the genesis of *The Human Mind* and summarizing his professional interests, concerns, and philosophy at that time.

To Frank Peers,[1] Constantinople, Turkey, May 10, 1919

Dear Frank:

The world is so full of rapid transits and wonderful changes, particularly in this century, that it does not seem strange, as it once might, that I am addressing you, whom I saw recently here in Boston, in the Orient in answer to a letter which I received from you two thousand miles west of here. I am deeply chagrined that I allowed so much time to elapse since the receipt of your letter of February in New York City, but it has been a rather eventful time, as I shall proceed to relate.

About the time you were writing that letter, Grace [Gaines Menninger][2] and I were getting established in Topeka, where we had just arrived. We are temporarily living with Father[3] and Mother[4] at 1251 [Topeka Boulevard]. The next thing was Father and I moved our offices up to the Mulvane Building, where we took a suite of six rooms. Father has restricted his work to internal medicine and diagnosis, and I am doing absolutely nothing but nervous and mental diseases. We have a young man assisting us.

The next most important event (I mean next chronologically, for it is far more important, as far as that goes, from anything else that has happened, or will happen for some time) was the birth of Julia Menninger on April 15th. This is quite an exciting event, both for the grandparents, parents and the said daughter, who still weeps to think of it quite frequently, according to Grace's letters.

1 A high school friend of KAM, Frank Peers was the son of a Topeka pediatrician; he became a painter and, after his travels, settled in Greenwich Village.
2 Grace Gaines Menninger was KAM's first wife; they were divorced in February 1941.
3 CFM was born in Tell City, Indiana. Originally an internist, after a visit to the Mayo Clinic in Rochester, Minnesota, in 1908, he decided to structure the Menninger Clinic along the same lines. He was chairman of the board of the Menninger Foundation at the time of his death in 1953.
4 Flo Knisley Menninger was CFM's first wife and mother of their three children.

You see I say letters, because the first of May, much against my will, but to meet unavoidable circumstances, I departed the banks of Kaw [Kansas River] and sped back here to Boston to assume my old haunts in the Psychopathic Hospital. I am assisting in laboratory work in Dr. Southard's course in neuropathology in Harvard Medical School. I came back chiefly for that reason. In about a month I will return home. . . .

Now, I have told you all about myself and our little, trivial home affairs, not because I think they are comparable in importance with the magnificent adventure through which you are passing, but because I know that these little trifles are of much more interest when one is away from home than they might appear from face value.

Dr. Southard,[5] whom, as you know, I admire immensely, came into the sitting room last evening to play chess, and he saw a copy of the *Topeka Journal* lying on the table. I half apologized for the rather small town and rural postscripts of the front page, which were not even up to the *[Topeka] Journal* standard. This provoked from Dr. Southard a dissertation on the beauty of things rural, and the advantages of living in a town as opposed to living in a city. You and I have been over this so many times that I suppose you know about what a strong second I would make.

Now, I am coming to your letters—one in New York and one from the Mediterranean Sea. Edwin told me about your stay in New York. It was fine that you could be with Esther [Peers' sister]; in fact, I think I will send this letter to Esther, because I am not sure I have recalled your address correctly. I left your letter with Grace in Topeka, but I certainly enjoyed immensely your description of your trip through Europe and around the islands of the South inland sea. I find it almost impossible to get more than a very fantastic and very likely wholly erroneous image of the scenery through which you must be passing. Your description is very beautiful and very vivid, so that I think I see a great deal in my mind's eye, but I daresay I am not conceiving half the beauty or half the interest which is really there for you to see. . . .

Always your Friend,

To E. E. Southard, Boston, July 5, 1919

My dear Chief:

It is with a certain feeling of deferential humility and even of diffident reticence that I address a letter to the chairman of the Neurological section

---

5 Elmer Ernest Southard began his career at Harvard Medical School, becoming Bullard Professor of Neuropathology in 1909. From 1912 until his death in 1920, he was director of Boston Psychopathic Hospital, where, with Mary Jarrett, he established the first school of psychiatric social work. KAM, who had served his internship at Kansas City General Hospital, met Southard while doing postgraduate study at Boston Psychopathic in 1918.

A.M.A., ex-president of the A.M.P.A. [American Medico-Psychological Association], editor of the *A. J. of Abnormal Psychology*, editor of the *Archives*, etc., director of the Industrial Mental Hygiene stunt, to say nothing of such minor matters as the Bullard professorship, the directorship of the Psychiatric Institute and originator of the Southard classification of Mental Disease.

Nevertheless a certain native buoyancy enables me to overcome this natural timorousness, and inspires the temerity to write vapid and perhaps airy notes to this same exalted but lovable chief.

First I must tell you that in writing my reports to the physicians referring me cases, I am detailing differential diagnoses which thrash the Southardian classification, nomenclature and terminology across many a weary page. I just wrote Smith[6] that I was inflicting upon a startled medical public a frightful barrage of logomachical ammunition. Yesterday I began the campaign of a medical meeting comprising the doctors of about fifteen counties. I played no French opening but played P to K P 4.[7] The next move is to promulgate a simplified nomenclature for your eleven disease groups in order that it may be put across with the Kansas medicos.

Things have been happening thick and fast. In the first place patients have been coming in too fast for one man to handle. I am utilizing a makeshift hospital at present for nervous cases, with something better in the way of a psychiatric hospital vaguely in view.

In the second place His Excellency the Governor has sent me a thing that looks like a high-school diploma which commissions me as secretary of the State Mental Hygiene Commission. All the men whom I named and some that I thot of later have been appointed as my confederates. More than that he has told me that the State Printing Plant is at my disposal which means that anything that I want to write in the way of Mental Hygiene propaganda will be printed by the state free and if my present plans go thru, enveloped and mailed by the state. What do you think of that?

Thirdly, the influenza papers[8] seem to have gone thru and more are on the way. I shall be writing Lawson [Lowrey][9] in a few days about certain

6 E. Roger Smith, a psychiatrist, was a resident at Boston Psychopathic with KAM. He later practiced in Indianapolis.

7 Both KAM and Southard were avid chess players; here KAM indicates through his chess analogy that he made a standard opening move rather than attempting a less common opening.

8 In a letter of February 17, 1919, to KAM (Menninger Archives: Topeka, Kansas), Southard had suggested that he, KAM, and Lawson Lowrey publish a collection of papers on influenza.

9 Psychiatrist and longtime friend of KAM, Lowrey persuaded KAM, in 1918, to study psychiatry, especially neurosyphilis, at Boston Psychopathic. From 1930 to 1945 Lowrey was editor of the *American Journal of Orthopsychiatry*, which he had founded. Lowrey spent

details of the book. Perhaps Lawson is too busy to get into this with us—I guess I had better wait until I hear from you as to that. Finally, there are a lot of things that I would certainly like to hear from you about. Thus I would like to make a formal request for a price estimate on, say, fifty of those brain photographs, large size. I have thot of one dozen uses for the "Southard brain prints." Then again I am wondering what you have decided about the association or corresponding membership in the Boston Psychiatric Institute. I suppose Raeder[10] has already talked to you about this idea. I suggested that with various depots and representatives across the United States to promulgate or at least to carry on and disseminate Southardian principles (which might have to masquerade for the time under the pseudonym of the Boston Psychiatric Institute), we could soon accomplish something in the way of a national school which while not quite as the Cushing[11] model would at least be something for them to reckon with who talk psychiatry. I for one will say that I shall esteem it an honor to subscribe myself associate member of the Boston Psychiatric Institute and as soon as you give me permission I shall do so.

Before I run on into any of the other dozen things which I have jotted down to mention writing to you, I think I had better come to an abrupt but pregnant close.

Sincerely yours,

FROM E. E. SOUTHARD, BOSTON, SEPTEMBER 11, 1919

Dear Dr. Menninger:

. . . I saw your paper on "Influenza Psychoses" in the *Archives*. It looked very good to me. It seems to me that your vivacious style was held properly in leash and not too restrained in that paper. You know that you and I suffer from the charge of being flippant and I do not want you to lose as much vogue as I have lost through the charge. I think you got away with it beautifully. I am making so much progress with my book on *The Brain and Mental Disease* (that is the book with Dr. Canavan)[12] and also so much progress with my book on psychiatric social work (with Miss Jarrett)[13] that I feel that I am

the majority of his career in New York City as a member of the Child Guidance Institute (1927–33).

10 Oscar J. Raeder, a Boston psychiatrist.

11 Harvey Cushing, professor of surgery at Harvard and surgeon in chief at the Peter Bent Brigham Hospital.

12 Myrtelle Canavan, pathologist at Boston Psychopathic.

13 Mary Jarrett and Southard, paradigm for other psychiatrist-social worker teams, wrote *The Kingdom of Evil* (1922), a collection of one hundred histories of psychiatric social work cases and a "classification and social division of evil."

beginning to learn the tempo of book writing as against article writing. Accordingly, I feel a bit encouraged about the influenza book.

My regards to the wife and to your family.

As ever,

To E. E. SOUTHARD, BOSTON, OCTOBER 12, 1919

Dear Chief:

I feel impelled to write you today, aware as I am of my comparatively long silence. I have not failed to receive and enjoy your occasional letters and my response to Mr. Hunter's[14] stimuli may be enclosed or follow shortly.

While I have not forgotten your interest and professed affection . . . for things rural, or I mean rather semi-urban . . . at any rate contrasted with metropolitan, nevertheless I refrain (not without some exertion of my probably-rather-hypo-boulic faculty) from narrating to you all the adventures of a western town, or little western city, as you will. We gracefully elude pursuing misfortune, either in the epiletoid style of Omaha mobs[15] or the schizophrenic (negativistic!) manner of Bostonian police. But despite this pacific mixture of urban-ity and rurality, our little world is quite full of the spice of existence, to paraphrase an old one, and busy enough to prevent (as you have seen) even respectably prompt correspondence.

And so while I may not tell you of our fair, and our boulevards, and our paved roads thru the counties, and the oil-rush just south of us, and the money everyone is making (except the poor capitalist!) nor the concert series . . . I shall tell you of a few things from the private office of K.A.M.

First let me confide, as penitent to priest, that the whole darn business[16] is beginning to bore me frightfully. The state hospital people, whom I fairly dragged and flogged into it, are suspicious, cantankerous, and apathetic. They do not turn their hands to do anything, intra- or extramurally, except try to swing the expenses to fit the cradle of the budget. There have been two rather ordinary articles in the state medical journal by two of the superintendants . . . and no original work has been published from here since Hector wagged his tail behind his master's chariot. They seem to think I am trying to show them up, and sometimes I feel like doing so.

14 F. T. Hunter was one of Southard's students. Southard had sent KAM a paper in which Hunter graphed "psychological conceptions" using a model drawn from calculus.

15 A reference to the so-called Omaha Riot of September 28, 1919. In that incident, a mob besieged the Douglas County Courthouse where Will Brown, a black man, was being held as the accused rapist of a white woman. The mob set the courthouse ablaze, took Brown from police custody, and lynched him from a lamppost. This was only one of a series of racial episodes that received sensational coverage in the Omaha press. Reformers argued that the Omaha "machine" had orchestrated these incidents in an effort to discredit the reform administration then in power.

16 KAM is referring to the labor of establishing the Menninger Clinic.

After Herculean exertion, I think we pushed over a plan for a convocation of ALL YE PEOPLE in November,[17] at which time I hope Beers[18] will send you, himself, and others if possible to convert a few of them to M. H. [mental health] and organize a state society. No sooner had this plan [been put] across than Beers wrote me that we ought to raise 5,000 simoleons before organizing a state society, and furthermore he doubted if they could find anyone able to come on the date set for our meeting. Summum in summa: I am going to execute the favorite military maneuver of PASSING THE BUCK just as soon as possible and let someone else push this. The president of the Commission, after I had done all I could . . . in fact all that was done . . . pocketed the credit, etc. in order to save me the trouble and to further his efforts at keeping me under cover, announces that he thinks it would scarcely be modest for him or me to publish anything or speak regarding the subject publicly! . . .

This leads up to something I have been meaning to tell you for some time, namely, that I think I shall try to get ready for the practitioners of Kansas some stuff that they can read and understand explaining what the various forms of mental disease really are. I sent you the first of my 3 preparatory articles. Then I thot I would take up one group after another explaining and illustrating them.

And by the way, I have decided on two more alterations that ought to be introduced in your 11-group (you notice I make it a 12-group) classification. I shall prepare the paper and send it to you before submitting it for publication anywhere. I know they will not break your heart by any means. And anything to kick up a little interest in classification, especially Southardian. (Sic!) Just to anticipate previous communications, I will tell you that I think GROSS BRAIN DISEASE should follow Neurosyphilis, chiefly because it is actually the second thing that a practicing neuropsychiatrist has to think of. And secondly, I think there ought to be a group of psychoses accompanying neurological diseases, not clearly encephalopathic; hyperthyreosis, multiple sclerosis, etc.

Perhaps we should just let these cling to their maternal stock . . . the former in Somato- and the latter in the Encephalo- group. But it stretches the point, a little anyway, to think of them so, or at least to try to get others to see them so.

(I admit the latter of these two suggestions is still somewhat tenuous. I'm still groping a bit, trying to work a sphere of neurology into a psychiatric classification.) . . .

17 KAM had worked unsuccessfully to convene a meeting of mental health professionals in Kansas.

18 Clifford Beers, longtime secretary of the American Foundation for Mental Hygiene. In 1909, after his recovery from a serious mental disorder, described in his autobiographical *A Mind That Found Itself* (1908), Beers founded the mental hygiene movement.

And now (after the manner of Lew Wallace[19] et al.) to my friend from thy friend, farewell (pro tem.)

FROM E. E. SOUTHARD, BOSTON, NOVEMBER 18, 1919

Dear Dr. Menninger:

Weisenburg[20] thinks that your paper is too long and ought to be cut down one half. I have requested him to send it back to you to see what can be done but I do not know that I entirely agree with Weisenburg. He has a neurologist's view, naturally, of the meaning of the small psychiatric details. It occurs to me that we might like to send the paper to the *Journal of Nervous and Mental Disease*. If so, I think all marks suggesting that it has been looked over by the *Archives* should be removed. But of course Weisenburg does not see what you and I know, namely, that these articles are going finally to be put in book form.

I have yours about general psychiatry for the general practitioner and note your insertion of the paranoid group. Will you not write a little paper upon that point and send it to some journal or other? I think Meyer's[21] article on "The Aims of Psychiatric Diagnosis" in the 1918 *Transactions of the A. M. P. A.*[22] mentions a paranoic reaction type in a list of other reaction types. Of course, my own feeling would be that a paranoic sub-group amongst the psychopathias would include practically all we need for the purpose and it seems to me that the resolution of the eleventh group into its major forms will be one of the next tasks. If you will write this note as I suggest, I can then counter in an article taking up Lowrey's suggestion of a change in order, Richard Cabot's[23] suggestion that the senile psychoses be omitted

19 Author of *Ben-Hur* and other historical novels.

20 T. H. Weisenburg, a Philadelphia psychiatrist and an associate editor of *The Archives of Neurology and Psychiatry*. KAM's paper "Influenza and Hypophrenia: The Interrelation of an Acute Epidemic Infection and a Chronic Endemic (Brain) Affection" was first submitted to the *Archives*, but when Weisenburg asked him to shorten it, KAM submitted it to the *Journal of the American Medical Association*, which published it in the October 1920 issue.

21 Born in Switzerland, Adolf Meyer, a specialist in neuropathology, arrived in the United States in 1892. In 1908, at Manhattan State Hospital, Meyer began utilizing psychoanalysis regularly. His first clinical studies focused on dementia praecox. He promoted the shift within American psychiatry from a neurological to a behavioral model, emphasizing the influence of the social environment on the individual. From 1910 to 1941, Meyer directed the Henry Phipps Psychiatric Clinic at Johns Hopkins University Hospital. Although KAM sometimes spoke disapprovingly of Meyer's influence on American psychiatry, Meyer's concept of the *life chart*, a diagnostic history of each patient, influenced KAM's own view of diagnosis.

22 The *Journal of the American Medio-Psychological Association*, which became the *American Journal of Psychiatry* in 1921.

23 Physician and philosopher, later professor of clinical medicine (1919–33) at Harvard Medical School.

and distributed amongst the other groups, and your suggestion that the grouping be extrapolated with the paranoic group. This will give an instance of every possible kind of alteration of my grouping. I could then call attention to the fact that the principle of the grouping remains untouched and that all such changes, additions, and subtractions are entirely welcome. You may note in an editorial in a current number of the *Journal of the A. M. A.* an approving statement concerning the Southard method of orderly exclusion. Can your father publish his account of the order of patients in the diagnosis of anemia somewhere so that it can be a matter of record and of reference?

We are just now trying to arrange the endocrinoses in such an order. As there is no real scientific basis of an order of the endocrinoses, I have attempted to use the space method, placing the endocrine disorders in a sequence in accordance with the amount known about each as indicated by the number of papers in the literature. I see how the wolves will fasten on this space method for their pabulum of ridicule but they will, I think, undoubtedly be beaten in the end. Why do you not with your recent interest in epilepsy undertake an orderly exclusion list of the epilepsies? Of course, I put one into my paper on the "Genera in the Great Groups of Nervous Diseases" but I did it very tentatively on your mature consideration. So far as I know, the course in neuropathology is going to occur in January but I have not been able to get the exact dates as yet.[24]

Sincerely yours,

FROM SMITH ELY JELLIFFE,[1] NEW YORK, FEBRUARY 15, 1920

My dear Menninger:

It was pleasant to get your letter and both Mrs. Jelliffe[2] and myself thank you greatly for your courtesy.

Southard's death was a terrible shock and it was a keen personal loss as I

24 This refers to a second-year course to be taught by Southard at Boston Psychopathic. Earlier, Southard had suggested that KAM serve as an assistant in the course, and KAM had accepted the offer.

1 A prominent New York neurologist, psychiatrist, psychoanalyst, and editor, Jelliffe earned his M.D. degree from the College of Physicians and Surgeons, Columbia University. He was managing editor of the *Journal of Nervous and Mental Disease* from 1902 to 1945 and an editor of the *Psychoanalytic Review* from 1913 to 1945. He and William Alanson White edited *The Nervous and Mental Monograph Series* between 1907 and 1945. As confidant and advisor, he was one of the most important men in KAM's professional life.

2 Belinda (Bee) Dobson Jeliffe was the second wife of Smith Ely Jelliffe. In 1936 she published a novel, *For Dear Life*, whose heroine, Belinda Dan, migrates from North Carolina to New York City, as Bee Jelliffe herself had done. After Smith Ely Jelliffe's death, she maintained a prolific correspondence, seeking rectification of what she deemed the neglect within the profession of her husband's ideas and increasingly championing right-wing causes.

liked him immensely. I never could get right up close to him, his defenses were so busy, but I enjoyed him, appreciated his brilliance, and really warmed to him. It leaves me very unhappy.

I am glad you wrote me of the services. Mrs. Southard had wired about them but I was unable to attend, much as I would have liked to. Mrs. Jelliffe and I called that Sunday night but she had gone, probably to friends, before going on to Boston.

I feel sure Southard was coming to his own rapidly, but he must have had a terrible conflict all of the time between his monistic idealism and absolutism—a fearful power complex, and his more pluralistic pragmatic, live and let live aspect. I cannot but feel he never quite got into the other fellow's skin in spite of his empathizing phantasy. Intellectually he did no doubt, but it was not a real commingling, a real pragmatic recognition of the other man's functional reality. This certainly kept him keyed up all of the time and when the pneumococcus came he did not have a ghost of a chance. The localized vagotonia was profound and he was swamped in 24 hours. Timme[3] tells me he was unconscious Sat. morning when he saw him and although alcohol and pituitary lifted him a bit there was no chance from the beginning.

I think it would be very profitable if we knew more of his unconscious—he always quibbled about his dreams and was really always afraid to tell them—or wittily ran away from them—to couple that up with our understanding of the rapid shock that really killed him. His intensity made him productive—it also finished him.

I trust you will have a very profitable time in Florida and if you work out any papers there let the *Journal* have one or two—or if you have any suggestions as to profitable inquiries as to other workers, I would like your ideas. Who are doing things worthwhile and where are they. . . .

With cordial regards,

To Adolf Meyer, Baltimore, June 10, 1920

My dear Prof. Meyer:

I shall not soon forget your courtesy to me and that of your assistants at the time of my visit to the Phipps Clinic.[4] My brief stay only made me more desirous of returning to stay longer at some future time. I am using an abstract of the case of C., which you so graciously furnished me in an article

3 Walter Timme was chief of clinic and director of the neuroendocrine department at Vanderbilt Clinic in New York and later professor of clinical neurology at Columbia.

4 KAM had visited Meyer to gather information about the management of a psychiatric clinic.

on the relation of influenza and epilepsy. You will recall this case as one of petit mal apparently precipitated by influenza.

This phenomenon has been observed at various times during the past hundred years and no very good explanation has been made, owing in part no doubt to our essential ignorance about both influenza and epilepsy. You may have seen certain correspondence between L. Pierce Clark[5] and myself some months ago in the *Journal of the American Medical Association.* . . .

I am bringing this subject up because I would like to have from you an expression of your general attitude toward this phenomenon of apparent epilepsies apparently precipitated by influenza which I could quote along with the opinions of a few other psychiatrists in my paper dealing with the subject. I should appreciate very much if you will have time to give us your views on the subject.

Sincerely yours,

FROM ADOLF MEYER, BALTIMORE, JUNE 16, 1920

My dear Dr. Menninger:

I remember your visit with great pleasure, and also the shock of hearing, practically the next day, of the death of Southard. His passing away leaves on our shoulders the burden of a great deal of work which Southard might have done for us.

With regard to your inquiry, I can give you my general conception of the relation of epilepsy and infectious diseases. A large number of infectious febrile disorders and toxic disorders tend to lead to deliria and to convulsions. I am in the habit of connecting deliria with conditions which show also through the presence of edema of the membranes and perhaps also of the brain itself. This same condition is observed in epilepsy. To what extent miliary hemorrhages play a specific role in the production of epilepsy, I would not be able to say. I do not, however, consider them essential and specific. In the main I would say it is probable that any cortical damage, either by poison or other injury including arteriosclerosis and circulatory disorders, can be the potential foundation for epileptic attacks.

I may say that I am very much surprised to see so few of the encephalitis cases of the present epidemic with epileptic attacks. For the role of influenza, it might be of value to inquire whether the cases that later developed epilepsy showed any special tendency to delirium or any cerebral involvement during the attack. . . .

Believe me

Very truly yours,

5 A Jungian psychiatrist in New York.

TO ADOLF MEYER, BALTIMORE, JULY 19, 1920

My dear Dr. Meyer:

I appreciate very much your letter of June 16 dealing with my question of epilepsy and infectious diseases. I am very proud to incorporate part of your letter into my little article which I think will appear soon. *(American Journal of Medical Sciences).*

How can one get closer to the whole subject of delirium? It seems to me we suffer immensely from the vagueness of terminology in nomenclature. Have we any license for restricting the name delirium to the mental symptoms obviously dependent upon somatic diseases? On the other hand have we any license to apply it to anything but such conditions? As I trace the word from the time it meant leaving the furrow to the time that it is applied to Bolshevism, it seems to have connoted at one time or another almost every psychiatric symptom and syndrome. How could we best arrive at some general agreement over the country so that delirium would mean the same thing for all of us and so that we could abolish forever those miserable connatives "toxic infectious psychosis" and "infectious exhaustion psychosis"? My verbalistic interests are incited to insurrection whenever I come across them. Your conception of delirium as representing the mental symptoms of cerebral and pial edema offers us something concrete, which, if universally accepted would make us a firm stepping stone. But the question arises as to the possibility of determining from the psychic picture the presence or absence of this pathology. Can it be done? Can it always be done? How shall we regard the schizophrenic elements in pictures that would seem to be precisely such instances as "deliria"?

Rather than bore you with further ramblings of this sort I shall stop precipitatedly hoping that in your busy life you will find time to give me some stimulations for further pursuit or satisfactory conclusions on these most interesting and to me very bewildering matters.

Sincerely yours,

TO SMITH ELY JELLIFFE, NEW YORK, JULY 21, 1920

Dear Dr. Jelliffe:

I feel as if it had been many moons since one of your welcome blue letters arrived and I assure you that I read them when they do come with the greatest interest and wish you had time to make them come more frequent.
. . .

Don't you think considerable damage is done to the cause of dynamic psychiatry *à la Freud* by such ambiguities as Farnell's[6] given on the second

6 Frederick J. Farnell, a psychiatrist who practiced in Providence, R.I., and New York. His "Personality and Disease" appeared in the second volume of *Contributions to Medical*

page of his contribution to the Osler Memorial series? My copy is at the house and I am writing from the office, but you will easily find the line I refer to. Perhaps no one takes it seriously.

With Orton[7] and Lowrey both at Iowa don't you rather look for a growth of psychiatric things out this way? Personally I am inclined to think that Boston's prestige in psychiatry will rapidly fall for I do not believe it can withstand the shock of Southard, Putnam,[8] and Lowrey leaving within twelve months. I do not know that any of the men now active in the State Service are particularly known as psychiatrists. Of course the light of things has gone out there for me.

Remember me to Mrs. Jelliffe. . . .

Sincerely yours,

FROM SMITH ELY JELLIFFE, HULETTS LANDING, NEW YORK, AUGUST 5, 1920

My dear Menninger:

Many thanks for your letters and your patience with my slow responses. I have finally gotten away to Lake George where I have a quiet den and am reading your last. Here is a wonderful spot and should you be east this summer, before Oct. 1, I would be very happy to show you what roughing it is like here in the Adirondacks. . . .

I read Farnell's paper rapidly and enjoyed it as I share the belief that it is necessary to include the "soul" in all our dynamic interpretations, but I am away from the book just now and can't discuss the passage you refer to.

It seems to me there is a great opportunity to push psychiatry in the West and you ought to get a real live bunch together. Meyer is going to lose Campbell[9] as you know. He gets Southard's place I learn, but you maybe can tell me more of the gossip than I am in touch with. Maybe Campbell

---

and Biological Research: Dedicated to Sir William Osler (1919), 659–64. The passage to which KAM objects discusses a case of sclerosis of intestinal vessels leading to hemorrhaging. Farnell finds the organic disease a product of "body and mind, vegetative system, instinct, emotion, and personality" (660).

7 Samuel Orton was the director of the University of Iowa Psychopathic Hospital, where Lawson Lowrey was a member of the neuropsychiatry section. Orton was widely (and correctly) regarded as an enemy of psychoanalysis.

8 James Jackson Putnam, pioneering neurologist and Harvard professor, died in November 1918. One of the most distinguished American converts to Freudianism, Putnam was the first president of the American Psychoanalytic Association (1911). His correspondence with William James, Freud, Ernest Jones, Sándor Ferenczi, and Morton Prince was published in *James Jackson Putnam and Psychoanalysis*, ed Nathan G. Hale, Jr. (1971).

9 C. Macfie Campbell, Adolf Meyer's colleague in Baltimore, shared his interest in mental hygiene and, like Meyer, was an important participant in the National Committee for Mental Hygiene. In 1920, he became professor of psychiatry at Harvard and director of Boston Psychopathic; he remained there until 1941.

will really do something [once out] from under the restraining hand of Meyer. At all counts he is a most lively man and I am glad he has the appointment.

Tell me what can I do for the *Jl.* [*The Journal of Nervous and Mental Disease*] to make 'em sit up.

Cordially,

Mrs. Jelliffe says by all means come up and help her milk the cow. She is cook and cow milker and is thriving.

To SMITH ELY JELLIFFE, NEW YORK, AUGUST 23, 1920

My dear Dr. Jelliffe:

Your welcome letter of August 5 deserves immediate reaction and here she comes. . . .

Did you ever do an autopsy in a country farmhouse? It is certainly an experience. One has to provide for many exigencies unknown to the hospital pathologist. For example the saw rasping on the skull, not an esthetic sound at any time, is far from pleasing to the family clustered in a little group in the adjoining room. One has to provide against keyhole peepers, moreover. And the devices used by country undertakers to support the corpse are fearfully and wonderfully made, and it is very distressing to have the darn thing break down while you are working with a horrible thud sufficient to bring the family rushing to the door to ascertain what has happened. . . .

Sincerely yours,

P.S. I think the *Journal* [*of Nervous and Mental Disease*] is right now making them "sit up," particularly by the splendid array of abstracts. Last time I discussed the *Journal* with Dr. Southard . . . he said, "It's better now than it ever was" or something to that effect. The abstracts department of the *Archives* is certainly a weak point.

FROM SMITH ELY JELLIFFE, HULETTS LANDING, NEW YORK, SEPTEMBER 6, 1920

My dear Menninger:

It is a showery day, the lake is all in clouds, the sun comes and goes; we cannot play tennis nor do any outside work and yours of Aug. 23 lies invitingly on top of my pile—so here goes. First with thanks for your letter, and Mrs. Jelliffe's comment, Thank God there is someone who can do something useful. Long life to Biddy, the cow, and may Dr. Menninger have the chance to milk her.

I have done many autopsies but none quite in the difficult surroundings you describe. I once did a funny one on a Negress in a hall bedroom. Formalined the brain intracarotidly and had the joy of seeing two sides of the face of different color. It took some explaining.

I don't think Campbell will do very much that is really new. He may, but I fear he has been too long with Meyer. He will always be "sound," but hell, anybody can be sound with a little caution and much reading. I do hope he will develop a vigorous reaction and get a lot of men about him—he is really a fine chap but a little dour I fear from his Scottish ancestry. I admire him immensely and hope he can carry on some of Southard's brilliant work— but I doubt if we shall get a worthy successor to Southard for a long time. He was a fine flower of the James-Royce culture period[10] and when shall we find another? His 40–50 year period would have been tremendous I think and he would have put psychiatry on the map in an astounding manner I feel sure. . . .

Now I must put the lamb roast in the oven and peel some potatoes and get some baked apples started.

Good luck to you and let me hear from you again.

Cordially,

To Smith Ely Jelliffe, New York, November 19, 1920

My dear Dr. Jelliffe:

. . . I am trying to get the folks out here to see the importance of teaching mental hygiene in its broader connotations in the colleges. . . .

I have tried to show that any attempt to apply normal psychology to human life is doomed to failure unless the equally important considerations of the abnormal in psychology be included. How many of our college students know the meaning of complex, rationalization, delusion, paranoid, and for that matter of feeblemindedness? If we did nothing more than provide a means of attacking that sense of inferiority which eats like a worm into the heart of the sensitive personality a course in mental hygiene would have proved itself worthy. . . .

You will wonder when I am coming to the point. Well it's just here that they objected that one would have to wait a while until such a course could be carefully and cautiously prepared. And I came back with the insistence that this overscrupulousness in insuring a good subject well taught was certainly a new note in the pedagogical chord, and what was more to the point it is practically equivalent to laying the idea on the table.

In others words we can be "safe" by avoiding being progressive. An idea

10 William James (1842–1910), American pragmatist philosopher and psychologist. Josiah Royce (1855–1916), the finest exemplar of "absolute realism." In 1882, James, a professor of philosophy at Harvard, invited Royce to join the department on a temporary basis; in 1885 Royce obtained a regular appointment. From then on, until James's death, the "golden period" of the department, James and Royce—both prolific writers—maintained an amicable debate concerning the merits and deficiencies of absolute idealism.

perfected before it is begun is in the end usually neither begun nor perfected.

Meanwhile I am having a great time with my young folks at the college
and next semester we will have a course in Mental Hygiene as well as a
seminar in Problems in Abnormal Psychology. The whole bunch wants to
go into psychiatry at present. . . .

Sincerely,

FROM SMITH ELY JELLIFFE, NEW YORK, NOVEMBER 28, 1920

My dear Menninger:

Many thanks for your favor of Nov. 19, 1920.[11] The state hospital gets
most of them [the mentally deficient] because when the first wobbles begin
about 13 or 14 or 15 the general practitioner only sees a limited organ and
not the functioning organism, and furthermore all of our doctors are taught
static conceptions. The flow of energy through a transformer they never get.
Their anatomy starts there and they never get below the sensori-motor nor
above, either, for that matter.

So we get them when the break in compensation is already almost un-
modifiable, i.e., the patients, and then try to tinker them up as best we may.
Still, the signs are not wanting that show the sky is clearing a bit and we all
go on our way working out our own problems as best we may and trying to
help others.

If cowardice was not so universal, if we were not so full of the many
things that are not so, because we fear to offend John and Bill and Harry,
and Mary especially; if we could see the functions of social agreement—
logic—as differing from those of the unfolding of the individual unconscious—prelogic—art, intuitions, etc.—then I feel sure we would all be more
sympathetic and learn something from everybody. Even the college professors—hardboiled as many of them are. You are absolutely right. This cau-
tiousness, laying on the table, playing safe, is an aspect of this cowardice
that needs the "logic" approval of his neighbor. In the psa. [psychoanalytic]
terminology—and here I am giving you a long shot—it is the working out
of the "Castration Complex" in social institutions. Just as the "Circumcision
Rite" bound a certain historic people together as a safety device, a protection
of their potency, so the "University Cliques" and other related types of logical bindings, terminologies, etc., work in a similar manner, and behind
much of it, the economic needs stick out. . . .

I know I shall like Bergson's Mind Energy—see editorial in last week's

11 KAM had recommended that Jelliffe contact a Kansas City physician who directed a
successful school for the retarded in order to solicit an advertisement for Jelliffe's *Journal
of Nervous and Mental Disease;* KAM supported the national dissemination of such advertising because he felt that state care of the retarded was inadequate.

N.Y. Med. Jl. on the Free Association method—although I have not yet read it, its phrases are floating around the place. One of my assistants wrote it, I imagine, and as a son-in-law [12] edits the sheet, I know about where they get it all. An aside—Be sure to get Kempf's new *Psychopathology*.[13]

With cordial regards and best wishes,

Very sincerely,

To Gregory Stragnell, New York, August 29, 1921

My dear Dr. Stragnell:

. . . I am head over heels into this psychoanalysis business. I am going to give it a fair trial which is more than I have ever really done. To tell the whole truth I think I have made considerable progress in the few cases I have already started.

Of course I have already run up against many stumps and I wish I had someone like you near at hand to tell me what to do. For example I have a little boy who has phobias particularly in regard to dying and in regard to Negroes. I rather quickly traced his phobias of dying to an unfortunate affair in which a beloved uncle died followed by the suicide of his wife all of which was discussed in front of the little boy to his great astonishment. This occurred when he was six. He is now eight. I got his free association by touching his eyelids with my fingers and asking him to tell me what he saw and then talking with his mother about the results.

Now, I know it is the feeling among psychoanalysts that the treatment of the mother in this sort of a case would be of help to the little boy. I am not sure that I see clearly why. But as a matter of fact I should like to know what I ought best to do next. Having had a session with the little fellow in which I rather thought I made some progress in straightening out his fear of death I thought we might gradually go on and take up the fear of Negroes, his bed wetting, and other symptoms. Perhaps on the other hand I ought to do something with the mother and if so you could show me what logic to use in presenting it to her and how to connect up the complexes which I am sure she has and which in fact I used to illustrate to her what I should try to do for the boy, with those of the boy?

Sincerely,

12 Gregory Stragnell, a psychoanalyst in New York from 1919 to 1932 and then director of research and executive vice-president of the Schering Corporation in Bloomfield, New Jersey. He married Jelliffe's eldest daughter, Sylvia, in 1920 and worked with Jelliffe as an associate editor of his journal.

13 Edward J. Kempf, an early advocate of psychoanalysis, joined Adolf Meyer at Johns Hopkins in 1913. From 1914 to 1920 he was affiliated with St. Elizabeths Hospital in Washington, D.C. In 1915, he became the second president of the Washington Psychoanalytic Society. In 1920 Kempf published *Psychopathology*, which delineated his treatment of schizophrenic patients.

From Gregory Stragnell, New York, September 4, 1921

My dear Dr. Menninger,

When you next come to N.Y. you are going to get nailed on the psa. cross if I can get hold of you. Before you come I am going to ask you to read Dr. W. A. White's[1] *Outlines of Psychiatry* or more important his *Foundations*. It is in the monograph series. Also Dr. Jelliffe's *Technique* in the same series. Then, by all means, you must read Freud's *General Introduction to Psychoanalysis*. There are many other similar works that I am sure would be worthwhile to you aside from the pragmatic works. I am in your pet territory at present in Royce's *Good and Evil*. I enjoy it. I use it as, indeed, I use most everything I get hold of. I feel that I understand Royce, Wundt, James, Butler, Schiller, (F.C.S.) [Ferdinand Canning Scott], Frazer, Hobhouse[2] and a host of other "worth whiles" the better for my knowledge of the workings of the unconscious mind and the phylogenetic layers which can be traced through the comparison of the neurotic's symptoms and the anthropological records.

You cannot be a pragmatist and ignore the unconscious. Now I want you to do me a favor and yourself an especial favor and read just a short article (the leading article on instinct) in the last issue of the *Journal of Abnormal Psychology*. Perhaps Narcissus speaks in full glory but this man[3] so fully and artistically expresses my full views that I shall feel neglected and abused if you do not read it *carefully*.

In regard to the boy. If you feel that his troubles are due to environmental difficulties then it would be well to have a talk with the mother and give her some light on the psychology underlying the boy's difficulties so that she can aid you in making an adjustment. Frequently neurotic boys of this type have many of their symptoms in order to *gain attention*. They gain their strength (attention) through manifestations of weakness, just as a hysterical woman will frequently manifest somatic symptoms in order to gain her goal

1 Born in Brooklyn, William Alanson White received his medical degree from Long Island Medical College. In 1903, White became superintendent of St. Elizabeths Hospital in Washington, D.C., where he remained until his death. His insistence that humane treatment of the mentally ill was necessary to ameliorate their problems helped make St. Elizabeths one of the world's foremost psychiatric institutions. As president of the APA (1924–25), White appointed KAM to chair the Committee on the Legal Aspects of Psychiatry.

2 Josiah Royce (1855–1916), Harvard philosopher; Wilhelm Wundt (1832–1920), influential German psychologist; William James (1842–1910); possibly Samuel Butler (1835–1902), British author (*The Way of All Flesh*) or Nicholas Murray Butler (1862–1947), educator, author, and president of Columbia University; Ferdinand Canning Scott Schiller (1864–1937), philosopher and author of *Humanism: Philosophic Essays* (1903); Sir James Frazer (1854–1941), author of *The Golden Bough* (1915); and Leonard T. Hobhouse (1864–1929), British political and social philosopher.

3 William Ernest Hocking, "The Dilemma in the Conception of Instinct, as Applied to Human Psychology," *Journal of Abnormal and Social Psychology* 16 (June–Sept. 1921): 73–96.

(attention of her husband or family). This comes from an initial inferiority feeling, on account of a comparison with older people at a very early age.

The Negro fantasy in children is a common one and has a very archaic background. At times it assumes a foster parent fantasy, again a phobia. The boy undoubtedly feels inferior to his father; feels that he does not get as much attention from the mother as he should (although he may be getting more than is good for him); sees his father getting this attention, etc. The result in these cases is an unconscious rivalry and hatred of the father and the mechanism of attaining his goal through various symptoms. This process is entirely unconscious. This must not be forgotten. The underlying inferiorities and cravings are also in the unconscious and they are suppressed, finally coming through in vicarious channels. The suppression is due to the painful affects and the conversion is an economic mechanism preventing the real conflict from coming to the surface.

The boy should be taught that he cannot attain his goal except by self-reliance and standing on his own "feet." He must be shown that his infantile mechanisms (when they are sufficiently revealed) are destructive and will not bring him the things he is seeking.

With kindest regards from us both

Sincerely,

To WILLIAM C. MENNINGER,[4] NEW YORK, DECEMBER 5, 1921

Dear Bill:

I am tremendously busy but I am almost ashamed to begin my letter that way because if I am not mistaken I have begun practically every letter I have written to you the same way.

Well, as a matter of fact it's true. The last two months were the busiest and biggest from all standpoints that I have ever had. And business is still coming our way in spite of the fact that times are very hard.

I am not looking at this just with the idea of seeing how many patients I can see or how many dollars I can drag in. I think I am getting a little more out of it than that. I am trying to take the point of view that if I discipline and keep myself up to snuff and deliver the goods as the saying goes, . . . which I suppose . . . means giving something to the people that they need

4 WCM, the youngest of the Menninger sons, received his M.D. degree from Cornell in 1924 and interned in medicine and surgery at Bellevue Hospital in New York City. He then worked at St. Elizabeths before returning to the Menninger Clinic in 1927. In 1930, he was appointed medical director of the Menninger Hospital. During World War II he served as a brigadier general in charge of psychiatry for the army. In 1957 he was elected president of the Menninger Foundation and actively engaged in promotional endeavors for the foundation.

which others are not supplying. I have forgotten how I began this sentence but anyway I hope that the fact that we are extremely busy means . . . that we are able to help a good many people. I am sure we are able to help quite a few of them and some I think might have gone quite a little longer without help if we hadn't seen them. . . .

The joy you're going to get out of your work is not directly related to the amount of money you make. If I thot you were making any sacrifice by going to China[5] I would certainly advise you not to go. As a matter of fact I don't think you are making any sacrifice but I think you have the vision of spending a magnificent exhilarating life at a splendid sort of work. Nobody but the ignorant conceives of the missionary in the camp meeting as a camp-meeting, hands-on-the-shoulder-of-the-wayward-sinner sort of fellow. That sort of thing is extinct. I know very well that you know this but I am just reminding you that the man that goes into foreign missionary work belongs to a moral aristocracy which doesn't need anybody to apologize for it. I told the students at Washburn College chapel (and incidentally I provoked a dickens of a row when I spoke in chapel, altho not on this particular point) . . . that they would some day see the silliness of the shallow aristocracy of Washburn[6] and see on the other hand that the great thing of the world is the intellectual and moral aristocracy. . . .

The fact that I am trying to get at and which I seem to be getting to very slowly is that I think you have everything to gain and not a great deal to lose by selecting the work you are going into. I say not a great deal to lose and that isn't literally true because the world is so constructed that we can't have everything. It is a pluralistic world and there are so many good things in it that one simply has to make a choice and do that for all he's worth with no regrets and no misgivings. I think your choice is a good one. It's not the only thing in the world worth doing but it's one of the great things worth doing and it's particularly worth doing from the standpoint (please get this now) that the greatest pleasure in life is particularly that which we derive from the work we do.

Now, you are going into a great work but you are not going into a particularly well-paying work. I can't go into the work you're in just now. The work I am in, however much I may make of it, has the disadvantage that a good deal of the pay instead of coming in the form of gratitude and joy and sense of having advanced the cause of Christ, etc., comes in the form of money.

And to make a long letter no longer I will tell you quickly what I mean. Don't choose your job on the basis of how much money there is in it but on

5 WCM was considering becoming a missionary in China.
6 KAM, while a student at Washburn, had been rejected by a fraternity; this may explain his characterization of the Greek system as a "shallow aristocracy."

the basis of the one you think you would enjoy. And accept my written promise that Grace and I will be glad to help educate your children as part of our contribution to the cause you are representing. It might be wise to put some numerical limit on the number of children we are to educate and aside from the smile I have a serious meaning: I don't recommend that you have a large family of children because I want to tell you that entirely aside from the expensiveness of the children in money there is the expensiveness in time and energy. I would advise you to have some children, two for example, but I certainly would not have a family of six if I expect to do work that will take as much of your time as yours and Virginia's[7] will. In fact you may decide to have no children at all. At least for the first five or ten years of your married life. In either case you may depend upon it that you will get some financial support from me whenever you want it and whenever you need it. In fact if the Lord pleases me with any means I expect to see that it is all spent before I die and I consider no finer way of being represented in China than being represented by my brother.

Sincerely yours,

To Lawson Lowrey, Iowa City, Iowa, December 27, 1921

Dear Lawson:

. . . The Mental Hygiene Society, however well intentioned, is distinctly erratic (I really am referring to the National Committee). As far as I can see it is almost entirely in the hands of exceedingly cyclothymic[8] individuals like Clifford Beers and Frankwood E. Williams,[9] and while I admire them both I have insight enough into the cyclothymic temperament to appreciate their fundamental weaknesses, one of which certainly is distractability. Neither you nor I know what they are going to do next and I am not sure they do either. Consequently your future, it seems to me, would be rendered somewhat tenuous.[10] They might be tremendously pleased by you and they might

---

7 A girlfriend; she did not become WCM's wife.

8 Cyclothymia is a bipolar affective disorder involving recurrent cycles of mania and depression.

9 Williams was a New York psychiatrist who applied the methods of psychoanalysis. In 1932, he cofounded the *Psychoanalytic Quarterly*. After Otto Rank's defection from Freud, signaled in 1924 with the publication of Rank's *Trauma of Birth*, Williams became known as the leader of the Rankian group in New York City.

10 The National Committee for Mental Hygiene had asked Lowrey to take a leave of absence in order to direct a "demonstration psychiatric clinic" to be staffed by a psychologist and a psychiatric social worker as well as by Lowrey. They were to serve in an advisory capacity to judges of juvenile courts to help prevent conduct disorders. The plan was that this clinic would operate in three or four different cities within a year. Lowrey turned down the offer on the grounds that he was indispensable at the Iowa Psychopathologic Hospital.

be tremendously displeased. In either case they might do anything. For example they sent me down to St. Louis to make them a speech and I made them a peach of a speech and got more applause than anyone else on the program and had the audience flock up to me to an embarrassingly flattering extent and had people give me their addresses and ask for reprints until I was black in the face. Well, since then they have never asked me to make another speech and when I submitted my manuscript for publication in *Mental Hygiene* they informed me that it was perhaps somewhat too popular for that dignified periodical and so it was published in an outdoor journal, and *Mental Hygiene* instead accepted such slop as "What is a Nervous Breakdown?" and "Inadequate Social Examinations" (altho this latter is really pretty good, but the title is characteristic of a lot of them in that journal which get my goat). . . .

And in my opinion most important of all there is this consideration, Lawson, if you stay where you are you are almost sure to get an offer of a professorship and the directorship of a psychopathic hospital in one of the surrounding states before many years. Even if that offer were not to come for five years you would still be the youngest director in the United States. If you back off now and give up your associate professorship I don't think you will help your chances and you may hurt them. My advice to you is that you work like the devil right now reading everything there is to read, studying as hard as you can, evolving a few ideas on the side and for the most part devouring the literature and getting some practical experience from a little different angle than the Boston life on running of a psychopathic hospital. You can get all of this at Orton's expense now, whereas a little later it will be altogether up to Lawson. . . .

I have other things to tell you about but I know your mind will be so taken up with that that you can't listen to them. One thing that we are quite interested in just now is a profit-sharing scheme which we have arranged whereby our employees will have an interest in the firm at least as far as profits are concerned. I don't think Christianity and business have very much in common but as near as possible I think we ought to help along the ideal of improving the relation between employer and employee by applying some psychology whether it's called Christian or not. As a matter of fact I don't believe it is because I think if your employees are not too feebleminded to grasp the point participation should be the spur to efficiency. However, I hate that word so much and hate the idea so much that I don't like to use it. However, I find I am rambling along on something that I didn't intend to discuss so guess I'll quit here.

To Smith Ely Jelliffe, New York, April 18, 1922

My dear Dr. Jelliffe:

I am anxious to ask a lot of technical questions. For example, do you find it advantageous to start your patients off at reading some elementary psychoanalytic matter first, or after you have gotten along pretty well with the analysis *or* never? I have about a score of such questions and so do a number of others who are in the same state of metamorphosis as myself and I wish we could think of some way to get you before a crowd of us either in person or in print and get some of these things straightened out. You are one of the few men who has frankly espoused Freud who does not have such a sense of inferiority that he shuts up like a clam and refuses to divulge any of the material which he has found to work so well. I could amaze you by a list of some of the western neuropsychiatrists of well-known organic leanings who manufacture a sort of psychoanalytic home brew and quaff it with a sparkle in the eye and a good deal of indigestion and hide the product under the shades of night and the university club mate's friendly and confidential ear! (mixed metaphor!)

I still insist that the most interesting psychiatric study would be an analysis of psychiatrists—myself and yourself included. Now that I have said that I think I recall your having made that remark to Ernest Southard once at a New York meeting.

When I come to New York you can rest assured that you will know it and one of the reasons for coming to New York is yourself. I shall never forget that at a time when my *Selbstverstandung* [self-understanding] was tenuous and my sense of inferiority very healthy indeed and my psychiatric acquaintanceship not very large you reached out with a very gracious and a very strong hand and gave me a pull which was a kindness that it would take a Herculean effort on anybody's part to equal. At a time when Southard's loss was so acute to me your bigness was an unforgettable thing.

Sincerely yours,

To SMITH ELY JELLIFFE, NEW YORK, NOVEMBER 25, 1922

My dear Doctor Jelliffe:

I want to tell you a secret and solicit your help. In fact I am going to tell you two secrets. One is that you have completely persuaded me, I frankly espouse Freudianism. I am going to tell you all about my conversion, which actually occurred nearly two years ago, when I come to New York next month. I am only hoping that you will not be too busy to let me see you a little while as you are one of the chief things I am going East to see.

My second secret is that I have been invited to review for a very orthodox journal some psychoanalytic material. Of course I want to present the best, the newest, the truest and the most important. You know that they who assigned me this job didn't know how big it was, but I have to do it anyway and I want to do it well. Nobody in this country could give me the right sort of pointers better than you. Therefore please write me what, and who, and where, and any admonishments that you will take time to give. Mind you I don't promise to take them, but I do promise to come and see you altho I must have this stuff in before I will get the opportunity.[1]

Sincerely yours,

To Henry Mitchell,[2] Warren, Pennsylvania, December 26, 1922

My dear Dr. Mitchell:

I am certainly a heck of a correspondent to write you so late as this. But I just had a fine letter from Dr. Brush.[3] It seems that he lost the letter that I wrote him long ago and therefore never answered it but we are gradually getting things straightened out now. I am not yet sure where my paper is but I presume he has it and if so with your permission, or I should say with your recommendation, I will revamp the thing and prepare it for the Detroit meeting. As I wrote Dr. Brush I have had scads of new ideas since then and I think I could write a better paper on another subject but I do think Southard's nosological theories ought to be developed for what they are worth and if we wait many more years they will be forgotten in the rush of things and perhaps be superseded by something much less valuable. Consequently I feel as if I perhaps should do as Brush suggests, revamp my paper as I told him and stand on my hind legs presuming to defend Southard against his friends (friends such as Orton for example). . . .

Our meeting of the Central Neuropsychiatric Association was a whiz bang. We had about forty or more there from all over this section and we had a marvelous clinic in neurological surgery. You will be happy to hear that the only criticism we received was that there was not enough psychiatry represented. Did you ever hear that kind of criticism of a neurological meeting before in your life? I tell you that the signs of the times are unmistakable and psychiatrists may be elected to the supreme council of the world's government yet.

You are foolish enough to take some personal interest in me so I shall bore you by telling you that I am having a splendiferous time always and that all is going well in all directions. I have two healthy children and a devoted wife and a new house and some fine college students and a blooming practice and excellent health and I am amusing myself by dabbling in a lot of things such as running a University Club, practicing criminology, studying psychoanalysis and discussing art and literature with my betters.

---

1 In his reply of December 2, 1922, Jelliffe lists a number of books, including James Jackson Putnam's *Addresses on Psychoanalysis* (1921), Oskar Pfister's *Psycho-analysis in the Service of Education* (1922), and Kempf's *Psychopathy*.

2 The president of the APA.

3 Edward N. Brush, a Baltimore psychiatrist and editor of the *American Journal of Psychiatry*, had read KAM's paper that was to be presented at a Detroit meeting of the APA. In it, KAM defended Southard's eleven-category nosology of mental disease.

Now that's how I spend the 365 days. How do you spend them? I am wondering if you took the job the government offered you and if you didn't why didn't you? Also I wonder if you went to the Research Association? My reason for not going is that I am coming East next month and if you will be home I will call on you and spend a day or so if you will treat me nice and perhaps I should add if you will let me in the door.

Sincerely,

To Lawson Lowrey, Dallas, Texas, April 23, 1923

Dear Lawson:

. . . This week the Public Health Association of the state is having a meeting in conjunction with the School for Health Officers. Mental Hygiene gets one day and I am enclosing a program gotten up by John Stone.[1] . . . I have put him in my office now and he is getting along famously. He is secretary of the Kansas Mental Hygiene Society and also business manager of this office. Besides that, he makes himself generally useful in various ways and is a great help to us all.

My present objective is to get every doctor in Kansas wholly imbued with the idea that neuropsychiatry and myself are for the present synonymous and build up around myself a machine for helping people that no one else pays much attention to or succeeds in helping very much. I don't remember whether I told you in my last letter that we got hold of a very fine young woman from Phipps Clinic,[2] Baltimore, a graduate nurse who spends her time developing the patients from a Meyerian standpoint, a sort of intramural social work, also occupational work, etc. We have also expanded in several other ways which I will let you see when you come.

I only mention all this because I want you to know a few personal details about myself, being as how you have told me so many about yourself. It sounds sort of pale to me beside the magnificent program that you are carrying on but I know we are both having a lot of fun. I envy quite a bit your opportunity for first-hand contact with the problems of delinquency, provided as you are with all the equipment for perusing the matter so much deeper than I can. I keep changing my point of view so much that I wish I could feel settled on a good many points that concern that whole problem, but I suppose that would take away a lot of the romance of it. I hope you have time for some scientific investigation of some things about delinquency that no one has ever done. For example, what is the relation between re-

1 John R. Stone, one of the original investors in the clinic, was its business manager. In 1930 he became a partner in the Menninger Clinic and Sanitarium. Over the next nineteen years he held various administrative posts with the foundation.

2 Frances Hoy, who returned from Phipps to become a nurse at the Menninger Sanitarium.

peated petty larceny and compulsion neurosis? Also, what is the relation between hysteria and prostitution? Also, in how far is morphine addiction a symbolic compulsion? Also, how can you increase inhibitions in regard to social offenses in people of defective intelligence? The corollary of this question is, what should be the objective of an institution for the feeble-minded? What physical or mental compensatory mechanism can be called upon to increase the value of the individual to society? Is every hypophrenic potentially an idiot savant?

I am more interested in psychoanalysis than ever, but I warmly recommend to you a book that I have always neglected because of its miserable title, *Morbid Fears and Compulsions* by Frink.[3] It is positively the best thing in psychoanalysis I have ever read. There have been several good popular books lately which you will find helpful to read to people, including your social workers. One is *Psychoanalysis and the Classroom* by Green,[4] and another is *The New Psychology and the Teacher* by H. C. Miller.[5] Don't fail to have them read Salisbury and Jackson's book, *Outwitting Our Nerves.*[6] It is an excellent sugar-coated presentation. This prompts me to tell you what I may have already told you, that I wrote up the psychoanalytic section of Bassoe's[7] yearbook and am writing a few reviews for the *Archives*.

I have been distressingly crowded for almost six months. First, because I was trying to get away for my trip to New York, and then because I had just been away. I have practically every hour engaged now for the next ten days, or a little longer in fact. Beginning the second week in May I am going to take one or two days a week and see no patients and simply do a little scientific work, writing, and so forth. Of course everyone is glad to have a lot to do, but it gets to be sort of an obsession, nagging at you all the time. I started this once before but gave it up when I went to New York.

Some of the interesting things I have seen lately are: a man who had had one testicle destroyed in childhood who had the hobby of collecting stones all his life and became a mineralogist, but his mine ventures were always a failure. Now he has developed a neurosis around the theme—"I am not

3 H. W. Frink, 1918. As early as 1911 Frink was reporting cures from psychoanalytic treatment at the Cornell University Dispensary. Frink was, with A. A. Brill and C. P. Oberndorf, a leader in the nascent New York Psychoanalytic Society. Despite this enthusiasm for Freudian theory, he was also influenced by and borrowed from behaviorism, especially in his explanation of transference.

4 George H. Green, *Psychanalysis in the Classroom [sic]* (1922).

5 H. Crichton Miller, *The New Psychology and the Teacher* (1922).

6 Helen M. Salisbury and Josephine A. Jackson, *Outwitting Our Nerves: A Primer of Psychotherapy* (1921).

7 Peter Bassoe, associate professor of nervous and mental diseases at Rush Medical College, had edited *Nervous and Mental Diseases* (1921), the last volume in an eight-volume series, *The Year's Progress in Medicine and Surgery,* under the general editorship of Charles L. Mix.

man enough to do so and so." He is a rather way-up man in [a local business]. Another thing is our old friend, Hypertrophic Muscular Dystrophy. I have seen about eight cases of epidemic encephalitis in the last three weeks including two bulbar palsys; a cerebello pontine angle tumor; [and] a brain abscess which I fortunately localized correctly, helped operate upon, stuck my finger in the abscess, and the man seems to be getting better.

This sounds again as if I were running off in a stream of stuff about my own work when I have actually much more interest in discussing your work. I tell you the best way to do it is for you to come up here to Topeka this summer and spend a few days with us. I say a few days because that's all I have the nerve to ask for, although I hope you can stay a few weeks. Of course you will bring Mrs. Lowrey with you. Give my love to Ella [Mrs. Lowrey] and assure her of our interest in the new little girl, in addition to Lawson [Jr.] and Ernest.

Sincerely,

To LAWSON LOWREY, DALLAS, TEXAS, JULY 30, 1923

Dear Lawson:

I do not know whether you will get this letter or not inasmuch as you are running to Galveston and where not, but I want you to know that Grace and I are very enthusiastic about your heralded arrival. We will look for you then about the tenth of September, and your wife and baby with you.

The plan of your work looks good to me and I think you are having marvelous opportunities and realize them.

I am so pleased with your letter that I am sending it to my friend R——[8] whom you very greatly resemble not only extrinsically but also in the relation you bear to me. I think R—— is getting along pretty well although I am not sure and I think I really ought to go to New York and find out. I can't afford to go, however, unless he and his relatives pay for it and they haven't volunteered to do that and I don't know exactly how to get them to do so.

All goes very well around here. You will be surprised to know that I have about five manuscripts more or less completed, some of which may see the light of day before long. I once asked Southard if the phenomenon of a private practitioner indulging in research was known to psychiatry and he recalled first of all Weir Mitchell.[9] You see I have worthy footsteps in which to follow.

8 A Topeka banker and fellow member of the Naked But Unashamed Club, an all-male Topeka social club. At R——'s expense he and KAM traveled to New York, where R—— was briefly analyzed by and became friendly with Smith Ely Jelliffe.

9 Weir Mitchell (1829–1914) was the most prominent neurologist of his day. This Philadelphia doctor devised and advocated a rest cure for nervous diseases. He wrote several popular novels (e.g., *Hugh Wynne, Free Quaker* [1899]; *Dr. North and His Friends* [1900]) utilizing a psychological approach.

There are once more faint echoes of the sanitarium question. A very wonderful opportunity here in the way of a house and grounds falteringly presents itself. I don't know yet how I shall deal with it. . . .

Hopefully thine,

TO SMITH ELY JELLIFFE, NEW YORK, FEBRUARY 15, 1924

My dear Doctor Jelliffe:

Much has happened of late, although the most expected thing has not happened which is the birth of my coming heir which is somewhat overdue and has given us some suspense. Mrs. Menninger is relatively comfortable, however, and there are no adverse indications. Anyway this explains one reason why I haven't written.

In addition I have had a tremendous amount of work, fortunately or otherwise, some of which has been very interesting indeed. Some of my psychoanalytic patients have interested me more than anything I have ever met and I should like to tell you about them. I won't, however, because it would take too much time, except one fellow who had had a psychotic episode lasting only a few weeks at the age of sixteen in which he expressed a belief, for reasons which he would not assign, that he should be castrated; subsequently he always denied having any idea why he should have had such a theory. Anyway he went on and became the most sexually promiscuous man I have ever met or even heard of. In the course of a few years he met, with or without any courtship, and had sex relations with over two hundred women. Curiously enough, or rather characteristically enough, he was not at all particular, and as he himself said he was not adverse to Negresses or chambermaids if other opportunities failed. He married an attractive and talented woman who shortly died. Once more he began running around over the country drinking heavily and having many affairs. Suddenly he broke out into an acute, severe psychasthenic state of agitation and depression, with many disturbing fantasies. One of the things which disturbed him most was an incident with his father in which they had quarreled and he had thrown a bottle at his father, striking but not injuring him. He was greatly concerned for fear this might have killed his father and he was equally concerned over an episode in his drinking career which symbolically reproduced this father murder. There are many exceedingly interesting points about the case and I scarcely know what to say or what to leave unsaid in this brief summary. Among other things he was one of those people with an encyclopedic memory who could tell you the date of most anything from the birth of Schiller to the first performance of some actress in New York.

He also had a lot of fantasies about a jinx or evil spirit which was his unseen and unknown enemy, and he would have dreams about slaying the dragon or the crocodile or whatever particular form he chanced to clothe his father in. He had an amazing array of color symbols and his dreams were always exceedingly complex with various synesthesias.

Well, the point of all this is that he really never identified or understood anything of it. Of all the resistant, fighting, tell-the-world-I'm-sick individuals I ever met, he was certainly the king. Withal he was one of the most agreeable and interesting chaps imaginable. Unfortunately the case was terminated by the father coming to town and deciding the boy was no better and taking him home.

Is it true that the more obvious the symbolical situation, the greater resistance the patient is likely to develop in seeing it? This lad certainly ought to have recognized without much difficulty the fact that one of his chief struggles was whether to sacrifice his penis and be like his mother or to possess all the women in the world in the hopes of finding her. When Woodrow Wilson died he was much disturbed in his dreams, but in spite of this and all the other symbols of his father's death he never did really see it, nor when, as a last resort I intimated that I knew he did see it, did he show anything but intense antagonism to the idea. I suppose it was merely a matter of time but he was here three months and while I learned a lot about him and psychoanalysis I don't think he got anywhere. . . .

Next Mrs. B——. She was really the first case upon whom I undertook a definite psychoanalytic study. I made many mistakes, one of which was that I went to see her at the hospital instead of making her come to see me at the office. Another was that I tried to defend her from a fiendish mother when I think I should have allowed her to persecute her instead of persecuting me. In the third place I let her return home for awhile because she was so much better and I should have insisted upon her staying here until she was independent or at least I should have so advised and told her it was up to her. I probably made other mistakes, too, but these are some of them. In spite of this, however, I got a great deal of information about her and the thing I remember most vividly is that she was the first woman patient who told me, without any prompting because I thought I knew nothing of it, of a castration complex in almost textbook words. As I remember she said something like this: "I remember masturbating and I associated the idea of cutting, blood and penis. Couldn't I have had a childish theory that as a punishment I had my penis cut off, leaving this wound (vulva), and maybe that's why I feel so badly every month when I bleed from this wound."

Anyway she did discover it and a whole lot of other things, one of which was her tremendous interest in feces. As you have no doubt found, she has an aversion for brown foods of all kinds and she has, or at least did have, frank fecal dreams.

Her husband is a peach and I am glad they came to you. I had her read your book, *The Drama*, and a number of other things on psychoanalysis. I told her about you when she was under my care but it has been a year or two since . . . and I have been wondering how she escaped her tyrannical mother and how she remembered to come to you. Didn't someone else give her a shove in the same direction, or did she give me any credit for it? She is a sweet girl and comes of a good family of the old New England type.

I thought I had done her some good; she seemed a great deal better and her husband was apparently delighted and promised me that he would consummate marriage immediately. *She,* likewise, expressed a desire for intercourse and I thought that had all been settled. Of course, as I say, she slipped away from me and I didn't know. She is a great girl to hold down the bed and call for the heart specialists, the skin specialists, superintendent of nurses and everybody else. Anyway I am exceedingly interested and you must tell me more about her progress. . . .[1]

Sincerely yours,

FROM SMITH ELY JELLIFFE, NEW YORK, MARCH 13, 1924

My dear Menninger:

I am sorry I shall have to answer your last rather shortly as I am really up against it for time. I have only had about three hours in the last two or three months when I could dictate a letter. It was very good of you to write me such a long one.

I should like very much to be able to discuss the history of the patient which you sent me, especially his terrific insistence on chasing the women. There is no doubt about the encyclopedic memory being an anal-erotic factor and that the homosexual retreat was the cause of the heterosexual urge. . . .

Mrs. B—— is by no means easy. She is one of those compulsion neuroses which have a tendency to either develop a psychosis of the depressed type or sometimes break into a catatonic. She could not remember having told you about the castration complex as you reported to me, but she certainly is full of material. As yet no consummation has taken place and her fear of people being poisoned by glass and other things is very pressing. She made a suicidal attempt about ten days ago—luminal and veronal—and got about three days' sleep. At any rate she has come out of it with apparently a defi-

1 The letter concludes with Menninger's recounting of three particularly vivid dreams: "climbing a long hill westward with some man, with a sense of pervading thrill; "playing a duet on the piano with some man"; "I dreamed of medical school . . . with complicated arrangements as to schedule, rooms and the like, my only clear recollection being that I was somewhat apprehensive that the teachers would think my grades were deliberately sought." He added: "The darned thing doesn't need much interpretation because it is all according to Hoyle and for this reason perhaps it deserves a whole lot of interpretation."

nite change in the conscious attitude. Whereas heretofore she has not wanted to get well, she has for the first time said that she does want to get well. The insomnia is fierce and she has a number of somatic mild catatonic signs. Her husband certainly is a peach but she has him almost dead.

As to your own dream I will have to take that up some other time. . . .

With cordial regards and best wishes, believe me,

Sincerely yours,

To SMITH ELY JELLIFFE, NEW YORK, MARCH 17, 1924

Dear Doctor Jelliffe:

I appreciate your letter of March 13th the more in view of the fact that you have been so crowded. Nevertheless I am going to write again about certain matters which I want to get cleared up even before I see you, as I shall in June. This is by way of harbinger that Mrs. Menninger and I hope to spend the first few days of June in New York City.

The first question is the one made on page 2 of my previous letter as to whether there is any relation between the obviousness of the symbols and the intensity of the repression on the part of the patient. The old maid, for example, is usually the last one to see what the most naive of the general public can see in regard to her fear of snakes and of a man under the bed. I have repeatedly observed patients to be obsessed by a fear of killing a parent or something of the sort thinly disguised, with a tremendous repression, which is not nearly so great in those who come upon it by chance, as it were, in the course of dream analysis. . . .

Your psychoanalytic restraint in making no comment upon my dream until I get there has, of course, whetted my appetite and increased my admiration for your technique. I can't help but laugh to myself at the (I assure you unconscious or at least inadvertent) attempt on my part to prevail upon my psychoanalyst by stealth. The fact that it amuses me so much as it seems to this moment is that I should have been so blind as to the obvious indirection of it is a sort of a mild abreaction.

Sincerely yours,

FROM LAWSON LOWREY, MINNEAPOLIS, MAY 6, 1924

Dear Karl:—

. . . For nearly three months I have been wondering a great deal what has happened to you to produce the general air of submission and gentleness, which has been so definite in your letters, and to some extent, it seems to me, in your writing. Your letter leaves me even more puzzled. I don't know whether it is because you feel so desperately poor or whether it is that your narcissistic complex has been overwhelming you a bit. At any rate, I like the restrained air, which so well characterizes you at the present time, but I dread the notion that it might go too far. . . .

Yours

To William C. Menninger, New York, September 3, 1924

Dear Bill:

I read your interesting letters each week but don't write as often as I ought to. We have had a very interesting summer up here but not as interesting as yours, I know. You are having fine work and enjoy it, I can see, very much. I am sure you will enjoy medicine more than surgery, for while it is somewhat less spectacular and exciting it requires much more head work. Get all you can out of your surgery, however, as whether you go into surgery or not it gives you a great deal of help in understanding the surgical implications of a medical case.

I am getting more and more interested in a particular phase of psychiatry which we are calling orthopsychiatry and which concerns itself with conduct disorder. Of course most psychiatric cases show more or less conduct disorder, but antisocial conduct disorder at various times is apt to precipitate a crisis in a patient's life and there is an increasing tendency on the part of the public to turn to the doctors and particularly the psychiatrists. We are studying several cases right now which have been referred to us by the chief of police of Topeka and we have under our care cases from Denver, Iowa, Chicago, Kansas City, and tomorrow afternoon we are getting one from Minneapolis. These in Topeka have done all sorts of things from forging checks to exhibiting their genitals. The one from Denver stole automobiles after having graduated almost at the head of his class at the university. The one from Kansas City lies and steals although neither are necessary, and the one from Minneapolis is said to have assaulted a teacher among other things.

The present tendency is to try to keep these people out of institutions if there is any hope for them, or put them into the right kind of institutions if that is the best treatment. A good deal can be done out of the institution. Sometimes of course it is done without the aid of a psychiatrist, but we think we can do it a great deal more expeditiously. . . .

Our three children are well and happy.[2] Bobby grows quite conspicuously. Just at present he is having a phase of shouting NO to everything that is said to him. He knows what it means although he may not know what the question means. He arches his neck and holds his head stiff, bats his eyes and shouts NO with great emphasis. He can also say quite a few other little things and is very amusing in his play. He runs trains of one kind

2 KAM's three children from his first marriage are Julia (b. 1919), Robert (b. 1922), and Martha (b. 1924).

and another all over the house. Last night he was choo-chooing around and I thought I would help out in the railroading and did some choo-chooing on my own account. But this seemed to be strictly forbidden and he would jump up and shout NO at the top of his voice and come over and spank me and then go back to run the train a little further. This was repeated four hundred and seventeen times without change. He is much trouble to his mother by persisting in taking a sitz bath in the crow's dishpan. When he gets up with his little pants sticking to him like rubber and dripping all over everything, he is much pleased by the effort. The crow is one that strolled up on our front yard not long ago with a wing clipped and we have kept him since in spite of a variety of decorations deposited on the front steps and elsewhere.

Sincerely yours,

To Abraham Myerson,[3] Boston, September 24, 1924

My dear Abe:

I shall look forward eagerly to your new book on heredity. I like the title.[4] I read carefully your paper before the Boston Society. I am glad somebody with authority is at last going to say something we can refer to and you can rest assured that several copies of your book are already sold as I am teaching several hundred students at Washburn College.

Mrs. Menninger was glad you remembered her. We have three children now who have not so far developed dementia precox or endocrinopathy.

. . .

What would you think if I burst forth with a book on failures, from the standpoint of personality defects, and so forth? You see I still have a strong transference to you of the so-called father identification and I come now for advice.

By the way, you are dead wrong on psychoanalysis unless you have changed your mind since your personality book. I long since changed mine and so will you if you get a correct understanding of it. I blush to think how often I damned it with incorrect quotations and the like. You ought to take a hint from the fact that all the neurologists past sixty are opposed to it whereas most of the psychiatrists under forty are for it.

Sincerely yours,

3 Abraham Myerson came to America from Russia in 1882 and received his M.D. degree from Tufts in 1908. Except for a year's residency in neurology in St. Louis, he spent his entire life in Boston, where he was affiliated with a number of hospitals. Myerson and Menninger were longtime friends, though Myerson's antipathy toward psychoanalysis caused friction between them.

4 *The Inheritance of Mental Diseases* (1925).

To William C. Menninger, New York, September 24, 1924

Dear Bill:

Before we use much of this stationery, which just came from the press, and which was only decided upon after about ten proofs and much discussion and argument, we want to show it to you and get your permission to use your name as shown.

The way of it is this. Father and I have felt for some time that we ought to try to educate the doctors and people to the fact that neuropsychiatry, as now conceived (and practiced by us), is a difficult, complicated branch of medicine which requires the interaction of a number of persons expert in various phases of the subject. We have been materially helped in formulating our plans by the fact that the National Committee for Mental Hygiene has sent so-called psychiatric clinics over the country and the old plan of Southard has been more or less universally adopted, namely, the grouping together of a psychiatrist, a psychologist, and a social worker, which we have elaborated a little bit, thus. We have pushed out the medical and neurological and endocrinological ends with the assistance of Father and Mildred[5] and cut down on the field work (social worker), substituting for it physiotherapy and psychotherapy, which Miss Lindquist[6] and John [Stone] and I do.

Our work has evolved so that practically speaking what happens is that people come in here for the same sort of group clinical study that they go to the Mayos for except that we attract a little different type of case which is practically what we want to do. We are advertising by sending reprints to four thousand doctors in New Mexico, Texas, Oklahoma, Kansas and Nebraska and we are prepared for their patients when (and as) they come. In the first place, we have taken on additional rooms here so that we now have ten rooms. We have put in a fine X-ray outfit and have ordered a high-frequency outfit which will provide us with the diathermy, and so forth. We have sent John [Stone] away to get special psychological training and will probably send him away for more yet. We are considering now employing a business manager because John's time will be pretty well taken up with psychology. We have drawn up the articles of incorporation for a sanitarium company which we will practically control and in which all the employees [will] have stock as well as Father and me. . . .

Thus you see we are trying on the one hand to provide the facilities for

5 Mildred Law joined the Menninger Clinic as an X-ray technician in 1921; however, from the beginning of her employment she worked intimately with CFM, WCM, and KAM as an administrator. She became clinical director and then planning director for the C. F. Menninger Memorial Hosptial. In 1942, she was elected to the Board of Directors of the Menninger Sanitarium, and in 1944 she became a member of the executive committee of the clinic. She retired in 1965.

6 Ingeborg Lindquist, masseuse and physiotherapist.

the best possible study and treatment of certain types of patients and on the other hand to get it spread abroad that we have such facilities so that the people who need them will know where to come or be sent.

What are the types of trouble that we feel best qualified to handle? They are all the diseases which might be roughly classified as neuropsychiatry if the endocrine system be understood as included. Where we are particularly strong here is in the study of conduct disorders, personality defects, and so forth, because there is practically no one west of Chicago that does this work at all. We are getting cases from Minneapolis, Denver, Chicago and the Far West although not as many as we will get as soon as I put out some advertising on the subject. As I wrote Harry Bone[7] recently to kid him, he may behold in us the anti-Christ if he likes, who comes to compete with the Y.M.C.A. and other organizations already extant in saving the sinners, although of course we do not take the attitude that they are sinners. Wayward, if you please. In addition, of course, there are all the more obvious somatic things that come in the field of neurology and endocrinology—diabetes, tabes, goiter, neuritis, tumors, and so forth. But there are many men who do these latter things well and so the thing for us to develop is that which the mental hygiene movement is making increasingly possible, namely, the study and scientific treatment of conduct disorders. . . .

We need at least three doctors and ultimately we will, of course, have to have more. For the time being at least we want to think of you as belonging to the group. You really are doing some work for us that has helped us a great deal and I think it is more than possible that you will come back to be with us a little while before or after you go abroad.

This leads me to say that the whole matter of your going as a foreign missionary is a sort of taboo subject because it is a project which is an expression of a religious conviction and we all recognize the right of everyone to have his own religious convictions. I feel particularly reticent about the matter because I once felt exactly as you do and laid my failure to realize my plans on other circumstances and other people, but as I look back on it I think that was merely an excuse; I think I was already realizing that I did not really want to do it enough. There is much I could say by way of explaining my present opinion and by way of advice to you, but all I will say is that I certainly adjure and exhort you to do *whatever appeals most to you*. I think the so-called sense of duty is usually a fake—an excuse for putting ourselves through a painful process and hoaxing ourselves by saying we don't like it but feel we should, when really we want to suffer. . . .

Sincerely,

7 A friend of KAM at Washburn, Bone received his doctorate in psychology from the University of Paris. Bone cofounded the Psychological Center of Paris and later practiced in New York.

To David Levy,[8] Zurich, October 6, 1924

Dear Dave:

It was a great joy to have your letter of two weeks ago which was received this morning. . . .

I am immensely interested to hear that you have gotten six weeks of analysis already and are going to stick it out. Oberholzer[9] is fine—far better than Jung.[10] You will doubtless get in touch with Jung for a chat or lecture or something and that will probably be enough. I feel that his stuff is so ethereal and vague as to be of little value practically.

I was very interested indeed also to hear about the other men you are working with and I wish you would write me more about it all. I admire your capacity for studying neuropathology. As far as I am concerned it is work for my next existence possibly but certainly not this one. I think it should be done just as I think there should be electricians and lawyers, but I think it is a long way from the study of personality. Most of this is a defense reaction because I am so stupid in it.

I am having John Stone, the lad who has been associated with me for four years and who has quite a native psychological genius, go to Chicago and work with Adler[11] for a few months and pursue a psychoanalysis with Blitzsten.[12] I want him to improve his technique. He has been doing a little analy-

8 From 1923 to 1926, Levy was attending neurologist and director of the Mental Hygiene Clinic for Children at Michael Reese Hospital, Chicago. In 1927, he cofounded (with Lawson Lowrey) the New York Institute for Child Guidance. He was a lecturer at the New York School of Social Research from 1928 to 1939 and an instructor in the New York Psychoanalytic Institute from 1936 to 1941. From 1935, he practiced privately in New York City, and in 1945 he became attending psychoanalyst of the Psychoanalytic Clinic for Training and Research.

9 Emil Oberholzer was cofounder (with Oskar Pfister) and first president of the Swiss Society for Psychoanalysis (1919), a group which admitted lay members. Later Oberholzer turned against the admission of lay analysts and abandoned this society in order to establish the Swiss Medical Society for Psychoanalysis, which restricted membership to physicians. This society eventually disintegrated when many of its members returned to the Swiss Society for Psychoanalysis.

10 In a letter of September 20, 1924, Levy had written of his plans to be analyzed by Oberholzer rather than Jung, saying that he preferred to be analyzed by a Freudian and adding, "So far I should say that a psychiatrist should go through it—and with a medical analyst."

11 Herman M. Adler, a Chicago psychiatrist, was professor of criminology and head of the social hygiene, medical jurisprudence, and criminology department at the University of Illinois Medical College. Before moving to Chicago, Adler was assistant professor of psychiatry at the Harvard Medical School and chief of staff at Boston Psychopathic Hospital.

12 An emigrant from Russia in his youth, Lionel Blitzsten grew up in Chicago and became one of the first psychoanalysts in that city (where he established a private prac-

sis here . . . under my supervision and doing it quite well, but I thought he should have the experience. If you think this is advisable, knowing Blitzsten as you do, I wish you would write me in detail immediately and I will promise to destroy your letter or keep it inviolate, as you wish.

Nothing exciting has happened over here . . . except that Washington beat the Giants yesterday.

I am enclosing a few splurges [articles] of mine in the local *Mental Hygiene Society*. If you will write a longer letter, I will reciprocate.

Sincerely yours,

To WILLIAM ALANSON WHITE, WASHINGTON, D.C., FEBRUARY 4, 1925

My dear Doctor White:

Your letter of January 31st is of such immediate importance that I am rising up from my sick bed—literally—to dictate a short reply.

I feel exceedingly honored by your request that I serve as chairman of the medico-legal committee [of the American Psychiatric Association] and I accept with the assurance that I shall do everything possible to produce something of a progressive, forward-like sort to report at the Richmond meeting.

With your permission, I shall think over very carefully the names of the persons you suggest and possibly a few others for membership on the committee and send you a memorandum in a few days.

It has occurred to me that the first thing to do, as soon as you have appointed the committee, would be for me to get out a letter to all of them and ask for their view of the situation, their ideas of the best thing for the American Psychiatric Association to do as a body, etc. My head is too hot to do much thinking this afternoon, but I will get up some sort of a letter and get it out as soon as I have your official list of membership.

In the meantime won't you give me your own personal feelings as to what the American Psychiatric Association *could* do and what it *should* do in this regard. My own spontaneous feeling is that we should do something to impress the lawyers with the fact that we are interested in amelioration rather than justice and in facts rather than evidence, but the question is, How can we get this across tactfully and expeditiously?

In the second place I want to explain the reason for my failure to turn up in Washington to see you as I had planned and promised. A few nights after you left New York, when we had that memorable chat in Dr. Jelliffe's office, I had a telegram in regard to the daughter[1] concerning whom you will re-

---

tice), as well as a founding member of the Chicago Psychoanalytic Society and Institute and the first president of the Society.

1 KAM's daughter Julia had had a mastoid operation.

member we had a phone call that night. They asked me to take the next train home and I did so, not in time, however, to be present at the mastoid operation, from which she has gradually recovered. I found that my wife was ill in bed and my two other children also, and my stenographer and clinic manager were both in bed, the former in the hospital, and after I had run around getting odds and ends together and awaiting Nature to exhibit her vismedicatrix, I got the flu myself and was in bed nearly a week and really don't seem to have recovered since as I have been back in bed now for four days more. The disappointment of being unable to visit you and other plans I had made in the East was partially countered by the gratification over my daughter's recovery, but things have not been very cheerful.

All of this pales into insignificance in comparison with the terrible catastrophe that Dr. Jelliffe, and all those who love him, have experienced in the death of Leeming.[2] . . . You probably went to New York, and when you have time I wish you would tell me how Dr. Jelliffe is weathering the night. I don't see how it can help but take the morale and spirit out of him forever, but I am certainly hoping that something will avert this.

Sincerely yours,

FROM WILLIAM ALANSON WHITE, WASHINGTON, D.C., FEBRUARY 7, 1925

My dear Dr. Menninger:

. . . You ask me what the [American Psychiatric] Association can do or what it should do in this particular. Of course I suppose that is what the Committee is for—to find out. I am very doubtful myself. Inasmuch as the Committee [on Legal Aspects of Psychiatry], however, has been authorized I suppose it ought to try to carry out some kind of a program in response to the feeling that brought it into existence. It would seem, in the first place, . . . with all the hue and cry about expert testimony and allied subjects, that a representative association such as ours could not remain absolutely silent without taking any position whatever or at least without even considering matters of such importance, and so perhaps the most important thing is to have a committee which at least will be in existence and can function like similar committees from other organizations, for example the bar associations, in contact with us as they may readily do. It would seem rather strange if they had such a desire and could not find any way of making such contact.

As you know, I have some fairly definite opinions about this whole matter and I think you know pretty generally what they are. I feel that your Committee should, as far as possible, develop a constructive rather than a destructive program. I do not think, in other words, that there is much use in

2 William Leeming Jelliffe, Smith Ely Jelliffe's youngest son, died of a self-inflicted gunshot wound; the death was ruled accidental.

ranting against an institution with as extensive an historical background as the criminal court. The practical method of procedure, I think, would be to build up such agencies as the juvenile court as are conceived in something like the spirit of our own thoughts. In other words, instead of trying to beat down the criminal court, which I think would be a perfectly useless effort, I would support the institutions that are growing up more in the spirit of the times, such as the juvenile court.

Another thing which should be emphasized I believe is the necessity for getting into court with an adequate psychiatric study of the case. To this end medical men might, though very probably they won't, resist efforts to get them to testify which do not include placing every opportunity before them to become acquainted with the personality of the defendant. In general this proposition might be reduced to saying that it constitutes a tendency to discourage the hypothetical question.

I have been very much impressed with the arguments that I have seen here and there for and against capital punishment that have been published since the Chicago case [Leopold and Loeb] and it is perfectly obvious to my mind that these arguments, pro and con, are dictated, almost one hundred percent, by the temperament of the individuals, certain types of temperament being constitutionally for and certain types constitutionally against capital punishment, and in each case the argument is but a rationalization to support the emotional attitude. Our Committee might, I should think, divest itself of at least the crudities of such an attitude and undertake to investigate and present the facts. For example, I have seen it somewhere stated, and I have not the slightest idea that there is not the slightest suspicion of what I believe to be a fact, namely that crime is essentially a manifestation of the adolescent period of life and that the largest number of criminals who are charged with capital offenses are mere youths. I have in fact read a statement recently that 75 percent of the prisoners going to Sing Sing Prison are under 21 years of age. You see how much strength this lends to my position of building up the juvenile court, which is constructed more nearly in line with our own ideas of enlarging its field of operation, by extending its age limits. Doing this would automatically withdraw from the operation of the old, antiquated, worn-out and largely useless system the material with which it can no longer deal adequately. These are my suggestions.

Poor Jelliffe was hit pretty hard. I went right up to New York and brought him back to Washington with me. I spent several days with him and tried what I could to soften the blow, but at best of course it was pretty bad. He will come back all right in time, but it isn't going to be an easy matter by any means. . . .

Let me add one thing: In making up committees I think it is always a good plan, as a matter of showing your good feelings, etc., to include a member from Canada. There is at least one member who has had a good deal of medico-legal experience, but I am sorry I cannot think of his name. The principles the association needs to stand for are not such that differences in law in the two countries would separate the members materially, it seems to me.

Very sincerely yours,

To the Committee on Legal Aspects of Psychiatry, Washington, D.C., March 10, 1925

My dear Doctor[s:]

As the committee appointed by President [William Alanson] White "to study and investigate the legal aspects of psychiatry with special reference to difficulties arising in the field of psychiatric expert testimony, and to report to the [American Psychiatric] Association," we have before us a rather complicated task. We have not only the theoretical and philosophical aspects of medicine and law to harmonize, but we have the necessity of proposing and recommending a practical scientific solution and a possible medico-legal compromise. We must determine, as the chairman sees it, first of all, what *should* be done. We must in the second place decide as a matter of pragmatism what *can be* done by this particular committee. In the third place we must determine which of these possibilities we will follow up: i. e., what this committee *shall* do. It is our task to weigh the *issues* involved and try to formulate specifications; it is also ours to discover and suggest the *avenues* for a remedy of the present unsatisfactory situation and to recommend such steps to our association as would appear to be most practical in beginning the reformation.

There is probably no dispute but that the present medico-legal situation is unhappy and no member of the medical profession is more concerned in this than the psychiatrist. Not only is the psychiatrist brought conspicuously into disrespect and distrust because of the spectacular nature of the cases in which he testifies, but the changing conception of psychiatry into that of a medical social science has greatly increased his importance in the courtroom. It has brought what was formerly a matter of ignorance into what is a matter of polemics. In a day and age when no less a person than Lord Chancellor Haldane[3] can give as his opinion that he "does not know any more vague science than psychology is at the present and thinks that it is a most dangerous science when applied to practical affairs," it is time for the

3 Richard Burton Haldane was a British statesman and lawyer, lord chancellor from 1912 to 1915 and again for nine months during 1924. He was cotranslator of a three-volume edition of Schopenhauer's *The World as Will and Idea* (1883–86), as well as author of five books of philosophy.

psychiatrists as a body to rise to a correction of such evils in the system as should permit of such misunderstanding of its function and purpose.

The chairman of the committee feels that it will not be in keeping with the spirit of science to limit the consideration of this committee to any single point in the problem such as was suggested in the original motion, any more than it would be possible to scientifically discuss with pragmatic advantage any one symptom of a disease entity. The problem must be considered as a whole. It seems to divide itself into certain legal changes or reformations which we feel are presently imperative, certain scientific projects which must be undertaken before we can speak with as much authority as we would like, and the problem of propaganda and education of the public and the legal and medical professions.

I. *In re:* Specific Legal Amendments. 1. In regard to the laws and legal opinions regarding criminal responsibility. A criminal responsibility bill has been proposed which has certain pros and cons (see White's book, p. 142).[4] 2. Laws in regard to expert testimony. Suggestions have also been made here (see White, page 143). 3. The chairman feels that a very determined effort should be made by this organization to unify and harmonize the commitment laws in the various states.[5]

In order to effect these changes, which are now impossible in most states because of legal barriers and public misinformation and professional ignorance, it seems highly advisable to the chairman that we first agree among ourselves as to what is most desirable and then that we consider the calling of a special joint meeting of a committee from this organization and a committee from the national bar association and any other representative bodies who are in a position to come to definite conclusions and take definite steps in regard to the needed requirements. Members of this committee should not fail to acquaint themselves with the Massachusetts law[6] recently passed through the agency of our fellow-member, Dr. Briggs.[7]

II. *In re:* Scientific Research in Criminology and Penology. As for scientific projects, it would seem that the American Psychiatric Association ought perhaps to include in its program for research the collection of reliable sta-

4 *Insanity and the Criminal Law* (1923).

5 Menninger's footnote here reads: "It is a determining corollary that the conception of 'insanity' should be unanimously relegated to legal definition and legal usage, and that all medical use thereof be abolished. Insofar as it means commitment, there should be unanimous criteria determined by the statutes for use in civil and probate procedure only."

6 The Massachusetts law was "the first piece of legislation making the mental examination of those indicted for a capital offense (or those known to have been indicted for any other offense more than once, or to have been previously convicted of a felony) a *routine procedure,* not dependent upon the alertness, knowledge, opinion, or caprice of those in charge of the accused" (Sheldon Glueck, *Mental Disorder and the Criminal Law: A Study in Medico-Sociological Jurisprudence* [1925], 55–56).

7 L. Vernon Briggs of Boston.

tistics in regard to certain psychiatric aspects of crime. To some extent this has already been undertaken by the National Committee for Mental Hygiene, but there is reason to believe there is plenty of material for this body to assist in correlating.

Also a penological technique should certainly be considered by the American Psychiatric Association. So far as the chairman is able to discover, the very remarkable psychiatric operations in such representative prisons as Joliet and Sing Sing have never been adequately presented at a meeting of the American Psychiatric Association and it is more than possible that the majority of our members are largely ignorant of the psychiatric procedure that is already in vogue at some of these better prisons.

III. *In re:* Propaganda & Education. Most important of all, in the chairman's opinion, is the development of a definite philosophical attitude and an informative educational campaign concerning the psychiatrist's medico-legal situation. The American Psychiatric Association has been exceedingly conservative in its self-expression. It will be felt by some that the majority of propaganda is the duty of the National Committee for Mental Hygiene rather than of the American Psychiatric Association. Nevertheless the former can scarcely be expected to take any direct steps to eradicate the opinion held by the public of the expert, and particularly of the psychiatrist, which has been so widespread and which seems to increase rather than decrease. This organization might do something to promote the study of criminology in the law schools to be taught by a competent psychiatrist. It could also give a somewhat more definite support to the juvenile court. It could very definitely and vociferously emphasize the total disinterest of the scientist in matters of punishment, responsibility and justice (a scientist is, of course, interested in none of these but merely in the problem of amelioration, social and individual). A scientist collects certain facts (not "evidence"!) and upon these facts attempts to establish a diagnosis, prognosis and a line of treatment. This treatment may or may not mean confinement, but it certainly never means punishment; it certainly never concerns itself with "justice" and it is totally innocent of sophistry about "responsibility." This point of view should be gotten across to the laity, to the legal profession and to the medical profession; and certainly every member of our organization should be so imbued with this gospel that it would never again be possible to put the psychiatrist in the unholy light of a medieval argument between two lawyers about someone's "responsibility" or someone's "punishment" or someone's "insanity."

It is not the duty of this committee to consider the prevention of crime; this is a task for the Committee on the Prevention of Juvenile Delinquency and similar organizations. It is not its task to consider the treatment of the misbehaved, as is essayed by the American Orthopsychiatric Association. It is our task to consider the general medico-legal situation in the United States from a psychiatric standpoint and offer suggestions for its amelioration. If we do no more than summarize the problem and so report, we shall have made a start. (In some instances we can probably do more.)

The chairman does not wish to foist his personal opinions on any member of the committee nor flatters himself that this were possible. For the purpose of discussion he has outlined the problems as they have appeared to him upon relatively hasty reflection. As you know, the committee was only appointed recently and the time has been very short. It will be necessary for every member of the committee to act immediately.

You will find attached a questionnaire with page headings which are, by reference to the contents of this letter, more or less self-explanatory. Will you, as a member of this committee, kindly set forth on the respective pages with as much more paper as you wish to add, your views on the various topics?

The chairman will then attempt to correlate the various opinions and with the assistance of members of the committee formulate a report based on all the replies, and before this report is submitted to the association it will be returned to you for a correction of your contribution, and any further notes you may wish to make.

Sincerely yours,

P.S. This letter and questionnaire are being sent to a number of men over the country who, although not officially members of this committee, are recognized authorities in this field. The committee will appreciate it if they will cooperate with us by participating in this discussion.

To WILLIAM ALANSON WHITE, WASHINGTON, D.C., MARCH 11, 1925

Dear Doctor White:

I have gotten to work on this medico-legal committee to which you appointed me and I am about to spring the trap. I have drawn up a statement of the situation as it appeared to me, trying to be as noncommittal and as judicial as possible, and have followed it with a skeleton questionnaire. I want to have a few of these multigraphed and sent to all members of the committee. I have tried to word it in such a way so as to stimulate some valuable replies. I will also, as you suggest, send the questionnaire to numerous other people who might contribute something of advantage to the discussion, including the original list of people which you sent me some weeks ago.

I have not yet had it set up to multigraph because I want you to go over it carefully and make any amendments and corrections, curtailments or enlargements, which you think would help the cause or the clarity.

I know you are busy but I know how much stock you put in this work and I want to leave nothing undone to do a good job of it.

Sincerely yours,

To WILLIAM ALANSON WHITE, WASHINGTON, D.C., MARCH 27, 1925

Dear Doctor White:

First, let me acknowledge the return of the questionnaire, and your kind complimentary letter.

Secondly, let me tell you of my great interest in your article on the "Significance of Psychopathology" in the March number of the *Journal [of Nervous and Mental Disease]*. I have read it very carefully and I think it is a very important contribution because it more or less boldly champions in round, philosophical terms a point of view which up until this time has been rather falteringly advanced by a few scientific pioneers.

There are a number of questions I should like to ask if I thought you had time to answer all of them, but perhaps I should defer them until I get to see you. I think you know how thoroughly I am convinced of your farsightedness and the correctness of your vision and so you will not take offense if I say that I think you leave some points unclear; for example, I don't feel quite satisfied with the explanation that "mental reactions are total reactions." It must occur to a reader to wonder what has been totaled. Of course you say in various places that you refer to the reactions of the individual as a whole and therefore "total" must mean all his reactions. Now I can visualize this even to the extent of regarding a knee-jerk or an inflammatory reaction as being part of what is meant by "mental," but I think it is a little confusing to insist upon using the word in just that way. The pseudo-problem which you refer[8] to has been with us a long time and even those of us who grant that it is the earth that moves and not the sun, still go on speaking of the sun rising and setting. In the same way don't you think it might be more easily understood if you would elaborate this a little bit more and explain just what that sentence means?

I hope you won't think that I am so stupid as not to see that your whole article is in a sense an explanation of it, but I still think that explanation is much less clear than, for example, the explanation on page 263—"that the fine pattern of the psyche is backgrounded by a specific pattern of somatic structure and energic investure." The latter sounds more complicated but is actually more clear to me.

8 White had written, "the discussion of the relations of mind and body implies a separation which does not in fact exist and . . . therefore the body-mind problem is not a real problem at all but, as I prefer to call it, a pseudo-problem" ("The Significance of Psychopathology for Somatic Medicine," *Journal of Nervous and Mental Disease* 61, [March 1925]: 246).

At the American Psychiatric Association I am to present some more influenza studies this year in regard to schizophrenia. The upshot of the cases seems to be that most of what we thought dementia precox, according to the old terminology and the old conception, failed to materialize as such, or at least after more or less schizophrenic fireworks lasting all the way from a month to a couple of years, the majority of them cleared up and the patients are as well as ever. Such findings indicate either that our diagnoses were wrong or that our conceptions of dementia precox are wrong, or that influenza produces a curious and atypical type of dementia precox which tends to recover. It has been my contention for several years, as you may or may not recall, that there is no essential difference from a psychopathological standpoint between simple delirium and dementia precox except chronicity, or as I want to call it for individualistic reasons, reversibility. It seems to me that what influenza does is to scrape off enough of the superficial or tangle up enough of the superficial associations to permit the naked, unconscious skeleton (to mix a few metaphors) to stick out in a disjointed, grotesque way which we have labeled schizophrenia. I thought I would follow this up further in a subsequent article on influenzal delirium in which I would analyze the content of some delirious cases, but in the meantime I am writing for some suggestions and comments and stimuli from you.

Sincerely yours,

FROM WILLIAM ALANSON WHITE, WASHINGTON, D.C., APRIL 4, 1925

My dear Menninger:

Thank you for your very appreciative letter of the 27th ult. [March]. I have read it with a great deal of interest. I have no doubt that a critical examination and discussion of some of my concepts might be clarifying. I think my general proposition is all right. In detail I can see how you might be confused in thinking of mental reactions as total reactions. Of course I may have in mind a little different concept from what that phraseology gets over to you. Whether a reaction is a total reaction in the sense of being mental or a partial reaction in the sense of being physiological has perhaps, oftentimes at least, as much to do with the point of view as with the mechanism of the reactions themselves. For example, to the engineer in the ship the movement of the machinery is analogous to the functions of the organs in the body—in other words, it is physiological—but to the navigator on the bridge the course of the ship from port to port is more analogous to a total reaction in the sense of mental. In neither case has there been any change in what is going on so far as the ship is concerned. It is the viewpoint of the engineer in the one case and the navigator in the other. The engines are not going to a definite port, but the ship is going to a definite port. Such situations as this of course would tend to make the two types of reactions, partial and total, come closer together. On the other hand, if the ship tried to make a five-thousand-mile trip with fuel only sufficient for three thousand miles the general tendency of the ship as a whole would be frustrated by certain internal conditions. I wonder if this is not the point that you are making, in which case I regard it as a legitimate one, and one for argument and clarifications. Perhaps we may thrash it out in Richmond.

Very sincerely yours.

P.S. Get this concept. I am approaching the question of the definition of the psyche from an entirely different point of view from that ordinarily utilized. I have an abiding belief that things cannot be defined anyway, much less such highly complex affairs as the mind, so I have done this: I have said to myself, What kind of activities of the organism are those with regard to which, when describing them, we necessarily use psychological terms? Now it is perfectly obvious that when we are talking about a part of an organism, such as when we say, for example, about the liver that it stores up sugar for release upon certain occasions, that we are talking in physiological terms, but that when we ask what the man is doing we are talking in psychological terms. Of course, on the other hand, with reference to any particular organ, such as the liver, when we say of it, as we might, that the liver as such would, if it could, absorb the entire energies of the organism so that the organism might, so to speak, become entirely liver if it was not opposed by other organs with similar tendencies, then we are talking about the liver in the same way that we are talking about the organism as a whole, and therefore are using psychological terms, and with reference to this tendency of the liver; therefore, the liver may properly be said to have a psyche, which is not an incredible thing, because from my point of view and that of the biologists everything living has a psychological aspect, etc., etc.

FROM WILLIAM ALANSON WHITE, WASHINGTON, D.C., SEPTEMBER 12, 1925

My dear Menninger:

I have read Glueck's book[9] and will try to reply to your letter. Of course I think I must express your feeling as well as my own when I say how highly I value the book. It is, I think, a magnificent contribution to the subject by and large, and taken as a whole I find myself in agreement with him. But that is one thing. And now as to details, I will try to make myself clear. In the first place Glueck makes some specific suggestions. One is a suggestion for the adoption of the doctrine of partial responsibility, and I think this suggestion goes to the root of my entire critical attitude toward his book. The adoption of the doctrine of partial responsibility only dilutes the present situation. It does not fundamentally change the attitude toward the criminal

9 Sheldon Glueck, *Mental Disorder and the Criminal Law.*

in any specific way, nor will it have any particular effect upon the total situation so far as I can see except that a lot more people will be held irresponsible. The defect in the present situation is basic and I do not believe can be cured, at least without an objective that is more basic than that even though that may be adopted ultimately as a means.

The difficulty with the present situation with regard to crime and the criminal law and criminal procedure is essentially this: We are trying to deal with twentieth-century conditions with tools that were forged in the nineteenth, the eighteenth, the seventeenth century, and so on, and even though all these tools are reforged into one, they remain antiquated and inefficient. Suppose you and I should endeavor to form a partnership and conduct a corporation according to the laws and practices of a century ago, where do you suppose we would land? For my part I have not the slightest idea. Now, institutions and laws and *ways of thinking* are tools with which we find our way about in this world of things and events and people, and the law and the practice and the way of thinking about it are the tools with which we must find our way about in this field of criminology. The mental tests are one of the tools that were developed in the last century and have hung over into the present. The present availability of these tools has been pretty well demolished by Glueck. The question of whether we should invent other ones to take their place remains a practical issue. Personally I have doubted its advisability because I know, as you know, that psychiatry has been forging ahead with such rapid strides lately that it might easily happen that by the time we had anything formulated it would be no good.

If we do leave the door wide open in this way how are we going to practically deal with the situation? My suggestions are as follows: The recognition of the psychological basis upon which the personality of the criminal can be understood will never be gained by any pronouncements to the jury by the trial judge or any formulation as a basis for the jury. I do not see any way of reaching the jury, but I do feel very strongly that the fundamental objectives of the criminal law are wrong. They are wrong to the extent that they discuss at all the question of responsibility, because this opens the whole question of guilt and innocence or right and wrong from an ethical or a theological sense, and in the twentieth century such questions have no place in criminal procedure. The outstanding fact of the present century, so far as these matters are concerned, has been the birth of a social consciousness, and what the courts and the law should be interested in is the sole question of whether the prisoner at the bar is such a type of individual as can be safely trusted with an attempt to lead a free life as a member of society. If his conduct has been such as to negate this assumption society has a right to be protected from him and . . . can exercise this right by locking him up in an appropriate institution. The minute they do this, however, the rights of the individual come into the foreground and then society is bound to consider them. It is inconceivable that any present-day society would sentence a man to prison for twenty years and then insist that throughout those twenty years he shall be made to suffer continuously, and yet that is the implication of many of the criticisms of the criminal law and of the conduct of the modern prisons. Vengeance, punishment, suffering are in the main destructive agencies. Society should take hold of the incarcerated criminal and give him every opportunity consistent with his safety to live the rest of his life with the maximum benefit both to himself and others.

If I have put over to you what I mean in the last paragraph the following implications will be clear. In the first instance we are confronted by the absurdity in our present procedure that a man is either guilty if responsible or innocent if irresponsible, and if innocent because irresponsible a verdict of not guilty has to be rendered, the irresponsibility being understood to apply only to the period of the alleged crime, which may be a year or two back, and the individual is turned loose. The impossibility of constitutionally neglecting the question of irresponsibility is due to the fact that the guilty mind is an essential ingredient of guilt—that irresponsibility means a mind so altered by disease that it could not be guilty and therefore the whole question of guilt and innocence revolve about the question of responsibility. Now it would seem to me that this matter might be fixed by legislation that would regulate some of the matters involved. For example, if a criminal who actually committed a homicide is found not guilty because of insanity, which implies of course that he did do the deed, legislation ought to compel his immediate incarceration in a proper institution for the care of the mentally ill. That is the first step. Now the second step is that legislation should safeguard his discharge from this institution to the extent at least that upon habeas corpus the presiding judge should not be allowed to discharge the petitioner solely upon some legal technicality, but that in every instance the actual merits of the situation should be inquired into; in other words, before a person, of whom the state has full notice of the fact that he has been and may be dangerous, is discharged into the community, the merits of the situation should be thrashed out. Thus, think for example of the outrageousness of a presiding judge who calmly discharges a murderous, homicidal lunatic from custody on the sole condition that he will get out of the jurisdiction, thereby saying as plainly as words can say that he may kill as much as he pleases so long as he does not kill in a certain geographical territory. This is the maximum absurdity of technicalities where living social issues cry for solution.

Now in my book [*Insanity and the Criminal Law*] I made certain concessions to what I considered to be practical. Glueck has made certain concessions in his book to what he considers to be practical. His suggestion of adopting the doctrine of partial responsibility is such a concession. I have no objection to concessions, but I believe we should have, if it is humanly possible, a fairly clear objective. Having that objective, if we are practical-minded at all, we will find that it is essential to ally ourselves with the foci of social change as they exist and not endeavor to bring about a change that is so radical that an attempt to do so will defeat the ends aimed at. This suggests some further remarks.

Unfortunately some of the trouble with the present situation must rest at the door of the medical expert. Medical experts, when they take the witness stand, are either so fully cognizant of the criminal law and fit so well into it in their opinions that they do nothing to change the situation, or else are so confused in their attempt to find some pathway between an antiquated law and a modern scientific concept that they make a mess of the situation in another way. My objective for the expert is that he should not undertake to decide, if he can avoid it, any question which I regard as purely legal; namely, whether the defendant is insane or not, or whether the defendant is responsible or not. These are both concepts that seem to me to be of a nature that renders any opinion upon them worthless, if not impossible. They belong to the concepts that have survived their usefulness which should now be recognized for what they are, namely pure fictions. In the Chicago case [Leopold and Loeb], when the district attorney asked me what responsibility was, I told him in my opinion it was a legal fiction. The matter stopped there and I was not asked any further questions on that point. If I were asked to define insanity, and I think I was too, I told them that that was a matter for the lawyer, and that I did not know—that insanity was a legal term. My idea [is] that it is solely the province, or should be solely the province, of the expert to lay before the court and the jury a longitudinal section of the defendant's personality so that they can understand, as far as it is understandable, how he came to do what he did do, what were the motives for his conduct, their nature, their strength, their source, and their objectives. And then the jury, representing society, will do what they will do, and they will do that anyway. I see no place in such a scheme for mental tests. I see no place in such a scheme, so far as the expert is concerned, for concepts of responsibility, partial responsibility, or irresponsibility. I see only the function of the expert reduced to what it seems to me was its original intention, to bring his expert knowledge to the assistance of the issue so that the court and the jury will have a clearer idea of what they are dealing with, and God knows, so far as I can see, they need it.

Life is short and time is fleeting. I have given you a hint of my point of view in as short a space as I can. I will only add that it suggests itself to me that it might not be a bad idea to communicate with other committees, such, for example, as that now being formed in New York for an analysis of the crime situation, and offer to cooperate with them if they feel that they might be helped by such cooperation in any manner.

Very sincerely yours,

To the Committee on Legal Aspects of Psychiatry, Washington, D.C., July 21, 1926

Gentlemen of the Committee:

With the approval of one or two of you whom I was able to locate by wire, I dashed out of Denver to lay this thing before the bar association, which I found to be convened in this close proximity.

By means of some personal friends and communications, I got in touch with the president of the bar association and had our report considered by their executive committee. It was referred to the Section on Criminal Law, which in spite of the timeliness of the subject, seems to me to be a rather sluggish and desultory section. They did, however, extend to me the courtesy of asking that I speak on the matter for a few minutes and I did so as seductively and at the same time [as] frankly as possible. I took the position that we had no favors to ask but that as sanitary engineers might feel in the midst of a great plague of cholera we felt that if the doctors (lawyers) were not too busy to consider some suggestions which we could make . . . on the basis of our past experience with sewage, we should be glad to cooperate.

If you have ever attended bar associations, you know that they have a curious way of sitting very silently and discussing none of the papers formally, but a goodly number of them did discuss the matter with me informally afterwards, and I think we have perhaps made a point in that the report is now definitely before them for consideration and will probably be referred to in their next session. I took the names of a good many of the lawyers who wanted copies of the report and have mailed it to them.

It occurs to me that it would be excellent publicity to send a copy of the report to every lawyer who attended that meeting because the subject was frequently touched upon in the various speeches. I could send with it a form letter saying that this is the report which was presented to the American Psychiatric Association in New York and to the Criminal Law Section of the American Bar Association in Denver, July 13th. If you approve of this, let me know.

I am also taking the matter up with Mr. Henry Taft [of New York], who is chairman of a committee on law reform and who made a number of suggestions in his committee report in Denver touching on the futility of the hypothetical question and other matters in which we are interested.

Finally, I wish to direct your attention to a report made by Mr. Hadley[1] on behalf of one of the committees of the American Bar Institute and released apparently through the National Crime Commission as publicity

1 Herbert S. Hadley, chancellor of Washington University, St. Louis, presented "Criminal Justice in America: Present Conditions Historically Considered." It was published in the *ABA Journal* 11 (1925); 674–79.

agency. It is a model code of criminal procedure. Insofar as it concerns psychiatry, it seems to me to have a very vicious defect in that although it purports to be a progressive and modernized instrument, it perpetuates the convention of insanity and prostitutes the psychiatrists in the same old way as regards the issues of responsibility, punishability, etc. I earnestly direct your attention to it and request that you write me whether or not we should officially address the National Crime Committee or the bar association on this particular point, and if so in what language you would voice the protest.

Sincerely yours,

To E. K. Wickman,[2] Cleveland, September 23, 1926

My dear Wickman:

Your letter of September 7th was of immense interest to us just at present because we are in the very act of starting a little school ourselves. Our school is to be much different than the one that you project, however. It is to be limited to children, and probably for the most part actually deficient children, although we want to get all the behavior disorders and superior children that we can. We are having lots of fun working out plans for advertising it and launching it.

The plan which you suggest for superior children only, of a rather more advanced age, seems to me to be one for which there is a very definite need. Of course you and I both know there is a need. The difficulty is to get the people who have such cases in charge to realize the need for the kind of treatment which you have outlined. Then you have the additional problem of getting the fact disseminated among that minority which should recognize the value of your school, that you have such a school. This advertising game is a mighty complicated one. I have spent seven years now trying to understand it and I still feel like a man trying to take a walking trip around the world; it is slow business and it is a long road, with many troubles.

I doubt if you can afford to run your school for fifteen hundred to two thousand. You might just as well make it two hundred and fifty a month, because one of the advantages of being in the East, and particularly there near Asheville, is that you have access to a lot of wealthy people. You won't make your money off of the wealthy people, but you will get quite a few students who have more money than any we have out here. That is one reason why I doubt if I would be able to send you many students, if any. To make that kind of a school pay as it should, you will have to charge more than my people out here can afford as a rule. At the present time I don't know of a one.

This leads me to make another philosophical remark that you can take for

2 Wickman was one of the founders of a child guidance clinic in Cleveland, Ohio.

what it is worth. Strange as it may seem, your business won't come from your friends. I don't know why this is, unless it is that most of your friends are people trying to do the same thing you are doing and if they are any good at all they are working as hard as they can to develop their own efficiency and production. Because neither one of us is sensitive about it, I might refer you to the situation of Lawson and myself. Lawson is the most intimate friend I have in the world and I have never sent him but one patient and he has never sent me but two. I suppose I know three-fourths of the neuropsychiatrists in the United States and the total number of patients received by reference from these other fellows over the country in the past year—with one exception, the Mayo Clinic—wouldn't pay our postage bill for two months.

The thing you have to do is to impress the people with the value of your school who are in a position to refer you cases from the immediate vicinity. This will build up the reputation of your school and give you more basis for advertisement and gradually you can increase your capacity. I think our frontier advances about fifty miles a year. The first year of my practice I got patients for the most part within a radius of fifty miles and we now get patients within a radius of about four hundred miles. I certainly hope that the increase keeps on at this rate. We have had several patients this year from a thousand miles away but this isn't the average. In the East you will have matters better, of course, because the population is thicker and people have more money. The kind of a school you project is needed. If you can convince people of the need and of your ability to fulfill it and will charge enough for your services, your school will succeed. I shall be interested in whatever happens.

Sincerely yours,

To Ludvig Hektoen,[3] Washington, D.C., November 24, 1926

Dear Doctor Hektoen:

I was glad to have your letter of October 18th in regard to the matter of cooperation of the American Psychiatric Association, enclosing a letter from Prof. E. N. Morgan.[4]

Prof. Morgan's letter interested me very much. It is one of three typical lawyer's reactions: The first is a reaction of indifference such as characterizes most of our own profession. The second is one of hearty approval, with the reservation that we are probably ahead of our public. The third is an an-

3 Chairman of the division of medical sciences of the National Research Council and member of the Board of Trustees of the Chicago Psychoanalytic Institute.

4 The letter from Harvard law professor E. N. Morgan has not been preserved. Morgan was directing a legal survey of the medico-legal situation in large American cities.

noyed stirring of resentment against the frank junking of some of the re-vered old shibboleths.

Prof. Morgan says, first, that our report is discouraging because it is too top-lofty; then he says our analysis is entirely mistaken (because) it will not do for us to say we have no interest in responsibility. I don't see why we can't say we have no interest in responsibility if it is true, and I think most of the modern school of psychiatrists will assure you that it is true. Mr. Morgan has evidently some notion of public policy; he implies that we must not say we are not interested in responsibility, for someone might hear us and go out and commit a crime. As scientists, we can't possibly have any such tricks up our sleeves. It is quite true that we can't overturn the present system immediately, but a man living in Massachusetts should be the last one to say that very radical changes may not be made in criminal procedure in such a way that psychiatrists rather than politicians and jailers pass on the problem of whether or not a given individual is likely to profit by a given type of treatment. . . . [Morgan] says that the present machinery for admin-istering justice (whatever that is) is at best crude and rough; our report in-dicates that we believe it will be made less crude and rough by the applica-tion of scientific rather than historic methods. I know how it offends the legal mind to question their conception of justice and responsibility, but for a medical man they are just so many words, entirely divested of all the historic richness and philosophical significance with which they are imbued by those having had a legal training. As far as I know, no medical man considers that anything that happens in nature is particularly just, or for that matter, unjust.

Sincerely yours,

To WILLIAM ALANSON WHITE, WASHINGTON, D.C., DECEMBER 18, 1926

Dear Doctor White:

I heartily congratulate you upon the report of the investigating commit-tee. . . .

If you have time give me a little counsel on the matter of going to Europe. I am thinking of leaving here the latter part of March and going to Rank for analysis. I haven't the money to spend more than a few months, and Frank-wood Williams thinks that ought to be long enough with Rank's new tech-nique.[5] Do you think I should better go Ferenczi, or someone else? Smith Ely seems to favor the Berlin bunch but they want you to stay so long be-cause they still follow the old orthodox technique, which is what I have been

5 Otto Rank, one of Freud's earliest disciples, challenged the Freudian tenet that psy-chotherapy must be of long and indefinite duration by limiting therapy to three months at the most.

using. My friend Lowrey is going to Rank, and I am sort of waiting until he has completed his analysis so that we wouldn't have any spiritual clashes. Otherwise, we might have gone over together on January 15th.

Finally, I want to find out just how my brother Will should apply to spend a few months with you at St. Elizabeths. I think he could come next month, or he could wait until I got back from Europe, although the former is preferable. The money is no particular object if he could find a place to eat and sleep, but what I want him to do is to get some contacts with you and Nolan Lewis.[6] I have thought over the situation many times and I am sure there is no place in the United States I would rather have him go to get some psychiatric information and stimulation. He is a splendid fellow; I told you this before, and you will not be disappointed. I am sure you will want him to stay longer. As soon as he has saved up a little money here I think he will come back to you but I want him to have a few months right away. Have you got a niche to stick him in, and if so what are the motions I should go through to get him there?

Sincerely yours,

FROM SMITH ELY JELLIFFE, INNSBRUCK, AUSTRIA, SEPTEMBER 6, 1927

My dear Menninger:

Just a word to tell you a little of the 10th Internat. Congr. of the Psychoanalytic Society here at Innsbruck. Delightful weather after a lot of rain and cold which we knew nothing of. About 200 people there. 150–160 members—very cordial—good feeling and quite a satisfactory meeting everything considered. Politics about the same. Wiener Gruppe Berliner Gruppe: always watching each other and barking for $—from the shores of America—or growling, if not barking. The Teaching Commission—or Committee—arrived at some understanding concerning the training of analysts, but the lay-analyst question was not decided. It was held over for another year. In the meantime we want to get all the dope we can on the snide [?] analysts.

It would have been very nice if you came. Rank is apparently dethroned and is in disfavor. He was not there. The "ladies" were not in as great evidence as at "Bad Homburg"[1] but there is a bigger contingent of women in all of the European societies.

---

6 A psychiatrist and neuropathologist, specializing in schizophrenia. He was director of St. Elizabeths Hospital in Washington, D. C., from 1923 to 1933 and a charter member of the Washington-Baltimore Psychoanalytic Society, formed in 1930. He later became professor of neurology and director of the psychiatry department at Columbia University. He was a personal friend of KAM.

1 The Ninth Congress of the International Psychoanalytic Association was held in Bad Homburg, Germany in 1925. Karl Abraham presided. This congress signaled the shift from

The papers were not *hervarragendes*[2] but interesting. I got a lot from meeting the different men and will read their papers with more understanding in the future.

In a week or so the Irrenaerzte and Nervenaerzte[3] of Germany meet in Vienna. I shall take them in and enlarge my vocabulary.

'Tis raining now—as I write for the first time since I struck Europe 9 days ago. On to Vienna tonight for another 10 days or more—

[Best regards from house to house. On the side of the last page of the letter, Jelliffe has noted: "(Isador) Coriat, (Lionel) Blitzsten, (Frankwood) Williams, (William) Silverberg, (Abram) Kardiner, (C.P.) Oberndorf, Jelliffe—the USA psa. bugs there."]

To Editor, Lincoln, Nebraska, *Star*, October 20, 1927

Dear Sir:

I have just read your editorial in the issue of October 11 and I regard it as ignorantly or maliciously misrepresenting my remarks at Beatrice.[4] I used a manuscript, and an advance copy of what I said was given to the Associated Press, so there was absolutely no excuse for your false and libelous statements. The American Psychiatric Association has taken a very definite stand directly contrary to the position implied in the third and fourth paragraphs of your article. We have expressly stated that it was our opinion that individuals suffering with criminal propensities should be locked up indefinitely for the protection of society, and for you to write an editorial implying that we are desirous of evading or subverting the protection of society is a deliberate and vicious misrepresentation. I think you should make immediate retraction and I should be glad to transmit your apology to the American Psychiatric Association.

Very truly yours,

From Lawson Lowrey, New York, December 11, 1927

Dear Karl:

I am supposed to be hard at work today, but the things I have to work on cannot be located either here or at the office, so I have some time which I propose to spend in writing to you. Your name in the paper in connection

---

relatively casual standards in regard to the training of analysts to establishment of more rigorous standards, and the First International Training Commission was created to govern psychoanalytic training. In America, A. A. Brill was instrumental in effecting this change (he was president of the American Psychoanalytic Association from 1929 to 1935).

2 Outstanding.
3 Mental health specialists and neurologists.
4 Site of the Nebraska State Hospital for the retarded.

with some murder[5] has been a particular reminder of the fact that it is a long time since I wrote you in any detail. So here goes.

Things are going on very well here. I have the feeling that we are at last under way, because so many difficult situations arise which must be straightened out. I believe I have already sent you a copy of the announcement we sent out about the Institute[6] and its purposes and limitations. That gives a clear picture of our responsibilities, but not of the complexity of the job, because the latter hinges so much on variations in personality, training and experience, not only of staff but [of] students as well. Not to mention the infinite complexity of New York and its social agencies, schools and other resources. So far, of course, we have not gotten things well systematized, and yet sooner or later *everything* about the place must be systematized. The biggest part of the job is to get satisfactory case work going in such [a] way that the interests of the patient are conserved and the students get their training. Some task, I can tell you. . . .

Rank comes over every Saturday night and meets with the group of psychiatrists he has analyzed to discuss the lectures he is now giving in Philadelphia. I don't get much out of it, but go just the same. Last night he sprang a new idea on us. Apparently someone has made him an offer here on teaching and lecturing, and he proposes to run off immediately to Europe and return to New York in January to form a group who will do analyses for those who can afford to pay very little, they to be parcelled around; he to work with the several analysts using his methods in what is called a "controlled analysis." I rather hope the idea goes through, as I want to start analytic work in February and certainly need help and supervision. As I think I have said to you before, the lack of any such arrangement has seemed to me the weakest point in Rank's development of workers. Something has apparently happened so that he sees an opportunity to start here in NY something like the Berlin Psychoanalytic Institute. In any case, it now seems that he will be here from January to some time in the fall. Don't you think therefore that you ought to come on to NY and be analyzed while he is here? As soon as I know anything more definite about his plans I'll shoot them on to you. Which reminds me that you have been quite hurt over the fact that I couldn't give you a job if you were to be analysed in NY. I repeat what I said before—I can give you a place in which to work; some interesting research problems to work on; a limited amount of case experience; but I can't give you any salary. As a matter of cold, impartial fact, I wouldn't give anyone a salary while they were being analyzed because my own experience with analysis indicates that no one is worth a salary during such periods. A salary means definite and fixed responsibilities, and the person being ana-

5 KAM had recently testified at a murder trial in Kansas.
6 Lowrey was now director of New York's Child Guidance Institute.

lyzed is about as irresponsible as it is possible for anyone to be. Of course the real reason I can't give you a salary is that I have no money with which to give you one. But I should love to have you around for a few months, even if you become, as most of us do during analysis, a hermit. The fact remains that I should see you from time to time, and we could have some of our famous quarrels. . . .

At present I am doing almost nothing in the way of creative work. My speeches are (from my point of view) rotten; I can't write a decent paper; I am unwilling to fight about anything; I don't give a damn whether school keeps or not, either at the office or here at home; I am months behind in certain sections of my work and don't care; I'm not happy in my job, merely indifferent; I run along from day to day without thought for the morrow; I refuse to speak unless I'm paid $100 and am none too anxious to do it then: yet I am terribly sought-after for speeches; my board thinks I am doing a marvellous administrative job. . . . All this seems to me rather terrible, and the only explanation I can give is that I am in some sort of post analytic state. This is, I think, the true explanation, since during the last three weeks I have been able to get off sleeping 12 hours a day and back into the swing of things. The curious thing is that no one seems to recognize all this except myself. But I certainly am taking a passive part, to my own great advantage. And boy, how much kudos I do get from it. So much so that it may become a fixed habit of reaction. I hope so. . . .

There. As near as I can make out, I have talked about job, your situation, mine, that of several other people, the possibility of your coming on to NY, and many other things, some of them entirely too personal ever to be repeated, so I sign off.

Always yours,

To Lawson Lowrey, New York, December 14, 1927

Dear Lawson:

I have just received the finest letter from you that I ever got in my life. I am not going to answer it now, however, because I want to thoroughly digest it and I have two or three other minor matters to mention.

In the first place, there is absolutely no way to change the date for our darned opening [of the Menninger Sanitarium]. We are taking advantage of the fact that it is the established date of the district medical society, which has met regularly for thirty years on the first Thursday in January, and the local county medical society is scheduled to join in with us. Henry Woltman[7]

7 Henry Woltman was a Mayo Clinic neurologist who helped KAM establish the Menninger Clinic and Foundation. Woltman received his M.D. and his Ph.D. degrees in neurology from the University of Minnesota. He joined the Mayo Clinic in 1917, later becoming chairman of the Section on Neurology and Psychiatry.

is coming down to talk on some neurological topic and Pete Bohan[8] is going to talk on medical economics, and I wanted you to talk about progress in psychiatry, or some such thing as that. Then we are going to have Logan Clendening, whose marvelous book [*The Human Body*] you have probably seen, introduce about twenty or thirty local neuropsychiatrists and other guests of honor. He will do it in a very witty and fetching fashion. We expect about two hundred doctors and perhaps more. The building is a beauty. It is fireproof and looks like a big beautiful home and not an institution at all. Several prospective home purchasers have driven in to see about buying it. In spite of that, it holds twenty-four patients, hydrotherapy, storeroom, etc. We are going to buy a moving picture machine and have weekly shows and a weekly dance. We are installing occupational therapy just as soon as we can be assured of the money and already have a worker lined up. . . .

I wish to heaven you could come because I don't know anybody in the world who can do what I want done except you.

While bragging, I must tell you that our [Southard] school has grown to the point that we have moved into a beautiful old mansion downtown with room for the teachers and cook and ten little pupils. We have lost money on the darned thing since it has started, but it is so much pleasure and so gratifying that we all enjoy it very much and I think ultimately we are going to make a little money; in fact I know we are, and it is growing faster than we supposed it would. We moved in day before yesterday and feel very gratified about that, too. We have a wonderful director.

I am enclosing an announcement of an alumni dinner we had last night which would have done your fraternal heart good to have seen. I actually believe there were a hundred and twenty-five or more men present at this alumni dinner. I was astonished. I helped organize the thing and I have gone regularly for months and it has grown by leaps and bounds. . . . Please notice that I am an officer of the organization [the Central Neuro-Psychiatric Association] and taking an active part.

The American Orthopsychiatric Association has, as you know, elected to come to New York the latter part of February and I am coming at that time to stay a week and maybe two weeks. I hope we accomplish a lot of things, one of which I might as well tell you about right now. I am about to spring a book on the unsuspecting world. I will show you the manuscript and everything and in fact I will probably want you to go over to the publisher with me, although I already have my entree and credentials arranged. Logan Clendening has written *The Human Body,* as you know; I am writing a companion volume to the called *The Human Mind,* and he and I are writing a third volume together to be called *The Human Soul* from a physician's

8 An internist in Kansas City and a professor at the University of Kansas Medical Center.

standpoint.[9] These books will probably not set the world by the ears, but they afford us a great deal of phantasy gratification and may get written and even published—who can tell?

In addition to seeing the publisher and attending the Orthopsychiatric Association meeting and some theaters and your institution, I would be willing to do anything else that turns up. I note, for example, in an enclosed pamphlet of the Child Study Association of America, that all my old friends are giving lectures and I should be perfectly willing to fill the vacant date of February 21, if they would give me a few hundred dollars for doing it. You probably know all these birds by their first names, and I hereby commission you to call them and tell them that for the small sum of a thousand dollars I will do most anything from an evening of original verse to a dissertation on why girls leave home and end up in sanitariums. Just at present I think I am most expert on delineating schizoid characters and I have gotten hold of a book of biographies which enables me to flip off with amazing facility the various schizoid manifestations of a score of gentlemen all the way from Isaac Newton to Napoleon Bonaparte, bringing in such estimable details as their necking technique and eating habits. I hope you realize that I am serious insofar as I would like to get some speaking engagements in New York which would help to defray my expenses. With your munificent salary this may not appeal to you, but it means a lot to me.

Furthermore, if you can pause in your mad career long enough to give me some additional advice and help—how do you think I might proceed to grab hold of this twenty-five-thousand-dollar job as director of the psychiatric investigation of criminals recently recommended by your governor Al?[10] I feel confident that Dr. White and Dr. F. E. Williams and yourself and others would all recommend me, in spite of the fact that I haven't the slightest idea how I would begin to handle it, and I would like to hold the job down for a few years in New York. Among other things I could see you oftener and keep you away from the wild women with whom I am only too well acquainted.

Answer all these questions and then I will write you a real letter in answer to the fine one you just sent me, but I wanted to get these things off of my chest.

Sincerely yours,

To J.E. Lawrence,[11] Lincoln, Nebraska, December 15, 1927

Dear Mr. Lawrence:

I have been in Texas and various other parts of the country since the

9 *The Human Soul* was never written.
10 Gov. Alfred E. Smith.
11 Managing editor, Lincoln, Nebraska *Star.*

arrival of your letter of November 23rd and I hope you will pardon my delay in not responding sooner.

I appreciate your frankness in acknowledging your error, but I cannot help but feel a little out of patience with you for persisting in the same error, even in your letter. Your position seems to be that since different people have different ideas it is all right for you to say that we believe something which we have specifically said that we don't believe. You say, for example, that "seemingly we have differed with you only in that we have felt there has been too much coddling of those who commit crimes." Well, I don't see why it seems that we differ in this matter because we agree precisely. If you will look at the center heads on the story that your own newspaper ran on September 22nd, you will see that we are specifically opposing the release of criminals, as is now being done simply because they have served a few years of a sentence. Our point of view is that if a man has a make-up which indicates that he will be antisocial all his life he ought to be in prison all his life without the necessity of his having committed murder. On the other hand, we can conceive of a man who commits a murder for whom it would be better for all concerned if he served no sentence at all. This isn't a matter of coddling prisoners; it is a matter of treating them scientifically instead of coddling, which is now being done.

In other words, what I have been protesting about is that in your editorial you have set us up as holding a position which we have loudly proclaimed we do not hold; you have put the onus of the present situation on psychiatrists, when as a matter of fact the psychiatrists agree precisely with your point of view and are bitterly opposed to the present inefficient and incompetent system.

You ask me to check through the Associated Press story, from which you said you got the idea, and you have underlined a sentence which says that "the scientists frankly avow the aim of protecting society rather than achieving justice." In other words, we want prisoners locked up indefinitely rather than letting them out in a year or two just because someone feels that it is not just to keep a man in so long when he has only done this or that little crime. We would base long detention on the fact that indications of his personality trend are that he will always be a thief or forger, or whatever he is.

I would say that the Associated Press report of my speech was excellent; so also was your reporter's report in the Sunday *Star* for September 22. Anything that you would say in your editorial based on those reports I am sure would be well said.

I have an aggressive way of speaking and writing and I hope you will not take offense at my frankness. I think like many newspaper men—one of whom I once was myself—you read our stuff hastily and using it as a text and the psychiatrist as the goat you expressed yourself vigorously and somewhat harshly in a direction which you have been thinking and feeling for some years. I think in your haste you carelessly overlooked the fact that the people you are attacking are endeavoring to give support to the very view that you have. In this way you unintentionally gave us offense, not because of what you said against us so much as by reason of the fact that you completely ignored what we had said.

I appreciate very much the gentlemanliness of your letter and I trust that we both understand each other better.

Sincerely yours,

FROM LIONEL BLITZSTEN, BERLIN, FEBRUARY 1928

Dear Karl:

Just a line to let you know that I am still in the land of the living. The work here has been extremely interesting and engrossing. I have been analyzing five patients—four Germans and a Russian—and doing my control work with Dr. Karen Horney.[1] She is a whiz and I am happy to say that she has never had to correct my technique once—in fact she is most complimentary. This isn't a bit of narcissism for I have had most of that knocked out of me during a rather stormy analysis to which I have submitted myself at the hands of Dr. Alexander.[2] This has been going on for the last five months and I believe I shall be finished with it in a few weeks. There are other Americans here. George Mohr,[3] George Daniels,[4] and a woman whom I

1 A native of Hamburg, Germany, Horney received her M.D. degree from the University of Freiburg, Berlin, in 1913. She was an instructor at the Institute for Psychoanalysis in Berlin from 1920 to 1932. She came to the United States in 1932 at the invitation of Franz Alexander and became Associate Director of the Chicago Institute for Psychoanalysis. While in Chicago, she analyzed Grace Gaines Menninger. She left the Chicago Institute in 1934 and became a lecturer at the New School of Social Research in New York City, where she built a practice and a school. She resigned from the American Psychoanalytic Association in 1941 and organized the Association for the Advancement of Psychoanalysis and its teaching extension, the American Institute for Psychoanalysis. She was dean of the institute from 1941 to 1952.

2 Founder of the first psychoanalytic institute [Chicago] in the United States, Alexander conducted KAM's first longterm analysis and analyzed many of KAM's other correspondents as well. Son of a Budapest philosophy professor, Alexander received his M.D. degree from the University of Budapest in 1912. He subsequently became the first student at the Berlin Psychoanalytic Institute. In 1930 he came to the University of Chicago as the first university professor of psychoanalysis. In 1932, he established and became director of the Chicago Institute for Psychoanalysis (commonly known as The Chicago Psychoanalytic Institute or merely as The Chicago Institute), which he insisted remain separate from the Chicago Psychoanalytic Society. In 1956 Alexander accepted a position as clinical professor of psychiatry at the University of Southern California and as training and supervising analyst at the Southern California Psychoanalytic Institute.

3 George Mohr trained in Vienna with Anna Freud. Affiliated with the Chicago Institute, he became director of child analysis there in 1956.

4 A New York psychoanalyst, Daniels applied psychoanalytic concepts to the under-

don't know—all with Alexander. . . . Mrs. B[litzsten] has been in London since November where she was being analyzed by Glover.[5] Unfortunately she developed a thyrotoxicosis a few weeks ago and almost passed out of the picture. I have just returned from London to complete my work. Those weeks in London were a nightmare. If I didn't go stark mad then, I never shall no matter what the circumstances. However, she is on the road to recovery—slowly, and I hope surely—and I shall take her to Sicily for a few weeks as soon as I am finished here and she is able to travel. I'll tell you the details when the conversation is vis-à-vis.

The series of lectures and the seminars at the polyclinic have been quite remarkable—especially those of Rado[6] and Simmel[7] and the Fenichel[8] seminar. In addition, I, together with George Mohr and two others, are taking a series of lectures from Dr. Jaensch,[9] the psycho-physiologist. He's a top notcher and has absolutely the right idea about the whole subject of constitution. Kretchmer[10] can take a back seat. Incidently, his ideas coincide ex-

standing of certain physical diseases at Columbia University Presbyterian Hospital. In 1945, dissatisfied with the restrictiveness of the educational committee of the New York Psychoanalytic Instititute, Daniels, along with Nolan D. C. Lewis, Abram Kardiner, Sandor Rado, and David Levy, created a psychoanalytic training and research center at Columbia University, the Association for Psychoanalytic Medicine. He chronicled this split from the New York society in an unpublished essay, "History of the Association for Psychoanalytic Medicine and the Columbia Clinic," sent to John Weber, president of the Association for Psychoanalytic Medicine, on January 29, 1969.

5 Edward Glover, British psychoanalyst, trained at the Berlin Psychoanalytic Institute.

6 Sandor Rado was born in Hungary in 1890, received his M.D. degree from the University of Budapest in 1915, and from 1913 to 1923 was secretary of the Hungarian Psychoanalytic Society. Between 1923 and 1931, he was associated with the Berlin Psychoanalytic Institute. In 1931, at the invitation of A. A. Brill, Rado moved to New York to organize a psychoanalytic institute on the Berlin model. In 1944 he was appointed professor of psychiatry and head of the Psychoanalytic Institute of Columbia University, the first such institute within a university.

7 Born in Germany, Ernst Simmel practiced medicine in Berlin until World War I. During the war he treated psychiatric battle casualties and was instrumental in founding the Berlin Psychoanalytic Institute. In 1926, he established the Schloss Tegel sanitarium on the outskirts of Berlin. Sigmund Freud came there for rest three times during his treatment for carcinoma. In 1934, Simmel came to America and, after considering an invitation from KAM, settled in Los Angeles, where he founded a psychoanalytic study group that evolved into the Los Angeles Psychoanalytic Institute.

8 Otto Fenichel began his training at the Vienna Psychoanalytic Institute and completed it in Berlin. In 1937, he came to Los Angeles and led the training program at the Los Angeles Psychoanalytic Institute. Classified as an orthodox Freudian, he nonetheless allied himself with Wilhelm Reich in a dissenting Marxist faction within the International Psychoanalytic Association in the 1920s and 1930s, before Reich parted ways with the analytic movement in 1932.

9 E. R. Jaensch, professor of psychology at the University of Marburg, author of *Eidetic Imagery and Typological Methods of Investigation* (1930).

10 Herman Kretschmer was a Chicago urologist. In 1941 he was elected AMA president.

actly with psychoanalytic theory. You might tell [Leo] Stone[11] that the discourse I once gave him about schizophrenia and its reversibility—in bases—of a retrograde psychophysical integration is the foundation of Jaensch's idea. However, that was four years ago and I have never heard of Jaensch. I am not patting myself on the back but there is much to discuss when I see you.

Alexander seems to be the man of the hour. He gets three New Yorkers in August—all psychiatrists. Why don't you come over also? T'would do you some good I am sure. I can be reached via American Express Co., Berlin. My regards to Stone and any of our mutual acquaintances you may chance to meet.

Yours,

To Lawson Lowrey, New York, February 6, 1928

Dear Lawson:

I have a whole sheaf of letters from you in my hand to answer, so here goes.

In the first place I want to tell you what I think I shall bring up in my presidential address to the American Orthopsychiatric Association. I think I shall sound some of the dangerous shoals for orthopsychiatry, as I see them. You know that I think one of them is that you folks [of the A.O.A.] are going to institutionalize the thing to death. I am not going to bear down very hard on this because you and a lot of my best friends are tied up in some of these big machines, but I think the whole tendency of civilization in the direction of machinery such as these [child guidance] institutes is a suicidal trend. I think it exemplifies in medicine what mass production and similar things are doing in the economic and business world. You have probably seen the play *Marco's Millions* [by Eugene O'Neill]. If not, you ought to see it. And whether or not you see it, you have seen *R.U.R.* [by Karel Čapek][12] and similar plays and you know what I mean. Furthermore, you are tremendously speeding the arrival of a more generalized state medicine. In spite of my socialistic inclinations, I think state medicine would be a dreadful thing. Perhaps I am biased because of my personal connections. I think, however, that the tendency should be away from state hospitals instead of toward them and toward any extension of them. I cannot see anything in these child guidance institutions and other similar institutions but an extension of the same principles. It is not a medical problem but an economic problem and I

11 A neurologist and psychiatrist. In 1933, he became the first resident to enter training at the Menninger Clinic after its recognition by the AMA as a training center.

12 KAM worried that the medical profession was moving toward overregimentation. He found a parallel in the political situation depicted satirically in the O'Neill and Čapek plays.

think that once given a grant or a fund of money you folks assume that you are no longer dependent upon the economic laws which govern the rest of the populace. You concentrate upon a system of machinery aiming at an exemplification and application of certain techniques and you forget entirely that after all you reach but a small fraction of sick people, whereas the hundreds of thousands of doctors, and let us frankly include Christian Scientists, osteopaths, etc., who are really treating sick people, would not in any conceivable way benefit by your program, your teaching, your lectures, your classes, or your discoveries.

I am purposely making this somewhat argumentative and challenging because I want you to react to it. I submit the thesis that a thing as economically unsound as your institute and all child guidance institutes and all these free clinics which George Stevenson[13] is fostering cannot be scientifically sound. There is growing up a tremendous and very bitter antagonism on the part of physicians, to whom I talk every day, against these free demonstrations and free ministrations which these clinics represent. A lot of us in private practice feel that you are not only condescending and superior in your attitude, on the basis that you have seen so many thousands of cases in your institute or have had so much more experience than anybody else, but also because we feel that you are directly attacking our bread and butter. Your institute in New York, for example, doesn't in any way help me solve the problem of college students at Washburn. . . . Neither does it inspire any of the doctors or teachers connected with these people to consult me to help these patients. It does, on the other hand, disseminate the idea that such cases should be treated by free public institutions of some sort, equipped elaborately with many social workers and psychologists and lie detectors and reaction measurers, all of which—as I have repeatedly emphasized—is to be done free. We read about it in the magazines and medical journals and we doctors get the idea that such things are thus to be done, and clubwomen get the idea that such things are thus to be done. We mental hygiene fools go out and make speeches telling people about these fine things and further spreading the idea that such things are thus to be done.

I am giving you fair warning that this is the sort of speech I am going to make unless you convince me that I am wrong, or that even if I am right I shouldn't make it, which is probably true.

Having delivered myself of all this, I hope you will believe me when I say that I have no conscious homosexual panic at the present time and feel very friendly and kindly toward you, but I do have a good deal of antipathy for the prevalent spirit of let-the-state-take-care-of-the-crazy-people attitude on the part of the general public. I suppose you know the private psychiatric hospital owners have formed an organization and are prepared to battle this

13 Medical director of the National Committee for Mental Hygiene.

thing through to a finish. We are beginning by cleaning house and we are standardizing psychiatric hospitals on the same basis that general medical hospitals are standardized. . . .

I am glad to know that your psychoanalysis has left you so human. We now have three or four photographs of yourself on our walls. No one can be in doubt of our friendship who visits this institution. We are thinking of putting one or two on the walls of the halls of the new sanitarium building.

Don't take offense at this mild raillery because I really am proud to have them. I have quite a few others now including Timme, Jelliffe, and in fact about twenty or thirty of the fellows. Oh, yes, Adolf Meyer.

Furthermore, don't imagine that I don't realize that a photograph like this costs as much as a new Ford. However, if you are going to indulge in having them taken I want you to continue to indulge me in sending them to me.

My conscience hurts me for kidding you about this so I must tell you that I get bawled out about it so frequently on the part of friend wife [Grace Menninger] that I take glee in it. If I want to torment her particularly much, I suggest, in a sober and serious tone of voice, that it would be a nice thing for Father and Will and me to have a halftone made of ourselves and use it in sending out advertisements, on Christmas cards, etc., with announcements of our office hours and telephone number below. She nearly goes wild at this because she thinks that I mean it.

Reverting again to that Ortho address, I am going to attack two words with all my might. One of them is your confounded word "adjustment," or rather the verb "adjust" used intransitively. The other is the word "systematized."

I hope you and Ella are happier now in your new location and that the boys have a good school and like it.

I want to talk to you a long time when I see you about my own psychoanalysis. It is indefinitely postponed. . . .

Sincerely yours,

FROM WILLIAM ALANSON WHITE, WASHINGTON, D.C., MAY 21, 1928

My dear Menninger:

I have just finished reading your report, which I am returning herewith. Before making any comments let me tell you how splendid I think it is. You have done a fine piece of work, as you always do, and I think the [American Psychiatric] Association will be very fortunate in having the situation so ably presented.

You ask for suggestions. I think the report as it stands is splendid and I don't think I have any suggestions. It shows an advance in the acceptance of the psychiatric viewpoint which is far greater than I had any idea existed, and I think our Association ought to be tremendously gratified at learning this in detail. The Association might be interested in knowing that the Harvard Crime Survey is trying valiantly to write a psychiatric chapter into their report; and it might be of further interest to know that the National Society of Penal Information under a grant from the Laura Spellman Rockefeller Memorial is conducting a survey of the health and hospital work in the prisons, both state and federal, throughout the country, and that this work is near completion. It will undoubtedly furnish a mass of information which will be exceedingly valuable. The committee conducting the survey is under the chairmanship of Dr. Frank L. Rector.

Very sincerely yours,

FROM H. L. MENCKEN,[14] NEW YORK, AUGUST 21, 1928

Dear Dr. Menninger:

Unluckily this article[15] leaves me in doubt, chiefly because I have a violent antipathy to the psychiatrists' treatment of criminals. That it may do some good in certain cases, I by no means deny. What I object to is the banal theory that crime is merely a pathological matter. It seems to me that this is not true. Many criminals perform their occupations in a highly logical and realistic manner. They are not crazy but decidedly intelligent and their intelligence is shown by their success. It is my conviction as an old police reporter that not more than five percent of the criminals in America are ever punished at all. I am sorry that I have these doubts about your article, but there they are. What else is in the book? If you care to let me see any parts of it I'll certainly be delighted to read them.

I remember meeting you very well and very pleasantly. This morning came a letter from Clendening showing him lolling under a pine tree in California with a highball at least eighteen inches high in front of him. What a gaudy life!

Sincerely yours,

TO H. L. MENCKEN, NEW YORK, AUGUST 25, 1928

Dear Mr. Mencken:

I appreciate your frank rejection of my manuscript on the grounds that you opposed the psychiatric attitude toward criminals.

---

14 In 1906, after being editor at the Baltimore *Morning Herald*, Mencken began a thirty-five-year association with the Baltimore *Sun*. In 1908 he became literary editor of the *Smart Set*. With George Jean Nathan, he founded the *American Mercury* in 1924 and remained editor until 1933. He was a contributing editor of the *Nation* between 1921 and 1932. From these positions and in his numerous books Mencken lambasted the follies and prejudices of the American "booboisie."

15 KAM had submitted an article on psychiatry and crime to the *American Mercury*.

I accept the rejection in the best of humor, but I don't accept your mis-judgment of psychiatrists because you are too important a man to go on talking such bunk. Look at the carbon copy of your letter of August 21 and tell me what intelligent psychiatrist you ever heard say that criminals were not often logical and realistic and intelligent. You are the last man on earth to put up a straw man and knock it down and blame the psychiatrists for it. Psychiatrists don't even claim that crime is a disease—which you imply. What they do say is that crime is one of the symptoms of a disorder of a sort which they understand because of their familiarity with queer people. As an old police court reporter myself, my only point of difference with your com-ment on the punishment of criminals is that five percent is too high; it is considerably less than one percent.

The psychiatrists have been trying their damnedest to get the idea across to the public that to get some satisfaction out of punishing one percent of criminals is not worth the trouble it costs, and that to regard the whole hundred percent as being socially impossible and turning them over to the psychiatrists with instructions to keep them out of trouble or lock them up for good would achieve more results. If you can think of anything less sen-timental than this, what have you? The sentimentalists are those who keep shouting for more punishment when no one knows better than you and I that with this objective in view we are never going to catch one-tenth of the fish in the stream for the pan.

Forgive me for any too great acerbities. I'm sorry my article didn't make the grade, but I would rather think it was because of its literary deficiencies than to have you continue in an illusion which neither the article in question nor the position of psychiatrists in general justifies.

Sincerely yours,

FROM H. L. MENCKEN, NEW YORK, AUGUST 29, 1928

Dear Dr. Menninger:

I dare say you are quite right. I wrote that letter after emerging from a book written by two gentlemen whose names I forget. It came out a few months ago and is devoted to the thesis that all criminals are diseased and that all of them may be cured. This seems to me to be rather a tall order.

Do you ever come this way? If so, I hope you let me hear of it next time. I'd like very much to see. you. Clendening reports that he is having a roar-ing time on the coast.

Sincerely yours,

TO WILLIAM ALANSON WHITE, WASHINGTON, D.C., NOVEMBER 17, 1928

Dear Doctor White:

I have just had a letter from Dr. Orton, now president as you know of the

American Psychiatric Association, dated November 13, 1928, which after a preliminary apology contains the following paragraph:

"I have been thinking very critically of the work of the Committee on Legal Aspects of Psychiatry of the American Psychiatric Association and have discussed the situation at length with the Executive Committee of the Council, and while I value very highly the tremendous energy and enthusiasm which you brought to the chairmanship of that committee and appreciate to the full the great amount of work which you have done there, yet I feel that a committee whose work is of so great dynamic danger should have as its chairman someone with a little less of the manic component in his make-up. In other words, I am very anxious to have you remain on the committee not only as a member but as an active worker, but I want to place at the helm someone who is by temperament of the strictly judicial turn of mind."

I have spent a day or so in trying to decide just what my attitude ought to be and I am writing to you before I write to anyone else, or say anything to anyone, because I very much want your personal guidance and counsel.

I have felt for a year or so that I ought to resign from the chairmanship with a suggestion to the president that he appoint you, instead of myself, as a much more logical person for that office. I am hoping with all my heart that it is you whom Dr. Orton intends to appoint. More important, however, and knowing his distrust of what he disdainfully regards as radical clinical psychiatry, I feel almost certain that he will not appoint you.

I am not as evangelical as Dr. Orton and consequently I am not as concerned about the future of the work as I am about my own hurt pride in the matter. I am not sure Dr. Orton has any right to demote the chairman of a committee who has been appointed by a previous president for five years. I am not inclined to contest this point, but on the other hand I am additionally irritated by the probable illegality and unconstitutionality of such a move. I am even more concerned, however, by the fact that Orton feels that he can ride over me and those who have backed me and supported me, including of course first of all yourself.

Of course I am psychiatrist enough to understand Orton. . . . I can see the justifiability of appointing an older and wiser man for this committee, but I don't see the justifiability of . . . Orton, acting under divine inspiration for the good of the cause, pouncing on me as being a dangerous manic.

Many of us had hoped, perhaps yourself included, that the series of failures which Dr. Orton has engineered in the past few years[16] might have succeeded in rendering him somewhat less anxious to humiliate and wound

16 In 1927 Orton had lost his position as director of the Iowa Psychopathic Hospital. The next year he secured a position as neuropathologist at the New York Neurological Institute.

the feelings of others. Apparently, at least so far as I am concerned, he is the same old Orton. There are a hundred tactful ways in which this might have been accomplished if his evangelical zeal demanded it. I am wondering if it is not the more pleasant to have this opportunity by reason of his jealousy of Lowrey, whom he did his best to ruin a few years ago and who has since then so definitely passed him by. Lowrey, as you know, has always been my most intimate friend among the younger men. He and I started in psychiatry together, he a year or two ahead of me, and in spirit we have been together ever since. Orton thoroughly disliked Lowrey and his behavior toward him almost resulted in an acute depression.

I have been running on to you in an informal sort of way because I want you to tell me how to take this thing and what to do about it. There is one other thing I ought to tell you. Last winter, you recall, I visited you in the early part of February and told you how Dr. [Herman] Adler had attacked me for having stood up loyally for the American Psychiatric Association. Dr. Adler said at that time that I was in a temporary elation owing to the fact that the chiefs of the American Psychiatric Association had set me up, and warned me that the American Psychiatric Association would let me down just as hard and I would come to realize that they (most of them—not you) were not interested in having any progressive, youthful activity. You will recall that I was rather disturbed about the insistence of the various men in the American Orthopsychiatric Association that it was useless to try to pay wholehearted devotion to the American Psychiatric Association and that we should have a separate group. You will remember that my simple soul was somewhat torn at the time because I was so single-heartedly devoted to what you had started me at doing and to what I was trying to carry out. The first man I saw after I left the rooms at the meeting in New York was Sam Orton and I told him all about it and he was very interested and congratulated me on being loyal to the mother organization. It passes my psychoanalytic insight why the irony of fate should be such that it should be none other than Orton himself who should verify their prediction.

Now, I don't want to go off half-cocked about this thing. I suspect that old spitfire Woodward[17] of Chicago wrote Orton a letter and Orton felt the strivings of God within his soul and . . . utilized this opportunity to do what he sincerely believes to be a fine stroke of presidential wisdom. I think I can understand in a way how it is, but I am thoroughly upset about it. You appointed me in the first place and I think I have been doing what you think I should do. I have never done anything that I did not consult the older and wiser members of the committee about. So far as I know I have never gotten

---

17 William C. Woodward, physician and professor of medical jurisprudence at Chicago's Loyola University Law School. At this time, he was executive secretary of the AMA Bureau of Legal Medicine and Legislation.

the committee into any serious trouble. I don't think I have a lot to lose by being demoted, but it hurts me like the devil and it has stirred up all sorts of unholy feelings within my heart. I know only too well that it will be hailed with glee and acclaim by the radical members of the association who will tell me a hundred times that they told me so and warned me and hope to God I've learned my lesson. I don't want to learn the lesson which it appears to have taught. I think something is not right and I still think that your ideal of a central national psychiatric body is the right one and I am not interested in rebellion in spite of this colossal incentive to join it. Please don't use that word rebellion to anyone. I am writing to you confidentially. I don't think any of the other members would call it rebellion. But that's what it is and you know it. I did my level best to fight for unity. Now Orton comes along with his battle axe and hits me on the head. I don't know what to do and what to think and I want the counsel of one who has lived long and wisely and who has always been particularly kind to me, namely, yourself.

Sincerely yours,

To Lawson Lowrey, New York, November 19, 1928

Dear Lawson:

I want to tell you how glad I am that you have taken up so enthusiastically the idea of writing an article for us. You didn't say anything about how proud you were of me for editing such a fine series,[18] but you can be assured that I am pretty proud to have you write for it. . . .

Now I want to tell you about something else. Think back a few years and recall that you came to me several times in great perturbation for some psychiatric counsel in connection with Iowa City, etc. And I am now coming to you in pretty much the same state of perturbation and with much the same desire for some psychiatric counsel. There are times, you know, when even a psychiatrist gets upset. . . . In this particular matter I am not so very much upset. I was at first, however. It is more a matter now as to what I ought to do to be more politic and to achieve the greatest end results.

The situation is simply that our friend Sam Orton has fired me as chairman of the Committee on Legal Aspects of Psychiatry of the American Psychiatric Association. He does so in a letter dated November 13 . . . saying something about "a committee whose work is of so great dynamic danger should have as its chairman someone with a little less of the manic component in his makeup." Now . . . Orton, acting under divine inspiration for the good of a mystical cause, talking about my being a dangerous manic is a kind of a comedy. Nevertheless, there is something to what he says. Con-

18 KAM had recently begun his series of advice columns for *Household* magazine.

fidentially, I think he was moved to do it by a fellow named [William C.] Woodward, who is the legal light in the offices of the American Medical Association, who took offense at a misunderstanding he made of a word in one of my letters and blew up in a tremendous temper tantrum about it which [Herman] Adler and Sleyster[19] and a few others have been trying to straighten him out on. I think he probably wrote Orton and told him that I had insulted him, etc., before the boys got him pacified. I didn't insult him but he thinks I did and that's too long a story for us to go into here. Anyone is likely to have jams like that.

I am the youngest member of this committee and I have thought for some time that White ought to be made its chairman, but I resent like holy hell Orton kicking me off in this way. I think it is illegal and unconstitutional because I was appointed for five years and I think it is tactless and hazardous. You see after that meeting of the American Orthopsychiatric Association in which you and Adler and the rest of you told me that my loyalty to the American Psychiatric Association would meet with a jilt, that the same chiefs who had put me up would later let me down just as hard, I talked with Orton about it. He was at the meeting and had gotten some of it and I told him that I was convinced that the American Psychiatric Association deserved my loyalty and was going to have it in spite of the warnings I had received from men who felt that it was hopeless from the standpoint of the utilizing of the young and more progressive men and ideas. So he knew precisely how I stood and he pretended to think my loyalty very fine, etc. Consequently it disturbed me all the more to find out not only that you and Adler were right, but that even Orton, who knows precisely how you and they and I feel, should be the one to verify your prediction.

Of course I know you are saying "I told you so; we told you so." I know you did and I didn't believe you. And I'm not yet sure that you are right, although I have had about as convincing a demonstration of it as anyone could have. . . . I had hoped, as had many of us, I guess, that the series of failures which Orton had engineered during the past few years might have succeeded in rendering him somewhat less anxious to humiliate and wound others. I think he gets all the more satisfaction out of this particular stroke because . . . he knows you and I are so intimate and I think he is burning with jealousy of you, whom he once tried to ruin. I want to write and tell him that. I want to write and tell him that his enviousness of you and his chagrin at not having succeeded in demolishing you were presumably having a little satisfaction in [his] jumping me as hard as he can. I want to write and tell him that we had supposed that some of the defeats he had had to take himself had softened him a bit. But I am psychiatrist enough to know

19 Rock Sleyster, director of the Milwaukee Sanitarium in Wauwatosa, Illinois.

that it won't do any good and it might do some harm. So I probably won't do that. But I don't know what in the devil I *should* do.

I have thought of lots of things. I have thought of writing all the members of my committee and telling them what has happened, or letting someone else write them and suggest that they resign as a protest. I realize that this is kind of narcissistic, but I know that two or three of them would be glad to do so. I haven't gotten quite that crazy, however, and I realize that the committee is going to go on and accomplish something even without my magnificent efforts, and I also realize that I ought to be putting some of my energies into other things now that I have done what I could in that capacity, but I'm just trying to think how I can turn this disaster into a good end. I've about decided the thing for me to do is to admit to you and Adler that I am licked and turn my energies in the fullest measure in the direction of the American Orthopsychiatric Association. I'm about to concede that you were just that much smarter than I was in seeing all this before it happened. I still think that your wisdom is dependent upon some complexes of your own, but whatever it depends upon I think you could see it better than I could. The fact that the American Psychiatric Association is organized in such a way that one man, possessed of a notorious propensity of pouncing on people, is in a position to attack the chairman of an important committee who has done all the work of that committee for three or four years—a work which has been unanimously accepted and endorsed by the association and repeatedly complimented by many individual members of that association—without a trial, without any charges, and without any patent reason, is strong reason for making me believe that you were right when you said that from the standpoint of science in which we were interested the American Psychiatric Association is hopeless. If you will remember that I have been directing all my energies for the last three or four years in . . . a conviction that the American Psychiatric Association was a great and noble organization, you will realize how much of a concession this is for me to make.

Now the question is, what should I do about it? I can assure you that I am in a position to listen very earnestly and eagerly to your advice. I have not written this letter very well. I have not tried to be eloquent. I don't want you to think that I'm as much upset as I would have been some years ago when I was younger and more mercurial. I found out with a mighty jolt that I was wrong about some things; my pride has been hurt; I feel as if all my efforts have been in vain and unappreciated, and what hurts me worst of all I feel as if I were a kind of a failure—not so much in what I was doing as in the way I was handling it. I may be simply kidding myself when I say that it was simply the clash of a cycloid and a schizoid temperament. This is probably a little too simple. I don't know just what it is and I should like you to tell me. And tell me what to write Orton.

Sincerely yours,

FROM WILLIAM ALANSON WHITE, WASHINGTON, D.C., NOVEMBER 21, 1928

My dear Menninger:

I have your letter of the 17th instant and feel deeply with you regarding what has happened. I do not really know whether the president has the right to appoint a chairman or not. Ordinarily, as a matter of practice, the first man named on the committee appointed by the president acts as chairman. Certainly the members of the committee are not to be disregarded in this matter, in my opinion. Personally I have been entirely pleased with all the work that you have done and I cannot see for the life of me how it has done the slightest harm to anyone or to any cause, and I do not believe Dr. Orton has any authority to demote you or change the make-up of the committee. The Association, as I have often said, ceases to exist when it adjourns its annual meeting so far as doing anything is concerned, except for some of the things that the secretary does and some of the things which the president has been charged to do at the meeting. My immediate reaction is that I would not pay any attention to Orton's letter. I do not see how you could possibly write him without starting a controversy which might be endless, and while it is not a very courteous thing to disregard a letter from the president of the Association, on the other hand it was a very tactless thing for the president to write such a letter. I think the committee can take care of itself and if he does not get an answer what is he going to do? I think it would be rather disarming. In any case he can't do anything, except what he has threatened to do and he will do it under much greater disadvantage, at least that is my present feeling.

Very sincerely yours,

FROM LAWSON LOWREY,[20] NEW YORK, NOVEMBER 23, 1928

Dr. Karl A. Menninger:

Had expected the lightning to hit somewhere but not you despite the fact that Sam [Orton] has never liked you, this next year is one merely to be borne until he takes another magnificent failure not even his adroit unscrupulous wife can pull him through here write nothing until you receive my letter I sympathize with all paranoids because of their helplessness in the grip of grandiose delusions but he is beyond sympathy think you were right about the association but who could imagine that such terrible presidents could be chosen believe I know how to defeat him on this special point and convert it into victory for progressives send me by air mail actual copy of his letter am now ready and willing to make open fight if necessary and documents are at hand we still like and trust you even when you go wrong which is not often.

20 Telegram.

To Lawson Lowrey, New York, November 23, 1928

Dear Lawson:

Your telegram actually moved me to tears. I mean the feeling that you were so loyal and ready to fight about it gave me a great kick. I am mailing this exact copy on the next air mail East and I will send you a photograph of it if you want me to. I don't know what you propose doing, but it doesn't matter. You know I like nothing better than a fight, although I had just about decided that the thing to do in this matter was to take life calmly and sweetly and let come what may. I know you have some very heady ideas and I shall be very interested in knowing about them.

You ought to know one or two additional things. I have not said anything to Adler about it. I did write Dr. White a letter. I am sure that White—who is the one who originally appointed me—is a very positive friend, and I think that Earl Bond[21] is. I do not think that Cheney[22] is, although I do not know that he isn't. [Adolf] Meyer and Haviland,[23] who were on the executive committee last year, would be for me. . . . I feel certain that White was not at the executive committee at which Orton sprung his bomb.

Since I don't know what you are going to do, I think I ought to tell you a little more about this [William] Woodward affair in Chicago. Several years ago we exchanged some correspondence. It ended with a very pessimistic and discouraged letter from him. Last year I pointed out that we had not received very much help from the A.M.A. and the members of the committee . . . said I ought to give them hell more vigorously than I had done. Being suggestible, I wrote a letter when I got home and told Woodward that it was regrettable that the A.M.A. wouldn't give us as much help as the American Bar Association at least and reminded him that the *J.A.M.A.* had not even printed our report or acknowledged it. He ignored nine-tenths of the letter and pounced on one word. I had said that the program was one which no honest man could criticize, or something of that sort. It wasn't a wise sentence, but you [should] have seen the three-page reply I got from him. . . .

He just tore up the earth over three pages about my accusation that the A.M.A. was not honest, etc. I sent the letter to White and he said it was an unjustified sort of explosion and that I had better try to mollify Woodward without apologizing and show him that he had misunderstood me. I showed it to Adler and he said he would go to see Woodward personally, as Woodward was a good scout but a little hot-headed. I talked to Rock Sleyster about it (he is on the board of the A.M.A.) and he said Woodward was a

21 Philadelphia psychiatrist, affiliated with the Institute of the Pennsylvania Hospital.
22 Clarence Cheney, a New York psychiatrist; after 1931, he was director of the New York State Psychiatric Institute.
23 Floyd Haviland, a New York psychiatrist.

good Indian but had at several times gone off half-cocked like this and needed a little soothing and that he would look into it and let me know. In the course of his letter Woodward said that I had done the A.P.A. a great injustice by writing such a letter to him, as a representative of the A.M.A. I told the damned fool it was not an official letter, and if you could see the letter you would realize it was a very informal personal kind of communication without any nastiness in it. I wasn't trying to be disagreeable to the buzzard; I was sincerely trying to find out why the A.M.A. council wouldn't pay any attention to us. Neither White nor Adler thought my letter was much amiss, although of course we all realize that I could have found a much better adjective than *honest*. That's the only thing in the letter which Woodward took seriously. I'm telling you all this because I think that Woodward may have written Orton and told him that I was insulting the A.M.A. and compromising the A.P.A. and Orton may have flourished this letter around at the council meeting and made it out to be worse than it is. If you will talk to Dr. White on the telephone, at my expense (I shall certainly charge it up in my committee expenses), you will find that this is a fair summary of the situation. White saw all the correspondence. I never answered the correspondence because I never took the letter any too seriously, in view of what these men told me. The only thing I ever did for which I deserve some criticism is something I doubt if Orton knows about. . . .

At the Minneapolis meeting the newspaper reporters, before the meeting, asked for some early releases. The National Crime Commission had just released their broadside which quoted our previous year's report. One of the reporters came up to George Pratt[24] and myself and asked where they could get some more information about our attitude. George said that no publicity committee had been appointed but that I was chairman of the committee. The reporter said, "Will you talk about it?" Of course I should have said that I would wait until the publicity committee had been appointed. Unfortunately I didn't; I talked with him along the usual lines. Because they were short of news about our Association, however, they played this up on the front page that evening with some big headlines about the head of the organization saying that the legal point of view was passé, or something of this sort. It was bad, there is no doubt about it, but it wasn't wicked. It was just unfortunate. It was not the mistake of a manic; it was the combined mistake of George Pratt and myself and the newspaper reporter, but it was chiefly referable to me.

I don't know how important this thing is. I've never given another thought to it since the meeting. . . . Since Orton has bumped me so hard, naturally I have thought of everything, and this is the only thing I can recall that I have any regrets for whatsoever. If you will look back in the transactions,

24 We have been unable to find any information on this individual.

you will find that we have never had anything but praise from everybody concerned. No committee reports have ever been received with as much complimentary remarks from members of the Association. Dr. Healy[25] never missed an opportunity to get up and say nice things about me personally in connection with the report. It was Adolf Meyer who reappointed me as chairman for five years. I'm telling you these things for what good they may be and also because your telegram very much stimulated me. It was read to me over the phone and I will have to wait until it comes out so that I can study it.

We are running about 20 to 24 patients in the sanitarium, some of whom are very interesting, and we are doing a little investigation with pituitary. Our school is running over with about 13 students coming from five or six different states. We have half a dozen neurological patients over at Christ's Hospital. We are not making much money yet, but things are looking pretty for 1930. . . .

Sincerely yours,

To WILLIAM ALANSON WHITE, WASHINGTON, D.C., NOVEMBER 24, 1928

Dear Doctor White:

I am very much gratified by your reassuring and comforting letter of November 21st. I shall do exactly as you say. I have had some very vigorous suggestions from Dr. Lowrey, but I shall be guided by the advice of my very loyal friends and counselors, among whom I certainly consider you at the top.

Sincerely yours,

To WILLIAM ALANSON WHITE, WASHINGTON, D.C., AUGUST 12, 1929

Dear Doctor White:

I see that Mr. Hoover has recognized the desirability of improving the prison situation at Leavenworth, Kansas, which is, as you may not know, about fifty miles from here on a concrete road.

I have long had my eyes on the federal prison at Leavenworth from the standpoint of being made a psychiatric consultant to the government for that prison. They have never had a psychiatrist there. There are three prisons at Leavenworth—a state prison, this federal prison, and the disciplinary barracks of the United States Army. The latter has a full-time psychiatrist. The state prison has a very experienced man, although not a duly qualified psychiatrist. The federal prison has no one.

25 Wiliam Healy was a Boston child psychiatrist and psychoanalyst, director of the Judge Baker Foundation. He published *Roots of Crime* (1935) with Franz Alexander.

I don't know enough about politics to know how to go at this, but I do know enough to know that you can tell me. I should appreciate very much all the help that you can give me. I feel sure that Mr. Hoover will ask you something about matters and I know you will be in favor of having some kind of psychiatric work done there. I think they need a full-time psychiatrist and of course I couldn't be that, but I should like to be the consulting psychiatrist whether or not they get a full-time man. Will you tell me how to proceed?

Sincerely yours,

To NORMAN FENTON,[1] WHITTIER, CALIFORNIA, SEPTEMBER 2, 1929

Dear Fenton:
. . . Because of our mutual memories, you will be happy, I know, to learn that I am publishing this winter a sort of case book in psychiatry [*The Human Mind*] which was originally suggested to me by Doctor Southard. Ten years have passed since then and my ideals have changed and the world has grown a little older and we have—thank God and Doctor Southard—a few new ideas in psychiatry. So it is not just as I thought it would be when I last talked it over with him, but I think it would please him if he were here. I am sure that no one but you can realize how much I have had him in mind while I have been writing it. Fortunately for me, and I hope for the cause, the publishers have been very kind about it and it is probable that the Literary Guild will distribute it as their January offering. Be that as it may, I hope it meets with the approval of my friends and the disciples of our old chief.

Sincerely yours,

To GEORGE NEUHAUS,[2] OMAHA, NEBRASKA, OCTOBER 16, 1929

My dear George:
I have Doctor Farrington's letter in regard to the admission of the Southard School to the Special School Association, and it was very courteous indeed of you to write me about it. They had asked Miss [Stella] Pearson for most of this dope also, but I will tell you about it so that you can write him direct. I will also have a catalog sent to you.
I thought you saw the school when you were down here. It is a small place as yet but a very promising one. Most of our students have been re-

1 Director of the Bureau of Juvenile Research, Whittier, California, and former colleague of KAM at Boston Psychopathic Hospital under Southard.
2 An Omaha, Nebraska, psychiatrist. E A. Farrington, director of the Special School Association, had asked him for an appraisal of the Southard School at the time of its application for admission to the association.

ferred to us from psychiatrists in various parts of the country. I believe at one time you tried to get one or two people down here and they may come yet. At present we are practically full up which means fifteen students. We have them from about nine different states if I am not mistaken. Miss Pearson, the director, had her training at Vineland, New Jersey, and then was educational director at the Connecticut State School for four years, and then conducted a private school in Oklahoma and was persuaded to come up here by us because we wanted a school of this sort in conjunction with our clinic and she wanted to conduct her school in connection with psychiatrists. For these reasons we made a very good combination.

Miss Pearson is a quiet, dignified woman who is very patient and long suffering with these children and has a great deal of interest in making a success of the school. Technically she knows very little about child guidance techniques that Lowrey and the rest of the fellows are using in the East, but intuitively she knows how to handle children. Of course she has had training in the special educational care of these particularly handicapped children. I think she is making a wonderful success of it. We have actually sent back into the public schools several children for whom a few years ago I should have recommended permanent state institutional care. In other words, she has helped us to learn what we should have known without having had to learn it from her, that the hopelessness that we ordinarily associate with feeble-mindedness is a mistake. We take a very different attitude toward our handicapped children now than we did a few years ago before we had this opportunity at hand.

I think you could commend the school quite highly. Its faults, I believe, are chiefly that it is still small, that it has not some of the elaborate equipment that some of the older schools have, that the playground space is rather limited. All of these things, I hope, will be remedied as we grow a little older. So far I think Miss Pearson has done remarkably well. I think I told you something about the school when you were here. As you have noticed, we named it after the dear old chief.

I certainly wish I could see you. I am looking forward to the trip you have in mind for me later in the year.

Sincerely yours,

To FRANCES WHITING,[3] NEW YORK, NOVEMBER 15, 1929

Dear Miss Whiting:

I have been thinking a good bit about your letter of November 5 asking me for some dope for advance publicity.

---

3 A publicist with Alfred A. Knopf, KAM's publisher, who had solicited information about KAM's background prior to the publication of *The Human Mind*.

I find it very difficult indeed to put together the material that you would want about me. I am sure you would get a very much more objective and more valuable account by writing to some of our mutual friends; for example, Mr. Elrik B. Davis, book editor of the *Cleveland Press*, Cleveland, Ohio, or Mr. Ray Yarnell, editor of *Capper's Farmer*, Capper Publications, Topeka, or Mr. Nelson Antrim Crawford, editor of *The Household Magazine*, Topeka. They all know me very well and I think would be glad, and perhaps even pleased, to give you just what you want.

I have already sent you something which I got together for the *Kansas City Journal-Post* some time ago. You no doubt have that on file.

I am glad to answer the particular questions you ask, however. I will tell you how I came to write the book. It is a rather complicated matter. You see there was a group of us gathered about the feet of Ernest Southard, professor of psychiatry at Harvard, during the war. We thought then, and I still think, that he was one of the greatest minds in American medicine, and besides that he was a very inspiring personality. I think perhaps I was one of his most beloved disciples, although I should not want to be quoted as saying that. I was certainly the youngest one, but on the other hand I think he was more intimate with me than with any of them. He wrote several books, one of which is a compilation of cases illustrating shell-shock, and another is a compilation of cases showing the opportunities and necessities for social work in psychiatry. He said people like to read about people and so he was fond of the case-history method, as was also my other professor, Richard Cabot, the author of *How Men Live* and numerous other books. I think I learned from them the idea of the great dramatic power which the actual histories of people in trouble contain. The further I got into medicine and the further I got into psychiatry in particular, the more I was convinced that the tragedies and comedies of their lives were far more fascinating than ordinary stage dramas. Of course I was interested in the scientific principles of behavior which underlay them all.

As I say in the preface, Southard commended me when I talked to him about writing a book about psychiatry. You see psychiatry was even then rapidly becoming popular, but there were no very competent textbooks. There are some textbooks, to be sure, but they are very abstruse and technical and the result is that most physicians don't read them and in fact very few physicians are even acquainted with them. You see we have always taught psychiatry wrongly as I view it; we've approached it from the rear end. We have shown a few extremely crazy individuals locked up somewhere in an asylum. We have told them that these are people with mental diseases, and the study of mental disease concerns itself with these lunatics. Well, naturally it is only an occasional student whose perspicacity and penetration are such that he can see that this lunatic wasn't always a lunatic and be interested in the way in which he came to be what he is. But psychiatry never taught much about that. It spent all of its time describing these end states and expected people to be interested in them. Of course psychiatrists, including myself, are interested in them in a way because they are theoretically very interesting and they have certain points of practical interest. There are certain individuals that we have to arrange about locking up. But there are a lot of other individuals all around us who are not going to be locked up—at least most of them are not going to be—and they are just as full of evidences of psychiatric principles. And they are a lot more accessible to treatment, too—some of them at least.

Now, all the time I was studying psychiatry I suffered, as every other student does, trying to find a textbook that would tell me about it without confining itself to a detailed technical description of these end conditions. I found that some psychiatrists were interested in these end conditions and some were not, and those who were not were interested in other aspects—for example, the psychoanalytic aspects, or the abnormal psychology of the thing, or the sociology, or what not. These were all to be found in various books written by various competent authors. My notion has always been to view the thing in a simple but comprehensive unitary way. Human beings show their humanness by getting into trouble in their contacts with one another. What are these troubles and how far does the fault lie with the psychological, the physical or chemical makeup of the one individual or the other?

Then I had another inspiration from the fact that I was brought up to be very bitter against psychoanalysis. By being "brought up," I refer to my medical school attitude at the time I got my first training. I came to see in time, however, that psychoanalysis was one of the great intellectual contributions of the twentieth century and I began to see that I could only understand psychiatry by knowing more about it. So I studied as much as I could about psychoanalysis and applied it as much as I could. I found out how very wrong my early prejudices had been. Then I began to try to find a reason for those prejudices. Of course we know that most of such prejudices arise within us, but I am convinced that they had been made more insuperable for me and for others by the unhappy way in which psychoanalysis was and has been, and perhaps I should say still is, presented to the medical readers and lay readers, too, of this country. It is as if a surgeon would hand out a platter of bloody fragments of human tissue to ignorant laymen and say—this is the result of surgery. One can imagine how shocked the laymen would be at seeing a platter of gore. As a matter of fact, that isn't surgery at all but merely the end results of the surgical operation. The psychoanalysts used to fling before the American public horrible extracts of this person's or that person's mind and call it psychoanalysis. This, they say, is the result of psychoanalytic delving—just see what we found! No wonder people were shocked by it. I think psychoanalysis can be presented to people in fairly complete detail without shocking them. I think I have done so, in a measure, in this book. It isn't that I object to shocking people, but I object to shocking people whom I expect to enlist in support of the idea I am promoting, that's all. I just think it's poor salesmanship, if that's what you want to call it, although there again I think I should not like to be quoted as using that word.

Another source of the book is probably to be found in my teaching. I have been teaching at Washburn College for nine years, altogether undergraduate students. I have been teaching them mental hygiene, abnormal psychology, and criminology, all of which are in a sense treated in my book. I found no good textbook for them and so I used my own syllabi and then I conceived putting together something of a textbook for them, and that, too, was one of my objectives. That's about all I can think of in the way of motives for having written the book.

Now as to some remarks about my travels, etc., I have never traveled outside of this country but I made it a point to get acquainted with every neuropsychiatrist of note in the country as far as I could. I have visited the clinics or hospitals of most of them. I used to spend several months a year going from one large city to the other visiting each man and getting personally acquainted with him. The result is that I know a good many of them. I helped to organize the Central Neuropsychiatric Association about ten years ago, which is an organization which comprises the leading neuropsychiatrists in the central states of the nation. I was also one of the eight charter members of the American Orthopsychiatric Association, at whose annual convention last year there were over a thousand people. Yet it is only four years old. I really am personally acquainted with a good many neuropsychiatrists and a good many medical men who are not psychiatrists but who live in this part of the country and refer cases to me. This leads me to say that another reason I wrote the book was for the reading of the general practitioners with whom I come into contact so much in my daily work. All of my clinical practice is referred to me by the general practitioners over the states of Kansas, Oklahoma, Missouri, Nebraska, New Mexico, etc. I wanted to write a book that they could read and which I could send them if I wanted to say, "see page 314 for description of this condition."

The thing I am most proud of is my association with my father and my brother and Mr. John Stone in the so-called Menninger Clinic. It has been our ambition to centralize as much as possible the methods of diagnosis and treatment of nervous and mental diseases and limit our work to nothing else. Consequently, without any capital to start with, we organized our clinic and a little later our hospital and a little later our school—the Southard School for nervous and backward children—and all of these are centrally controlled. We also have a neurological department at one of the local hospitals where we take our neurological cases. In this way we are equipped to handle all kinds of nervous and mental diseases, with the exception of brain surgery. But before you send out any publicity touching on these matters I earnestly request that you let me see it because it is very easy to offend doctors by mentioning personal facts about other doctors, particularly in regard to their clinical practice. Please construe this as a direct request, that you send out nothing about me which touches upon my professional work without letting me look it over.

Sincerely yours,

Part II
1930–39

The year 1930 was crucial in Dr. Karl's career. In January *The Human Mind* was published. It received a largely favorable response from both professional and lay readers, eventually becoming the bestselling book on psychology to that time. In it, Menninger illustrated through case histories the concrete operation of Freudian principles in everyday life. After debating whether to take his father to Europe with the proceeds or invest the money in the partnership, Dr. Karl chose to begin psychoanalysis with Franz Alexander in Chicago. Three years later, in a letter not published here, Dr. Karl said of the analysis with Alexander, "It was certainly the greatest experience of my life and marked, I think, a very definite turning point" (October 13, 1933).

That year was also a critical one in American psychiatry. As psychoanalyst and historian of psychiatry John A. P. Millet notes, three important psychiatric events occurred: "The First International Congress on Mental Hygiene—organized by Clifford Beers, with the help of distinguished American and foreign psychiatrists . . . was held in Washington, D.C., in May; the second was the organization of the Boston and Chicago Psychoanalytic Societies; and the third was the invitation from the University of Chicago to Franz Alexander . . . to become the first professor of psychoanalysis appointed in the United States."[1]

Even though Otto Rank's advocacy of a non-negotiable three-month term for analysis had been rejected by the majority of American analysts in favor of a longer, indefinite period, most analyses lasted only twelve to eighteen months, a far shorter time than their duration in later decades. In 1931, his analysis with Alexander completed, Dr. Karl returned to Topeka and to the concerns that would absorb his attention during the next decade: the clinic, the sanitarium, the Southard School, the criminal justice system, and the

---

1 John A. P. Millet, "Psychoanalysis in the United States," *Psychoanalytic Pioneers,* ed. Franz Alexander, Samuel Eisenstein, and Martin Grotjahn (New York: Basic Books, 1966), 544–45.

teaching of psychoanalysis. Always an advocate of psychoanalysis, Menninger made a commitment to explicate and defend certain key psychoanalytic concepts and practices that he considered misunderstood by both the public and the psychoanalytic community, and his letters attest to his willingness to cajole and correct those in any community—medical, psychiatric, political—who had failed to accept Freud's theories.

Jeanetta Lyle, who would later become Dr. Karl's second wife, joined the staff of the clinic and sanitarium in July of 1931 as Dr. Karl's collaborator on a column of psychological advice for the *Ladies Home Journal;* independently, between 1929 and 1942, Dr. Karl, as a member of the Topeka-based Advisory Council on the Mental Health of Children, also contributed articles to a *Household* magazine column, "Keeping Your Child's Mind Healthy."

In 1932, the AMA Council on Medical Education approved the residency program in neuropsychiatry of the Menninger Sanitarium (one year's training for doctors who had already had a year of internship and were seeking to specialize in psychiatry). The first residents were Robert Knight and Charles Tidd from Chicago, Leo Stone from New York, Frank Abbey from Kansas, and Ralph Fellows from Missouri. Another milestone was reached in 1932 with the founding of the Chicago Psychoanalytic Institute by Franz Alexander, assisted by Lionel Blitzsten, Ralph Hamill, Thomas French, and Karl Menninger. Dr. Karl was the first graduate. Earlier in the year, he had commented in a letter on the dissensions within the Boston Psychoanalytic Institute: "I wonder if someone couldn't pour oil on troubled waters if they went about it in the right way" (April 20, 1932). As in the Boston group, factionalism, friction, and politics destroyed harmony in the New York Psychoanalytic Institute. In a letter to Jelliffe a year later, Menninger observed, "Fortunately, things are going smoothly in Chicago so far," then added prophetically, "but we are young yet" (April 12, 1933). Indeed, rivalry and strife seemed endemic to these young institutes, and Menninger himself was soon embroiled in controversy related to the proposed hierarchy within the fledgling Chicago organization. The tone of his letters to Alexander regarding, on the one hand, the titles to be assigned to individual faculty members connected with the institute and, on the other, Alexander's criticism of Menninger's unauthorized use of material from his letters in an article on suicide exhibited a new assurance. That article became the first chapter of *Man Against Himself.*

Letters to Karen Horney and Ernst Simmel, analysts who would acquire further significance in the later correspondence, first appeared in 1933. Grace Gaines Menninger, Dr. Karl's first wife, commenced analysis with Horney in that year. Although the relationship between Menninger and Horney appeared to be cordial, Menninger soon came to regard her advocacy of self-analysis, her rejection of the dual instinct theory, and her emphasis on the role of society in personality formation as disloyal to Freud's cardinal precepts, and after Horney's rejection by the Chicago Institute, Menninger and Alexander united in their attacks on her. Simmel was one of the first of many German analysts to emigrate, and his fortunes in America became one of Menninger's persistent subjects of contemplation.

Rivalry in the Chicago Psychoanalytic Institute recurred in a 1934 exchange between Dr. Karl and Lionel Blitzsten. Blitzsten prided himself on frankness, a word repeated in his letters. Using frankness as his own rationale, Dr. Karl attempted to defuse the charge that he was displaying aggression. Thus the psychoanalytic tenet that challenges repression of thoughts and exalts candor was marshaled in the rhetorical strategy that Dr. Karl was increasingly to use to his own advantage in these arguments.

In 1934 Menninger traveled to Europe with Alexander to attend the Congress of the International Psychoanalytic Association in Lucerne. It was during this trip that Menninger had his singularly disappointing encounter with Freud.

The letters from the mid-1930s indicate that the various Menninger enterprises were prospering. Despite their unlikely setting in a small city remote from the major concentrations of population, the Menninger institutions had succeeded in attracting an international clientele. This prosperity may clarify Dr. Karl's wish to purchase both the library of Smith Ely Jelliffe and the prestigious *Journal of Nervous and Mental Disease,* which Jelliffe edited. (Both offers were rejected: the library was sold in 1941 to the Hartford Psycho-Analytic Institute, and Jelliffe retained control of the *Journal.*)

In 1935, at the request of physician friends, the Menninger Clinic staff offered its first postgraduate course in neurology and psychiatry to twenty-five practicing physicians. The goal of the course was to familiarize the general practitioner with techniques for understanding and handling the mentally ill patients who constitute a difficult portion of every doctor's practice. The Menninger Sanitarium captured national publicity that year through an article by Dwight Macdonald in *Fortune* magazine.[2]

Three innovative and enduring accomplishments of 1936 were the establishment of the *Bulletin of the Menninger Clinic,* edited and managed by Jeanetta Lyle (the first issue appeared in September); publication of the first entry in the Menninger Clinic Monograph Series, *Juvenile Paresis,* by William C. Menninger; and the organization of a psychoanalytic study group modeled after Ernst Simmel's group in Los Angeles. California was on Dr. Karl's mind for other reasons as well. In 1936 and 1937, the Menninger brothers considered locating a branch of the sanitarium in southern California, a site

2 Jeanetta Lyle went to New York to check the accuracy of this article; in conversing with its author, she was introduced to the notion of a nonprofit corporation. Subsequently, she discussed the idea with other Menninger staff members, and it became a catalyst for the transformation of the clinic, school, and sanitarium in 1941 into the Menninger Foundation.

that promised to complement the Topeka setting. California must have looked particularly appealing as the residents of Kansas suffered record-breaking heat and drought during the summer of 1936, "some fifty days with a temperature over 100°," as Dr. Karl noted in a letter of August 24, 1936 to Franz Alexander. In a trip to the West Coast in 1937, he sought an attractive location for this western extension of the Menninger Clinic. Santa Barbara was given serious consideration, but ultimately the plan was abandoned, and the Menninger partners decided instead to further develop the Topeka facility.

Concurrently, Dr. Karl made final modifications in his book *Man Against Himself* and completed the first revised edition of *The Human Mind*. These labors sparked controversy with Zilboorg, who was also conducting suicide research, and renewed conflict with Alexander. With Alexander the outcome was a permanent and eventually intractable disaffection, but the disputes with Zilboorg did not spoil their personal relationship. Zilboorg stated: "We shall continue to be intellectual, scientific adventurers . . . in the desert of clinical darkness. It is this that I admire in you and I don't care whether you and I ever are of the same mind as to suicide. And because I don't care I find it possible always to consider myself your friend" (letter of April 6, 1937).

Man Against Himself went on sale in February 1938. In an unpublished letter to Heinz Hartmann, Menninger would later write, "It is, as you know, the first book and so far as I know still the only book that came out wholeheartedly accepting the destructive instinct as a workable hypothesis and attempting to apply that to psychiatric and psychoanalytic data" (November 3, 1949). From the many positive appraisals by literary critics, Dr. Karl singled out the review by Joseph Wood Krutch in *The Nation*, which commented: "It makes the reader feel as if he had always known this but had not known how to express it" (letter of March 31, 1938). A dissenting note occurred only in Abraham Myerson's review; he and Menninger were old Boston friends but had had a sharp exchange earlier in 1938 over a survey Myerson was conducting to determine psychiatrists' attitudes toward psychoanalysis. Antipathies reignited after the appearance of Myerson's review, but the two soon resolved their differences and proclaimed mutual friendship and esteem.

At the year's end, Menninger ruminated on future projects; pondering the increasing American hostility toward foreign analysts and other refugees, he speculated in a letter to the League of American Writers that antisemitism might be a factor in the lack of acceptance of psychoanalysis and suggested that it be studied "exactly as we proceeded in the study of those other epidemics—yellow fever, typhoid, and the plague" (December 20, 1938). The American Psychoanalytic Association faced much the same problem, exacerbated by the fact that many of the refugee analysts were not physicians. American psychoanalysis had always been considered a branch of medicine by native practitioners, and the majority of them had opposed the European tradition of lay analysis. Although Dr. Karl had battled with often antagonistic state licensing boards for the accreditation of refugee medical analysts, he also objected to admitting lay analysts to the American Psychoanalytic Association. One reason for Menninger's opposition was that the Topeka Psychoanalytic Institute still had official jurisdiction over new institutes west of Topeka, including those in southern California where Simmel and Fenichel, both immigrants themselves, challenged the authority of the parent organization by supporting lay analysis. (Ironically, in the 1940s and early 1950s, the Topeka Institute changed its position and allowed the practice of lay analysis.)

The year 1939 was distinguished by changes in Dr. Karl's personal life. He interrupted his career in Topeka to live in New York City; there he saw a few patients, but the primary cause of his relocation was his decision to undergo further analysis, this time with Ruth Mack Brunswick, Freud's disciple and analysand. His letters to his family in Topeka during this period are some of the most entertaining in the correspondence. Although he commented on and interpreted such international events as the Civil War in Spain and the portents of World War II, more commonly he remarked on less grave matters. A celebrity in his own right, he reported in the manner of an observant tourist, at once awestruck, acerbic, and humorous—a kind of traveling correspondent providing graphic vignettes of New York society nightlife.

Despite Dr. Karl's absence, the Topeka Psychoanalytic Society was organized, and Dr. Karl was elected its first president. Moreover, the draft of an article on the Southard School written by Fred Kelly prompted Dr. Karl to enunciate again the principles of the school: "Everything we do is based on psychoanalysis, on the science, theories, and practices of Freud" (letter to Fred Kelly, July 10, 1939).

To Lawson Lowrey, New York, January 8, 1930

Dear Lawson:

. . . [something] I would like to bring out if I ever made another presidential address and which I shall try to bring out if I am your critic, is that the real spirit of orthopsychiatry is utter objectivity. It is an objectivity of a kind not found in any other psychiatric field that I know of. What we try to do is to objectify the patient for himself and for those who study him. Ordinary institutional psychiatry while it appears to be objective is really not so; it is paternalistic, it is machine-like, it is very superficial. . . .

I got interrupted here. By the way, do you use your dictaphone much? We use dictaphones here now exclusively. They are a great help, aren't they?

One trouble is however that you can't see what you have just said and when the telephone rings and you get interrupted you know how it is.

What I most wanted to write you about was to discuss this Europe business.[1] I am very grateful for your suggestions. I have read your letter several times. How long do you suppose an analysis by Alexander would require? I don't feel that I can afford more than a few months at this time, four at the outside. I thought I would take a low-power survey of things this trip and an oil-immersion concentration [a metaphor from microscopy] next time. On the other hand I'm going alone this time and a couple of years hence or three I thought I would like to take Grace and perhaps the children also with me, and of course if I did that there would be no psychoanalysis. I realize that. Then I also have some misgivings about the cost of an analysis. I suppose that would run the expense up another $1,000.00 or so.

You see I don't know what I want. I haven't the slightest idea what I want. I thought I wanted to kind of look around Europe so I wouldn't be quite so ignorant when Europe was being talked about and get acquainted with a few men etc. and so on. But of course the fundamental thing I ought to be trying to do is improving my vision and getting more depth and inspiration and so forth and I presume that an analysis would be far more likely to be of an advantage to me in this way than a mere scrutinizing of various cities and various clinics and meeting various doctors and having dinner with them, etc. I haven't done either one, however, and I don't know which would come first. I seem to be drifting along in the direction of taking this tour which will last about eight or nine weeks and then spending a month or so more looking around more carefully in London and Berlin, perhaps Vienna. . . .

Won't you please look somewhat critically over the enclosed *Household* column for February. Tell me if you think we are doing a good job. We get thousands of letters. We answer a hundred or more a month. . . . I am going to write an article on how parents mistreat their children in the name of correction.[2]

Affectionately yours,

To Lawson Lowrey, New York, January 22, 1930

My dear Lawson:

Well, old top, the book [*The Human Mind*] is out and the die is cast and I'm expecting to get hell from you most any day now. I hope you are not too disappointed with it. I feel a little better than I did while it was still in

---

1 KAM was debating whether to use his royalties from *The Human Mind* to travel to Europe, to invest in the sanitarium, or to begin analysis with Alexander.

2 KAM answered many letters in which mothers had remarked on their use of corporal punishment.

galley proof. It seems to me to be a little better written than it did then some way or other but there are still plenty of flaws in it God knows.

I'm glad that you have helped me with my *folie de doute* in regard to going to Europe. I think myself that the best thing to do is to go and look things over this time and then go back later and stay longer. And don't worry, I shall be right there in Washington with bells on the 1st of May.[3] As far as I know I'm not on the program but I expect to have a good time running around meeting people, etc. Grace will probably come with me. . . .

I'm glad you like the *Household*.

As soon as you have had time to look at my book tell me what you think. You can see from the number of times I return to this theme that it is much on my mind. Bookstores are loading up with it here and I am expecting a lot of fun soon. I had a nice letter from Jelliffe today. He seems to think it's all right, in fact gets a bit extravagant.

I asked them to send you a free copy. I hope they did. If they didn't I'll see that they do but in the meantime you might blow yourself for $5.00 and charge it to the Institute for Child Guidance, address 145 East 57th St.

The real reason for my writing at the present time is that I expect to be in New York from about February 10th, maybe 15th, to and including February 22nd. If you hear of anyone who wants a speech made on psychiatry bad enough to pay me something for it, tell them that you will use your influence and persuasion to get me to do it. What leads me to think of this is the announcement in the current number of the Mental Hygiene bulletin that you and Ed. Strecker[4] are about to make a million dollars apiece addressing somebody I can't find out just who it is at Romford Hall. Knowing that you wouldn't be doing this for nothing I thought you might be declining a few insignificant lectures at $100.00 or $200.00 a shot which I would be glad to fill in for you if possible.

Bill [Menninger] says to tell you that I am slightly manic at the present moment, which is a good thing because I have been quite depressed. Not really depressed, just jokingly so.

Best wishes and hope to hear from you soon.

Sincerely,

FROM SMITH ELY JELLIFFE, NEW YORK, JANUARY 25, 1930

My dear Karl:

The Herald-Tribune has just asked me to review your book and I have said "Yes." So what with all the other things here I am just having gone

---

3 KAM was going to Washington for a meeting of the White House Conference on Child Health and Protection; he was a member of the subcommittee on problems of mental health in childhood.

4 A Philadelphia psychiatrist, consultant at the Institute of the Pennsylvania Hospital.

over it rapidly. Before I warm up to the job I thought I would call your attention to some minor mistakes and also a misstatement of fact or two and also express a small gesture of disapproval so as to get over the resistances.

'Tis a damn good book—even if a bit too big, but then it deals with lots of things and you do it very well—exceedingly well. It is graphic and accurate—reporterese, but of the best—scientific yet not pedantic.

As to a few small errors. . . . On p. 264 you make a mistake. "It came about in this way—Freud (1885 should be put in) was studying in Paris. The great French neurologists Janet, Charcot and Bernheim were demonstrating, etc." Now this is all wrong. Janet was never in Paris when Freud was there. Janet did not get his A. B. until 1886. He then taught philosophy in the Lycées of Chateaurouix and Havre, 1886 to 1890. Got his Ph.D. in 1889. In 1890 came to Paris and began to study medicine with Raymond. Charcot died in 1891. Raymond had the chair. Janet got his M.D. degree in 1893—so this is all applesauce and should be corrected. Bernheim was in Nancy and not in Paris and was a bitter antagonist of Charcot. Freud went to see Bernheim about 1889—I am not sure of the date. Janet did not do any of his work in Paris until five years after Freud had left.

"A little later, Breuer died." Breuer died only two or three years ago. This whole paragraph is incorrect and gives a false impression. Freud had associated himself with Breuer in 1880–1881 and Freud when he went to Charcot (1885) tried to interest Charcot in the things Breuer and he were interested in but Charcot was too much taken up in hypnosis. (See Freud in Grote's Darstellung.) When Freud later (1895) with Breuer published the *Studien uber Hysterie,* Breuer took over the Janet hypotheses much to Freud's discontent and thus they began to separate, and when the transference situation of Breuer's patient was so evident that she accused Breuer of giving her a child, then Breuer ran away from the whole sexual situation, and that's why Breuer never joined in. This is a very unsatisfactory page, in my opinion—the only one I totally disapprove of. Whether to mention it or not in the review I do not know.

I think the footnote on p. 265 could have been phrased differently about "nonoriginal." See Freud's *Introduction to the Dream* where nearly all the predecessors are mentioned, which makes this kind of a footnote not quite gracious.

Then I don't quite like the frequent citation of Frink. He was a fourflusher. Someone else wrote his book and he is no good and could not himself adjust because he was a crook and grafter and those of us who have worked hard don't relish such a number of his citations pushed down our gullets.[5] I don't

5 In 1923, after a visit to Freud, H. W. Frink rankled the New York Psychoanalytic Society by his arrogant assumption that he was Freud's appointed disciple in America and by his caustic criticism of Brill's *Fundamental Conceptions of Psychoanalysis* (1921). After a second visit to Freud, Frink suffered a psychotic breakdown.

care for psychasthenia. Janet's psychasthenia was a jumble of precox, manic depressives, brain tumors, paretics, etc., etc., as the long section history later revealed. It was a "no good" clinical syndrome.

This is enough of a holler for this time.

With sincere regards,

To LAWSON LOWREY, NEW YORK, JANUARY 30, 1930

My dear Doctor Lowrey:

I'm answering herewith your letter of January 6th asking two questions in regard to fundamentals.

1. What is mental health? I recently defined mental health as "the adjustment of human beings to the world and to each other with a maximum of effectiveness and happiness. Not just efficiency, or just contentment—or the grace of obeying the rules of the game cheerfully. It is all of these together. It is the ability to maintain an even temper, an alert intelligence, socially considerate behavior, and a happy disposition. This, I think, is a healthy mind."

Would you make a distinction in such a definition for children and for adults? Theoretically, no, practically yes. Children are in a formative process, with a rapidly changing base, so to speak. They are obliged to sever primary libidinous fixations and make new ones. This is a difficult task but a very necessary one and one which is not necessary for the adult; consequently, one might add to the requisites of mental health "a proper progress in the emancipation of the child from his parents."

If so, what is the distinction and why do you make it? I've already answered this.

2. What, in your opinion, would constitute the best constructive program for the development and preservation of mental health?

The dissemination of correct information about the nature of the mind and the nature of so-called mental disease and a correction of the erroneous public attitude that the symptoms of mental ill health constitute an exception to be regarded with terror, revulsion, or amusement.

If these are not answered sufficiently in detail I shall be glad to supplement them.

Sincerely yours,

To CARL VAN DOREN,[6] NEW YORK, FEBRUARY 7, 1930

My dear Mr. Van Doren:

I want to thank The Literary Guild of America for their very courteous

6 A member of the advisory board of the Literary Guild, critic Van Doren was influential in persuading the club to choose *The Human Mind* as one of its main selections.

treatment of me in every respect. I think the binding you put on my book was very attractive. The one hundred copies have arrived, and most of them have been distributed to various friends of mine. The past issues of the Guild are on the way so that I will have duplicates of nearly everything, to my immense satisfaction.

Let me tell you again how very much I appreciate the honor of having had my book selected by the Guild, how very enthusiastic I am about the Guild itself. I shall continue to be a member indefinitely. And in spite of the fact that I observe that you have never taken two books by the same author it will be my ambition to write something else so good that you can't resist it.

The issue of "Wings" which you sent out with the book seems to be a very nice issue. My own objections pertain to the first page. I can't imagine who gave the information to the editor.

In the first I am not over six feet tall as it states; my skin is very fair rather than dark; as to angularity in features and general appearance I only wish this were a little more true. I weigh 200 pounds, and 200-pounders are rarely angular.

I do not recall that I ever said I have never been out of the United States, I have been to both Mexico and Canada, and that's something, isn't it?

But most of all I was astonished to read that "in spite of the K in his given name, Dr. Karl Menninger is not German." My middle name is Augustus and I have never had the slightest reason to apologize for my German ancestry; on the contrary, I am very proud of it. I have retained the "K" in my name very happily because of this fact. My grandparents came from Germany, and one of my ambitions is to go back to Germany and see their birthplace and old home. I have the greatest admiration for the German people, and I have always had, even when it was not so popular to do so. My mother's parents were part German, part Welsh, and part English. But no one in our family ever made any claim to Revolutionary ancestry. Please assure your public of that. I detest such emphasis on glorious old-line stock; I think that conceptions of heredity have done far more harm than good in the world, and I certainly never boosted my sense of inferiority by wistful gestures in the direction of Colonial ancestry. Please understand me; I don't decry the old stock. I merely disavow any necessity for comforting myself with the notion that, bad as I may turn out, I came from the good old pioneers.

My mother was indeed a pioneer, but a pioneer on the Western plains. She came from Pennsylvania as a little girl ten years old, the oldest of eight children. The first year was a bountiful one and they thought Kansas was all that Heaven had been described. The next year there was a drought and they nearly starved to death. Many of the experiences described by Rolvaag in *Giants in the Earth* and other stories of that sort my mother experienced. If my heredity must come in for discussion I refer you to her.

It also is incorrect to say that when I finished my preparatory medical work I returned to Topeka. I returned to Kansas City for a time and worked in the hospital there and then went back to Boston and taught in the Harvard Medical School. I came back to Topeka when my chief, Dr. Ernest Southard, died in 1919.

Sincerely yours,

To WILLIAM ALANSON WHITE, WASHINGTON, D.C., MARCH 6, 1930

My dear Doctor White:

Item 1. Thank you for the comment on the problem case of *The Household*. I shall modify your adjectives slightly for editorial purposes and publish the letter along with the other comments if you don't mind.

Item 2. I agree with you that the Orthopsychiatric is getting pretty large. The program this year I think was not quite so good as last but the audience was just as large and apparently just as enthusiastic. For the first time in seven years I am no longer one of the officers, and I think that ought to help the organization providing God will come and reign in my stead. Dave Levy is going to be president and I think he has rare good judgment and all ought to go well with him. At any rate it shows that a lot of people are interested in getting together and talking over about their troubles in saving the world.

Item 3. I am told that your review of my book for the *Survey* is wonderful. I heard that in advance from the editor, Miss Ross. I am deeply grateful to you for saying nice things about it but I am in great ecstasy over the fact that you see good in it and that you think so well of it. It pleases me of course that the *New York Times* and so forth and so on have published nice comments coming from literary people and the like, but to have you and Dr. Ruggles[7] and Dr. Jelliffe and other psychiatrists look it over and pronounce it satisfactory does me an awful lot of good. I think you know what I mean. I tried hard to be honest with myself and honest with the thing I was trying to represent. I tried to be fair to psychiatry, and that's a big order. I realize that if the book is popular it's going to be because psychiatry is great stuff and not because of any creation of mine. If I have helped to put it in simple and assimilatable form for public consumption I'm not sorry, of course, but neither do I overestimate my part in it. Anyway, I'm glad you think it was all right.

Item 4. I'm sending you under separate cover a Literary Guild copy of my

7 Arthur H. Ruggles was physician in chief and superintendent of the Butler Hospital, Providence, R. I.

book. I've had a good deal of trouble with Knopf about sending out copies, and I'm sending you a Literary Guild copy for several reasons. In the first place you can't buy one, and it will be a little different edition for you. In the second place I happen to have two or three on hand. In the third place, with Dr. Jelliffe's assistance, I have revised my erroneous remarks about Freud on two pages at the opening of the "Motives" chapter, and when the third edition[8] comes out with Dr. Freud in his proper position and incidentally some remarks about Dr. White, I will send it to you if you would like to have a copy of this third printing. It ought to be out in a few months, perhaps sooner.

Item 5. I have just within twenty-four hours returned from New York to Cleveland and also stopped off at Columbus to look into an interesting murder case that I had heard about for scientific reasons only.

Item 6. While I was in New York the question came up about writing for some magazines. Of course Dr. Jelliffe feels rather strongly opposed to it. He thinks it would have a bad effect on my morale and be somewhat cheapening, etc. I feel on the other hand that if I say exactly what I think and refuse to have any editorial changes made for the sake of policy and go on the point of view that there are certain members of society who have to have general principles explained to them in very simple and practically applied ways that I would not sacrifice anything. As for dignity I never aspire to that anyway. Frankwood Williams and Lowrey think I would be foolish not to take on some of these jobs and go to it. Perhaps I shouldn't have told you what these other men said as it may complicate your view of the matter. If you have time to express an opinion however I should be very happy to listen to it.

Sincerely yours,

FROM WILLIAM ALANSON WHITE, WASHINGTON, D.C., MARCH 8, 1930

My dear Menninger:

Thank you for your very interesting and full letter of the 6th instant with illustrations on each page of the Menninger Sanitarium. Every time I see the picture I feel as if I would like to come there and rest. The trouble is I won't be in the Topeka jurisdiction when the time arrives.

I hope you will like my review of your book, but I assure you that it was through no friendship of mine for you that I made a good review of it. It was solely because I thought the book deserved it. You have turned a trick for psychiatry, and I can't help but believe that you have done psychiatry a service as well as all the various people—of whom I hope there will be many—who will read your book. It usually takes something more than a scientist to

8 He means the third *printing*, which incorporated some minor changes.

write a book and something more than an author to present a scientific view. It is the same old story. If you get a work on psychiatry translated by a German into English it isn't worth a whoop if the German isn't a psychiatrist. He can't get over the finer nuances of meaning. I think you have been able to do that.

What I have just said leads me to add that I think by all means you should write some magazine articles. I think the day is passing rapidly when the doctor has to sit in a dark corner of the world off by himself, secluded and hidden in every possible way, and wait until he becomes famous. The physician who has a message for the people owes it to the people to deliver it. I have written barrels full of stuff for the newspapers in my nearly forty years of medical life but it has almost all been written by proxy—that is, by reporters who have interviewed me—and for the most part the whole bunch of it hasn't been worth a damn. Occasionally I try writing something myself and whereas I think what I write is better, yet I haven't had the journalistic training, and despite the fact that I write clearly for a certain type of audience I doubt if I am a good writer for the general public. Now I think you have this gift, and I don't see why you shouldn't use it. You know how James Harvey Robinson has put it—how important he has said the popularization of science is; if the scientist insists on talking a language nobody else can understand after a while they will jump the scientist. The scientist has got to maintain contact with the great mass of people who, after all, support him, and I think he owes it to them. It is the same old story over again. The man of wealth not only is privileged to give certain of his moneys for public welfare purposes but by the great Lord Harry he comes pretty near having to in these days if he wants to be respectable. Of course that doesn't mean that you are going to have your name stuck up on all the filling stations or that you are going to write for the *Police Gazette*. I don't have to discuss such details with you. But selected articles in the proper magazines, as informative as you can make them, cannot help but be worthwhile. The only trouble is that psychiatry is so oversold now that you will probably sink what little is left of the ship afloat. But never mind—go ahead.

Thank you very much for your kind offer of sending me a Guild copy of your book. I assure you I shall be more than pleased to have it and shall treasure it. I hope you will be so good as to inscribe it to me, that it may have still further a personal value.

And by the way, before I stop writing a letter which is about to compete with yours in length, let me add that I have just finished reading a book on mental hygiene, under the title however of *Love in the Machine Age*, by Floyd Dell if you please, which to my mind is as good a piece of work on the mental hygiene subject as yours is on the psychiatric side. In fact if I were a plutocratic publisher I would like to put two books out in the same set. This may be overenthusiastic but at any rate you see that you get the book and read it and let me know what you think about it. I have written a review of it for the April number of *Mental Hygiene*.

Very sincerely yours,

FROM FRANZ ALEXANDER, BERLIN, APRIL 9, 1930

Dear Dr. Menninger

Dr. Oberndorf wrote me about you and I shall be very pleased to undertake your analysis. Of course, three months are not sufficient for a thorough analysis, and it would be advisable for you to finish it up on a later occasion and to consider these first three months only as the beginning.

I shall be in Berlin in July, leaving August for a summer place, and be back again in Berlin in the middle of September. You could of course spend August in the same place and work with me. Only the first fortnight in September will be somewhat problematic as to our working because in these two weeks presumably I am going to travel around.

I hope to see you in Washington where we will have opportunity to discuss the details.

Sincerely yours,

TO FRANZ ALEXANDER, NEW YORK, MAY 22, 1930

Dear Dr. Alexander:

I am very hopeful that you have decided to be in Chicago this fall so that I may begin my analysis. I have burned all bridges so that my resistance will have a hard time getting me away from it now. I am sure I shall be much the better for the experience, to say nothing of the advantages accruing to my patients.

Won't you drop me a line at your convenience and give me assurance that you will be in Chicago and tell me approximately when and where.

Sincerely yours,

FROM FRANZ ALEXANDER, CHICAGO, JUNE 4, 1930

My dear Dr. Menninger:

I was very pleased to receive your letter saying that you definitely decided to undertake an analysis, and I hope that I shall be able to start to work with you in the first part of October. I beg to tell you that in Chicago I shall take $20 for one session because I shall not be able to take more than five or six cases. Please address me [at the] University of Chicago.

Very sincerely yours,

To Lawson Lowrey, New York, October 30, 1930

My dear Lawson:

Well, old fellow, I wish you were here being analyzed by a real psychoanalyst along with your friend Barty [Leo Bartemeier][9] and myself. We are having a wonderful time of it with ups and downs, of course, but on the whole it is an amazing experience which I am so glad I finally brought myself to. Barty and I live in the same hotel together altho he flies home for three days a week and I go home once every two weeks. If anything should bring you to Chicago, remember our address and let us know at least two quarts in advance.

I am also doing a little private practice here to the extent of two or three psychoanalytic patients a day, and I am trying to do a little writing. You may have seen the *Ladies Home Journal.* Two articles have now appeared therein. They have raised my salary and I am still going strong and am now working on the February issue. I am getting my stride and doing somewhat better. I think you will like December and January even better than the present ones. You will recall that you were probably instrumental in my having done this. What I mean is that I am sure it is a good thing and am glad I am doing it for I think it will do a lot of good. I don't like the way the editor ended up the article and put the little center affair in saying that we stood ready to save the world and all they had to do was to write Dr. Menninger and he will solve all their problems.[10] I have written him to cut that out. However, we haven't gotten a great many letters so far and of those I have got, I am answering most of them by telling them to consult their nearest psychiatrist and I am suggesting whom to consult.

Could you take the time, old fellow, to give me a list of some of the men in New York whom I can refer psychiatric cases to? Now I know the New York fellows perhaps as well as you do, but I don't know the younger fellows or who is doing private practice or who has time to do it, etc. So please

9 Leo Bartemeier and KAM became companions and friends while they were both analysands of Alexander's in Chicago. Bartemeier was the first psychoanalyst in Detroit and a charter member of the Detroit Psychoanalytic Society. Between 1924 and 1926, Bartemeier studied neurology and psychiatry with Adolf Meyer in Baltimore. He then moved to Detroit and entered private practice. In 1938 he became a training analyst in Chicago. He was elected president of the APA in 1944. At the close of World War II, in 1945, he accompanied KAM and three other psychiatrists on a tour of the European theater of operations.

10 The editorial material that KAM dislikes begins: "Upon mental hygiene rests the ability to maintain an even temper, an alert intelligence, socially considerate behavior, and a happy disposition. It is of inestimable value in family life where contacts are so intimate and young lives so impressionable" (*Ladies Home Journal* 47 [Oct. 1930], 109). It continues in this vein for three more short paragraphs.

take the time to sit down and make out a list of a dozen men or six if you like to whom I can conscientiously refer these problem cases. I would refer them to you if you were doing private practice, you old rascal, and whenever you get ready to open up that branch office for the Menninger Clinic, let me know and I will finance it and make you the director and everything else and send you some patients besides.

Give my love to Ella and I am sure Barty would want me to remember him to you if he were here. I am going to see him at lunch at the Quadrangle Club in a few minutes. Dr. French,[11] formerly of Bloomingdale, also analyzed by Alexander, is locating here and is lunching with us today.

Sincerely yours,

To ELIZABETH M. HINCKS,[1] DETROIT, MARCH 9, 1931

My dear Dr. Hincks:

I appreciated very much indeed your inquiry of February 27.

The Southard School is the outgrowth of a conviction that I had about seven or eight years ago that something of the sort ought to be started in this part of the country. As it has turned out, however, most of our children have come from other parts of the United States. It is a small school, and incidentally it has always been a financial liability. We are not running it for the sake of making money but for the sake of providing scientific care for these children who so much need it and who are so often so greatly neglected.

The chief advantage of the school is its small size and the direct personal attention which it enables us to give our little patients. We have a capacity of fifteen and we are considerably below that number at present.

The age limit is roughly, three to fifteen. At the present time we do not have anyone over twelve, but we have had children as old as seventeen. We think on the whole, however, that the younger group would be better since that constitutes the majority of our children.

We take all types of problem children, both the feeble-minded and the behavior-problem types. We can do this because we are so small that we do not try to group children according to their diagnostic catagory but rather

11 Thomas French, a Chicago psychoanalyst. With Alexander, he conducted studies on brief psychotherapy and psychosomatic medicine. A member of the original staff of the Chicago Psychoanalytic Institute, he became its director of research in 1956. "Bloomingdale" refers to Bloomingdale Asylum for the Insane, established in 1771 in New York City. It was moved to White Plains, New York, in 1894, and in 1936 the name was changed to the New York Hospital, Westchester Division.

1 Director of the Wayne County Clinic for Child Study, Wayne County Juvenile Court, Detroit, Michigan.

deal with them individually or in small groups on the basis of their play and learning capacity.

We have had a few psychiatric and neurotic problems in children who have not been feeble-minded. In fact, I think our most brilliant and satisfactory results have been in these children. We have one such at present.

The expenses, concerning which you ask, are approximately one hundred dollars a month. I say approximately for the reason that we occasionally take children who plan to stay several years for as low as ninety and in some instances we are obliged to charge one hundred and twenty-five and even one hundred and fifty in cases of exceptionally difficult children. We ordinarily say that one hundred dollars is our standard minimum.

We would be glad to consider taking the fifteen-year-old girl whom you mention, providing her parents would be satisfied with the school. If they are socially ambitious and the child is the mental age of eleven, I am not certain that they would be satisfied since we do not have facilities for teaching cooking and other things which girls of this age probably should know. On the other hand, we have had several girls at one time or another of about this age level who rather took it upon themselves with our encouragement and assistance to act as assistants to the teachers and the director and felt very important in so doing and thereby achieved a considerable degree of self-reliance and self-assurance which combined with restraint, which the home training had never achieved. We should be very glad indeed to have the parents of this child communicate with us if they are at all interested. We should not like, however, to have them understand that the school is a large or pretentious institution such as can be found in many places in the East. Our purpose has been quite the opposite, developing a modest home school in which the children were in daily contact with each other and with the teachers and with ourselves and try to develop in them not only a certain educational attainment where possible but also a certain degree of poise and self-control, which are so likely to be lacking in these individuals.

We shall appreciate very much any children whom you may send us to the school. We depend entirely upon our professional friends, and, as I have said, the school has never been and probably will never be anything but a certain amount of financial liability, but on the other hand it gives us an opportunity to take care of some of the many children whom we see in our clinic and concerning whom we are consulted by our friends in various parts of the country and cares for them in a way which I have not felt that most of the schools for backward and problem children have done. We are trying to make it better all of the time and in some degree I think we are succeeding.

I am exceedingly interested in the clinic which your stationery announces and hope that you will tell me a little more about it when you next write.

Sincerely yours,

To Gov. Harry H. Woodring,[2] Topeka, March 30, 1931

My dear Governor:

I wish to add my tribute to the many which you must be receiving for your courage and intelligence in vetoing the bill in regard to capital punishment.

I am quite convinced that the capital-punishment measure would have defeated itself in actual practice. I am opposed to it for the reasons that you mention in your very able discussion of the problem, and also because I think it has a very bad effect on public opinion, but most of all because I think it gives a false sense of security and destroys the only material from which we will ever get at a scientific understanding of crime. I have elaborated these views in an article which I should be very glad to submit to you were I not fully aware of the enormous work which is before you and the impossibility of reading everything pertaining to your diverse interests.

What I most admire is your intelligent understanding of a problem from a psychological standpoint, which most people understand so very little. I also admire your courage in living up to your convictions. I am not one of the many thousands of people who voted for you, or at least tell you they voted for you. As a personal friend of John Hamilton, I voted for your opponent. But I am very glad indeed that you were elected.

I have been very much interested in these problems for a long time. It is still my hope that Kansas will some day take some forward steps in regard to the scientific examination of the prisoners whom it is called upon to deal with. I am quite certain that the difficulties of decision in regard to parole, as well as those in regard to sentencing, could be considerably simplified by the study of the mental condition of the offender, not with an idea to proving him insane but with an idea to discovering something of the psychiatric indications as to what he is capable of or is not capable of in the way of social adjustment.

Sincerely yours,

From Alan Finlayson,[3] Cleveland, July 28, 1931

My dear Dr. Menninger:

Your letter of July 8, enclosing a copy of your letter to Mrs. B—— of Lakewood, Ohio, was referred to me today on my return from my vacation. I wish to thank you for referring this patient to me.

I believe that one who is doing psychiatry labors under the delusion that it is much better known than it really is. Many of the people that I come in

2 The governor of Kansas, who in 1931 vetoed a bill authorizing capital punishment.
3 KAM's colleague at the Chicago Psychoanalytic Institute; after he finished his training, he practiced in Cleveland.

contact with, who are very well informed along other lines, have in many instances heard the term psychiatry or psychiatrist, and if they have, they have only a vague notion of what it is all about, and as far as psychotherapy is concerned it might just as well be a word in Choctaw, as far as their having any appreciation of its meaning. It will only be through contacts handled through such men as you, who will get word to the public, that will make it better known and help people to avail themselves of its benefits.

As I said when I saw you in Chicago, there is a great deal of opposition from certain people here in Cleveland to psychotherapy and those are the people who are in positions of influence and that make the public listen to what they say. The only way to overcome this opposition is to demonstrate that psychotherapy does have something to offer in a remedial way.

I hope I will have the pleasure sometime in the not too distant future of seeing you and talking with you again. With very kind regards, I am

Sincerely yours,

Boston

To C. F. MENNINGER, WILLIAM C. MENNINGER AND JOHN R. STONE, TOPEKA, OCTOBER 17, 1931

My dear partners:

It is Saturday noon. I am back from the C.N.P.A. Convention, having caught a fast train last night at midnight. Buffalo is twelve hours west of here. I don't think it was worthwhile to stay over because most of the program was yesterday and I have a lot to do here, especially my two patients[4] whom I don't want to neglect.

It was a pretty good convention. A large attendance, and a few good papers, although as usual neurologic things were overemphasized. Many of the doctors asked about Will.

Having been secretary for ten years I thought it was probably wise for me to insist upon resigning and did so, suggesting Henry Woltman in my place. I was made president. The next meeting will be in Rochester [Minnesota] and I am going to give them a bang-up paper on psychoanalysis.

Have several ideas as a result of the convention which I want you to earnestly consider:

1. Dehydrating an individual who has had a brain injury or who has had a brain lesion, particularly an acute one, is the routine treatment in Philadelphia, and it is done not only by administering glucose intravenously but more especially by holding the fluid intake down to about one-fourth of the usual amount. The patient gradually gets accustomed to the thirstiness. This is continued sometimes for months.

4 KAM saw two patients in Boston during his analysis with Alexander.

2. They showed us some encephalograms and the Association decided that one case had been killed by the encephalogram, which was rather embarrassing for the speaker. He used the usual method of sucking out some fluid and then injecting air and taking the pressure each time. Blackwenn[5] has invented a needle device whereby this can be done simultaneously, which is theoretically safer and seems to have wide approval. I suggest you write to him immediately and get one.

3. This cortin described in the Associated Press dispatch which was in all the newspapers, and you may have seen it, is really quite a discovery, I guess. You understand, I think, that it is the extract of the cortex of the adrenal. It has distinctly different effects from adrenalin. Chiefly they seem to be in the direction of giving pep and endurance. They have tried it out on progressive muscular atrophy and Addison's Disease with great success, although it gives no results in Myasthenia Gravis. I think it ought to be tried as an experiment at least in neurasthenia. But it is very expensive and hard to get. There seems to be little storage of the substance in the gland. It takes many bushels of glands to get a small amount of hormone. Nevertheless, I think it would pay us to correspond with Dr. Hartmann[6] and see if we can't exchange some raw material purchased by us from the Morrell Company there in Topeka for some finished product, or perhaps Mildred [Law] could follow his technique and make it. I suggest that Will write him immediately as I think more of such research as this should be going on in our institution all the time.

4. Timme gave a very stimulating talk on calcium deprivation, the substance of which is that he thinks many cases of obscure nervous disease are really due to this cause, running from headaches, gastrointestinal and pseudo-tuberculosis syndrome symptoms to behavior disorders, but particularly those in which a reaction is made too suddenly, indicating a hyperirritability of the nervous system, familiar of course in tetany. He had some rather astonishing tales to tell about temper tantrums and off-the-handle reactions in children which were immediately and marvelously cured by calcium administration, relapsing as soon as the administration was discontinued.

Because I think this, too, should be a matter for research and experimentation at the school as well as in the hospital, I made careful note as to the technique of diagnosis and treatment. In diagnosis Timme stresses a low

5 Probably W. J. Blackwenn, a Wisconsin physician associated with the development of drug therapy to treat psychiatric disorders. In 1930 he published "Products of Sleep and Rest in Psychotic Patients" (*Archives of Neurology and Psychiatry*), reflecting ten years' experience with the use of barbituates to treat mentally ill patients.

6 Frank A. Hartman, who, with Katherine A. Brownell, had developed cortin at a Buffalo, New York, laboratory. The hormone extract from the cortex of the adrenal gland was used to treat palsy and Addison's disease. Leonard G. Rowntree and C. H. Greene of the Mayo Clinic were independently conducting similar experiments.

blood calcium and high blood sugar (occasionally also high blood pressure, which of course he thinks is due to the same cause, namely overreaction on the part of the sympathetic system). X-rays of the skull he considers very important and he says there are two types—those in which lots of calcium seems to have been laid down so that the skull is thick, has numerous calcium deposits in evidence, often shows pineal and other calcifications, etc., and the other is just the reverse, the skull being very thin and there being many recognized areas of insufficient calcification. Now he thinks the majority fall into the former group, and that the latter group, namely the thin-skulled people, may also show the opposite kind of blood findings from the former group. The former and commoner group of about 85% of cases he thinks represent calcium deprivation occurring in sympathicotonic individuals and the latter smaller thin-skulled ones represent calcium deprivation occurring in vagotonic individuals.

Both should be given calcium—for example, calcium lactate in tablet or powder form—five days a week. In order to activate this calcium, the former or first group should be given parathymone 5 to 10 minims three times a week hypodermically for two weeks and then rest for one week. The dose is slowly increased but one must look out for kidney injury.

The second group should be given the calcium plus viosterol or vitamin B in some other form.

This sounds rather simple, almost too simple a formula, but it could do no harm to try it out, for example on Mrs. H——. . . .

As an interesting corollary Timme says that calcium administered during the week prior to menstruation would often greatly relieve the discomfort of women subject to dysmenorrhea.

I hope things continue to go well there and I should like to hear all about it frequently. I hope Dr. Fellows[7] is enjoying his work.

Sincerely yours,

Boston

To C. F. MENNINGER, WILLIAM C. MENNINGER AND JOHN R. STONE, TOPEKA, DECEMBER 5, 1931

My dear Will, Father, and John:

I was glad in one way to have John's informative letter and I share with you the concern over the financial status, although as usual I cannot but take an optimistic view of the situation.

By this I do not mean to disapprove of anything you have done, least of

7 In August 1931, Ralph Fellows had become the first psychiatric resident at the Menninger Clnic. Ultimately he became medical director of the Milwaukee (Wisconsin) County Hospital.

all of the salary cuts. I have thought for some time that we were rather pretentious in trying to pay our employees what we would pay them if we were prosperous instead of facing the fact that we are losing money every day. I think they should understand very clearly these facts and then if they think their own personal advantages would be better served by leaving us they should certainly be permitted, in fact, encouraged, to go, as in that way we will get rid of those whose narcissism would interfere with their usefulness to us sooner or later anyway. I think it ought to be made clear to the employees that we are not reducing their salaries because we know how easily they can be replaced and therefore feel that we have them at a disadvantage but it is really they who have us at a disadvantage because, actually, we cannot replace them except at a great inconvenience to ourselves. I think it should be made clear to them that we consider we have a considerable financial investment in them which we cannot save for ourselves in any way except in preserving their loyalty. I think it is legitimate to remind them also that $50 a month today is equivalent to about $80 two years ago so far as purchasing power is concerned. It occurs to me that since the kitchen force voluntarily reduced their own wages they should be exempted in this present cut.

It seems to me exceedingly important that these things be put before the employees in a frank and friendly manner and that they be made to understand clearly why it is necessary and how much we esteem them and hope that we can raise their salaries again soon. I don't think it would do any harm to remind them that they have not done so badly by staying with us and that no one so far has been dismissed in order that we might economize, which is true of scarcely any other business I can think of. I think we have let our employees get the notion that we are too comfortable and too prosperous. It is the old problem that we have been up against so often— the better you are, the more growling you have if things aren't perfect. I think we have always treated them too affectionately, i.e., like the spoiled child. Tell them that the logical consequences of continuing the present plan are that they all go broke and that we are all out of a job.

As far as Miss Lyle[8] is concerned she says she will willingly accept her cut in salary but in view of the fact that she has been and will probably continue to work much overtime and is improving in her functioning I think I will personally make up the difference to her for the balance of her six months' period at which time we will make a new arrangement with her of some sort. I am not only working her overtime but I am employing an outside

8 Jeanetta Lyle, KAM's second wife, joined the staff of the Menninger Foundation in 1931 and during the early 1930s served as an editorial assistant to KAM. In 1938 she was appointed executive secretary of the Southard School and was secretary to the board of trustees until 1944, traveling extensively to promote the school. From 1936 until 1970 she edited *The Bulletin of the Menninger Clinic*. In 1939 she entered analysis with Irene Haenel in Los Angeles; in September 1941 she married KAM there.

stenographer two hours a day, which I suppose will be greeted with groans on your part but for which I hope to have something to show in the course of time. . . .

Another thought occurs to me about the employees. It might be good psychology to urge them to get a better place if they can. Let them take time off (at their own expense) to find out how difficult this will be. If they are fortunate enough to get something they consider more valuable, let them take it by all means and not store up any grudges against us. Yes, I think we should urge them to do so. It may help give them a true perspective on the present situation. The $3,000 we owe is much more than most of them can visualize and they don't know what it means to be faced with that kind of a debt. . . .

I am sorry to hear about Bess; I am sure that I will have to face some hostilities on this account, but I don't see what else we could justifiably do unless you folks think you could put up with her as sanitarium stenographer at a salary of $75 a month.[9] I don't urge this, but in view of Mrs. Clark's leaving I think the advantages of having someone who is familiar with things, someone who is as capable as Bess is technically, and someone who would be willing to work at $75 a month might outweigh the disadvantages of her disposition. You might offer it to her. She has been out of work for 18 months or more and walked the streets and has perhaps learned a little humility and appreciation. As I think it over, under the circumstances, I think you could do worse. . . .

I approve of eliminating state medical journal ads.

I think business is a little better, although the stock market looks pretty sick to me. And I am out about $350 on my very small investment in it. Opinion here is both ways, optimistic and pessimistic. I tear around from early morning till late at night dictating to my two stenographers—lunch today with Dr. Lowrey, dinner at 6:30 with the mental health counsellor of Harvard and the dean of the graduate school, seminar at Alexander's at 8:30, seminar Sunday night with Lewin[10] of New York, conference Saturday night with discussion group of psychoanalysts and psychiatrists, meeting of psychoanalytic society Tuesday night for a long struggle between Rank and Freud, inspect Butler Hospital Thursday afternoon and speak at meeting of the Rhode Island Nervous and Mental Disease Society Thursday night; zip out to Detroit on the 15th but to save time and money will not come further west. You might cite my great self-sacrifice as an incentive to the employees.

One more cheerful item is that a new patient comes from Detroit to begin analysis the first of the week.

Sincerely yours,

9 Bess Cowdrey, a sister of Grace Menninger, had been a secretary at the clinic. Her position was eliminated to cut costs.

10 Bertram D. Lewin, prominent New York psychoanalyst, was a friend, teacher, and colleague of KAM.

P.S. Seriously and earnestly, I hope you will all keep in mind the fact that pessimism is as unsound as undue optimism, and if you continue to do what we have done with the utmost scientific thoroughness, we nor anyone else will starve to death.

To John Taylor,[1] Boston, April 20, 1932

My dear John:

Well, you gave me a lot of news and I'll try to respond. I just got back from Chicago where our Society had Brother [Hermann] Nunberg in from Philadelphia. We had a regular seminar in the afternoon and in the evening we had a formal presentation from him which we all discussed.

The seminar was very good but the evening meeting was rather dull. Nunberg is no Alexander, I'll tell you that! We have a very active and lively society, and I'm afraid Nunberg got a too realistic impression of the wild and wooly West. Not that it was so wild, but it was certainly frank enough to startle anyone not used to it.

Out here at our clinic we are having a busy time and a very enjoyable one and we are delighted to hear there is a faint possibility of having you as our guest this summer. I have given up all ideas of being able to go to Europe and shall be here all summer without fail and should be delighted to have you come and stay as long as you will. We have several nice golf courses here if you like golf—to tell the truth I have forgotten whether you said you liked it or didn't like it—but I remember that you do like tennis and we have a court on the place, also tennis courts at the country club, etc. I am really quite worked up with enthusiasm about the possibility of your coming and if you will let me have just a little notice we shall make it as agreeable as possible for both you and Mrs. Taylor if she decides to come also.

Mrs. Menninger and I leave the last week for California. It is a hurry-up trip because I am carrying seven psychoanalytic patients in addition to our daily psychiatric conferences and conferences at the school and a few other things I am working in on the side. I am going to speak to the State Medical Society out there and hope to be able to convert a few of them to psychoanalysis. If much speaking will do any good I should be successful because they have me lined up for a lot of spouting.

It is really too bad that you are having so much trouble in the Boston Society, and I feel as if it were my holy duty to return and see if I can't make bad matters worse or something of the sort. Seriously, I wonder if someone couldn't pour oil on the troubled waters if they went about it in the right

1 Boston psychoanalyst and member of the Boston Psychoanalytic Institute (formed in 1932).

way. Surely Coriat[2] needs only to have his feelings soothed a little bit. Surely Ives [Hendrick][3] will not really resign, he is only bluffing. Perhaps Sachs[4] will be able to bring everything to rights because he will have less analytic carryover in the way of hostility from some of the brothers. I forgot all about his not being a doctor, and I suppose that will cause some difficulties but not among the analysts surely.

Please give my regards to Mrs. Taylor, and to any of the brothers and sisters who would not be too pained to hear that I have not passed out of the picture and am enjoying life increasingly and would like very much to see you all again.

Sincerely yours,

To Leo Bartemeier, Detroit, April 26, 1932

Dear old Bart:

It is late evening. Poor Jean [Jeanetta Lyle], weary and worn, is sitting beside my desk writing notes while I am eating my supper on my desk, answering letters, dictating analytic notes and all the other things you are familiar with. We are having very hectic days around here, lots of patients coming, lots of them going, including that tic case that I was so interested in. He wrote his mother to come, that I didn't love him, etc., and then next day wrote her to stay home, that he was mistaken, but she had already jumped on the train and here she was. She gave me a great line about his life being ruined by his father's evil spirit but she stayed here long enough to blow up his analysis anyway. It was a very curious thing how he feared and depended on her. After she came he got so he couldn't say a word in the whole darn hour.

Grace and I are about to take off, leaving Wednesday noon, arriving in Los Angeles Friday afternoon, and speaking Friday night at the Hollywood Academy of Medicine and Saturday night at the Catholics' Delight (Birth Control Clinic), Monday at the Conference of Social Work, Tuesday and Wednesday at the Medical Association and Thursday at the Federation of

2 Isador Coriat was an American-born psychiatrist and neurologist. A pioneer New England practitioner of psychoanalysis, he helped establish the Boston Psychoanalytic Society (1930) and served as president for three terms (1930–32 and 1941–42).

3 Hendrick earned an M.D. degree from Yale in 1925. From 1928 to 1930 he studied at the Berlin Psychoanalytic Institute. He joined Harvard's psychiatry department in 1943 and remained there until 1965. He was professor emeritus until his death in 1972. Hendrick had a private practice in psychiatry and was an important member of the Boston Psychoanalytic Society.

4 Hanns Sachs, an early psychoanalyst and friend of Freud. He was Franz Alexander's analyst at the Berlin psychoanalytic Institute. In 1933 he began work at the Boston Psychoanalytic Institute, following Alexander as a training analyst. As a nonphysician, he was attacked by Hendrick.

Women's Clubs. I have told you this several times before but if I can't be a little exhibitionistic to you, who can I?

After a certain amount of discouragement I think the old bean is beginning to work again because I had some swell ideas last night which I think are original and even if they are not they ought to be in regard to my suicide stuff. I have to rewrite my entire papers, that is how radical it is. . . .

I have definitely settled with Brother Rado on May 21 for our next [Chicago Psychoanalytic] Society meeting although I have told him that the 22nd would do. It is for you to decide whether the 19th and 20th or the 22nd, 23rd and 24th would be most suitable for your visit. We want you to come in May because the flowers here are really worth speaking about with baited breath providing you come while they are menstruating. Miss Lyle says she doesn't mind these shocking letters but they don't make any sense. She didn't really say that but she thinks it.

I almost disgraced analysis today by getting so amused at something one of my serious-minded patients said that I nearly fell off my chair restraining loud laughter. He has been giving me hell for ten days because of the heartlessness, duplicity, unscrupulousness, hatefulness, wickedness, etc., etc., etc., of my going off and leaving him for two weeks. He is thinking of sending me a bill for lost time and bringing suit against me for "taking away my beloved masochism and also for trotting off on a pleasure jaunt in the midst of my analysis."

I am delighted to hear of the possibilities of your taking on an estate in Bloomfield Hills which I have heard about *one or two times*. I hope you do it.

PLEASE WRITE ME FREQUENTLY AIR MAIL, ADDRESS HOTEL HUNTINGTON, PASADENA, CALIFORNIA. I shall leave there about May 8.

TO FRANZ ALEXANDER, CAMBRIDGE, MASSACHUSETTS, MAY 18, 1932

My dear Dr. Alexander:

The night after I wrote you that letter [from] California[5] I had an acute attack of gastric pain in the night and felt quite depressed the following day with some notions that I had painted the picture more rosy than it really is, and some conscious feelings of hostility toward [name deleted in the original]. It passed away however and Grace and I had a pleasant tour of northern central California which we liked very much better than the artificial, superficial, sunshiny southern part, and arrived here [Topeka] a few days ago, since when I have been extremely busy. I took on a new case for analysis yesterday and another one today, which makes me eight cases a day, and I can't possibly take any more along with my other work.

Tomorrow Bartemeier and wife arrive and we expect to have three very

5 This letter has not been preserved.

active days around here, inasmuch as Bartie has never been here before and I want him to see our school, hospital, sanitarium and clinic. We are also expecting Dr. Ulrich,[6] who has just returned from a didactic analysis with Helene Deutsch[7] and control work with Anna Freud.[8] We may take him on here as an additional analyst.

Sunday Bartemeier and I go to Chicago to attend the Society meeting and have some control work. Rado is the speaker.

I am enclosing another check which reduces my account to $480.00, I believe, and I will send more at the earliest possible moment.

I have just had a letter from Dr. Eitingon,[9] regretting exceedingly that I can't come and accepting with pleasure my suggestion that one of my friends read my paper for me. Of course, I should like very much to have *you* do this if you will. If you are going to be too busy with various things tell me so frankly and suggest who I might have read it but I hope you will do it.

Another matter I wish to ask you about is this: I am president of the Central Neuropsychiatric Association, an association of Midwestern neurologists and psychiatrists which we organized about eleven years ago and of which I was secretary for ten years. We meet this year at Rochester, Minnesota, as guests of the Mayo Clinic, the outstanding medical organization in this country. They put on the program. I am going to give a presidential

6 Carl Ulrich, a psychoanalyst then practicing in Cleveland.

7 Helene Deutsch, a graduate of the Vienna Medical School, was analyzed by Freud from 1918 to 1919. During that year she became the second woman (after Helma von Hug-Hellmuth) admitted to membership in the Vienna Psychoanalytic Society. After a year's work with Karl Abraham in Berlin, she returned to Vienna in 1924 to found the Vienna Psychoanalytic Institute, which she directed for ten years. In 1935 she emigrated to the United States. She wrote numerous papers, including a classic essay, "Some Forms of Emotional Disturbance and Their Relation to Schizophrenia" (1934), on the "as if" personality and the two-volume *Psychology of Women* (1944, 1945).

8 Youngest child of Sigmund and Martha Freud, Anna Freud practiced analysis in Vienna betwen 1923 and 1938, although she had received no academic degrees. In 1938, she emigrated to London with her father, her mother, and five siblings. She was a child therapist at the Hampstead War Nursery from 1939 to 1949; in 1947 she founded and became director of the Hampstead Child Therapy Course and Clinic. She and Melanie Klein were the first child therapists and headed the two factions of child analysis in England. In 1955, a grant from the Alfred P. Sloan Foundation established a series of visiting professorships to be awarded by the Menninger Foundation to outstanding psychiatrists; Anna Freud was named Sloan Professor in the Menninger School of Psychiatry in 1962. In September 1962, she lectured in Topeka as part of the commemoration of the twentieth anniversary of the Topeka Institute of Psychoanalysis. She paid a second visit to Topeka in conjunction with observances surrounding the twentieth anniversary of the Menninger School of Psychiatry.

9 Max Eitingon, Swiss-born psychoanalyst who studied with Freud; with Karl Abraham and Ernst Simmel he founded the Berlin Institute in 1920. In 1926 he pioneered a psychoanalytic sanitarium near Berlin; later he served on the advisory board of the Chicago Psychoanalytic Institute.

address which will deal with psychoanalytic topics. Each year we have one outside speaker. I have conferred with the secretary and he has asked me to invite you to be our outside speaker this year. It will meet in October, so it will only be necessary for you to make an overnight trip. We will pay your expenses. Informally I think you could also announce the institute as they will all be interested. This will not only give you an opportunity to represent the cause before a large and representative group of Midwestern neuropsychiatrists but will give you an opportunity to visit the Mayo clinic which is well worth doing and will amaze you.

Give my kind regards to Mrs. Alexander and if you aren't too busy write me pretty soon and answer these questions.

Sincerely yours,

FROM FRANZ ALEXANDER, CAMBRIDGE, MASSACHUSETTS, MAY 23, 1932

My dear Dr. Menninger:

I read both of your letters with great interest. So far as it is possible to pass judgment from a distance, it seems that your postanalytical period is taking a desirable course; especially your California experiences seem to me of importance. . . . I would not pay too much attention to the acute conversion symptom which you have mentioned. That happens even in the best families.

Naturally I shall be very glad to read your paper at the Congress.[10] Please let me have it as soon as possible. I could perhaps make some remarks or suggestions before I leave. I am sailing from New York on June 24th on the *Vulcania*.

Your proposition to go to the Mayo Clinic in October to read a paper is very convenient for me and I shall be very glad to go there. The California plans do not seem to be quite crystallized as yet. As I have already told you, I should not mind going there once in connection with some lectures, because this part, especially San Francisco, is the part of the country I should like to see the most.

I shall write to my publisher to send you four copies of my book [*The Criminal, the Judge, and the Public*] as you ask in your letter.

I received your check and thank you very much for it.

I met Dr. Nunberg, who told me about his Chicago experiences. It seems your and his impressions were mutual. How was Rado's debut? I hope that you have seen Mr. Stern[11] while you are staying in Chicago and should like

10 The Twelfth International Psychoanalytic Association Congress, held on September 4–7, 1932 in Weisbaden, Germany, and presided over by Max Eitington.

11 Alfred K. Stern, president of the Board of Trustees of the Chicago Psychoanalytic Institute. He had been analyzed by Freud.

to hear from you your latest impressions about the development of the institute plans.

Cordially yours,

P.S. Just now we received a wonderful bouquet of flowers with your card attached. Thank you very much for it. Mrs. Alexander left yesterday for Chicago and probably you have met her there. Thus she does not know of your kind attentiveness.

To Franz Alexander, Cambridge, Massachusetts, May 24, 1932

Dear Alex:

I am busy as hell and haven't got time to write this but I think I should. I just got back from Chicago where we had a very nice meeting of the group with Rado but I learned of some things which I think you should know immediately.

It seems that our zealous friend Al Stern has let his zeal get ahead of his judgment (a propensity with which I can sympathize) and he has gotten out some kind of a tentative prospectus [for the Chicago Psychoanalytic Institute] which has raised the devil of a lot of trouble. In the first place he made the mistake of submitting this prospectus to a few people for their opinion. Blitzsten, Bartemeier, myself, and others who did not see the prospectus wondered why one had not been sent to us. When it was explained that they were merely submitted to a few people for an opinion it was only a case of fat in the fire. Blitzsten, for example, wondered why someone else's opinion was solicited and not his. But that wasn't the worst of it.

It seems that on this prospectus the regular faculty and staff is listed and also some kind of a consulting staff, and Dr. Blitzsten and I learned that we were not on the regular staff as we had gained the impression that we were to be, which aroused considerable feeling as you can imagine, the more so when we learned that Dr. Bacon[12] was listed on the regular staff along with Tom [French]. Furthermore Dr. Blitzsten was much annoyed that he should be put in a class with such non-analysts as John Favill[13] who has the same position and rank as Dr. Blitzsten and myself.

With my characteristic impetuousness I blurted the matter out to Tom only to learn that he was equally annoyed and offended that he should have been put with Dr. Bacon in what he regarded as an inferior status to those of us who are on the consulting staff. Of course I see the humor of this as I am sure you will, but I also see that we are going to have some very unnecessary friction and hostilities if Stern continues to take upon himself the responsibility of deciding on such arbitrary distinctions as this. Blitzsten,

12 Catherine L. Bacon, a psychoanalyst affiliated with the Chicago Institute.
13 A prominent Chicago psychiatrist.

Tom and I chatted together about it and agreed that you could not possibly have had anything to do with it since you had given us an entirely different understanding and would not have allowed this unfortunate episode to have occurred had you known of it. If you will permit me to suggest, I think you should restrain Brother Stern a little bit and give him to understand that you will arrange this faculty and not he, and that if you want advice about the prospectus you will get it and not he. If Blitz, French or I had had a letter from you, either asking our ideas about a staff or else telling us what you had decided, there would have been no trouble about it whatsoever; if there were any dissatisfactions about it we would have expressed them to you before the matter came out in this printed form. Mr. Stern has never conferred with Blitzsten or myself about the institute or for that matter about anything else. I have never seen him since you and I parted from him at the Standard Club that evening. It isn't necessary to consult me, although I shall be glad to be helpful. I think it is highly desirable, however, for reasons which I need not elaborate to you, that Blitz be given some consideration; he is president of our group and you know his unconscious self-distrust of something that makes him sensitive about such matters. Of course Tom is also sensitive and I don't think Tom should be ignored either but Bartemeier and I are doing everything we can to promote peace and harmony by being absolutely neutral toward these two friends, pursuing the suggestions that you gave me.

I hesitate to intrude these suggestions into your very busy life; I have some notion of how heckled you must feel because I myself have eight hours of analysis now—one or two conferences daily, some consultation work and my teaching—and while I enjoy it I feel a little hunted, as you once put it. Nevertheless, I think it is probably desirable that you try to straighten this little tangle out, at least to the extent of checking Stern in some of his ambitious steps.

Things are going fine with me; I hope no less so with yourself. Please give my regards to your wife and tell her we are awfully glad she is coming back West with you and we shall all see much of each other this winter.

Sincerely yours,

From Franz Alexander, Cambridge, Massachusetts, ca. June 1, 1932

Dear Dr. Menninger,

I was glad to hear that things are going fine with you. The rest of your letter would have disturbed me very much if I wouldn't be sure that much of a postanalytic reaction is behind your unnecessary worries. The [Chicago Psychoanalytic] Institute is not planned to be a place either to hurt or to flatter narcissistic claims. Indeed, I should like to have once a little analytic community without the usual personal sensitiveness, friction, etc. We won't have titles, ranks and similar attributes of the [illegible]. The staff consists of those who will do work in the Institute, giving their whole or a part of their time, and receive salary. We have no definite arrangements except with Dr. Horney, with Dr. French, Dr. McLean,[14] Dr. Bacon, and yourself. I understand that you are willing and able to come for a quarter of the year to Chicago and spend a part of your time in the Institute. Naturally you will then belong to the staff. But there was no definite prospectus in this respect; the tentative prospectus deals with the aims and the organization, the by-laws of the institute but not with the personal arrangements, at least not in a definite form. You will receive a copy as soon as it is in a presentable shape. Dr. Blitzsten's status depends upon him. The last time I saw him, he thought that he will not analyze in the Institute but participate in the work in another form. It depends upon the work he is going to do what a title he will have. It depends upon his choice. You write about "ranks" and similar things. *They do not exist* in the Institute. I asked Mr. Stern to communicate with you last Sunday; evidently he did not succeed to reach you. I am very glad that you and Bartemeier are doing everything to promote peace and harmony and I am sure that you will succeed if you do not let yourself get involved emotionally in the narcissistic anger of the problem. I want your cooperation and a real collective work, all aggression directed against the external problems and resistances and not against the brothers.

Cordially yours,

I am expecting your Congress manuscript. Please write me your plans regarding the time arrangements of your work in the Institute.

To Franz Alexander, Cambridge, Massachusetts, June 8, 1932

My dear Doctor Alexander:

I have gone over very carefully what you wrote me and I think that you are partly right in that some narcissism may have hidden behind my interest in Dr. Blitzsten's and Dr. French's injured feelings. I did not myself feel very much hurt, chiefly because I felt it was an honor to be connected with the Institute in any capacity and thought that if you had felt like changing me from what you had first told me to the rank of consultant, it was for some good purpose.

However, I have taken to heart your reproof very kindly because I realize that if you were mistaken it was because of your anxiety to have me as free as possible from such concern; that I truly think I am, to a degree surpassing my own expectations and perhaps even yours. I still think it is unwise

14 Helen Vincent McLean was psychoanalyzed by Franz Alexander in Chicago during the same period when KAM and Leo Bartemeier were undergoing analysis with him. She was an original staff member of the Chicago Institute.

for Doctor Stern to consult some members of the Chicago Psychoanalytic Society and not others, particularly when such jealousies are so likely to flare up.

I already promised you that I would give several months of my time to the Institute. You had not yet decided whether I would come back and forth every two weeks or whether I would come and stay two months or even a little longer or just what I would do. Nor did you tell me just how much they felt they could pay me. This is not essential but it is something that I want to consider.

I think you may find it desirable to work me in at irregular places, or perhaps you know already just where and when you want me. Three months is a little longer than I should like to come but perhaps it could be shortened a little bit.

As I read over your letter again I see you say that there was more definite agreement in regard to my coming; this I must remind you is inaccurate as I definitely promised you that I would do whatever you wanted me to do. We talked with Zilboorg[15] about one possibility and then you said you would let me know just what could be worked out. I repeat my willingness to do whatever you want me to if it is at all possible.

I am enclosing a copy of my letter to Mr. Stern and I will try to see him Thursday when I am up in Chicago for the Analytic Society.

I am still very busy here, working at night on my manuscript[16] which I will mail you in a few days. In case you do not have time to mail it back with certain suggestions you have my permission to make any changes or omissions you wish in reading it and then before it is published I will make any changes you recommend, or you can make them for me when you hand it in to Doctor [Ernest] Jones.[17] It is my impression that it would be wise for me to have it published in the *International Journal [of Psycho-Analysis]* rather than in the *American Journal [of Psychiatry]*. Do you not agree with me?

15 Born in Kiev, U.S.S.R., Gregory Zilboorg received his M.D. degree from Columbia in 1926 and joined the psychiatric staff of Bloomingdale Asylum. From 1929 to 1930 he was an assistant at the Berlin Psychoanalytic Institute. From 1931 until his death in 1959 he had a private practice in New York City. Zilboorg shared with KAM an interest in suicide and in 1936 helped organize the Committee for the Study of Suicide, becoming its secretary and director. (See part 3 introduction concerning a charge of impropriety against Zilboorg.)

16 A preliminary version of chapter 1 of *Man Against Himself*, which Alexander had agreed to present to the International Psychoanalytic Congress.

17 A British physician, Ernest Jones was a friend of Freud and his fervent advocate. His three-volume *Life and Work of Sigmund Freud* (1953–57) remains the definitive biography. In 1911, Jones advised American psychoanalysts during the organization of the American Psychoanalytic Association, and in 1913, he was a founding member of the British Psycho-Analytical Society. He was also editor of the *International Journal of Psycho-Analysis* (1920–39), twice president of the International Psycho-Analytic Association (1920–24; 1932–49), and its honorary president (1949–58).

I am carrying nine patients a day besides a psychiatric conference, numerous conferences with employees, a little tennis, a little interest in my wife and children.

We have been exceedingly busy around here in spite of the depression and have rather more patients than we can take care of. We have been trying to get another analyst to come and join us who appears to be a very good man, Carl Ulrich, who did control work in child analysis with Anna Freud and Helene Deutsch. I have made him a final proposition and am waiting to hear whether or not he would come. He lives in Cleveland and may develop his career there altho we should like to have him work with us as I am sure it would stimulate me a great deal to have another analyst here to argue with me. At present I have things too much my own way and there are many points on which I am undoubtedly incorrect. I have a study group which meets every Thursday night at which we take up the psychoanalytic aspects of certain cases, certain novels. . . .

In case I don't have any opportunity to write you again before you sail for Europe, please tell me where I can reach you over there by mail, give my best regards to Mrs. Alexander and your two little girls. Have the best possible rest this summer and count on me to meet you in Chicago October 1st or whenever you plan to return.

Sincerely yours,

FROM FRANZ ALEXANDER, CAMBRIDGE, MASSACHUSETTS, JUNE 16, 1932

My dear Dr. Menninger:

I am sending back your manuscript, which I have read through very carefully and made all my remarks on the margin. I hope you will be able to read them. In general, I find the paper somewhat diluted, but the main concept of distinguishing the three motives in suicide is very sound and interesting. In your place, I would make a distinction between the first two motives in contrast to the third one (wish to die), because the first two motives (the wish to kill and to be killed) can be psychologically established, whereas the last one is only an assumption. I find the many newspaper clippings superfluous and not very illuminating, with the exception of two or three. I think the paper can easily be shortened even for the publication. There are many parts which are of no interest for the trained psychoanalyst, only for the lay reader. For example, when you discuss in many pages the phenomena of ambivalence, jealousy, etc. Indeed, they are out of place in a technical article such as this. Furthermore, I think you took too literally the leadership of the death instinct, which shows the way for the Eros. I do not think that we have any right to assume some mystical connection between the two. Positive cathexis of objects develops rather independently from the aggressive tendencies and overshadows and neutralizes them. But a kind of magnetic attraction between the two never has been assumed and I do not see in your paper any evidence of it. You simply assume it.

Many parts of the article are very well written and very clear. I have also put the positive criticism on the margin.

I hope that your shortened and revised manuscript still will reach me in New York, from which I sail June 24th.

I hope the question of the denomination of the different members of the staff is now satisfactorily solved. I eliminated the word "instructor," because neither Dr. McLean nor Dr. Bacon will be instructors, but clinical associates; whereas Dr. French will be both clinical associate and lecturer. You and Dr. Blitzsten are called lecturers. I hope you won't construct any differences of rank now between these different denominations, for there are none.

Very cordially yours,

To Franz Alexander, On Board Ship, New York, June 21, 1932

My dear Dr. Alexander:

I am deeply grateful to you for the suggestions about my manuscript. I have gone through it carefully tonight and altered it radically in the directions you suggested. I doubt if my stenographer can get it finished in time to reach your boat but she will try. This copy we are mailing you is the final copy, the one for publication. I am having a separate copy prepared for you to read which is much shorter but I doubt if we can get it down to fifteen pages. What you can't read you can't read and that is all there is to it.

Most of your criticisms were obviously correct. I don't see why you take issue with my exposition of the way in which destructive and erotic instincts accompany one another outside the ego and oppose one another inside. I didn't think I was saying anything particularly new here. You will find a discussion of this subject in *The Psychoanalysis of the Total Personality*, by Dr. Franz Alexander, page 140 ff. and also was it not Freud who first spoke of the death instinct as the pathfinder for the erotic tendencies?

I am a little ashamed that I did not cut out of my first manuscript some of the popular elements; I really mean to say that I am sorry that I did not cut all of them out for I can assure you I did cut out many. I have a plan as you know for writing a book on the self-destructive tendencies and the original manuscript will do very well for my original purpose. I hope in this modified and abbreviated form it will not seem too elementary for the Congress.

You have my permission as always to make any changes at the last moment.

Be sure to let me know as soon as possible where to reach you in Europe so I can mail this abridged copy to you. I will also send you a copy of the abstract which I will mail Dr. Eitingon in the next day or so.

I am going to read the paper to the Society in Chicago at our last meeting this year which will be June 29.

I had a slight emotional flurry about you going to Europe, so far out of reach; I had a slight gastric attack last night but on the whole I am sure things are going better all the time. I am deeply moved by your kindness in having gone into this manuscript with so much pains when I know how busy and rushed you must be. I think I should confess a slight evanescent paranoid reaction for a few moments after your letter arrived while my narcissism was getting adjusted to your very fair criticism.

I hope you have a grand summer and please give my regards to Mrs. Alexander. We will be looking for you in Chicago in October.

Sincerely yours,

To Lionel Blitzsten, Chicago, August 31, 1932

Dear Blitz:

I hope your long silence doesn't mean anything ominous such as a marriage or a fit of indigestion or a late consequence of Kansas heat or rain, but knowing your tabu on writing I thought I had better hope for the best and send out this little feeler to see how you were. I am afraid my death wishes toward you are getting rather weak because I haven't seemed to worry much about you but my narcissism would like the satisfaction of a letter from you now and then and I can't stand the strain any longer.

Things are going along in pretty good shape here both in the matter of clinic business, clinic relationships, psychoanalytic activities and domestic adjustments. We have radically revised the matter of presenting cases at the staff conferences which is one of the results of your visit. We now make the chief focus of interest a study of the attitude patterns manifested by the patient toward the dramatic personae of his life in the six or seven basic situations from early home, the school, etc., on up to the present illness and the hospital situation. I never thought before how neatly it works out that employers, for example, represent parents and employees represent children or offspring, and again in the hospital doctors represent parents, the nurses sometimes children, sometimes teachers, sometimes siblings, the other patients represent siblings, etc. My analytic work seems to be going along pretty well, thanks to your patient tutoring and I am not in any particular trouble just now but I will be very glad when I can come up and have another conference with you.

This brings me to the point that I wish we could have a meeting of our [Chicago] Society before October. I don't see any point of waiting that long before getting together. Must we have Brother French present in order to have a meeting? I think we ought to get together and discharge the slumbering hostilities accumulated during the summer. Also the unsatisfied homosexual libido.

Sholem Aleckum,

P.S. Miss Lyle says where the hell are those carbons you were going to send back with comments?

To FRANZ ALEXANDER, CHICAGO, OCTOBER 10, 1932

My dear Dr. Alexander:

Use as much of the following as you like in the announcement of my seminars:

PSYCHOANALYTIC PSYCHIATRY

The study of psychiatric cases from the psychoanalytic standpoint. Cases to be presented by members of the seminar analyzing the data as to personality patterns, traumatic experiences and their effects, unconscious psychic mechanisms, libido investments, technique and focus of aggressions, therapeutic indications. The Socratic method will be used with special reading assignments and brief summarizing lectures as to special significances and pertinent psychoanalytic theory.

Cases illustrative of the established psychiatric syndromes will be taken up in the following order:

Simple and reactive depressions (2 sessions)
Melancholia (4 sessions)
Mania (2 sessions)
Paranoia (3 sessions)
Schizophrenia (7 sessions)
Delirium and the toxic psychoses (2 sessions)
General paresis (2 sessions)
Epilepsy (2 sessions)
Special syndromes, depersonalization, hypochondriasis, Korsakoff's folie-
à-deux (1 session each)

As arranged the work falls into one quarter each, devoted to the introjective psychoses, the projective psychoses, and the organic psychoses.

The course is especially planned for psychiatrists, but psychologists with psychiatric interests and psychiatric social workers will be admitted. The physicians, however, will be given preference in the presentation of cases.

Sincerely yours,

To WILLIAM ALANSON WHITE, WASHINGTON, D.C., NOVEMBER 6, 1932

My dear Doctor White:

I have been slow in answering two of your nice letters, partly because I have been in Chicago off and on, to help with the inaugurating of our Institute. As one of the officials you know all about it so I shall not enter into a discussion of that. I am teaching what we call psychoanalytic psychiatry or psychoanalysis in psychiatry, which is probably better, and we have a surprising amount of interest on the part of physicians in Chicago and on the outside. Things are going off, on the whole, very well indeed.

I don't know exactly what to say about this suicide research except that I wish you would have a translation made and published of Ferenczi's *Genital Theorie*, and Hesnard and LaForgue's *Les Processus d'Auto-Punition*, and Neufeld's *Dostojewski*. I think these all throw light on some of the less obvious and direct forms of suicide which is what interests me most just at present.

As I told you in a previous letter I am trying to get together some general and particular ideas about the unconscious self-destructive tendencies. It was nice of you to offer to publish them. I don't know what to do about that yet, but should like to bear your kind offer in mind.

You might also tell me if your fund[18] would apply to such a case as the following: Last week Dr. Alexander called me from Chicago to say that he had a wonderful example of a certain kind of self-destructive process in a woman who needed analysis *in an institution.* Her husband could afford to pay $20 a week, which would be of course only a fraction of what it would cost to keep her here with analysis thrown in free. It was a wonderful opportunity for some psychoanalytic research but it couldn't be used because the people couldn't afford to keep her here and we couldn't afford to foot the bill either. We would be perfectly willing to keep such people at cost and donate the professional services of the analyst to boot, but we have no endowment or outside help of any kind. For some inexplicable reason we seem to be thriving and getting ahead a little bit but we are not in a position to take charity cases, not even such fine research cases.

Then there is another way in which we could use help, and help which would be directed exclusively to the suicide problem. We have many interesting cases with suicidal propensities which we would like to have studied psychoanalytically but for whom the immediate problem is one of hospital care, and whose financial status is such that they couldn't afford to pay anything extra for psychoanalytic study. I should like to employ an additional analyst on a salary and ask him to devote four hours a day to research work if you want to call it that—I mean to the application of psychoanalytic technique to the investigation of suicidal tendencies in psychotic or near psychotic patients who cannot afford to pay anything extra for this treatment. For example, I would like to get . . . one of the younger men from the Chicago Institute and put them at this. If your fund would pay half their salary or even one-fourth of it I think I could manage the rest. What I had

18 White had grant money to distribute for research on suicide.

in mind by focal self-destruction is this: that many times suicide appears to be attenuated or diluted in point of time or in a special way; that is, the self-destructive attack, instead of being upon the personality as a whole or the body as a whole, is focused upon one of the constituent parts of the body. I took up in particular malingering, psychotic and religious mutilations, poly-surgical attacks, and some purposive accidents and tried to show the similarity in the unconscious motives in each case; how these individuals punish themselves, locally, for the purpose of continuing the indulgence for which the punishment is inflicted.

Sincerely yours,

FROM WILLIAM ALANSON WHITE, WASHINGTON, D.C., NOVEMBER 17, 1932

My dear Dr. Menninger:

I have your very good letter of the 6th instant. . . .

Now to be brief and to the point. In the first place, I can help you. I am very anxious to make a study of suicide and we have already started one here. I am enclosing an outline of the study as we are going to undertake it, and as I say have already begun. We have had pass through our institution nearly forty thousand patients and have their records, and we thought it would be worth while to make an orientation study of the subject, examining the records for doing so. Then I thought, in order to supplement such a study, it would be highly desirable to have yours, for example, working at the matter more intensively and individualistically, as you indicate you would like to do, dealing not only with the subject of suicide in general perhaps, but with the special problems which come to the surface as you investigate the matter psychoanalytically in each patient. I may intimate also that the donor is very much interested in the manic-depressive type of reaction and the suicides that come from this source.

Now as I told you, I haven't a great deal of money, but I should say that money could perhaps be spent to best advantage, not only in the matter of the research that we are talking about, but also so far as you are particularly concerned in the work with your patients, by paying part of the salary of an analyst. Finally, as to the matter of translating books, we came to no conclusion. One reason I think is that you did not express yourself regarding the translation of the books other than to say that you would like to have them translated. Of course we would all like to have everything in English. If you can give a little better reason why these books should be translated I will take it up further the next time I have an opportunity.

Now finally, will you let me know at your convenience when you can get hold of a good man [and] how much of this salary you will want me to pay. You suggested a half or a quarter.

What I intend to do and what I would like to have you look forward to is that finally we will get up a little monograph series in which we will publish the results of all of the work that is done by this fund, having a special format and binding, and my own idea at present is that these volumes should be presented to a certain number of outstanding libraries.

May I add also, in order to be thoroughly disconnected, that I am personally very much interested in what you call focal self-destruction, and what I call attenuated suicide. Will you let me hear from you again when you see fit and tell me whether you can cooperate in accordance with the plans suggested. I have no doubt you can.

In the meantime, Greetings!

Very sincerely yours,

FROM LEO BARTEMEIER, DETROIT, NOVEMBER 17, 1932

Dear Karl:

There are no hostilities of which I am conscious, but as for constructive criticism, I might make the following suggestions regarding your seminar. Horney is correct.[19] I agree to that. It must have seemed that we were making long guesses. If you have no material from your own psychoanalytic cases which would be suitable for seminar presentation, why not borrow some from other sources—*Psychoanalytic Journal*, Alex's books, etc.? The work there should be kept up to the highest possible standard, but I would tell Mrs., Madame or Mr. Horney that it is equally important not to bewilder the nonpsychoanalytic audience, which is what might well happen were you to follow out her suggestion. For the seminars to be successful from the audience's point of view, it does seem to me they must leave with the feeling they have really acquired something worthwhile, which they in turn can use to advantage in their respective fields. Horney overlooks the complexion of your audience and makes her criticism only in terms of herself and other trained analysts. Personally, I felt I had learned considerably from you that afternoon and had it not been for Wilson's[20] contradiction—a manifestation of hostility which broke out so unexpectedly—the poor frau would probably never have suspected that your cases had not been as thoroughly investigated as she had thought. There is a further light on her criticism. You have unusual abilities as a teacher, which obviously Horney does not possess—at least, no one started falling asleep during your presentation, as was the tendency during her seminar, which to me was a sorrowful affair.

19 Horney, who attended KAM's seminars, had criticized them as insufficiently documented by case material. Beginning on October 22, 1932, Menninger gave a series of five seminars at the Chicago Institute on "Psychoanalysis in Psychiatry."

20 George W. Wilson, a Detroit dermatologist, who began analysis with Thomas French at the Chicago Institute in 1932. After completing his analysis, Wilson became a member of the institute.

Doctor What's-her-name, who presented the case in Horney's seminar, had not prepared her material, which was jumbled and perplexing and which left many of us in a fog a good bit of the time. If you want proof that I am right about this, listen in to Horney's next seminar and hear Finlaaaaaayson [sic] present something which he plans to dish out for the simple reason (according to his actual statement to me) that he is badly confused about the material.

You are altogether too sensitive to the carping old mother. Talk to Alex, or get him to sit in at your next seminar, which I positively will not miss. You did yourself well and when I praised you immediately after it was over, this was because I meant it. Once or twice while you were talking, I must admit that I thought some day I would have to buy you a circus hoop to better dramatize your performance, because momentarily you had become a little too frivolous and too excited, but here it occurs to me to say that even in these instances you were making your hearers love you all the more, and you and I both know that love and learning go hand in hand.

You ask me why I am not controlling with Alexander. You are largely responsible for this because for more than a whole year you have exhorted me to control a case with Blitz, whom you have persistently praised as an excellent teacher. Now the facts are that I haven't analytic cases ad lib; in fact, I am controlling, as you know, three with Tom [French], and one with Blitz. There are no others available to control. The next time I get one, I will undoubtedly ask Alex to help me. Furthermore, you must realize by this time that I do not possess the yearnings for Alex which you find in yourself. I doubt that I ever had more than a very thin transference to him. This is the only way in which I can explain my ability to leave him so easily and to think of him so seldom. Some day I would like to discuss this whole problem with you, but I do not wish to interfere with your progress in any direction. There is something about the last meeting which some day I would like to speak myself out. This may never happen. It all depends very much on how I think you are. At the time of the next meeting, may I have an appointment with you? I am glad to pay for this if it is necessary. If you ever act so stand-offish toward me again as you did the last time, I will quickly chop off your rudimentary penis. . . .

I did not have an opportunity to tell you in Chicago that at the time Barrett[21] came here to see Mrs. S——, he and I had a long visit, in the course of which he informed me he was planning a trip to California during the Christmas holidays to attend a meeting. He had also remarked that he had had a very sad experience by sending patients to private sanitariums. He then spoke about a patient we both know and said he planned to send her to Wauwatosa, that he sent some chap to Bloomingdale, that there really were no good

---

21 Albert Barrett, professor of psychiatry at the University of Michigan.

places. This gave me an opportunity to speak about our Topeka institution and I almost persuaded him on the spot to stop off via Santa Fe and visit you and see for himself what was happening in the best sanitarium on earth. I wish I could give you some notion about the number of wealthy patients with whom he deals privately and how kindly he feels toward you. All of this leads me to say that I think you should write him that I had told you what an enjoyable visit he and I had had together, how helpful he had been to me in a particular consultation, that I said he had told me he was planning to go West, and that this gave you opportunity to express a long standing desire to have him become acquainted with your outfit.

I am deeply grateful, dear bozo, for any patients you may send to me. My present fifteen-hour-a-day schedule is not to last much longer. Your lady[22] leaves here Saturday or Sunday, much reluctantly I understand and with much resistance. Mr. W—— [her husband] was somewhat disappointed in the physical equipment and in your father, whom he thought was quite unkindly and not very human, but he praised you personally to the skies, and on the whole, seemed well pleased. Tell father I put in some good words for him, and told Mr. W—— that you people spent your money buying well trained intellectual equipment rather than putting it into brick and mortar. My suggestion is that you build a Southard School on your sanitarium grounds and get Saarinen[23] and myself to plan it for you. I'll make a success out of you yet even though it takes my life to do it.

To Ives Hendrick, Boston, December 14, 1932

My dear Ives:

I was delighted to have a second letter from you. You are quite right that were it possible for you to come here we would have most interesting times as we have a daily staff conference at which psychiatric cases are presented and discussed from a psychoanalytic viewpoint. All treatment is directed by psychoanalytic principles, the recreational and occupational directors are all interested in experiments which carry out these ideas, etc. We have a psychoanalytic seminar every other week, and every other week, also, I go up to Chicago and participate in the seminars and discussions up there.

For such an interesting life, however, we have to make some sacrifices, and it is quite apparent that you overestimate the prosperity of the West. None of us receive any such income as $800 a month net, in spite of the fact that we have been working together many years getting together our practice, so you rather took our breath away when you suggested that you come in here without any acquaintances except myself with a beginning salary so

22 A patient Bartemeier had referred to the Menninger Sanitarium.
23 Finnish-born Eero Saarinen was a prominent Chicago architect.

much above our scale. Even the guarantee of $500.00 a month is quite out of the question. Had you suggested a straight salary of $400.00, say, a month, over and above your office expenses, which as I have indicated are rather high here because they include so many things in the way of scientific activities, etc., and the cost to us of getting the patients for you, we would have leaped at the opportunity to have so capable and stimulating a person as yourself with us.

It would be hypocritical for us to pose, however, as being in a position of having more money than we really have. I could elaborate, of course, about the fact that living expenses here are much less than you are accustomed to, but I think it is evident from your letter that your situation in Boston is satisfactory except for your wish to make a considerable amount of sure money immediately and unfortunately that we cannot offer. A fair income we could probably provide you even although we have three analysts on our staff, if the other assets of the place in the way of study, discussion, research, etc., appealed to you sufficiently to join with us for these purposes, rather than for purely financial remuneration of an amount more nearly commensurate with your wishes and worth.

I have an unusual opportunity to do some research work now if I could give about two or three hours a day to it. To do this it is necessary that I transfer some of my work to another analyst. In addition to this emergency, there are several persons in Topeka who wish to be analyzed but whom I cannot take because of my long personal acquaintance with them. Such patients would welcome an analyst of your standing and ability.

It was kind of Martin Peck[24] to speak so enthusiastically of my seminar. I am conducting it on lines very similar to the plan we have worked out in conducting our staff conferences daily. The [Chicago] Institute is going very well and has enrolled some promising candidates among the younger men. The Chicago Psychoanalytic Society has had some interesting seminars this winter. Harry Stack Sullivan told us of his work with schizophrenics last week.

Sincerely yours,

To Franz Alexander, Chicago, January 3, 1933

Dear Alex and Mrs. Alex:

The cocktail mixer is very tricky and we have already used it upon several pleasant occasions, mixing up Alexander cocktails in the Alexander cocktail mixer and drinking to the health of the Alexanders. This is an exceedingly agreeable form of cannibalism. I wish you could join me and commit autophagia.

24 An early Boston psychoanalyst, originally analyzed by Otto Rank, later by Hanns Sachs. Peck was the second president (1932–37) of the Boston Psychoanalytic Institute.

We had a very nice Christmas here and hope you did. I am looking forward to our next visit on the 14th and let's agree now to all take dinner together at another new restaurant. We might try that better Hungarian restaurant we heard about, or perhaps we can go to Cicos. Anyway save the evening of the 15th for us.

Margaret Ribble[1] has arrived and I think she looks fine and is going to enjoy her work here very much. She thinks she is going to like it and we have already started her on two patients with more to come. She wants to run controls with both Alexander and Horney, so tell Miss Moore to save time for her. Dr. Ribble would be perfectly willing to go over to Dr. Horney's house on Sunday if that would be more convenient.

Sincerely yours,

To Smith Ely Jelliffe, New York, March 8, 1933

Dear Chief,

We have had some correspondence from Dr. Archambault of Albany, N.Y., who transmitted your high commendations of us, for which we are exceedingly grateful but not at all surprised as you have done it before. I asked the girls to send you a copy of my letter and since then Dr. Archambault has written again saying he agrees with that point of view fully, which is no doubt through your analysis.

I think your attitude toward the petty politics of the New York Psychoanalytic Society is only another indication of your extraordinary healthy-mindedness and objectivity. I feel exactly as you do except that it disturbs me slightly to think that analysts must still carry out their infantilisms and their narcissism by this sort of undignified pettiness. Reflection reassures me, however, as it evidently did you long ago, that analysis is so much bigger than any of us that even such pettiness can't do it any lasting harm.

I am working like the devil carrying nine or ten patients and trying to keep my finger in the psychiatric work to the extent of attending the daily conferences and contributing some psychoanalytic viewpoints. I gave my lecture in Chicago [on] Saturday to the little group of psychiatrists that comes in, going over the S—— case and expanding the old paranoia ideas a little bit. I am interested just now in seeing just how far we are justified in applying our psychoanalytic ideas of psychiatry, not in the rather confusing way that Schilder[2] does nor the cobwebby way that [Edward] Glover does, both

1 Margaretha Ribble was a child psychiatrist with psychoanalytic training who had come to the Menninger Clinic from New York. Unhappy in Topeka, she left in 1933 to work in Vienna with Anna Freud. She popularized the expression "tender loving care" in her book *The Rights of Infants* (1933).

2 Paul Schilder, a neuropsychiatrist and psychoanalyst, emigrated from Vienna to New York, where he taught at Bellevue Hospital, and was affiliated with the New York Psychoanalytic Society.

of which I think leave the psychiatrists pale and gasping. I don't know how far I will get with it because I haven't had enough experience but I am keeping my eyes open and studying a few cases intensively. For example, a professor of English who wrote smutty rhymes on the wall with feces during her illness.

Blitzsten and I were discussing your multiple sclerosis idea[3] last week and we both have a hunch that 20 years from now the boys are going to wake up and see that you were right about it all the time.

Mrs. C—— is quite a little better, judging by the fact that she talks much more and a good deal of it seems to relate to realities even if somewhat confused as to time and place. I was greatly encouraged when I saw her last week, although I have said from the first that since she had survived these many months the life instinct must be pretty determined and we might again see a surprising remission. I proposed last week that we might have you come and see her and while the time is not yet ripe, I am still working in that direction.

Perhaps you will show this letter to Bee. At any rate, tell her that I think of her very often and her sincere, frank, sensibleness and wish I could sit down and talk with you both in a quiet way for many hours and drink some of your nice cordials and have the comfortable feeling that I was talking to people who are very honest with themselves as well as with me. Perhaps we can do this in June when I am coming on to the Psychoanalytic Association. I have a kind of notion that I will bring my wife and three children and give them a glimpse of New York as well as New England.

Things are going very well in the family at present, in fact the best for many years. You can tell Bee this and she will understand it as I know you do.

Sincerely yours,

To SMITH ELY JELLIFFE, NEW YORK, APRIL 12, 1933

My dear Smith Ely:

The *Psychoanalytic Review* came today and I stopped in the middle of my work to read your article on the death instinct, which is in my opinion by far the best thing you have ever written. It is clear, stimulating, has broad implications, excellent case material and the idea of organ suicide is exactly what I myself feel, following of course the lead you gave us many years ago. You probably know my expression "focal suicide" which I referred to in my Congress paper which ought soon to appear. I am now working on surgical operations and with your permission I shall certainly quote from your penetrating suggestions as to the function of surgery in this article.

3 Thirteen years earlier in 1920, Jelliffe had published an article on "Multiple Sclerosis, the Vegetative Nervous System, and Psychoanalytic Research," *Archives of Neurology and Psychiatry* 4:593–96, suggesting a psychosomatic basis for the disease.

There are many other things I should like to talk to you about. I have just gotten back from Chicago where Zilboorg addressed our society meeting and he talked to me about the New York situation. Apparently he has the utmost respect for you but he seems to regard the situation there as very hectic. Fortunately things are going smoothly in Chicago so far but we are young yet.

I want you to plan to come to Chicago and speak at our society meeting and also at my seminar and also see the Institute. Then come on to Topeka and spend a few days with us here in the spring when we have flowers and lovely weather. Could you take a week off and do this? It would do us all a lot of good. Bee would come too of course.

Perhaps Alexander and wife will spend a week with us here in May. Would you and Bee like to come at the same time?

Remind your secretary to send me the Dupuytrens paper.[4]

Mrs. C—— is slightly better but she has such a long way to go that it is rather discouraging. The fact that she holds on to life, however, ought to give us some hopes. I think she is getting a little more aggressive and vocative. When you come I will see that you see her professionally and that will also help with the finances.

Archambeault's case turned him down but you helped us to make a friend and we hope he will send us a patient later.

Tell Bee that Grace finally decided to go to Horney for an analysis which augurs well for the future.

I don't think the family will come with me but I am coming down to see you in June at the time of the Boston meeting. Once before we went to a Boston meeting together, do you recall!

We are developing things here rather rapidly as you can see from the enclosed announcement. We also have a school for the affiliation of graduate nurses who want special training and I will enclose a copy of that so you will see what we are doing. Dr. Ribble and I are giving a course to the nurses on how to handle institutionalized patients who are undergoing analysis. We may want to submit something to you for the *Monograph* series.

Sincerely yours,

FROM SMITH ELY JELLIFFE, NEW YORK, APRIL 17, 1933

Dear Karl:

It was balm to my soul to read your last. I really like my death instinct paper. It read well, was clear and really said something.

Freud wrote me he liked it as "a part of the medicine of the future" and I

---

4 A paper by Jelliffe from the same period as the one on multiple sclerosis, published finally as "Dupuytren's Contracture and the Unconscious: A Preliminary Statement of the Problem," *International Clinics* 41, series 3 (1934): 184–99.

feel quite set up. I hope others will like it. Use it TID in maximum dosage wherever and whenever you wish to.

As to Z.'s [Zilboorg's] ideas of "hectic" matters—I think they are mostly in Z.'s own bonnet. He is a stormy petrel himself. I like it myself as he stirs things up intellectually—though a bit Jehovistic himself.

I would like very much to get West and if the situation clears, I shall certainly come along. . . .

I will remind Miss Cohen of the Dupuytrens paper. I shall rewrite it with more of the sadistic material to clinch the argument. I have reams of it. Pounding, killing, stabbing, shooting, even some archaic stuff that indicates a myelopathy will come out of the freed sadism after the surgeons cleared up the hand disability partly.

Am glad to know Mrs. C—— is progressing. I send her my best wishes.

Sincerely—with regards to all,

To Ernst Simmel, Zurich, May 5, 1933

My dear Dr. Simmel:

The cable sent you by Dr. Alexander and myself a few days ago must have seemed surprising and strange and is to be explained as follows:

I am one of Dr. Alexander's students and completed my analysis with him a year and a half ago. Since then I have returned to my own clinic here, but have also been conducting a seminar at the Chicago Institute for Psychoanalysis, of which Dr. Alexander is the director. Last week when I went up to give my seminar and to hear Dr. Felix Deutsch,[5] a visiting lecturer, I asked both Dr. Deutsch and Dr. Alexander about the possibility of getting one of the European analysts who had been discommoded by the Hitler psychosis to come to our clinic and sanitarium in Topeka. I had some names in mind but Dr. Alexander immediately told me that you had only recently left Germany and might possibly be persuaded to come to this country and he and Dr. Deutsch both agreed that for the particular kind of work we were trying to do you would be the best possible choice and that our institution would most probably be most nearly in line with your own interests. Because we thought you might be making plans to accept another offer, Dr. Alexander thought I should cable you and suggested that since you did not know me I should add his name to the cable. Dr. Alexander is fully cognizant of my plans and will read this letter before it is mailed to you and will perhaps add a note of his own at the bottom.

I shall give you a brief sketch of our clinic:

---

5 Husband of Helene Deutsch. Originally in internal medicine, Felix Deutsch became a psychoanalyst, published widely on the relation between physical and emotional states, and was a pioneer in psychosomatic medicine.

It is located in a quiet attractive small city of 75,000 population, exactly in the middle of the United States, an overnight journey from Chicago and 36 hours from New York. I go to Chicago regularly every two weeks to conduct my seminar, and sometimes oftener, as these distances seem much less formidable to us than to you.

Our clinic is composed of my father who was originally an internist and who is still in active practice, my younger brother and his assistant who are in charge of the hospital and the sanitarium, and a group of six or eight physicians whom we have associated with us, most of them in the past year or two. One of them is a child analyst, trained by Anna Freud, and there is also a lay analyst well trained in Chicago, and another medical analyst. In addition there is a pediatrician, an internist, a neurologist, a pathologist and a dentist. Our work is limited entirely to neuropsychiatric cases. We handle some of these in the outpatient clinic, but we have available also a very modern psychiatric hospital for the acute mental cases and a less confining institution, "The Sanitarium," for milder mental cases, including the neurotics who need to be cared for intramurally. We take all types of cases.

At the present time we are running 20 psychoanalytic cases, 15 hospital cases, 10 sanitarium cases, about 10 outpatient cases which are nonpsychoanalytic and in addition we have a school for backward and handicapped children in which we have six patients. I am telling you this precisely so that you will not overestimate the size of our institution. It is only seven years old but fortunately we have the good will of a very large number of physicians and have been growing very rapidly.

Prior to my own analysis I did general psychiatric work, employing psychoanalytic principles to the extent that I understood them. Since my analysis, however, I am doing almost entirely psychoanalysis and my brother is directing the hospital and sanitarium. We work in very close harmony, however, and have a daily staff meeting at which a case is presented and thoroughly discussed or else some particular problem in the administration of the institution is discussed. We also have a psychoanalytic literature seminar once every two weeks and we have courses of lectures for our younger doctors and for the nurses. The latter are given, to the best of our knowledge, instruction in the particular handling of sanitarium cases undergoing analysis as well as general psychiatric nursing principles.

From what we know of your work I am sure that the particular problems that we meet with are well known to you and I am sure that you could be of the utmost help to us in developing our work along these lines. We hope to take an increasing number of severe neurotics for analysis and also to apply psychoanalysis increasingly to the milder psychotic cases. We are trying to carry out some controlled research in various directions. For example, on two of our cases who are undergoing psychoanalysis in which there have been somatic afflictions we are having certain clinical measurements made by the internist each day, with sufficient regularity, we hope, to preclude any special influence upon the findings. There are doubtless other details which would interest you and perhaps some that you would like to know about specifically. I am sure you will feel free to ask me about them.

We should like very much to have you consider coming to us as a member of our staff and working with us with patients and also with the lecturing and the training of physicians and nurses. It has the advantage of being close to Chicago where there is a larger group of analysts. We have understood that what might deter you most from considering the position is the question of your use of English. We have gained the impression that you do not feel confident of your English or that you do not speak it fluently. If this is true it would, of course, be an enormous handicap because, although we ourselves are Germanic and most of the members of our staff can understand German, very, very few of our patients speak German. In case it is true, however, and the opportunity is at all interesting to you would it be possible, do you think, for you to concentrate on the development of your English to such a point that you would be able to join us later in the year?

We shall be glad to hear from you as soon as possible and if you are interested in coming to America and in joining our staff we shall try to work out some definite arrangements which will be mutually satisfactory.

Sincerely yours,

To SMITH ELY JELLIFFE, NEW YORK, MAY 16, 1933

My dear Chief:

One seldom sees more beautifully demonstrated some of the various possible defenses which are set up by the unconscious against the incest guilt than in the A—— family which you so kindly referred to us recently. The older brother whom you interviewed defends himself as you discovered by an extraordinary series of compulsions including a daily visit to his sister and much atonement to his brother, uncle, aunt, and others in the way of masochistic nobility. The younger brother, whom you did not see but with whom I had several long interviews, has enveloped himself in a narcissistic armor and exploits his great sense of inferiority by the technique of passive aggression, clinging helplessly and dependently to the older brother and blaming him for both his virtues and his vices. The sister, who directed attention to the mess by her breakdown, wrings her hands and whines, begging to be taken to her husband, whom she "loves with all her heart," who "loves her more than she deserves," etc., almost saying in so many words that the guilt she feels for her death wishes toward him and for her wish to return to the incestuous brothers is more than she can bear. It is a fine family mess in which the hostilities are so unconscious because bathed in this rank, lush growth of denatured incestuous love.

The sister is here as I have said, and we have told the brothers that after she has recovered from her acute illness it would be time to begin on some psychoanalytic treatment for her. The younger brother is really seriously involved in his narcissistic neurosis. We have recommended that he, too, consider analysis. He is sacrificing everything to an ambitious illusion of success, which, of course, is compulsive. The older brother probably suffers more than any of them, and it is only a question of how long he can continue to erotize this suffering. I suggested to him that he see you again when he returns to New York next month and discuss with you some of his own personal problems, which I purposely refrained from going into with him. You made a great impression on him because of your frankness and the way in which you swept aside his customary superficialities of thinking. He is a sincere fellow and quite likable, I thought, and I believe he will come.

Secondly, I want to speak about Mrs. C——. You will be delighted to hear that she is immensely improved. She is definitely conscious now and talks rationally and sensibly about most everything. I talked at length with her about you and she said laughingly, "Tell Dr. Jelliffe his worm is still wriggling." (I didn't interpret this!) She was quite amusingly direct. She told me that she had read a book that I wrote which was very interesting but had a weakness in it. She wasn't sure what the weakness was but thought it might be mother fixation or homosexuality. She spent most of the time telling about the masochistic fantasies of her delirium which the nurses are jotting down for me so that I can send them to you later. I am pretty sure that we will have her back to you by fall. Her daughter came to see her the day after I was there and I haven't heard the result but I think things probably went all right. She can use her legs but neither one of her hands. If you have time I think it might be nice to drop her a note now. Send it to the Riviera Apartment, Kansas City, Missouri, or send it to me and I will take it down when I go.

Her fantasies interested me very much because they seemed to have to do largely with devouring children and others and I could see how her oral sadism was projected onto these monsters, etc. Almost in the same breath she said "I want to be a different woman and give up my greediness, and my badness." My impression was that the whole delirium was a terrific sadomasochistic orgy in which she was punishing herself for her oral "sins." It is premature to guess at this however until I have seen more of these fantasies which I will get hold of and send to you.

In the third place just what are your plans for Boston? I am not sure I will go but if I did one of the chief reasons would be to have a little visit with you and Bee. The possibility is that I could be there Monday, Tuesday, and Wednesday or I could be in New York on Monday and go up to Boston on Tuesday and Wednesday but then I think I must come right back. I have several patients who are about to end their analysis and you know what a trying time that is for the analyst as well as the patient and I don't think I should be gone longer. Nor can I afford it. It would help me a lot in making my plans if you would tell me what you are going to do.

Thank you again for sending the A—— case to us.

Sincerely yours,

To ERNST SIMMEL, BERLIN, JUNE 23, 1933

My dear Dr. Simmel:

We have not had a reply to our letter of some weeks ago but recently Dr. Alexander handed me one just received by him from you in which you express interest in the possibility of coming to our clinic to do psychoanalytic work. We are delighted to know of your interest in the project and we should like to make it possible. I feel sure we can get together on the financial question. The only problem that has worried us is the question of your speaking English fluently which is absolutely essential.

It happens that my brother, who is my partner in the business and who has immediate charge of the sanitarium, is leaving for Europe this week and will be in Germany shortly after you receive this letter. He has your address—that is, he has the address given on this envelope—and will come immediately to see you when he arrives in Berlin. That will enable you to get a better idea of the nature and extent of our work. We are hoping that it will be possible to have you with us by fall.

Sincerely yours,

FROM LEO BARTEMEIER, DETROIT, JULY 20, 1933

My Dear Brother Karl:

You have my best congratulations for a happy birthday and I hope the enclosed pipe serves a purpose and that it will be added to your collection. As you sit on the throne in your psa chamber please use it and think of me—it should serve for oral sucking and biting and above all I hope you really like it and have as much fun out of it as I want you to have. I think of it as an intimate gift—and you know what I mean. It was smuggled out of Canada so it has something of the necessary forbidden significance—and it just occurs to me that it is a pipe of peace from one Indian to his brother. May it bring you many happy free associations!

Life moves on rather monotonously with some patients off on vacations and others about to go—very little new work and I'm just as happy because I have more time for myself & Bess & children. My father underwent a prostatectomy a few days ago in D.C. and is said to be doing splendidly. Somehow I feel much less dependent on analytic father people this summer than I did last year. And I marvelled at your nonchalant manner of taking off for the entire summer with no prospects of control work till September. How much longer will you do controls? The good old libido is swinging in fairly definite grooves these days and life has lost much of its flair and also much of its former uneasiness. I sometimes wonder whether "our life of sin together"[6] was not the really effective force that has brought all this marvelous change in our lives—You are still the dearest friend I have and you always will be—so go on and smoke your pipe and then drop a note to your own Bart. Best love and good wishes.

FROM WILLIAM ALANSON WHITE, WASHINGTON, D.C., JULY 21, 1933

My dear Menninger:

I have your letter of the 19th instant.[7] In the first place, with regard to Dr. [Nolan D. C.] Lewis not giving you credit for the material on page 254. I have just finished talking with him about this, and he has no recollection that anything on that page was quoted from you. The only possible way in which anything like a verbatim quotation from you could have been made without his realizing it is as the result of the way in which he accumulates his material. He jots down notes in a notebook of different things that strike him as important with reference to the matter that he is working on. It is possible that he may have done this and neglected to indicate the source, which is his habit, however, and which he is not likely to do. You will note on subsequent pages 262–63 he does cite you fully and give you full credit, and as for his having gotten this quotation that you mention on page 254 from anything that you wrote me, I may say that he never saw any of your letters until today when I went over this matter with him. I did not show them to him. Therefore, if the quotation is a verbatim one it must have come from one of your printed articles. I can assure you that Dr. Lewis is innocent of any intent to ignore you, as I have already indicated he has cited you at least once in the article and once in the bibliography.

As to the matter of cooperation, you will see from the article by Lewis on suicide what the scope of the work is and how it is proceeding here. I had hoped from your communications to me, in which you stated you had been working on this subject for a number of years, that you would have some accumulated psychoanalytic material or that you would be able to supplement our work by detailed psychoanalytic records. You have written me brief reports of some cases which are interesting so far as they go, but of course we have notes of such reports in our records. Naturally we cannot psychoanalyze everybody in a great big place like this, and our records must

6 Bartemeier refers to the heady period when he and KAM were both undergoing analysis in Chicago.

7 This letter has apparently not been preserved.

necessarily be keyed to a largely descriptive level. What we need of course is the deeper significance of what on the surface are obviously castration phenomena, for example. We would like to get concrete, detailed evidence for or against many of our speculations. Particularly I am especially interested, and always have been, in one of the things in which you are interested, namely the particular portion of the body attacked: throat cutting, wrist cutting, shooting in the heart, etc. The method of suicide used, the part of the body which is attacked are to me very interesting, and if this idea were followed still further, what is the relation of suicide, the death instinct, and somatic disease? These are the types of things that require analysis and the elucidation to which I was in hopes you might contribute. If some of your papers which you have in preparation deal with these aspects of the subject I should love to have them. Personally I feel that the suicide problem very easily gets very much larger than the individual problem of any particular patient. It is for that reason that Lewis had outlined such a broad research. We shall never understand the suicidal problem without certainly going as far as he has planned in the above direction. The one direction in which I wanted you to contribute was in the psychoanalytic because I knew of no one else who was so deeply interested in that particular aspect or had a better opportunity to study it, because these cases have to be studied for the most part in institutions.

While writing this letter Dr. Lewis came in with his notes on suicide showing the above description as to how the matter happened to be exactly what took place. He copied his notes into the article and the notes did not show from what source he had obtained them.

Sincerely yours,

To WILLIAM ALANSON WHITE, WASHINGTON, D.C., JULY 23, 1933

My dear Dr. White:

Thank you very much for your letter of July 21. I appreciate your taking the matter up with Dr. Lewis. I do not impugn his motives; the ideas advanced in that paragraph happen to be some pet ideas of mine which have never appeared in print but which I did write you in my letters, for example on page 2 in my letter of November 6, 1932, in which the exact wording of Dr. Lewis' paragraph appears. Where he says that some investigators consider, etc., he can refer to no one but myself since this idea has not been definitely set forth with regard to this particular group of things by anyone but myself. I have no feeling about the matter any further, because I am taking your word for it that it was simply carelessness on Dr. Lewis's part. My article containing this material will not appear for several months anyway.

In the second place let me assure you that I want to cooperate with you in the research which you are helping to finance. What this money enabled us to do is briefly this: it has enabled us to get definite concrete evidence regarding the self-destructive behavior of several individuals and as we go further with it I think we shall get increasingly pertinent data. What I should like to know, however, is how you want the report on our work made to you, say at the end of the year. Do you want me to write up the particular cases we have or am I correct in assuming that what you want is an article on some phase of the subject which is based, in part at least, upon this work? If this would meet with your approval it would be a very fruitful way to summarize the findings of the analytic work we are doing with these two patients and I could also include some other material.

Another very unexpected thing which we have discovered in this work is the way in which the suicidal and manic depressive patient interprets his hospital environment. We think we have almost enough material from this aspect alone to draw up some suggestions for psychiatric nurses with reference to the special handling of psychoanalytic patients. . . .

If my idea about these other things is all right, give me the high sign.

Sincerely yours,

From William Alanson White, Washington, D.C., July 27, 1933

My dear Menninger:

I have your letter of the 24th. With further reference to the Lewis matter, I have no recollection of having shown him your letter, and so if you never published it and I never showed him the letter there must be some occult affairs at work. Probably, however, the solution is a simpler one. Personally I no longer trust myself any more than I do anybody else, so that everybody being equally unreliable, it rather puts us all in the same boat and at least ought to make for a tolerant attitude toward other's faults, if they are faults.

As to what I would like you to do in relation to choosing one of the several alternatives which you present, I think it would be much more satisfactory to have you present an article. I feel that I ought to present some concrete evidence of value received for money expended, and an article will do that in much the best way.

Your article on "The Common Cold" thankfully received. It is very interesting. Might I suggest one thing which I have no doubt you thought of but did not mention? Assuming that you are correct—that this cold was psychogenically determined—then I think it is fair to assume further that one of the reasons that it occurred was due to the very fact that was at the bottom of the tradition prevalent in the family regarding this young woman, namely that she never did have colds; in other words, the cold-producing psychogenic factor was under severe repression. Because of that fact it had accumulated a great deal of energy, and when finally, owing to the stimulus of the analytic situation, it escaped repression, it produced an abundant symptomatology. How about it?

Sincerely yours,

To HELEN McLEAN, HENNIKER, NEW HAMPSHIRE, AUGUST 2, 1933

My dear Helen:

Doggone it, I wish you had kept Mrs. W—— and psychoanalyzed her at $25 an hour, because I believe she could pay it and I would like to have you have it and I don't know who else but Dave Brunswick[8] to send her to in Los Angeles, but if she has gone back [to Los Angeles] I suppose that's the best thing there is to do. I admire your objectivity in deciding why it might not be best for you to take her, but I have a feeling that some of those difficulties might have been analyzed out. Perhaps, however, at the expense of arousing great hostility on the part of the parents. I haven't heard from them since, even to the extent of paying my bill. I hope you had better luck.

Now I will make a report on my summer activities. I had to call upon all my psychoanalytically acquired self-control and restraint in order to avoid commiting murder. The object of the murder was the judge who owned the farm I told you about, who will always be to me on outstanding example of anal-erotic resistance. The old codger stalled me off for eight or nine months and then had the audacity to write my agent that he had never had an offer from me. My agent . . . carefully handcuffed himself and then went to see the old boy and reminded him that we had made this offer over and over, and the poor senile old chump just looked at the ceiling and said he hadn't realized it was an offer and he would think it over again, but for the next few days he had a very important law case he had to give his mind to, etc. If you can imagine the anxiety which this kind of thwarting stimulates in such an avid person as myself you will be surprised that I haven't developed diabetes or goiter. But it all goes to show that Freud was right when he said that he who can wait need make no concessions.

What should develop but that I should find a new farm which is ten times better than the other one in the following respects. It has beautiful, delicious, very cold water in limitless quantities (I mean in a well and not tumbling over the rocks. This is Kansas and not Colorado). Second, it actually has a pretty good-sized creek with enough water in it to fall over some rocks and make a splashing noise like halfway between Niagara Falls and the bathtub, and said creek flows on around the place over a pebbly beach and into a swimming hole which, while far from clear, does not seem to deter my children.

8 A lay analyst in Los Angeles, whose brother, composer Mark Brunswick, was the husband of Ruth Mack Brunswick. David Brunswick was instrumental in persuading Ernst Simmel to emigrate to Los Angeles.

In the third place it has about ten acres of virgin forest (virgin of 1885, not 1933); in fact, it was virgin when the man who now owns it homesteaded it fifty years ago. There is black oak, white oak, red oak, hickory, walnut, sycamore, and to my surprise quite a number of sizable redbud trees, which are mostly bushes in these parts. Where this "forest" has been nicked out there is a little orchard (not much good but I can improve it) and a lot of second-growth hickory, and what is especially intriguing to me, a great many prolific wild grapevines and hazelnut bushes. This is pretty thick but it has paths thru it made by obliging but somewhat careless cows, but contrary to Marc Anthony the good that the cows did is going to live after them and we will use these paths as a basis for getting about without getting lost or acquiring chiggers. The tall stately woods on the other side of the place really look very Canadian. There are some other features but I can't seem to get enthusiastic writing you about a little Kansas woods when you are located there in the most beautiful place in the world and feel a little foolish for trying to and I am going to stop. However, I am quite enthusiastic about this new place and it is smaller and less expensive and by the time you get out to see us we will probably have a place to lodge you.

I would like to come East and spend some time with you there but there is no use kidding myself, what with my brother being in Europe and my wife going back to Chicago next month and with no housekeeper in sight and my Thoreauvian ambitions, etc. I will have to begin to plan on it for next year instead.

I haven't heard a darn word from any of the brothers or sisters except yourself and Bartie and for that matter I don't even know where they are. It would look as if they all wanted to get rid of one another for the summer, which is probably a good idea.

Sincerely yours,

FROM ERNST SIMMEL, BERLIN, AUGUST 7, 1933

My dear colleague Mr. Menninger:[9]

For many reasons which I do not wish to go into here, I am just now getting around to thanking you most gratefully for your most cordial letter and invitation. In the meantime, your brother looked me up and discussed the situation with me. In and of itself, the prospect of serving as your psychoanalytic colleague, as your brother described the position to me, is very attractive. On the other hand, as you know, I received an invitation at the same time from Los Angeles. Thus, for the time being, I'm still in a quandary as to which of the two offers I should accept. Naturally, the whole

---

9 Originally handwritten in German; translated in 1933 by an unidentified member of the Menninger staff.

thing depends upon monetary considerations, since I am responsible for a family of five. I have assurances from Los Angeles of an income of $7,000 per year from my private practice and from teaching. Would my income in Topeka be approximately the same? Would we be talking about a position with a fixed income and free board and lodging? On the other hand, are you considering profit-sharing, and would a private practice in addition to institutional practice be possible and permissible?

I might note that because of the economic collapse of the psychoanalytic clinic in Tegel of a year and one-half ago, I lost my savings and my personal debts which remain after the liquidation of the project have prevented me from saving any money in recent years.

Nevertheless, I have still, despite the general economic difficulties, a quite extensive practice and an adequate income. Yet, as a result of the circumstances mentioned above, I am dependent upon my day-to-day earnings and therefore cannot permit myself more than one or two weeks away from my work. That means I would be giving up an adequate and secure existence here if I should move over there; on the other hand, I would require monetary assistance from you in order to take care of the costs of moving to America.

In closing, I should like to note that as a result of the heavy professional load I have here, I haven't managed to keep up with my knowledge of English, although I am currently having instruction in English.

However, I am convinced that after moving to America I would be able to acquire the necessary proficiency in two months. For the first two months you would have to have a certain amount of patience with me, dear colleague; that is, you could not count on a fully productive partner in therapeutic practice for this reason. Your brother advised me, despite my reservations, to write to you and advised me further that I didn't need to worry that I would write to you in German.

I'm looking forward to hearing from you in the near future. Again many thanks and my best wishes—

Most sincerely yours,

To Karen Horney, Locarno-Monti, Switzerland, August 14, 1933

My dear Karen:

I feel very guilty for having waited so long to write you. Perhaps I have been a little too envious of the grand times I know you have been having running about Europe leading a happy, normal existence while I have had to listen to free associations ten hours a day, six and seven days a week. But a very pretty postal card arrived from Capri with a nice note from you with an appended note from your daughter whom I will be very glad to get acquainted with this fall. This really did not remind me to write you as I have been planning to do so for a long time. I am only afraid now that you will have started back before this will reach you.

What I have to tell you will be very dull compared to your adventures. The most excitement I have had has been connected with trying to get a little woods on a stream nearby on which to build a little house. Grace has been quite interested in it, too, and perhaps in the course of the next few days we will begin building our cabin. It will be very beautiful and I shall be proud to show it to you when you come to visit us.

Our clinic has been rushed with patients all summer. In fact, we have been the busiest ever in our existence. I am carrying ten patients which is too many but several of them come only four days a week now and two of them are near the end of their analysis although it may require a blow on the head with an axe to terminate the analysis successfully. Another nice young fellow has joined us who is doing very capable work—Dr. Robert Knight,[10] perhaps you have met him. And I am also happy to report that a few days ago in a cloud of dust . . . Margaret Ribble left us taking with her a small retinue of patients to Vienna, where I hope she plans to continue with her analysis with Anna Freud. One of her patients whom she had persuaded to go with her attempted suicide the day they were leaving and had to be left here in the sanitarium; she is going on very nicely with another analyst so that is all smoothed out and Dr. Ribble was, I think, very lucky.

My brother was taken to Europe by one of his wealthy friends and is over there now running about visiting clinics and hospitals. He went to see Simmel but it appears that Simmel has almost a phobia of trying to speak English and so they used an interpreter during the interview and it is not yet definite what Dr. Simmel wants to do. I don't think there is any use in his coming to America at all if he cannot master English. My brother had the impression that he almost had an inhibition against it.

I haven't been up to Chicago but I have sent a few more applicants up to the Institute with which you and the chief [Alexander] will probably deal when you come back. I think my brother himself expects to be analyzed, perhaps by you.

Grace is doing pretty well, in some ways remarkably well. She is inclined to be rather moody and erratic and she is entirely disinterested in me, but who can blame her? She has raised some arguments against returning in the

10 A psychiatrist and psychoanalyst, Robert P. Knight was one of the earliest members of the Menninger Clinic; he came to Topeka as a resident in psychiatry in 1933 and remained until 1947. From 1946 to 1947, he was chief of staff of the Menninger Clinic and senior consultant to Winter Veterans Administration Hospital. In 1947 he left the Menninger Clinic to become medical director of the Austen Riggs Center in Stockbridge, Massachusetts.

fall but she will be there all right whenever you are ready for her.[11] I have tried to carry out what you suggested.

The brothers and sisters are scattered far and wide. Helen [McLean] is in New Hampshire, Blitz [Blitzsten] in Wisconsin, Alexander I think in Maine, French somewhere in the East, Kiffie [Catherine Bacon] I don't know where. Bartie and I are working every day and trying to pay the rent and feeling very righteous and, I must add, very envious. If I get my farm, however, I mean my woods, I won't envy anybody but I will invite you all down to it this fall and then you will be envious, because it is really very pretty and quite wild.

Give my love to the new little sister[12] whom I don't promise to treat as a sister.

Sincerely yours,

To LIONEL BLITZSTEN, CHICAGO, SEPTEMBER 4, 1933

Dear Lionel:

Your letter delighted me except for the bad news that you have been ill again and I am glad to know that the internists are on the trail of something concrete and will be getting you straightened out. I had some FA [free associations] about psychogenic factors but I am afraid you wouldn't have much patience with them.

Mildred [Law] reported very briefly about her conference with you. She seemed to be completely satisfied with it. Just yesterday (before your letter came) she told me about the new developments in her life. I made some comments at the close of which she said, "I see you have heard from Blitzsten." Evidently our noble minds run in the same channel and I seem to have used some expressions and made some comments that exactly coincided with yours, which pleased both Mildred and myself. That afternoon your letter came, but of course you didn't make any reference to it.

We still think as much as ever of Knight, and I think he likes us. He will be coming up with me this fall. He took over one of Ribble's cases and I took one and both of them are going along better than they were with Ribble, so far as I can judge. I think one of Dr. Ribble's faults was one which you thoroughly drilled into both Knight and myself, namely, to bear down hard on the real situation and the ways in which the patient is using the analysis as an alibi and a device for further aggressions.

If I didn't restrain myself I'd fill six pages with bubblings over my farm

11 Grace Menninger was in analysis with Horney at the time.

12 Probably Gertrude Jacob, a German psychoanalyst. In April 1933 she left Germany and settled in France, where she taught psychoanalysis to staff members of an Alsatian sanitarium. In 1935, she became a staff member of the Menninger Clinic, but a relapse of tuberculosis forced her to leave five months later.

stimulated by your generous sympathetic enthusiasm. We really have a beautiful place. Everyone says so who sees it and I am exceedingly interested in it and think it is the best sublimation I ever developed. It is about 10 acres of a high crowning hill covered with grass, about 10 acres of virgin timber 60 or 70 years old, very solemn and quiet, and about 7 acres of second-growth trees and shrubs which is very intriguing and pretty, and then about 4 acres (this should add up to 30 but I see it doesn't) lowland in which there are many big specimen trees of many different kinds with about 250 yards of good-sized stream skirting this and our property line runs down the middle of the stream. The water is muddy and unattractive, like all Kansas streams, but it has a nice waterfall at one point and a rocky ford at another point, and the kids think it is wonderful and given a certain amount of moonlight it really is pretty. Our present plans are to do exactly as you suggest in regard to a house but I doubt if we will begin building until spring because I think what we lose in higher prices we'll gain in reflection. As Blitzsten, Menninger and others often say to their patients, psychoanalysis ought to make it possible to endure the pain of waiting a little while, which I shall try to do.

We have spoken many times of Dorothy [Blitzsten] this summer and are glad to know that she is getting along so well and is so near to the realization of her motherhood. Tell her we are thinking of her and hoping for her continuing health.

Bob Knight and I are just about to discuss some cases and he asks to be remembered to you and Dorothy.

I have had an interesting summer with Sister B—— [a patient who was also an analyst]. She had a dream some months ago that she was encased in silver armor and we have been trying to get the silver armor off that girl ever since. She came to realize after about 20 or 30 dreams of the same sort that she has always taken the attitude that because she is rich she can get away with anything and doesn't have to give anything or do anything and after she got quite sick of dragging her silver armor around and began to think of ways to get rid of it she realized she had enormous resistance against making restitution to anyone. She talked of paying me $50 an hour and felt terribly guilty because she hadn't; she counted up what she had spent for her analysis and was surprised to find it was less than one-third of what she had supposed it was; made some small whispers about couldn't she pay me more, but gave no real evidence of wanting to pay anyone anything. This gave us an opportunity to discuss how she had always salved her conscience for these money- (and penis-) snatching propensities by giving trivial gifts, flinging alms with her eyes shut, etc. She realizes that she has been staying here for some months just because she does feel so guilty on this score of not paying me as much as she felt she could and wanting to make restitution to somebody by shutting her eyes to the fact that she should make restitution to her husband, children and take some responsibility for this money toward less fortunate people in the world who really don't seem to exist in her consciousness at all.

It seems to me I just have to let her find her own way of making restitution, declining of course to take any more money per hour than was originally agreed upon. I thought I would wait until she really offered it, however, before I made any such announcement, and to date she hasn't made it with any real intention in her voice or manner and she is making plans to stay here indefinitely as far as I can see. I believe our original hunch of telling her she must saw off on a certain date may be necessary after all, but I don't believe it is time yet.

C—— is going along pretty slowly, faced more and more with his feminine tendencies and paying me back with ridicule, jeering, etc., in the dream of the subsequent night whenever an interpretation is made. His chief resistance seems to be that he plays around, especially in his daily golf rounds, and gratifies his narcissism, homosexuality and passivity in the analysis, but I have just about got that stopped now and things are going better. I forgot to tell you that Mrs. B—— has recalled recently that her mother and sister repeatedly told her that she wasn't pretty and never would hope to be and this ugliness humiliation was one of the original traumata which resulted in the extra-strong yen for money.

Grace and John [Stone] are going up [to Chicago] about the middle of the month. My brother is still in Europe. I go out to my farm every night and have a glorious time sawing down dead trees and imagining things I can show you when you come.

Sincerely yours,

To Ernst Simmel, Berlin, September 5, 1933

Dear Dr. Simmel:

We have given careful thought to your letter of August 7. We had a letter about the same time from my brother, who had had the pleasure of an interview with you.

If we understand your letter correctly, you are weighing the advantages of the two offers you have had from this country, a Los Angeles offer and our offer.

Perhaps it will help you if I make somewhat more clear the distinction between the work you would do here and the work you would do in Los Angeles. Los Angeles is, as you know, a large city 2000 miles west of Topeka; Topeka is about 1000 [miles] west of New York and about 500 miles west of Chicago. If you go to Los Angeles you are almost in a different country as it is only occasionally that California colleagues feel that they can afford the expense in time and money to come east to Chicago and New

York. It takes three days and two nights on the fastest trains to come from Los Angeles to Chicago and 20 hours more on to New York. From that standpoint Topeka has, as you will see, a great advantage. It is only an overnight trip from Topeka to Chicago and the trains are very comfortable and convenient. My colleagues and I go to Chicago very frequently, as often as several times a month, for conferences with Alexander and the other analysts up there and also for attendance at the Psychoanalytic Society meetings which are held there. In other words, if you come to Topeka you will be associated in your daily work with a number of psychoanalysts and you will be only a night's trip away from 15 to 20 more psychoanalysts. In the entire state of California, on the other hand, there is, as you know, not a single member of the International Psychoanalytic Association, and only one or two men who do any psychoanalysis whatsoever. You would in other words be isolated geographically and also psychoanalytically.

As to the nature of the work, I do not know what they have in mind in California except as you mention it in your letter but evidently it would be quite different from our work here. If you will refer to my letter of May 5 you will find a description of our clinic which includes a sanitarium and hospital and school as well as the outpatient work which I believe you call in Europe the ambulatorium. We work as a unit by which I mean that no physician, analyst, technician or other employee of the Clinic receives any income direct from outside sources. Each of us depends upon a salary which is paid monthly in cash. No one except the nurses receives board and room as a part of his compensation. On the other hand, no one pays any professional expenses for himself, by which I mean that the clinic pays the entire overhead of the office including secretarial, insurance, advertising, postal, telegraph and similar expenses, and we also pay transportation of members of the clinic to many medical meetings. In all probability, we would pay your transportation expenses to and from Chicago once a month. You could, of course, go more frequently if you desired to do so at your own expense. The medical journals, books, and society dues, etc., are also included in the overhead expenses paid by the clinic. In other words, we would pay you a salary and in addition we would pay all of your professional expenses. In return you would work full time as a member of our staff and all receipts would go into the clinic treasury.

It is our idea, as I wrote you on May 5, that you could take some ambulatory patients, some hospital patients, possibly some didactic analyses, and certainly some control analyses. In addition, you could help us with the training of our nurses and in the general staff discussions which are held daily.

The amount of salary we can offer under present conditions is $500.00 a month. If the difference in the costs of living are taken into consideration this is equal to or greater than $7000.00 a year in Los Angleles. In fairness to you we should remind you, however, that this is a small city and not a large metropolis but it is also fair to add that the advantages of a large city in the United States are not what a European is accustomed to expect in a large city and that in most respects Los Angeles has a beautiful climate all the year around whereas we have two months of rather severe cold and two months of rather severe heat. The other eight months are usually delightful.

We still hope that you will decide to join us. I think we both recognize that we have some common interests, particularly the development of intramural psychoanalysis. Alexander has told me that he hopes very much that you will be able to join us. I shall be quite frank and tell you that our only misgivings are in regard to the language difficulty, which, of course, would apply equally whether you come to Los Angeles or to Topeka. Our impression is that even after diligent study for the next few months in Germany it will require several months here before you will feel at ease with the language, and naturally that impairs your earning capacity considerably. If you found, after a month, that you could not carry on analytic work with English-speaking patients and preferred to play only a passive role for a time while you improved your language we might make some compromise on the matter of your salary during that time, e.g., 50%. It may be that you underestimate your proficiency in English, but I think we could soon determine that quite definitely and I feel sure that if you associated with English-speaking people daily, as you would here, you would soon increase your vocabulary and fluency.

In regard to the matter of your transportation, if it would help you to have a salary advance of several hundred dollars to help you make the trip, we could easily and gladly arrange that.

Sincerely yours,

To Lionel Blitzsten, Chicago, September 23, 1933

Dear Lionel:

. . . For your forthcoming paper[13] may I contribute the following illustrations:

A patient (Mrs. B——) had a dream about being a golddigger. She analyzed this with reference to contemporary and ancient manifestations and then added, "I see that, but what does all that get me?" "Get me!" I echoed. "Oh, I see what you mean. I am still talking about getting me something instead of about giving me something. Oh, I mean instead of about my giving somebody something."

To another patient (H——) it had just been pointed out that he was ero-

---

13. We could find no record of Blitzsten's ever having published a paper on slips of the tongue.

tizing his aggressions. "I see that," he said; "Yes, I must do my best to erotize these aggressions. I mean *analyze* these aggressions."

Sincerely yours,

To CATHERINE [MRS. WILLIAM C.] MENNINGER, EAST ORANGE, NEW JERSEY, SEPTEMBER 27, 1933

My dear Catherine:

You have heard from the folks now and then and have been kept fairly well posted on matters here and so you will be wondering why you should receive a letter from me. There is no special reason except that I sent a cable to William C. [Menninger] the other day urging him to make the most of his splendid opportunities he now has to get some more postgraduate work either in Europe or in this country. I thought I ought to tell you this and lay the matter, as I see it, before you too so that you could reinforce our suggestions with him. Things are going along so well here that he can continue his leave of absence without detriment to the business. Everything has progressed fine in every way here this summer and so far this fall. Dr. [Ralph] Fellows is doing excellently in William's place. Therefore I felt I ought to urge William to do this while everything is going along so favorably. In his last letter from Vienna he said he was coming on home to America, perhaps stopping at London before he sails. After coming to America he intends visiting several institutions, especially one at Hartford, Conn. Here he leaves us in somewhat of an uncertainty as to his future destination. But one somehow draws conclusions from what he does not say that then he will come on to Topeka and later thinks he will go to Chicago to take up his analysis. If such conclusions drawn are correct I believe he would make a mistake. If things are going on so nicely here and you are so nicely situated in East Orange with the children in school why waste so much energy, time and money to come back to Topeka, unsettle you and the children at East Orange and resettle you here in Topeka and then go off to Chicago or N.Y. for study and analysis, thus again being away and being separated from you and the children? It would have an unsettling effect on the doctors who are doing their best to carry on his work in his absence, not to say anything of the effect it would have on the patients.

Bill has realized that he has a tremendously great responsibility in handling the clinical end of our hospital and sanitarium and has often felt the need of further study in this line. This trip to the [Boy Scout] Jamboree[14] aside from the opportunity he has had to very casually see and examine a

14 Throughout his life, WCM was active in the Boy Scout movement, beginning as a troop leader at Topeka's First Presbyterian Church and later recognized at the national level. He was awarded Scouting's Silver Buffalo Award for his service to the organization.

few of the hospitals and sanitariums in Europe has not been an opportunity to do any real studying in neurology and psychiatry. It has been a great sightseeing itinerary and of course very stimulating but as far as learning more about the nerves and brain and their disease states it has added very little to his already existing knowledge. So I want to write you so that you can aid him in helping himself when we here at home are so anxious to have him do so for his own good and for the benefit of all of us. And now how best to do that remains to be decided. According to my idea it would be best for him to make trips to the very best private and public sanitaria and hospitals like ours and stay there long enough to make real intensive study of them and their methods. Then write detailed reports to us giving us the benefit of any improvements observed. And if at the same time he can put in real study of neurology and psychiatry and possibly also psychoanalysis then he will be really accomplishing something for his own and our collective benefit for all time to come.

Give me your reaction to these suggestions and do so at your earliest and let me help you in any way I can.

Lovingly,

To WILLIAM ALANSON WHITE, WASHINGTON, D.C., OCTOBER 6, 1933

Dear Doctor White:

I have been somewhat remiss in reporting to you recently in regard to the suicide research but I will now try to summarize what has been going on for the past several months. Dr. Ribble's departure has really been a fortunate thing for the work. She took one case with her but the important material with regard to the suicide had already come out and we were able to replace him with other cases.

One girl, a college student, attempted suicide right here and it was possible to study her analytically for a month or two following the attempt. This was instructive. We expected a good deal from the case of a poor farmer's wife who was not so depressed but insisted that she was impelled to commit suicide at any minute and was not only distressed herself but managed to distress the family a good deal about her. We carried her for a month only to learn, however, that her intellectual level is so low and her resistance is so high that she was not likely to furnish us with much that was valuable or at least that she was so difficult that other cases seemed much more promising investments. One, in particular, for which we have high hopes which I think will meet with your unqualified approval is the case of a young woman whose suicidal tendencies have tended toward the structural and organic forms and who now appears to be developing multiple sclerosis in a relatively early form. The psychogenic factors are so clear, however, even superficially that even our neurologist, who has a strong organic leaning, endorsed the idea of psychoanalytic investigation. It is too early to make any report except that things have begun but I will let you hear more abut this next month.

Finally, there is the case of the manic depressive student about whom I have reported several times. I have carried him myself and I have already gotten what I think is a very clear demonstration of a factor in the self-destructive tendency of melancholiacs which has not previously been emphasized in psychoanalytic studies. It relates to the reason that these patients take the loss of a love object so hard. Of course we all know that as Freud says the loss of the love object precipitates the depression and that the depression is severe because of the underlying neurotic attitude of the melancholiac toward the lost object. I am getting some evidence, however, to show that the loss of the object may be actually brought about, or forced, by the melancholiac himself so that he justifies his depression in advance, so to speak. This relates to the suicide directly because, of course, it relates directly the destructive wish toward the love object with the destructive attack on the self. I will write this up in detail after we have gone along further but I thought you would like to know and hence this report.

Sincerely yours,

To William C. Menninger, London, October 26, 1933

Dear Will:

Now that you are settled in London for four or five weeks I thought I would write and tell you how glad I am that you are planning to see all you can there. I have left the letter writing to Dr. Fellows, because he seemed to cover the news so thoroughly and also because I have had a number of added responsibilities and duties both at home and at the clinic. But now I want to set down a few free associations.

I have read all your letters with a great deal of interest and wish you had had time to write more but no doubt you have been keeping some memoranda which you can use to refresh your memory when you come home and tell us all about it. I have not written you many of the details about the business because there is not much you can do about it and we have made our own decisions about it and gone on the best we could. The most satisfactory things have been the splendid way in which Dr. Fellows has administered the hospital. I think his work has been excellent from every standpoint—the scientific treatment of the patients, the educational development of the staff, the training of the nurses, and most important of all, his handling of the relatives. He has made all the relatives feel that we are extremely interested in their loved one and are trying our best to help him. I have made a slight increase in his salary but I think he should have more because he is getting distinctly less than he is really worth to us.

Dr. Perry[15] took occasion to tell me one day at luncheon that our weak spot here was the fact that none of the Menningers were good contact men; that I was too abrupt with the relatives, that you were too evasive and vague, and I have forgotten what he said about Father, and that he thought such men as Phelps[16] and Fellows were extremely valuable to us.

Having said this much about Phelps I want to digress a moment on another point. I detected in your last letter what I think is an overreaction to our telegram where you say that you will only be here a very short time, which is a marked contrast to your previous letter in which you indicated that you would be home [for] several months. I have the feeling that you alternate between thinking you are not wanted simply because you are not so strongly needed at the present time and the feeling that you aren't needed at all and can't contribute anything. Now the facts are, as nearly as I can put them, these. You had been considering the fact that you needed to go for a period of study and observation to build up your self-confidence and to stimulate your old creativeness, etc., so that you could help to develop the Menninger Clinic to what you and Father and I want it to be. You had planned to go off for analysis this fall. Then came this offer from your friend to go to Europe which should, I think, be regarded as a wonderful stroke of luck, because it gave you these tremendously increased opportunities at a time when it has been possible for us to get along temporarily without you. We have been able to get along because you gave the training and responsibility and authority to Dr. Fellows, and by now he has gotten onto the hang of it, as I have indicated, very well. Now for you to come back for a few months would have what effect? On the patients it would once more renew their emotional conflicts as between you and Dr. Fellows, something which, as you know, stirred some of them up when you left quite a bit. That, I think, is not so important, however, as the fact that it would be necessary to get Ralph readjusted. He would have to surrender the authority that you gave him only to have it thrust back on him in a few months, and this giving somebody something and taking it away from them is apt to be very disturbing. Furthermore, the situation is so adjusted so that there are no imperative things here that demand your presence. That doesn't mean that we don't want to see you, and I think it would be a mistake for you to make too hasty a visit here. I don't think you should deny yourself any opportunities in Europe or New York, but I think you should plan to stay long enough to

15 M. L. Perry, superintendent of the Topeka State Hospital.
16 Glen Phelps was business manager of the Menninger Clinic.

see how your work and our work is going on here, tell us about your European experiences in detail, etc.

Just before an analysis is always a disturbing time for a fellow and I have a notion that you are quite apprehensive about it. Like everyone else, you have some fears about what you will discover about yourself. Now you can rest assured that whatever you discover about yourself will be much better dealt with after you see it than before you see it. One of the things that I think you are puzzling about is just what your function in this clinic should be. Certainly it should be what you enjoy doing with your whole heart and not something that you do compulsively because you think I want you to or because it is the only way you see to make a living or something of that sort. An analysis will help you on this very point. You have an excellent mind and you have had excellent training but you don't always use it. That comes from some inhibition which an analysis should serve to remove. Then you will be able to find out what you really want to do around here. As one of the partners you are in the extremely fortunate position of being able to do about what you want to do once you discover what it is and to do it with much pleasure and satisfaction to yourself. There isn't the slightest possibility in your case of the danger that confronts many patients with great horror—that is, of losing your place altogether. You know absolutely that you have a place here that you can take or leave about what you want. You thought our telegram was harsh, I think, because you felt at that moment that there was no place here for you and you must come home and assure yourself that there was one. Obviously that is neurotic and not true to fact. For my own sake I often wish very much you were here, but for your sake I think you should finish what you have started to do which is not merely to get a training analysis but to analyze out some of the inhibitions which have kept you from doing as fully as you would have liked to have done what you think you want to do.

I forwarded your letter to Alexander. I read it before sending it and was amazed to learn that it was going to be possible for you to be analyzed and also to pay for your seminars and other training for as little as $2,000. I think this is another great stroke of luck and, while unconsciously I may envy you in recalling how many more times this I had to spend, on the other hand I am glad for your sake and in the long run I know it is to my own great advantage, also. Alexander asked me last week if I had heard from you, saying that he was expecting you in January or February. I told him you had written me rather seldom and I had had no word about your plans in that regard. The training facilities in Chicago are wonderful and I think you can look forward to an extraordinarily interesting year. I remember how much panic I had about it myself prior to going and if you have half as much I can sympathize with you but I can also assure you that the anticipation is much worse than the experience.

I want to go on now and tell you about many other details about here. Leo Stone continues to be conscientious both scientifically and professionally and is, I think, an invaluable asset to the institution. . . . Knight is also a good man and is much more than earning his salary with his analytic cases as well as proving very helpful in the sanitarium. Tidd[17] is a good intern. He is going to begin an analysis at the institute a year from now. . . .

Mother seems pretty well. Father seems exceedingly well. Grace is still in Chicago but I believe will finish her analysis quite soon. Julia fell and broke a front tooth. Ben[18] continues to be a mainstay of the institution in many ways. Personally I have had a wonderful summer except for the fact that because I can't get rid of them I have had more patients than I wanted to carry. The big fun I have been having is with a little 30-acre tract of land over on the north side which has some big woods on it, a thick second growth, a stream (Soldier Creek) and some other advantages which I can show you when you come. I am out there every spare moment I have. I don't believe I would even trade it to you for a trip to Europe. It is a wonderful bird refuge and I am putting up bird feeders and it will be the utmost joy for me if you will come out next summer and help me identify some of the species. Some of the wild ducks land on my creek so that you can also see the waterfowl to some extent, I believe.

Did I tell you or did you know that Mildred Law got herself engaged and was about to leave us but changed her mind, broke her engagement, and is going to stay with us permanently, I believe and hope? All our other good boys and girls are still with us.

My dear brother, I hope this letter conveys to you better than any formal declarations would that you and your future are very dear to me. You say so little about your real feelings, thoughts and plans that I am not very certain how you do feel, but I get a little impression from your last letter that you had a little anxiety and doubt. I am writing to do what I can to dispel any conscious necessity for either. My ambition is for us to work happily and fruitfully together as long as we live. I think you must help to find the best way in which to do this so that you will not have any feeling of inadequacy or inferiority or disappointment but rather the feeling that you are doing what you love to do and doing it better than anyone else could possibly do it, in which I would want to help you and in which you would be helping me.

17 Charles Tidd was among the first residents at the Menninger Clinic. After leaving Topeka, he practiced psychoanalysis in Los Angeles and became a charter member of the Los Angeles Psychoanalytic Institute (1946), headed by Ernst Simmel.

18 Ben Boam, chief engineer of the Menninger Clinic and Sanitarium and brother of Pearl Boam, CFM's second wife.

To Franz Alexander, Chicago, October 28, 1933

Dear Alex:

You will have had my brother's letter by now and I hope you will write him immediately that you are expecting him by such and such a date, in January. I have also written him, because I detected in his last letter a certain amount of anxiety, that the anticipation of analysis is usually worse than the experience itself and also assuring him that he had nothing to fear in the way of losing his position here with me or on the financial basis. I don't want to have you consider postponing his analysis for the sake of giving me some help. I think this would overwhelm me with guilt feelings because I am sure that I already have some unconscious feelings about my brother's analysis by you, as I told you. I think I would feel better if I got it out of my system to tell you that I have not yet quite reconciled in my mind the fact that these fellows are being analyzed for $2,000 when some of them could very well afford to pay much more than this and still pay much less than those of us who came earlier. I don't know that this has come out in the discussions we have had about private practice and the Institute. Although I am subjectively affected by it with thoughts of the well-known infantile type that my brothers can have from Father what I paid much more to get, that perhaps now my brother will replace me with my father, as indeed happened in my childhood, as you know, that I am being charged for seminars, etc., when I have already paid for my analysis, whereas these brothers get seminars free along with paying less for their analyses.

These subjective thoughts I don't defend rationally at all, as I know intellectually that the development of the movement is the most important thing and that this is conducive to it. I do feel, however, that were I in Chicago it would trouble me to have men paid a salary as high as George Wilson, for example, of $6,000 a year when I was unable to earn that much after years of experience. I can't possibly offer a man $6,000 a year, even a man who has much more experience than George Wilson, and at the same time I know that George has not finished his analysis nor his controls but is paid a salary for material which he then works on controls. This seems rather petty of me, but as I told you I would feel better if I said it. I like George Wilson very much, but it seems to me that such a man as George might be paid a salary something like $2,000 a year for a year or two, and it seems to me it would then not be necessary for you to sacrifice so much or for us to make the sacrifices which we all must make to keep the Institute going. The Institute, for example, could not afford to pay me a much smaller sum to continue my seminars. I don't resent this at all, in fact I think I would be loath to give the time to it, but I have some resentments on this score and I must get it off my mind.

I have been thinking a great deal of continuing my analysis with you. I have an enormously strong temptation to do it but at the same time I think it would be a great mistake because I think I would do it to have the means of reestablishing a transference relationship with you—i.e., of prolonging an emotional dependence upon you which I ought to be man enough to get along without. I find it hard to distinguish between the irrational elements in my attachment to you and the rational elements, and I like to think that it is mostly the latter which determine it, but I cannot avoid looking at my very obvious efforts to let you down and to show you that I can't stand the burden of responsibility you have placed on me. This means to me that I still want to maintain a passive rather than a cooperative attitude toward you. Even as I am writing this I have pains in my stomach! I think your intuition was entirely correct when you said that the burden of my responsibilities weighs too heavy upon me. But I think I can carry them. I think I will let no one down except you. Of course, I have let my wife down pretty badly in the past but I think that will be changed when she gets back. I think I can measure up to that responsibility. I don't know if it was consciously in your mind the other night, but when you were telling about Rank and how he was overwhelmed by the confidence Freud put in him I thought of myself and you. I was afraid to mention it for fear you would think it was a narcissistic overestimation of your regard for me, but as I reflect upon it I am sure it was not.

I think the best way for me to show that I am not like Rank, that I can endure it without guilt feelings, is to refrain from yielding to my impulses to carry on my analysis with you, which at the present moment I feel that I would like to fling everything else away and begin with. I am sure that there will be a time a little later when I must do it and can do it but at the present time the only thing I feel alarmed about is my strong impulse to do it, even though in so doing I confess to everyone the failure of analysis in my case and thereby the inadequacy and incompetence of Franz Alexander. I don't like this ascetic solution of life and this substitution of Mother Nature for more human females, but I think it is better than surrender and I think once my burden is lightened a little by the return of my wife and the definite program of my brother that I can hold a steady keel. Perhaps I am mildly depressed but that is better than being manic.

I have rambled on in a free associational way, conscious of these feelings of trust and admiration and the sense of guilt for my evidences of inexplicable hostility. I have even tried to make some elements of this conscious in the diatribe about the institution finances. Don't try to clarify it because I don't think they have much conscious justification.

Sincerely yours,

P.S. Miss Lyle says that recently I appear to be fearful of people and things that ordinarily I would not consider as serious at all. She mentions patients, finances, the future, unfriendly colleagues.

To Robert Yerkes,[1] New Haven, January 11, 1934

My dear Doctor Yerkes:

We are very much interested in this clinic in some experimental work on animals which might tend to support or contradict psychoanalytic theory and psychoanalytic observations in human subjects. We have a psychoanalytic seminar here and also a journal club, and numerous discussions have arisen concerning the subject at one of which Professor J. F. Brown[2] of the University of Kansas suggested that we write you for some suggestions, advice and references.

Theoretically we would like to see how much artifically induced trauma to an infant chimpanzee of certain specific kinds would affect his subsequent characterology and behavior. Again we should like to carry out certain experiments of the nature of continuous thwarting with particular reference to the subsequent physiological and possible anatomic alterations that might be related to it. I think this might contribute something to our as yet tenuous but persistent impressions of the psychogenic production of organic disease.

I realize that chimpanzees are very expensive and that baby chimpanzees are very difficult to obtain and Dr. Brown thought perhaps monkeys might do or even white rats. In our high degree of inexperience in this work we feel sure we should start with the rats but even with these we would like the benefit of your advice and suggestions and also such comment on our ideas as to the practicality of the work as a whole.

I am also interested in knowing more than I do about the comparative sexual behavior of animals, which I think should throw some light on some of the psychoanalytic theories of even more intensity than that offered by anthropology. . . .

I was working at [Boston] Psychopathic Hospital just about the time you

1 An American psychobiologist and early student of animal behavior, Yerkes held positions at Harvard (assistant professor of comparative psychology, 1908–17), at Boston Psychopathic Hospital (1913–17), at the University of Minnesota (professor of psychology and director of the psychological lab, 1917–19), and at Yale (professor of psychology, 1924–29, and professor of psychobiology, 1929–44). At Yale he directed the first primate laboratory. The laboratry in Orange Park, Florida, was named for him upon his retirement in 1942. He wrote *The Great Apes* (1929, with Ada Yerkes) and *Chimpanzees: A Laboratory Colony* (1943).

2 J. F. Brown, a prominent psychologist who participated in a symposium sponsored by the *Journal of Abnormal and Social Psychology* on "Psychoanalysis as Seen by Psychoanalyzed Psychologists" (1940; published by the American Psychological Association in 1953). In 1939 he was a member of the University of Kansas psychology department and was a research associate in psychology at the Menninger Clinic. In 1940 he established a private practice in clinical psychology in Los Angeles. KAM collaborated with Brown on a section of a textbook by Brown, *The Psychodynamics of Abnormal Behavior* (1940).

left but I heard so much about you that I always felt as if I knew you. Of course we have many mutual friends and I only regret that I have never had an opportunity to visit your laboratory in Yale or in Florida and see some of the actual work represented by your well-known publications.

Sincerely yours,

To WILLIAM C. MENNINGER, CHICAGO, APRIL 21, 1934

Dear Bill:

I want to congratulate you upon the fine letter you wrote for Mr. [Al] Stern. I think it is a splendid presentation of our work and our needs and I can't imagine how it could have been better written or better done. I think it is fine that you have been able to enlist Mr. Stern's good offices in getting us a hearing with the Rockefeller Board. I suppose he thinks he might as well represent two or three institutions as one and I hope he is able to put it across.

I notice one of the medical journals—I can't remember which one—had an announcement that the Salmon Memorial Foundation was parceling out a little money to people, which I think we ought to be able to get in on. I believe it was in the *Psychoanalytic Review* news notes. You might investigate this while you are at it. If you rewrite your letter I would increase the special aides from six to nine, because I think the women at the school or at least two of them ought to be counted and I would increase the accommodations from forty to sixty since we really could take that number if necessary. The special interest of Dr. Knight's is the Treatment of Paranoid Syndromes by Psychotherapy, in which he has been amazingly successful in two or three cases here lately.

Grace is home and says she had a wonderful time, thanks to you. I think it was mighty fine of you to be so good to her and I am also glad to know that you are enjoying yourself and getting around so much.

We have filed the C—— case and will look for them.[3] May I suggest that in the future when they call you up like this tell them your minimum fee for the first interview is $25. If they are worth seeing they will pay this, and if they won't pay it they usually aren't worth fooling with. I can tell you this on the basis of a lot of such experience. Incidentally, they will appreciate what you tell them more and your time is well worth it.

We are having a picnic for the clinic group to keep up the morale and good spirits out at my place, which is very pretty at present with redbud, fruit trees and hawthorn in bloom.

For the first time in several weeks I have had an opportunity to work steadily this afternoon on my self-destruction thesis. . . .

3 WCM had referred C—— to the clinic.

I am reserving a large hole in the middle of my book[4] for your diabetes paper and I hope before the book goes to press you will have been able to analyze one, although I think as it stands it is very satisfactory. I suppose you kept the carbon copy and if you want to I wish you would let me have the carbon copy and if anything happens to the original I would always have this and could pluck it out of my book if you needed it.

I think Alexander had a good time and he certainly got to see many aspects of Topeka's life. He made a very fine impression on the people who met him at the Leonardo Club[5] and elsewhere. He boosted the staff meetings and I think he got an excellent impression of the quality of our work here. He said it was better than anything he had seen in the East.

We are pretty busy here at the hospital and will be glad when Fellows gets back. We are running around thirty patients, although we have had three commitments in the last few days. John [Stone] is working very diligently. He works a good many evenings. I believe the Chicago announcements go out this week and Leo Stone's reprint is still being mailed hither and yon. A new child comes to the school today.

I leave next Wednesday night for Evansville, Indiana, and then DePauw University at Greencastle and will be in Chicago Saturday afternoon in time for the meeting and will probably leave that night on the 9:15. If you don't have other plans let us take dinner together.

Sincerely yours,

FROM LIONEL BLITZSTEN, CHICAGO, APRIL 23, 1934

Dear Karl:

I think you are under some misapprehension about my collaborating with you on the paper on skin lesions. I remember that you mentioned the possibility of this when I discussed my case material with you, but at that time we came to no definite conclusion as to collaboration: As a matter of fact, I think that I prefer to take the sole responsibility for the publication of my case reports if I eventually decide to publish them.

Anent the paper for the *International Journal* about which you requested opinion. I am willing to send it on to Jones if you wish it but I think you should consider the following facts before you take this step: first, that the case material is for the most part not your own and you are not prepared to back it up from your own observation; second, none of these cases are analyzed cases: therefore, one's viewpoint can scarcely be sufficiently objective, and offers neither you nor your readers sufficient basis for a scientifically

4 The book was never completed.
5 At Flo Menninger's suggestion, KAM organized a group of ten Topeka couples who met monthly for a dinner and a talk or presentation. WCM and his wife, Catherine, were included in the group some years later.

critical attitude. I feel that the paper might well be published in a non-analytical medical journal such as the *Journal of the AMA* or the *American Journal of Dermatology*. I hope you will take these comments in the friendly spirit in which they are offered, and if you still wish me to do so I shall send the paper to Jones immediately. Hoping to see you on Saturday, and with kindest regards to Grace and you. I am

Cordially

To Lionel Blitzsten, Chicago, April 20, 1934

Dear Lionel:

I was very comfortable when I left your home Saturday night because I thought you had been very frank and agreeable about the skin matter and also about the paper for the *International Journal.*

I still agree with you about both and I wish you would return the malingering paper and I will follow your suggestion about it and send another one to the *International Journal.*

You pride yourself on your frankness and often say that you appreciate the attitude in other people, and so I am going to tell you that I didn't like the letter that I found on my desk when I got home at all. You say I am under misapprehensions, that you "remember that you (I) mentioned the possibility of this when I discussed my case material with you." You never discussed your case material with me, and it was you, not I, who proposed that we collaborate with a dermatologist in Philadelphia; and thirdly, because I wondered when we would get together and do this and you spoke of doing so when you visited Topeka, but we were too busy with other things at that time. I don't hold it against you that you want to withdraw from this proposal. It suits me just as well either way, but since you did propose it I was afraid to go ahead with my own plans without mentioning it to you for fear you would take it as an aggression, since you had proposed it and since I had agreed to it.

This isn't very important, Lionel, but you like me to be frank and since I have said this I don't feel angry any more, but your letter is so haughty, perhaps unintentionally, in spite of the very good criticisms which I think it contains and which I appreciate.

It was very nice of you to invite me to dinner, because I really wanted to come and I hope you will do so again.

Sincerely yours,

P.S. I gave your message to Grace and she asked if I had been careful to tell you that she came away unexpectedly before she had time to carry out her intention of coming to see the baby.

From Lionel Blitzsten, Chicago, May 10, 1934

Dear Karl:

I'm sorry you found my letter haughty. It was not so intended—nor have you ever found me so previously either in our personal contacts or in our correspondence. I still pride myself on my frankness and I still appreciate that attitude in other people. Ergo your frank expression in your letter was decidedly acceptable to me. However, I see no need to argue with you whether I did or did not discuss my case material with you or whether I asked you to collaborate with me or merely discussed the possibility. You will say you remember distinctly and I shall remind you that I also have a fairly good memory, and how will it end? It's really of no great moment. I appreciate your mentioning your own plans to me—but I see no reason why I should take your going ahead without me as an aggression and to understand the motives behind either kind. I really am not going around with a chip on my shoulder. If I expect loyalty and a modicum of consideration from people who have received both from me, is that being too unreasonable?

I for one don't want anything to disturb our friendship of many years— so just forget about the haughtiness and don't ever be afraid to come to me and tell me frankly whenever I've done anything which you consider unfair or unwarranted. I've always been open and aboveboard with you even at the expense of incurring your wrath and antagonism. Am looking forward to seeing you on the 19th.

My best to Grace and you from

Dorothy and me—
Yours

Remember me to the Knights and to Jean Lyle.

To Karen Horney, Chicago, May 12, 1934

My dear Karen:

We haven't heard from you and we are wondering whether you are feeling well again. We hope you are out of the hospital and have your usual cheerfulness and freedom from pain.

Grace has asked me several times if I have heard from you and I haven't and in fact have heard from no one, except a letter about a case from Alexander and a letter from George [Wilson] with a line at the bottom which I think is your handwriting, but I am not sure. It is in Latin and I think it says "Love and kisses" or something of the kind, so if you didn't write it I am in a tough spot.

Particularly I want to remind you that we are having a party for the psychiatric social workers to whom you are going to speak in Kansas City later this month. They have chartered a train for May 24 and a hundred of them are coming down here immediately after you finish speaking to spend an afternoon and evening. We are going to have a scientific program followed by a tea and then a little automobile ride and a picnic. The picnic will be out at my country place in the woods. It will end in time to get them to a train back to Kansas City at 9:30. You, however, we hope can stay over and spend Friday the 25th with us at least, if not also Saturday and Sunday. Grace joins me in this invitation.

We are going to try to show these girls a grand time and you included. If you want to make a little talk to them formally or informally there will be time to do so and they would appreciate it but our chief aim is for you to have time to look around and enjoy yourself and get a line on us.

Sincerely yours,

To WILLIAM C. MENNINGER, CHICAGO, JUNE 8, 1934

Dear Bill:

Father and I made a sudden change in plans because we had an opportunity to go up to Lake George with Jelliffe and his younger son in their car and so we gave up the North Carolina trip and went up to Lake George and started home from Albany. We called you in Chicago, but you were on the way home from Topeka and so we missed you. We spent a forenoon in the Kohankie nursery in Ohio and then we spent Tuesday going around Shaw's Garden[6] and the more recently established experimental gardens just outside of St. Louis.

We have just come from a conference where we presented a summary of some of the papers and our visit in New York. Father contrasted it with a meeting fifteen years ago attended mostly by older men. This was attended by both young and old but mostly by younger men. He thought one of the most interesting things was the general acceptance of their interest in psychoanalysis. There were a large number of papers dealing with psychogenic factors in physical symptomatology. They were rather disappointing, however, upon close study as they all evade the real problem almost in the same way that the medical men do. Quite a number of fellows are working at Columbia and elsewhere in the medical wards but they only spend a few hours with each patient and reporting that you have cured someone of goiter by getting them to tell you about a fight with their mother-in-law does not seem to me to contribute anything to our real problem. There was a lot of that sort of slipshod work. On the whole, I came away with the impression that we are doing very much better work here than that represented by

6 Shaw's Gardens in St. Louis are now the Missouri Botanical Gardens.

the papers at the meeting. We met an awful lot of people and made a few good political moves, I think. . . .

We visited the World's Fair the evening we were in Chicago but were very much disappointed in the foreign villages and of course were also disappointed in not finding you.

I have looked over the record of I——— N——— which you left and I can well imagine your state of perplexity. I couldn't improve on your diagnosis. I have not seen the child but have heard from the parents that aside from the vomiting attack yesterday she has seemed to be much better.

Mrs. Nuzman[7] has shown me your first juvenile paresis paper and says there will be eight of them. My suggestion would be that you get these together in book form and let Williams and Wilkins publish it or else Jelliffe and White in the *Monograph* series.

I am not coming to Chicago Saturday because I am tired of traveling and think I ought to stay home and work a little, but I will be up on the 23rd. I may even be up on the 22nd because I speak in some little Iowa town on the 21st.

Father had the time of his life and it was a very fortunate and happy thing that I took him. He enjoyed the meetings and the people and the parties and the gardens that we visited. Everybody liked him very much. A few of them thought he was you. Quite a lot of people asked about you.

For reasons I told you I think Ralph Fellows will leave Sunday night to go to the Cleveland meeting. I don't know whether he plans to see you in Chicago or not. (Miss Lyle says he plans to be in Chicago Monday morning and will see you.)

It was very hot here but it was hot almost all the way home from New York and not quite so dry here as it was some other places both East and West.

Should you want to discuss D——— with Leo, his address is 887 Ocean Avenue, Flatbush, Brooklyn, care of Dr. Frederick Stone. Just at this moment he may be at Atlantic City attending the neurological association.

One thing I learned at the meeting was the desirability of more careful planning for our residents. My present idea is that we should each take them under our wing for one or two months. I mean each member of the staff so that they can go over their work with a more experienced person.

I am about to have a conference now with Tidd. All of my time in the afternoons is taken up with these conferences with various members of the staff. I'll be glad when you get back and can help with these and other things.

Sincerely,

7 A member of the Menninger secretarial staff.

To William C. Menninger, Chicago, November 2, 1934

My dear Bill:

I forgot about your going to Minneapolis and shall be awfully sorry to miss you but I will write this letter and you will get it immediately upon your return and can think it over.

I have given quite a little thought to the nurses' training school and have come to the tentative conclusion that we would be much better off without it. My reasons for thinking so are as follows:

What is happening is this. We keep training girls and no sooner get them fairly well instructed than we dismiss them and off they go to supply other institutions with our ideas and techniques. In this way we lose some fine girls—Miss Dunlope, for example. I understand that three of our girls have gone to Livermore. Well, that in itself is not so serious although I don't think it is of much value to us as advertising, but it occurs to me that the effect on our patients is very bad and in this all of the doctors agree. The patients are subjected to a constantly shifting personnel. Of course, some of the patients are shifting too, but on the other hand, the shifting of nurses goes on much more rapidly and it is very disturbing to some of the patients who no sooner get some transference to a nurse than they are obliged to give it up. I think this is very bad for Miss P——, for example. Furthermore, we are never quite certain of how much confidence we can put in our nurses. We know we can depend on our permanent staff of nurses because we have selected them carefully, and it seems to me self-evident that we would have a far better nursing corps if all of them were permanent, a carefully selected, highly trained group with whom we were very familiar and who were very familiar with what we believe and want.

Moreover, the kind of teaching we are giving the nurses seems to all of us here dubious. We are teaching them psychiatry and psychoanalysis instead of psychiatric nursing. I think we are overdoing the intellectual side and underdoing the practical side. Instead of trying to go over and over with these new classes of nurses the elementary principles of psychiatry, etc., it seems to all of us that it would be better to have less intensive but more persistent training of small groups—lecture courses, special speakers, etc., planned in conjunction with the training of fellows rather than the training of green nurses. Such lectures and courses would be attended by all of our regular staff of nurses, or at least all who could get off duty to attend.

Furthermore, the whole business of training nurses is being taken away from doctors and being put more and more into the hands of nurses, and I think we ought to let the nurses handle their own psychiatric education.

We have some excellent nurses now who could be retained for permanent duty and some of those whom we have had could probably be employed.

There are additional difficulties which you know about—the uncertainty about getting candidates, the difficulties with the administrative head, the antagonism from other hospitals.

For all these reasons, as I say, it seems to me foolish to continue the training school, ideal and progressive as the plan is. In this everyone here is now in agreement except Miss Erickson,[8] whose real objections we have not yet learned. The only two objections to it are these:

1. it may cost a little bit more (Latest figures show us to save about $2200 a year by having it!) to hire a sufficient number of permanent nurses to be ready for all emergencies and special duty requirements, etc. Mr. Stone and Mr. Hoover[9] are endeavoring to determine this exactly.
2. There is a prevailing feeling that this graduate school is very dear to your heart and that you are going to feel badly about it.

I don't know how much the latter is true, because it was dear to my heart also until I began to realize that our best girls keep leaving us and the patients are subjected to this shifting personnel. Furthermore, I thought it was too expensive to do anything else.

But I am perhaps overlooking some other reasons why it would be a bad idea to make such a change aside from our sentimental satisfaction in it. Naturally our greatest satisfaction is going to be in getting the best work and most dependable and satisfactory machine. It might even be possible to combine the two systems and take two or three girls here for a year's training or something of that kind. . . .

Think this over and write us in detail about it as you see it. Perhaps you will agree with us and perhaps you will be able to change our minds completely. Furthermore, Mr. Stone may find it too expensive to do anything else but he will know about this in a few days.

I am going to see George Hall[10] in Chicago [on] Sunday about bringing the C.N.P.A. here next fall. We do not think the dining room is going to be a large enough or suitable place for the meetings. I think we have nothing to be ashamed of in the interior of the gym for the meeting. The exterior, however, seems to me to be bad. I am dropping a note to Ross[11] to tell him to have some practical suggestions to give us about changing this when we meet with him in the middle of the month. If you have any special ideas you can write him. . . .

8 Head nurse at the Menninger Sanitarium.

9 Merle Hoover, the chief bookkeeper.

10 G. Stanley Hall, a New England psychologist, philosopher, and educator, who helped introduce psychoanalysis into psychology. He published a classic work on *Adolescence* (1904). As president of Clark University, in 1909 Hall invited Freud and Jung to present five lectures on psychoanalysis. Hall wrote an introduction to the American edition of Freud's *Introductory Lectures* (1920).

11 Ross von Metzke, an architect and landscape designer, designed several of the early buildings on the Menninger campus as well as KAM's home at Karlyle Woods.

We are making some important changes about the laboratory which consist in turning over a large amount of it to Waraich[12] so as to permit us to do more laboratory work without increasing the overhead. I'll give you the details about this when I see you. Too rushed at present. . . .

Sincerely,

To Leo Bartemeier, Detroit, November 10, 1934

Dear Bartie:

I am going to ask your advice about something concerning which I have asked no one else's advice and concerning which I wish you would please tell no one else for the present. I am sure you will do this if I ask you.

Recently Zilboorg asked me to take Frankwood Williams' place on the editorial board of the *Quarterly*. The editors own the *Quarterly* and it costs them about $500 apiece each year to have the honor and prestige of being editors. That is what it would cost me. It would give me a rather powerful political position which I think it is desirable for one of us Westerners to have so that we can keep things somewhat evenly balanced and prevent unnecessary jealousy and friction. I don't particularly care for the work it involves, and God knows I could spend $500 in other ways, but possibly it is something I ought to do, not only for the sake of the cause but for the sake of my own reputation here and abroad. I think you can advise me about these things from your position of calm detachment. At least you can give me some free associations which will undoubtedly be helpful.

I have been rather eagerly looking for some word from you all week about our friend Ophuijsen.[13] I am sorry for that poor devil. He certainly stepped into trouble.

I shall not be in Chicago this weekend, as you know, because I leave for San Antonio Tuesday morning.

Sincerely yours,

From Leo Bartemeier, Detroit, November 13, 1934

My dear Karl:

Since receiving your letter yesterday morning, I have been doing a great

12 Gurbrux S. Waraich, a laboratory physician who later went to Rochester Medical School in New York.

13 J. H. W. Van Ophuijsen was an analyst who came to Detroit from Holland in 1934 to escape Nazi persecution. He irritated the Detroit psychoanalytic community by inviting other European analysts to emigrate without clearing the invitations with the local analytic community.

deal of thinking about the question you asked me, and the following are my free associations.

My Hebraic tendencies immediately lead me to ask myself, why is Frankwood Williams resigning his position? You and I are alike in that we are always flattered by offers of this sort. We are inclined to spend the money and do any amount of work for the sake of a bit of vainglory. Were you to accept Zilboorg's offer, you would be the only editor on this board outside of New York. The vote would be three to one. I have no evidence, and wonder whether you have, for believing that such a post would give you any political position of any strength.

Five hundred dollars is a great deal of money, and you are not in any position to keep on spending and spending. Your reputation in this country is well established. While I am not in possession of the facts, I doubt that you have any particular reputation abroad. It does not seem to me that you are doing anything for the cause by becoming a member of this board. My advice is to reject the offer.

Dr. Van Ophuijsen called upon me, and we had a very pleasant visit together. We talked about the International Association, his membership in the Central Committee, his interest in the discussion of the difficulties of the American Psychoanalytic Society, the activities of the Dutch analysts, the question of lay analysts, the nature of my practice, the Chicago Psychoanalytic Society, his statement that he had met you this past summer in Europe, my invitation to him in the name of the Society to attend our meetings and to address our Society, and everything else in the wide world except Van Ophuijsen's plans for the future. I did ask him if he intended to do private practice here, to which he replied not exactly yet. He would have to first get a license and become familiar with the local situation. A few days later, I invited him and his wife to a dinner party at my home and a musical concert afterwards, but he had to decline because of his wife's illness.

I like him very much, and I have the intuition that he intends to deal with me as he finds me, and not in the manner in which I have been described to him by others. I stand by to watch the unfolding of the various acts in this psychoanalytic tragedy. I quite agree with Alex, that he is the unwitting pawn of another man, who is the unsuspecting tool of an outraged woman, and I do think that the less anyone says to Van Ophuijsen the better.[14] It

14 During this time, Harry August, a psychoanalytic candidate, had analysis with Van Ophuijsen five times a week. On the fifteenth day Van Ophuijsen announced to his analysand that he had to leave the city. He gave no specific reason, but, according to August, the speculation was that a rival psychoanalyst, later determined to be psychotic, had become delusional and reported Van Ophuijsen to the FBI. Allegedly, Van Ophuijsen panicked and fled to New York, where he practiced for a number of years. August knows nothing of the rumors hinted at in this letter (Personal communication with the editors).

would strengthen my own position if he were to come to his own conclusions, without advice or suggestions from yourself and Alex and others about my integrity, or any remarks pertaining to treachery on the part of anyone else.

Sincerely,

P.S.: Dear old Pal—Let us always keep all these things we write to each other just to ourselves so that we may always be of real help to one another—

As ever—

To FRANZ ALEXANDER, CHICAGO, DECEMBER 5, 1934

Dear Alex:

There are three matters which I wish to mention to you. The first is the request that you tell Miss Moore to remind Doctors Finlayson and Harrington [15] that they are on the program at the Literary Seminar this coming Saturday. She should do this immediately so they will get word in time.

The second one is that Doctor Bierring [16] of Des Moines, Iowa was here Monday and attended one of our staff conferences which impressed him very much. It was a case of convulsions in which a psychogenic origin was suggested. This led him to describe a patient of his at some length who . . . turned out to be John B——. He was telling us that an exploratory operation had been deferred until the patient elected it, but stated that the patient had now come around to the point of requesting it and that he, Doctor Bierring, was to make an appointment with Doctor Penfield, the brain surgeon, next week. Doctor Knight and I told him we were well acquainted with the case and Doctor Bierring earnestly requested our advice and recommendations. We told him that it was our impression and conviction that the boy had been doing very well under psychoanalytic treatment and was probably considering surgery only as a kind of resistance and that we would strongly advise him not to allow the boy to use him (Doctor B[ierring].) as a means for escaping his analysis. We told him that several years of analysis would not be a surprising necessity for such a difficult case and that in view of the futility of other methods of treatment and the amount of money they had already put into this it was strongly advisable, even if viewed in the light of a scientific trial, to make no change in the type of therapy for a year or two. Doctor Bierring expressed himself as highly gratified to receive this information and indicated his intention to act on that basis. In other words, Doctor Knight and I think we saved your patient for you and want you to be duly grateful. . . .

15 Possibly G. Leonard Harrington, a Kansas City psychoanalyst.
16 Walter L. Bierring specialized in internal medicine in Des Moines. He was president of the AMA from 1934 to 1935.

The third point was a strictly scientific one. I have just had some confirmatory analytic material in regard to psychogenic factors in convulsions in a man who has had them only about once every ten years. That is not quite accurate; he had them about once a year for three years and then no more for ten years. This began before he was twenty and he is now forty-one. He had an attack here the other day and I was able to get very convincing evidence that the attack was in the nature of an unconscious suicidal equivalent related to conflicting feelings of hopeless inferiority and boundless ambition. As a matter of fact, he had mentioned the possibility of unconscious suicidal motives the day before his convulsion which was in the evening and the following day brought me the details so far as he could recall them of the earlier attacks. In the first one of all he was swimming in a race with his best friend and greatest adolescent rival. A few yards form the shore he realized he was beaten in spite of prodigious effort and straightway lost consciousness and would have drowned had he not been rescued by the friend with whom he was contending. This circumstance in itself seems to me to be eloquent. If you are interested I should be glad to make a brief report of the matter some day, in connection with your case seminar.

I should be glad to learn what results you had from the tea party and such other news as you can tell me about the Institute affairs. I shall be on hand at 10 o'clock on Saturday but unfortunately am obliged to leave at 8 o'clock the same evening. My former publisher, Mr. Knopf, has come West and insists upon having a conference with me in Kansas City.[17] If you have any very positive notions about publishers I should be glad to hear them. Mine are mostly negative.

Sincerely yours,

FROM IVES HENDRICK, BOSTON, JANUARY 11, 1935

Dear Karl,

. . . I remark . . . your interest in "how thing are really going in Boston." I should have been glad to have given more frank expression to it if I had realized your interest. In brief, the analytic group is maturing and is developing some competent analysts and teaching. I am participating in the scientific and pedagogic functions of the society, but have withdrawn from all committee and organization work because of my resentment at the other older men who left it to me to assume the leadership and bring about a progressive solution whenever facing an issue was involved and then exploited the resulting ambivalence toward me for their own political ends, at

17 KAM had quarreled with Knopf after KAM had privately discussed a Literary Guild edition of *The Human Mind* with Carl Van Doren without first conferring with Knopf. Knopf did not publish any of Menninger's subsequent works. (See the letter of August 24, 1936 for KAM's opinion of Knopf).

times without either integrity or ordinary courtesy. In spite of my friends' supplementing the wishes of my enemies, I have maintained a fairly decent practice, though without complete security for the future, and a reputable position in the professional community. Nevertheless, in both respects I recognize that I have not nearly the success which was assured if I had attended to my own interests and not that of the psychoanalytic movement in years gone by. I have learned a lesson but I can't go back. There is no desire to disclaim that my strong anti-Semitic and anti-Viennese tendencies, and an inclination to promote the notion that Americans who carry a philosophy of democratic liberalism too far are not infrequently going to get bitched by those they help, are entirely the product of subjective experience. I do, however, deny that they are entirely the product of envy and jealousy of more successful rivals. Sachs' escape from German anti-Semitism and assurance of American prosperity and prestige are the result of my work in creating a need for a teacher in analysis here and my cooperation in inviting him here. In a general way he has shown himself to those who really know the situation to be entirely unworthy of these privileges. In a personal way, he has very cunningly contrived to imperil my success in every way he was able. Kaufmann,[1] in days when he was more obviously a Ghetto product than today, I made a friend of. I asked him to dinners when told I should be damaged in Boston by intimacy with that kind. I set the wheels in motion for his appointment at McLean when the immigration authorities were after him; I put him across with the superintendent, who offered the objection that the trustees had never thought Jews were acceptable to their clientele. In 1931, when my opponents (Putnam,[2] particularly) wanted to straighten things out by putting me in charge of things, Educational Committee Chairman, etc., I would not accept what was otherwise agreeable on the ground that Kaufmann's ability made it unfair to leave him out, and they would not accept that. When he was fired from McLean I helped him emotionally and helped him get started again. In 1932, he tripped me up, accepting the seductions of Sachs to advance himself and leave me cold. The hypocrisy became more clear to me in a number of acts—why go on? I am anti-Semitic because Sachs and Kaufmann and others who have touched my professional life less definitely do not know the American meaning of play-fair— loyalty is considered a neurosis if one's own advantage, and particularly

1 M. Ralph Kaufman, Boston psychoanalyst and president of the Boston Psychoanalytic Society (1937–39). When WCM was chief of psychiatry for the Surgeon General's office, Kaufman was a psychiatrist for the U.S. Army. He was later known for his psychosomatic research at Mt. Sinai Hospital in New York City.

2 Tracy Putnam was a Boston neurologist and professor of neurology at Harvard University Medical School (1934–39) and later at Columbia University. His wife, Irmarita, was an analysand of Freud and was influential in bringing Hanns Sachs to Boston.

getting ahead of a Gentile, is sacrificed. My Id's probably as aggrandizing and envious as theirs, but I have a different ego-ideal.

The only reason all this bothers me is that it has left me with a certain bitterness and hostility which at times affect my enthusiasm for my work. It produces an obsessional-depressive tendency to hate analysis, doing analysis, and thinking analysis, and to phantasy that I should be happier if I threw it up; fortunately, thanks in large part to Marie, the twins, and earning my living, this neurosis is only intermittent and mild. But it's enough to spoil a lot of fun and the vitality of my work after hours.

I allow myself this indulgence only with the confidence of an intimate friend. I do not think it is good stuff to quote me about, because I can expect others to see it largely in the light of my neurotic tendencies and the present situation, and can expect it to be interpreted to my advantage by those who do not know the whole history well.

I agree that this was one of the best scientific sessions. Your paper was an important part of it. I look forward to reading it.[3] I do not know whether the essence of what I was driving at was clear in public discussion, but it was the fact that to me your work on psycho-physiologic relationships avoids the pitfalls of most similar work, of identifying somatic symptoms and sexual symbols. The relationships are much deeper, and I do not think it is generally much more than metaphorical to analyze physiologically expressed complexes in terms of the mechanisms of transference neurosis and transference dreams. . . .

Marie and I are sorry your trip was so busy and filled with professional activities. A dinner and talking around the fireside without the hurly-burly would have been so much more to our liking, and we wish you could find the occasion for a personal visit.

Very sincerely,

To Dwight Macdonald, New York, February 22, 1935

My dear Mr. Macdonald:

I think your article[4] is one of the most intelligent and comprehensive dis-

---

3 "Psychogenic Factors in Urological Disorders," which KAM had just given at the American Psychoanalytic Association midwinter meeting held in late December in Chicago.

4 Writer, critic, and editor. He wrote an article, "The Nervous Breakdown," for *Fortune* (April 1935) after an investigation of sanitariums for mental disease. He described the Menninger Sanitarium as the outstanding mental hospital west of the Alleghenies and as one of the five best in the country. His most important book was *Against the American Grain* (1962).

cussions of the subject I have ever read. I have made numerous corrections and comments interlinearly where there is actual misstatement of fact. I have not appended any footnotes because I do not differ essentially by way of opinion from those expressed.

The one exception might be with regard to the threadbare misstatement about transference which says that the patient "falls in love" with the analyst. If this occurs the psychoanalysis is already mishandled and blown up. A patient may think for a short time that he is in love with his analyst, but he soon sees that he is only using the analyst as a convenient symbol or representative of someone for whom he had an earlier attachment. Moreover, it would be more accurate to say instead of falling in love with his analyst that he uses his analyst as an object upon which he may vent his hates and other emotions arising in early childhood and up until this point indiscriminately expressed toward innocent victims in the outside world. An analyst can stand it (for one hour a day) whereas a wife, a child, a business colleague, or customer cannot or will not stand it. The patient either explodes at these individuals unreasonably or he restrains an impulse to do so with great mental strain, and both of these are expensive. When this happens with respect to the analyst, however, it is possible to trace them back to their earliest origins so that the neurotic, suffering as he does from an inability to separate himself from a pattern of emotional reactions determined in childhood by overindulgence or overthwarting, is enabled to free himself from this pattern and grow up emotionally.

I think you give a little too much credit to Adolf Meyer; Ernest Southard of Harvard inspired a great many more people in this work and is equally responsible for the increasing popularity of psychiatry. You can get firsthand information about him from Dr. Frederick F. Gay of Columbia University there in New York.

I wasn't quite able to see the connection of this article with sanitariums. Most sanitariums do not use psychoanalysis. We have three psychoanalysts at present, including my brother, Dr. William C. Menninger, who is doing some special research work in Chicago just at present but who will return to Topeka in a month or two. We also have a child analyst who does a modified psychoanalytic technique with some of the children in our school (the Southard School). We are interested not only in the treatment of the neurosis by psychoanalysis but in the treatment of the mild forms of more serious mental disease and in the psychoanalytic treatment of some medical conditions formerly treated only by drugs and surgery.

I must say that on the whole your discussion of psychoanalysis is unusually fair. I assume that you have read Zweig's description of Freud in his book, *Mental Healers*. You might find very helpful Freud's own autobiography and discussion of psychoanalysis in a rarely mentioned book, now out of print but undoubtedly available to you, called *The Problem of Lay Analysis*.

Don't be deterred by the title. I might add that Jung has practically no standing in this country in spite of his considerable clinical skill and his followers are a lonely handful. I suspect you have fallen under the pleasant influences of Beatrice Hinkle[5] but I must warn you that, outside of New York and a few friends of Mrs. McCormick's[6] in Chicago and academic psychologists, Jung is almost unknown. Alfred Adler[7] made his appeal through a series of dull and repetitious books addressed to schoolteachers, but he has absolutely no clinical adherents in this country to my knowledge. The Freudians correctly maintain that there is only one form of psychoanalysis, namely Freudian analysis. In this they are concurred with by all the other so-called schools of psychological analysis. Jung, for example, is interested in "individual psychology"; Rank now speaks of his work by some new phrase which I have forgotten, etc.[8]

You have gone so far with this discussion of psychoanalysis that I would suggest that you have a talk with one of our New York members or with Dr. Brill himself, who will give you a list of the constituent societies and tell you a little about their work. Dr. A. A. Brill would undoubtedly be the one to talk to and you will find him very cordial and direct. . . .

In looking over the paper I hope you will not take offense at my somewhat sharp-sounding corrections of technical and definitive errors in the first few pages.

I see on page 11 that I promised a footnote. Freud does not believe what you say about anxiety states. Thirty-five years ago was his first impression but later he came to feel that anxiety was a psychological means of defense against the conscious acceptance of something considered dangerous by the ego. This dangerous thing may be a sexual temptation but it is very frequently something nonsexual—for example, the wish to hurt a loved one. Even such a *wish* is a terrible and disturbing thing, but it is sometimes stimulated by certain experiences and comes near to entering into consciousness. This causes anxiety somewhat similar to the way in which a sharp instrument pressed against one's flesh causes pain in proportion to the pressure. This leads me to add that the past ten to fifteen years of Freud's researches have developed the importance of the aggressive or destructive

5 An American psychiatrist and follower of Jung. She established a psychotherapeutic clinic at Cornell University Medical College (New York City) in 1908.

6 Ada McCormick was a wealthy Chicagoan who championed Jung's cause; she later moved to Tucson, Arizona, and edited the journal *Letters*.

7 One of Freud's early associates, Adler resigned from the Vienna Psychoanalytic Society in 1911 to establish his own school, which he called Individual Psychology. Whereas Freud, in his libido theory, emphasized biological determinism as well as the predominance of the sexual factor in psychological development, Adler stressed the influence of the social environment on the individual. Adler coined the terms *inferiority complex* and *superiority complex*.

8 Rank used the term *dynamic relationship psychology* to characterize his theories.

tendencies within the individual as being of equal significance in the production of neuroses as the sexual or erotic impulses. I think this point might be enlarged upon in your article. It is probable that no one is made seriously sick by his sexual impulses, no matter how forbidden they are or how deep or how close to consciousness. That which makes him ill either in the form of anxiety or in the form of guilt feelings, depression, etc., is the unconscious wish to hurt someone, a wish which is sometimes turned upon the individual's own self. My own particular research has been along the line of exploring the ways in which this destructive impulse, which Freud thinks is related in its deepest origins to what he calls the "death instinct," is turned into forms of modified—sometimes complete—self-destruction.

I think you have made an extraordinarily thorough and competent study of your subject and I am looking forward to reading what you have to say about sanitariums. So far as I am concerned you are at liberty to use any of the case material in my book, *The Human Mind,* and in my brother's article, if you wish.[9]

Sincerely yours,

P.S. In connection with what you have said about Russia, may I refer you to p. 91 of Freud's *Civilization and Its Discontents,* where he expresses the conviction that cohesion among the members of a group is made easier by allowing the aggressive instinct to find outlet against a common enemy outside the group. He thinks the communistic type of culture in Russia has found this psychological support in the persecution of the bourgeois and wonders, with some concern, how the "Soviets will manage when they have exterminated their bourgeois entirely." He says, "It is always possible to unite considerable numbers of men in love toward one another, so long as there are still some remaining as objects for aggressive manifestations." I cite this to show that Freud was not wholly optimistic about the future of Russia, at least not at the time he wrote this.

To Dwight Macdonald, New York, February 25, 1935

Dear Mr. Macdonald:

The paper on our sanitarium has just arrived and we are hastening to return it to you. We have had some minor corrections, as you will note. We think you have been most kind to us and that, to quote your own words, you have "made an exceptionally serious and intelligent effort" to present our ideas and aims.

At the risk of seeming inconsistent, I should like to ask you to omit the

9 Although it might sound as if KAM was usurping a prerogative of his brother's, since the article was about the sanitarium, in which KAM and WCM had mutual interest, KAM felt free to give permission for both of them.

reference to state hospitals in the first paragraph of the story, at least in connection with our sanitarium. I believe this states the case too strongly to be quite fair. Such a statement in connection with a description of our institution would undoubtedly stir up a great deal of hard feeling among our medical friends in state institutions and among Westerners in general. The committee to which you allude is not organized to fight state institutions but to study conditions and to make suggestions to medical men. We have many staunch friends among state hospital men and often find them quite cooperative. The system is one which arose because psychiatry has advanced slowly in the West as compared to the eastern United States. It is a matter for tactful public education rather than open attack. I appreciate your espousing our cause so warmheartedly; but you will realize, I am sure, how such a broadside on state hospitals in connection with our sanitarium would greatly embarrass us.

You might like to follow your very nice opening sentence with something we think is distinctive about our sanitarium and clinic, namely that, although situated in a part of the country distant from the great centers of population, we draw patients from an unusually wide geographical range—from Maine to California and from Canada to Mexico, as well as from Europe. I believe we have a wider range in this respect than any other psychiatric institution in this country with the possible exception of Phipps Clinic at Johns Hopkins. . . .

On page two you speak of seven doctors, which is according to the information we furnished you. Actually we have eight full-time physicians, one of whom is a resident fellow in psychiatry. In addition we have a dentist and a consulting staff of physicians in Topeka. We purposely omitted mentioning these in order to avoid ostentatiousness. If there is any reason for more exactitude, however, you are welcome to this information.

The last paragraph, of course, pleases me very much. I have always liked the idea of modern psychiatry that I set forth in the last two paragraphs of *The Human Mind*—the idea that mental sickness is not hopeless, that most of its victims recover. Whether it has any application in this section or not, I do not know.

Sincerely yours,

To Leo Bartemeier, Detroit, May 28, 1935

Dear Barte:

. . . I haven't heard from you or written you for quite a long time and I'm going to give you a little account of myself. I want to tell you a few things that are on my mind first tho. One of them is that I wish you would put down on the tentative program possibilities for the Chicago Psychoanalytic Society for next year the following: Dr. Leo Stone—Contributions to the

Relations Between Psychoanalysis and the Organic Structure of the Nervous System; and second, Miss Leona Chidester [10]—a report of some psychoanalytic work with retarded children. I know the content of both of these presentations and they are extraordinarily good and will refresh, stimulate, and inform the members of our Society in a way which will be mutually satisfactory I am sure to the chairman of the Program Committee and the present.

I have just written Alexander a letter to which I shall eagerly await his reply in which I have suggested that we ought to consider a new plan about our meetings. I can't afford to go up to Chicago every two weeks, and in addition to myself there is my brother and Doctor Knight. I can assure you it is rather expensive for three of us to make a jaunt up to Chicago every two weeks, as you can recall; imagine, if you recall, that it is over twice as far as from Detroit to Chicago. Furthermore, it seems to me a little absurd that all of us take the same seminars every time. I have a notion that the Institute ought to arrange a course of seminars and other programs desirable for the more elementary students, and then again seminars or sessions of some other sort for the more advanced students. These might come on alternate fortnights, or again we might arrange to have meetings every three weeks. What I am getting at is this: that I think our society should possibly meet about once a month and meet for a much longer period than our present 4:30 to 5:30 sessions, which I think are too short to get anything done. I know this won't strike you favorably at first but I am very dissatisfied with the casual way in which our meetings go on at present. We attend these meetings all day until we are pretty tired, then we play ping-pong or whatnot and then sit down at 4:30 and hear a paper and have a brief discussion and then jump up and run home. That isn't my idea of the way our Society ought to meet at all. I don't think it is dignified enough, or that it lasts long enough, or that it contains enough meat. It costs me a good deal of money as I have already said to go dashing up to Chicago, and much as I appreciate the honor of being president, and the responsibilities thereof, I can scarcely afford the time and money to do this unless I get a greater scientific return.

What I have in mind is that our meetings should last three hours at least, if not four, and should contain several papers. I think there should be a thorough discussion of the matter and that the Society rather than the Institute should be the chief forum. In other words, instead of attending a Society meeting for an hour or two after the day of seminar meetings is over I think the main thing ought to be the Society meeting with the seminars on the side if we can work them in. I have in mind that it might be better, for example, to have a meeting once a month and have a two-day session at

10 The first clinical psychologist at the Menninger Clinic.

that time, so that we come Friday morning, let us say, and have our meeting all Friday afternoon, and then have a social affair Friday evening which now most of us can't have because we have to take the train back right away, then spend Saturday with some additional seminars and some control work if anybody wants to do this. I don't think this control work will interest you because you and I are through taking controls, but some of the younger men will be doing this and you and I may have some other matters we want to take up in a conference, say, with one another or with someone else.

I wish you would give me your reaction to this. I know Blitzsten is going to be opposed to it because he likes short and snappy meetings of an hour or so, and without meaning it in any derogatory sense he doesn't take much satisfaction in group meetings unless he is presiding over them. His own seminars which he used to conduct some years ago in his home, and I guess still does, lasted well into the night, and I don't see why we should have Society meetings with any less dignity, formality, intensity, or content. . . .

Now a word or two about our trip: Father and I went together and went to Washington as arranged. Most of the rest of the [Chicago Psychoanalytic] Society were there [at the American Psychiatric Association meeting] except you and Blitzsten. We had a small representation on the program, however, which some ascribed to a certain prejudice against us in the East, but my impression is that they are so concerned with their own quarrels and fights that they are not very much interested in us. There is a terrible fight in New York which is of so complicated a nature I can scarcely tell you about it without filling pages and pages. The upshot of it is that there are at least three factions in the New York [Society] and Doctor Brill is so discouraged with the fighting, etc., that he resigned, but we talked to him and got him to realize that resigning wasn't going to help any and he is back in the fight. He is really a grand old man and must stay in that position and keep things level. I do think it might be better if somebody else were president of the New York Society and let Brill continue as International president, but he mustn't resign until they get thru with their present fight.

The American Psychiatric Association itself was well attended and I saw many of our old friends and made some new contacts. I also got a few new ideas, which is supposedly one of the purposes of these conventions. The program on the whole was rather poor, however, and most of my ideas I got in the bar or over the breakfast table. I wish you could have been there because I believe it would have been helpful to you and to the cause of psychoanalysis, and it would have been exceedingly pleasant for me, which is my chief motive in mentioning it. . . .

School is over but Grace and I have not yet moved our family out to Indian Hill because the children want to play around the neighborhood a little while before we go. Then Julia is going to a camp in Colorado, Robert is going to stay with me, Martha is going to Girl Scout camp and probably Grace is going down to Florida to get her mother. I am going to work without interruption all summer as far as I know. . . .

Sincerely,

FROM BELINDA JELLIFFE, NEW YORK, JUNE 10, 1935

Dear Dr. Menninger:

I regret that while you were in the East, you hadn't the time to come up and see me . . . I have many things to discuss with you; however, you are merely running true to the form of all the psychiatrists I have known; do exactly what you want, and to hell with anyone else . . . however, it doesn't really matter.

I don't know what Dr. J[elliffe] wrote you concerning the library, but I do know that I am worried about his finances. He says nothing to me, but I cannot help but realize that he is in pretty bad shape economically. I said to him one day, "Why don't you try to do some stuff for some of the magazines?" He seemed very angry and said, You know I can't write popular stuff. I said there are plenty of writers starving who for fifteen dollars a week could write whatever you tell them; all they need is the facts. But it only caused hard feelings, so why should I bother? He has only thought of his darling family, so why should I worry about him? Only when I see how other drs. make money—criminals, many of them, as you know as well as I—and then to see a man of his calibre worried, hard up financially, I can't quite stomach it. . . . You lovely scientific men sit back on your asses and let the rotters put it all over you. I said to him one day, "When the psychiatrists come out with some stand concerning the reason for the enormous increase in mental diseases . . . then I'll begin to have some respect for both medicine and psychiatry. The way drs. go pegging along, scratching for their daily bread, working on each little patient (who are of no importance even if they are put back into circulation) and lose sight of the enormous job that is theirs, I for one pathetic ignorant human being have lost respect for them. Why can't they have the guts to come out and say that . . . the great increase in mental ills is due to the system under which we live; to the rotten exploitation of the poor, and the rich also become ill, because they know that they are doing it, and cannot quite face it out . . . oh, it's all simple, but the drs. are owned also, and can't take an intelligent, humane stand. . . . However, I don't know particularly why I am vituperating on you like this . . . , I think it's because you were so goddamned rotten mean as to come on to a stupid vile old medical meeting where you didn't hear ONE new idea or learn anything you didn't know, but you couldn't take the time or spend the money to come back by here. . . . Well, anyway, I don't really care. I only know that I am worried because I know that Dr. J. worries about finances. However, I don't know what to do about it, so as the psychiatrists do, I will do . . . , not bother. . . .

With these few nasty remarks, and love to you and Grace, I am as usual.

To Smith Ely Jelliffe, New York, June 14, 1935

My dear Doctor Jelliffe:

We have thought very earnestly about the possibility that you and I discussed when we were in Washington, relative to the purchase of *The Journal of Nervous and Mental Disease*. I am a little confused as to what the final word was about it, but my impression was that you felt that something like $20,000 would be a fair price for the return in pay.

I wonder if you could discuss this a little more fully so I could put this before our Business Department. In case we were able to manage it, how fast would it have to be paid and how would you suggest that the transfer in editorship be managed? Would you like to go on helping us or would you prefer to make a sudden shift? . . .

It was nice to see you in Washington. I hope you found things all right when you got home. I have had a little letter from Mrs. Jelliffe in which she seems to be a little hurt that I didn't come to New York, but I am going to write and tell her where we went.

Sincerely yours,

To Thomas French, Chicago, July 5, 1935

Dear Tom:

Alexander was here yesterday and we had some rather serious words together, no quarrel to be sure, but Alexander feels that my interest in the Institute has not been as warm as he would like. I had to call to his attention rather sharply the fact that I am in no way apprised at any time by any member of the Institute of what goes on officially. He was surprised to know, for example, that I did not know the name of a single candidate who had come before our Training Committee for training in the Institute.

Upon reflection both of us felt that this was part my fault in that I had not asked you to make me a report. I have to say frankly, however, Tom, that you have not even apprised me of the fact that your Educational Committee was meeting or that you were about to consider certain applicants. I should appreciate it very much if you would let me know hereafter when you expect to have any meetings of this committee, of which I believe I am an ex-officio member. Not only that, but I should like to have a written report of those meetings which I am unable to attend and I should like to know at the present time just what candidates have been approved by the Educational Committee for training in the Institute. . . .

Please do not interpret anything in this letter to be written in a spirit of criticism or reproach. As a matter of fact, it is rather the other way; I feel after what Alexander said that perhaps a part of my ignorance of what goes on in the Institute is my own fault and I am blaming myself rather than you, although I do think you should let me know about these meetings.

Sincerely yours,

To Helen McLean, Chicago, July 15, 1935

Dear Helen:

. . . I agree with you utterly in your interpretation of the matter I wrote Tom [French] [11] about; he wrote me very promptly and with mild irritation, but I think it was partly justified because Alexander gave me the impression of a lot of candidates having been accepted which evidently have not been at all. I am sure, however, that that is just Alexander's general optimism. I do feel, as you say, that there should be a more businesslike spirit at the Institute but I don't think we can expect Alexander to put that into effect, and just at I told Alexander, while I am spiritually and intellectually interested in the Institute, I am practically and financially interested in my own clinic, and while I am willing to help the Institute I cannot take as active a role as he would like . . . inasmuch as I am not directly dependent upon it or it dependent upon me. After all I am in a different part of the country, paddling my own canoe, and have to keep it going too.

I would really like to see some kind of tie-up between our institution and the Institute, but frankly Alexander has always had a tendency to be a little patronizing and depreciatory toward American psychiatry in general, and I think that's a mistake. I think very strongly that a lot could be done with a psychiatrist in Chicago and vicinity, but while he says he thinks this too, he doesn't take any steps in that direction and regards such an audience as being rather inconsequential. I don't deny that many of them are stupid fellows but I do deny that they all are. I'm still not saying exactly what I think, which is that Alexander has always, with no intended unkindness I am sure, treated me as a friendly colleague who could be mutually cooperative with him and so forth but not as one who had any particular knowledge, as you put it so nicely in your letter, of the American field. I think this

[11] The letter to Thomas French has not been preserved, and the precise matter under discussion remains obscure.

hurts my narcissism and makes me a little annoyed when I shouldn't be. After all, he is running the Institute and is going to run it in his own way, which may be more successful than our more efficient American methods after all, and there can never be any doubt in the world about his essential friendliness, kindness, and bigheartedness. I shall always be loyal to him and I know that you are, and I think the great future of psychoanalysis is probably going to be in the Midwest, where we have started out with less of the hostilities and envies that exist in the more crowded [illegible] on the Atlantic.

I am so glad that you and your husband and son can be in beautiful New England this summer, and I wish that I were going to be with you. As a matter of fact, we have had a rather pleasant spring and it has been quite cool except for the last few days. Today it is cool again and we hope for the best. I may take my family through Yellowstone Park for a week or two, but in the meantime I am having a grand time, very busy, doing a little bit of work, trying to finish up my book, and the clinic is booming with a lot of interesting patients, nice doctors, and I wish you could be here.

My love to Frank.

Sincerely yours,

To Julia Menninger, Colorado, July 31, 1935

My dear daughter Julia:

I have seldom had anything which gave me greater pleasure than the sweet little telegram which came on my birthday from you. I had already written you a letter that day before I got your telegram which came rather late in the evening which was the nicest surprise I got.

We had a wonderful letter from you yesterday describing the various hikes you have been on and some of the difficulties you had had in getting adjusted to the regulations and plans of the counselors, but I am sure that you will enjoy and profit from these various experiences. In one way that is what happens all one's life; one keeps making new adjustments and getting new points of view and getting the attitude of different people, etc., and trying to adjust oneself to all of it. In addition, one has one's own internal wishes, thoughts and impulses to adjust oneself to and the kernel of all personality which has the job of adjusting all of these internal and external things is kept pretty busy but you have a good one and I know you are going to grow up a whole lot out there at that camp. . . . I love you very dearly.

Goodbye—

To Anna Freud, Vienna, August 3, 1935

My dear Fräulein Freud:

I am taking cognizance of your letter of July 18 which just arrived and have informed some of our members about the matter, including the chairman of the Educational Committee, although unfortunately none of them plan to be in Europe this summer anyway. It seems to me this postponement has the added advantage, however, of making us all feel the more responsible for coming to the Congress next year if it is at all possible. I for one shall try to do so and hope to see you again.

Your friendly personal note at the bottom of the letter encourages me to say that I very much hope to become better acquainted with the European analysts at the next Congress than I did at the Lucerne Congress. I look back upon last summer with considerable disappointment as I feel that I knew the European analysts better before the Congress than I did afterwards. I feel sure that very likely this is due in part to our extreme differences in social technique and in part to my own lack of familiarity with the European methods. Our own congresses are, as you probably know, conducted very differently.

Personally, I feel that the movement and the science could not but be benefited from some effort in the direction of greater friendliness and understanding between the members. Perhaps our psychoanalytic insight and experience should warn us that this is an unattainable ideal but perhaps it could be more closely approximated than is the case at present. I cannot for the life of me see why there should be any greater difficulty in this respect among psychoanalysts than other groups of scientists. Theoretically, we should understand ourselves better and should have dissolved some of our transferred hostilities. Fortunately, I can report that in the Chicago Society we have at present no either overt nor smoldering quarrels and I believe that in New York the situation is somewhat better than it has been. The American societies in general will, I believe, gradually become more peaceful.

I can make my ideas somewhat more concrete if I ask a question or two to which I am sure you will reply with your characteristic directness. Is it entirely contrary to European customs for the convention city to organize some sort of hospitality for the foreigners? I for one felt very strange and unwelcome at Lucerne. I could not bring myself to mention it to you sooner as I was not sure how much of it might be some subjective reaction for which no details of arrangement or personnel could be held responsible. I have reflected about this now for nearly a year and I am convinced that it would take relatively little effort on the part of those psychoanalysts who feel at home in the country where the convention is being held to make those who are relative strangers feel very differently. Some of my colleagues think this is chiefly a matter of expense; I hasten, therefore, to add that I do not imply the expending of a lot of money in the direction of hospitality but rather some effort at immediate personal contacts.

Perhaps I am entirely out of order and I shall be glad to have you say so.

FROM CHARLES FLOM,[12] BALTIMORE, AUGUST 17, 1935

Dear Doctor:

Your very interesting and excellent article on impotence in the August issue of the *Journal of Urology* prompts me to write you for advice on the case cited below. I have tried to persuade this individual to seek the aid of one of the local psychiatrists but to no avail as she definitely insists she could not again relate the details she told me during a state of great depression and anxiety. I have made an effort to find a solution to her problem in the usual texts and current literature but with very poor success.

The young lady who is twenty-four years of age is greatly upset by a fear of perversion and failure of orgasm. She is rather well educated, quite intelligent, of very passionate nature, physically in excellent health. She is keeping company with a young man of whom she is very fond and has had sexual relations with him. He is very much in love with her and has asked her to marry him but she is afraid the marriage will not be successful owing to the fears previously stated and has temporarily postponed answering him either one way or the other. The following are details of her case.

At the age of five or six following a manipulation of her genitalia by a neighbor, she started to masturbate, continuing the same for several years. Then she stopped until she reached puberty, when she again started the practice of onanism. When she was about seventeen she met some young man with whom she became very friendly. It was at this time that she experienced her first heterosexual relationship. She soon became aware of the fact that while she derived great delight out of the preliminary kissing, caresses, and fondling, she felt very little excitation during the act of intercourse. Furthermore there was no orgasm in the sense of attaining a high state of emotion and then the sudden sense of relief with feeling of languor and lassitude even though her partner continued titillating the clitoris for a prolonged time. Instead she would reach a tense state in which she could tolerate no more stroking of the clitoris and then was forced to move away from her partner for a few minutes, after which she would become calm. She stated that while the clitoris was her most sensitive erotic site, she experienced quite a degree of pleasure from manipulation of the labia and

---

12 Flom was a Baltimore, Maryland, physician who had emigrated from Russia; he was an innovator in developing techniques to transmit stethoscope sounds and later X rays by telephone.

stroking of the vaginal orifice but practically none after penetration, though the act was not distasteful nor was there fear of pregnancy.

Some time later she met another sexual partner who on two occasions practised cunnilingism and forced upon her once the act of fellatio. She admits securing an unusual degree of pleasure from the cunnilingus act but the act of fellatio was rather abhorrent and she could not repeat the act. In the passive role during these acts of perversion she didn't secure any orgasm, but on the other hand she was not forced to move away as occurred when the clitoris was stroked by the hand. Further engagement in the perverse act did not transpire as her partner was called out of town on business. Soon afterwards she met the young man with whom she is now keeping company and for whom she possesses great affection. He, though aware of her not being a virgin and having had sexual relations with her, is sufficiently attached to her to desire marriage. He, however, does not know of the reason for her failing to reply in the affirmative.

Close questioning of her elicits the fact that while she has been very friendly with two or three school girlfriends, there never has been any physical relationship beyond the usual kiss on meeting or parting company nor ever any desire for the same. In her work, which is professional, she has met one or two homosexuals but never showed the slightest inclination to respond to any advances. One fact that seems to disturb her greatly is the fear she would submit to almost any erotic practice once aroused sexually.

My opinion in her case is that there has been a failure of transition of the erotic zone from the clitoris to the vagina, possibly as a result of the practice of masturbation. But I am at a loss to explain the failure of an orgasm in the usual form. It is quite possible that a number of women never experience the usually described form of orgasm with its sudden discharge of pent-up feeling but instead reach a great emotional pitch after which there is a gradual release or relaxation.

I have succeeded in allaying her fears somewhat on the score of perversion but am at a loss as to how to produce a change in the erotic zones to the normally accepted type. There has been some pleasurable feeling since her partner has ceased using a rubber sheath, using instead one of the contraceptive jellies. I am considering strongly the idea of prohibiting any manipulation of the genitals but permitting the usual kissing, caressing, and fondling of the breasts. Do you believe that one may hope for success in this case? I see no objection to the marriage as they are interested in the same ideals, culturally have the same tastes being exceptionally lovers of music, drama, and the other arts. The question outstanding in her mind is will it work out on a sexual basis.

Hoping you will forgive my taking the liberty of writing you and thanking you for any help you may be able to extend in this distressing case, I remain
Yours obliged,

To Charles Flom, Baltimore, August 31, 1935

My dear Doctor Flom:

Your interesting letter about your patient came while I was away on a little vacation trip and now that I am back I am answering it immediately.

It was very nice of you to speak kindly of my article and I am glad you enjoyed it. I hope it will interest some of the men in a phase of human life in which they are all interested but sometimes a little inarticulate, if not actually neglectful.

In regard to your patient, I should say that your interpretation was very probably quite correct; namely, that the transition which normally takes place in the erotic zone from the clitoris to the vagina has not occurred. As a matter of fact, this is exceedingly common in American women, as you probably know. Perhaps the majority of them do not achieve it. Nevertheless, it is the normal thing, as you know, and when it does not occur it is very frequently the case that an orgasm is not achieved, even when the clitoris is stimulated. The usual reason for this is that the patient still has a strong sense of guilt connected with sexuality, usually arising from childhood masturbation. The situation might be worded like this—

"I have not grown up enough to give up masturbation and accept the adult female role with vaginal erotism, but cling to the earlier (clitoris) type of satisfaction, but this being equivalent to masturbation and masturbation being equivalent to death, I cannot indulge in it either."

This is all unconscious, of course, and one can't do much about it with conscious psychotherapy. You have done precisely the correct thing in assuring her that any kind of preliminary play such as she has indulged in is entirely innocent and should not be regarded as a perversion. By allaying her conscious fears in this direction you will undoubtedly make her a little less nervous and anxious about the whole business.

But in regard to achieving an orgasm, it is impossible to be very dogmatic. If she were my patient I would advise one of two things. If she was sufficiently disturbed about it and seemed to be really quite inhibited in regard to her relations with this lover I would strongly recommend that she be psychoanalyzed, as I think that would get at the bottom of the matter and would probably result in a cure. The reason I would consider this in her case is that many women who have the same difficulties that she does go ahead and get married anyway and the fact that she is so worried about it that she lets it keep her from marrying sounds a little as if she overemphasized or overevaluated the genital function, which is, of course, a neurotic mechanism.

On the other hand, if she was very much in love with a worthy love object, I do not know but what I would suggest (not urge) that she get married in the hopes that the matter would gradually straighten out. As a matter of fact, it frequently does, as you know, particularly after the birth of the first child. I would certainly ask her what she is waiting for. In short, if she can't be psychoanalyzed she might as well go ahead and hope for the best.

Sincerely yours,

FROM FRANZ ALEXANDER, CHICAGO, SEPTEMBER 27, 1935

Dear Karl:

This time I have a complaint to make. In letters and telegrams during the summer both you and Bart urged me to announce the title and topic of my paper in Topeka, which I did. At that time you knew that you yourself planned to speak on the same topic and had ample opportunity to notify me of this circumstance and ask me whether I still wanted to speak on this topic. Not only was I not notified that our topics were exactly or almost the same, but last Saturday *I could not get from you any information about the program!* Even now I have not yet received a program of the Topeka meeting, and received my information accidentally from Helen [McLean]

I think it is a very poor arrangement to have two speakers talk on the same topic, especially if they are so closely connected with each other in their work and have a detailed concept of each other's ideas which, in regard to the major issues, are related to each other. I would have been willing and glad to speak on some other topic if I had known that you had chosen the psychosomatic problem. Of course, the time now is rather late for such a change. I should like to ask you now to send me a detailed syllabus of your and [Leo] Stone's joint presentation to give me an opportunity to judge how far our two addresses are covering the same ground, deal with the same problems, and offer possibly to a large extent similar solutions. I do not think it advisable that the same group should be exposed twice to the same topic, the psychoanalytic approach to somatic problems. This would make sense only if we would offer fundamentally different concepts—for instance, in the form of a symposium offering controversial points of view. If you send me your syllabus, I will be able to form an opinion as to the extent to which our papers are overlapping. I assume they do to a great extent, and in this case I shall not give this address which would be superfluous after your and Stone's address given on the previous day.

If you will answer me promptly, there will be time for me to change my topic or, what I consider as much more probable, for you to find another speaker in my place. I am sending a copy of this letter to Bart.

Sincerely yours,

To Franz Alexander, Chicago, September 29, 1935

My dear Alex:

I have your letter of September 27 and I think you are unnecessarily excited. I say excited because you seem to feel a little provoked with me and spent a lot of words saying so. You have been frank, however, and I shall be equally so.

In the first place, our program at the C.N.P.A. has nothing to do with the program before the Chicago Society. In the second place, it was Brother Bartemeier's suggestions that you be on the program here in Topeka, a suggestion which I cordially welcomed. He and I together wired you for a subject repeatedly and we put down the one you sent. It is not our custom to discuss with each speaker what their subject should be or what other subjects are to be presented on the same program, as that would resolve itself into an endless amount of correspondence. It is difficult enough to get anyone to present anything.

However, all this argument is really beside the point because I am sure that the presentations that Doctor Stone and I have in mind will in no way conflict with, overlap, or diminish the importance of yours. They are presented from an entirely different point of view. I think you are entirely too modest in assuming that it would be superfluous for you to speak on this subject after Brother Stone and I have spoken. On the contrary, I had in mind the probability that it would supplement and solidify the whole business.

To reassure you, Doctor Stone and I are sending you herewith abstracts of our papers and, if you like, we can send you the entire papers, altho I am still working on mine. In short, as you see, Doctor Stone is pointing out the physiological anatomical possibilities for psychogenic somatic disease as he sees it in the light of his neurological experience and his physiological knowledge. I, on the other hand, intend to outline in some detail the psychological dynamics of conversion hysteria and show in what way hysteria differs from and in what way it resembles a psychogenic somatic lesion. I do not know exactly what you yourself have in mind but I am sure that it will not overlap.

As a final concession, however, if you still feel uncomfortable or anxious about the matter, I shall be glad to have the programs reprinted and a new title for your presentation substituted.

At any rate, don't be worried about it. I appreciate your eagerness to make the program as interesting as possible and while I think you are unnecessarily worked up, I can see how you might have thought we were careless in the matter. You are not quite justified in being troubled at not receiving a program because no one has received a program yet; the only reason Helen

[McLean] had a program is because I sent her an advance copy for the purpose of coming to a decision as to whom we should send out the announcements to. Even the secretary and president of the organization (C.N.P.A.) have not yet received programs, nor have any of the other speakers.

Everything is going fine and I remember very happily my last talk with you and am looking forward to seeing you next weekend.

Sincerely yours,

P.S. Since dictating the above I have been called on the phone by Doctor Bartemeier, who tells me you insist upon withdrawing. Honestly, Alex, I think this is absurdly unjustified. Bartie thinks I ought to explain that my own subject was chosen weeks before your title came in; when your title finally arrived after repeated telegraphing, I thought it fitted in excellently as a kind of symposium. As a matter of fact, you are addressing the Chicago Psychoanalytic Society, *not* the C.N.P.A., and I am addressing the C.N.P.A. and *not* the Psychoanalytic Society. (The audience will not be the same by any means.)

As to not telling you Saturday what the program was, I had no ulterior motives as you seem to think; it never occurred to me that you would regard our papers as in any way conflicting. This isn't a horse race, anyway; it's a couple of scientific meetings, and why shouldn't a dozen men talk on the same topic if they choose to? Please, now, for Heaven's sake, don't make unnecessary difficulties and frictions by withdrawing. We can replace you on the program if you insist, but we won't get over the hard feelings about if for months, and you know it. . . .

FROM FRANZ ALEXANDER, CHICAGO, OCTOBER 3, 1935

Dear Karl:

Referring to our telephone conversation, I repeat the main points.

1. I have no bad feeling whatsoever about the whole affair. I resented that you did not inform me earlier that we were going to speak on the same topic, but I understand now that you did not inform me, probably thinking or foreconsciously expecting that I would take offense, and that I would consider such a communication as a hint that I should not speak. This was an unfortunate misunderstanding on your part, because I was not eager to speak anyhow, and when I consented, I followed Bart's suggestion who wanted me to speak in such an open meeting: open to physicians. Now, when I withdraw this paper, it is a great relief to me, because, as I told you, I do not like to repeat myself so often and would like to speak on this topic at some later time when I have new things to say.

2. If you would like to have me on this program, I would be willing to give a paper entitled "Psychogenic Factors in a case of Petit Mal." I started to

write up this paper, but decided to finish it up at a somewhat later date when I shall know more about the further fate of the patient. However, I could give this paper even though in one respect it will be incomplete. This is the only thing that I would be able to prepare in such a short time.

3. I consider Bart's paper: A condensed repetition of the first part which we heard together with the second part a very excellent presentation for this occasion.

Summary: I have no bad feeling at all if I do not appear on the program at Topeka because subjectively I would prefer to come as a listener. However, I shall be glad to speak on the second topic if I can do you any favor, and in this latter case would do it very willingly.

I hope that with this clarification this affair will be eliminated from the annals of our friendship.

Cordially yours,

FROM FRANZ ALEXANDER, CHICAGO, DECEMBER 17, 1935

Dear Karl:

I shall be glad to substitute for you on Saturday, December 21.[13] Dr. Grinker [14] will discuss a good case. . . .

There is another matter which I feel I have to mention in this letter. Last Saturday in the Club you passingly mentioned your idea of considering organic diseases as one type of manifestation of self-destruction. I remember that you made a similar general statement several times in discussions, also last year at the midwinter meeting in Chicago. The more we study organic cases psychoanalytically, the more I see that this formula is not correct in most cases, although I cannot say that it could not be applied to certain cases. You know that this formula—to consider organic disease as a result of introverted destructions—I expressed in my *Psychoanalysis of the Total Personality.* If I were to rewrite this book, the only serious change would be to eliminate this formulation and substitute an essentially different one. Our experience with organic cases is that the dysfunction of organs and its secondary results—organic structural changes—are produced not by destructive tendencies in the first place, but in most cases through pregenital tendencies, in fact through the erotic component in pregenital tendencies which are repressed and cannot find gratification through the voluntary or the gen-

13 That fall, KAM had offered a monthly seminar for advanced analytic candidates at the Chicago Institute. Alexander was agreeing to substitute for him.

14 Roy Grinker, a psychiatrist and psychoanalyst, was affiliated with the University of Chicago and Michael Reese Hospital. Later he was in charge of neuropsychiatry for the Army Air Force in North Africa and, with John Spiegel, wrote an influential manual on the treatment of traumatic neuroses (*War Neuroses,* 1945).

ital system. The destructive results of such gratifications as a rule are a secondary result of disturbances of physiological nature which are brought about through the innervations draining pregenital tendencies.

As a matter of fact I think that the problem of psychic factors in organic diseases is a highly technical subject and one in which we have already passed the state where popular generalizations as speculations are permissible. I do not think that we should present to the medical profession such general statements, and base our explanations on such hypothetical concepts as the death instinct, if we want to explain by psychological mechanisms organic dysfunctions and resulting structural damages. This field must be very carefully investigated by our best analytical clinical methods, and it is far from being ripe for popularization. Especially, premature generalizations should be avoided. I would hate to see you do that. One of the main purposes of our Institute is to do careful empirical work in this field and in this way bring together psychoanalysis with organic medicine on a really sound scientific basis. Of course, I do not know your special findings in this field nor your ideas in full detail. Do not take these remarks as a general criticism—only a criticism of the above generalization which you spoke about at different times and expressed in several discussions. I shall be very glad to discuss with you these problems in great detail.

About seven or eight years ago I myself went through this speculative phase in this field (organic diseases), and I know definitely now that it is the wrong approach. The statement that an organic disease is the *sign that someone wants to destroy himself,*[15] *wants to die,*[16] or *at least to punish himself,*[17] is both a platitude and a false statement. It is false because probably in many cases the organic disease is the consequence of a too-zealous wish to live, though to live *in an infantile fashion.*[18] (That a tumor is much more the manifestation of extreme disproportionate *up-building*[19] tendencies within the orgasm is quite obvious.) Also, strong infantile wish to be nursed, to be *taken care of, to be loved.*[20] Of course, the introverted destructive tendencies do also enter the picture, but their importance is different in different cases. So far as I can see, the destructive tendencies are as a rule not directed against one's own person, but are merely autoplastic expressions of aggressive tendencies against external objects.[21] I see how your ideas lead from self-mutilation to organic disease, but what is true for self-mutilation is not necessar-

15 Marginal note by KAM: "rather an evidence that he is doing so."
16 Marginal note by KAM: "wants to live!"
17 Marginal note by KAM: "Never 'at least.' "
18 Marginal note by KAM: "which means to live and hate—i.e., hostility is implied."
19 Marginal note by KAM: "autonomic compensation."
20 Marginal note by KAM: "and hatred which they may not express, because they *don't* get it."
21 Marginal note by KAM: "what's the difference?"

ily true for psychogenic organic disturbances. As a matter of fact, I am sure that in a number of cases the instinctual strivings and the dynamic situation are entirely different.

Please excuse me for this long letter, but I felt that I owed it to you to express to you these critical ideas which I several times wanted to tell you, but never could persuade myself to do so.

With best greetings,

Very cordially yours,

To Franz Alexander, Chicago, December 19, 1935

Dear Alex:

Thank you very much for your long letter of December 17. . . .

Your ideas about what you believe my ideas of psychogenesis to be are I am sure kindly intended. Perhaps it would be better if you would wait and read the manuscript before you draw conclusions as to what I am trying to show. I don't think we ought to develop a feud about this, and it is just because I do not think we have exactly the same theories about this that I was so anxious to have you present your theories here in October and listen to my theories. You declined to do the former and you failed to do the latter, so we never got together.

I feel the Institute must develop its theories and conclusions and I will have to develop my own. Sometimes these may not agree. This is one reason, however, that I very much disliked the title and the opening paragraphs of Leon Saul's [22] paper that I saw up there one day. It looked to me as if Leon was going to set the world right about my mistaken theories, and I have a little the feeling that your letter is the same. I want to be set right if I am wrong, but I don't see how you know what my theories are. My associate, Doctor Knight, doesn't agree with all my theories but he has at least read them.

Please do not interpret this as resentfulness. I should like to have you look over the manuscript when it is finished.

Sincerely yours,

To Leo Bartemeier, Detroit, January 21, 1936

Dear Barte:

I am writing hastily to make the following point.

In the first place, I have just gotten a letter from Zilboorg saying that he

---

22 Leon Saul was then a teacher and clinician at the Chicago Institute. He later became professor of psychiatry at the University of Pennsylvania School of Medicine and helped found a center of psychosomatic research in Philadelphia. We do not know to which paper Menninger refers.

is coming west following the Orthopsychiatric Association and if we like could present a paper in Chicago on the 22nd (of February) on: "An Hypothesis on the Genesis of Suicide." He says it will contain some anthropological data on the subject in the light of clinical psychoanalysis. Much as it irritates me to have Zilboorg talk about suicide when I think I am the world's authority on the subject, and much as I would like to read the paper on hypertension which you have asked me to read on the 22nd, I think the tactful thing to do would be to surrender that hour to Doctor Zilboorg since he would be an honored guest and he is always interesting and we all like him and what I said about my irritation was a joke. . . .

As for Helene Deutsch, I personally wish you would cancel the invitation. It makes me so damn mad at these foreigners who act as if they were privileged characters who didn't need to answer letters and telegrams, etc. As far as I'm concerned, I don't want to hear Helene Deutsch and I'm telling you right now I won't come to hear her when you do get her to Chicago. She told me in Boston that she was coming on down to Topeka and if she wants to do so I will come in and listen to her but I think we ought to put a stop to this adulation of the Europeans just because they speak a broken English. . . .

I am delighted that you are so busy. Yes, we are still taking feeble-minded children into the Southard School if they are able to pay the price but we have increased the rate from $100 to $175 a month. This includes psychotherapy. . . .

We are working hard on the last chapter of my book [*Man Against Himself*] which I would like very much to have you read, providing you will read it critically and make me honest-to-God sensible, critical criticisms and not just tell me it's a nice book. . . .

Sincerely yours,

FROM GREGORY ZILBOORG, NEW YORK, JANUARY 27, 1936

Dear Karl:

That you are not interested in my damned trip to Denver unless I stop over in Topeka is only good testimony to our damned friendship. That I am spending nights pondering over blessed timetables in order to dope out how to arrange a blessed visit to your blessed place in order to see your blessed face is good testimony to our blessed friendship.

You are therefore hereby and herewith enjoined to study the proposed plans outlined hereunder, and immediately thereafter to telephone or telegraph and duly and fully inform me so as to enable me duly and fully to ascertain your choice.

The map of that West of yours is crisscrossed with railway steel in all directions and, as I hear, studded with triple combinations of the alphabet. As you well know, all this is unconstitutional, but since yours is the only state with a balanced budget and apparently no less balanced governor, I shall overlook the rest and shall limit myself to the very conservative statement, "To hell with everything! and down with everything that is up!" And by way of balance: "Up with everything that is down." This being the case, and looking cheerfully to the brightest of all futures: "in with everything that is out and out with everything that is in"—all connotations are purely philosophical, of course, and not practical. Turning now to the practical features of this grave problem of the State of the Union (Pacific)—Omaha or no Omaha—here is (at last) the consecutive series of my platforms (railroad).

You and I come to a murderous encounter on suicide in Chicago on Saturday, the 22d of February in the afternoon. The favorable or unfavorable winds of East Ohio[1] will then carry us (you and me) to Topeka, Kansas—no suicidal discussion while *unterwegs*. We shall behold the psychiatric spires and steeples and the psychoanalytic planes of Topeka on Sunday morning, the 23d, spend there a devotional Sunday on some disturbed or undisturbed ward (male or female) and continue in the same spirit on Monday the 24th. Some time before midnight of that day I shall reluctantly part with you and those and that around you, and shall depart for Denver leaving you cursing my plans, visit and memory. *Or*

We shall give one another a hearty suicidal handshake somewhere in Chicago in the wee hours of Sunday morning after a restless and disorderly Saturday night in the windy city, and I shall depart for Denver only in order to reappear most suddenly and most unexpectedly in Topeka, Kansas, on Thursday the 27th, around 6:25 a.m. I shall arouse you from a somewhat emphatic slumber and despite your attempt to wave me away as if I were a fly bothering your nose so early—almost before sunrise, I shall persist and stay right there (European plan—breakfast included) through that to be memorable Thursday and perhaps not so good Friday. Around 2:45 p.m. Friday, voluntarily or not, I shall be drifting back to Chicago to catch the Twentieth Century next day to be back in New York on Sunday morning, away at last from balanced budgets, balanced governors, western friendship, East Ohioan ambivalences, and strongholds of Republican headwinds.

And so, my dear Don Carlos, will you please use posthaste our modern telegraph and let me know at once your wishes. I shall await your pleasure and within twenty-four hours or less thereafter I shall confirm my plans.

In the meantime, I shall mount all my telescopes and look forward to our meeting, encounter, and visit—all at once.

As ever,

---

1 The Chicago Institute was then located at 43 East Ohio Street.

FROM FRANZ ALEXANDER, CHICAGO, JANUARY 29, 1936

Dear Karl:

I am sending you a copy of the manuscript of our Annual Report. I shall appreciate receiving your remarks as soon as possible. I am also expecting your manuscript. I will go over it very carefully and *undogmatically*.

I wish to add to our last discussion that there is really no reason why we should not have different concepts for approaches to psychogenic factors in organic diseases. However, I think that a mutual tolerance of each other's approaches is most desirable. The future developments will decide which line of approach is the more productive. I admit that I have quite a bit of skepticism regarding the theory that organs outside of the voluntary and sensory systems have the faculty to express symbolically highly individualized ideational contents. . . . Your feeling that I myself changed my opinion in this field is only true to a very small degree. I never committed myself in this field and have always been skeptical about the Groddeckian type of interpretation, but I admit that new observations and more precise thinking have clarified my ideas in this field considerably.

I do not regret that I emphatically expressed to you my skepticism about one or two general concepts and would only regret it if you would misinterpret and resent it. If, after hearing my critical ideas, you feel no valid reason for more caution, the only thing for you is to go ahead with it. After all, none of us can decide how these things really are, and your theory might turn out in the end as the valid one.

Cordially yours,

FROM FRANZ ALEXANDER, CHICAGO, MARCH 26, 1936

Dear Karl:

I started to read your manuscript and began to make a few remarks on the margin. Then, looking through the whole book, I noticed that you have there two different versions of the end of the gastrointestinal system in Section 4, that is to say two different editions of "Discussion and Critique" of our research work in Chicago. One of these versions is more extensive. Regarding this more extensive version I have a few important remarks to make.

You discuss here certain concepts which you attribute to me, referring to quotations on pages 34, 35, and 36 which you take from private correspondence (or conversations?) with me. You allow yourself to quote from my letters to you—for example, about changes I would make in my book *The Total Personality* if I could reedit it. You discuss isolated statements of mine which I have written to you in confidence in a personal letter, statements which were never intended for publication. These statements in my private letters to you have followed a long night discussion with you and are only intelligible as a part of the whole discussion. But apart from that you have no right to quote in your book the content of personal letters. You must concede to me the right to publish my ideas in a form suitable for publication. Isolated ideas referring to a long private conversation are not suitable for publication. You must wait to discuss certain ideas of mine until I formulate them for public consumption.

With this letter I formally protest against using the content of these letters for publication. At the same time I wish to tell you that you have to wait probably considerably longer to discuss with me publicly my ideas on this subject because I am far from having definite opinions about the general theory of organic diseases in their relation to psychological factors, on which I am engaged in most difficult and laborious research work. I have no desire to formulate my opinions because I do not feel that I know enough yet to do so, and what I feel I am able to say in this field at present has all been published.

I must therefore most definitely protest against using sentences from my private letters for discussion in a book or referring to ideas which I only told you in friendly and confidential letters. The same is true regarding your footnote on page 36. There you start a sentence, "Alexander believes wholeheartedly." . . . You do not know what I believe wholeheartedly in this respect because I never stated that specifically. I stated that I believe in inductive methods but I never said that I have anything against working hypotheses or deduction in general. I believe that it depends upon the status of a science, and on the type of material you deal with, which method is preferable. My whole scientific productivity is the best witness that I am not a sterile collector of data but also use working hypotheses, even in my very last work on vector analysis, which is in itself a working hypothesis.

The text from the last paragraph on page 33 until the end of the chapter is highly personal in its tone, but that is your business—what tone you use in your book. But you are not entitled to use my letters as if they were statements for which I assume the same responsibilty as for my publications. It is a great disappointment for me that on the basis of this experience I must feel most cautious about communicating to you certain ideas in their *status nascendi* in the future. If you want to quote me you have enough published material. So, for instance, the ideas about the instinct fusion, bribery of the superego, and the neutralizing effect of erotic tendencies, which are essentially similar to many of your ideas and which probably influenced you in formulating your own main thesis are such examples to which you can refer in your book in discussing my ideas [2] in relation to yours.

---

2 Below his signature, with an arrow to this point in the text, Alexander wrote: "(or more precisely my elaboration of certain ideas of Freud)." The postscript is also handwritten.

I am waiting with going on to make remarks in the margin until I receive an explanation for your procedure in picking out sentences from personal letters and describing from that a scientific attitude of mine which I myself never have stated comprehensively and perhaps never will. You must understand that in the field of science everyone has the right, so long as he lives, to express himself, his own ideas, and nobody has the right to reconstruct somebody else's ideas except on the basis of what he has published. My ideas on the whole field of organic disease are in a process of development and continuous change. After I have stated them I will welcome your criticism or discussion of them; and the same is true as to my views toward scientific methods in general, my attitude toward induction and deduction, working hypotheses, etc.

Sincerely.

P.S. After having written this letter it occurred to me that perhaps you yourself have seen how impossible it is to take out sentences from personal letters and use them as targets of critical remarks in a scientific book. I thought you saw this and therefore you wrote the second shorter version of your "Discussion and Critique." Since I don't know, however, which is the first and which is the second version, very *unwillingly*, I must send you this letter. You may understand the severity of my disappointment when you make clear to yourself that I discussed with you these questions and wrote you my letter (which you quote!) because of my great interest in your work, to caution you against the danger of a naive or uncritical application of the "death instinct" theory or any psychogenic theory on organic-pathological processes. And now you use the content of these *private* discussions and letter to drag me into a public argument on a field on which I do [not] wish to make general and final statements before I come to more definite conclusions. I am *investigating* this field and not speculating about it, though I have no objection that other people should speculate about it. I hope you will respect my standpoint and my desire not to be quoted beyond what I have published!

To Franz Alexander, Chicago, March 31, 1936

Dear Alex:

I have just received your letter and I think you are quite unnecessarily disturbed. I think you have some justification but, on the other hand, you ought to know me well enough to know that I am very open to suggestion and wouldn't for the world do anything to embarrass you. I am willing and anxious to delete any of the passages you disapprove of for personal reasons. In fact, I would like for you to delete them yourself so that there will be no mistake about it.

I think that if you reflect a little bit you will recall that the whole thing arose as a reaction to what I still think was a premature and indiscriminately critical attitude on your part toward my book. It was quite a severe blow to me that you voiced such a decided opinion about the book before you had seen it, especially since you did not stay to hear it discussed here in October and had never given me any opportunity to present the material in any systematic way to the Institute group.

I can quite understand your amazement at being quoted on the basis of some remarks which you made to me personally and at having your whole philosophy summed up by me before it was clarified in your own mind because I feel that this is exactly what you did to me in passing judgment on my entire book on the basis of more or less unconsidered remarks which I may have made informally in your hearing.

I have thought all along that, in essence, we believed the same thing and were approaching it from two directions. Your energetic barrage of criticism the last two times I was in Chicago, therefore, was a great surprise to me and perhaps caused an entirely unnecessary and unprofitable artificial barrier to arise between us.

This feeling that you had condemned the entire book without a hearing probably led me to take a somewhat haughty and defensive attitude in the discussion which I am very glad to have called to my attention and which I wish to correct.

I shall appreciate your comments upon all or any part of the book which you have time to cover,

Sincerely yours,

To ESTHER EVERETT LAPE,[3] NEW YORK, JUNE 15, 1936

Dear Miss Lape:

On November 22, 1935, you addressed a letter to us [Karl Menninger and William C. Menninger] asking certain views, which was answered by one of us on December 11. On January 8 we received an acknowledgement of this reply, asking for a further statement of views which was not at that time forthcoming. On May 12 you addressed another of us (Dr. William C. Menninger) asking, if we are not mistaken, the same questions proposed to us in the original letter of November.

The present reply, then, is from both of us. We operate here as a clinic, a closely cooperative group of physicians, all of us neurologists and psychiatrists with a basic training in internal medicine, and while the views of various individuals composing the group might show some variance, what I shall say represents not only the views of us two, the brothers Menninger;

3 Member in charge of the American Foundation Studies in Government. She sent a questionnaire to KAM concerned with the relation of psychotherapy to hospital care.

I think it is fair to say that they do not depart radically from those of the rest of the group.

We believe, and we show by our method of practice, that a cooperative attack upon psychiatric problems is the preferable method today—we think the only method. Whatever the case may be in general medicine about which we have our ideas if not a large experience, the fact is that psychiatry involves an extremely complicated and broad view not only of medical science but of psychology, sociology, and general culture. It is a little extreme, but perhaps fairly illustrative, to say that one cannot properly understand psychiatric cases unless he is familiar with an extremely wide range of subjects from English literature and the history of music to political developments in medieval Europe and the nature of action currents in the heart. So far as I know, no other branch of medicine requires such an extensive scope as a part of the professional accouterment. Now, as a matter of fact, for all that psychiatry, more than any other branch of medicine, emphasizes the importance of one individual to the other—that is, the importance of the physician himself to the patient—it is paradoxically true that in order to make this possible to any considerably wide group of patients, a high degree of cooperation among various men with an essentially unified point of view is necessary.

Our tendency is, like that of other physicians, to become more engrossed in the scientific problems before us than [in] the economic problems which surround us. Nevertheless, we are fully aware of the incongruity between our laborious and assiduous efforts to relieve a few unfortunate individuals who come to us and our powerlessness to change the conditions which contribute to the bringing about in millions of others suffering which neither we nor anyone else is likely to be able to relieve. We differ somewhat among ourselves as to the exact importance of these environmental factors, at least insofar as a therapeutic program is concerned; I think perhaps most of our staff follows my own conviction that self-destructive impulses implicit in the individual have more to do with his grief than the inescapable factors of the environment, deplorable as we know this to be. The practical upshot of the matter is, nevertheless, that many of those who need treatment, who need some help to overcome these self-destructive tendencies, do not, cannot, reach us. In the interest of science and in our own interest, as well as in the interest of humanity, we welcome investigations such as you are conducting to ascertain more definitely why this is and how it can be altered.

In my previous letter I said that we did not know the answer and I repeat it. As a matter of fact, we have a considerable distrust of broad programs of change and reformation in any direction, because we feel that they border too much on the Olympic or Messianic way of saving the world. It is a beautiful ideal but not one which the vast majority of us expect to fulfill. It would be easy, for example, to join in the chorus of the intelligent minority who feel that a radical change in the social fabric would bring about a Utopian situation and eliminate all of the present evils.

Some tendencies in that direction seem to us to have very definite disadvantages which I tried to indicate to you in my previous letter. For example, in those instances I have observed where state medicine is practiced, certain drawbacks are often apparent. These include political interference, gross discriminatory practice, lack of interest in scientific progress, and failure to promote therapeutic science. In the West, particularly, a strong and naive adherence to democratic ideals has persisted, which in a sense rather approaches the communistic idea. The state hospitals developed as a necessity for the care of socially obnoxious or dangerous individuals, but they soon developed into a kind of state enterprise which those responsible for them naturally took pride in attempting in every way to promote. Thus, they came into frank conflict with private initiative in a kind of dog-in-the-manger way. They do not themselves promote science or exploit to anything like its possibilities the opportunity they have for research. On the other hand, by their active competition they handicap and retard the development of private institutions and make those institutions more expensive for the individuals who are fortunate and intelligent enough to prefer them to the state institutions. Our experience would prejudice us very strongly against the further development of state medicine in any form.

On the other hand, we cannot be said to have benefited or profited in the direction of scientific research as a result of those exponents of capitalism represented by the various foundations. Although we are trying to promote psychiatry, not only from the standpoint of pure science, we have not received a penny for research from any foundation, organization, state or federal source or any private individual with one exception, that exception being a matter of $3,000 received several years ago for a special research from an unknown party in the East, and this was received through the friendship of Dr. William A. White, who is familiar with the work we are doing here. We do not receive research funds because we are a private institution supposed to be attempting to further our own work and also because we are a Western institution and pure science is supposedly a matter of Eastern development.

This is merely a recapitulation of what I have previously written you and may seem to you to be a wholly personal matter. Naturally, it seems to us important because it is a pressing problem with us, but also because we feel that the future of psychiatry is at stake in the West. As you know, psychiatry has not made as great progress in the West as it should. We feel that this is largely because people in the West have been brought to feel that while physical illness is a matter for private concern, mental illness, perhaps because a few cases endanger the community, is a matter for public concern and that the private individual is not to be expected to undertake responsibility for its treatment. This has led to a crowding of the state hospitals and a dumping of patients on the state to such an extent that scientific individual treatment such as modern psychiatry is pledged to is impossible. We feel, therefore, that before any system of state medicine would be possible or tolerable to psychiatrists (at least to those of our own group and many others like us) the public would need to be educated to the point where it understood what proper treatment was. Otherwise between the present popularity of cutting the budget and holding down expenses at the cost of our educational system and public institutions, the care of the mentally ill by the state becomes nothing more than custody.

Perhaps a time may arrive when the public is sufficiently aware of what psychiatric treatment means and what their friends and families should have in order to recover from a mental illness, to consider a plan whereby everyone who needs it might receive proper psychiatric treatment at state expense, but at present the public is far too ignorant and some relatives too hostile and shamefaced toward the unfortunate patient who has a mental illness to care what becomes of him. . . .

If it [state medicine] comes it should follow a program of public education which would insure the retention of the personal relationship between patient and doctor. I believe this to be absolutely essential to the practice of psychiatry and I have never seen or heard of a substitute for this relationship of confidence which implies that the doctor is responsible to his patient first of all.

This is so important in psychiatry that I am skeptical of any attempt to work it out on a broad national policy under our present political set up. Whether it would be possible under any government I do not know.

Under our present political and economic set-up in the United States it seems to me that the logical way to see that everyone receives adequate medical care is to subsidize private enterprise, just as railroads were formerly subsidized and as the aviation industry is subsidized because its value is recognized. There would have to be better control and supervision of the expenditure of government funds than occurred with the subsidizing of the railroads and aviation enterprises, however. Such a plan, if it could be worked out, and I do not know that it could be, would not destroy the patient-doctor relationship. In our own case we have hundreds of inquiries from people who have achieved worthwhile things in the world but who are ill and cannot finance treatment. Some of these persons we treat free but many we cannot afford to, because we have difficulty in making ends meet (and also because we have sustained a free clinic in our own city for poor people for two years). Occasionally some of these people are lucky enough to find a wealthy, benevolent individual who will finance their treatment, but in most cases they do not. If we had a sum of money which we could use for treatment of such individuals we could accept many more than we can afford to now, and thus valuable members of society might be saved.

Not only individuals might be treated but scientific research might be furthered by the use of government funds judiciously administered. To refer again to our own institution, which we know best, we have a half dozen or more projects in research under way here and we expect to add to these. All of them, however, must be financed entirely out of what in most institutions would be called profit, used for individual purposes. We believe that under a system of government subsidy we could show that our research work was worthy of note and support. I do not need to tell you that since we are a private institution and prefer to remain so in order to preserve our scientific freedom, our research efforts are considered either a personal hobby or a form of promotion of our practice. We have been advised many times that if we devoted more time to personal promotion and less to scientific advancement we could secure funds. No doubt this is true, but it seems that most people at present believe that the time has passed when private wealth alone can cope with the ills of our civilizations.

Of one thing I am convinced: that one can never obtain the morale in a large impersonal organization that one depends upon to obtain results in a small personal group. The cooperation between staff members, nurses, therapists, and all employees, the loyalty to an ideal, and the concern for each patient that is all important in his treatment cannot help but be lost, in part, at least, in the tremendous overcrowded institutions with which state medicine is meeting the demand for care for the mentally ill at present.

Sincerely yours,

FROM LEO BARTEMEIER, DETROIT, JULY 1, 1936

Dear Leo:

I am deeply grateful for your criticisms of the chapter [from *Man Against Himself*]. Upon reflection, I think they are fully justified. For one thing, I think I should bring in a few martyrs other than religious ones—Gandhi, for example. Then, I think you would be relieved to know that the self-mutilation among savages has been very carefully described in an earlier chapter and will, as you suggest, dilute considerably the criticism which is otherwise aroused by the reading of this chapter all by itself. I am also grateful to you for reminding me that the Catholic church discourages and disapproves of any actual mutilation of the physical self, thus making a more subtle type of self-attack necessary rather than the more brutal and primitive attacks of more primitive religions.

I will make some changes in this and I believe when you read the article in the light of the entire book, which deals with self-mutilation and self-punishment in all kinds of forms, in fact, even in normal people, you will not have quite so much the feeling that I am being provocative toward the religious people. However, the religious martyrs are so dramatically described and oftentimes were so extreme in their behavior that they make excellent clinical material, and it is tempting to use more of them than perhaps is entirely balanced.

I am very glad to hear that you and Bess are going to be able to attend the International Congress in Marienbad. I am sure you will enjoy it.

Sincerely yours,

To Helen McLean, New Hampshire, July 13, 1936

My dear Helen:

I am writing to welcome you to your own home in New Hampshire. It was nice of you to invite me to visit you there, but it rather looks as if I were going to pick up my son in Michigan and drive to Canada and possibly as far west as Glacier National Park, make a few speeches at the Utah State Medical Society, and get back home by the 5th of September. That doesn't look much like New England, does it? My son, youngest daughter, and their mother are now in Florida visiting Grace's mother, and Julia is out in Colorado and I am here alone. I have a good time staying out at Indian Hill at night where it is really quite cool in spite of the generally hot weather. By the way, our weather hasn't been as hot as most of the rest of the country's this summer. It's hot enough, however. . . .

I received a note from the Educational Committee [4] June 26. I sympathize with you in the difficulties you have with Blitzsten; you know how it irritates me to have him continually badgering and attacking Alexander behind his back.

However, something happened recently which I think will give you a little better impression of just why he feels as he does. I am going to go into it in some detail and then you can digest it and present it to Doctor Alexander any way you like. Doctor Alexander irritates me sometimes by his assumptions. For example, I was a little irritated that he invited Zilboorg to speak on suicide and then wrote and asked me if I want[ed] to speak on something. Zilboorg has treated me rather shabbily about this suicide matter and while it doesn't worry me, I don't see why my own institute should favor him in the matter. However, that's water under the bridge. He dic-

4 The education committees of the psychoanalytic institutes controlled assignments of teaching and training and were often resented by those who felt that these committees had too much power. The Chicago Institute was frequently troubled by disagreements between Blitzsten, who had complained about his assignment, and his rival, Alexander. McLean, who then chaired the education committee, was aligned with Alexander. Here— although KAM begins by sympathizing with McLean—he ultimately attacks Alexander.

tated some notes to the education committee in which he talked about what he was going to do "in Chicago" and I corrected these notes to make them read "in the Chicago Psychoanalytic Institute" because it may be clear enough to some of us that that is what he means, whereas some of the rest of us might have a good reason for being very irritated that Alexander should attempt to speak for Chicago. Chicago is a rather big place and it is getting bigger.

Now, here is the incident that I want to tell you about. I am addressing you as Chairman of the Education Committee. I got a letter from Doctor Alexander a couple of months ago that a certain Doctor M—— was there for analysis but that the Institute couldn't take him yet and that he, Alexander, has suggested to Doctor M—— that he might come down to the Menninger Clinic for some psychiatric work while waiting for analysis in the Institute.

(2) I get up to Chicago and have an interview with Doctor M—— and he tells me substantially the same thing.

(3) I attend a meeting of the Education Committee and Doctor Blitzsten tells me that he has recommended to Doctor M—— that he (Doctor M——) come to Topeka and have his analysis down here with me. Doctor M—— also asked me if it might be possible for him to do this.

(4) Doctor Blitzsten adds that it was he, not Alexander, who suggested that he come to Topeka. Alexander, hearing this, chimed in and said, "Yes, why not take him yourself for analysis? That is what I recommend."

Now I don't know if Alexander recommended this prior to this time. If he did, neither he nor Doctor M—— told me about it. I don't know if Doctor Blitzsten mentioned it prior to this time because if he did Doctor M—— never told me about it. Be that as it may, both Doctors Alexander and Blitzsten suddenly announced that they were urging the patient to come to me for analysis.

I decided to wait until we had observed Doctor M—— a little while here. He tried to rent a fourteen-room house, saying that he had several servants and would need lots of space. We got the impression during the first few weeks that he had a great deal of money. He is a good worker and pitched in bravely, saying that he didn't want any salary. We gave him a small salary notwithstanding this. Nevertheless, as time went on it appeared that he had somewhat less money than he had at first pretended. He began to make inquiries about the cost of analysis by Doctor Simmel. It was suggested that he write and find out. He got a letter from Doctor Simmell saying that he could be analyzed there for $10.00 an hour. Then he talked to me. I told him that I could not take him for less than $20, that my rates were $25.00.

Doctor M—— told me at this time that Doctor Alexander had promised to take him at $5.00 an hour; he said that Doctor Blitzsten had offered to take him at $15.00 an hour; he now has an offer from Doctor Simmel for $10.00 an hour and from me at $20.00.

This is a perfectly absurd state of affairs and should not be allowed to continue. I thought we all generally agreed that the cost of analysis should be determined somewhat on a patient's ability to pay. One would gather then that Doctor Alexander estimated his ability to pay as being about one-fourth of what I estimated it to be. I don't believe that is the real cause of the difference. Nevertheless, you see that Doctor M—— is trying to decide whether he wants an analysis at $5.00 some time in the future or an analysis at $20 an hour right now. However, he can get analysis at $10 an hour by going out to Simmel. The whole thing has become for him a question of bargains or shopping around. Furthermore, it isn't his fault; it's largely the fact that that he has been told by one analyst that an analysis costs so much and by another analyst that it costs so much, etc.

Frankly, I don't want him. I would much rather have him stay here and work a little while and then go somewhere else and be analyzed so that I wouldn't have the responsibility of the inconvenience and the embarrassment of having a man on the staff also having analysis with me. But the principle of the thing is really quite bad, Helen. It is very bad for Doctor Blitzsten to have in his possession the information he does (and information which I also have) that Doctor Alexander offered analysis to this man who is perfectly able to pay much more than $5.00 an hour, a $5.00 an hour analysis. Doctor Blitzsten interprets this as being an attempt on Alexander's part to stop all of the training cases before they reach anyone else. I think this is a delusion on Doctor Blitzsten's part. I think Doctor Alexander is merely a very poor businessman, very enthusiastic about analysis, very easily taken in by people, very apt to be overoptimistic and try to make things easy for people to get in at the Institute, etc. This leads him to go exactly contrary to Freud's carefully expressed dictum that we should discourage rather than encourage psychoanalytic prospects—point out the difficulties, the deviousness, the expense, etc. It is one of Alexander's errors, however, which I do not interpret as malicious or malignant but which does have serious consequences, and Alexander's greatest aggression is that he fails to seriously consider this point. He refuses to see how it does hurt Doctor Blitzsten. I'll go further and say it hurts me. It doesn't hurt me very much because I have never expected to receive much business from Alexander. It is a good thing that I haven't because I have never, to my knowledge, received a single patient from him.

Al Stern did send one alcoholic to me, and you have sent several, but Alexander, never. I tried to point out to Alexander once that I wasn't dependent upon the Institute and really didn't expect him to send me patients but that if I were working in Chicago as Blitzsten is, and as numerous other men are, I would expect the director of the Institute to send me patients. As a matter of fact, I believe Alexander and the rest of you do send a lot of the other analysts patients, and this is as it should be. However, it is not as it should be for Alexander, as representative of the Institute, to offer people analysis at a rate far below what they can afford to pay when other analysts in the same city (I mean Blitzsten, for example) need the patients and must charge more if they are going to maintain their positions and pay their expenses. . . .

Anyway, in the cool retreat of your new Hampshire home, think it over and do what you wish. Send this letter on to Alexander if you like. I have not said anything which I intended to be antagonistic to him because I know that at heart he is a generous, sweet, kindly fellow, and his only aggressive-. ness is in a certain obtusity or a certain blindness to facts which he is apt to brush aside as being unimportant while to some people they are of great importance. Anyway, I think you are the most objective of any of us children and I think you can reflect on these things and do as you like with them, especially since now as head of the Educational Committee, you are in a position of authority. I do believe that one of the important things to be done is for the Institute to establish a more definite policy about charging for these patients and once established let us all know about it. I think it is ridiculous to have an Educational Committee which decides the candidates only to have the Institute have a certain financial policy which none of the rest of us know about.

Give my love to Franklin and tell him I have decided to put out my book in two different sections. One is purely a book for laymen and deals with the more sociological and psychoanalytic details. The other is a book for physicians and deals with attempts at hypothesis about the possible relation of organic disease to the self-destructive tendencies in general. I think the latter will be so conservative as to be accepted by all medical men and the former will be so radical as to appeal to all of the laiety.

Sincerely yours,

To Robert Knight, Traveling in Europe, July 25, 1936

My dear Bob,

I feel like a skunk for not having written you more frequently, so I'll start in and relieve my conscience by giving a few excuses. In the first place, it was 114° here yesterday breaking an all-time 100-year record. We are not the only place, but that is poor comfort. H. L. Mencken is in town on account of the big celebration. He said it was 108° when he left Baltimore and that he was nearly suffocated. He wore his coat yesterday and insisted that he wasn't as hot and was enjoying Kansas aridity. The poor old United States is getting an awful sock in the eye this summer, and you are lucky to be over there in Europe. Personally, I am not enjoying the aridity at all because my trees are dying, the grass is dried up, and everything is so dry that yesterday there were a dozen fires in Topeka and twenty or thirty fires in

Kansas City, grass fires. Five or six branches of the fire department were out in Westboro yesterday trying to stop a grass fire that killed a lot of trees, burned up a part of a house and a good many acres of lawn. So you see it really is something. On the other hand, the heat really doesn't bother us very bad as a rule, but yesterday and today it is about to get us down and we are glad you're over there out of it. Possibly a little envious. . . .

Clinic business is quite good and we are working hard in spite of the heat; Sanitarium business has fallen off considerably but with your return and the return of the cold weather I am sure it will improve.

We have enjoyed your letters immensely, and each of us reads whatever we have received at the lunch table so that we all can enjoy it. I have read your last letter several times. Everybody sends greetings and I my special love to Florence.

Sincerely,

To JULIA MENNINGER, COLORADO, JULY 30, 1936

Dear Glorious:

Your letter of July 25 was very sweet and your advice on the new car settles it. We shall get a maroon Cabriolet. Since I wrote you, however, I have changed my mind a little about just when to get it. I rather think that instead of getting it in Chicago I shall get it here and I shall wait a little while, too, because with Mother back we have the other new car and the old Buick will make out a little while longer. I think I can rent a car in Kalamazoo in case I go up to Michigan for Bob but I am not certain I will do that because we are terribly busy here at the Clinic. . . .

The plan I am concentrating most on now is to tear out of here the day before your final day there at Estes Park and get up there to see the final ceremonies like I did last year. I enjoyed that so much and I would like to be with you on that final day. . . .

I was interested in all you told me about the goings-on at the camp. Yes, I am quite interested in stealing because of course I see a good many people here who come because they steal or feel like stealing. It is a curious impulse that comes over some people. I suppose deep down in our hearts we would all like to take things because it would be nice to have everything if we could just lay our hands on it, but most of us would rather have the good opinion of others and conform to their expectations than to have the things that we could gain by snatching. However, I have observed that many times people take things that they don't want at all, or at least don't need. This must mean that the things they steal have some symbolic value to them, or else that they actually want to get themselves in bad by doing something mischievous that will make other people angry. A lot of people are like that. We call that provocative behavior because such people want to provoke other people. It is more normal to want to please other people.

Well that's enough psychiatry for the present. I think it is wonderful that you go clear up to the top of Long's Peak and back in one day. I never heard of the like. I don't think I could get half way up in one day. . . .

The dogs are enjoying the summer and so am I, in spite of having my family scattered to so many different parts of the country. The weather has gotten cool now and I am kind of sorry because when it was hot it was pleasant to go out and drink a cold beer or cold Coca Cola and take cold showers. Now it is so cool that the cold showers are not pleasant and nobody cares for cold drinks. I imagine, however, we'll get a little more hot dry comfort a little later.

I am expecting your Sunday letter today but it hasn't come yet and I'll get this off without waiting for it.

Sincerely,

To Franz Alexander, Chicago, August 24, 1936

Dear Alex:

Bill and I were glad to have messages from you and I am taking this occasion to sit down and reply to them and write you a little letter about the news of the summer. First, let me say that I am glad to hear that you have been so pleased with the California climate and so happy in your new little home there in California. It must have been a very interesting experience to have dined with Chaplin. It speaks great skill on your part in gaining entré to an exceedingly difficult place, a place in which many people envy you, including myself.

Bill and I have both been very busy this summer working on our books. He is working on his *Outlines of Psychiatry for Nurses* and I have just finished up my self destruction book [*Man Against Himself*] and am about to send off a copy to Doctor Fishbein,[5] who has been kind enough to say that he would read it and advise about publishing. I have a strong notion to send it to Knopf in spite of the difficulties I had with him before. He is disagreeable and ill-mannered and has a terrible wife who butts into his business, but in spite of all that he puts out beautiful books and he already has my *Human Mind* and he might do well by it. However, it seems to me I recall your saying that you have had a little trouble with him recently (which I also remember telling you that you would have) and if you've got some ideas about this, let me know. I am not going to commit myself to any publisher until I have had Fishbein's advice and until I have heard from several publishers as to what they would be willing to do in regard to promotion, translations, royalties, etc.

5 A physician, author, and editor, Morris Fishbein was an editor of the *Journal of the American Medical Association* from 1913 to 1949. He also edited *Hygeia* and the *Bulletin of the Society of Medical History and Medical World News*. He and KAM met in Chicago in the early 1930s and became friends, despite their differing attitudes toward psychoanalysis.

I think I already told you that I gave up the idea of writing a book that was good for both the medical profession and the laity. This book is written primarily for the intelligent laymen and such doctors as care to give it any attention. . . .

We have had a tragic summer here in that not only has it been terribly hot--as high as 115° one day and some fifty days with the temperature over 100°—but the nights have been pretty warm too. This sounds pretty bad and it is pretty bad, but we could stand this heat if it wasn't for the terrible drought which has killed our flowers, our lawns, our shrubs, and even our big trees, trees 100 years old that have withstood all kinds of damage prior to this. We thought 1934 was a terrible drought and it was the worst that had ever been known but this summer has been even worse. It has a discouraging effect on us and it has a bad effect on business too. Our business has fallen off very badly this summer and we have lost money right along with no signs yet of any pick-up.

In addition to this, Dr. Leo Stone, upon whom we depended very much for our neurological work, suddenly decided for reasons best known to his future analyst to return to New York. He says he wants to make a trial of private practice there and then perhaps he will come back to us. We were awfully sorry to lose him because he had a good influence on us scientifically. In addition, Dr. Ralph Fellows, who had been with us for four or five years, was offered the position of superintendent of a state hospital near here, and while we think that may work out very much to our benefit in many ways, we were very sorry to lose him too. However, it must be added that we feel very fortunate in the addition of Doctors Kamm[6] and Grotjahn[7] of Berlin. We have the highest recommendations for both of them and Doctor Knight has met Doctor Kamm and his wife and writes us that they are splendid people. They are having some little trouble in getting their visas but we are hoping that they will be here within another thirty days. In the meanwhile, we haven't been at all shorthanded, even with Doctor Knight being gone, because of the slackened business. . . .

My real vacation begins tomorrow and even it is not entirely a vacation. I am taking the whole family to Yellowstone Park where we shall spend two or three days and then I drop down to Salt Lake City where I address the Utah State Medical Society three times, once on the "Relations of Psychiatry and General Medicine," once on "Alcoholism as a Form of Self-Destruction as a Psychiatric Syndrome," and once on "Masked Forms of Aggressiveness

6 Bernard A. Kamm, a German psychoanlyst, joined the Menninger Clinic staff in 1936 and left in 1939 to practice in San Francisco.

7 Martin Grotjahn, fled Germany and came to practice at the Menninger Clinic in 1936. He left in 1938, settled in Los Angeles, and became clinical professor of psychiatry at the University of Southern California and a training analyst at the Southern California Psychoanalytic Institute.

in Children and Others." Immediately following the convention we drive directly home which will take us about three days and plan to be back here September 8 to begin work again. Altogether I will take about two weeks vacation this summer. However, I don't need one very much because I have had a very pleasant time evenings out at my cabin keeping cool with cold showers, cold watermelon and cold beer, comforts which I have been happy to have been able to share with visitors from time to time. I wish you could have been one of them.

You mention in your letter to me that Doctor Simmel had spoken to you of our plans. I don't know exactly what he mentioned to you but perhaps it was that we had invited him to come here and that he had declined, saying that he had too many obligations in California and felt the field in California was too good for him to desert it, but, on the other hand, suggested that we establish a branch of the Menninger Sanitarium in California. This idea is not a new one for us but he has perhaps brought it to a head. His idea is that we establish a psychoanalytic sanitarium out there, like this one here, only perhaps more strictly limited to psychoanalytic cases and that it be a branch of the Menninger Sanitarium which would be run by us and carry our reputation, etc. He would join us and we would have the advantage of his reputation also. We feel that there might be many advantages in this, chiefly the advantage that many people in the East who have the money for psychoanalytic and psychiatric treatment are much more easily persuaded to go to California for a winter or for a year then to come to Topeka, Kansas, a place they never heard of, so far removed from the urban conditions which most of them are familiar with that they are reluctant to come. They can easily say to their friends, "My doctor has recommended that I go to California for the winter," or they can say, "I am going to California for my health," or they can say, "John Smith has gone to California to spend the winter," whereas it sounds a little peculiar to explain one's going to Topeka, Kansas, and makes it necessary to come out with an explanation which many neurotic patients don't want to make and their relatives still less so. Then there are some other advantages: Los Angeles is a large city and there are many well-to-do people there who could go on with their work and have analysis, whereas in Topeka we must rely upon those who are sufficiently well-to-do to give up their work and come here and stay which greatly adds to their expense.

On the other hand, it involves many problems; we are well established here and I don't know if our reputation is as strong in California as Doctor Simmel says it is and I don't know what difficulties might arise in an attempt to promote the branch clinic. I don't know just what would happen to the Topeka branch. I should be sorry to move so far away from Chicago but there seems to be little interest in Chicago in financing us in the development of a branch there so we have practically given up that idea. Prospects of getting financial aid in California seem very good from several quarters.

Reflect on these things and, if I may ask you to do so, please keep them confidential for the present, but write me your reactions. I should like very much to know what your impression is of the possibility of our developing a place there. Incidentally, I might make it clear that we should do so partly with the idea of making more money for the amount of labor expended than we can do here. I should think that we ought to be able to limit our work to people with a good deal of money, who could, for example, pay $25.00 per hour and even more for analysis and who, if confined in the sanitarium, would pay very liberally for that, perhaps $100 a week. In short, I have in mind making an ultra-fine place which would incidentally be very expensive, but this, on the other hand, would enable us to do the things we would like to do with a small number of patients adequately and well. Of course, I don't know what difficulties we might have in cooperating with Simmel but we got along with him so well here that we are rather optimistic on that score.

Please let us know rather fully your ideas and impressions about this as Bill and I will both be very interested. Please don't say that you will wait and talk them over with us in Chicago. We want to know sooner than that. . . .

Our regards to Anni,

Sincerely yours,

To Leo Stone, New York, September 8, 1936

My dear Doctor Stone:

We are all pouncing upon the opportunity to write you and welcome you in your new office and to tell you "Good Luck" and "Congratulations" and "God Speed." We miss you like everything out here and your long silence since you left has made it seem like years. You see our hearts are with you, Leo, and we think about you a great deal more, I am sure, than you realize.

I just got back from my jaunt out to Salt Lake City to the Utah State Medical meeting. It was interesting but in many ways disappointing. There is a total absence of neuropsychiatry in that region, almost total absence. Strangely enough, however, there is a young neurosurgeon named Reed Harrow there who is doing some neurosurgery, some neurology, and perhaps a little psychiatry, although he doesn't have much confidence in himself in the latter respect. He is an earnest young fellow and has promise, I believe. The Mormon religion was extremely interesting to me and my time was profitably spent in investigating it. The best old families there are Mormons, but now that they have got it established and are growing up in it, they don't know just what they think of it themselves. My most pleasant interview was spent with Dr. Clark Young, a grandson of Brigham Young, the founder of Salt Lake City and the dynamic head of Mormonism; and yet, strangely enough, my friend Clark is no longer anything more than a nominal Mormon. It caused him enormous inner struggles, however, to "become a Gentile," as they call it. He really hasn't become a Gentile, but he is no longer eligible to enter the Temple. To do this you have to have a conference with your Bishop and be certified to have kept the faith in the proper spirit for the past few weeks, etc., etc. It is really very interesting. They believe in a preexistent state, on a different planet, and they also believe in a postmortal state in which one is reunited with his wife and children. Some of them, especially some of the doctors' wives I talked to, are just as devout and credulous about all this as a child is about Santa Claus. They are really extremely singular. Then when you see the results of the whole thing in the way they have beautified that marvelous valley out there, it is really quite impressive. It makes you think that the trouble with some of us is that we aren't crazy enough.

We hope you have lots of practice and lots of things to interest you and that you and your family are well and that you will overcome your writer's cramp in the near future.

Sincerely yours,

To Walter Freemen,[8] Washington, D.C., September 22, 1936

Dear Doctor Freeman:

A week or so ago a local physician, Dr. A—— B——, called me in regard to his mother-in-law, who he said was in your care. Of course, I was glad to tell him how well we knew you and how highly we regarded you. He said that you had contemplated an interesting brain operation for the relief of what I took to be an agitated depression. Since than he has called and told me that visitors have found her much improved immediately following the operation. Naturally, I am extremely interested in this and would appreciate it very much if you would have time to write me a little more in detail about the theory and practice of this new treatment.

I hope things are well with you. Bill joins me in sending best regards and congratulations on the success of this interesting work.

Sincerely yours,

8 A Washington, D.C., psychiatrist who pioneered prefrontal lobotomies in the United States.

FROM WALTER FREEMAN, WASHINGTON, D.C., SEPTEMBER 25, 1936

Dear Dr. Menninger:

The operation on Mrs. H——,[9] mother-in-law of Dr. A—— B——, was carried out about ten days ago and consisted in making subcortical section of some of the fiber tracts in both frontal lobes according to the technique recently devised by Egas Moniz.[10] As you may have heard from Dr. B——, Mrs. H—— was suffering from an agitated depression of a year's duration with constantly increasing restlessness. Upon recovering from the anesthetic this agitation was much reduced and there was steady improvement for a period of a week without obvious impairment of memory, judgment, or attention and with considerable improvement in her emotional reactions toward her husband and others, so that we were congratulating ourselves upon a brilliant result.

Last Sunday something went wrong, I suspect a further degeneration of the tissues in the frontal lobe, and she became confused, developed perseveration in speech and aphasia with other symptoms indicative of frontal lobe deficit but no paralysis or disturbance of sensibility. There has been some improvement since then so that she is beginning now to look at books and magazines and to draw pictures but she cannot yet write legibly or carry on a conversation. She is calm and almost too placid.

You will find an account of the first 20 cases that Moniz operated on in his monograph: "Tentatives operatoires dans le traitement de certaines psychoses." Whether Moniz's theory is correct that the destruction of the fibers in the prefrontal zone stops the pathologic activity of certain cellular complexes, or whether there is merely a generalized reduction in the initiative, hardly seems to matter since this procedure is reported by Moniz to have cured five out of six patients with agitated depression and to have relieved the sixth to some degree. We have been intensely interested in the procedure and expect to try it out on some younger individuals hoping to obtain the good results without complications.

Very sincerely yours,

TO FRANZ ALEXANDER, CHICAGO, OCTOBER 8, 1936

Dear Alex:

Just to keep the arena clean, may I bring up a few things that I have noted?

In the first place, I have never received *The Vector of the Psychoanalytic*

9 Marginal note by KAM: "This was Dr. Freeman's #1 lobotomy."
10 Pen name of Antonio Caetano de Abreu Freire Egas Moniz, a Portuguese neurologist who developed the technique of prefrontal lobotomies, for which he won the 1949 Nobel Prize for medicine.

Institute,[11] of which I am *supposed* to be a member. I see that a copy was sent to Anna Freud and that her reply was mentioned in volume I, no. 2. I am curious to know just whose oversight this was.

In the second place, at the bottom of page five I discover a reference to a *Bulletin of the Menninger Clinic* which is described as "promising." I should be very interested to know who was inspired with this damningly ambivalent word.

The "promising" *Bulletin* had some very nice complimentary words from Dr. Adolf Meyer, Dr. Peter Bassoe, Dr. Harry Stack Sullivan, and perhaps one hundred others from all over the United States and Europe, but we prize each little compliment and we are glad to know that our Chicago colleagues regard it as "promising."

I was very much interested also in the announcement on page one of our friend Gregory Zilboorg's cooperation with the Institute in further investigating Zilboorg's ideas of suicide. You must have more confidence in him than I do and also more influence with him. He asked me to be on his committee, and he also promised me funds, but that is the last I ever heard of him. However, if you do consider me a member of the Institute staff, knowing my interest in suicide, you might have flattered me very much by asking me to have some interest in this research. Least of all you might have told me about it before making it public knowledge in a bulletin which apparently goes to many but *not* to me. I resent your having made this deal with Zilboorg without consulting me, in view of the fact that I am associated with you as a member of your Institute and am supposed to have some interest in what goes on there, and in view of the fact that you knew perfectly well of my interest in suicide and of Zilboorg's curious attitude toward it and me.

You have thrown up to me repeatedly the fact that I am not warm enough in my support of the Institute. I haven't thought this to be quite accurate and I have been anxious to help the Institute and have repeatedly made suggestions in regard to it, most of which have not been followed. I am loyal to the Institute and I will never stoop to say nasty things about it to other people or to retaliate against you in any way. But I begin to feel, as I wrote Helen [McLean] very frankly, something of the desperateness and hopelessness of the situation that Lionel and Bartemeier feel, although this does not imply my approval of their activities. I am in the unpleasant position of appearing to them to be lined up with the Institute against them when, as a matter of fact, I am not even receiving from the Institute what I would con-

11 The *Vector* was a short-lived publication edited by Bernice Saul, who wrote to KAM on November 15, 1936, "The *Vector* is not an official organ of the [Chicago] Institute but is something taken extremely lightly, and therefore things are not thought over very carefully, but written spontaneously and I am the one to blame if the *Vector* conducts itself awkwardly."

sider courteous treatment. The patronizing reference to our *Bulletin* made us all mad as hell down here. Similarly, as I have already said, I think the deal with Zilboorg over my head without my knowledge (or even with it for that matter) was an act of disloyalty to friends that I personally would not want to be guilty of.

We all see things different ways and perhaps there are many facts that I don't know about. The whole business makes me so angry that I just don't care to be stirred up so, and for that reason I think I shall come to Chicago seldom this winter. It has always seemed to me that it is your business as director of the Institute to keep enough in touch with those of us who have supported the Institute and who have been, in a measure, dependent upon it to understand our feelings and make allowances for our personal reactions instead of going ahead ruthlessly and inconsiderately as if whatever you did ought to be all right. You know I haven't been rebellious in the main, that I have been loyal to you, and I have supported what you have done, but you don't seem to recognize a reciprocal obligation on your part. I don't mean that you are disloyal to us in big ways, because I know you are not; I know you are essentially friendly and kindly and mean well, but that isn't enough. These little things get under our skin. You can call it paranoid if you like, but the fact remains that it hurts us and we react about it, and I don't want to do that, and the best way for me not to do it is to stay away.

Sincerely yours,

From Franz Alexander, Chicago, October 12, 1936

Dear Karl:

This time I must ask you very seriously that, before you write to me both complaining and aggressively accusing letters, you inform yourself about what you are writing. I feel that I have the right to demand this from you as a sign of minimum respect which colleagues working together for long years owe to each other. It cannot go on that every time you blow up about some imaginary injury or trifle which hurts your sensitiveness you write me a letter of redundant unjust accusations. This time the facts upon which you base your complaints and accusations are so simple and undebatable that I almost feel ashamed to write you this answer, and put you in the embarrassing position of making you see on what a ridiculous basis you are attacking someone whom you always emphatically call your "friend."

The *Vector* is a toy of Bernice [Saul, the editor]. It is not only not an official publication of the Institute, but is edited under the sole responsibility of Bernice. The articles are not censored by me. I make no suggestions as to content. My only relation to the *Vector* is that I have permitted Bernice to publish it, in an unassuming way as her own responsibility, as a forum where everything that is unofficial around the Institute may appear; opinions, suggestions, perhaps even complaints of the candidates and the friends of the Institute. Until she gives me reason not to, I am going to let her go on with this little private enterprise of hers, which might have some place in our little community. Most of its articles are supposed to be based on personal interviews. I am sure that, if you had happened to be here before this issue appeared, Bernice would have published a personal interview with you, which would have flattered your narcissism. But to complain to me that the *Vector* has called your *Bulletin* "promising" is simply comical. Since at this moment I am lying sick in bed, I have no opportunity to ask Bernice about it, but I assume that she wanted to make some friendly remarks about the *Bulletin* as one of the important news events, and, since the *Bulletin* was just received, she had not yet the opportunity to receive from somebody or from you some more relevant remarks about it. Not even I as yet have had an opportunity to read the *Bulletin,* and therefore you have not received "nice complimentary words" about it which will put me in a role with Drs. Meyer, Bassoe, Sullivan, and "one hundred others from all over the United States and Europe." I sometimes begin to become resigned and give up the hope that such complimentary words will ever cease to be so close to your heart.

Your remarks about Zilboorg are almost incomprehensible to me. Zilboorg dealt with you before he did with me. You never consulted me about that. Not you, only Zilboorg told me about it, and, when I last saw him in the spring, he told me that he was planning to give some money to you the same way as he was to the Institute. Just a few days before I left Chicago we agreed to accept his offer to the Institute. What happened to his deal with you I did not know. What kind of injury against yourself you see in this I simply cannot comprehend. I accepted Zilboorg's offer since in our controlled work we deal repeatedly with cases with self-destructive tendencies and symptoms. We keep anyhow records about these cases, and Zilboorg's offer made it possible to give financial support to some excellent young men. How your interests are endangered by that I do not see.

I feel rather hopeless in writing this letter. If you wish to find some reason for aggression, you will always find something. I come to the conclusion that there is something wrong with your attitude toward me and the Institute. I cannot escape from recognizing how you feel (of course, not consciously) about our relations. According to your feeling, there is an arena in which the two gladiators—the Menninger Clinic and the Chicago Institute— are fighting a struggle for life and death. That might be true for you; it is not for me. I am teaching here peacefully the candidates and conducting a modest, but intensive, research work. These activities possibly cannot give reason for such violent outbreaks of emotion. You know perfectly well that I am always eager to have your cooperation. You know that you can teach here always, whenever you wish and whatever you wish. You know that constructive contributions on your part to our research work are highly welcome. Why are you then during the past two years always looking for some trouble and reason for such emotional outbreaks? *I* am not competing with the Menninger Clinic or with Karl Menninger, neither scientifically, financially nor narcissistically.

Your repeated veiled remarks about Lionel and Bartemeier are unfortunately symptomatic. I wish you would tell me what is "desperate and hopeless" in the situation regarding the Institute—perhaps that the Institute has created in Chicago in an unprecedented short time a healthy, lively, and rapidly developing psychoanalytic life, and helped the existence *without exception* of all younger and older analysts? Shall I consider these remarks of yours as a threat, or do you want to make me feel that God should save me from my friends? I hope not. But all this is symptomatic of something being wrong with your subjective feeling. You should like to feel toward me as a friend, and yet it seems you cannot help seeing me as a gladiator and the plains between Kansas and Chicago [as] a gigantic arena. Should not this picture of an arena serve as a memento to the author of self-destruction?

Sincerely yours,

To Franz Alexander, Chicago, October 21, 1936

My dear Alex:

Bill says he had a very pleasant time at your house but at some time during the day he tried to explain to you some of the matters which you do not seem to understand. Today I get your letter saying "Bill also told me you planned to talk over different matters with me which I shall be glad to do."

Bill tells me that he did not say this: I do not have any plans to talk over things with you, although I appreciate your friendly gesture in the direction of doing so if I wish to. I will tell you why I do not wish to. You are always so charming and so kindly in personal contact that it is absolutely impossible for me to talk these things out with you. When I get there you are so friendly that my previous feelings become suddenly repressed and I just say to myself, "Oh, skip it; I'll overlook it and we'll go on from here." The trouble is we really don't solve anything: you so often don't seem to understand what I am talking about. You didn't, for example, in your letter of October 12.

I have tried, therefore, with the advantages of distance, to analyze your letter of October 12 very carefully in one last effort to help you to understand what it is that you do that hurts our feelings. I have rewritten this letter several times in an effort to make it as clear, objective, and free from emotionalism as possible.

You say in your letter that I should inform myself about what I am writing. The purpose of my letter of October 8 was exactly that, and if you will reread it you will see that I asked you specifically about most of the points therein. Others did not need any further information than I already had.

You say that the facts upon which I based my complaints and accusations are so simple and undebatable that you are almost ashamed to write an answer to them. My dear Alex, one difference between you and me is that you almost never admit that you are in the wrong about anything. Consequently, no facts upon which anyone bases any complaints ever seem to you to have any justice or any foundation. You ask me in the last of your letter just what it is about the Institute which gives me and others the feeling of hopelessness. I will tell you in a few words. It is simply that you never seem to realize that you are mistaken about some things and that your position is not absolutely impeccable. It seems utterly impossible for us to get across to you the fact that you hurt other people's feelings. You always assume an air of astonishment as if any such occurrence were preposterous. This naive astonishment and amazement on your part that people react to having their feelings hurt gives one the hopeless feeling that there is no use to try to tell you about it. One must either take the position that since you are the head of the Institute and since you have this curious blindness about yourself, one can either take your aggressions and forgive you for them, nursing one's feelings the best one may, or else one can simply withdraw from you and the Institute. You are, in the main, so good at heart and so generous and have so much to teach all of us that no one wants to do the latter (withdraw) but at the same time no one likes to be kicked as you repeatedly kick all of us and have you assume this air of being amazed that anyone could have considered that you do so.

I agree with you that I overreacted to the description of our *Bulletin*. After all, it is true that we hoped and expected considerable approbation from our psychoanalytic colleagues in Chicago and it happens that not a one of you except George Wilson (and at the time I wrote you, not even he) had shown any indication of liking it and the first word we had was this accidentally observed remark in the *Vector*. You are right that it shouldn't make so much difference to us what you or any of the Chicago people think of our *Bulletin*, but whether or not the *Vector* of the Chicago Institute is official or not has absolutely nothing to do with my objections, and this reply was provocatively evasive.

But concerning repeated references to the narcissistic basis of my appreciating comments on our scientific efforts, I want to say that this is not only poor sportmanship on your part but it is, in my opinion, bad psychoanalysis. It is one thing to interpret to a patient that certain difficulties of his arise on the basis of an overnarcissistic sensitiveness; it is quite another thing to accuse one's colleagues of narcissism every time they react to your aggressions. I could talk about your narcissism if I wished; I could remind you that you were very anxious to have yourself given credit for what you have done;

you were very anxious to have favorable comments for the *Reports* of the Institute, but instead of hurling this fact at you as a weapon, I tell you I think it is considerably in your favor. I think the narcissism which is represented by the satisfaction in the approval of one's scientific colleagues or one's scientific work is not a reprehensible type of narcissism and you don't think so either, at least you do not live as if you thought so. Furthermore, even if it were, you would not be justified in replying to my letter by talking about my narcissism. Two people can always say to one another, "You are narcissistic," and it will always be true; so what? I could say, for example, that your narcissism made you so emotional in the letter of yours of October 12, but I am not your analyst and if I were I would try to make more accurate interpretations and point out just what it is that disturbs your narcissism. Perhaps what disturbed your narcissism was a painful and entirely unnecessary injury. It happens that I am now trying to point out to you that you inflict painful and unnecessary injuries upon people which understandably hurts them—hurts their narcissism, if you like, but hurts.

About the Zilboorg matter—I don't object to your taking money from Zilboorg. I said I thought you should have told me about it—first, because I am on the Institute staff; and secondly, because I am interested in suicide and talked up suicide research there. For you to let a New York man come in and cooperate with you in pursuing research on suicide without even mentioning it to your colleague, myself, whom you know to be interested in the subject and with whom you had conferred with about the subject is the kind of disloyalty of which you are repeatedly guilty and yet always astonished that anyone should feel as such. It may be (and I really believe it is) entirely inadvertent disloyalty and therefore you feel so aggrieved to be accused of it because it may be true, as you say, that you have no personal hostilities about it. I don't accuse you of having any. I only accuse you of being clumsy in such matters in a way that hurts my feelings, and I have been under the impression that it is our psychoanalytic conviction that if our feelings were hurt we ought to talk them over with the people who hurt them. I have tried to do this and I get only a stormy, blustering, evasive letter from you. I tried to reply in a different tone. I don't know how you will take it but I earnestly hope that you will not regard it merely as a narcissistic squawk, or consider that so designating it settles everything.

Sincerely yours,

FROM LIONEL BLITZSTEN, CHICAGO, NOVEMBER 1936

Dear Karl:

I am not going to apologize for not writing you upon receipt of the *Bulletin* a few weeks ago. You know me and writing. So—I'll just begin this letter by saying I think it's just the swellest thing I've ever received from any institution, which should justify you in throwing out your chest. By sheer accident I espied the latest concoction of the C.I.P. [Chicago Institute for Psychoanalysis] called, humorously enough, the *Vector*. As it happened to be in the hands of Peggy Gerald[12] the moment I espied it, I asked her if I might glance thru it. It served two purposes—1st, it enabled me to divert my attention from the irritating [?] mental B.M. which Tom [French] was trying to achieve to the accompaniment of many ehs—ahs—ohs, etc.; the end result being only a feeble fart: the 2nd, well, if you perchance have seen it you'll know what I mean. Comparisons are odious I know and this one might be called odorous. All of which is my awkward way of telling you that your *Bulletin* is ace high and the *Vector* is somewhere else. Or if I must stick to comparisons—then your opus is Casin's [?] Sweet Pea—the *Vector* what the other fellow's crap smells like to anybody but the crapper. Ye Gad. I'm waxing anal-ytic.

Now for your invitation to give my paper on dream interpretation. Let me hasten to make two corrections. 1—it isn't a formal paper but a two-hour seminar. 2—It's on the role of dream-meaning—the purpose to which patients use dreams in analyses—and the uses the analysts can have for the patient's dreams. Of course techniques will be discussed, especially my variations and differences from the usual misinterpretations of Freud's technique. I might tell you that the especial stress I shall make in this seminar on dreams has something to do with the widespread misconception of the true meaning of free association and something more about the psychoanalytic cliché "abreacting," which for most of the analysts I've met around these parts remains a beautiful term capable of much magic.

You know that very early in my career as a psychiatrist I began to distinguish between the theory of psa and the technique of psa, the latter so far removed from the former. If you recall, I dubbed the former—which I repeatedly recognized *in statu flagrante* at the C.I.P.—"The penis-penis-who's got the penis" brand of psa. I have hopes that some day my voice will be heard in the outer darkness so when I receive a letter like yours my hopes rise. . . .

By the way I'm very interested in your idea of moving your institution to a real center of population. Dorothy and I have discussed it at length and we have some ideas on the subject for you when next you come to Chi. In advance let me tell you—we think it's a swell idea.

Also—since it's of interest to you—I think that [Charles] Tidd is showing a great increase in maturity over what he had.

So—old top—many thanks for your kind letter. . . .

P.S. Put me on your mailing list for the *Bulletin*, will you?

12 Margaret Gerard was an analyst who, along with George Mohr and Helen Ross, had journeyed to Vienna to train in child analysis with Anna Freud. She had been invited to the Chicago Institute by Alexander.

FROM WILLIAM ALANSON WHITE, WASHINGTON, D.C.,
NOVEMBER 23, 1936

Dear Menninger:

Yours of the 21st duly received. I believe the letter was intended for me, but you have addressed me as William Allen White. Will you please tell me why I am followed all over the country by all sorts of people with that designation? Is it a compliment or an insult, or symptom of aggression, or what is it? In any case, to the question at issue:

Of course you have undoubtedly quoted me correctly, although I have not verified it, but it isn't quite my idea. I am pessimistic but I am pessimistic only for the now. I have faith in the future. The trouble is the future in which I have this faith is too far off to be of any particular use to you or to me. You remember it was Nietzsche who said that mankind has a poor ear for new music, or words to that effect, and what you say about the lack of faith in the psychiatrist is just as true as the lack of faith in economists and bankers, and I have no doubt many other kinds of people. The average individual is a long ways from home, from our point of view, and it is going to take him several generations to get there. Our faith should not be placed in making the world over out of the material of the present generation— men who have made successes of their lives teaching what we believe to be outmoded principles. If we are to make the world over it has got to be with the youngsters. I do not think that things are quite as bad as you say they are. Prisons have improved. The fact that committees exist is after all a step towards the light. We never will correct any errors until we know they exist, and when the machinery exists for informing us of that fact we have taken the first step. I think you would find, too, that the net result of all these ancient and honorable methodologies and ideologies of the law, etc. have improved in practice, or had until recently, for in the past few years there has been, in my opinion, a great slump in the morale of the whole world. And so I would say that we must not lose heart but must keep on. There is no other direction for us to go.

Very sincerely yours,

TO SIGMUND FREUD, VIENNA, DECEMBER 12, 1936

Dear Doctor Freud:

I still remember with deep pleasure my short visit with you on the porch of your home in August 1934. Last summer my colleague and associate, Dr. Robert P. Knight, had the pleasure of a short conference with you during which you very kindly autographed some photographs of yourself, one of which now hangs on the wall of my office. I feel very grateful to Doctor Knight for this gift and grateful to you for having autographed it for him and for me, because he tells me he told you for whom he intended it.

Your photograph now hangs in numerous places about this clinic because we already had a large-size copy of the Pollok etching, and Dr. Ernst Simmel very generously gave us a very large photograph, which we prize highly. These pictures remind Doctor Knight and myself of the inspiring opportunities we have had to talk with you, if only for a few minutes, but more significant than this, they remind all of us of your spirit, which, I believe I can truthfully say, hovers over this place and inspires all of us to strive toward the patience and objectivity in which you have set us such a great example.

When he was here, Doctor Simmel mildly reproached us for not having written you more fully of the way in which we have tried to apply psychoanalytic principles in all departments of our work here. He was very generous and enthusiastic and said he was going to write you about it; he said he had always dreamed of carrying out psychoanalytic principles in some such way as this with both children and adults and did not know that he would discover his dream so nearly realized here so far away from Vienna and Berlin and even from New York. We use psychoanalysis in the standard way with both in-patients and out-patients, and those sanitarium patients not accessible to psychoanalysis are prescribed for (by my brother and his associates in the hospital) according to psychoanalytic principles.

In addition to the practical application of psychoanalysis and psychoanalytic principles in our daily work, we have a weekly seminar which all staff physicians and some others attend, devoted to theoretical presentations of psychoanalysis, psychiatry, neurology, and psychology. We have also a psychoanalytic study club which we hope will ultimately become a branch society; at present the six analysts on our staff constitute the membership of this, but we shall probably soon have one or two child analysts, and, in addition, there are some analysts in training in some neighboring cities who may affiliate with us.

We publish some of our work in a small bi-monthly, *The Menninger Clinic Bulletin,* which I believe you have received. We plan to dedicate the May issue of this *Bulletin* to you and wish to print the picture which Doctor Knight of our Clinic brought back from his trip. We also intend to publish an account by Doctor Knight of his interview with you. In addition, there will be some psychoanalytic articles.

Before we proceed, however, we should like to have your permission to use the picture and we should indeed feel very proud and honored if you would write a few sentences which we might use as a foreword in the journal. (I hope that you do not consider this request too presumptuous.) If, for any reason, you do not care to comply, we shall understand your position, but if you can do so, we shall be deeply appreciative.

We earnestly hope your health and strength remain equal to the many tasks you have set for yourself and for the continued inspiration you are to all of us.

My regards to your daughter, Anna Freud.

Sincerely yours,

To Joseph Wood Krutch,[1] New York, February 8, 1937

My dear Mr. Krutch:

I was very pleased with the castigation that you gave Paul Schilder on his absurd scriptures relative to "Alice in Wonderland" in the current number of *The Nation*.[2] I was in New York and attended that meeting, but I left just before Schilder spoke. As you know, Doctor Schilder is not a member of the Psychoanalytic Association and, while he is regarded by some as a psychoanalyst, I have personally a good deal of fault to find with some of the things he does in the interest of psychoanalysis. It isn't that I want to keep psychoanalysis from appearing ridiculous; psychoanalysis must stand or fall on its own merits, in spite of its friends and foes. But, I object to the scientific accuracy of Schilder's stuff.

As a matter of fact, even granted that what he says is true (and some of it most certainly is not, to my notion), a child is prodigiously satisfied by reading somebody else's fantasies of this type, and is thus saved certain direct and personal expressions which might be disastrous. Furthermore, Schilder entirely misses the point of the book as a whole, which you very succinctly indicate in your article; I refer to the satirical way in which she [Alice] (he) [Carroll] caricatures the inanities, pseudologic, pomposity, patronizing of children, and all of the other things of which her (his) parents must have been guilty. I thought of writing something about the matter myself, but you have said it so well here that I doubt now if I shall have the energy to get at it.

My manuscript, *Man Against Himself*, is with Harcourt-Brace. They are

---

1 An important American social and literary critic, Krutch taught at Columbia University and was editor of *The Nation*. His interest in and sympathy with psychiatry led to an extended correspondence and friendship with KAM.

2 Schilder, then research professor of psychiatry at New York University, had given a talk at the winter meeting of the American Psychoanalytic Society warning of "exposing children to the dangerous corruptions of Lewis Carroll." Krutch answered: "It ought to be evident that his nonsense, like so much nonsense and so much wit, was a device by means of which his intelligence protested against various kinds of cant which his priggish and conventional temperament would not permit him to flout openly. . . . Why, of all people, should a psychoanalyst be shocked to find complexes in an artist, or afraid to have children . . . introduced at an early age to a literature, the very secret of which is its successfully playful cartharsis of certain all but universal obsessions?" ("Psychoanalyzing Alice," *The Nation* 144 [January 30, 1937]: 129).

going to publish it and I think Mr. Pearce[3] is going to see that the manuscript is put in your hands very shortly, if it has not already reached you. I am making some modifications and improvements (I hope) in one or two chapters and it may be that he is waiting to get the revised copy before sending it to you.

Sincerely yours,

Los Angeles

To WILLIAM C. AND C. F. MENNINGER AND JOHN STONE, TOPEKA, FEBRUARY 27, 1937

Dear Will, Father, JRS,

If this trip was for the purpose of getting rest it is a great failure. We have been on the run with no prospect of peace. We get up early every morning and immediately after breakfast I come back and see Mr. S——[4] and Miss Lyle works on manuscripts and correspondence and answers the phone, which is quite a job in itself. The I——s and the K——s call us every day and want to schedule us for various events. And others.

Thursday the I——s took us to lunch at a restaurant, the Vendôme, which is quite a popular movie star retreat, and we saw quite a few of them at close range. Miss Lyle had to wait in Earl Moore's[5] car in front of Bullocks-Wilshire yesterday for half an hour and she said she saw more of them than she did at this restaurant. Trying to see these movie stars in the flesh is a game here and seems to be related to the impulse to see Mama getting out of the bathtub in the nude. Anyway they all do it and we follow suit. The I——s subsequently took us riding through Beverly Hills, Bel Air and Westwood to Santa Monica. In spite of the drizzle it was very beautiful, although the white architecture gives you a feeling that the whole town is a movie set of a World's Fair which will crumble away in a few months.

That same evening I went out to the county hospital to a neurological case demonstration by Ingham[6] and his associates. The county hospital is as big as the Merchandise Mart in Chicago (not really, but that's the impression it gives you) with many different colored stripes in the floor which visitors are directed to follow toward their various destinations. The nurses' lecture hall was literally as big as the Florentine room at the Jayhawk [Hotel in Topeka]

3 Cap Pearce was KAM's editor at Harcourt Brace at the time of the publication of *Man Against Himself* (1938). In 1939, he was one of the founders of Duell, Sloan and Pearce and became editor in chief.

4 The deleted names are all those of patients or former patients.

5 A resident at the Menninger Clinic who accompanied KAM on the trip to Los Angeles.

6 Samuel D. Ingham was professor of neurology at the University of Southern California Medical School.

and this was only one of several nurses' lecture halls. About forty neurologists, interns, and nurses were clustered in one corner and four or five typical neurological cases were brought in, briefly presented, and discussed by Ingham and some of the others. It was interesting but not extraordinary.

I don't want to wax philosophical but someway or other that vast hospital, that huge room with a little cluster of neurologists in one corner, seemed to me so typical of this place. The idea of bigness and of making a grand show whether you've got anything inside of it or not seems to be the prevalent spirit. They have ten new psychiatric cases a day in this hospital besides all the neurological patients which are even more numerous and all the out-patients which are still more numerous. But the psychiatric cases are merely held long enough to be committed or released. So what? There is apparently no scientific study of them at all. I looked over a medical and neurological history and there are forms and indexing systems and reports of the laboratory examination of the bacterial content of the stools that would knock your eye out but the actual physical neurological examination is about what you would expect in a county hospital. They certainly wouldn't get by at the Menninger Clinic.

I am still a little philosophical. These people out here are really damn confused with the comings and goings, the automobiles dashing crazily all over the map, the races here and the movies there, the oceans and the mountains and this and that, that they really give relatively little concentrated interest to their special work. The neurologists all feel terribly inferior and the psychiatrists simply don't exist. I have talked with numerous doctors, including Ingham, who sat with me for two hours over a couple glasses of beer purchased by him, and as one fellow put it, there is lots of wealth out here but the thing is to try to get it. The quacks and cults have a strong hold and everybody is on an equal footing. In other words they carry democracy to its extreme degree of degradation. Think of old floppy-pants, baby-faced Ingham being the head of the whole thing out here and steady open-minded fellows like Glen Myers[7] being kept off the university faculty in spite of recommendations from Adolf Meyer, Ebaugh,[8] Macfie Campbell,[9] and others. Think of the county hospital having a large unit called the "osteopathic department" run by the osteopaths. Think of one-fourth of all the chiropractors in the world being located in this county! The point is the country is so new that expansion is easy, everyone is taken at his face value,

7 A psychiatrist who owned the Compton Sanitarium, Compton, California.

8 Franklin Ebaugh was a psychiatrist affiliated with the University of Colorado Medical School and with the Colorado Psychopathic Hospital in Denver.

9 C. Macfie Campbell was a student of Adolf Meyer at Johns Hopkins. Like Meyer, he was interested in mental hygiene and was involved in the National Committee for Mental Hygiene. In 1920 Campbell was named professor of psychiatry at Harvard; he became director of the Boston Psychopathic Hospital after Southard's death.

and face value counts for a lot. Organized medicine is not very strong, they have a nice little library and lunchroom building, and several doctors' buildings, but none of them compares with Kansas City, Dallas, or Fort Worth, in spite of the fact that this town is three or four times as large and probably has much more money. . . .

They announced a little roundtable luncheon for me yesterday at the medical building which was a washout. Somehow I can't convey the feebleness of the neurological interest here better than to tell you that after all the announcing of this, leading you to think it was an important affair, about a dozen people showed up, some of them women analysts, and we sat very stiffly around one of the tables in the place and after a 40¢ lunch which tasted 10¢ cheaper than that, we adjourned and that was that. Here is a city of two million people, or call it a million, and in the medical library restaurant where you would expect hundreds and hundreds of doctors to be coming to lunch there were perhaps a total of forty at lunch and twenty-five more playing bridge downstairs.

Myers drove me on out to Compton and we picked up Miss Lyle and made a tour of the sanitarium. It looked even prettier than when I was here before. They have two private cottages and one pavilion that takes four patients. The rates remain low. The furniture in some of the rooms is nice, in most of the rooms mediocre. They have disturbed patients well isolated from the others. Their dining rooms and kitchens are on the first floor, in fact everything is on the first floor. The occupational therapy room is one big airy sunny room, not very well equipped. They have no recreational therapy. . . . Earl Moore is having a good time, thinks if we could run the place we could double the rates and collect more of what we earned than they do. All the people like Dr. Meyers because he is gentle and reliable. Many people asked to be remembered to Dr. and Mrs. Tidd. . . .

Miss Lyle's impression of Compton was that it was much nicer than she had expected from everyone's reports. The surroundings are pretty bad but the grounds themselves and the general atmosphere of the place is very agreeable.

On the way to the psychoanalytic society meeting I talked with Myers about our coming out here, because I thought he would probably have heard it. I told him there were four disadvantages in Topeka that he didn't have to combat out here—its bad reputation for summer climate, small size of the town for outpatient residents, with few amusements, etc., no university connection, and no way to disguise the purpose of patients coming there. Also the lack of wealth. I told him we had been urged to start a psa. sanitarium at pretty high rates and therefore would not compete with his and might even help his, but that I was not very enthusiastic about all the work it would entail.

He said he would personally welcome us. He was sure it would help his business. He told me his income for every one of the past ten years. It is of course, far better than ours, but like all other doctors I have seen, he thinks purely in terms of money and not in terms of psychiatric prestige or scientific accomplishment. He thinks the latter are difficult to develop here. He thinks we would make money, but he says the amusements and other attractions here hinder rather than help, and that people are willing to spend their money for everything rather than medical treatment and that all medical fees are very low. He thinks it would be fine if I would come out here alone but thinks it a little strange that we should want to give up the wonderful organization we have built up in Topeka which is the more outstanding just because it is some way isolated and not complicated by distractions. He would like to sell us his sanitarium at a huge price, perhaps $200,000 or $300,000, but he realizes it is a bad location. . . .

On the other hand, this city is growing rapidly and is full of people from all over the world, and I believe if we would put the promotion effort to getting started here that we have been putting into Topeka we would rapidly have an international reputation and an international business. It would take a psychological shake-up to want to do it, and I think we'd have to proceed on the assumption that what help we would get from L.A. doctors would be minimal, not because they would fight us, but because they are so weak. The point is that mediocre men like Myers, without any promotion, with a mediocre establishment, are nevertheless getting along well and if we stayed true to our ideals we could do ten times better scientifically and probably several times better financially. I'm going to have a long talk with Earl Moore.

Last night we went to the psychoanalytic meeting which is held in what Simmel calls his office, which is a little bungalow, five rooms, gorgeously furnished. About forty people, most of them lay analysts, psychologists, but a few doctors were present and asked questions till midnight.

. . . Tonight Myers is giving a party and inviting eighty people and tomorrow we will watch Eddie Cantor broadcast. Sunday evening we have dinner with Simmel.

Jean will be very helpful to me and if it is not causing too much inconvenience at home I think she will stay until the end of the San Francisco visit, starting from there Friday or Saturday night and arriving in Topeka Monday or Tuesday morning.

Sincerely,

To Edythe Tate Thompson,[10] Los Angeles, April 5, 1937

My dear Edythe:

Well, that was a charming pair of breakfasts we had with you there in San Francisco and about the high spot of our entire trip. . . .

10 Born in Concordia, Kansas, Thompson was named chief of the California Tubercu-

Anyway, we got back [to Topeka] and, in the meantime, our friends and scouts had thoroughly investigated Samarkand [a Santa Barbara hotel]. I am afraid our dream is busted up. In the first place, there is more wrong with the hotel, we suspect, than appeared on the surface. I mean there are a good many architectural and other errors which would make it far less of a bargain at $75,000 than I had supposed. In fact, the most reliable estimate we could get would bring the value down to just about $75,000 or $100,000, assuming that the land values in Santa Barbara continue to rise, which I understand they are doing very slowly. We also learned that the beaches in Santa Barbara have been spoiled recently by the Los Angeles breakwaters or something of the kind, so that swimming isn't what it used to be there. I can't go on and list a lot of faults to find with it, because I still think it is one of the most beautiful places I ever saw in my life and one of the most attractive little hotels I was ever in in my life. The real thing isn't so much the matter with the hotel as the matter with us. We think that with a house full of patients here, running over in fact, our reputation pretty well established as being Middle-Westerners, with our contacts pretty well made, and our knowledge of the laws and customs here in the Middle-West much better than the laws and customs of California, etc., etc., and most of all because of the enormous difficulty entailed in busting up an institution of 150 to 200 employees, fourteen or fifteen doctors, and several hundred thousand dollars worth of investments, and starting on a new venture when we're doing fairly well right here (the new venture might do well and might not) the whole thing is too appalling. We have decided that it is all right to have pleasant dreams about moving to California, the South Sea Islands, or somewhere else, but that in the meantime we had better settle down and tend to our knitting. . . .

Anyway, it was nice to see you, and I may be all wet about not moving out to your lovely state, which I do really like in many places very much, but I think maybe we had better stay here where we know the county attorney and could get bailed out of jail, if necessary.

Sincerely yours,

FROM GREGORY ZILBOORG, NEW YORK, APRIL 6, 1937

My dear Karl:

Time and again during my visits to Chicago I have been hoping to see you come in the way you had appeared the first time, and I expected to have a talk with you and thrash out fully the essential points of differences in our points of view on suicide. It is a matter of great regret to me, my dear Karl, that in a matter so purely scientific you always seem (in relation to me at

losis Bureau, State Board of Health in 1915. She was instrumental in the passage of tuberculosis legislation in California.

least) rather subjective and rather disturbed. I disagree with you on some not very major points. I agree with you on many essentials, but our respective approaches are fundamentally different: Yours is metapsychological and dynamic, mine is ethnological and historical. As a result our ways of telling our respective stories must be couched in different terms, and colored by the vastly different materials we are dealing with. Our points of departure being always the same, i.e. clinical material, you are looking for a psychoeconomic formula of a given suicidal (overt or disguised) reaction, while I am looking for the psychological embryology as it were and I temporarily refrain (or I think I do) from making any final formulation as to the psychological economics of the given individual case. Hence, I am working on the foundation, the cellar floor, etc., while you take these things as they are and you study the windows, the roof, the heating system, etc. No wonder I talk about cement and gravel and sand while you are talking about vents, sashes, risers, etc. There is no misunderstanding between us and least of all is there any disrespect, or as you suspect—deliberate misunderstandings.

You are right, I have a great deal of affection for you and you for me; among us psychoanalysts there are truly few who are still restless enough, adventurous enough to seek for new things, to plunge into uncharted waters and to risk thinking and formulating our thoughts even if we are going to be wrong. There is an old saying that only dead men and idiots are never wrong because they never do anything. You and I happen to be among those who will always have a number of mistakes to our great credit because we are both alive and still have some brains. Why then, my dear brother, consider my mistakes as an attack on you and my misunderstanding as a dislike of you? Why not view the whole thing as an honest groping for something neither of us know yet instead of an aggressive thwarting of one another's trends? I for one am very distressed when I hear from you by word of mouth or by letter that you are angry, offended or what not. As I told you on many occasions I am deeply interested in your work, I don't always understand it fully and at times don't agree with everything you say. Your attitude toward my work is exactly the same. This is how it should be and it will be a pleasure to see you in Pittsburgh, have a good talk while fully sober and a good time with or without a few drinks. The rest really doesn't matter.

We shall continue to be intellectual, scientific adventurers, roamers who know how to remain sedate when we get hold of true facts and how to become happily nomadic when we look for facts in the desert of clinical darkness. It is this that I admire in you and I don't care whether I agree with you or not, I don't even care whether you and I ever are of the same mind as to suicide. And because I don't care I find it possible always to consider myself your friend.

As always,

To Franz Alexander, Chicago, April 15, 1937

Dear Alex:

It may flatter the members of the Chicago Psychoanalytic Society to learn that the Atchison, Topeka, and Santa Fe Railroad, learning of their visit to Topeka, arranged for a special Pullman to be added to your train going back to Chicago last Saturday night and that is one reason why you found it possible to get so many reservations with such ease. They placed this special Pullman out for your convenience without telling us they were doing it, and we learned about it accidentally later.

I am supposed to review Horney's book [*The Neurotic Personality of Our Time*] for the *Nation* and for the *Survey* and I want to do a good job of it. I have only read the first three or four chapters, and I am amazed at the way she is willing to betray her own ambivalence by first praising Freud and then telling what is wrong with him. There are a couple of technical points that I have encountered so far that I want to straighten out. I wish you would help me.

On page 77 she says, "A third point in which I find myself at variance with Freud is his assumption that anxiety is generated only in childhood." If I am not mistaken, Freud said that the pattern of anxiety is formed in childhood but tried to make it clear that anxiety is generated by situations in adult life which threaten to recreate anxiety-producing situations similar to the original one. In other words, this is a straw man of a very patent nature. Am I correct?

On page 63 she puts in italics the statement that hostile impulses form the main source of anxiety and goes on to say, "I am afraid lest this *new* statement should sound . . ."

Is this something new? Isn't this something which has been an accepted part of psychoanalytic theory for a long time? Was this something that you first pointed out, or did Freud, or just what is the history of it? I should like to be accurate in referring to the matter.

I may find some further points as I go along and I will let you know. Thus far I am amazed at the naïveté of the book.

Sincerely yours,

From Franz Alexander, Chicago, April 24, 1937

Dear Karl:

I have just returned from a short vacation connected with a trip to Washington, and I am hastening to answer your letter concerning Dr. Horney's book.

First, regarding your definite questions: (1) What you say in the third paragraph of your letter regarding Horney's misstatement of Freud's position regarding anxiety as generated in childhood is fully correct. Freud never made such a statement, and what you write in this paragraph is the right interpretation of Freud's concept. (2) What you mention in the next paragraph about Horney's "new" statement that "hostile impulses form the main source of anxiety" is really quite a serious matter. One cannot call this anything but arrogance combined with either ignorance or with intellectual dishonesty. Freud, in his book *Inhibition, Symptom and Anxiety* [1926], makes distinction between real fear as a reaction to external danger and neurotic fear originating from *repressed destructive tendencies*. This is the central idea of the whole book. But even earlier in his *Civilization and Its Discontents* [1930] Freud already explains the origin of the sense of guilt from repressed hostile impulses. He uses the sense of guilt pretty much as an equivalent for neurotic fear (fear of conscience), which, according to him, develops exclusively from hostile and aggressive tendencies. Of course, the statement as Horney puts it that aggressive impulses are the main source of anxiety is only true for anxiety which comes from internal sources and not for anxiety which is in reaction to real danger. However, it might be true that a dangerous situation evokes first hostile aggressions and then fear, but nobody has proved this as yet. Regarding my own contribution to the clarification of the source of neurotic anxiety, already in *The Psychoanalysis of the Total Personality* [1930] on page 74 I describe the development of fear of conscience as a reaction to hostile aggressive feelings. The essence of this description is that fear of conscience is essentially retaliation—fear of one's own hostile aggressions. On page 148 again I describe fear of conscience as deriving from hate. Even in the index on page 171 you will find: "Anxiety—its origin from hate." Of course, in those days these were quite new statements; today they are commonplace and generally accepted. I do not know any author of consequence who has any doubt about the intimate relationship between anxiety and hate.

I also call your attention to Jones's writings on this subject, especially his article "Fear, Guilt and Hate," *Inter. Journal of Psychoanalysis*, 1929, in which he explicitly derives anxiety from hate and hostility. I cannot imagine that Horney does not know all this. If she claims this insight as discovered by her, I simply cannot explain it otherwise than dishonesty or such an extreme conceitedness and arrogance which blinded her judgment entirely.

I am sorry to say that I was unable to force myself to read the whole book. From what I have read its tone is so repulsive and arrogant and it contains so many platitudes that I am not eager at all to waste much time on it. The sad part of it is that what she considers her most original discoveries are all taken from others. The importance of the conflict: Ambition versus [the] love-seeking attitude she learned from me here in the Institute from the study of peptic ulcer and criminal cases, in which, as you know, I describe the vicious circle—how ambition and striving for independence increase the wish for dependence and love, which latter attitude drives the individual to enforced competitiveness. She snaps up these things and then brings them out as her original contributions. This alone is bad enough but would not be so bad if at the same time she would not bite those from whom she learned and took all these things. The whole thing seems to be pretty pitiful, but of course Horney is smart and an able clinician, and so perhaps the book also contains some valuable things.

Anybody who reviews this book should not let all her misstatements go unmentioned and let her get away with the arrogant attitude by which this smart but rather shallow woman impudently takes credit for deep and creative insights of Freud. If I want to convert my distaste to an aesthetic reaction, I visualize a small female dog (b . . . .) yapping in impotent rage at a giant. I think that finally someone should put her in her place.

Cordially yours,

To World Peaceways,[11] New York, April 26, 1937

Gentlemen:

I appreciate very much your sending me the various bulletins and releases in regard to the work of your organization.

You ask my opinion and I can only repeat that I am very much in sympathy with your purposes and ideals. I might add that from a scientific standpoint I do not agree with the article by Miss Mary West on "Substitutes for Death Toys and Games." From our point of view, we think it would probably be better for children to act these things out in play when they are children than to carry this play into adult life in the form of war. To put it another way, the aggressiveness of children must have some kind of release; it is unreleased aggressiveness, in my opinion, which later leads to provocativeness and even the aggressiveness of war. I have spent about five hundred pages in a forthcoming book discussing this, so I won't labor the point now, but I think Miss West's assumption that because children play war games they will want to play real war games when they grow up is not entirely justified from the psychological standpoint. It may do some good, however, in calling the attention of the public to the way in which we pretend to be against war, but keep on tolerating it in these various small ways about us.

Sincerely yours,

11 In a letter of March 31, 1937, KAM had complimented World Peaceways, an antiwar organization located in New York City, for an advertisement depicting a family—a father, mother, two sons, daughter, and dog—all wearing gas masks. The copy under the picture concluded with the claim that war could be stopped if enough people supported a peace movement.

To Smith Ely Jelliffe, New York, May 17, 1937

My dear Smith Ely:

It was very kind of you to write us immediately upon the appearance of the May *Bulletin;* in fact, I got your letter before I had seen the *Bulletin* myself. I was delighted to think that it pleased you. We worked hard on it and feel rather proud of it, and if it seems good to you, I am sure it will seem good to others, because I know you look at it critically, even though tempered by your kind indulgence toward us.

I shall, as you suggest, ask Miss Lyle, our editorial secretary, to prepare a notice of it and send it to you for the *Journal.*

I did not go to the Pittsburgh meeting, and I was not surprised to hear from the boys that you did not go either. The chief reason I would have gone would have been to discuss the paper which you so kindly asked me to take part in since I was the only non-New Yorker to do so, and I wanted to put a western flavor into it, but I couldn't go. Will, Father, and two of the other men went, and they said it was an interesting meeting although no particularly epochal contributions were made. Apparently the insulin shock business is going the way of all sudden enthusiasms, based on unsound psychological premises. I was opposed to it from the start.

In regard to Doctor [William Alanson] White's death, my first impulse was to write you because I knew that more than anyone else in the world you would miss him. You who had worked so long with him and who had done so much to give him ideas which he was able to popularize, and to talk over with him ideas and plans which the two of you worked out together—I knew what a great blow it was to you and I thought at once that I should write you. Then I postponed it, partly through those reasons of hesitation and procrastination which do not submit very well to scrutiny, and partly through some feelings that I did not know exactly what to say. There really isn't anything one can say at such a moment, except that I loved him, too, and I know that his loss saddens you more than the rest of us can know.

Doctor White was very kind to me and helped me several times, but I always knew, Doctor Jelliffe, that it was really because of you. I am sure that it was you who commended me to him, and while I do not mean to say that he was not capable of forming opinions of his own, I'm sure it was your friendliness for me that was communicated to him which he expressed in numerous very kind ways. You know he gave a grant once of $2,500 from some woman who wanted to bestow it on someone for some research, and he appointed me chairman of a committee in the American Psychiatric Association, from which they "bumped" me later, but through no fault of his. Once, too, he wrote me in regard to accompanying a patient to Europe, and although this did not pan out I was grateful for his thoughtfulness. I never got to talk with him as long as I should have liked, but I have some faint realization of the great debt that American psychiatry owes him and which it pains me to see some painfully and foolishly ascribing to Adolf Meyer.

Finally, in regard to the organ suicide[12] which I know is a concept you have recently used and for which I gave you full credit in the book from which this little article is only a small excerpt: I think you can get no feeling that I have forgotten that you, more than any other American, have promoted this idea. In fact, I have a little surprise for you which I was going to keep until my book appeared, but perhaps it will give you a little pleasure to think about it before it happens.

I am dedicating the book to Freud, to Southard, and to you.

Sincerely yours,

To FRANZ ALEXANDER, CHICAGO, JUNE 1, 1937

Dear Alex:

We've got a pretty serious problem with these two Germans, Grotjahn and Kamm. As you know, there is a gathering feeling against the foreign physicians, especially the German physicians, in this country. I don't know just what stimulates this, although I have some ideas about it which I will discuss with you over the bar some day, but just now there are some practical questions.

Doctor Knight went to Berlin and saw these men and invited them personally to come to this country. They were not refugees and were not obliged to leave. They came to Topeka and made their application for citizenship promptly. Then they made application to the secretary of the State Board of Registration for examination and licensure for the practice of medicine in Kansas. To our astonishment, they were declined. The Board wouldn't even give them the examination. Reason: They are not American citizens.

There is no use filling several pages in telling you all the things we did to try to get around this. It was pointed out to the Board that they had made application for American citizenship and would have to wait five years before they would be full citizens. We emphasized that if they were not allowed to practice it would work an injustice upon them and upon us and upon their families, etc. We made the point that they were not in competition with anyone. We pointed out all sorts of things to them. But the Board remains adamant.

For the present, we are going to let the matter drop and hope that the Board will not see fit to bring action against us, but we are under the impression that we are not violating the law if we permit these men to do psycho-

12 Organ suicide is a form of what Menninger in *Man Against Himself* calls *focal suicide,* in which man's self-destructive energies cause disease in an organ of the body.

analysis and make examinations under our supervision here at the hospital. Very likely no questions will be raised about the matter, but, of course, if a question were raised and the Board was successful in showing that these men were practicing medicine in contravention of the law they could make them stop practicing and cause considerable trouble besides.

Probably the worst they could do would be to make them go elsewhere to earn their living, but at the present time they are not licensed in any other state, so we thought it wise for their own protection to urge them to obtain licensure in some other state which did not have this ruling against foreigners. Missouri being close they immediately made application there, which to our knowledge has recently been admitting foreign physicians, providing they successfully pass the examination. To our dismay, we got a letter saying that they declined these applicants because they could not ascertain whether or not the university medical schools from which they graduated fulfilled the standards required by the state of Missouri. Of course, this is simply an evasion; they don't want German doctors either, and instead of passing a ruling against them or against any foreigners they refuse to examine them on this flimsy basis.

Well, anyway, our German doctors still remain unlicensed and, naturally, they feel a little insecure. Consequently, we are going to get them licensed somewhere so if they were not permitted to practice in Kansas or if they became dissatisfied in our clinic they would not be at the mercy of charity. My impression is that more and more stringency will be exercised against Germans in the next few years, and I feel that it is very important that these men get themselves licensed immediately somewhere.

I am writing you for several reasons: In the first place, you will undoubtedly be sympathetic with their problem; in the second place, you have probably had some experience with some of your physicians there at the Institute. You will know exactly what the possibilities are for these men to be licensed in Illinois. It would be very helpful to them and indirectly to me and the rest of us here if you will give us the facts about the situation fully. What did you do in regard to Doctor Benedek,[13] for example?

Our idea is that if the state of Illinois is granting licenses to foreign-trained physicians, Kamm and Grotjahn will make [application] for licensure in Illinois immediately and take the examination as soon as they will give it to them. . . .

It further occurred to us it might save a good deal of trouble if you would permit them to give 43 East Ohio Street [the address of the Institute] as their address. They can also give Topeka as their temporary address, but I think

13 Therese Benedek, a Hungarian medical analyst, initially trained in pediatrics. She was analyzed by Ferenczi and became a member of the Berlin Psychoanalytic Institute. In 1936 Alexander invited her to the Chicago Institute and she emigrated to the United States.

it will look a little peculiar to the Illinois examiners to have an application from Topeka, Kansas, while, on the other hand, it would be perfectly understandable to them that they should be registered at 43 East Ohio Street, Chicago. However, if this would embarrass the Institute in any way, we would naturally not want you to do it. I don't see how it could, however, and I am sure you are anxious to help these fellows as much as I am. Let me make it clear again, that for Kamm and Grotjahn to be licensed in Illinois is no assistance to the Menninger Clinic whatsoever, but we do feel that in justice to these men we should help them get licensed somewhere so that in case the clouds get darker and things get bad here they will not be utterly without a place to go and practice medicine legally.

I hope to be in Chicago for the next meeting of the Society on Saturday.

Sincerely yours,

To Mrs. John Boettiger,[14] Seattle, August 11, 1937

My dear Mrs. Boettiger:

I am taking the liberty of writing you because of having met you in the home of Mrs. Burt Cochran[15] in March.

I want you to use your good offices for me with your mother [Eleanor Roosevelt]. I think I told you when we were in Seattle that I am a great admirer of your father and I should have added then, as I will now, that I am also a great admirer of your mother. I admire her catholicity of interests and her highly developed humanitarianism. It is because I have need of her influence to support some projects that will appeal to these qualities in her that I am writing you.

All over the United States there is a great interest in physically crippled children. This has been enormously supported, very deservedly, by the interest your father has taken in it. But all over the United States there is another type of crippled child who receives very little attention, although he is in even greater need of it than the physically crippled child. I refer to the mentally crippled child. I am not talking now about feeble-minded children but about children whose minds are normal or even superior to the average but upon whom the blows of fate have fallen too hard or too rapidly and who either because of misfortune in the family, or because of the stupidity, cruelty, or inadvertence of their parents develop psychological traits which make them unhappy, unadjusted, incapable of learning or living in a normal way. These children are unhappy at home, misfits in school, and subse-

14 Anna Eleanor Roosevelt Boettiger was the daughter of Franklin and Eleanor Roosevelt.

15 Burt Cochran and Jessie-Lee Wyatt (Mrs. Cochran) were prominent Seattle socialites. In 1937 he managed the Seattle office of the advertising firm of H. K. McCann Co. (now McCann-Erickson).

quently add to the list of neurotic and psychotic individuals or to our criminal population.

These children form a part of the professional interest of every psychiatrist, especially of his charity practice. As a general thing the maladjusted child of well-to-do parents is sent to exclusive private schools where he is tolerated (not treated) because the school needs the money and support of the parents, regardless of the fact that such a school is not the best place for such a child. If it becomes impossible for the child to remain there, he is sent on a trip to Europe or to a foster home, or to a ranch, etc. But middle-class people and poor people, finding that their child is unhappy and incapable of public-school adjustment, really do not know what to do, and their children are more apt to end up in a reformatory or eke out a miserable and hectic existence until they are old enough to run away from home or get themselves into some other kind of difficulty.

Perhaps I have put too much emphasis upon misbehavior; I am not so much interested in the delinquent child as I am in the unhappy child. It is for these that we founded the Southard School twelve years ago. I felt very strongly that such children as these were neglected and that for every thousand dollars spent on the physically crippled child there is less than one hundred spent on the emotionally handicapped child. Whether this is because their problem is unrecognized or whether parents feel so guilty and ashamed on behalf of such children that they refuse to admit the problem exists I am not sure, but, at any rate, there are very few schools like ours in the world, and ours is a very small, unpretentious one. We have conducted it as a private enterprise until recently, in spite of the fact that the deficit ran around $5,000 annually and members of my family made it up privately. The school, however, was restricted in size, and upon advice of some friends in New York and locally, we converted it into a nonprofit institution. I am enclosing a press clipping telling more of this move.

What I want to ask your mother to do is to become a member of the board of directors. I know she receives many requests to serve on this and that board, probably far more than she can investigate. We don't want her merely to lend her name to what we think is a very worthy scientific piece of work; we want the benefit of her advice. We want her to visit us and see for herself what the school is doing.

Last fall we had a conference to which no one but scientific people—psychologists, social workers, child psychiatrists, and educators—were invited. We had an all-day session with lectures and demonstrations by some of our own people at the Southard School and a few invited speakers. We wish to have another one this year with not more than one hundred guests, and we would like to have Mrs. Roosevelt head the list of speakers. Since the group is so small (necessarily so, as we do not have room to accommodate many) it can be very carefully selected. Last year we had several from New York, more from Chicago, and still more from the Middle West. I am sending you under separate cover a *Bulletin* which contains some of the material presented and describes the research we have started. We want to further this by annual postgraduate sessions and conferences to which those who are interested in the training and treatment of these children may come to discuss common problems and to learn the most recent discoveries in child psychiatry. We can have this meeting almost any time this fall that would suit your mother's convenience.

I wish you could get this message to your mother in some way. We'd like very much to have her here, and I think it would be the support of a very greatly neglected matter in which she may be more interested than I know. I'll appreciate anything you can do for me in getting this to her attention.

Please give my regards to your good husband, who I imagine is very busy with the many problems involved in the rapid economic changes taking place not only in Seattle but everywhere.

Sincerely yours,

To Albert Deutsch,[16] New York, October 26, 1937

My dear Mr. Deutsch:

I was very glad to have your courteous letter of October 13 in which you speak kindly of my review and ask certain pertinent questions. . . .

I am also glad to know that you feel inclined to give Lowrey and his associates more credit in the next edition.[17] I think the Child Guidance Clinics have been a very important movement in this country and that Lowrey's work as a pioneer is very significant. However, as I indicated in the review, I think the most serious omission in your otherwise excellent book is the omission of a full discussion of the influence of Ernest Southard. You refer to him in three places, it is true, but you refer to another American psychiatrist in nine places, a psychiatrist whose disciples have until recently been far less active in American psychiatry than Southard's. Southard had a prodigious influence. Frankwood Williams, Lowrey, [Samuel] Orton, [Abraham] Myerson, [Myrtelle] Canavan, and many others were inspired by his indescribably stimulating personality and intellect. A book on his life is soon to be published, written by Professor Frederick P. Gay of Columbia University, and I earnestly counsel you to look this book over carefully before you complete the revisions for your second edition.

I should like to answer the final paragraph of your letter in which you

16 Author and journalist. Menninger reviewed Deutsch's *The Mentally Ill in America* in *The Nation* 145 (August 28, 1937): 225.

17 In his review of Deutsch's book Menninger wrote, "The work of the legal committee of the APA is quoted without credit or reference, and the work of Lawson Lowrey and David Levy in developing child guidance clinics is not mentioned."

explained your emphasis on state hospitals by the fact that only 2.4 percent of mental patients in this country are in private hospitals. I see your point but I do not quite understand how it answers my objection. It might be shown, for example, that only two percent of the cancer patients of the United States are in cancer hospitals. This would not justify one in ignoring cancer hospitals as a place for research in the diagnosis and treatment of cancer, and, granted that this illustration is not exactly parallel, let me come back to my original contention: Most psychiatric research in the United States was originally done in private psychiatric hospitals and I think this is still the case. The work of Earl Bond and his associates, of Ross Chapman and his, . . . Bullard of Rockville, of Sleyster,[18] etc. is certainly worth mentioning. I challenge you to show me any state hospital in the United States that has done more research into scientific aspects of the care of the mentally ill in America than that indicated by the articles which I am enclosing. In addition to these, I have contributed some investigations myself, but I am leaving these out of consideration. My brother's work in the analysis and direction of the care of the individual patient is not mentioned in your book, but this is understandable if the latter part of the book is frankly only a description of state hospital care. The state hospitals follow, they do not lead in these things; in the first part of your book you point out leaders and present them, and in the latter part of your book you discuss the followers.

I have written you as objectively and scientifically as possible. I cannot deny that I have some subjectivism in the mention of private psychiatric hospitals. I am not one of those who opposes some great social change. I am a New Dealer and I believe that Communism is dangerous partly because it has so many attractive features. But state hospitals are not socialistic and they are not democratic. They are a compromise and an insincere form of state medicine. I say insincere because they are not conducted on a sound financial basis, they compete with private hospitals, and they do not define their purpose clearly as being custodial, therapeutic, or prophylactic, or all three. They do not seriously compete with a hospital like ours, but they do compete with the smaller, middle-class private hospitals in a way which I think is not necessary or desirable. By "compete" I do not mean financial competition, or not that alone. I mean that they represent and promote mass treatment as opposed to individualized treatment in which I think our best hopes lie. This is off the subject. The point is that there is some psychiatry outside of state hospitals and I think your otherwise excellent, almost encyclopedic book should take cognizance of this fact. I think it is a "swell"

18 Earl Bond was a psychiatrist at the psychiatric hospital of the University of Providence; Ross Chapman was a psychoanalyst at Sheppard and Enoch Pratt Hospital, Towson, Maryland; Dexter M. Bullard, a psychoanalyst, was medical superintendent at Chestnut Lodge, Rockville, Maryland; Rock Sleyster, director of the Milwaukee Sanitarium in Wauwatosa, Illinois, was president of the AMA in 1937.

book; in addition to the review copies, of which we received several, we have bought three or four copies, and we require our residents and postgraduate student nurses to read it. I feel very honored that you should have consulted me in regard to some revisions. I hope some of the things I have said will prove useful.

Sincerely yours,

To H. Flanders Dunbar and Theodore Wolfe,[19]
New York, November 10, 1937

My dear Friends:

I remember as the highlight of my visit to New York the pleasant cocktail hour at your home on Wednesday. I have communicated to my brother and others the good news that you are likely to come a little ahead of the special train to San Francisco and spend a day with us. This will give us the utmost pleasure and we are making our plans now. They were delighted to hear of it. . . .

It was thoughtful and courteous of you to come to the evening meeting at the [New York] Academy [of Medicine] which I notice most of my analytic friends skipped. I can't blame them, but I certainly do appreciate your coming.

Be sure to see Henry Murray's excellent article in the current number of the *Journal of Abnormal and Social Psychology.*[20]

I have talked with our librarian about books for Doctor Wolfe. The one I had in mind is: Thoinot, L.: *Medico-Legal Aspects of Moral Offenses.* Translated and enlarged by Arthur W. Waysse, Philadelphia: F. A. Davis Company, 1921. In addition to this, I would suggest Stekel's various books on the subject, about which I am sure you already know. Also, there are, of course Kraft-Ebing, Havelock Ellis, etc. I am trying to recall whether you asked me about interpretative books or merely descriptive ones. Stekel attempts some interpretation, as you know, as does also Kempf in his *Psychopathology.*

A set of books which I think would interest you very much indeed because they appear to be honest attempts at description of the variations in the so-called *normal sex life* of people are the books by one W. F. Robie, an inconspicuous zealot who lived in a small town in Massachusetts and published his books himself. They are somewhat hard to obtain but they are extremely frank and quite illuminating. I would particularly recommend the

19 Dunbar and her husband, Theodore Wolfe, were New York physicians. She helped establish the American Psychosomatic Society, edited its journal (*Psychosomatic Medicine*), and wrote the standard text on psychosomatic disease, *Emotions and Bodily Changes* (1935).

20 Henry A. Murray, "Visceral Manifestations of Personality," *Journal of Abnormal and Social Psychology* 32 (1937): 161–84.

one called *The Art of Love,* although there are several, one of which is called *Sex and Life* and another *Rational Sex Ethics.*

Don't forget Hamilton's *Research Into Marriage.* Hamilton is a wild analyst now practicing in California. I believe he is the one who analyzed (?) Eugene O'Neill.[21] Don't fail to see Alexander's chapter on perversions on page 138 in *The Criminal, the Judge, and the Public.*

I feel that you have a very valuable opportunity to clear up the idea, which is widespread among psychiatrists as well as among laymen, that any non-genital sexual pleasure is a perversion. In spite of the fact that I repeatedly mention in our staff discussions that any preliminary activities terminating in normal copulation should be regarded as normal, we still have occasional evidences (as must be expected from nonanalyzed residents) that some forepleasure techniques are confused with perversions. Also, I think a psychoanalytic text should make clear distinctions between perverse objects and perverse methods.

My own feeling is that perversions in the sense of aberrant techniques or objects pursued for their own sakes and as an end rather than as a means to an end represent frantic attempts to eroticize over-great hostility incurred at a pregenital level. It is my impression that those who adopt perversions, whether happily or under protest, are always self-destructive. Hence, I think Freud's original remark about a perversion being the opposite of a neurosis should be revised in the light of his later theories. Perversions are *similar* to neuroses to the extent that they are self-destructive reaction formations to hostility; they are the opposite of neuroses only in respect to the form of expression, and even here I do not think opposite is the best word.

What is the difference between one who is in love with his own rectum (as in constipation, enemas, etc.) or in love with the rectum of someone else; or what is the difference between a preoccupation with one's own eyes, let us say, and a fetishistic interest in the eyes or nose or big toe of someone else? In the former the consciousness of sexual interest is represented and in the latter instances it is unconscious, but in both cases there is a focus of hostility sharply neutralized by eroticism. Whether the eroticism is conscious or not is important socially because of our social attitudes toward sexual consciousness, but this is one of the mechanisms which is partly *socially* determined, whereas the fundamental mechanisms arise, I think, in the special experiences of the individual.

I have been writing all of this extemporaneously and I do not know if I

21 Gilbert V. Hamilton was indeed Eugene O'Neill's analyst. His *Research into Marriage* (1929) was a precursor of the Kinsey report: it analyzed the responses of 100 married women and 100 married men, including Eugene O'Neill and his wife, Agnes Boulton O'Neill, to 300 questions about their sex lives before, during, and after marriage, with each other and with others.

believe all I have said, but I know when one is writing a book, as you are, it is helpful to have a few ideas scattered along the way, even if they are wrong.

Sincerely yours,

To Ives hendrick, Boston, January 10, 1938

Dear Ives:

I was delighted to have your letter of December 31 and have read it several times and have shown it to Miss Lyle, who was also glad to hear from and about you. . . .

It's nice of you to invite me to Boston. I expect to be in New York in February at the time my book *[Man Against Himself]* comes out, and then I'll probably be back in April for the Jelliffe dinner, about which you have probably heard or will soon.

I don't know Harold Jones, of whom you speak, and I know nothing of the work of the Institute of Child Welfare. I do know that in general psychiatry in California is at the very lowest ebb. As you know, there is an analyst in San Francisco by the name of [Bernhard] Berliner, who I understand is not getting along very rapidly, and there is also our old friend Bernfeld,[1] who is very able but a lay analyst. I didn't know of your special interest in children, but it sounds as if this would be a wonderful opportunity for you to find out about things at least and if you were especially interested in children it might prove to be extremely interesting. I am sorry to hear that you feel the opportunities in Boston are not what you had hoped. I agree with you, however, that private practice is a little discouraging and lonely. I wouldn't want to practice by myself now that I have had the experience and joy of practicing in a group. Every one of us in this group could make a good deal more money individually than we make in this way, because a good deal of our present income goes into group activities of various kinds, which individually we would not attempt to support. I think I could go to a number of cities and treble my present income, but I wouldn't think of doing it. I wish very much that I had some kind of a university connection, but that has never been forthcoming and probably never will be and I'm pretty happy here, and I wouldn't give up the association for anything.

1 Siegfried Bernfeld, a socialist and a Zionist, was a friend of Martin Buber. He received his Ph.D. degree from the University of Vienna and became a member of the Berlin Psychoanalytic Institute and underwent a training analysis with Hanns Sachs. He was especially interested in mental disturbances in children and wrote two classic studies, *Sisyphus, or the Boundaries of Education* (1925) and *The Psychology of the Infant* (1929). He was one of a number of analysts who attempted to reconcile psychoanalysis and Marxism. In 1937 he left Europe and, at the urging of Simmel, Fenichel, and Frances Deri, settled in San Francisco.

To go back to San Francisco, the leading psychiatric spirit, if there is any, is a man named Johnson,[2] who is one of the victims of [Franklin] Ebaugh and who was in turn one of the victims of Adolf Meyer. I say victims because I feel that the Johns Hopkins training had a tendency to confuse people in regard to psychiatry and to put emphasis upon superficial descriptive things rather than upon dynamic things. Johnson is a nice fellow personally, and I think he considers me his friend, as I do him mine, but I am afraid he is not very stimulating to the students. . . .

It would give us all a great deal of pleasure to have you visit the Menninger Clinic, and we are going to begin looking forward to it. Harry Stack Sullivan was out here a couple of weeks ago, and if he can be believed, he had the shock of his life. He said it looked as if we had an institution with a three-million-dollar endowment instead of an institution with none at all, and he said a great many nice things about us which did our hearts a lot of good, and I hope it stimulated us a little into trying to be better than we really are.

Finally, let me congratulate you and Marie both on the prospect of a third child, whose birth may have occurred before you receive this letter. I hope things go well for Marie and that her happiness outweighs her pain by far.

Sincerely yours,

FROM ABRAHAM MYERSON, BOSTON, JANUARY 21, 1938

Dear Dr. Menninger:

I am making a survey of the reactions of the men in the field of psychiatry to psychoanalysis, and I am anxious to have your classification of yourself in this report. For my own convenience I have divided the reactions into four groups:

1. Those individuals who completely accept psychoanalysis. The term "completely" need not to be taken too literally. One may substitute "wholeheartedly" or "in general."
2. Those who feel very favorably inclined towards it but do not wholly accept it and are, to a certain extent, skeptical.
3. Those who, in the main, tend to reject its tenets but feel that Freud has contributed indirectly to the human understanding.
4. Those who feel that his work, on the whole, has hindered the progress of the understanding of the mental diseases and the neuroses and reject him entirely.

If you feel that this classification does not meet your needs or sense of fitness, please feel free to state your own reaction and your classification of yourself in your own way.

2 George S. Johnson was a psychoanalyst at Stanford University Hospital.

Thank you very much for your cooperation.

Sincerely yours,

To Smith Ely Jelliffe, New York January 27, 1938

Dear Smith Ely:

Some time ago I asked my publisher, Mr. Alfred A. Knopf, to send you a copy of the new edition of my book, *The Human Mind*. I hope you have had a few minutes in which to glance through it because I should like very much to have your impressions with regard to its present form and content.

I made a serious effort in the revisions not only to represent modern psychiatric opinion fairly but to present it in such a way as to appeal to medical men. The history of the book is rather peculiar in this respect: I wrote it originally to appear as an unpretentious manual of information for some of my general practitioner friends who had become more or less interested in my work and had referred me a few patients and to whom I wished to return these patients with some suggestions as to subsequent treatment. I wrote it with these doctors in mind but it was turned down by a medical publishing company or two who did not think doctors would be interested. Then the Literary Guild and Mr. Alfred Knopf got hold of it and sold one hundred and sixty thousand copies, showing that the laity was interested in the subject whether the doctors were or not.

I think the doctors *are* interested in psychiatry and I think the medical publishing companies just guessed wrong. But the fact remains that it was *and still is* intended for doctors; if the laymen can get something out of it also, I am glad, of course. As a matter of fact, a number of psychiatrists, neurologists, and even general practitioners have written me that they prescribe the book frequently and think they have very good results in some cases from this particular bibliotherapy. I get a lot of letters from people saying that it has helped them this way or that but fan mail of that type is less reliable I think than the more objective opinions of other physicians who have tried the experiment.

There are many things in it which still do not suit me; I do not believe much in typology, for example, but I retained the personality types because they are conventionally used and serve as convenient pillars about which to group some descriptions and discussions. There are other things that I would like to improve but I think we cannot rewrite psychiatry too rapidly and I have tried to keep it in contact with prevalent psychiatric opinion at the same time introducing modern viewpoints and ideas wherever possible. To do this and still make it interesting enough and readable enough for the medical man to lay down his book on surgery or obstetrics and read a little in our field was one of my chief objectives.

If you have had a chance to look at it, I wish you would tell me what you think about it or tell my publisher, Mr. Knopf, and send me a copy of the letter, because I really want to know. Mr Knopf might become enthusiastic and quote something you say, if you don't mind, but if you want to say something not to be quoted, just indicate that fact. Personally, I sometimes have day dreams about the book being accepted as a text in psychiatry in more medical schools because I think it would interest the medical students in a way which more formal treatises do not; but perhaps this is too much to hope. Meanwhile both doctors and others keep buying it a little here and there, and I hope they will keep on.

Sincerely yours,

To Harley Williams,[3] London, January 27, 1938

My dear Doctor Williams:

It is evening; I have returned to my office to do a little work because I have been swamped recently with a sudden burst of new patients after a long period of less than the proper number. In addition, I have a few extra things on hand, such as a contribution to a rather silly and futile book called *A Symposium on American Civilization, 1938.* I am supposed to write the chapter on "Psychiatry" and I feel it a hopeless task to say anything proper about anything so fundamental. On the other hand, I think it is a correct gesture for them to want to include psychiatry for the first time in the history of the world, and so I am going to try to say something, but I declare I don't know what. . . .

Please let me know if and when my book *Man Against Himself* appears in England. It has not yet appeared in this country, nor will it for about a month yet. I would like to have you have a copy also of the revised edition of my book *The Human Mind.* I think the revision has considerably improved it; I tried to make it a little less popular style and more likely to appeal to medical men. It had a huge sale, something over one hundred and sixty-five thousand, I believe, and so a good many Americans think of psychiatry in terms of my book, which pleases me in one way and terrifies me in another. I had planned to dispatch a copy of the book to you but find that the express charges to England are more than the book itself costs, so I guess you'll have to get a copy over there. . . .

The feeling against Japan is pretty strong in this country, but not strong enough I am afraid to compel the government to get together with England and France and Russia and say to these gangster nations, "We disapprove of this and we mean what we say." I am an extreme pacificist, but I do believe that an economic boycott would have more advantages than disad-

3 Williams was a British physician, writer, and barrister. His books include *A Century of Public Health* (1929), *Doctors Differ* (1946), and *The Conquest of Fear* (1952).

vantages. England and the United States have both had their cotton manufacturing taken away from them by Japan, and the people in the south of this country who are getting a little satisfaction out of the fact that Japan is buying their cotton at a high price just now will feel pretty sad two years from now when Japan is raising all its cotton in China. I can't settle those things, however; I have enough trouble trying to keep our own clinic heading in the right direction, and the patients well taken care of, etc., etc. I expect we doctors ought to take more interest in international affairs than we do, however.

This brings me to the fact that you mention Dr. J. R. Rees.[4] If I am not mistaken, Doctor Rees is interested in an international psychotherapeutic meeting to be held in London this coming summer. I have heard quite a little discussion of this among American psychiatrists. There is a prevalent feeling that this meeting is a masked effort on the part of the German Nazi scientists to get back into the good graces of their international colleagues. At any rate, the fact that Jung is at the head of it is enough to make many of us lose interest, since we cannot have confidence in his scientific opinion or judgment since his celebrated paper in support of the Nazi regime which distinguishes between Aryan and Semitic psychology.

I shall be interested in hearing from you whenever you find time to write.

Sincerely yours,

To Abraham Myerson, Boston, February 4, 1938

Dear Abe:

I have your grandiloquent letter of January 21 beginning with "Dear Dr. Menninger" and ending with "A. Myerson."

If I didn't know you so well and like you so well and respect your honesty so much, I'd be inclined to kick you in the pants for this letter. I don't mean because it is so formal, nor do I mean that for you to make a survey is pretentious or overly ambitious, but I think it is absurd to think that one can classify one's feelings toward a scientific method. Why not make a survey as to how we all feel toward physics or toward chemistry or toward psychiatry? I am sure you would find some doctors who do not "accept" psychiatry. You and I just smile at them, but we would not take seriously their opinion as to its validity or their opinion or vote as to its acceptability. In other words, what in the name of Heaven is your idea of conducting a survey after the

4 John Rawlings Rees was a British psychiatrist. From 1932 to 1946 he was medical director of the Tavistock Clinic in London, and from 1939 to 1955 he was consulting psychiatrist to the British army and a brigadier general. In 1945, he was one of the British psychiatrists who escorted the five-man American psychiatric team on their fact-finding visit to Europe.

fashion of one of these popular opinion estimates that one reads in the newspaper, or a political campaign vote?

Of course I accept the fact that psychoanalysis exists; so do you; so does anyone else who isn't asleep or psychotic. We know that psychoanalytic technique exists; we know that psychoanalytic theory exists; we know that psychoanalysis as a body of knowledge exists. We may not fully understand the knowledge, we may not use the technique, and we may not agree entirely with the theory. But, the word "accept" is a pathetically unfortunate word, and I am the more astonished that it should come from you, Abe, as you are always so careful and clever on such matters.

As I look through the letter again, I wonder whether you mean by skeptical, etc., etc., to indicate some skepticism as to the therapeutic efficiency of psychoanalysis. But I must reject even this as not being worthy of a mind like yours. Is one "skeptical" of surgical therapy? In inoperable carcinoma of the stomach I should say that we would be skeptical of surgery, but in the average case of appendicitis, I think we should not be skeptical. Similarly, I think our present psychoanalytic techniques are more likely to succeed in some cases than in others, and pretty apt to fail in some. I don't know whether you call that skepticism or nihilism, but it certainly isn't a question of political preference.

The last line "reject him entirely" might have been taken out of a revival circular; "do you accept Jesus, or do you reject him entirely?" Abe, my dear fellow, I don't know what you have in mind, but this is pretty bad and I wish you'd get back to the field in which you have done such magnificent and stimulating work, that of heredity. I was proud to refer to you several times in my revised edition of *The Human Mind* and also in my *Man Against Himself*.

Sincerely yours,

From Sigmund Freud,[5] Vienna, February 14, 1938

I welcome your book especially because the death instinct has become rather unpopular among analysts.

Very cordially,

To George S. Kaufman, New York, March 14, 1938

Dear Mr. Kaufman:

I just saw *The Women* last night. I have heard rumors that you had something to do with the script and having seen it I am more convinced than ever

5 Handwritten in German.

that your influence is present.[6] The intelligent references to psychoanalysis, in which I believe you are interested, add to this conviction.

I think it is an extremely clever play. Perhaps I think so because it so excellently illustrates a theory of mine on the self-destructiveness of people. It shows how deftly women destroy themselves as well as one another by their hostilities and by their blindness to the essential aggressiveness that their behavior toward one another represents. These women pretend to be friends with one another but a mixture of hypocrisy, envy, prudishness, greediness, stupidity, and a few other traits ruin their own possibilities for happiness and contribute to the self-destructiveness of their friends as well.

It does occur to me that it might have been possible to have introduced one or two really admirable women into the play because to omit them rather furthers the theory that all women are vicious and are capable only of vicious techniques. This theory seems to be highly approved by the American public, if the popularity of that gynecidal film *Snow White and the Seven Dwarfs* is any indication.

Sincerely yours,

FROM E. V. ALLEN,[7] ROCHESTER, MINNESOTA, MARCH 19, 1938

Dear Karl:

It was very thoughtful of you to send me your book, *Man Against Himself*, and I have been reading it with a great deal of interest. It has provoked a good deal of comment here, all of which is favorable except that those of us who have very little grasp of psychiatric matters cannot quite go all the way with you. I myself have enjoyed it tremendously and have found the presentation of the material very helpful in interpreting various situations. It is not surprising, I suspect, that I, who know a little bit more about psychiatry than the average doctor's wife, also cannot go the entire way with you in some of the interpretations. He who has very little knowledge of music is, of course, greatly handicapped in understanding the presentation of a symphony. However, even he who has little knowledge of the technique of music can enjoy presentations of a symphony. So I have enjoyed the presentation *Man Against Himself*. My feeling that sometimes the interpretations exceed the available information is probably quite characteristic of those who are not steeped in psychiatry. I have a feeling sometimes that coincidences are interpreted as cause and effect. The assumptions seem along the same general lines as if I were to say that the reason why I am wearing a red tie

6 Clare Boothe, wife of Henry Luce (publisher of *Time* magazine) and later ambassador to Italy, wrote *The Women* (1937), but Kaufman, an accomplished playwright, was a frequent visitor at rehearsals, and there were rumors that he helped write or actually wrote several scenes.

7 A Mayo Clinic internist.

with white dots today is because the sun rose. One cannot deny that the sun did rise and that I am wearing a red tie with white dots. Therefore, the rise of the sun possibly influenced me to wear this type of tie. One has a feeling also that if one probed superficially into the subconscious and conscious life of an individual, he might always find some mechanism to explain that which has occurred quite normally. For instance, a surgeon, a friend of mine on the staff here, recently cut his finger in the course of an operation. About two years ago he had prostatic abscess. This man is to all intents and purposes quite normal but I suspect that if a psychiatrist were to have a session with him, he might find things which were interpreted as attempts at self-destruction. If he believed that emotional conflicts caused organic disease, he might even develop the thesis logically that the prostatic abscess was a direct result of emotional conflicts. I may remark parenthetically that I am afraid you will find little agreement with internists or pathologists on this phase of your presentation. Another thing which one feels when he reads your book is "What's to be done about it?" I anticipate reading this part of the book to which I have just now come. I would like to know much more about neurotic invalidism, the neuroses, and the so-called nervous exhaustion states, etc., but these subjects, of course, would not be in place in *Man Against Himself.* My opinion (it is worth little) is that you have done an excellent job. . . .

Kindest regards,

To E. V. ALLEN, ROCHESTER, MINNESOTA, MARCH 28, 1938

Dear Ed:

I was very much pleased with your letter of March 19 in which you went into considerable detail in regard to your reactions to my book, *Man Against Himself,* and the reactions of some of your colleagues. I fully understand your skepticism about some of the points made; in fact I am skeptical about some of them myself. On the other hand, I think you are very open-minded to be willing to read it at all and to assume that some of it may be true, even if it is not to you entirely convincing. I agree with you that the medical section is the most hypothetical of all and the most open to question, but, on the other hand, the logic and the deduction is there, and it is a tantalizing theory, which if it ever works (I don't even suggest that it always works) means something entirely new in our scientific thinking, or at least in our medical thinking. That's why I think it is so important.

In this connection, I can also answer the questions that you raise toward the end of the first page, "What's to be done about it?" As you will have discovered by now, I feel that there is something to be done about it in the very recognition of the existence of these self-destructive trends, and already I have had several letters from people, one from a doctor, one from a newspaper man, reporting the sudden and considerable improvement in certain afflicted individuals who read the book. Now I know that that can happen after reading everything from Mary Baker Eddy's nonsense to the *Arabian Nights*. But the point is, I have postulated in the book [that] a certain amount of insight and a certain amount of recognition of the fact that we ourselves are to some extent responsible for what happens to us constitute the most effective therapeutic tools. One of these cases was a case of multiple sclerosis, and you know that is organic enough to suit anybody's taste. It was a medical man too. According to the reports I got, he suddenly began to think that maybe he had something to do with the production of his own symptoms, silly as that sounds, and he took up his bed and walked, so to speak. Now I know that multiple sclerosis has remissions and so do you, and I don't know but what this fellow is back on his bed flat as a pancake, but I do know, because I have seen it, if a person can actually get an emotional realization as well as an intellectual realization of the way in which they themselves are hurting they themselves (excuse the bad English), they can *sometimes* throw the thing into reverse.

Here I want to put emphasis upon the fact that whether or not the thing can be thrown into reverse, to repeat that rather inept metaphor, has nothing to do with the main theory. What I am trying to say is that the fact that self-destructive trends, which can be recognized psychologically as well as physically, may or may not be concerned in the production of a particular organic disease has nothing definitely to do with the fact that some of these cases can be approached clinically from the psychological standpoint. I have made these points in my book and I am probably not making them a bit clearer in this letter, but your letter just started me to thinking and rambling on.

Anyway, I am delighted that you think well of my book and that you are taking the trouble to read it and I shall be very interested to hear your final reactions when you have finished the chapter on reconstruction. . . .

Sincerely yours,

To JOSEPH WOOD KRUTCH, NEW YORK, MARCH 31, 1938

Dear Mr. Krutch:

I had already received reports from several friends in the East whose copies of *The Nation* had arrived before mine of the swell review you had written of my book, *Man Against Himself*. I was not prepared, however, for the high appreciation which you accorded it. And I would rather have your estimate of my book than that of any other critic I know, so you can imagine how pleased I am.

I believe that the last sentence of your review was the finest compliment that I have received or that any author could receive upon his work. It appealed to me because to say of a book that it makes the reader feel as if he had always known this but had not known how to express it and had not seen it stated so plainly before is to imply that the content of the book has been accepted emotionally and incorporated into the person's thinking. To a psychoanalyst this means that the tremendous resistances which we all have to accepting unpleasant psychological facts about ourselves has been in some way circumvented—the "censorship" which Freud mentioned has been eluded. You mention that this has already happened in the case of the entire theory of psychoanalysis and I think that this is in no small part due to Freud's genius as a writer and psychologist. You can see, therefore, why it delighted me so for you to apply this very significant compliment to my own work.

It is often said that psychiatry is an art rather than a science, and certainly the delicate technique which is required of the psychiatrist every day if he succeeds in undermining, dissolving, or somehow outwitting the considerable resistances to accepting any therapeutic idea which is found in all patients, and indeed in all human beings, can be described in no other way. Perhaps the whole problem of helping people through books comes back to this idea of in some way or other making them feel that the idea is their own and thus enabling them to accept the thought.

I said that yours was the most complimentary review that I have received. About a month ago I yielded to an invitation to review some of the main points of the book before a small literature club in this town of which I am a member. This was the first time they had ever asked me to present anything, and if you have ever lived in a small community you know how difficult it is to feel that what you are saying is met with either understanding or sympathy. However, it received, this time, a number of kind and really very intelligent discussions. One of the chief solicitors of the Santa Fe Railroad, for example, said his department was convinced from their own experience with railroad accidents that some people were bent on unconscious self-destruction. A factory manager told how an employee had cut off a second and third finger demonstrating how an accident had happened to his first finger. A doctor and an engineer got into an argument about the psychosomatic question in which both went much further than I do. Finally, near the end of the circle, the manager of the Nash Motor Car Agency, if you please, one of those uneducated, somewhat uncouth, totally unpredictable fellows who likes to philosophize, spoke up. Everyone had wondered what he would do with material as abstract, or perhaps I should say as complicated, as this, and to my surprise he said, "I have had so many thoughts while I was listening to this that I can't say any of them. It seemed like Doctor Karl was just saying things that I had known all my life, that all of us had always known but never could quite say because they sounded so strange; yet when he said them they didn't sound strange at all, just perfectly obvious. That's all I can say now."

To me this was the most significant reaction that came from any of the men. To have the most penetrating critic of letters and ideas in America say the same thing in a published review gives me the highest satisfaction.

Sincerely yours,

FROM FRANZ ALEXANDER, CHICAGO, APRIL 11, 1938

Dear Karl:

You have probably received all the circular letters from the Emergency Relief Committee of the American Psychoanalytic Association dealing with the Austrian situation, but in case you have not, I am sending you a copy of some of the pertinent material.

In discussing these problems of relief I have come more and more to the conviction that those Austrian analysts who wish to immigrate to this country should be urged to settle down in the large cities in the Middle West and South, where there are no psychoanalysts as yet and where there is a very definite need for them. Our Eastern, especially our New York, colleagues seem to me very much concerned about the possible invasion of a large number of Austrian analysts who all will want to settle down in New York or Boston. They want to help, and yet they are concerned because from correspondence with [Ernest] Jones it became evident that the most desirable analysts are planning to go to England and France, leaving the less desirable ones (mostly difficult personalities) for us to help. However, at the present moment it is very difficult to establish who wants to come to this country.

In face of the terrible plight of our Austrian colleagues who after they leave the border will be exposed to real need and misery, I feel that we should give them as much help as possible. Since the State Department in Washington shows a very cooperative attitude, it should not be difficult to gain admittance for the Austrian analysts. There are already many affidavits prepared in New York, and also funds amounting to six thousand dollars have been raised in New York, Chicago and Boston. However, the main problem seems to me to be the future existence of the immigrating analysts. This probably can be solved best if we find places for them where there is a need for a psychoanalyst. I thought that you could be especially helpful in this regard on account of your extensive acquaintanceship with Western and Middle Western psychiatrists and other physicians. Would you kindly take the trouble to inquire among your friends and acquaintances in the different large cities of the Middle West regarding the chances of psychoanalytic practice? There also might be some state institutions or universities which might be interested in obtaining the services of a psychoanalyst.

I am not quite sure whether I can go to New York, but will wire you in time. If I cannot go I hope that you will be able to stop over in Chicago for a while to discuss the coordination of teaching activities in Topeka and Chicago.

As ever,

TO FRANZ ALEXANDER, CHICAGO, APRIL 13, 1938

Dear Feri:

I was glad to have your letter of April 11 and sorry to hear that there is some doubt about your going to New York. Let me know just as soon as you can if you can go and when you want to go. I think I'll leave here Tuesday night.

We are all very sympathetic with the terrible plight of the Austrian colleagues and we have taken up a small collection which Doctor Knight is forwarding to Lewin.[8]

Just what to do to help the German and Austrian psychoanalysts I am sure I don't know. I must say, however, that I have grave doubts about the advisability of the plan you mention. Let us analyze it carefully.

The New York analysts are alarmed, first, because so many new analysts are coming to town; second, because some of these analysts are difficult people; and, third, because some of these analysts are not as good analysts as they ought to be, and not as good analysts as those who are going to want them to be. If one simmers these various things down, it amounts to this: that the New York analysts are alarmed at the competition of the colleagues from which they ran away and left. I still don't seem to be saying quite what I mean. Most of the New York analysts were once Europeans themselves. They came to America because they thought there was a wider field for their efforts. Most of them have done well. Now some more European analysts want to come, and these former Europeans who are established in America do not want them to come. It seems to me this is a pretty familiar situation to anyone who has been a psychoanalyst and listened to the outpouring of emotion which was generated by the arrival of more siblings. You go ahead and make it clear that you don't think they ought to be in Chicago either. Therefore, you say, let us put them in the Middle-West. I believe you suggested Texas at the last meeting of the society.

Well, now, as a Middle-Westerner, I say, "Why wish them off on the Middle-West?" Is it your point that they are not good enough for New York

8 New York psychoanalyst Bertram Lewin was in charge of collecting the contributions from the various institutes around the country.

or Chicago, but they are plenty good enough for the West? It seems to me that the man who has to defend psychoanalysis all alone in a city should be a better man, not a weaker man, than the average. It is much harder to practice psychoanalysis faithfully, honestly and scientifically when one is all alone than it is in a city where one can always get his mistakes corrected to some extent by discussion with other analysts. Above all, I don't see why you should take the lead in trying to help the New York analysts from having too much competition from their European colleagues. Furthermore, I do not see why you should want to scatter them among the cities of the Middle-West, or, for that matter, the Middle-East, or the Northeast, or the Northwest, or any other part of the country.

Of course you have other ideas in mind besides this and I well realize this, but I am not just sure what those ideas are. Is it your idea that these people are more likely to make a living in some of these Middle-Western cities other than Chicago? Or is it your idea that it would help psychoanalysis to have psychoanalysts working in these cities? Or is merely your idea that it would relieve the anxiety of Chicago and New York [analysts] if the people did not settle there?

I raise these questions because I can't cooperate in this plan unless I understand it fully. On the surface of it, the idea seems preposterous. What I mean is that for the average European Jewish psychoanalyst, accustomed to urban life and with a total ignorance of small-town life, accustomed to Jewish cohesiveness and separatism, with the existing prejudice present and the probably increasing prejudice against Europeans, against Jews, against alien doctors, to say nothing of the prejudice against psychoanalysis—I think the idea of trying to transplant a person with that background into a middle-sized, ninety-nine percent native-born, Middle-Western city is inconceivable.

Alex, you can't take one of these Austrian or German Jews and put him in Little Rock, Arkansas, or Wichita, Kansas, or Sacramento, California, or Columbus, Ohio, or Roanoke, Virginia, and expect him to adapt himself with any degree of success. They are far more inflexible than you seem to imagine. You mustn't compare them with yourself; you are a very flexible person, an international person; furthermore, you are not aligned with the Jews and you are not aligned with the recent immigrants, etc., etc. It is very different with these fellows. They aren't going to be welcomed with open arms by everyone simply because we analysts are fond of some of them.

No, the only place for these fellows is in a large city where there are lots of foreigners, lots of Jews, and I might add lots of psychoanalysts. It is their only chance in the world. We've had a terrible time with Kamm and Grotjahn, neither one of whom are Jews, neither one of whom are difficult persons, neither one of whom were forced out of the country but came voluntarily, and came to a group already established, etc. In spite of that, we have had lots of trouble. We can't get them licensed to this day. There are lots of these Western states who do not license foreign doctors. They must be American citizens and that means five years. We've been all over this together, but you suddenly got this inspiration of scattering psychoanalysts all over the country, and, well-meaning as I think it may be, I think it is a futile plan.

And, furthermore, even if all of these things weren't so, I have learned from experience that it is absolutely useless to try to give advice or to give invitations to these foreigners. You will think I am a little hard-hearted and unsympathetic, but I have simply learned that they have been so embittered and so shocked, or something, that they do not take advice. I don't think there is any use in trying to advise them where to go. If they ask my advice, I shall certainly tell them what I said above: go to the largest cities and try to get under the protective wing of someone with whom you have some bond of affiliation.

You may think this is a reversal on the part of one who has long been an assimilationist, but I don't think you can begin to assimilate the Jews by putting a European Jewish psychoanalyst in the midst of a native-born population who will regard him as a cross between Rasputin and Morris Fishbein.

Sincerely yours,

FROM MERRILL MOORE,[9] BOSTON, MAY 17, 1938

Dear Karl:

You are certainly good to take time to answer. I know how busy you are but I did want to pass along a few random notions that came to mind. First of all, you are very kind to state that the work we are doing is important but I am afraid it is really low-grade research, mostly statistical. The reason for that is that we have no other facilities for working at present other than pencil, paper, and hospital records.

The Boston City Hospital is very much agin psychiatry and we have not been able to get a psychiatric ward or service started, though I have worked there ten years with that aim in view and hope ultimately to accomplish something. One by one the roses fall. It seems to me that every big general hospital would be an excellent place to study suicide intensively or extensively, and one thing about your book that impresses me so much is, it is extremely stimulating in opening up many ideas that even surgeons or internists could follow in studying the problem of suicide, which after all is basic among human problems.

Without meaning to flatter you (I really don't) there is no question that

9 Moore was a Boston psychoanalyst and published poet who shared KAM's interest in suicide research. He wrote *M: One Thousand Autobiographical Sonnets* (1938).

your book, *Man Against Himself* is the first and best book on the subject that really is comprehensive and deep as well as wide. When you look back over the early literature, it is really amazing to see what has been done and what good shots in the dark some people have written on the subject. I know you are familiar with the early books, but did you happen to know that there are four hundred and seventy-five books on the subject of suicide in the Boston Medical Library? These were collected by A. Warren Sterns and bear his name as a separate collection on the subject of suicide. It might be nice if you would send them a copy of your book inscribed. The Librarian is Mr. James Ballard, 8 Fenway, Boston, Massachusetts. . . .

One thing that interests me more and that is the actual careful, thorough reporting of cases of suicide as case reports. It seems to me that there is a great deal of interest and a great deal that is stimulating just in the case reports themselves. I had thought of the idea of writing a book called *X Plus Y Equals Z*, X representing personality, Y a given situation, and Z the suicidal attempt.

If I myself had the time to do it I would like to go through the series of 1,147 cases at the City Hospital and write them up from a literary point of view, but that would take another reincarnation.

Although we have a hundred fifty alcoholics who attempted suicide in connection with a spree I still don't know how to work it up and am now reading the case records carefully with the view of putting them together in the form of a paper to read next year somewhere. What we really need at the City Hospital is a psychiatric ward and service; then, of course, we need more intensive study of individual cases.

Here is just a little idea but I pass it along to you for what it is worth. Whenever a child learns about someone having committed suicide the first question the child asks is, "Why did they do it?" That basic reaction on the part of the child mind seems to me to bear most directly on the whole problem of suicide. The real problem is motivation, as you point out in your book, and it is only by the study of the deep psychology and its relation to social and psychological factors that anything can be made out of the difficult tangle.

You are very kind to mention speaking to Zilboorg. I would be only too glad to cooperate with the group but I don't think I could do any more than what I am doing at present, and I could of course do that without any contact with the group. I go along in my rather patient pedantic way looking for things of interest and trying to write up and report in a factual way what I come across, but not being trained as an analyst I can only approach it from the psychiatric point of view. It is quite possible that the research is more along the psychoanalytic line than I would be qualified to cooperate with, but whatever you do about it, I will be only too glad to help in any way I can. . . .

It is my feeling that *Man Against Himself* is going to take hold and dig in and will of course be a book of permanent value . . . I find that *The Human Mind* and *Man Against Himself* are more valuable for people who are not being analyzed and most valuable for family, relatives, friends, and people who want to be helpful and just don't know how to do it. I find that after people read *The Human Mind* they are able to give much more important and useful observation and history and additional information that is helpful regarding the patient, and I am constantly being surprised over the extraordinary shrewdness and helpfulness of nontechnically trained minds in dealing with psychiatric problems. . . .

One of the disadvantages of having an Ediphone is that one writes letters to one's friends as if they were there and as if one were talking to them. I am afraid I had better sign off out of respect for your other appointments.

With best wishes,

Yours sincerely,

To Smith Ely Jelliffe, Huletts Landing, New York, June 30, 1938

Dear Doctor Jelliffe:

I am answering your postal card request of June 23 to give you some of the dope about Schilder's book which most impressed me.

First, let me disclaim any of the witch-hunting spirit mentioned. I know full well how hostile New York analysts are to Schilder, and formerly I regarded this as an example of a pettiness which characterizes some psychoanalysts. As I have gone along, however, and watched Schilder and heard him make a fool of himself, I have had to revise my views. His asinine attack on *Alice in Wonderland*, for example, did psychoanalysis an immense amount of harm, in my opinion. *Alice in Wonderland* has many friends and for it to appear in every newspaper in the land that "a prominent American psychoanalyst" or just "these psychoanalysts" disapprove of *Alice in Wonderland* because it stimulates sadistic fantasies in children gave rise to a lot of ridicule against psychoanalysis which was in my opinion entirely justified. Even if it were sound science, which I do not think it was, it would have been unsound policy. Schilder is a European, not an American, and he does not understand English very well, in spite of his pretentions of doing so. I think the sadistic fantasies expressed in *Alice in Wonderland* relieve children rather than excite them, so that I do not even think his science is sound on that point.

Furthermore, it has always seemed to me that Schilder was making a grand effort to impress the neurologists with the fact that he was one sound psychoanalyst, not to be confused with unsound, nor [with] orthodox fellows like Smith Ely Jelliffe and Oberndorf[10] and Lewin and George Daniels[11] and [Flanders] Dunbar and all the rest. He has toadied to Adolf Meyer and all of these fellows who are at heart bitterly opposed to us. Because of some of Schilder's stuff, which they can't understand but which sounds pretty neurological and pretty sound, they think he's all right. Personally, I think most of these articles are a mixture of philosophical confusion and psychoanalytic ambivalence. Not entirely, I grant you; I know he has some good ideas and I'd like to give him credit for them if he would express them in intelligible English and without these political connivings that he indulges in, but I must confess that his wretched, his abominable, his atrocious English nearly slays me. I can stand his squeaky voice, but I cannot stand to hear him murder the English language as he does without some emotional reaction to it which blunts my capacity to grasp his thoughts. I am told by competent German-speaking people that he is equally ungrammatical and uncouth in his German usages. . . .

The point of all this is that I heard in San Francisco from some of the psychoanalysts that if it weren't for the support of good old Doctor Jelliffe, Schilder would have passed out of sight some time ago except among the strict neurological friends with whom he consorts. The impression was that with your big, generous spirit you thought that he was a somewhat persecuted and misunderstood fellow and, therefore, extended your blessings to him. All I can say is that anyone who writes a sloppy, unrepresentative book of this type and talks about writing two or three more books at the same time and advises his readers to depend solely upon European psychoanalysts as authorities, describes these as "more or less" loyal to Freud, and ends up by saying that he doesn't consider psychoanalytic training necessary for psychoanalytic therapists is unworthy of your support, and I deplore the fact that so many physicians will buy and read his "psychotherapy" and think they are getting the *real dope.*

To MERRILL MOORE, BOSTON, JULY 6, 1938

My dear Merrill:

I have purposely delayed answering your letter of May 17 until I could sit down and take time to answer it properly. Since it came I have been in Chicago to attend the American Psychoanalytic Association meeting and on

10 C. P. Oberndorf, an eminent New York psychiatrist affiliated with Bellevue and Mt. Sinai hospitals and later professor of psychiatry at Columbia University. He was president of the APA in 1936. He wrote *A History of Psychoanalysis in America* (1953).

11 A New York psychoanalyst. Originally a member of the New York Psychoanalytic Society, Daniels, along with Sandor Rado, Abram Kardiner, and David Levy, withdrew and in 1945 established the Association for Psychoanalytic Medicine and the Psychoanalytic Clinic for Training and Research at Columbia University. The defection violated the established practice of allowing only one psychoanalytic society in a city and marked the first institute in an American university.

to San Francisco where the American Psychiatric held forth for five days and then after a two-day interval the American medical meeting began, and I stayed out through that. I have come back now and after a week of nice cool weather we have begun to have some good hot weather. I am up here at my office Sunday afternoon with everyone gone and it is pretty hot but cool here in front of the fan with a nice ice cooler in the offing and I feel very much in the spirit of sitting down to a contemplative reply to your nice letter.

You mustn't be discouraged about developments in Boston City [Hospital]. The things one wants to accomplish in his immediate environment always seem to go a little slower than they ought to. The accomplishments that other people seem to be achieving always seem to be going faster, more successfully and more smoothly than they have any right to. I think it is really marvelous the way the Boston City has developed since I was there, and I think you have had a big part in it, and I think you shouldn't be discouraged at any time. Personally, I am not absolutely sure that a psychiatric ward is as desirable as a psychiatric service, but that is a mere detail. I know you are going to get something there and I know you are going to get more and more ideas across to the younger fellows even if some of the older ones won't absorb them.

It was awfully kind of you to say all the nice things you do about *Man Against Himself*. I keep having new ideas every day that I wish I had included in the book and I see some new case material every now and then that seems infinitely better than any I had collected at the time I wrote it, but that is the way one feels after he has written a book, I suppose. At any rate, I hope to revise it sometime and include some of this, and, in the meantime, I have some new ideas which I am working on and which I'll tell you about before long. In essence, they are a better way for us to organize the immense amount of material that accumulates when one studies a personality thoroughly. As I put it in one of my discussions, the surgeons don't have enough data but they do a lot with what they get; the psychiatrists get so much data that they can't do anything with it. Of course, this is only a general principle, some of them do a lot with it.

I was extremely interested to learn of the suicide library in connection with the Boston Medical Library, by which I suppose you mean the one over on Fenway. I have spent many happy hours there. . . .

I think your idea to go through the 1,147 cases of attempted suicide at the City Hospital would be an excellent one. Perhaps you could get one of your students or associates to do some of the routine work.

Just now I am studying a number of records of an insurance company of fairly well-to-do people who had large policies who committed suicide without very definite reasons. I don't know what this may come to, but you'll be hearing about it one of these days perhaps. . . .

I can't report any progress in regard to the suicide research committee of Zilboorg's. In fact, believe it or not, I don't know yet who the members of the committee are, except that I am supposed to be one. I don't know what our duties are, what our prospects are, or anything else. Zilboorg has the most amazingly curious way of telling me a little dab of information here and there, but I can't put it altogether, and I don't get to first base discussing any suggestions with him, although I did mention your name. One of these days perhaps there will be a meeting of the committee and then I'll have a chance to find out who they are and what they plan to do and why you shouldn't properly be one of them.

I wonder if you happened to see Ed Strecker's[12] review of *Man Against Himself* in the *Public Health Journal*. He doesn't like the alcohol chapter and I think I can understand why. Personally, I am very disappointed in his book on alcohol, and I think it is much the poorest thing he has done. I have great respect for Ed and like him immensely, but he has a curious hostility for psychoanalytic ideas; a part of this, of course, is his Catholic background, but there is more to it than that.

I was very much interested in your comment about the intuitive helpfulness of some shrewd, nontechnically trained person. I too have a great respect for this and for a long time we thought we might be able to get by using individuals like this for nurses. Unfortunately, however, their lack of training militates against their successful adaptation to the needs of a psychiatric hospital. They are helpful in individual situations in which they happen to be but it is very difficult for them to learn to adapt themselves to anything that comes along and also to adapt to the rules and regulations that necessarily apply in organized medical practice. For this and other reasons we have given up entirely taking anyone but graduate nurses in the sanitarium and in addition to that we require that they have a postgraduate training in psychiatry. My brother Will has worked out this course in great detail. For the few male attendants whom we have to have we take only college graduates. In our therapy departments we have college graduates and frequently those with Master's and Doctor's degrees. They do the educational, recreational and occupational therapies, etc. . . .

Sincerely yours,

FROM MERRILL MOORE, BOSTON, JULY 11, 1938

Dear Karl:

It is certainly good to have your nice long newsy and chatty letter of July

12 Clinical professor of psychiatry and mental hygiene at Yale from 1926 to 1932, professor of psychiatry and head of the psychiatry department at the University of Pennsylvania from 1932 to 1953. His books include *Discovering Ourselves* (1931), *Practical Examination of Personality and Behavior Disorders* (1936), and *Alcohol: One Man's Meat* (1938).

6. I can't imagine how you really found energy and time to write it after going to all the meetings. It comes to me at a time when I am particularly glad to hear from you and to get your comments on the ideas in it. You must have an Ediphone or you couldn't possibly get out such long thorough letters. I am impressed and appreciative.

I am really not discouraged about developments at the Boston City Hospital. Things are actually moving along. I am giving a one-month course in psychiatry to the interns during August. It is very informal but it might be of some interest. . . .

May I pass on to you some gossip about myself? I am having trouble with the local Analytical Society. I was psychoanalyzed by Dr. [Hanns] Sachs and he recommended me to the Training Committee to do some control work. I was flatly refused by the Control Committee with a great deal of emphasis and effort put into the refusal by our colleague, Dr. [M. Ralph] Kaufman. The Committee feels that I am "characterologically and by personality" unfit for becoming an analyst. There has been a great deal of discussion and talk including considerable indulgence of personalities.

I don't know what is going to happen. I am complaining to the Training Committee that I feel that my case has not been given due consideration and that factors of personal prejudice (manifestly present) have operated in a way that is not favorable to my application.

I am waiting to know what the Committee will decide. I hope very much to be able to do control work.

I mention this to you because in discussing it with some of the analysts who are friends, several of them have said, "You haven't any business in analysis. You are a psychiatrist and ought to stay in psychiatry. You will be more useful there. You are just like Karl Menninger. He is one of those overactive persons like yourself. He has good ideas and does lots of things but he can't be an analyst." About six people have said that to me and have made me wonder if there is any truth in it or is it just one of those "pseudo-doxia epidemica" that drift around. I appreciate the compliment of being compared to you and apologize to you for the comparison to myself but thought you would be amused at my passing along this fragment.

There has been a great deal of talk about the fact that I am "publicity minded." I certainly am and expect to remain so. It seems to me that it is important for a doctor who is interested in psychiatry, public institutions and the psychiatric aspects of social medicine (God forbid the term) to be interested in public reaction as well as in public action.

I am not calling for sympathy or asking for any partisan expression of ideas but I have encountered a great deal of hostility to the type of work I am doing and am trying to do and hear along with it criticism of yourself and Zilboorg as "publicity seekers." My feeling is that this criticism is nonsense and sheer gossip and usually comes from people who are envious or inactive and apt to be on those accounts critical and reductive.

No doubt you hear a lot of this sort of thing but I wanted to mention it to you so that if and when we ever do have time to sit down for an hour or two, we can go into this problem in a general way because it interests me a lot and I hope to do something about it in the time that is to come.

Personally I admire the sort of thing you do and the sort of thing that Alexander does and the sort of thing that Zilboorg does. That type of analyst and psychiatrist represents my ego ideals much more than the passive and critical type. I think that psychiatry has done a great service and is much forwarded by activity of this sort.

If your hospital were in the East where it would economically threaten some of the more stupid and older institutions, you would find yourself in for a very severe kind of economic warfare based on criticism. . . .

As a general statement I would say that *Man Against Himself* is the best book ever published on the subject of suicide. It really summarizes all that has ever been said. I think it would be well worth further study, further research and some rewriting. It might even be expanded in larger book form. It is the sort of book that ought to be in the new *Modern Library Series* of the so-called Giants. You have seen them. I think they are splendid.

Please remember that at the Boston City Hospital there are about twelve hundred cases of suicide that are available to you any time if you want material from them. They are not easy to get out and require a good deal of time and digging and when one gets them out they are not in particularly good shape but they are one thousand or a little more *Arabian Night* stories that all end tragically. . . .

They have a copy of your book in the Boston Library, so you shouldn't bother about sending one. . . .

You have no idea (maybe you do) of the latent ambivalent hostility toward psychoanalysis. I often wonder what the future of psychoanalysis is going to be. I personally would like to see it broad and liberal.

It is interesting to note that you take only graduate nurses in your sanitarium. That is a splendid idea and will do a great deal in raising standards in the course of twenty years. . . .

With warmest regards and every good wish,

Sincerely,

P.S. I forgot to thank you for the reprint "The Cinderella of Medicine." It is very very delightful. Why don't you meet Disney and cooperate with him in producing a really good psychiatric movie? He could help a lot. I've often thought that his charm lay in the successful sublimation of his anal and schizoid character components. If you notice the three little pigs are very anal.

When he got his degree at Harvard the applause was tremendous. There is no question about how the public feels.

To ERNST SIMMEL, LOS ANGELES, JULY 25, 1938

Dear Doctor Simmel:

I have just received your letter of July 19 and as I am leaving tomorrow for New York I must respond immediately or else defer it longer than you may want to wait.

I have taken due notice of your announcement that you intend to found a psychoanalytic institute and sanitarium. The Institute sounds to me most promising. There will be some technical difficulties, of course, but within the next five years or so these should smooth out. We should regret losing the California members from our society, but for the present there is no reason why our society should not sponsor an institute in Los Angeles. I think it is good news and I am anxious to help in any way I can.

In regard to the sanitarium, I am a little reluctant to express my opinion frankly for fear my motive will be misunderstood. Let me begin by answering the latter part of your letter. Indeed we shall be glad to help you in discussing your plans of organization, and our business department joins me in assuring you that we should be glad to welcome one or two representatives who might wish to come here and study our institution.

Next let me say that although it may sound paradoxical, I believe that such a sanitarium founded by you would be of great indirect benefit to us here. At present you send us many patients and we are grateful; in the future it would probably be that we would be able to send you more than you would send us. But I believe the ideas, originally yours, which we have been trying to carry on here would be forwarded in the development of another such institution and very likely there would be a considerable interchange of staff members, employees and perhaps also patients. From this standpoint I like the idea and I hope you go through with it.

From what I have said I hope you will believe me that what I am about to say next does not come from any feelings of ire, envy, professional jealousy, etc. Whatever my unconscious may be, I do not consciously entertain such objections. I do suspect, however, that your self-destructive tendencies may be entering into your notion of complicating your work in Los Angeles by the development of a psychoanalytic sanitarium. In the first place, you are already so busy that I do not see how you could carry on the additional responsibilities that this entails; in the second place, your relations to the medical profession in Los Angeles are such that you could be sure of encountering additional opposition and resistance for yourself and for psychoanalysis by the founding of anything so nearly resembling a hospital. In the third place, I must tell you that it is my conviction that the private psychiatric hospital and, for that matter, the private general hospital is doomed. No new ones have been founded in several years and many old ones have gone out of business. Bernard Glueck[13] wants very much to get rid of his sanitarium in New York. It is plain to see the handwriting on the wall, I think; medicine will be socialized and the private institution has no chance at all in such a program.

And finally I can assure you that whether it is your money or someone else's money, the financial burden of conducting a psychoanalytic sanitarium is enormously disproportionate to the financial gain. Our sanitarium has every advantage and yet we either run at a loss or show such a pitifully small profit as to be the despair of our directors and stockholders. Even if you did not expect it to make money, you would expect it to break even, and this it will not do unless it is managed with an astuteness and personal devotion which it is very difficult to hire or buy. I do not know of any colleague in Los Angeles or, for that matter, anywhere in the United States who would be willing to put the hours and hours and hours of patient detailed work into the management of an institution that my brother Will and our business manager, Mr. Stone, have been and still are doing. It must literally be the life work of several individuals, and these individuals are very hard to find.

I cannot encourage you in the idea of a sanitarium, therefore; nevertheless if you go through with it, I shall be of whatever help I can. . . .

Sincerely yours,

To Abraham Myerson, Boston, July 27, 1938

My dear Abe:

I have been urged by many colleagues to reply to your bitter, captious review of my book, the revised edition of *The Human Mind.* I have declined to do so largely because I felt it would be useless. I feel sure that you do not regard it as an unfriendly diatribe against an old friend, a friend and student who learned much from you and who is and always has been grateful for the help you gave him.

Several of the points made in your review were good ones and I shall profit by them in my next revision. I could only wish that you had shown a friendlier or kindlier spirit in making them, and I regret too that you did not bring the sharp focus of that keen intelligence of yours upon some of the more important defects of the book instead of making yourself somewhat

13 A psychoanalyst who played a significant role in the development of psychiatric social work. In 1918 he became head of an innovating psychiatric clinic at Sing Sing Prison. He was also affiliated with the New York School of Social Work, later renamed the Columbia University School of Social Work.

absurd and certainly very petty by exploding over details concerning which we have a difference of opinion.

I am fond of you, Abe, and your public exposition of hostility has not embittered me in the least; I see too plainly, or I think I do, that in attacking me and more particularly Freud as represented by me, you are giving vent to anti-Semitic feelings which your present circumstances do not allow you to admit to consciousness, let alone public expression. I do not mean that this is all there is to it. Knowing you as intimately as I do, or rather as I once did, I know how prone you have always been to attack your friends and regret it afterwards. I remember the bitter remorse that you suffered and voiced to me on the way to Southard's funeral. I have done the same thing myself sometimes, and I owe it to psychoanalysis that I am no longer quite so dominated by these provocative impulses.

I write you, therefore, to assure you that your various gestures of unfriendliness, disguised as scientific zeal and conviction, in no sense reduced my feelings of friendliness and appreciation toward you.

Sincerely yours,

FROM ABRAHAM MYERSON, BOSTON, SEPTEMBER 9, 1938

Dear Karl:

Your letter of July 27 has remained unanswered for the simple reason that I was in Europe when it came and did not return until a day or two ago, during which time I have been cogitating on what answer I should make to you.

First, I welcome your statement of esteem and friendship and assure you that I reciprocate your feeling and I have no personal animus against you whatsoever. I am not conscious of any bitterness. As I look over my review of your book I see nothing in it that can be styled bitter or captious criticism. It is severe; so far as I am conscious of my own feelings it is honest; and I do not believe that I have exaggerated my reactions at all. Furthermore, nothing in your letter meets my criticisms. If I were to take them up point by point I would still say what I said, and the final statement that the book oversells psychiatry still holds good in my opinion, 100%. So that I cannot apologize for the review nor do I feel that I should retract any of it.

Moreover, I must take serious exception to certain phrases of your letter. In the first place the statement that I am, unconsciously of course, an anti-Semite is, in the present state of the world conditions of the Jews, almost insulting. At the present time I have in my laboratory three men who are refugees from Europe. I have taken them in there in the face of hostility which to a certain extent threatens my own position. My laboratory staff is, in large measure, made up of Jews, to the point where definite criticism has been made of me as being too pro-Semite. Like all Jews my social life is largely Jewish. Your statement that I am anti-Semitic runs true to psychoanalytic form. You pass judgment on the quick and the dead without the slightest personal acquaintance, since you cannot say that you now know anything by direct experience of my inner life and your conclusion is, frankly speaking, glib and without any basis. These are hard words but they are not as hard as your statement that "you are giving vent to anti-Semitic feelings which your present circumstances do not allow you to admit to consciousness, let alone to public expression." I have never been accused of being afraid to give vent to what I thought. In fact I think my reputation is rather that of a person who does give vent to very unpopular opinions, let the result be what it may. Of course, if all this is unconscious to me and you have access to my unconsciousness in some mysterious fashion, extrasensorially, so to speak, why that is that.

You take the attitude of other psychoanalysts I have known, one of complacent superiority. *You* have been purged of bitterness by psychoanalysis and *I* have not been, since I have not been psychoanalyzed. But the facts do not bear you out and I am a stickler for facts. The psychoanalytic societies have at least as much if not more struggle, quarreling, bitterness, and schism as any other scientific group in the country. I know, because I have been apprised of the situation in psychoanalysis by leading and important psychoanalysts. Moreover, the psychoanalysts I know personally show no evidence either in general personal relationships, in the marital state, in freedom from neurosis and psychosis, of any purging process. They are human and all too human. So am I, and I must say that I am rather amused by your rather condescending attitude toward my inner life.

They who write books must take it—*it* meaning criticism. Some of my books have been very hostilely criticized. I have never attributed that hostility to anything but the honest opinion of the reviewer. I have often questioned his judgment and his learning. I have never analyzed his inner motives and found that he was actuated by something that he did not know anything at all about. I have never written a letter of remonstrance, protesting my friendship at the same time.

I am very sorry if I have hurt you. If my very best friend were to write a book which I was asked to review (remember, I did not solicit the job of reviewing your book), I would write as frankly and as freely as I did about your book. There is no captious bitterness in my attitude towards you as a man, as a person of whom I have very pleasant memories and whom I still hold in affection.

Very sincerely yours,

To Abraham Myerson, Boston, September 24, 1938

Dear Abe:

Thank you very much for your letter of September 9. I agree with you that a reviewer should not be influenced in his judgment by any feelings of friendliness. I am sure no one would accuse you of that. Just as I said of your review, I must say of your letter, that you make *some* very good points.

I should like very much to give you my point of view in regard to many of your statements, but I have the feeling that we could never meet on any common intellectual ground. I deplore this. You do not like my book; you do not like my letter. I liked some of your review and some of your letter, but if everything I say is only another challenge to you to defend yourself, I should cease.

But you are such a warm-hearted fellow under the surface, Abe. In a world so full of belligerency, should we add to it?

Best wishes, really.

Sincerely,

From Abraham Myerson,[1] Boston, September 27, 1938

Dear Karl:—

This being a Jewish holiday, my sec'y is away & I am answering your letter at once to let you know some things which your very, shall I say, sweet letter evoked.

The world *is* too full of belligerency, as you say, for old friends to quarrel about such unimportant matters as their differences of opinions and even the gaps intellectually between them. Let me say again, I am sorry I hurt you, and I say so because I believe that if men are sincerely striving to understand human difficulties, then that is more a point of great union between them than the different roads they travel to that goal constitute a point of departure. You and I are fellow workers in psychiatry; you follow a road which I cannot follow at least in sufficient degree to be a fellow pilgrim of yours. I follow a road which you think in the recesses of your mind is superficial and while useful is not the direct one to our common goal. So be it, and yet we may wave cheerful and kindly greetings to one another and we may say out of the fullness of our hearts, "God speed, comrade!"

It is a fault of mine to be sharply critical, and perhaps unkindly so. Mine is, I think, a very direct nature, I overvalue proof, experiment, statistics, and have a streak of intolerance which because I have the gift of clear expression may cut like a sword. And yet I am warmhearted, so you say and so I believe. Out of that warmheartedness, then, I call out to you Karl that however divergent our views may now be, and may continue to be, that I do not really feel that such divergence is nearly so important as the fact that as men we are friends and that we are both psychiatrists.

Yours

To Franz Alexander, Chicago, December, 1938

Dear Alex:

. . . I have been giving considerable thought to a course of lectures that I will give at the institute if they want me to. I thought I might have an informal hour twice a week reviewing systematically the works of Professor Freud and developing some discussion along the way. I think all of us would profit by going over this again.

Another thing I thought of is a somewhat more formal series of lectures on the psychoanalytic significance of certain fairy tales, myths and Biblical incidents. This interests me very much and would require somewhat more work on my part than the mere reading of Freud but perhaps has less practical value. Still a third thing I thought of was the presentation of some psychiatric cases with some psychoanalytic discussion because my impression is that most of the cases that your staff members get to study are neurotic rather than psychotic. This would be exceedingly easy for me to do but I don't know if you want it. It seems to me this is valuable but I feel somewhat dubious as to the demand for it since Mr. Stern's decision that it wasn't even worth carfare.[14] You must assure him that under the circumstances there will be no cost to the institute—not even postage.

Sincerely yours,

To the League of American Writers, New York, December 20, 1938

Gentlemen:

I am responding to your letter of November 22 asking what I think might be done to oppose antisemitism in this country.

I am in complete accord with the purpose which impels your Committee to solicit suggestions in this direction although I recognize, as I am sure you do also, that your appeal is a sentimental rather than a scientific or a political one. It is obviously impossible to obtain a scientific solution to so tremendous a problem by the mere expedience of obtaining an expression of the feelings of a selected number of persons, who are urged by airmail to tell you "by an early post" what we think should be done about it.

To say that this appeal must be primarily sentimental is not to damn it, except in the eyes of those who are so unfortunate as to be incapable of giving credence or attention to their feelings or to the feelings of others. It is probably just these who make up large numbers of the professed antisemites. You may record my feelings as being profoundly sympathetic with the revulsion that you and all other civilized people feel toward the infliction of brutality upon a weaker group by a stronger group, and toward the feelings which dictate such brutality. Similarly, my heart is with you fully in your feeling that something should be stirred within us to protect ourselves against an outbreak of the same disease in our own country.

14 As president of the Board of Trustees of the Chicago Institute, Alfred Stern had refused to pay for KAM's travel expenses to Chicago for this presentation.

But if we put our heads at the service of these ideals as well as our hearts, I think we shall have to recognize at the very start that we do not know exactly what antisemitism is. It is nothing new that strong people, or people who feel strong, sometimes torture those who are weak, and justify it by specious sophistry. How this phenomenon is related to self-punishment and self-destruction has interested me for many years, as you know from some of my published work. Why the Jews should be singled out at the present time, as in the middle ages, is not at all clear in spite of many explanations which have been offered.

These questions will suggest the answer I have to make to your inquiry. Antisemitism is one very poignant symptom of a widespread social disease. One can scarcely speak of a symptom as being epidemic or endemic, but it is certain that antisemitism is both. Scientific training and convictions would tempt me to proceed exactly as we proceeded in the study of those other epidemics—yellow fever, typhoid, and the plague. I would propose that the subject be studied scientifically by a research committee composed of sociologists, anthropologists, psychologists, and psychiatrists—in short, a committee composed of men qualified to make an objective study of the exact nature of this social affliction, the determining factors of its inception, and the conditions which permit or encourage its growth. The politicians, editors, writers of columns in the daily press, and speakers from public forums seem to assume that it is merely a matter of German brutality versus Hebraic meekness. This is certainly too oversimplified a version. And yet, these voices speak with such self-assurance that I am afraid that the suggestion of a committee on research with appropriate financial support will seem to them, as perhaps to you, a visionary scientific supererogation. Such a research into the matter of man's hates *might* have embarrassing extensions; we might find, for example, that our educational system is really as rotten as we suspect it is, and that the children who are told to extract cube roots but who still believe in myths like the Jewish race, the guilty nation, and the freedom of the press are often *taught* to be antisemitic, antiliberal, antiscientific, antisocial, and anti-a-good-many-other-things, through the ignorance, incompetence, neuroticism, and official repression of the "educators." Such a research *might* indicate that some of the politicians, newspaper columnists, ministers and rabbis, who are now loudly lamenting, as they should, the anti-semitic explosions in Germany have in the past contributed very materially to the cultivation of ideals and attitudes among those whom they influence, which led directly to the thing which they now deplore.

Please notice that I have said *might*. I do not know what such a research would discover. But I must repeat that while I do not deny that the stimulation of emotional realization of and reaction against this malady may have some temporary benefits, in the long run our greatest reliance should be placed in scientific investigations, so that an intelligent prophlaxic may be undertaken.

Sincerely yours,

New York

To WILLIAM AND C F. MENNINGER, JOHN R. STONE, JEAN LYLE, AND MILDRED LAW, TOPEKA, MARCH 23, 1939

Dear Dr. W.C.M., Dr. C.F.M., John, Jean & Mildred and all:

I thought you might be interested in my excursion into the realms of the controllers of public opinion. I went to dinner last night at the home of Mr. and Mrs. Arthur Sulzberger. Mrs. Sulzberger was the only daughter of the late Mr. Ochs, who built up the *New York Times*. She is a sweet, quiet, gray-haired, brown-eyed little woman who isn't a bit pretentious or smooth in that polished New York way that one dislikes. Her husband is a very handsome manly looking fellow, has iron-gray hair parted in the middle, and looks a good deal like Bill Kercher[1] used to years ago.

They live in a beautiful big house of several stories just off Fifth Avenue on Eightieth Street. The rooms are very large, and the staircases are very broad and winding, and it is very swanky, not quite as much so as the Ogden Reid[2] home, but a good deal warmer and more human.

When I got there, Mr. Sulzberger was mixing up drinks, and one of his four children was helping him and talked to me over her shoulder about going to Smith next year. She is now in high school.

There were fourteen guests, the most important of which was Mr. Matthews,[3] who has been one of the two *Times* correspondents in Spain. I think he is considered the crack *Times* correspondent, just as Knickerbocker is for Hearst. He is a tall, thin-faced, sensitive-looking, quiet-speaking fellow, very modest, a little frightened by all the attention, I thought, but kept his poise very well. Then there were three or four bankers and lawyers of the obviously very wealthy sort; the one next to me an aristocratic, Bostonian, Republican Gentile; and the one across from me an almost identical character, except that he was a Jew and a New Yorker (I think he was a Jew, but these people all look alike, and except for their names, one can't tell whether they are Jewish or not). As a rule, they don't mention the Jews; to my sur-

---

1 Bill Kercher, KAM's cousin, worked for the telephone company in Topeka.

2 Reid was editor of the *New York Herald-Tribune* from 1913 until his death in 1947.

3 Herbert L. Matthews went to Spain in November 1936 to cover the Loyalist front for the *New York Times*. With journalists on both sides of the war (William Carney covered Franco and the Republican forces), the *Times* carried on its tradition of impartial reporting. Matthews later became the Rome correspondent. After Germany and Italy declared war on the United States in December 1941, he was arrested and incarcerated in Siena until May 1942.

prise, however, Mr. Sulzberger told a story involving the imitation of the Jewish accent of Dr. Brill, which I thought was in very bad taste. As a matter of fact, it was the second time he had told it in my presence, and he admitted that he had told it at his office when he made a speech to the employees a few days ago. He is such a cultivated, dignified fellow that it is amazing to hear him come out with this ridicule of the accent of other Jews. . . .

To go on with a few other guests, there was a Mr. Marcossin, who writes a good deal for the *Times.* Then there was a Mrs. Anderson (I think that's her name), who runs the *Town Meeting of the Air* program, and takes it seriously, too, believe me. The woman at my left was a homely but cute little thing, the wife of a lawyer who wasn't present. She had apparently grown up with Mrs. Sulzberger, and had been taken all over Europe as a child by Mr. Ochs, and seemed almost like a relative. She was violently pro-Loyalist, and she was very clever too, and kept throwing some of the Franco boys into confusion, but I am getting ahead of the story.

After the usual cocktails and shrimps with stuff to dip them in, we all went into a very large dining room and found our places. Mr. Sulzberger was sitting at one end of the table, and Mr. Matthews at the other end of the table, with the hostess at the guest-of-honor's left. This worked out very well because later he spoke as I shall tell you. There was nice turtle soup followed by filet mignon planked, with fresh peas, beans, etc. The dessert was this very fancy looking dish which is very expensive in French restaurants and not very good. It is ice cream surrounded with a large gob of this spun-sugar candy, so that it looks like an immense bird's nest. There was wine and later brandy and whiskey, but no champagne.

It might interest you that in spite of what Emily Post says about serving the guests first, at all the dinners I have attended in New York this has never been done but once, and the old custom of serving the hostess first has been therefore almost invariable. The lady next to me said that in spite of Emily Post, the custom of serving the hostess first seemed immovable.

There was the usual dinner-table conversation, and then Mr. Sulzberger rapped on his tumbler and said that he did not want to deny the ladies the opportunity to hear Mr. Matthews, so we would all have our coffee here together, and could ask Mr. Matthews some questions.

I shall try to give an impressionistic picture of what happened. In his quiet, deliberate way Mr. Matthews described the terrible conditions that existed during the war, and told facts that are pretty well known to all of us. Someone asked him why he had been so optimistic, and he defended himself quite well by saying that had American supplies been allowed to come through, or had the excellent Russian equipment continued, or had the Italians not gotten so numerous, or had the food situation not gotten so bad, it well might have turned out the other way. He thinks there is no doubt now but that Franco will execute thousands of people, and the people know it, and that is why they will not surrender Madrid. He says that the Loyalists are not antireligious, as many people think, but that they were strongly antichurch because the church had become very rich, very monopolistic, very corrupt. He said that the original communistic fervor had decreased, while at the same time it had increased in numbers of adherents. At the beginning, there were perhaps 15,000 Communists, and now he thinks there may be 300,000 Communists, but the general spirit is not communistic any more. The Germans were good soldiers, but there weren't many of them. The Italians were very numerous but poor soldiers. Russian equipment, which is American bought, was the best by far. Germany and Italy were paid for all the material and all the services they rendered. The Loyalists shipped a lot of money out of the country some months ago, and Franco is probably planning to get hold of this if he can.

No one wants the refugees who are in France; France doesn't want them and Franco doesn't want them back in Spain because they are hostile, demoralized, and have to be fed and have no jobs, etc.

This was all very interesting as it was being told although I got so sleepy I almost tumbled off my chair once or twice. Mr. Sulzberger called for a vote, and to my amazement about one-third of those present were for Franco, and none of them were Catholics. I said I did not know that anybody except fanatical Catholics were for Franco, and Mr. Sulzberger and Mr. Marcossin both explained that they had been for Franco at first because the government had shot down people who wanted to go to church. Later Mr. Sulzberger admitted to me that were that same war taking place here, he would be on the Franco side because of economic reasons: in other words, because he was a rich man and felt that it was a class war. I told him I was sorry to hear that because while I thought a banker could take that attitude, a newspaper man couldn't. Mr. Sulzberger came around later in the evening when I was talking to an old dowager, and sat down beside me and talked to me about twenty minutes or longer about his policy in running the *Times.* He said he had to remember when he was an American that he was a newspaper man and that he was a Jew. He said he was suspect because of the latter, and therefore had to be very careful to print all the news and accept all the advertisements that were decent, even when they were against the general interest of the Jews. He said his ancestors were run out of Spain in 1490, and naturally he had sympathy with the Jewish and other minorities that were being made to suffer, but on the other hand, there was the newspaper whose business it is to print absolutely all the news. This is the reason that right beside Mr. Matthews' column he carried the column by Carney, whom the liberals in New York hate. . . . Mr. Sulzberger would not admit this, but he did say that he was a much weaker reporter and could not be compared with Mr. Matthews, but he was the best that they could get at the moment, and they felt that they owed it to their readers to print both sides, not only of this but of everything. He said he felt boycotts were dangerous, and he would not refuse the pages of the *Times* to German steamship companies because that only gave Germany more real grievance against us Americans and against the Jews. He said he probably killed plenty of Jews in the World War and German Jews killed plenty of American Jews, and he had no illusions about Jewish brotherhood.

I told him I did not see why he was so timid about being known to be a Jewish newspaper owner. He said the Germans had accused America of being completely in the power of Jewish newsmen, but then he went ahead and answered this himself by admitting that there were very few Jewish-owned newspapers in the United States, and very few Jewish-owned large corporations, and also that the great bulk of the *Times* advertising did not come from the Jewish firms as people sometimes erroneously thought, just because Macy's, Gimbel's, Saks, and Bloomingdales are so big. Well, I didn't learn anything new from all this except that it just illustrates again the class divisions in this country. In spite of all he said, Sulzberger is more of an economic loyalist than he is a liberal Jew. Nominally, he is a Democrat, but at heart I think he doesn't want to be anything. I really can't quite make him out. It seems strange to say so and hard for anyone to believe, but my impression is that he is an exceedingly inhibited, exceedingly intimidated man, who feels (as he actually said) that his only duty is to print all the news and let the people draw their own conclusions. He says this is because he has the newspaper instinct, but I think it is because he is so scared and so uncertain as to which side he ought to be on. He would like to be a Tory Republican Gentile, and he won't face the fact that Torian Republicanism is forever irreconcilable with liberalism and religious minorities; that is, the Jews. His wife is a staunch pro-Loyalist, and like all women, is in this sense much closer to reality.

Another thing that impressed me about this party was the stiffness of it. Mr. and Mrs. Sulzberger are not stiff, but there is something about the formality of the service, the rapid succession of beautiful big service plates, the dodging in and out of the butlers, the fact that so many of the guests don't know each other (which is always the case at New York dinners), and something about all these which combines to make the party not quite come off. My friend Alex Gumberg,[4] who is about as graceful as a turtle, can get a bunch of people together and everybody has a grand time no matter how many bigwigs are present. I had the feeling that nobody was feeling quite honest at the Sulzberger dinner. . . .

I forgot to tell you that the one thing Matthews told us that was very

4 Alex Gumberg was a Russian émigré who conducted an import-export business. He and his wife, Frances Adams Gumberg, lived in the same hotel (One Fifth Avenue) where KAM resided during his New York stay.

startling was that the bombing didn't do a great deal of damage, and therefore the thing which Chamberlain and Daladier feared most from the Germans bombing London and Paris was probably unsubstantiated. The bombs were terrifying but they are extremely expensive and do relatively little damage. The most terrible bombs, of which there were not very many, were apparently an experiment tried out by the Germans and the Italians. It is believed that their contents were liquid air. These shook the ground for acres around.

Sincerely yours,

New York

To William Menninger and John R. Stone, Topeka, March 30, 1939

Dear Bill and John:

This letter is for recreational purposes only.

I thought you might be interested in my expedition of last night which began at 7:00 with a dinner in a Greenwich Village apartment (which means a dark, dirty doorway and a couple of flights of dingy steps, and then stepping into a really very charming three- or four-room suite.) This was Lorine Pruette's, who reviews books for the *Herald Tribune* and writes a page or two for the *London Bystander* called *A New York Letter,* and does other such things. She is a nice girl, and had a noisy woman physician, a very Bohemian girl who had two or three boyfriends call in person during the dinner, a professor of economics from Columbia, a Ukranian, and Colonel and Mrs. McCormick. He is the Commissioner of Corrections, and told an amazing story about his childhood in Maine, where his father was a preacher and had eight children, and the whole family lived on about $50 a month. They were so cold in winter and had so little food. They used to have one soft-boiled egg for the entire family, and each one would take a taste of it out of a spoon. He talked to me afterwards for quite a while, and told me how he became so masochistic, and identified himself with that character in *If Winter Comes* who took the blame for everything, etc. . . . He has charge of all the prisons in New York and is a curious mixture of sweetness and softness and hard-boiledness and realism. He won't allow any jailer to so much as raise his hand against a prisoner, which is in sharp contrast to the way the police treat them. I could run on about him for several pages, but I will pass on to the next act, except to say that he said the Police Department was very sensitive about the high suicide rate, but that the way to study it would be to get a friend of mine, who influences the Mayor, to have the Mayor do it. Of course, I am not going to do this. . . .

Oh yes, you would be interested to know that McCormick has the greatest admiration for Wilson and the Wichita police system, which I told him more about, and he is very generous in his praise of others and very modest about himself, although he could have almost any federal job in the country, but prefers to get a state prison job later in a university town where he can lecture on Penology.

I had to bust out at 11:00 to keep an appointment with Alex Gumberg, who has been working like mad in the past few days since returning from California trying to accomplish certain things in Washington. As I suppose you know, there is an almost mythical character, Tommy Corcoran, who is supposed to be extremely influential with the President. Well, Tommy has a fiancée who is a pretty little Irish blonde who had to come to New York to have a good time with a friend of hers. . . . Anyway, it was very important for Gumberg to give these girls a nice time, so she picked up Bruce Lockhart, author of *British Agent* and in reality a member of the Intelligence Services for the British government, a charming Scotchman who speaks about five languages and is very cute, but afraid of women, which they love of course, and the five of us went down to a night club called Twenty-One, where we saw Robert Benchley and had a long talk with two of the editors of the *New Yorker*. Then we went over to the Stork Club. The Stork Club is on the whole the most interesting and lively place, I guess, although others are more aristocratic and attractive, and have more socialites. It is very difficult to get a table at the Stork Club unless you have a pull of some kind, but we had a very nice table, and Alex kept supplying everybody with champagne, and we had a string of visitors, chiefly on account of the pretty blonde, I think, but partly because of Gumberg and this woman lawyer whose name I forgot.

Heywood Broun sat down with us for quite a while. He is as big as a mountain and really almost flows over the chair, and his hand is like a bear's paw. . . .

Franchot Tone and several friends were sitting at the adjoining table about three feet from me, but I did not ask to meet him because he looked kind of wistful and pale, and I think all this divorce notoriety has made him feel a little on the spot. He told one of the columnists who was with us that he was not going to do another Guild play, but was returning to Hollywood this summer and then coming back to New York in the fall. He had several boyfriends around him, but no girls.

At the next table was Schnozzel Durante, who was having a gay time, and later took the microphone and entertained the crowd. He is an ordinary-looking pug in everyday life. . . . He nodded and smiled at me, so I went over to talk to him for a minute or two, and told him I liked his show.

There was a columnist there by the name of Leonard Lyons, who is a kind of rival of Walter Winchell, getting stories from Gumberg. My business seemed to be to dance with the girls alternately. While I was dancing with one girl, Gumberg was doing politics with the other girl. I don't know how far he got with the politics, and the dancing wasn't much because the floor was too crowded. However, this fellow Lyons is a charming, wistful, earnest fellow, who is apparently on good terms with Walter Winchell and who had the management remit the entire bill for all evening, but Mr. Gumberg insisted on paying it. These newspaper columnists are very powerful in places like that. Lyons sat with us most of the evening, which was a great compliment. He told me quite a little of how he worked. He begins at 10:30 in the evening, and makes fifteen nightclubs every night to see who is there and get some stories. I told him that one night of it nearly killed me, and how he stood it I couldn't imagine. He smiled wanly, and shook his head. He gets to his office by 4:30 in the morning and writes his story, and by that time it is morning, and he plays with his little son for a while, and then goes to bed, and gets up in the middle of the afternoon. He said the Stork Club was usually the best place for seeing people and for his work. He's got a friend he wants me to see professionally, and he is supposed to call me today or tomorrow. I told him I would send him a book if he promised not to give it any publicity, my reason being that I didn't want him to think I was bribing him. I also asked him not to mention my name in his column.

Walter Winchell came over and sat down with us, and I talked with him quite a while. He is really a nice gentlemanly fellow, and responded with evident pleasure when I told him I thought his column was getting better all the time. He said he had always wanted to put in some of his social ideas and ideals, but that Hearst would not let him. He is still afraid that Hearst would fire him although I told him that I thought that was practically impossible, but that he ought to know more about it than I. I have heard before that he has this phobia. He said he had been wanting to meet me, having heard of me through Frank Norris of *Time,* and asked if I wanted to ride around with him some night in his little police car. I told him that I would, and he said we ought to wait until the weather was a little better, and then that I should pick him up at the Stork Club any night I could come. He said it might be exciting or it might be dull, that one never could tell. I said it did not matter, because we could talk anyway. He was very pleasant, but left us rather shortly to go back to a rather uninteresting group of men, with whom he sat for the next two or three hours. Lyons told me that he had said that there wasn't any use of his talking to me because he knew that he was crazy. I hope this won't appear in his column.

There were several other notables sitting around, but these were the ones that would interest you the most. I got dead tired toward morning, and told the crowd I was going home whether they were or not, and I think they were pleased that somebody had the courage to do this, and we charged out into the rain about 5:00 a.m., having smoked 500 cigarettes, having drunk 4 quarts of champagne, and eaten 50 sandwiches and bumped into 200 people on the dance floor, and talked to I don't know how many people.

This was my first nightclub experience this year, and I think it will be the last one, but I think it was rather interesting. Many people know or wanted to know these two important women (because anyone who wants to influence anything that is happening in Washington thinks they can do so by influencing this girl, but they are wrong). This blond girl is a typical little snappy blue-eyed Irish girl who is smart enough to keep her mouth shut and pretends to be a dumb innocent little girl when really she knows her way around and realizes her power but is very modest about it. She and this woman lawyer, who kept telling me that it was her ambition to be more feminine, were much more interested in one another than they were in any of us men. I never realized before how night clubs, which are supposed to be shot through with heterosexuality, and the place where people get up and dance as if their life depended on it, are really motivated by the combination of narcissism, exhibitionism, unconscious homosexuality, curiosity, a wish to escape from boredom, and the fear of going home to be alone (Franchot Tone, for example). If the people were really motivated by heterosexuality, they would go home before the night club instead of afterwards. I got so darn sleepy that I almost fell off my chair several times (this was fatigue, not alcohol, believe me), and to make matters worse, I did not count on this dancing, and had taken a four-mile walk in the afternoon.

But don't get the idea that New York life is all beer and skittles. This was an interesting evening, but I have had lots more pleasurable ones, and in spite of getting home toward dawn, I had to get up this morning a little past 7:30 and get to work.[5]

I attended the Psychoanalytic Society meeting Tuesday night and heard a very literary but nonscientific, nonpsychoanalytic paper by Zilboorg on Proust followed by a long-winded discussion participated in almost exclusively by some foreign Jewish analysts, to the annoyance of the American Jews and Gentiles, followed by a business meeting that gave me a pain in the neck, but in which, fortunately, a strong movement to limit the number of analytic candidates was overridden by a slight majority vote.

Sincerely yours,

To Harry Levey,[6] Chicago, June 15, 1939

My dear Harry:

Last night I read very carefully your "Critique of the Theory of Sublimation," in the current issue of *Psychiatry*. It interested me very much, and I want to say that I think you have done us all a great service in making this

5 KAM was seeing patients in New York while undergoing analysis with Ruth Mack Brunswick.

6 A Chicago psychoanalyst affiliated with the Chicago Institute.

survey. I have long wanted to know just what you here so painstakingly point out for us.

I, myself, have a notion that sublimation is not something that happens to the sexual instinct, but something which the sexual instinct does to the aggressive instinct. In other words, I think the erotic instinct is never sublimated but does the sublimating, or tries to. You don't say what your own theory is, and I am not sure that we fully agree, but I would like to know your impressions of this brief statement because no one that I know has thought as much about it in modern terms as you have.

I should appreciate it very much indeed if you would send me at least one, and preferably two, reprints of your fine article.

Sincerely yours,

To Harry Stack Sullivan and Ernest Hadley,[7] Washington, D.C., June 20, 1939

Gentlemen:

In the article by Erich Fromm in the current issue of *Psychiatry*, the criticism of Rank's theory is interesting and pertinent, but the first half of the article contains many serious inaccuracies which will undoubtedly arouse the suspicions of careful readers as to the validity of the latter half. One cannot help but react in astonishment to the author's expressed conception of psychoanalytic theory and practice.

On the second page, he states that the most important philosophic premise of Freud is his belief in the effectiveness of *reason*. He adds that Freud's method depends upon curing people by helping them to *know* the truth. In the first place, Freud has never expressed any great confidence in reason, nor does the psychoanalytic method depend upon it philosophically or practically. The naive assumption that reason is synonymous with knowledge, as indicated in the author's own words, is almost incredible in so well-oriented a student as Dr. Fromm. This error invalidates most of the succeeding discussion.

It is equally inaccurate to say (on the following page) that it is also Freud's premise that by changing the conditions of living one can change human character. Freud's conclusion (not his premise, an inappropriate word) was exactly the opposite, that change in the conditions of life does *not* effect a change in the personality structure which was erected as a result of instinctual and reality conflicts in infancy.

In the next paragraph, Fromm's discussion of psychoanalysis as based

7 Between 1938 and 1945, Sullivan and Hadley edited *Psychiatry*, a quarterly published by the William Alanson White Psychiatric Foundation, which the two men had established.

"on the sexual instinct" would indicate an unfamiliarity with the developments of psychoanalysis in the past fifteen years, were it not for the two final sentences of the paragraph mentioning the destructive tendencies without discussion.

It seems amazing that Fromm in the year 1939 should choose to perpetuate the tiresome misstatement that "To Freud [the enjoyment of life] means essentially to enjoy sex." After setting up this ridiculous straw man, Fromm can indulge in the familiar pious deplorings about the narrowness of such a view.

His implication on page 232 that the psychoanalyst makes no effort to "reach out toward the person whom we want to understand" is likewise an untrue statement, the refutation of which is similarly pointless.

Fromm uses the example of Nora in Ibsen's *Doll's House*. He states that if the analyst to whom Nora might have gone "believed in the conventional values of marriage," he would have regarded her reasons for wanting to leave her husband as neurotic "and would have primarily psychoanalyzed these," but if he shared Ibsen's belief that for her own sake she must leave her undesirable husband "then the analyst would have focused on psychoanalyzing those fears which would make her put up with an unbearable situation."

What kind of psychoanalysis has Dr. Fromm been exposed to, in which psychoanalysts *elect* what they will analyze, in which there is a *primary* psychoanalysis and presumably a secondary and tertiary analysis, an analysis in which there is *focusing*? That such procedures take place in the name of analysis one is obliged to believe, but that they can be called psychoanalysis in the scientific concept of the term no one can assert.

I am not sufficiently familiar with the writing of Rank to know how accurately he has been interpreted by Fromm, and his conclusions seem significant and important, but I can easily imagine that a student of Rank's might find the misrepresentations of psychoanalysis in the first half of the article very convincing.

Sincerely yours,

To Fred Kelly,[8] Peninsula, Ohio, July 10, 1939

Dear Fred:

Laura Knickerbocker[9] and I are having lunch and are looking over your

8 A journalist whose story on the Southard School appeared in both the *Reader's Digest* and *Kiwanis Magazine* in 1939.

9 Laura Knickerbocker was the wife of H. R. Knickerbocker, a traveling war correspondent for the International News Service, and a professional writer herself. She first came to Topeka to enroll her son Conrad at the Southard School and later represented the Menninger Clinic in New York City.

article with a critical eye, not very critical though because we like it very much in the main.

First of all we do not like your title very well because we do not like to be called experts and we do not like to have our children called bad even in quotation marks. We do not think any children are bad. This question of a title is a worrisome one but does not have to be decided this minute. We think the illustrations at the first part of the article are very good, and Laura has a few additional ones which are as follows:

You do not develop the idea, although you mention it, that some of the children are of superior intelligence. We feel that superior intelligence is frequently an indication of a child's inordinate striving to please someone and at other times it is a weapon which he uses aggressively in what he feels to be a battle against the family (the brothers and sisters as well as parents). For this reason we never put any great stress on intellectual achievements of the superior child, but put more stress on their evidence of improved social adjustment, greater kindness to other children, willingness to please the teachers in other ways than by getting high marks. You can make up a little illustration along these lines if you like, and if it won't do we can cross it out.

Here is another illustration in connection with the court showing that it does not always work out the way it is intended to. One day the children had baked a cake and later it was found that a large piece had been eaten out of the center. The court session was summoned and a highly intelligent little boy was chosen as judge and carried the whole proceedings through with logical technique and some mental pyrotechniques. He asked each child if he or she had stolen the cake, and when finally one admitted that he was the aggressor, the judge in a fatherly manner decided that since it was not such a great offense they would let the offender off with a reprimand, and then closed the court session upon an amicable note. Later it was discovered that the extremely intelligent little judge was the one who had stolen into the kitchen and eaten the cake and had carried through the court proceedings. . . . In addition, this is also an incidental illustration of false confession, since the boy who was sentenced admitted the guilt. This is something we see frequently. You would be surprised how many children confess having done things that they never did just in order to get punished. We had one child who not only did this but when he found that it wasn't effective used to go and deliberately do provocative things, prohibited things, and then come and tell the teachers about them. He would be very disappointed if they did not scold or punish him. "Aren't you going to spank me?" he would say. "I really did it. Why don't you punish me?" He realized what many punishing parents do not realize—namely, that punishment gave him the right to repeat his "crimes," and of course the crimes that he felt most guilty about were the crimes that he never confessed. In reality these unconfessed crimes were much less serious than the ones he did merely as a device for getting himself punished and relieving his sense of guilt. Freud has described a criminal character type on this basis called "criminality out of sense of guilt." The penal system never takes this into consideration, and that is what psychiatrists mean when they say that prisons increase the crime rather than decrease it. They remove the inner restraints of the individual and give him objective justification for renewing his onslaught on society.

There is a sequel to the court case above which you may want. The way we found out that it was the judge himself who committed the crime is that some time later he asked to have a special session of the court called so that he could make a confession. With a good bit of aid from the counselor who sat in on the court session, he told the other children that he had been the thief and he added in a whisper, "And I think I told a lie too." This was the healthy thing for him—that it all came out. It wasn't so much that he had been the thief, but he admitted that he had lied too. It was very difficult for him to do it, but he did.

You may wonder how we knew which of these two confessors to believe. In the first place we do not consider it important for us to know because we do not feel that we should take an active part in detecting or punishing misbehavior. In the ordinary sense of the word, we do not do any punishing whatever. It is purely up to the children, although, of course, we do counsel them. It is sufficient that the children believed the second confession. As a matter of fact, we had other evidence that it was the correct explanation. But this is interesting only theoretically and not practically because we make (made) no use of it.

Another incident about a superior child is a highly intelligent little girl came bustling in in rompers which had been made by her overly socially conscious mother. She had flowers on her hat and was a picture of fluttering femininity. Everything she saw she said, "How charming, isn't this marvelous?" in an affected and irritating manner. It was obvious from the first that the child was playing a role which had been imposed upon her by an unfortunate family situation. Her own personality as it developed through the observations of several months was that of a strong, original girl with mental development and talents far in advance of her years. After a few weeks she laid aside the rompers and the hat with the flowers and began to be extremely active, and instead of lying as she had in the past about the smallest incident learned to tell the truth rather flatly. When she was able to tell us things she did not like about the school and was able to express deep resentment against some of the teachers, we felt that she had made progress in developing some of her own capacities. Instead of encouraging her to be too lovely we encouraged her to speak out because we knew that when she returned to the unfortunate family situation she would have built up a sufficient bulwark of self-confidence on the basis of this new technique. When she said, "I do not like this old school," we were very proud of her. We encouraged this little girl to be a tomboy.

In another case which shows the opposite technique we encouraged a girl to work out her resentments in a feminine way rather than a masculine. For instance, this second girl was very pugnacious and always wanted to have fist fights and to indulge in physical combat. One Sunday morning when she had the radio turned on listening to some hymns being broadcast one of the boys in the room said in a demanding voice, "Turn down that radio," whereupon the girl jumped up and proceeded to punch the boy. The fight ended in a draw with no bad penalties exacted from either side. Later in the week the cooking teacher explained to the tomboy girl that we were going to have a tea and that since she liked to cook but had never had the opportunity to learn, she would let her help make the cookies for the tea. It was interesting to note that she brought exactly the same emotions to the kitchen when she made the cookies that she showed when she gave the boy a punch. She was not content to make a small batch of cookies but made four hundred, and kneaded the dough and beat the eggs and worked with tremendous energy. She produced good cookies and from that time on showed great interest in cookery, which seemed to be as good an outlet for her as fights.

One little girl had a strong urge to continue the role of being a baby although she was ten years old. She continued her baby talk and gave many evidences that her highest ambition in life was to be "daddy's baby." Curiously and incidentally, "daddy" was one of the words that she couldn't say. To overcome this pathologically prolonged need the technique used was to direct every effort toward giving her some satisfaction in *having* a baby rather than being one. She was given numerous dolls and encouraged in their care. In the workshop she was assisted in making dolls. The phenomenon of maternal care in domestic animals was illustrated. She was given pets and encouraged to take care of them. This is about enough of such illustrations— in fact, probably too many—but you can take your pick.

Going along now in the article you will note that at the bottom of page 2 I have made some pencil marks with reference to what you say about the teachers. You say they are highly trained, but I think you might make more of a point of the fact that they go on being trained. There are not only daily conferences of teachers, doctors and psychologists, but there are evening seminars at regular intervals at which not only cases are presented but systematic studies are pursued. In the summer an institute is given which all the teachers attend and which some outside teachers are invited to attend. You know something about this. But you may have gotten the idea that it was a missionary effort only. To my notion, the greatest value of it is the education of our own teachers although this is continued, as I have just said, throughout the year.

In this connection, but jumping to page 5, where I have made a note about it, I think you might make much more definite both early in the paper and throughout the paper the point that the school is organized along psychoanalytic principles. In this it differs radically from all other schools. Everything we do is based on psychoanalysis, on the science, theories, and practices of Freud. We made a fundamentally different presumption at the very start. Most schools and 99% of the half million teachers in the United States, or whatever number there are, believe that the child is hungry for facts and that the chief duty of the teacher is to marshal these facts in some interesting way with the proper gradation of difficulty so that the child seizes simple facts and the more complex facts as the teacher doles them out—something like a cafeteria. Now, we have no conviction that the child is so hungry for facts as all this. We do not think of him as going through life eagerly seizing such morsels of information as he can obtain from more or less skillful waitresses. We think he only accepts facts and reality, information, knowledge, learning, etc., as the lesser of two evils, you might say. He accepts them because he wants to please the teacher and wants to please her because he wants her to love him. In ordinary education the love of the child for the teacher and vice versa is considered incidental, unimportant, and often something of a nuisance. In our school we think it is fundamental. But we think it has to be controlled and regulated and profitably directed. The whole school is based on this principle, helping the child to learn by helping him to love. You asked me once what I would say to be the fundamental difficulty with the children that require special help, that is, help from us in a special school. I should say that these children are those who have had unusual difficulties in obtaining or realizing love from their parents. Parents frequently think they love their children when they do not, and the children know it. So I do not expect you to be able to get this point across very well in your article, but at the same time I think it is quite fundamental. You will find it to be the basis of my article in the *Atlantic Monthly*, a manuscript copy of which I am going to try to send you.

Please understand that this use of psychoanalytic science is quite apart from the specific use of psychoanalysis as a therapeutic method in a given case. Many people are confused about this, and perhaps you are. Psychoanalysis is in the first place a treatment technique and we use it that way. In addition it is a theory of psychology, a scientific discipline. It is a body of principles and laws. In this sense it can be applied to things like education, as we are trying to do. It can also be applied to anthropology, art, etc., but this is not our immediate concern.

On page 5 you make reference to our clinic as being the largest in the country. I think you are wise in soft-pedaling the clinic, and I am glad that you make only this one reference to it. But I do think you could say something better than calling it the largest in the country. In the first place, it is not the largest one, it is the largest *private* one. There are some public clinics in New York which are much larger. I do not know exactly what you should say here. Anything I suggest sounds a little immodest to me, but to be as objective as I can I believe you might do best by being somewhat vague and allegorical. You could either just say the "famous or well-known Menninger Clinic," which I do not like, but which has the advantage of being nonspecific, or you might say "the Menninger Clinic which is for psychiatry what the Mayo Clinic is for surgery." It happens that the Mayo brothers were Doctor Will and Doctor Charley, and my brother is Doctor Will and we sometimes are twitted in a complimentary way about this, but it must be done very delicately, and before it goes in I want Mr. [John] Stone to pass on it, because he is very strict in his ideas about this, and I think he is perhaps right, although I do not think it is as important as he does.

On page 4 I have indicated that what you call progressive education methods refer in the part that you mention only to the project method, which is actually used by some nonprogressive schools. To tell the truth the expression "progressive education" is a kind of polite racket, and while we have no objections to it we think they claim too much, and probably would want to take claim for everything that is being done at the Southard School if they knew about it.

I have forgotten that on page 7 you discuss punishment, but you can add some more about it from what we have dictated above.

As I have indicated in several places, I think it would be better not to nickname the school "Southard." It is "The Southard School," and while you can abbreviate it occasionally just to relieve the monotony, do not do it too much.

On page 9 I have made a note for you to see my *Atlantic Monthly* article about parents.

You asked me once how the school started. I think that is described in one of the pamphlets that they gave you, but I will describe it again (you might read these if you don't mind). I was teaching at Harvard when Ernest Southard, the youngest and one of the most brilliant professors Harvard ever had, was in his heyday. I was talking to him one day about my own future, and he said, "You are a son of pioneers and you must be a pioneer too. They need you out West. They will be more susceptible to new ideas than we are in the East. Go on with your plans to establish a psychiatric clinic but do not forget the children. Most of us do." Most psychiatrists forget the children too. And we are going to learn most about psychiatry and psychology and education from the studies of children, especially children who do not get along as well as others, so when my brother, father and I established our clinic we also started the Southard School. Southard died suddenly shortly after I had talked with him about this, and that is one reason I left Boston and went back to Kansas. What was more logical than to name the school after him? He was one of the biggest inspirations of my life and not only of mine, but many other contemporary psychiatrists. He was only forty-two when he died. A biography has just been published by Doctor Frederick P. Gay.

Do not put all this in the article, but these are the facts. The school was a financial liability from the start. We never expected it to be anything else. It has been supported by donations from friends, patients, my family, the Rockefeller Foundation, and, I should add, by many of the employees who have patiently labored at their very interesting work at salaries less than I should like to see them getting, which amounts to a donation and a very loyal and generous donation. The reason the school runs at a loss is that we regard it primarily as a research institution. We only take children that we think we can help and not children that parents want to get rid of because they are ashamed of them. We do not have a sliding scale. I mean, the rich children pay no more than the poorest child, and neither pay as much as it costs to keep them in school. As a matter of fact, and I do not know if you could or should put this in your article, one of the significant things we have all learned is that parents are not willing to pay much to help their children (Laura [Knickerbocker] thinks this should go in the article so I will tell you more about it.)

Parents brag about how much their children cost, but as a matter of practical economics they simply will not pay even what it costs for treatment. A wife will spend 10 times as much on the treatment of a habitual alcoholic husband as she will spend on an unhappy, neurotic child. Of course, this is partly due to the fact that adults earn money and such a wife often feels that she is only spending her husband's money to try to rehabilitate him. The truth of the matter is that few parents realize the seriousness of the personality difficulties in children. They keep encouraging themselves to believe that a child will "outgrow" it. Furthermore, they do not like the implied reflection upon their own bad techniques. Sometimes I think also that parents want to pay for medical attention like they buy clothes. They think because the child is little and uses less cloth in his suit, therefore his clothes cost less than his father's, that his psychiatric treatment should cost less than his father's. As a matter of fact, the psychiatric treatment of children takes more time and more skill than that of adults, not less. This is the reason that there are 100 sanitariums for adults to every one school of the type of the Southard School. There are only one or two or three such in the United States and in fact in the world, and the reason for this is not lack of vision on the part of the psychiatrists; the reason is that the parents who see the need are those who cannot afford the treatment. Parents who can afford it either do not see the need or will not spend the money. I could give you so many illustrations of this that you would have to write another article.

Laura says if I give you any more ideas you will have indigestion. So do what you can with these. In the meantime I am sending Laura's copy of the manuscript plus a copy of this letter to Miss Jean Lyle, who, as I told you, was associated with us for a long time, and having been a high school principal herself as well as a newspaper woman, she has always had an interest in the school and was materially responsible for building up its present ideals and structure. I will ask her to return the manuscript with notes of her own interlined and some additional suggestions that may occur to her. As I understand it you want these as promptly as possible, so I will air mail this today and ask her to attend to it immediately also.

Sincerely yours,

TO HARLEY WILLIAMS, LONDON, SEPTEMBER 2, 1939

My dear Doctor Williams:

Little you suspected at the time you wrote me on August 15 that such startling changes would occur within the next two weeks. I think you will realize now why we all felt so strongly that England should have acted at the time Czechoslovakia was taken, but we are proud of England for taking a firm stand now. Many of us feel that our Senate, in its childish resentment against some things Roosevelt had done, helped to precipitate this crisis by encouraging Hitler to believe that we would not support England, not only with materials but ultimately in other ways. Personally, I have no doubt but what we will support England in whatever way England needs us, although I must add that there is a great distrust in this country of Mr. Chamberlain and of all those associated with him.

You asked me to tell you a little about the feeling over here. The feeling has not changed here for a long time. There is almost unanimous disapproval of Hitler and of the Germans. Most of the people who dislike Roosevelt or disapprove of his domestic policy approve of his foreign policy. However, the Americans are determined not to get into the war, or at least they talk as if they were, and I think this is partly due to the fact that they feel it is inevitable and hate to think about it. People seem to be slow to realize there is no such thing as an isolated country any more, that all nations are interlocked. Personally, I think nationalism is a stupid device which propagates trouble. By the time this letter reaches you, England probably will be making great sacrifices of money and blood, and you will be intensely sympathetic and hoping for the best.

You and all the English probably think we are pretty smug sitting here thinking what England ought to do, etc., and hoping to keep out of it ourselves. I don't suppose I can explain this to you fully, but to put it briefly, I should say the American attitude is something like this: Most Americans feel that if Chamberlain had not been secretly sympathetic with Hitler he could have prevented this war by taking a firm stand at Munich. If he had not succeeded in stopping Hitler, he would have had the enthusiastic and loyal support of the Americans in his effort. At the present time we feel that he is reaping the consequences of his duplicity or fear or whatever it was that made him act in such a stupid way. Of course it is a human tendency to try to shut our eyes to our own responsibilities. I think, for example, we made a terrible mistake having not supported the Loyalist government in Spain (which England also fought against for some stupid reason) and the Chinese government. Don't think I am so chauvinistic that I think what we do is correct. It is always a lot easier to see what some other country does that you do not think is correct.

I am writing this letter in little spurts, almost like free associations, in the midst of various interruptions, frequent radio bulletins, etc., and just to complicate matters, we happen to be having our monthly psychoanalytic society meeting today. Furthermore, I leave Monday for New York, which, as you know, is quite a little journey, and as I expect to be gone a month or two, I have many odds and ends to finish up here.

I think it would be very interesting to have a little honest personal information and if you will write me rather frequently, I will do the same to you. Address me at 1 Fifth Avenue, New York, however, instead of Topeka. Thus far we have no censorship, and I don't believe you do either. The Americans find it absolutely incredible that Germans should be forbidden to listen to foreign radio dispatches. We listen to everything, but no one believes anything the Germans say. We are always impressed with the dignity and restraint of the English speakers as well as their excellent literary style.

We are very busy here at our Clinic; we wish we had the possibility of having you with us.

Sincerely yours,

New York

To Harley Williams, London, October 28, 1939

My dear Dr. Williams:

For the perfectly selfish reason that I hope to get another letter from you soon, I am going to answer yours promptly. I am still in New York. . . .

It happened that before your letter came, I had had dinner with an English friend or rather an American friend who had lived the first twenty years of his life in London and the past five years here. He is very objective, I think. He says the idealistic English citizens are rather provoked at us for not coming to the support of their program. He says it is hopeless to try to make them understand that America is so enormous and comprises so many different nationalities and so many diverse opinions that it lacks the solidarity of England. He says a few of them realize the distrust that Americans have of the fascistic elements in the British government. He distrusts them himself, but he agrees with you that at the present time Chamberlain is pretty mad at having been tricked, and all parties are solidly behind him.

Well, at any rate, I can assure you that the American people are 90% sympathetic with England and about 85% sympathetic with China. The newspapers are full of stories from England and speeches and opinions so that we think we hear a good deal about it. Nevertheless, I was glad to have your enlightening comments. Opinions about Russia seem to be very confused here. Some people think that Stalin was really doing us all a favor, and of course others think that he is an imperialistic grabber almost as dangerous as Hitler. As psychoanalysts, I suppose we should suspect that both things are partly true.

As a psychoanalyst, also, it is interesting to me to see, what you also hinted in your letter, that in spite of our fear and aversion, etc., there is something within us that slightly welcomes the idea of a war. A lot of doctors are talking about going to England in organized medical units, and it even tempts me a little, but of course we would have to have some wounded men to work on. This sounds ghoulish.

Roosevelt is steadily gaining in popularity, even with his enemies, on account of his intelligent foreign policy. Of course, I have always been strongly for him although reared in a family committed to the ideal of the opposite party.

When the Senate refused to repeal the embargo in the spring, I wrote violent letters to my senator and asked him what the hell, and I see that he has now switched over, which in my unconscious is, of course, entirely *my* accomplishment. At any rate, I think there is little doubt but that the embargo will be repealed. If it had been done sooner, I think it would have discouraged Hitler from starting the war, so I still feel a little bitter about it.

I am trying to get out a couple of books of my own, besides one by my mother about her early days in Kansas [*Days of My Life*]. I think you would enjoy it very much, and I will send you a copy if you want one.

Is there anything else you would like to have from over here? If so, I will be glad to send it to you. I am going to send you a copy of a memorial I wrote about Freud.

What is the British opinion of Chamberlain's book, *In Search of Peace?* I bought it but I haven't read it yet.

What is the British opinion of *Grapes of Wrath?* I think it is a wonderful book, slightly one-sided and its dramatic highlights emphasized, but essentially true.

I ought to be at work on my manuscripts, but I couldn't resist the temptation of chatting with you this morning.

Do the British write as many letters as we do? If so, I should think it would take half the population of London to examine the letters of the other half. I honestly believe that if we should ever have to have a war, the post office department would simply give up in despair at the thought of having to censor all the letters. I would estimate that I write about eighty letters a week, and I imagine that the number of letters that go out of our clinic would be in the neighborhood of a hundred a day, and of course we are microscopic compared to some of these enormous institutions. Hundreds of radio performers and movie stars get thousands of letters a day.

I apologize for the disorganized style of this letter, but, as you will see, it is just what I said it was: a kind of a morning chat.

Sincerely yours,

New York

To John Dollard,[10] New Haven, November 2, 1939

My dear John:

I have continued to admire your fine mind and your fine work ever since our all too brief contact in Chicago. I was deeply appreciative of your courtesy in having recommended La Barre[11] to our clinic. He is a fine man and we enjoyed having him.

Now I have got to tell you that it is up to me to review your book, along with several others, for *The New Republic,* and it pains me to have to pan it, as I feel compelled to do. Frankly, I am very disappointed in it and I think you have done yourself an injustice. I don't want to add to this by doing you a further injustice, and the least I can do is to send you a carbon copy of the review as it is framed at present. If I have made any errors of statement, I should appreciate it if you would correct them. I don't feel very good about speaking unkindly of a book written by a man whom I consider my friend and whom I hope to continue to consider my friend, and I suppose if I were less self-destructive, I would maintain a discreet silence.

The reason I shall do otherwise is not because of your book at all, John, but because of what I regard as a pernicious tendency for something that I consider unscrupulous and opportunistic exploitation of the present interest in the rapprochement of sociology and psychology by certain psychoanalysts. There are some traitors to psychoanalytic convictions and principles who will welcome your book, and because I am committed to irreconcilable opposition to their activities, which I do not believe are sincere, I am obliged to include your book in the condemnation because it appears to give them support.

10 A psychologist affiliated with the Institute of Human Relations, Yale University. KAM negatively reviewed his book *Frustration and Aggression* (1939) for the *New Republic.* Dollard believed that aggression is the result of frustration rather than an instinct of self-assertion.

11 Weston LaBarre was professor of anthropology at Duke University and clinical professor of psychiatry at the University of North Carolina Medical School; he is currently professor emeritus of anthropology at Duke.

You may be totally unaware of all this, and if so, you are an innocent victim, and you should not permit yourself to continue to be either innocent or victimized. On the other hand, it may be a matter of conviction on your part, and if so, I know it is honest even though I regard it as mistaken.

I don't believe psychology is something that can be picked up by clever fellows at cocktail parties, so to speak, and applied to sociological problems. Naturally, I am aware of the fact that you don't do this, but some of those who call themselves sociologists are doing it and are receiving support from some of those who call themselves psychoanalysts. I don't know who your psychoanalytic or psychiatric advisors are, but I think they ought to have spared you from what I regard as palpable errors in this book, so that instead of being a support to these superficial sociologists, it would have been a landmark in the broadening of psychiatric orientations.

The book appears to be successful, and I am glad my review is going to be too late to have any material effects on the sale. If I had not been concerned about your good opinion, in spite of my brutality, I should not have taken the trouble to write this letter, which I certainly hope you will take in the same spirit in which it is written.

Sincerely yours,

New York

To C. F. MENNINGER, TOPEKA, NOVEMBER 4, 1939

Dear Dad:

I feel remiss in not having written you more recently. I had such a nice letter from you about a week ago. I am delighted to know that you have a man to drive for you and to help out at Oakwood and do more work for you than you are getting from Richard.

I will give you a little report on my activities recently, which you can pass around to the boys if you want to, and I believe John Stone is keeping some of these for posterity. This reminds me to ask you how your work with the firm history is getting along.

A few days ago I went to Baltimore for the third time in a month. This time it was to address the welfare workers, that motley group of wistful men and women who look after the incompetents of the state, partly because it is a bread-and-butter job for them, partly because of some scientific interest in psychology and sociology, but partly because of some masochistic motives that perhaps all of us in the humanistic profession share but which is always very conspicuous in these groups. I have seen the same thing in a struggling organization of social workers in Kansas and in New York. I can't make up my mind whether they have this slightly pathetic coloring because of this neurotic element or because the public doesn't appreciate their work, pays them poor salaries, etc. Nevertheless, it was a good audience and an appreciative one. Near the end of my remarks, the governor of the state came in and shook hands with me and said a few words of encouragement to the audience. Dr. George Preston, an old mental hygiene friend, commissioner of the state hospitals there, is doing a fine progressive job. He is very friendly toward psychoanalysis although, of course, he is not a psychoanalyst.

After the meeting, I went over to a little party at the home of one of the Baltimore psychiatrists. All the young psychiatrists in Baltimore are very much under the influence and oppressive dominance of Adolph Meyer, and then Baltimore is, as you know, a slow, dingy, dull city where I should find it difficult to get much inspiration.

One of the men at the party, who is the psychiatrist to the Supreme Criminal Court, took me to a dingy restaurant where we went to a back room and met H. L. Mencken and his brother, who is an engineer . . . , a Catholic priest, who is a chemist, a Catholic judge, a Jewish lawyer, and one or two others. It seems that three or four of them sit down and drink beer and talk together every Monday night from ten to twelve, a pleasant custom. Mencken has lost all the fire and steam that used to characterize him. As you know, he used to be something of a misogynist, and then when about 40 or 45, he married this wife whom he loved very much. She died, however, after a few years, of tuberculosis. Perhaps his unconscious hostility for women made him feel guilty about her death. At any rate, he has been rather sad ever since. He used to be quite liberal, but now his tendency to be on the wrong side of questions is not very stimulating. He is rather typical of a class of persons who are small in number but whom one occasionally meets here, who feel very suspicious of England and rather inclined to think that the Germans have been more severely criticized than they deserve. Of course, no one defends Hitler, but the idea that the Germans are all wrong and the British and French are all right irritates these people into assuming a position that seems almost pro-German.

I told Mencken that I liked the book that he had written many years ago, *In Defense of Women,* and that I thought it was very intuitive and psychologically sound, and he professed to be very much pleased with these comments because he had recently been discussing with his publisher the possibility of revising the book and bringing it up to date.

I took the night train back from Baltimore, and the next evening I went to dinner with some rather aristocratic, wealthy Jewish friends, lawyers. One of them was the son of the famous economist, Seligman.[12] Many of these

12 Edwin Robert Anderson Seligman, who died in July 1939, was professor of economics at Columbia University. His son Eustace was a lawyer with the Wall Street firm of Sullivan and Cromwell; he was on the board of directors of numerous corporations, chairman of the board of trustees of the graduate faculty of political and social science of the New School of Social Research, and a contributor on legal subjects to various publications.

wealthy and brilliant Jewish lawyers are members of Gentile firms with very Irish names. I forget the name of this man's firm. I like the Jews very much as a rule. They are intelligent, cultured, and idealistic, and, of course, this wealthy group have very good manners and avoid many of the little irritating things that some of the less educated Jews do. Many of the things that we blame the Jews for are not Jewish so much as Oriental or Russian. One thing, however, that even these intelligent Jews do which irritates me and which I think they are quite blind to is having a dinner party with me the only Gentile present. They don't seem to realize how aggressive this is. The only Gentiles in the room were the maid that was waiting on the table and me. Anyway, their chauffeurs drove up and we rode to the theater in their private cars, which is a great luxury in New York. We saw Helen Hayes in a play which has been panned by all the reviewers but which I thought was a beautiful, clever, and extremely interesting play called *Ladies and Gentlemen of the Jury*. Helen Hayes herself is so sweet and natural and girlish and unaffected that the evening was delightful. I saw a number of my friends in the audience, as I nearly always do now that I am getting fairly well acquainted in New York.

After the theater, visitors to New York usually go to night clubs. The real New Yorkers generally go to quiet restaurants and have a simple drink or maybe some scrambled eggs, as in this case, and talk about the European situation or do some mathematical puzzles, as we did in this case, and go home a little after twelve. Of course, there is a set in New York, or several sets, the debutantes and the rich young people, and some of the livelier group of unmarried or divorced people in the late thirties who do a certain amount of nightclubbing, but in general, the nightclubs and aftertheater shows are for the entertainment of the vast number of visitors who come constantly on business or pleasure to New York.

The next day, which was Wednesday, I went to lunch with a businesswoman acquaintance of mine at the Colony Restaurant. This is supposed to be the swankiest restaurant in town because a great many society people come in there for lunch. Next to my table was Mrs. Randolph Hearst, who is much younger looking than her husband, but not very attractive. If she were not a Catholic, of course, she would have gotten a divorce long ago because of her husband's well-known love affair with Marion Davies. There was an ex-opera star, very fat and very homely, whose name I don't remember, and there were several socialites whose names I had heard but who mean nothing to me. The food at the Colony is excellent but not as good as Voisins, where I took Will when he was here, and which is probably the finest restaurant in the world.

That evening I went over to the Engineering Women's Club, which is a modest little house on East 35th St. which the wives of some of the engineers have made into a kind of rendezvous for the use of these women when they are in New York. You see, many of them live in the suburbs, and in New York, while there are lots of good restaurants, the thing you never get away from is the crowds, and for this reason people go to a lot of trouble to find any restaurants that are not very well known or form these little clubs where they can feel a sense of privacy and proprietorship. In addition, the club has formal dinners every two weeks with speakers, and on this particular night I happened to be the speaker. . . . The engineer who designed the Lincoln Tunnel was there and other engineers of different types, some of whom were quite intelligent and interesting, but most of whom were rather stodgy. In this respect, a little meeting in New York is no different from a little meeting of a similar sort in Topeka. The actual accomplishments of the individuals are usually greater, but the intelligence is no greater nor are they any more sophisticated and alert. I think they are rather more self-confident and they are a little more formal in their speech and a little less concerned with local happenings, but not only is human nature the same everywhere, but people are the same everywhere. There are always some queer ones, some pretty ones, some homely ones, and some self-important ones, etc. If someone had told me I was in Toledo or Topeka or Denver or San Francisco, I would not have known the difference. I think of this so often.

The following day I worked all day on Mother's manuscript, and in the afternoon I was called up by Mrs. Sam Lewisohn, whose father-in-law gave the Lewisohn Stadium to New York City, and she invited me to fill in at a dinner party where one of the men had sent belated regrets. This was a very interesting affair, and I was glad I went. They usually invite you to come at eight, and after cocktails, dinner is served about eight-thirty. The Lewisohns are extremely wealthy and have a three- or four-story home in the Gold Coast (upper East Side), and they have an elevator if you are too weak to walk up the grand, big staircase. Mr. Lewisohn is an art collector, and the house is literally full of modernistic paintings. They have what I believe is considered to be the finest of the Van Goghs plus many Renoirs, Picassos, etc. Mr. Lewisohn is a bland, boyish, leisurely man who has never had to work and who strolls about plucking the tip of his nose, laughing and telling you about the pictures in a very interesting way.

The editor of Harper Brothers was there, a man named Ordway Teague; he is also the superintendent of Higher Education in New York, which is just a hobby with him. This corresponds to the president of the Board of Education, except that he has some 50,000 college students under his general supervision. He is also the author of several books which I am going to get. I liked him very much. He had a keen mind and an incisive way of speaking and thinking, and we got along excellently together.

Another guest was Eddie Bernays, who is a son of Freud's sister. Bernays has made himself famous for being a shrewd . . . counsel on public relations, which means that he does for business firms about what Bill Kercher does for the Telephone Company [in Topeka]. There are quite a lot of these fellows in New York; some of them work on a salary basis and some of them on a fee basis. Some years ago, you will remember a famous Edison celebration, the first electric light, etc. Bernays was the fellow who thought this up and arranged it. Ostensibly it was a memorial to Edison but actually it was a big promotion for the electric light utilities. I have no exact way of knowing, but I imagine he got a fee of $25,000 or $50,000 for this, or maybe more. The psychoanalysts don't like Bernays very much because they think he exploits his relationship to Freud without being genuinely friendly and certainly not very generous. The private gossip is that he won't even give a few dollars to his poor relatives although he is well-to-do, and this kind of a sin is regarded by the Jews as little short of murder. The Jews are as a rule extremely generous, especially to their relatives. That is why the suffering of the German Jews was such a particularly bitter thing for them. Most of them don't like the German Jews, and they don't like to be accused of being more interested in German Jews than in American sufferers because these New York Jews are really very American in their ideals and activities, but the fact that the German Jews are remotely or sometimes closely their relatives made them feel absolutely bound to help, and they have contributed literally millions of dollars, often at a considerable sacrifice, to these funds.

Another guest at the Lewisohn party was Dr. Brill, and still another guest Karl Karmer, who wrote *Stars Fell on Alabama, Listen to the Lonesome Drum* (the folklore of various communities in New York State), and more recently *The Hudson River*. He is a silent man and said nothing all evening. His wife wears her hair too long and isn't very interesting; she sat next to me at dinner, and I gathered that, like so many authors, their moods rise and fall with their royalty checks upon which they depend for a living. The Karmers don't know yet how the last book is coming. Many of these authors, and I have met quite a few, do their writing at home, and their wives often do the typing for them. One of the great problems is to make themselves go to work.

The conversation at this party was unusually interesting. We talked a lot about education because of Mr. Teague, and then we talked about Freud's book *Moses*, because some of the guests were Jews, and then we talked a lot about psychoanalysis not only because of Dr. Brill and myself, but because one or two of the guests had been analyzed.

A little after midnight we went home, and Mr. Bernays sent me to my hotel in his car, which served to save me a one-dollar taxi fee. A comment in passing while speaking of the Jews and New York in general: most of these Jews employ only Gentile labor, which of course the poor Jews don't like a bit. This chauffeur was an Irishman and a very dumb one at that. He had been sitting out in his car for five hours. I don't know how long he had been waiting outside, but after he got me back to the hotel, he had to go to the garage and this would get him back at one o'clock. Then he was due at the front door of the Savoy Plaza at eight in the morning, where the Bernays live, to take the kids to school. This, by the way, is one of the chief functions of these chauffeurs.

Well, that brings me up to yesterday. I had lunch yesterday with the editor of *True Story* who is a very interesting character and runs a very interesting journal. His name is William Rapp. For six years he was a missionary with the WMCA in Turkey. He told me of the great extermination of the five million Armenians by the Turks which we hear so little of today. He has written . . .[13]

From John Dollard, New Haven, November 6, 1939

Dear Karl:

I liked your honest and heated letter [of November 2, 1939] very much, and I assure you that it gives me pleasure to conduct a discourse on this level. I wish that it were only possible to do it more often. I saw your little reference to the *Frustration and Aggression* book in your own *Journal* and thought at the time that it was far too harsh and indicated a disproportionate feeling on your part; I wanted to write and say this to you, but it is so utterly unconventional to squawk about a review, in my circles at least, that I did not do so. I did plan, however, to have a swing at you the next time we met.

You give me the opportunity now, and I am going to take it. My points would be somewhat as follows:

(a) I do not think you ought to punish us for "pernicious tendencies" in the field or for superficial pronouncements by some psychoanalysts and sociologists. I agree that there is a lot of trivial and sometimes dangerous hocum propagated nowadays in this field. I am committed to opposing it in every and any form, and to the types of researches which will give us unarguable knowledge about human socialization.

(b) I think if you are going to write such a derogatory review you should state your bias, i.e., that you have a more or less competing book in the field, and that we have not followed your hypothesis. I think that readers should know that we have had a chance to frustrate you in producing the book at all.

(c) As to the review itself, I think you should not state that the "stimulus-response" theory as a basis of scientific psychology was abandoned years ago, at least without stating who abandoned it and what they have in place of it. My impression is that it is more vital than ever before, and that it is

---

13 KAM has written at the bottom of the page, "continued in next letter."

getting an increasing body of relevant principles which are consonant with the findings of psychoanalysis. Such a statement itself indicates either that you are very badly advised on psychological movements in America or terribly stirred up about the book itself, and in either case you should be careful.

(d) You have not even read the book thoroughly. In the statement that you quote on the first page of your review, beginning "this study," you do not notice when you say that aggression is always a consequence of frustration that it is specifically denied shortly after that aggression is the only consequence of frustration. This oversight on your part takes away, for me, the main criticism that you have. On the third line of page 9 you will find a correct statement of our position. On the top of page 19 there is also a very careful statement on this point. If you claim that we erroneously state psychoanalytical concepts, which I do not believe because I did this work myself, I think you must give the correct Freudian statements or else say and underline that it is your unchecked impression that we misstate Freudian concepts, but that you have not specifically looked up the relevant writings of Freud. For example, if you can make anything else of "beyond the pleasure principle" except what we have stated, I would like to have the correct statement in Freud's own words. I worked like a dog on this, Karl, and I don't propose to be airily told what Freud's impression is. You must have really conceded the point when you say that under irritation or excitation "aggressive trends . . . have either been repressed, sublimated or directed elsewhere." Whence did they arise, then, if not from an instinct of aggression which both Freud, and you following him, have taken as your theory? Why is it treacherous to quote Freud correctly and not to agree with him?

(e) The statement on race prejudice is loose, as you have said, and I take the responsibility for this myself. What we meant, of course, and what a properly indulgent reviewer would see in it is race prejudice behavior. But in view of some virtues that the book has, I think this a rather petty point to make.

(f) I do not think that we have deplorably neglected Freud's hypothesis of aggression, as you have said. On the contrary, I think that we have given it with offensive clarity. If you had said that Freud did not operate on it, although you have tried to make it work in your book, I would have agreed with you; and if you had said that there is another theory of aggression implicit in psychoanalysis with which you did not hold, I would have agreed. I think on page 21 I have made it perfectly clear that we are adopting one of Freud's two theories of aggression, the earlier one and the one used in actual clinical practice by most of his followers. The fact that he has promulgated another dogma in *opposition* to his other theory of aggression is his hard luck and that of other analysts who do not think correctly about the problem. We just picked the one that seemed best to us and gave Freud full and flat credit for it, so I don't see where you get the "studied neglect." I think we have stated Freud's instinct theory correctly on page 22. At least it is the best that I could do with a theory that is not too admirably formulated by Freud himself, and I must say that I don't think that you had any better luck with it. It is true, by the way, that I have taken the route of cowardly silence in not reviewing your advocacy of Freud's death-instinct; I refused.

(g) With regard to the umbrella-poking example in which you distinguish between frustration and irritation and quote us to our great disadvantage, I want again to point out that you have not read the book carefully. We would define the state of an unpoked person as that of satisfaction. He is making a whole set of muscular responses which are interfered with by the umbrella poking which raises a painful tension and serves as instigation to behavior. There is an actual frustration, therefore, in the sense in which we are using the word. You may not like this way of using the term, but I do not think that you should misunderstand us or misinterpret us.

(h) You say that to the best of your knowledge none of the authors is a psychologist. The four whose names are on the book with mine are all members of the A.P.A., trained experimentalists, and members of the department here. I wonder if you are not taking sides in a private battle of psychologists on this point. Apparently you would consider Lewin a psychologist but not Thorndike,[14] on whom we draw so heavily; [J. F.] Brown a psychologist, but not Hull,[15] etc. Certainly you will not profit by any such side-taking and derogation of some of the most valuable persons in psychological science.

I think you have been both harsh and unfair in your view and that you ought to reread our book and rewrite the review.

I have been sent reviews several times before with the same request that you have made and have never taken the trouble to answer them. But it seems to me worth while doing with you, partly because I hope for a more vivid understanding of the work we are trying to do at New Haven, and I do not like to see you so prejudiced against it all in advance. I think a couple of days on the grounds here would put you in a much better mood to read the book and write a review.

Do I understand that you now have an office in New York, and if so that there may be an occasional chance to see you?

Yours cordially,

14 Edward L. Thorndike was a psychologist who taught at Columbia between 1899 and 1940. He was a pioneer in conducting laboratory experiments on animal behavior and applying the results to human learning. He was also a leader in the area of mental measurement. His major works include *Educational Psychology* (1903), *Animal Intelligence* (1911), and *The Measurement of Intelligence* (1911).

15 During the 1930s, Clark Hull held seminars on psychoanalysis and learning at Yale.

New York

Dear Dad:

Here comes the second installment in the report of my recent activities.

I believe I was telling you about the editor of *True Story,* and what he had to say about the Turks. He has written this up in a book which he gave me called *Osman Pasha.* Now he edits this *True Story Magazine* which has a bad name because it is a MacFadden publication and people think it is full of sensational stories. He, however, has a very high ideal about it, and says that it is not a sensational magazine full of yarns but a magazine which goes to people in the low-income group, who use it for a kind of mental hygiene. Not only do they read the troubles that other people are having, but they write their own troubles out and send them to him. He frequently gets as many as 15,000 letters in response to a single article in a single issue. I got very much interested in the material which he had collected as a result of the perfectly enormous correspondence which comes from his over two million circulation. I think he is in a good position to know what people are really worried about, not intensively as we do in psychiatry, but extensively in a broad survey. I got a great many ideas from talking to him, and he sent me a lot of statistics and sample stories and some of the questionnaires which they have used. I got a very different idea about the magazine than I had had before. As soon as I have read some of this material, I am going to do something with it and will probably write you about that again later.

On the way home from lunch I dropped into a movie on criminology that I had wanted to see, and although I only saw forty minutes of it, I got the idea. I came on home and wrote a few letters, saw a patient for an hour, and dashed off to a cocktail party.

I want to tell you a little about this cocktail party because it is very typical. It was given by an extremely wealthy woman . . . in her apartment at the Savoy Plaza, which is one of the swanky residential hotels. She invited me because I had met her at a luncheon. She has a compulsion for social activities and told me that she had not been to bed before four in the morning for ten nights, and I believe it. She had about a hundred guests there. I went in with Judge Pecora,[16] whom I know and happened to meet in the lobby. He and one or two others were the only ones I knew, although I did meet one or two people whom I shall try to remember. There was a Russian prince

16 Ferdinand Pecora, born in Italy, was one of the original members of the Securities and Exchange Commission appointed by President Roosevelt in 1934. He resigned in 1935 to become a justice of the Supreme Court of New York; in 1936 he was designated by the governor to preside over a special session of the Supreme Court of New York during highly publicized racketeering trials.

there whose name I didn't even catch but whom I enjoyed talking to. He just looked like any mature, intelligent, American businessman. I asked him about a few prominent Russians that I knew, and he disavowed any acquaintance with them or interest in them with considerable hauteur. Then he broke down and admitted that his cousin was an official in the present government, and although he despised the present government, he was very fond of his cousin. He said his cousin was a wealthy man who, of course, had lost all his property, but this cousin had made a hobby of social revolution and was very interested in it and believed in it, even at his own great loss. I was impressed by the incongruity between this man's hostility for the regime and his broadmindedness towards his cousin's interest in it.

At such parties as this, they usually serve champagne, scotch and soda, or any other drinks you want, and a few bites of food which, as a rule, are not very good. There are always a lot of very talky, talky women, who keep their hats and furs; a few rather bored-looking businessmen; authors; a lot of sissy-looking males from eighteen to twenty-eight, who are probably homosexuals; a few big, fat dowagers, who occupy the best chairs; and then a few celebrities to which the hostess always tries to introduce everybody. At this party they had Zasu Pitts, the movie star, and I never felt so sorry for anybody in my life. A lot of people were hanging around her and making inane remarks and expecting replies from her until she looked positively haggard. Then they dragged her over to one of these devices for recording your voice, and made her say something. Then they turned on the current and it bawled the thing out all over the room. If anything is more childish than this, what is it? I am sure that at a party in Topeka, she would have been treated with far more dignity and consideration. Meanwhile, she wanted very much to talk with me and asked me several questions which I never got to answer because people would interrupt with some damn silly chatter, or insist that she meet somebody or other whom it was obvious that she did not want to meet. She would smile and smile faintly at them and turn back to hear my answer to the question she had just asked only to be interrupted again. She did tell me that she had a curious interest in people who are in prison, and never failed to go through penitentiaries if she was in a town in which one was, and she also told me that it was so strange to her that people were so anxious to meet her and see her, but thought that that was only because they have the same interest in her as in anyone else in the pictures. She is really a modest, unassuming woman who is a little bewildered, which is the way she acts in her comedy roles. When she was introduced to this prince, she said, "What, a real prince!"—and she said it in such an innocent and naive way that no one could doubt her sincerity although, of course, she must have met lots of Russian princes before. There are plenty of them around.

Judge Pecora invited the hostess and myself and a fellow named Rubinstein, who was the financial advisor to Czechoslovakia at the time of its collapse, to go to supper with him. So about 8:30 we went over to have some spaghetti and other food at an Italian restaurant that the Judge likes, and he told me quite a few interesting things about libel suits, one of which he had just that day settled. They had awarded $25,000 to a magazine because a columnist had said that the magazine would probably fail, and four months later it did fail and blamed this remark in this column for having done so. The Judge said it is a common idea that these statements have to be malicious, whereas it is not necessary to prove that they are malicious in intent, but only that they are not true and do harm. He says the public has no idea how many of these libel suits against the newspapers are brought constantly because, of course, the newspapers never print any accounts of them.

Mr. Rubinstein, the financial advisor, had a great deal to say about the European situation, and there was a hot argument between him and another man as to whether or not the pro-German elements in England and the pro-English elements in Germany would manage to get together sufficiently to stop the war before long. Mr. Rubinstein did not think they would.

After the supper I took a taxi up to the Academy of Medicine where the Postgraduate Fortnight at which I spoke last year was in progress, and has been for two weeks. They have lectures every night in the amphitheatre, and the halls are full of excellent exhibits. I looked the latter over, and listened for a while to the lecture. There was a large crowd—a thousand or more I should estimate. I had a few reprints mailed to the clinic. The general subject of the two weeks was endocrinology, and most of it seemed to focus about the estrogenic and androgenic hormones.

I finally caught the subway back to my apartment, and read a little while and fell asleep. That was all for that day.

Nothing special happened Saturday, and Sunday I will have to write you about next time—a lunch, a speech at the International House at Columbia, a dormitory of 500 foreign students, and then the B and O train for West Virginia. All this in my next.

Love,

Part III
1940–45

$\mathcal{D}$r. Karl retained his quarters in New York City through May 1940, when he ended his analysis with Ruth Mack Brunswick. This year's correspondence was dominated by his continuing resentment over Horney's defection from Freudian concepts, an animus triggered by the publication of her book *New Ways in Psychoanalysis* in late 1939 and perhaps by Horney's analysis of Grace Menninger. Much of this dissatisfaction was vented in letters to Franz Alexander, whose review of Horney's book Menninger criticized as excessively tolerant.

In February 1941, Grace and Karl Menninger were divorced after twenty-five years of marriage, and in September Dr. Karl married Jeanetta Lyle. The idea that had intrigued Jeanetta Lyle, the reorganization of the Menninger Clinic and Sanitarium into a nonprofit organization dedicated to education and research, was realized in April 1941 when the Menninger Foundation was incorporated, with Dr. Karl as its first president.

In this year, Menninger was especially incensed about several war-related matters, such as the failure of the army to provide adequate psychiatric evaluation of prospective soldiers, the abolition of the Selective Service medical organization, and the dearth of psychiatrists in the military hierarchy. In June 1941 the staff of the Menninger Foundation offered a seminar dealing with various aspects of military psychiatry. The audience included physician and lay members of the local Selective Service Board, as well as area social workers. Data from this seminar were edited by Jeanetta Menninger and presented in the September 1941 *Bulletin of the Menninger Clinic*, a special issue dealing with military psychiatry.

The accusations of unethical behavior against Gregory Zilboorg (he had accepted the gift of a watch from a patient) came to a head in 1942 with an investigation conducted by the New York Psychoanalytic Society's board of directors. In his prolific correspondence with Zilboorg, Menninger counseled him on his course of action and assured him of his personal support but offered reasons for refraining from a more public advocacy. The majority report of the hearing concluded that Zilboorg had committed "technical errors" and gave him a reprimand, though a minority report declared Zilboorg innocent. Menninger worried that the reputation of psychoanalysis had been compromised by the precedent set by the hearing, especially by Alexander, who had testified against his former analysand.

Menninger's status within the profession was reflected by his invitation to become one of the editors of the *Psychoanalytic Quarterly* and by his unanimous reelection to the presidency of the American Psychoanalytic Association, the first president to serve two consecutive terms. Perhaps the judiciousness expected in this role was a key reason Menninger chose not to champion Zilboorg's cause publicly. A similar dilemma was posed by an invitation to review Horney's newest book, *Self-Analysis* (1942), a work which to Menninger reflected her characteristic contrariness to Freudian doctrines. Ultimately, Dr. Karl recommended that Otto Fenichel write the review for *The Nation*.

The concurrent publication in 1942 of Menninger's *Love Against Hate*, written with Jeanetta Lyle Menninger, and Alexander's *Our Age of Unreason* seemed to ease their rivalry temporarily and to moderate the ideological differences between them. "Our purpose is certainly the same," wrote Dr. Karl, "although our approach is quite different" (October 20, 1942).

Ernest Jones wrote to Menninger in 1943 to solicit information about the American psychoanalytic community and to complain about the uncommunicativeness of the American psychoanalysts. Although Dr. Karl complied with Jones's request, he proceeded to castigate him and the other European analysts for being equally stingy with information about their activities. From this response, it was clear that Menninger, who in the early 1930s had occupied a junior (albeit promising) position among established American analysts, now regarded himself as a member of the psychoanalytic elite. Moreover, he had become a mentor to such correspondents as Iago Galdston, J. K. Hall, and, of course, Zilboorg.

The war created a practical and immediate problem for Dr. Karl because of the imbalance between available psychiatrists to staff the clinic and the large number of prospective patients. Toward the end of the year, Dr. Karl's letter to the Surgeon General's office suggesting alternative uses for Winter General Hospital in Topeka revealed his farsightedness and contained a harbinger of the direction his future thoughts and activities would take.

Two notable letters were written early in 1944. In February, Dr. Karl wrote to his former colleague Robert P. Knight, then at the Austen Riggs Institute in Stockbridge, Massachusetts, citing the adventitious remark that had led to his choice of psychiatry as his specialty early in his medical career. This letter illustrated two recurrent dynamics in Menninger's personal and professional life, in his books, and of course in his letters: his proselytizing temperament and his fondness for the dramatic—the case history, the unexpected contradiction, the revelatory anecdote—as a teaching method.

In scattered letters in the early 1940s, Dr. Karl had predicted that the pressing postwar problem in America would be the treatment of its minority citizens. In March 1944, in a lengthy letter spurred by his reading of Lillian Smith's novel *Strange Fruit* (typically, fiction provoked this distillation of Menninger's thinking on the problem), Dr. Karl excoriated his country's, his city's, and even his own attitude toward blacks. "I have spent a good many years of my life championing the rights of people who are discriminated against," he wrote, but he concluded that he had done little about the biggest social problem of all: Our country's blindness, he declared, "is surely a form of passive suicide" (March 14, 1944)—and thereby he linked the problem to one of his most sustained interests. The concordance between the war against the Jews in Europe and the plight of American blacks also struck Menninger, and his readiness for commitment to neglected social causes was by then a familiar pattern in his letters as in his life.

In another long letter of 1944, Joseph Mankiewicz, the Hollywood writer, director, and producer, expressed alarm at the treatment of psychoanalysis and psychiatry in the movie *Spellbound*, then being directed by Alfred Hitchcock. Always sensitive to distortions of classic Freudian concepts and procedures, Dr. Karl corresponded with David O. Selznick, the producer, with Bartemeier, president of the American Psychiatric Association and official spokesperson for psychoanalysis, and with May Romm, psychiatric advisor for the film.

Menninger devoted much of 1945 to traveling. In California, he and Jeanetta tried their hand at fund-raising for the Menninger Foundation, attempting—rather unsuccessfully, he reported—to convince Californians that money was needed for the *training* of psychiatrists. This function was already important at the foundation, and at the Winter General Hospital it would soon require most of Menninger's energies.

Suddenly, he was summoned to Washington to begin his most important assignment and journey of the year. With Drs. John Romano, Leo Bartemeier, John Whitehorn, and Lawrence Kubie, he was dispatched to the European Theater of Operations (ETO) by the Surgeon General (and his assistant, William C. Menninger) to study war psychiatry in general and the syndrome of combat exhaustion in particular. The letters Dr. Karl wrote in 1945 from France and England to his family in Topeka were as lively and colorful as the letters he had written to his family from New York in the late 1930s. These letters were circulated among the family and selected clinic staff, and copies were sent from Topeka to Dr. Will in Washington.

When he returned to Topeka in July, he used some of what he had observed in Europe—such as group therapy in England—in his newest venture, the restructured Winter Hospital, which had been taken over by the Veterans Administration. This hospital became not only a sanctuary for veterans with psychological problems but, under Menninger's tutelage, an innovative experiment, a pilot training institute for psychiatrists and other professionals in the "helping" professions (social workers, psychologists, etc.), a prototype of the union between civilian and military psychiatry. The Menninger Foundation assumed responsibility for the teaching program at the hospital and staffed it with their physicians. In a letter of mid-July to the Office of Scientific Research and Development, Dr. Karl identified an indirect benefit of the trip, related to his latest ambitious endeavor: "[One] of the collateral values of the expedition . . . was the information gained with reference to the problems of psychiatric education, both for the immediate and for the more distant future" (July 14, 1945).

The final letter in this book is, fittingly, addressed to Anna Freud. In it, Karl Menninger expressed his enthusiasm for the impressive task to which he was now committed.

New York

To Lawson Lowrey, New York, January 2, 1940

My dear Lawson:

On the train returning here from Topeka I read your report on the Mental Hygiene Project at Kindergarten Level and the reprint of your article on Problems of Aggression. . . .

The article on "The Problems of Aggression in the Child" was interesting to me, most of all I think for the paragraph on page 9, in which you so frankly avow the "death instinct" principle ("As I see it, hostility is a part of man's innate biological make-up").

This and the following sentence are exactly what I believe. As you know, there are a few rather noisy psychoanalysts who reject all this and speak contemptuously of the "instinct theory" and deny the existence of any innate tendency of that kind. I think they do this largely to gain support from the sociologists, who seem to be coming into a big swing of popularity at present. See, for example, my review of Dollard's superficial book [*Frustration and Aggression,* 1939] and Horney's exasperating book [*New Ways in Psychoanalysis,* 1939] in the next (?) issue of the *New Republic.* From this statement of yours I should say that you are so nearly in agreement with the main stem of Freudian psychoanalytic theory that it is a pity you don't get into it officially. This doesn't distress my soul in the least, but rightly or wrongly I have a little impression that you are somewhat lonely professionally. Of course, this is none of my business.

Your friendly greeting recalled many days long past and made me wish that we might sit down and have a long talk together. I have been rather waiting for you to propose it and I suppose you have been waiting for me to propose it, so let's not stand on ceremony any more. I'll be the host if you will set the date.

Sincerely yours,

New York

To ANNA FREUD, LONDON, JANUARY 10, 1940

My dear Anna Freud:

Your letter of December 8 commending Dr. Redlich[1] came recently and was very helpful. We were glad to know of your favorable impressions, which we fully share. We have given Dr. Redlich a definite appointment for a residency with us beginning in July 1941. We are obliged to make these appointments a rather long time ahead because we have so many fine applicants and we like to select and make certain of the better ones as soon as we can. Dr. Redlich is well satisfied with this, however, because he wants to do some work in Boston in neurology and also, I believe, undertake an analysis. He has expressed himself as being very happy about the appointment with us, and we shall look forward to his coming.

I have had it in mind for some time that I should write you about certain developments at the Southard School, in which I am sure you would be interested. . . .

The actual administration of the school has been rather complicated, but we have now worked it out quite well. After many experiments, we put a young psychiatrist in charge and divided it up into various departments, including a psychoanalytic department, an educational department, a recreational department, etc. Perhaps you know something about this already from our *Bulletin* and other material that I assume you are receiving.

With the question of a child analyst we have had a series of difficulties. You will probably remember the difficulties that we had with Dr. Margaret Ribble. I am not sure that you were able to get an objective impression of the situation at that time, and I don't believe I ever wrote you about it because I did not regard it as a controversy so much as a result of the disturbed emotions of a woman whose father had just committed suicide, and who felt obliged to project the guilt which she felt for that event upon those with whom she had previously had amicable relations. I have never cherished ill will against Margaret in spite of the bitterness which she suddenly developed toward me and others. At any rate, she left precipitously, as you may recall.

---

1 F. C. Redlich, a psychiatrist who had published on schizophrenia and on social class and psychoanalysis, as well as coauthoring with Daniel X. Freeman the text *Theory and Practice of Psychiatry* (1966).

For a while we had no child analyst, and then we tried an untrained but intuitive psychologist, who had been analyzed, and she did some good work and some bad work, and she asked to leave. Again we had no child analyst for a time, and something over a year ago we received the application of a woman who was then living in Detroit. Mrs. H—— had apparently made a very good impression on several of our friends, but as we afterwards learned, some of them may have recommended her to us in an effort to get her further away from them. One of our staff members interviewed her and got a good impression of her, and I interviewed some individuals in New York, one of whom informed me that Mrs. H—— was a "pathological liar." I had some reasons to distrust this informant, however, and another informant told me that Mrs. H—— had fairly recently had some more analysis, or else some conferences with your father, and had been able to conquer some of her previous personality difficulties. My memory is a little hazy on these points now because it was over a year ago, and I am only sure of one thing, namely, that we did not investigate her as thoroughly as we should have. For instance, I certainly should have written you about her.

She began her work with us very auspiciously. She made friends with everyone rapidly, and expressed herself so enthusiastically about her opportunities and her satisfactions in her new work and took up her duties so energetically that we were all misled. She seemed to do excellent clinical work with some of the children. She read a very good paper to our Society.

Gradually, we began to have all kinds of difficulties with her. I will not bother you with an account of all of these, and no one of them is of major proportions, but I will give you some idea of them. She antagonized some people by reminding them frequently, especially when there was any difference of opinion about a case, that she was a relative of Freud, that she was a psychoanalyst of long experience, and that in Europe her opinion was considered important. When she was in the presence of some of the older analysts, including myself, she would be extremely unctuous and humble; she would refer to me as "the big chief" and appear to take every comment of mine with the utmost deference. I called her attention to the fact that she was a little paranoid and a little boastful, and she appeared to be immensely impressed by this, and declared her resolution to overcome these unhappy traits. Soon, however, we found that by subtle innuendoes and, in some instances, by outright gossip she managed to stir up a great deal of bad feeling among various members of the staff.

More serious than this, she insisted upon interviewing the parents of the children she was analyzing, saying that this is the way you always did and this is the way she must do, but when she would interview these parents, she would say in substance that she, the child analyst, was having great success with the child, and would have greater success were it not for the Southard School, which, in her estimation, was a terrible place. Since these parents had put their children in the Southard School and regarded the analysis as simply one of the treatment projects of the School, they would become much disturbed by this. In one instance, according to the psychoanalytic colleague who sent the child to us, Mrs. H—— told the very conservative grandmother that the child was ill because she, the grandmother, had taken so much pleasure in giving the child enemas and cleaning up her defecations. This shocked the grandmother incredibly and led her to decide that the school was a place in which indecent and immoral ideas were circulated, and she took the child out.

I do not know how convincing these piecemeal items may be to you, but I can only say that more and more clearly we realized that Mrs. H—— was an incessant troublemaker, a gossip, and, while I am not willing to say a dishonest woman, at least a very disloyal woman and a very indiscreet woman. Consequently, we were obliged to dismiss her early in December. I might add that she is one of only two or three employees out of over a thousand whom our organization has ever dismissed.

I want to say one more word about Mrs. H——. Her husband had made himself immensely popular in Topeka among businessmen, teachers, and others. Our business manager discussed his wife's personality difficulties with him quite frankly. His reaction to this was distinctly to his credit. He remained loyal to her and at the same time indicated that he could fully understand the reasons for our dissatisfaction with her. In other words, he acted the gentleman and expressed resentment neither toward his wife nor toward us. She, on the other hand, was quite bitter, as you can imagine. We allowed her to retain several of the patients whom she had begun work with who did not live in the school. I do not know what her future plans are, but I feel that she is not an asset to child analysis, and that you ought to know these developments in her career.

Her departure left the school in a rather difficult position, since five or six children need analysis and some of them had begun work with Mrs. H——. We immediately made vigorous efforts to locate a child analyst. We contacted Dr. Bornstein,[2] but she has now established herself in New York although she told me that at one time she would have liked to come to Topeka, but understood that we had Mrs. H——. Several other child analysts are prevented from coming to Topeka by reason of the fact that their husbands are engaged in work which keeps them in large cities in the East. Suddenly, we heard of Dr. Mary Hawkins,[3] and made immediate attempts to get hold of her. Dr. Bornstein gave her a high recommendation, saying that you and she had regarded her as one of your most promising students

2 Berta Bornstein, a Vienna-born child analyst.

3 Mary O'Neill Hawkins, a New York child analyst, was trained in Vienna. Later she assisted KAM and Jean Menninger in the adoption of their daughter, Rosemary, and became Rosemary's godmother.

in Vienna. We sent one of our most objective representatives to interview Dr. Hawkins, and our representative has a very favorable impression. Consequently, we offered her the position, only to learn that the day before this she had taken a position in San Francisco; she much preferred working at the Southard School and asked to be released from her position in San Francisco, but thus far has been unable to arrange this, to her great disappointment and ours. It looks, however, as if she might be able to come to us by the first of February. If you care to express an opinion about Dr. Hawkins, it would be very helpful to us, I am sure, in working out the most comfortable and effective situation for her at the Southard School.

I have given you this rather long resumé about the school partly because I wanted you to know something of the work we are doing and some of the troubles we are having in doing it, but also for another purpose. I scarcely know how to approach the matter other than very bluntly. We have been wondering if there might be any possibility of interesting you in coming to the Southard School. I am assuming that if you did so, there would probably be a considerable number of individuals who would want to study child analysis with you, and that a good deal of your work would be teaching. We are in hopes that, in the near future, we shall be in a position to develop a psychoanalytic training institute in Topeka, and of course you would be one of the prominent participants in such an institute. We are expecting Karl Landauer[4] to arrive soon; Edoardo Weiss[5] is already with us, as you may know, and in addition we have two other training analysts. We have probably the best organized and most highly developed psychiatric institution, private or public in this country, although it is much smaller, of course, than many of the large public institutions. I think our reputation for scientific work is high. We have an excellent panel of resident psychiatrists, who come for a minimum of one year and who usually stay longer for training.

Of course, the question will arise in your mind about the position of a lay analyst in this country. The general attitude at present is that child analysts need not be physicians, and, as you know, several of the European lay analysts are recognized teachers, Dr. Sachs and, to some extent, Dr. Bernfeld. On the other hand, I must admit that there is a more and more definite line drawn against lay analysts in the general practice of analysis—I mean for adults. This would not mean, of course, that you would not be able to take adult patients for didactic and occasionally even for therapeutic work, especially if you were in our clinic, which is definitely a medical organization (and this includes the Southard School).

I realize, of course, that you are probably now well established in London,

4 With Henrick Meng, another German psychoanalyst, Landauer had helped establish and codirected the Institute for Psychoanalysis at the University of Frankfurt.

5 A psychoanalyst who had been a staff member of the Chicago Institute; formerly he was a visiting professor of psychiatry at Marquette University, Milwaukee.

that you are doing a lot of teaching, and making a very good income. I really have no idea whether you have the slightest inclination to come to America or what would be likely to interest you in doing so. I assume that, like most Europeans, you would prefer to live in New York if you would come to America. In spite of these misgivings about the probability of your being interested, I still feel impelled to ask you to tell me what we might offer you that would be tempting because if it is within our power, it would certainly be our inclination.

In conclusion, let me express in writing to you personally what I have already expressed in print and in cablegram, my personal sympathy on account of your bereavement by the death of your father. We all know how much this must have meant to you, in addition to what it meant to all of us.

Sincerely yours,

P.S. I thought you might be interested in the enclosed article which I wrote for one of our weekly journals here.[6] I think it will be self-explanatory, with the exception of one point. I did not refer to Dr. Horney as "Miss." This unfortunate designation was inserted by the editors, who do not know that she is a physician. It makes my criticism of her book appear to be somewhat sneering and depreciatory, and for that reason I regret it very much. The book is terrible, which is all the more reason why the author should not be inaccurately labelled. An explanation of this mistake will appear in the next issue of the journal. I might also add that the book by Dollard, reviewed on page 58, is one of many varieties of the present Horney-Adler bunk which is appearing in the press. Both Horney and Dollard are pretty angry about these reviews.

New York

To C. F. Menninger, Topeka, January 12, 1940

Dear Father:

I will write you a little news about my general behavior recently, which you can pass on to the boys.

Yesterday I went at nine o'clock to meet Dr. Karl Bowman, who, as you know, is director of the Psychiatric Department at Bellevue. He spent the entire morning showing me around, guided by a diagram which I am enclosing. I was in every single one of these rooms, so you can see I did considerable walking.

6 In "The Year in Psychology," *New Republic* 102 (January 8, 1940): 57–58, KAM concluded that Horney's *New Ways in Psychoanalysis* (1939) "deliberately makes its appeal to an audience unprepared to recognize its many inaccuracies, distortions and misstatements, and will thus tend to give rise to further confusion about the 'psychoanalysis of Freud, Adler, Jung and Horney.' " In the same review he criticized *Frustration and Aggression* (1930), by Dollard et al., for its unsound "psychological tenets and for its erroneous statement of psychoanalytic concepts."

Dr. Bowman is an excellent administrator in the sense that things apparently go along smoothly and with a minimum of friction, and he has apparently selected very good young doctors to assist him. They have about a dozen interns, which correspond to what we call residents. Then they have another dozen of what they call residents and we would call Junior Staff Members. Above this they have what they call Junior and Senior Staff Members, who are appointed on the basis of civil service examinations. They try to keep their staff filled up in the same way as we do, by training their own residents. In spite of their competitive examinations, they get a far less desirable selection of men than we do. My impression is that the training of these men is very poorly organized, but, of course, they have a huge quantity of clinical material. I have forgotten exactly, but I think something like fifty patients are admitted daily. There are an average of three skull fractures a day, and something like twenty drunks every day.

The Children's Department surprised me because it was so large and because they were making such a commendable effort in the way of individual teaching, project work, recreation, etc., but it is the noisiest place I have ever been in my life. Everything is concrete, and the walls echo, and New York children are noisy anyway, and to cap the climax there is a steam vent from the engine room just outside the Children's Department which roars constantly like a tornado. The teachers have to scream at the children to be heard, and the children like to scream anyway, so you can imagine the din. This work is in charge of Dr. Loretta Bender, an earnest, energetic, intelligent, somewhat emotional woman of great homeliness, who married Dr. Paul Schilder a few years ago and has to look after him along with her children. He is supposed to be the brains of the place, running around giving off bright ideas, educational information, research suggestions, etc. At times I think he is very good, but he is very unsound and unreliable, and I find him personally unpleasant.

The doctors' living quarters are not very nice, but they will do. There are a lot of operating rooms, X-ray rooms, etc. because of the considerable number of medical and surgical complications which have to be taken care of in connection with these patients. In the laboratories they are particularly interested in questions related to coma and vitamin deficiency associated with alcoholism. The general psychiatric wards are just like those in any big state hospital, except that the public hospital smell is a little stronger. The library is very nice. The dining room is smaller than ours and very crowded because there are so many doctors.

The staff meeting was rather a disappointment. About 100 student nurses, many of them Negresses who are at the hospital for three months for training, occupied one side of the room, and about 150 doctors, psychologists, visitors, etc., occupied the central tier of seats, and Dr. Bowman sat up in front of all of us, and aside from introducing the doctor who was to present the case, he said absolutely nothing. Two cases were presented quite well, I thought, entirely extemporaneously, or at least without reading from any manuscript. The patient was brought in and questioned by the man who presented her, and a few people in the audience asked her a few questions. Then she was dismissed. The art instructor made some comments on some pictures the patient had made, and one of the psychological staff explained the Rorschach, not very intelligibly.

There was very little discussion except by Dr. Schilder, but his remarks were quite good insofar as the neurological symptoms were concerned. He made the point that we should not take very neurological symptoms in a hysterical patient too seriously (the presenting physician had thought one of the patients might be suffering from multiple sclerosis, in addition to hysteria). Dr. Bowman asked me if I wished to say anything, and whenever I am asked in this way I decline, except that I did say that I agreed with Dr. Schilder.

I asked Dr. Bowman later why he did not arrange for a more thorough discussion, and he said that that was one of the weaknesses of the place, and he knew it, but with such a large staff, he didn't know how to handle it. I could have told him, but I didn't.

After lunch, Dr. Bowman showed me the Mental Hygiene Department, which is simply an outpatient service, the physiotherapy rooms, which are large and airy, and the huge record room, which is something of a mess. Incidentally, the chief record clerk asked me how we were going to handle the problem of getting at old records when there were readmissions of patients, in case we followed out our idea of photographing all records. She thought it would be very inconvenient to have to review the case with a projector, and at Bellevue they would have to have a good many projectors to accommodate the many physicians who are obliged to look up the back records. I hadn't thought of that matter of convenience, and I refer this matter herewith to Miss Law.

Dr. Bowman insisted upon my sitting down and talking with him for about an hour after that, so you can see how leisurely and calm he is in spite of the pressure of many duties. Of course he is that kind of fellow, as you know. He still remembers you as one of his early and stimulating teachers, Father.

We talked about some of the complications of psychiatry today, one of which is that the neurologists insist upon calling themselves psychiatrists: Foster Kennedy, for example, at Bellevue, and even Israel Wechsler of Mt. Sinai, for whom I have had such a high regard, and of course all the neurologists up at the Neurological Institute of the Presbyterian Hospital—they all claim to be psychiatrists and do very poor psychiatry, but they have a lot of influence with people who do not want to admit that their problems are psychiatric or do not want their friends to know it, and they also have a lot of influence with the old line of medical practitioners and the Academy of Medicine. For example, recently when the civil service examinations for city psychiatrists and staff members at Bellevue were to be given, the civil service commission asked the Academy of Medicine to give them a list of examiners, and this list contained not a single experienced psychiatrist. Dr. Bowman protested, and they gave out a new list, from which two very good examiners were selected, but as Dr. Bowman said, this illustrates the trend.

Further illustrative of the trend is the fact that poor Dr. Wechsler has gotten himself into all kinds of ill-favor around here by having accepted a position on the Psychiatric Commission which examined a famous criminal, and he made a very bad report and some of the psychiatrists are now publishing an account of that whole affair, which I am afraid will reflect again on Dr. Wechsler. They all feel that he made a great mistake in allowing himself to be considered a psychiatrist, but several people have complained to me recently that he was doing this all the time.

Another illustration of the trend is the fact that Stanley Cobb, originally a neurologist although one with some psychiatric training, is likely to be made Professor of Psychiatry at Harvard next year. Dr. Bowman was associated with Professor Macfie Campbell and likes Dr. Campbell very much, but thinks it is regrettable that Dr. Campbell cannot extend himself a little to make people like him. The result is that the Rockefeller Foundation have shown far more preference for Stanley Cobb than for Professor Campbell, and considerable psychiatric work has developed in the M.G.H. [Massachusetts General Hospital] which ought to have developed at the Boston Psychopathic. . . .

I came away with the impression that the Psychiatric Department at Bellevue is very much more comprehensive in scope than I had imagined, as well as being much larger than I imagined, better organized, better housed, and better staffed. On the other hand, it smells even worse than I imagined, and has a dreary, hard-bitten appearance characteristic of many institutions in New York which are subjected to the ceaseless wear and tear of so many millions of people.

Last night I rushed up to this annual dinner of the New York Society for Clinical Psychiatry, which is a relatively small organization, and enjoyed a pleasant social talk with Dr. Brill and others, including the speaker of the evening, Dr. Malinowski, the great Polish anthropologist who lived so long in London and is now a professor at Yale. I enjoyed talking with him because he is a cultured, intelligent man, but I did not enjoy his talk, which was very dull and said in substance practically nothing. In private, he made some very complimentary remarks about my book, *Man Against Himself,* saying that he had profound respect for it, but in public he paid tribute to all the modern fakirs in psychoanalysis, Horney, Kardiner, Dollard, etc., my opinion of whom you will find recorded in the current issue of *The New Republic.* Incidentally, I received many congratulations from my colleagues at this dinner on account of this article, and a letter from Dr. Horney saying that she understood I had been slandering her. My satisfaction ought to be complete. . . .

Sincerely,

New York

To OTTO FENICHEL, LOS ANGELES, FEBRUARY 18, 1940

Dear Doctor Fenichel:

I want to congratulate you on the excellent review of Horney's book *[New Ways in Psychoanalysis]* which you contributed to the *Quarterly*. I admired the brave and unflinching way you called her on her misrepresentations, misstatements, and muddled logic. Personally, I am even more offended by her extraordinary lack of taste, presumptuousness, and arrogance, but naturally these are not things which one can bring out in a scientific review. You probably saw my review of her book in the *New Republic* for January 8.

I was requested to speak at the New York Society the other night by several officers of the organization, to discuss a paper by Jekel[7] attacking Horney, and I made the point that only the ambivalence of the members of our organization toward Freud could explain the obsessive persistence with which the New York Society devotes meeting after meeting to the discussion of Horney's heretical and nonpsychoanalytic propositions. I pointed out that the tone and content of her book were in contrast to her gracious and reasonable manner in everyday life.

In her speech of reply, she said that she did not understand why we got this impression, that perhaps it was because she envied Freud's penis, and perhaps, as I had suggested, she did not quite understand the English language, but that it didn't seem to occur to any of us (and here she began to shout) that she was obliged to tell the truth! At this point her voice broke and she almost cried and hurried off the platform. In fact, I think she was crying. It was a dramatic exhibition of considerable significance. I have had many kind, congratulatory words from the members since, and I was encouraged in reading your review to write you about this incident.

Sincerely yours,

New York

To JOSEPH HARRINGTON,[8] NEW YORK, MARCH 5, 1940

My dear Mr. Harrington:

We have been very much interested in your articles in the *Cosmopolitan*,

7 Ludwig Jekel was a German-born psychoanalyst. During the 1930s he regularly attended meetings of the New York Psychoanalytic Society.

8 A writer for *Cosmopolitan* magazine, which published a series of articles on the relative merits of state hospitals and private sanitariums.

and we believe your motives and purposes are highly commendable. You have made many excellent points which the people ought to know, for example, the falsity of the exaggerated claims for shock treatment.

In order to make your points, you have somewhat exaggerated the examples, or rather you have used extremes which are not exactly comparable. You are comparing one of the best private sanitariums with one of the worst state hospitals. Unfortunately, there are some poor private santiariums and there are some fairly good state hospitals.

The real problem is more complicated than you realize. The fact is that people want state hospitals, but they do not want to pay for them. They think they want state medicine, and that is what state hospitals represent. Considering the niggardly amounts of money allotted the state hospitals and the confused purposes to which they are put and the unsound economics upon which they are operated, the state hospitals do pretty well. You and I know that nobody gets something for nothing, and the idea that, if you get mentally sick, you are entitled to get something for nothing from the state is in itself very bad mental hygiene.

On the other hand, the care of the mentally sick, in a way that really benefits them, is an extremely expensive business, and relatively few people can afford to pay what is actually necessary to do the job right. There are a great many details about this which you do not know, in spite of your very thorough researches. You do not realize, for example, how much it costs to make sure that a building is fireproof. It costs so much that many private sanitariums do not attempt it. If they did, people could not afford to pay the prices they would have to charge. Very few hospitals, either public or private, use many graduate nurses. They pick up attendants without training, and usually give them very little training. I can't tell you offhand, but I think that, out of 602 hospitals for the mentally ill in the United States, less than half a dozen, if that many, use graduate nurses exclusively. Furthermore, in many hospitals both public and private, there are simply no funds available, either from the patients or from the state, to pay for the treatment that the patients need. Of course, this doesn't justify the hospitals mistreating patients or claiming that they are getting treatment when they are not, but it is a problem that I don't know the answer to, and I don't think anyone knows the answer to it. The truth is that the people do not have very much interest in the problem, and that is why I think your articles may do a lot of good. I think they would do still more good if you would point out promptly that, if people are going to expect the government to pay them when they are sick or to provide for them when they are sick, they are going to have to expect mediocre and indifferent treatment, *as a rule.*

One other point: Private sanitariums could be and would be a whole lot better if the state hospitals were not in direct competition with them. In spite of all the things you say about the state hospitals, the fact remains that some people who could well afford to go to private institutions wangle their way into state hospitals, or rather their relatives wangle the way in for them. You have no idea how frequently the children of well-to-do parents, who want to get their hands on the estate, take advantage of the parents' mental illness by putting them in a state hospital. If you think the state hospitals turn down well-to-do patients, you are very much mistaken. In one state hospital that I know of, one of the patients' chauffeur calls each day in a large Cadillac and takes her riding. Either the patients or their relatives want to save money, and they say the state owes them this care. Sometimes, the board of administration, or whatever it is, protests to these individuals, whereupon they use all kinds of political pressure. They think they are just doing the logical, natural, clever thing to try to get something from the state for nothing, rather than have to pay for it privately.

There is a very simple solution for this. That would be for the state hospitals to conduct their economics in an honest, rational fashion, and charge each county or each individual $5.00 a day for treatment. This would give the state hospitals the funds they need, and it would make the counties consider thoughtfully whether or not the patient was actually in need of that much financial aid from the county. In this way, the state hospitals would not compete with private hospitals; private hospitals would have a larger population, and hence a smaller overhead, and the rates would correspondingly fall. The best managers of private sanitariums could give you exact statistics on this, but I can assure you that there isn't a single one in the United States that could not lower its rates, and would be glad to lower its rates, if the population were developed. I can further add that I am sure its population would be developed if the state hospitals were not giving free treatment to patients who could well afford to pay for private treatment but who are exploiting the present system.

This letter is not for publication. I do not want you to use my name, but you are perfectly welcome to examine or use these ideas if you like.

I repeat that I think that you are doing a very necessary and valuable job.

Sincerely yours,

New York

To ABRAHAM MYERSON, BOSTON, MARCH 13, 1940

Dear Abe:

I am not writing this to revive an old feud because I have only the friendliest feelings, but I just read your article in the November issue of the *American Journal of Psychiatry*.

On page 624 you presumably quote me (I understood that to be the case from your previous letters). You quote me as having said (in quotation marks) "that practically all informed scientists accept psychoanalysis."

Since that statement makes no sense to me, as I told you in answer to the questionnaire, I took the trouble to look up yesterday exactly what I had said. In *The Human Mind*, page 359, I wrote as follows:

"Practically no intelligent and informed scientist today disputes the main thesis and findings of psychoanalysis. There is still much controversial matter. . . ."

You are a scientist, and we share a belief in the scientific method. Don't you think you ought to have quoted me correctly if you were going to quote me at all?

Sincerely yours,

P.S. My point is that my statement may have been incorrect, and had your questionnaire corresponded to an inquiry as to the truth or the untruth of the statement, I think it might have been very valuable.

FROM ABRAHAM MYERSON, BOSTON, MARCH 14, 1940

Dear Karl:

I don't see that there is any particular difference between your statement and mine: "Practically no intelligent and informed scientist today disputes the main thesis and findings of psychoanalysis . . . ," and then, "practically all informed scientists accept psychoanalysis." It would be hair splitting to mind the difference between the two statements as to actual meaning. I am pretty good at dialectics, but it would strain my ingenuity to find a difference between your statement and mine.

Moreover, the questionnaire did not finally have to do with your statement. By a series of plain questions to a group of representative psychiatrists, neurologists, and psychologists, the bulk of the American Neurological Association, many of whom are distinguished and informed scientists, leaned away from psychoanalysis and certainly did not accept the main thesis and findings, even though they may be grateful to Freud for his stimulus to human thought. This is true in lesser measure of the psychiatrists; and is true in greater measure of the most distinguished psychologists of America.

Furthermore, you had absolutely no warrant for making that statement. You sent out no questionnaire to intelligent and informed scientists. Your statement was made absolutely *ex cathedra* and, if you will forgive me for saying it, slightly arrogantly. The questionnaire shows you were definitely mistaken, and it goes farther than that I think.

I am not particularly a feudist, although I have the undesirable trait of saying what I think fairly plainly and without reservation. Meanwhile, I have no objection to the psychoanalysts continuing their studies and investigations. The horizon, however, is full of portents of a different day: Brain waves are coming along; new chemicals are being introduced; vitamins and hormones are proving their worth even in the field of mental disease, and

shock treatments do more for the depressions than all the psychotherapeu-
tics of whatever type put together. I'll lay a little wager with you that the
Menninger Clinic twenty years from now will say far more about chemo-
therapy than it will about psychoanalysis.

Very sincerely yours,

The tone of this letter is really more belligerent than I meant it to be—you'll
have to forgive the heat,—really I am much more peaceful than I seem to
be—So, there's no feud between us, and you'll go on your merry way as a
firm psychoanalyst and I'll go mine as a firm physiologist and organicist.[9]

New York

To Franz Alexander, Chicago, March 15, 1940

Dear Alex:

I was very glad for your letter saying you would write Simmel about his
violation of your express wishes about the use of your name.[10]

I finished your article. The first part of it I liked quite well, although I
thought you were a little too kind to Horney. I feel that the continued discussion of Horney's book and Horney's principles, such as has occupied the
New York Society so obsessively for the past year, represents an ambivalence on the part of all of us regarding Freud. As I said in the New York
Society the other night, Horney worked along with us in Chicago peaceably
and inconspicuously; she comes to New York and writes a scurrilous, arrogant, nasty, dishonest attack on Freud, and immediately she leaps into fame.
Meeting after meeting of the New York Society is devoted to a discussion of
her writings, in spite of her contemptible attitude. (I might have added that
the *Psychoanalytic Quarterly* devotes its leading article to a many-page review
of her theories by Franz Alexander.) . . .

So far as your article in particular is concerned, my reflection was, in short,
just this: Does one have to be disagreeable and attack Freud in order to be
taken seriously by his colleagues? In other words, I don't think that the

9 The postscript is handwritten. Marginal note by KAM: "Incorrigible—file un-
ans[wered]."

10 Simmel had announced plans to form a psychoanalytic institute in Los Angeles.
KAM and Alexander, among others, were to be sponsors of the institute, which, like the
institutes in New York, Chicago, and Topeka, they assumed would be approved by the
American Psychoanalytic Association. When they learned that Simmel was planning a
clinic-sanitarium, which he wanted to call an institute, KAM and Alexander withdrew
their support. After Simmel assured him that he would get approval, Alexander again
agreed to lend his name, but finally in April 1940 he denied his approbation once more.
The matter was further complicated by Simmel's not having a California license and by his
having surrounded himself with lay analysts, whom he had taught and trained. In 1946
Simmel became a charter member of the Los Angeles Psychoanalytic Society and served
as its first president (1946–47).

Horney book justifies the attention that your article gave it. Of course, I know your point was to emphasize that psychoanalysis does need more sociological orientation, but not in the way that she did it. Nevertheless, I think it is an error to assume that Horney is the only one who thinks so. The plain facts of the matter are that Horney felt rejected by the analysts and got enthusiastic about the reception the social workers gave her in Chicago. A lot of us were enthusiastic about social workers and gave full recognition to their point of view long before Horney came to America (see the original edition of *The Human Mind,* and see the work of Southard and many psychiatrists in this country, including Frankwood Williams, the psychoanalyst).

I did not find fault so much with particular statements you make as with this general attitude, although I don't think you should have said some things, as, for example, on page 4, that were again "written in a most conciliatory style." It is true that you make these compliments only to be followed by criticisms, but I don't see anything in it to compliment. If I said that some friend of ours was a nice fellow but a son of a bitch and then lied about him, I don't think anyone should write a 36-page article in the *Quarterly,* saying that Dr. Menninger is a very pleasant and conciliatory fellow, and says some nice things about his friend, but you don't agree with a part of what he says. If I said a thing like this, I would write myself down a rascal and a skunk, and not worthy of having one of the leaders of psychoanalytic thought make my remarks the subject of such honest, even though critical, consideration.

That is why I urged you not to write this article in the first place, and I still feel that it was a mistake, even though, as I say I agree in most particulars with what you actually say.

I am not emotional or disturbed about this, because I still know where my loyalties lie; they lie with you and with Freud and with everyone who has tried honestly to find out something about human beings; and they don't lie with anybody whose disloyalty and dishonesty are obvious, as I believe to be the case with Horney. I do think my book, *Man Against Himself,* has been slighted by the psychoanalysts, but I think it has been slighted for the same reason that I think Horney's book has been advertised, namely, because of the ambivalence of so many psychoanalysts to Freud, an ambivalence which they like to call objectivity. No one knows better than you that one can find philosophical arguments to justify any position, and just as I can find philosophical arguments to defend Freud, Horney, or someone who thinks more logically than she, can find philosophical arguments to attack him. The difference between us is that I don't pretend that this is entirely objective, and as soon as anyone pretends to be entirely objective, I distrust him. Freud did not treat me very nicely, as you know, but nonetheless, I think his ideas, his grasp, his formulations are so infinitely ahead of anything else that has been proposed, that I have nailed my banner to his mast, and I'll defend it against assault for the rest of my life. For this resolution I have you to thank, but no change in your views would make me change now.

In regard to speaking at the Institute, I'll be glad to give you my ideas on sublimation, if you wish, but I would not be willing to review the literature. [David] Levy has done this as well as I could do it or better, and I don't think it gets us anywhere anyway. I am more interested in the concept of sublimation that derives logically from Freud's theories, regardless of what tentative formulations were made about it years ago. I am still more interested in the interpretation I have of the structure of the maladjustment process as an expression of instinctual diffusion, an idea originally proposed by Franz Alexander, which I still think is sound and enormously fruitful.

I am somewhere near the end of my analysis. My plans for the immediate future are vague, so I must ask you to be somewhat vague about the exact dates of my lectures at the Institute, but you can count on something from me without fail.

Sincerely yours,

FROM FRANZ ALEXANDER, CHICAGO, MARCH 20, 1940

Dear Karl:

I wrote to Simmel but have not heard from him as yet. As to your remarks about my article, I wish to tell you that I never received more letters and opinions expressed about any of my writings than about this article. With the exception of yours, they were all extremely enthusiastic, so I really began to think that the article might be quite good and helpful. Kardiner[11] was the only one who thought I was too severe with Horney, and you were the only one who thought I was not severe enough, so far as statistics go.

My feelings about what you say is that one must differentiate between the personal issues and objective statements. The validity of a statement cannot be refuted on the basis that the author makes the statement not because he is in love with truth but for some ulterior motives. I tried in my article to take Horney's book as an occasion to discuss certain fundamental issues of psychoanalysis. It is not really intended as a book review. As you probably noticed, the last chapter does not deal with Horney's book at all. I feel that in the field of science, we must be extremely fair and set the validity of ideas above any personal issues. You know how I feel concerning Horney's motives. I refer repeatedly to her "polemic ardor" and give expression to this feeling in my article as much as it is at all possible. On the other hand, I feel

11 Abram Kardiner, an American psychiatrist, was analyzed by Freud in 1921–22. He taught at the New York Psychoanalytic Institute until 1946, when he left the institute to become one of the original members of the Association for Psychoanalytic Medicine and the Psychoanalytic Clinic for Training and Research at Columbia. He was a leader in the movement to integrate cultural anthropology with psychoanalysis.

that this "Freud or no Freud" attitude is an extremely undesirable one. The counterpart of Horney's anti-Freudian feeling is the emotional dependence upon Freud and certain traditional concepts which he introduced. . . .

As ever,

New York

To Franz Alexander, Chicago, March 27, 1940

My dear Alex:

I was glad to have your letter of March 20, and shall be very interested to learn what you hear from Dr. Simmel.

I was glad, also, that you wrote me frankly about my comments on your paper, although I felt you were definitely disappointed by my reaction. I think there is a great temptation among all of us to say only what we know our colleagues want us to say about such things, and I was rather reluctant to express any opinion about your article for just that reason. When you tell me that my letter was the only one you got that wasn't enthusiastic, I feel a little reproached, but I also feel that you ought to be discriminating enough to realize that it is a lot easier, simpler, and safer to write a few lines of enthusiastic endorsement than it is to write a careful, conscientious, and more critical estimate.

To answer the specific point made in the second paragraph of your letter of March 20, I think you misunderstood slightly the basis of my objections to Horney. I do not care what her motives are or how ulterior they are, and I did not attempt to refute her doctrines on the basis of her motives. If my letter sounded like that, I did myself an injustice. What I object to is her deliberate misrepresentation. I think this is reprehensible in the highest degree, and I do not think that deliberate misrepresentation, whatever its motives, ought to be accorded the dignity of thoughtful analysis.

You go on to say that you deplore the Freud or no-Freud attitude. I really don't know what you mean by this. If we are going to be Freudians, as we claim we are, I don't see how we can tolerate radical anti-Freudianism, and I certainly don't agree with you that the opposite of anti-Freudianism is an emotional dependence upon Freud. I think this is a *reductio ad absurdum*. If some member of the Chicago Society says in my hearing that Alexander is a rascal, a fool, etc., do I betray my emotional dependence upon you if I get angry at such a person and refuse to discuss it with him? On the other hand, would I be showing my objectivity if I write a long article saying that, while it is not true, as Dr. Smith says, that Alexander is a fool and a rascal, I want to be independent of Alexander and hence I will admit that he has a lot of faults? I don't think that is being objective; I think it is more objective not to discuss it with such a person and not to discuss what such a person says.

They are not worthy of it. Of course, Alexander may have faults and, of course, Freud made mistakes, but why should we give someone the credit for pointing out their mistakes who doesn't take the trouble to be either accurate or fair in his accusations? . . .

Sincerely yours,

FROM FRANZ ALEXANDER, CHICAGO, APRIL 5, 1940

Dear Karl:

Returning to your letter of March 27th, I wish to tell you that it was not at all meant as a complaint that you were not too enthusiastic about my article and that you wrote in detail what you thought about it. You are right that it is much more interesting to hear such a critical opinion than a simple expression of enthusiastic endorsement. As to the merits of your remarks, I still think that we have to distinguish between the motives and the validity of a statement. Furthermore, Horney did not say Freud was a rascal or a fool and therefore your simile does not hold. I am still getting reactions to this article of mine which shows me that probably I succeeded to clarify many of those issues which Horney has raised and much of the confusion which her book has caused. If this is true, then the article fulfilled its purpose.

Horney's anti-Freudian feelings belong to another chapter and are just as distasteful to me as they are to you. Her exaggerations, confusion and demogogic appeal to the public are the results of these emotions. But since much of her statements attack real scientific weaknesses of many so-called orthodox analysts her contentions must be dealt with on a rational basis, avoiding as much as possible personal issues. This is and remains my conviction in this matter. . . .

As ever,

TO LEWELLYS BARKER,[12] NEW LONDON, NEW HAMPSHIRE, JULY 30, 1940

My dear Doctor Barker:

It was very kind of you to take time to reply to my comments on our contribution to the Convalescence Conference. . . .

In regard to your comment that the orthodox Freudians are excessive, my comment would be that your bad impression of the analysts comes not from the orthodox Freudians but from the unorthodox non-Freudians. I think the distasteful, unscientific exhibitions in the name of psychoanalysis are not likely to come from anyone who emulates Freud either technically or in character. On our staff we have ten psychoanalysts, all of whom are quite

12 An internist at Johns Hopkins University Medical School, with which he was affiliated from 1894 until his death in 1943.

"orthodox." Such books as those of Stekel[13] and Horney shock and offend us no less than they do you, but these, I should like to emphasize, are not psychoanalytic, according to our conceptions. . . .

Sincerely yours,

To Franz Alexander, La Jolla, California, August 15, 1940

Dear Alex:

Thanks for your letter of August 9. . . .

I am amazed to read that Professor [J. F.] Brown "today" gave you some proof in his book[14] which you say you have not yet had an opportunity to see. This amazes me because for a month he has been writing me your opinion about the book, and I got a letter several days ago from him saying that you were reading it. I'm a little mixed up about all this, but what I imagine is that you dreaded the job of reading it so badly (as did I myself) that you put it off as long as possible and he thinks you have read it. . . . I don't object to him quoting you; I think he should, but I don't think he should lay himself open to the charge of merely mirroring your opinions and attitudes, especially inasmuch as this book is going to be interpreted by many as being an immediate reaction to his analysis. I do think it is a pity if you give him any encouragement to quote the bastards or the fifth columnists of psa. . . . I think you feel that you are tolerant in this respect, and I feel it is a weakness on your part, a neurotic complacency, which in Mr. Chamberlain caused a lot of trouble, as you know. I'm against appeasement.

I'd like to talk to you a long time personally but I don't believe I've got anything to say in writing.

Sincerely,

From Franz Alexander, La Jolla, California, August 22, 1940

Dear Karl:

Thank you for your letter of August 15th. I am sorry that I will miss you here. . . . As to your remarks:

13 Wilhelm Stekel was an Austrian psychoanalyst who had early been a member of Freud's Wednesday study group in Vienna and who was, with Adler, an editor of the *Zentralblatt für Psychoanalyse*. Like Adler, he broke with orthodox Freudian tenets in deemphasizing childhood difficulties as the essential focus of analysis. Stekel believed that the therapist and patient should be active and equal partners in the therapeutic situation.

14 KAM had collaborated on chap. 4, "Psychiatry," of Brown's *Psychodynamics of Abnormal Behavior* while Brown was doing research at the Menninger Clinic. Brown credits KAM for editing the chapter for "errors of fact and infelicities of expression" (Brown, ix). KAM's pique at Brown may also stem from Brown's esteem for Fromm, Horney, and Dollard as revealed in Brown's recommendation in his book that students should read their works (Brown, 249).

1. Tolerance is mostly the sign of strength and not of weakness. Intolerance, always the result of fear and weakness.

2. What you write about my "neurotic complacency" to me is okay. To write it to an analysand of mine is unwise, and very unkind toward a patient whose analysis might become disturbed by it.

3. To compare scientific life with politics is most unfortunate and misleading. In science and art the products count and not the person. Great products of art and science have been produced by persons who had great weaknesses. Who has not?

It was a pleasure hearing from you but would have liked very much to see you after such a long period.

Warmly as ever,

To FRANZ ALEXANDER, LA JOLLA, CALIFORNIA, AUGUST 26, 1940

Dear Alex:

I just had your kind and characteristic letter of August 22. My conscience has hurt me ever since I wrote Brown commenting on your attitude toward Horney, and now it hurts worse than ever. I don't justify my having spoken of you as I did at all, because I should not have done it, but I must tell you that Brown has at times worried me and annoyed me tremendously. He piles this manuscript in on me with rush orders to get it back to him immediately; I read it as fast as I can and find it is pretty terrible in spots and tell him so. Then he tells me he wants me to be his collaborator and I agree to do so, providing he allows me to make radical changes.

He says okay to all this and I make the changes or as many of them as I have strength to make (and it took a lot of strength too), and then he begins to bombard me with letters telling me to work up a bibliography for him and calls me up in the middle of the night . . . and tells me that you and he are going to take me down and put me in my place and that he is resigning from the clinic.

All this does not explain the present issue, however, but among other things he kept insisting on references to Horney, saying that you did not agree with some of my criticisms at all, and then I got your letter saying that you didn't agree with my attitude about Horney. . . .

Anyway, it was very nice of you to take such a gracious attitude toward my mistakes, but I still think you are terribly wrong when you recommend tolerance as an attitude toward rascals. Scientifically, we can say Hitler and Chamberlain are the results of psychological forces operating in their childhoods and, therefore, we should be tolerant toward them and try to understand them. I don't give a damn to understand Hitler and Chamberlain, nor Horney, as I think they are rascals who have not asked my scientific blessing or study, and I think defending any of them puts me or you or anyone else who does it in a wrong light. I have heard you very severely criticized for this by people whom you respect but who cannot understand why you persist in taking an ambiguous position. However, it is your privilege to do so and it does not justify me for criticizing you to your analysand. However, I do feel that if he wants me to collaborate with him he must respect my very strong feeling in regard to the psychoanalytic traitors and exploiters. I will not have her name or work mentioned as if it were to be taken seriously in anything that I have to do with. I wish to goodness I could persuade you to see it in the same light, but if I can't it will not change my fundamental feeling toward you and my wish to talk, drink and reminiscence with you at the earliest possible moment. I am so sorry you won't be in La Jolla when I get there.

Sincerely,

FROM FRANZ ALEXANDER, LA JOLLA, CALIFORNIA, AUGUST 30, 1940

Dear Karl:

I was glad indeed to receive your warm and sincere letter. I fully understand and know well the tactics by which Brown irritated you. It seems, however, that his analysis now really struck home. I hope that it will have a lasting effect upon him.

I fully appreciate your feeling about Horney and also that you are justified to try to ignore her as much as possible. I also agree with you that there is very little original in what she contributed. In what is valuable in her attitude and emphasis she was very much influenced by me in the first years of her stay in Chicago. She exploited the weakness of the psychoanalytic system and also the fact that much of the later developments have not been systematically formulated, and published and utilized all this for a destructive dialectical campaign. Personally she is a neurotic, unfortunate, aging woman animated only by one last impulse: debunking of father images. Both of us, you and I, know this equally well. On the other hand, she has an extremely clear mind[15] and her dialectical crusade had, in spite of her, some good effects. She showed up weaknesses and emphasized certain necessary reorientations.[16]

As I have written to you so often, I cannot subscribe to your comparing political personalities with scientific writers. Science is simply not politics. Its aims and methods are fully different. You can't appease anybody in science,[17] you can only show where a scientist is right and where he is wrong.

15 KAM has added in margin: "Nuts!"

16 KAM has added in margin: "He always evades my point which was (and *is*) that *he* should not appear to justify and support Horney!"

17 KAM has added in margin: "Alex is trying to appease Horney, medical men generally, and others."

Any other considerations, personal, moral, friendship, etc., are out of place. Their introduction in scientific writings has a corrupting influence. Loyalty to truth and your intellectual convictions is the only loyalty in science.

I am also sorry that we shall have to postpone our personal chat for a later date.

Cordially yours,

To Lewellys Barker, Baltimore, October 15, 1940

My dear Doctor Barker:

I delayed in answering your kind letter because I wanted to read your book[18] carefully. It came and I want to thank you for it. I have read it and have written a note about it in our *Bulletin,* a copy of which I will send you.

As I have said in that review, I think the most significant thing is the fact that a man of your experience and fame should have seen the necessity for a book on this subject at this time. It is a cogent indication of the trend of modern medical thought. You have always been known for your catholicity and for your clinical skill with patients, and I think you must have come to realize that your success with your patients did not depend entirely upon the physical and chemical measures which you instituted to combat their illnesses. In trying to organize the reasons for your success and to justify your position philosophically you wanted to develop the way in which psychological forces could be used by the physician in his work. Hence, you wrote the book and in doing so, you did medicine a great favor.

Since you are too astute to be pleased by an unalloyed commendation of the book, I will register my objections to it with the same candor with which I have expressed my appreciation. I think your condensed account of psychoanalytic theory is excellent; I think your objections to psychoanalytic practice are understandable. The high-priest attitude of some psychoanalysts is just as irritating as the former high-priest attitude of some surgeons was. I do not think you should have let this confuse you, however. Three times you refer to the fact that psychoanalysis is too expensive and twice to the fact that it is "time robbing." This repetition betrays your irritation and I share your irritation, but I do not think we can correct it by being captious. Psychoanalysis is still a very young technique; surgery in its early days certainly made many equally serious mistakes. Psychoanalysis is still further handicapped by the fact that the training is much more difficult than surgery; it requires more intelligence, more time and more money. It is unfortunately true that in the past it has not always attracted the most admirable and well-rounded personalities.

---

18 *Psychotherapy: Treatment That Attempts to Improve the Condition of a Human Being by Means of Influences That Are Brought to Bear upon His Mind* (1940).

Nevertheless, psychoanalysis is growing up to some extent in spite of the difficulties under which it was launched and in spite of the fact that the medical schools in a competitive effort to maintain a reputation for great conservativeness have introduced it only surreptitiously. . . .

If I may still further express myself about your book, I would say that one of its faults depends upon one of your virtues. Your essential kindliness and loyalty shows itself in your earnest attempt to support the theories of Dr. Adolf Meyer. Doctor Meyer contributed an important stimulus to the development of American psychiatry in his early days. His work in neuropathology and his introduction of the German nosological system and his emphasis upon the inclusion of psychological factors in personality study were of fundamental importance. In the creation of what he calls psychobiology, however, Doctor Meyer has, in my opinion, confused rather than clarified the field of psychiatry. His neologisms (parergasias, etc.) are used by few if any. Medical men simply do not understand what he is talking about. Some have confidence in him for the reason that they understand him to be a conservative, honorable, and earnest scientist who has little use for newfangled psychoanalytic nonsense.

Doctor Meyer is your friend; you want to be loyal to him and you try to explain his ideas but in this part of the book I think you are quite unsuccessful. Frankly, in spite of a good deal of study and many discussions with Meyer and his students and long reflecting I have not the slightest idea what the expression "distributive analysis" means, and I am utterly opposed to the use of expressions which are vaguely meaningful but specifically meaningless. To inspire a young physician to want to understand his patient's troubles and sufferings is to my mind a high goal; to tell such young physicians to "apply distributive analysis to the parergasias" of his patient seems to me to be almost valueless.

What I like about your book is what *you* tell us of *your* own long experience and practice which those of us who follow you and learn of you can well afford to study and try to apply.

Sincerely yours,

To Dorothy Thompson,[19] New York, November 5, 1940

Dear Miss Thompson:
I don't suppose you will get this letter what with all the mail you will be receiving these days, but I just wanted to tell you I am for Roosevelt too and I have admired your stand. It certainly took courage as well as intelligence and since you are not lacking in either I was not very surprised.

19 Newspaper columnist, lecturer, and radio commentator. The second of her three husbands (1928–41) was Sinclair Lewis.

The situation out here is that most of the solid, substantial people are going to vote for Willkie for a variety of reasons, one of which is their relative lack of awareness of the acuteness of the social conflict. In Kansas no one wants to be an ignorant, low-class farmer. Everybody wants to do what the upper crust seems to be doing in order to prove that one isn't a peasant.

The so-called upper crust here is not nearly as calculating and overtly selfish as many of the rich Republicans in the East; they conscientiously believe in things like tradition, middle of the road, no experiments, etc. Furthermore, they are far more naive than the New Yorkers and believe everything they read in the newspapers, which are of course 90% pro-Willkie, for reasons I do not need to explain to you.

Consequently, between the earnest people who believe the newspapers, the steady people who are alarmed by experiments, the professional people who do not know what conflicts are going on in the country, and the farmers who do not want to look like farmers, Mr. Willkie is going to get a heavy vote. However, as my housekeeper (a humble country soul) said the other day, "I ain't met nobody that's going to vote for Willkie. Have you, Doctor?" So Mr. Roosevelt may get a few votes from us humble people.

Best regards. I will be back in New York shortly after the first of the year and I wish you would take lunch with me, if you're not dated up ten weeks in advance.

Sincerely yours,

To Ruth Mack Brunswick,[20] New York, December 30, 1940

Dear Doctor Brunswick:

Last night after writing you I lay awake for quite a while and had the fantasy that I would not awaken the following morning, that I would not get up, and that I would not go to work. I would just drop everything and this would cause great concern and my brother would come out to see me. I would just let everything go and not care. I was not conscious of any feelings of depression so far as I can recall but I think I must have had them.

I slept very soundly, however, but recall the following dream which

20 KAM's analyst from 1940 to 1941, Brunswick was born in Chicago and graduated from Radcliffe College, where she studied mental psychology with Elmer Ernest Southard. She received her M.D. degree from Tufts Medical School in 1922. In Vienna, she was psychoanalyzed by Freud and eventually became a member of the inner circle of psychoanalysts surrounding him. Between 1925 and 1938 she practiced primarily in Vienna and participated in the Vienna Psychoanalytic Society. Her particular academic and clinical interests centered on borderline psychotic patients. Freud referred patients to her, including the "Wolf-Man." In 1938 Brunswick returned to the United States and set up practice in New York City. Complications of myocarditis caused her untimely death at 48.

I want to record before I forget it: I was apparently living in New York in a large apartment hotel called 1 Fifth Avenue but it wasn't the 1 Fifth Avenue in which I actually lived when I was there. Your business had become so good that you were moving into this same building; I thought this would be very convenient for me as I would simply have to go down a few floors or up a few floors and could have my hour without leaving the building.

It seemed that I was helping you move which was quite a job—there were a great many parcels, pieces of furniture, etc. You seemed to be carrying some and I was carrying some and you were very tired and your voice was tense and you were somewhat flurried, etc.

I can't remember just what happened next but the previous part of the dream seemed to be outside the building and in the next part of the dream you were established in a very large and sumptuous apartment and I was thinking how expensive it must have been for you to lay such luxurious rugs, etc., and what a great expense it had been to you to move; but then I reflected that you had so many patients, as you had told me over the phone, that you must be making a great deal of money and could well afford it.

Next I recall that I was just finishing a rather intimate hour on the couch and as I got up to leave I discovered that your secretary had been in the room all the time and I was astonished and somewhat disturbed about this. I was the more disturbed when I discovered that the secretary was none other than Anita Alexander. . . . You quickly explained, however that Anita had left [Franz] Alexander and was working for you now and it was perfectly all right, that she could be depended upon to be entirely loyal. In some way this relieved my feelings and I went on out the door.

I don't have a clear notion of what the dream means but probably you will be able to see something in it. I am impressed with the fact that immediately after our conversation I had this dream and then that I had the impulse to write you about the dream. I think it is noteworthy that in the dream I was continuing my analysis. I don't get the import of your moving into 1 Fifth Avenue but my association is that I think it is a better apartment house than 29 Washington Square and I used to wish that you had a little better office than you did over there.

I think the idea of the new secretary for you ties up with the secretaries I got for you, mentioned last night, but why I should have supplied you with Anita Alexander I do not know, unless I unconsciously blame you for bringing about my divorce. That is all that occurs to me about the dream at the moment and I will mail this off to you because it may be tomorrow before I can get around to writing you in detail about the present development of external events.

Sincerely yours,

To Henry Alsop Riley,[1] New York, April 4, 1941

Dear Henry:

Your letter was swell. I do not disagree with your conclusions at all; namely, that certain individuals are a burden to society and we would be better off without them. I also agree that many prisoners who should not be at large are released on parole.

The trouble with capital punishment, it seems to me, is that it deters convictions and gives us a false sense of security by leading us to believe that the serious criminals are executed and the non-serious ones might just as well be released. My idea is that if we would quit making such a big threat as capital punishment and make a more consistent threat of permanent detention of dangerous individuals, we would be less likely to excite the anxieties or emotions of one kind and another on the part of juries and judges and could apply some scientific principles to handling criminals.

What I am trying to say is that I am not interested in this thing from any sentimental reasons in the nature of saving the lives of the condemned. It is just a guess which is the most effective way to get science induced into criminology and I have always felt that capital punishment worked against us. Maybe I'm wrong, and I surely appreciate your taking the time to reply to my letter.

Sincerely yours,

From Gregory Zilboorg, New York, May 29, 1941

Dear Karl:

I too was very sorry that we did not have an opportunity to have a good talk at Richmond. The point is, I was not myself there. The political passions of New York reached the boiling point and behind the scenes and almost in the open the Rados and the Levys ganged up and concentrated their forces. Everyone who had an ax to grind pooled their forces and a campaign of blackening and knifing me was well under way. By the time I got back to New York it reached its peak. As a result I did not feel very happy then or now. The tragic stupidity of it all is that Alexander, Levy, Rado and Lorand[2] turn out to be one team. We had not heard the last of it. Elections were held in New York, and due to the campaign of slander and rot which had nothing to do with the real issues involved I was beaten for reelection to the Educational Committee by one vote.

1 A neurologist in private practice in New York City from 1916 to 1963; he and KAM met during KAM's stay there.
2 Sandor Lorand arrived in New York from Budapest in 1925. He became a member of the New York Psychoanalytic Society and later of the New York Psychoanalytic Institute. He was honorary president of the Psychoanalytic Association of New York.

This having been achieved by methods of knifing of which even Tammany would be secretly proud, did not make us feel badly—but the atmosphere is charged and stercoraceous [covered with dung]. . . .

About the American Psychoanalytic Association—of course I shall be glad to share with you some of the ideas I have,[3] if you want me to. I wish I could have a talk with you. Certain of the New York matters which degenerated politically into personal persecution do not lend themselves well to expression on paper.

Warmest regards.

As always,

To Morris Fishbein, Chicago, July 17, 1941

My dear Morris:

I'm all hot and bothered and I want to get it off my chest and get a little advice from you, perhaps a little psychotherapy.

When these Selective Service psychiatry seminars were first started by the men in Washington, Harry Stack Sullivan and others,[4] we were very much interested, and we were pleased when one of our staff members, Bob Knight, was invited to come down to Atlanta to participate in one. Subsequently other members of our staff were invited to come to Chicago and Dallas, and one of our members on leave as well as some of our ex-staff members participated in one in Los Angeles.

They brought home reports of the meetings and we were all very much stimulated. To realize that every psychiatric mistake made by the draft boards and the medical examining boards in the last war meant an average expense of $35,000 to the United States government seemed very impressive to us. The United States government has spent something over a billion dollars for psychiatric cases from the previous world war and this gave us pause. We visited some of the army camps around here, some of the induction board examinations, and some of the local draft board examinations, and, to tell you the truth, we were shocked. Man after man who should have been excluded because of psychoneurotic, psychopathic, or other psychiatric defects was passed along as if he were a 100% normal specimen simply because he had no heart lesions or broken arches.

---

3 KAM and Zilboorg had planned to get together at the spring meeting of the American Psychoanalytic Association in Richmond, Virginia. In a letter of May 13, 1941 to Zilboorg, KAM said that he wished Zilboorg could have told him "some of the things that were worrying" him, in response to Zilboorg's statement in an April 22, 1941 letter that there were "many many things I would like to discuss with you while in Richmond." That anticipated meeting didn't take place.

4 Sullivan and other members of the psychiatric community in Washington, D.C., had helped organize a series of seminars to advise selective service boards on ways to spot and avoid potential psychological problems among draftees.

We spoke with some of the doctors about it and got very friendly responses; they would be glad to have us come down and help, etc. So down we went, but we got nowhere. They didn't seem to realize that there was a cry from Washington and from the army and from various other quarters to exclude these psychiatric cases. We understand that the same thing is more or less true in many other parts of the country.

So we thought we'd do a little education, not only of ourselves but also of some of the local brothers. We put on a series of seminars for a week, two to five hours a day. We did a great deal of work on it and we gave a good deal of our time. We expected the examining boards not only of this county but of the surrounding counties and districts to show up in a mass but, with the exception of a few men who drove here from out of town, and two of the local brothers who came out for two sessions, we had almost no doctors in attendance.

Some of the local lay draft board men came and their attitude, somewhat loosely translated, was this: "We know you are right. We know these men ought to be excluded. We know the medical examiners are not excluding them. You say this is a medical problem but your own medical colleagues do not exclude these cases and it is up to us, as laymen, to try to do it." Of course we told them that was wrong, that it would upset the statistics, that it wasn't their duty to be excluding people on account of psychiatric problems, but their arguments were pretty hard to answer.

Now the local situation doesn't matter much. Kansas is a small state numerically, and a few psychotic soldiers from Kansas won't make any great difference one way or the other perhaps, but it seems to us to be a serious national problem, and we cannot find out whose fault it is. The army claims it doesn't want these cases. It encourages these seminars, it gives out these intructions, and yet the medical boards do not seem to have heard anything about them.

I have talked to some of these doctors and have tried to apply a little psychiatry and psychology to the situation and this is what I find: These men are practicing physicians. They are busy trying to earn a living. They are asked by the Selective Service Act to donate their services for the examination of men for the army. To save their faces, they don't want to refuse to do it, and they are probably as patriotic as anyone else. But, on the other hand, they feel that the army has its own medical staff and that the examinations which are done locally are not very important and not to be taken too seriously. "Let's rush them through and go back to work," they say. Consequently, although there is no law or rule or statute or anything else to the effect that the examinations must all be done in one day, they are nearly always rushed through in one day with great speed and everybody thinks he has done his duty when, as a matter of fact, it seems to me they have done something pretty terrible. They have admitted a lot of psychiatric prospects into the army who are going to disturb the army morale, and be sent out of the army at terrific expense after they have broken down or run amuck or alarmed and antagonized and distressed the officers and fellow soldiers and then they are going to come back into the community and be dependent wards of the government.

Now it seems to me the place you come in on all this is right there. This backfire is going to be a sharp reflection on the medical profession. Isn't there some way that the American Medical Association can bring some influence to bear to improve the wretched state of inefficiency, wastefulness, bad medicine, bad psychiatry, bad military preparation that is going on? You can reply perhaps that the induction board physicians will take care of all this, but I can forestall that argument. We sent some of our men up to an induction board examination and we say [. . .][5] bad medicine [. . .]. Examinations were inadequate in certain respects, particularly in psychiatric examinations, but the soldiers were handled in a way which is certain to increase our troubles rather than decrease them.

You've probably done a lot of thinking and talking and acting on this subject already, but while it was fresh in my mind—fresh because of my interest in these stimulating presentations at our seminars here and fresh also because of our disappointment at the lack of attendance and disinterest on the part of the local brothers—I wanted to get a line to you and ask you what you thought.

Sincerely yours,

To George Gray,[6] New York, July 18, 1941

My dear Mr. Gray:

I wrote you rather sharply last time because I was puzzled by your questions, and I get so many manuscripts and letters all the time from people who want to publish articles, books, etc. who have not made a thorough study of the subject.[7] I had forgotten our previous correspondence and I am glad to know that you have a commitment to publish [an excerpt from your book] in *Harper's*.

Insofar as the quotations from *Man Against Himself* are concerned, it is

5 Here and after "bad medicine" the words have been deleted from the carbon copy, and the original has not been preserved.

6 Author of *The Advancing Front of Medicine* (1941), which examined typical problems confronting contemporary medicine, including treatment of alcoholism.

7 Gray had earlier written KAM asking his permission to quote from *Man Against Himself* in that part of his book dealing with alcoholism. KAM responded tartly in a letter of July 10, 1941, admonishing Gray for not explaining why and for whom he was writing these articles and for relying on the work of Robert Fleming while ignoring that of Robert P. Knight.

perfectly all right with me for you to use them, but you should get the approval also of Harcourt, Brace and Company, since, although I hold the copyright, I think they consider it courteous for you to notify them.

The list of men you give in your letter as reading the manuscript is, if I may say so, very uneven. I have the utmost respect for Alan Gregg, but I have no respect for the last-named man in your list,[8] whose claims of course I know about, and from the quotations you have made from Fleming,[9] I am highly suspicious of him.

I gave the manuscript a hasty reading last night and marked a number of things that struck me. If I could talk to you, I could probably make my point a little more clear without running the risk of seeming sharp.

You are a little too much taken with your reading of Brother Fleming. Perhaps he is a personal acquaintance of yours, and I am reluctant to keep hammering away about it, but you are making a mistake to take his stuff so seriously. He is not considered an authority and he evidently knows nothing about psychoanalysis. Dr. Robert Knight, of our clinic, has gone very thoroughly into the question of the merits and demerits of psychoanalysis in the treatment of alcoholism. He read a paper at the American Psychiatric Association in which he gave the statistics of psychoanalytic efficacy in a lot of different conditions, including alcohol addiction. If you really want a scientific comparison of the efficacy of psychoanalysis you ought to study this paper as well as previous articles by Doctor Knight, who is undoubtedly the leading psychoanalytic authority on alcohol addiction in this country, if not in the world. You do not even refer to him a single time in your paper. He proposed a classification similar to the one you quote from Fleming long before Fleming used it, although I think Fleming's article was published first, to tell the truth.

The most serious error you make, however, in my opinion is not here, but in your failure to grasp what I regard as the deeper psychiatric conception of alcohol addiction. While I do not agree with the way he puts it, I think you might begin to grasp this if you would read Rado's article of about five years ago. I have made the point repeatedly in *Man Against Himself* and *The Human Mind*, namely that alcohol addiction is not a disease, or at least not a primary disease. It is a pathological exaggeration and abuse of a very available, relatively cheap, ordinarily useful drug by persons who suffer from

8 Frank Fremont-Smith, a physician associated with the Josiah Macy, Jr., Foundation in New York. KAM's hostile reaction here is a puzzle, since there is only a single reference in Gray's work to Fremont-Smith, an anecdote Gray had heard from Smith that suggests the power of repressed memories from childhood.

9 Robert Fleming, a physician who taught at Harvard Medical School, and Kenneth J. Tillotson published in 1939 the findings of a study of 124 alcoholics treated in a New England hospital. Fleming was convinced that psychoanalysis was ineffective in treating alcoholism.

a disease (a neurosis) in which anxiety threatens to overcome them. Let me put it another way:

Some individuals, for various reasons, develop instabilities of personality which make them constantly subject to intense anxiety, fear, etc. If alcohol did not exist, these individuals might develop hysteria, depressions, suicidal tendencies or criminal tendencies; but alcohol does exist and they get introduced to it early and they find that it relieves the psychic pain caused by the threatened emergence of these other tendencies. It betrays them, however, in that once its effect wears off, the anxiety returns in greater force, and they are the more liable to an outbreak of their real disease and must, therefore, take more and larger quantities of the anesthesia.

The use of the anesthetic thus becomes pernicious in a habit-forming way but the use of alcohol does something else. It enables them to express some of these very aggressions, the outbreak of which they so much fear, but in an indirect way. Instead of killing their fathers, they worry them to death, outrage them, humiliate them, disappoint them, etc., and they do all this with relative freedom from guilt. It is as if a German sympathizer in England who hated the British about him but at the same time feared that he would be arrested if he expressed his resentment was overwhelmed with his fears and began running, ostensibly to get away from the British, but actually knocking down women and children as he ran, thereby doing the very thing for which the British police would have a perfect right to arrest him.

I am glad you are quoting from my book and I do not retract anything I said, but that book was written as an illustration of a general thesis, and the self-destructiveness in alcoholism is somewhat confused because it is so obvious. Let me put it this way: I believe the deepest and most fundamental factor in an alcoholic, as in everyone else, is his self-destructive urge, and I believe that in the alcoholic this is less well controlled than in normal people. This self-destructiveness, however, gives rise in turn, on the second level of the personality as it were, to hostile impulses against others, aggressiveness; and this in turn gives rise on the third level (coming up) to fears lest this aggressiveness properly placed will result in retaliation, punishment, etc. Consequently (on the fourth level), as a defense against the anxiety which developed on the third level, the alcoholic turns to a device which at the same time inflicts the aggression he secretly yearns to inflict, numbs himself to the fear of the consequences, and gratifies the deep, primitive self-destructive impulses—all these simultaneously. The self-destructiveness which is so evident in the result is thus really related to the deepest motive, but there are so many important intermediary motives that the average person is somewhat thrown out of line if he emphasizes too much. In a particular case it is usually pretty obvious.

Well, I seem to have written more than I intended to. I wish you luck with your article.

Sincerely yours,

To Leo Bartemeier, Detroit, August 15, 1941

Dear Leo:

I guess I will just have to sit down and write you a long letter about this Zilboorg matter. I have received many, many communications about the Zilboorg problem,[10] and I am not sure I understand it yet. This much I do understand, however, that Zilboorg made a solemn promise that he would not engage in any public activity representing or associated with psychoanalysis, that he would resign all offices and positions and would confine himself very privately to his private practice. Apparently, this promise was given in the presence of witnesses.

Subsequently, it seems he allowed his name to be put up for the Education Committee, and because of this some of the brothers lost all patience with him and were going to bring action against him or did bring action against him—I am not sure which. The rumor came to me that he had been suspended from the New York Society.

As secretary and president, you and I are probably entitled to a complete report on this problem. I had thought of writing the secretary of the New York Society myself and asking just how things stood, but I was reluctant to get drawn into it, since I felt that some of the persons who were most active in trying to restrict Doctor Zilboorg were persons whose ideals and conceptions of psychoanalysis were different from mine, to put it mildly.

Nevertheless, in view of the fact that Zilboorg did make these promises, and about this there seems to be no question, I feel that it is very unwise for me to put him in the position of having to decline or else to accept by breaking his word. I am fond of Zilboorg in spite of his mistakes and I think he has rendered valiant service for psychoanalysis. I would champion him as a member against all comers. But, on the other hand, I am reluctant to make an official appointment in the face of his promises.

Another thing that complicates this matter somewhat is the fact that Zilboorg was chiefly responsible for the electioneering whereby you and I were elected. It was his suggestion that we be elected. We might have been elected anyway, but the fact remains that he talked it up, argued for it, and asked people to nominate us. Naturally, however, this is not a reason either why we should appoint him or should not appoint him. But we cannot be appointing people just to keep them from being hurt, or we will be in terribly hot water.

I am not sure I agree with you [that] he is the best qualified. Even assuming that he was, I think at the present time we cannot appoint him, and one reason I have been delaying the matter is in the hopes that the thing would clear up somewhat. . . . In the meantime, however, I think we should reflect on who else might be if not the best qualified at least well qualified. . . .

You might think it would be easy to simply write Zilboorg a frank per-

10 KAM was then president of the American Psychoanalytic Association.

sonal letter and ask him what the status of things is. The reason I do not do this is that I think it is possible that he would write back that he never made any such promises, that there is a conspiracy against him, etc., and then it would be his word against others. He is already charged by some with having lied flagrantly, and what I am afraid of is we would simply be stirring up more fire. It is a very difficult problem and I would welcome any suggestions you have for its solution.

Sincerely,

P.S. There is another consideration which I did not mention. I feel that it is a great mistake in our Society for one person to retain the same office or job year after year. Zilboorg has been chairman of the Program Committee for several years, and I think there are others who could do as good, if not a better, job. Upon reflection, I believe this is the most important reason why I should appoint someone else.

To summarize the situation, then: Zilboorg is our friend, Zilboorg has fought for psychoanalysis, Zilboorg is well qualified; but on the other hand, Zilboorg has had the job several years, Zilboorg's program arrangement has been sharply criticized by many members, other men are capable, and it would be more democratic to pass the job around, and, last of all, Zilboorg is under something of a cloud and has given a promise not to participate publicly.

To Franz Alexander, La Jolla, California, August 15, 1941

Dear Alex:

I must write you about the Zilboorg matter. There is strong pressure upon me to reappoint Zilboorg as chairman of the Program Committee. Personally, I am fond of Zilboorg, and I know that he would like the job, but I feel that it would be an advantage to the [American Psychoanalytic] Association to pass the job around and let others try their hand at it. For me to explain to Zilboorg that this is my chief motive in appointing someone else will only be received by him as additional trauma; he will not believe it.

You told me that Zilboorg had promised you in the presence of witnesses not to accept any public office or to participate in any public way with psychoanalysis, or to associate himself in any way with it. Of course, this would preclude his accepting the chairmanship of the Program Committee. You also told me, however, that I was not to reveal the fact that this information came from you. This puts me in a very difficult situation.

Of course, I have the right to appoint anyone I like, but I also like to discuss my appointments with my fellow officers. When I say that I was told that Zilboorg promised not to do these things but that I cannot say who told me, I am put in a weak position. I wish, therefore, you would release me from my promise to keep your name secret and would give me a letter signed by yourself and the other witnesses stating that this promise was made.

Sincerely yours,

To C. B. Pinkham,[11] San Francisco, California, August 15, 1941

My dear Doctor Pinkham:

I have had word from Dr. Ernst Simmel, of Los Angeles, of your hospitable reception of him some weeks ago and your courteous attention to his presentation of the outlines of postgraduate training required in psychiatry for the psychoanalytic technique. As I hope he convinced you, we are maintaining our requirements very high, the highest of any specialty, because psychoanalysis is particularly prone to be misinterpreted and misused by poorly or incompletely trained individuals. I commend your earnest consideration of the proposals and suggestions made by Doctor Simmel, and I now wish to write you in regard to a personal matter concerning Doctor Simmel.

Doctor Simmel was one of the outstanding psychiatrists of Europe and, because of his contributions to military as well as civilian psychiatry, he was in high favor until the Hitler regime, under which he was persecuted, imprisoned and forced to leave Germany by the Gestapo. You probably share with some of the rest of us certain annoyances at the presumptuousness and arrogance of some German scientists, not lessened by the behavior of some of them since their forced immigration to America. I can assure you that Doctor Simmel is not one of those who would arouse in anyone such feelings. He is a very loyal American and a very modest man, and his contributions to medical science and particularly to psychiatry have been of the highest order and we are all very much indebted to him. The medical profession of California is especially in his debt, in my opinion. It was he who from the first insisted upon the limitation of training psychoanalytic technique to physicians, something which we American physicians take for granted, but which was not in practice in Germany. He maintained a very high standard in teaching and practice among a small but growing group of men in Southern California, and in recent years he has had a supervisory relationship of great importance to the psychiatrists in San Francisco who are using psychoanalytic methods.

Let me sketch briefly some facts about his history in the teaching field. In 1922, nearly 20 years ago, he founded the first training committee for the adequate, controlled, regulated training of psychoanalysts in Berlin. Until that time psychoanalysis had been a haphazardly taught technique largely in the hands of a few who had apprenticed themselves, as it were, to Freud and to one or two of his associates. Doctor Simmel laid down the first reg-

11 Secretary-Treasurer, California Board of Medical Examiners.

ulations regarding psychoanalytic training, and it was one of his early principles which has been accepted in every American [Psychoanalytic] Society that a candidate should only be accepted for this special training after having been investigated by a committee to pass on his abilities and character.

One of Doctor Simmel's first students in Berlin was Dr. Franz Alexander, now Director of the Institute for Psychoanalysis in Chicago; this Institute, as you know, is largely supported by the Rockefeller Foundation, and it cooperates with the University Medical Schools of Chicago, where it is held in high esteem.

Doctor Simmel came to California about seven years ago. (I am not sure of the exact date.) We had invited and, in fact, urged him to join our staff here in Topeka, and we regretted very much that he felt the opportunities and needs of California were greater than ours. He did not appreciate the difficulties he would have in getting a license, and even after he learned of these difficulties, he anticipated it would be possible for him to arrange in some way to be licensed. Time passed, however, and these opportunities did not materialize; on account of his age and his preoccupation with teaching and maintenance of himself and a score of refugees whom he supported, it was not possible for him to get an internship. The phenomenon of a distinguished scientist of sixty following along with newly graduated medical students the routine of an internship would, I think you will agree, be pathetic, even if it were possible.

Doctor Simmel is very anxious to comply with the law in all respects and thus to show in practice what he believes in theory; namely, that psychoanalysis and psychiatry should be developed by the medical profession in a legal, orthodox, standardized way. It is a paradox that this man who has done so much to promote the development of psychiatry and psychoanalysis as a medical activity should, for technical reasons, be unable to obtain the legal status of a practicing physician in California, after having spent many years of his life in medical practice and teaching in Germany.

I am telling you these facts because I would like to incline you to favor the granting of a California license to Doctor Simmel as a special concession for distinguished merit without an examination and without an internship requirement. There are a number of other excellent German psychiatrists and psychoanalysts in California who do not have licenses, most because they have not had internships; I have urged all of them to get their internships regardless of the sacrifices in time, income and pride. In the case of Doctor Simmel, I think it is now impossible for him to get an internship, and I know also you have a ruling against granting licenses to immigrants from countries where Americans are not admitted to examinations, as is the case in Germany. But Doctor Simmel is a very exceptional person and I earnestly urge that consideration be given to the possibility of making him an exception in the matter of a license. As President of the American Psychoanalytic

Association, a medical body affiliated with the American Psychiatric Association, I can say that we consider Doctor Simmel one of the half dozen most eminent teachers and leaders in our specialty, and it would be a favor not only to Doctor Simmel but to American psychiatry and psychoanalysis if you would see fit to take this step. If it would strengthen your purpose or facilitate your action, I should be glad to have similar endorsements supplied to you by other officers in our organization, a step which we have never taken with regard to any other physician in any state in the country.

I hope you will not regard my request as presumptuous or importunate. I recognize the difficulties and complications of your job and I have heard of your reputation for efficiency and thoroughness, especially in your campaign to rid California of quacks, a program which I heartily endorse. This concession to Doctor Simmel would be helpful in that same direction.

Sincerely yours,

To GREGORY ZILBOORG, NEW YORK, DECEMBER 2, 1941

Dear Gregory:

I am just dashing off to make five talks in Houston, Texas, before a sizable bunch of the wistful but untutored. In the same mail as this letter to you I am sending in a review to the *Herald Tribune* of one of the most interesting books I have read in many a day.[12] I hope it pleases you. I tried to write the review with the same convincing restraint you yourself used in the book.

I wanted to indicate that I thought you were a great man and had rendered a great gift to psychiatry without laying it on so thick that anybody would say I was trying to whitewash you for your alleged sins. I refrained from making any criticism chiefly because I didn't find any to make, except the deplorable omission of Southard and what I thought was too much emphasis on Adolf Meyer and his bunk. I thought you were extremely fair to Brill and Jelliffe. I do not see why you added the unnecessary chapters by Henry and of course it irritates me that Henry did not look beyond the Atlantic seaboard for new developments in psychiatric-hospital ideas. It would have been more in line with what you wrote. Even my highly vulnerable narcissism was not injured by anything you wrote except possibly in a very slight degree by your credit to Mr. Norton on page 141[13] for something about which you will find mention in *Man Against Himself* on page 251, to say nothing of the fact that the general material of that paragraph (I mean on page 141 of your book) is discussed at length (and I mean at

12 Gregory Zilboorg and G. M. Henry, *History of Medical Psychology* (1941).

13 The footnote reads, "I am indebted to W. W. Norton for calling my attention to the self-torturing groups in New Mexico who even today inflict wounds upon themselves and others during their religious Christian ceremonies."

length) on pages 87 to 143 and pages 231 to 285 in the aforementioned *Man Against Himself*, which if you do not have a copy of I shall be glad to send you.

Seriously, Gregory, I think the book is wonderful and you have set us a great ideal for painstaking scholarly research. It contains so many ideas so brilliantly presented that I am afraid you will have excited great envy in the hearts of a few but you will have also excited great admiration, gratitude and affection in the hearts of many more.

We have four copies of the book in our library (Bob Knight thinks you promised to give him a copy, and sometime I think this would be a good idea), but will you please autograph a copy, the net retail, undiscounted, undecorated, unqualified remittance for which is enclosed, and send it to us for a woman who has generously supported our foundation and who will be delighted with your book as a Christmas present from us. Her name is Lucy Stearns McLaughlin of Santa Fe, New Mexico. She is a trustee of the Menninger Foundation; she has given generously to the support of psychiatry and to the carrying of the torch. I cannot recall whether or not you met her when you were here. I wish you would write something nice on the flyleaf and sign your name, and she will be tickled to death. Don't postpone this because we want to be sure to get it to her by Christmas and if you don't do it now you might forget it.

I am eagerly awaiting further details of the silly business—you know what. Every time I think about it I get mad.

Sincerely,

To Smith Ely Jelliffe, Huletts Landing, New York, December 4, 1941

Dear Doctor Smith Ely:

I have deferred a shamefully long time answering your letter of October 20 in which you asked me if I was sore about something because I wanted to sit down and write you a long letter. Now it happens I am going to Houston, Texas, for a series of addresses to a medical group and that means it will be another week or so before I can write, and yet I am under such pressure getting off that I cannot do justice to this.

I do want to tell you I am not sore about a thing in the world. I continue to think about you most affectionately as one who guided me, helped me, encouraged me and inspired me. I put this in the past but I will also put it in the present and in the future. I was delighted to see what Zilboorg said about you in his new *History*, and I feel as he did that you are one of the five great American leaders. He unfortunately omitted Southard to whom, as you know, I was greatly attached. Personally, I think you and Southard did more than any of the others.

The reason I have not written can be put in a very few words. Grace and

I were divorced last February and in September I was married to a girl I have loved for a long time. We took a trip through the Canadian Rockies and came back to Topeka and are living in a small house out in the country. This involves a great many readjustments of a great many different things, and I leave that to your imagination. I have three children in college and they take a good deal of my libido as well as my cash, and I have a former wife whom I must also support. For these reasons, my nose has been pretty close to the grindstone. Working in a group this way none of us makes as much money as is frequently imagined, but we are quite busy and I think we can carry on if things don't get any worse. I am a strong interventionist and think we ought to be over fighting both Germany and Japan right now.

We have also completed the establishment of the Menninger Foundation, details about which Dr. Robert Knight will send you under separate cover in case you wish to put a note about it in your journals.

I wish you would remember me kindly to Bee from whom I used to receive occasional stimulating postcards. Tell her I am still planning to bring my new wife and call upon you in your beautiful home upon the Lake, but it probably will not be until spring at the earliest.

Sincerely,

To Adolph Stern,[14] New York, December 30, 1941

Dear Adolph:

. . . My appearance at your meeting in New York was with the express purpose of being of some assistance in lightening the labors of the committee in what seems to me to be a needlessly involved and prolonged piece of business,[15] news of which has spread to the public even to the extent of being reported in the daily press. Because I feel that such things are extremely harmful to psychoanalysis, I had hoped to use my personal and official influence to bring this to a speedy conclusion. I was sorry not to have been able to convince the executive committee of the possibility of doing this. I must say that I deeply deplore the handling of the complaints of a patient lodged with the officials of the New York Society, and in so doing I do not wish to reflect in any way upon the sincerity and integrity of any of the members.

I repeat what I said to all of you in convention; namely, that this is not, in my opinion, an appropriate way to deal with such complaints, since it defeats the purpose of the constitutional provision, which was the protection

14 Stern came to the United States from Austria in 1886 at the age of eight. He became a psychoanalyst in 1921 after two years of studying with Freud. He was a member of the executive committee of the New York Psychoanalytic Institute during the Zilboorg hearing.

15 The Zilboorg hearing.

of the good name and repute of psychoanalysis. In addition to the bad notoriety and the unjust injury of an accused member long before he is found guilty (or not guilty), it also sets a very bad precedent and one which medical organizations generally have long since eschewed. Perhaps one good that will come out of it is a revision of the constitutionally provided procedure in cases of alleged unethical behavior. I shall be glad to have your recommendations in regard to this at the conclusion of the matter, so that I may incorporate them into my presidential address at the May meeting.

Sincerely yours,

FROM GREGORY ZILBOORG, NEW YORK, JANUARY 6, 1942

Dear Karl:

The enclosed is being sent to you because I don't know who the chairman of the Program Committee is this year.

I have been thinking about the Section on Psychoanalysis and the [American Psychiatric] Association. The war may necessitate some last-minute changes and I am sure you must have thought about it. Phil Lehrman[1] is chairman-elect of the Section. I understand that he has already been called (Med. Corp, U.S.N.R.) and should he prove unavailable this coming year (he is still around) the political fellows might try to put something over. I wonder what formal and constitutional steps one could quietly prepare to meet this eventuality. Should Phil prove unavailable and should one think of a New Yorker, Kubie might be a very good choice indeed. I think in this connection also of the American [Psychoanalytic Association]. It would be a good idea to keep the presidency in the hands of non-New Yorkers for a while to avoid further political complications. On the other hand, you probably know that Levy and Rado maneuvered Kubie[2] out of the presidency in Cincinnati and Rado later told Lewin that Kubie was shoved out by the "Zilboorg machine." Their boy is Daniels, who always played with them and the Horney people and who at the same time succeeded in playing the other side. As a result he is considered *safe*, but you know better I am sure.

Thank you for letting me have the carbon copies of your letter to [Adolph] Stern. I hardly need to make any comment on the substance of either. People are small and pompous—pompous and small.

The so-called hearings are over. This coming Friday, the 9th, the Board of

1 Philip Lehrman, a Freud analysand, was a psychoanalyst at the New York University Hospital. He helped develop the curriculum for the New York Psychoanalytic Institute.

2 Lawrence S. Kubie was a New York psychoanalyst and close friend of KAM. He was one of the five men appointed by consultant to the Surgeon General, WCM, to study combat exhaustion in the army in Europe in 1945. His books include *Practical Aspects of Psychoanalysis* (1936), *Practical and Theoretical Aspects of Psychoanalysis* (1950), and *Neurotic Distortion of Creative Process* (1958).

Directors will sit and decide. The last tidings were not glad. I hear that the majority are against me. They might change their minds by Friday, but I doubt it. Those people are too impressed with their sudden importance and they have no sense of perspective. They became very formalistic. They are impressed with the legal rules and the power they find themselves suddenly wielding. They do not realize that punishment is of no avail as a rule. Nor do they realize that punishment has already been meted out to an extreme degree: months of suffering, rumors, calumny and whatnot. They seem to have followed the advice of the Queen in *Alice in Wonderland:* "First sentence and verdict afterwards." If, as it undoubtedly will, the matter is brought up before the Society, the whole thing will spread through eighty mouths— many of whom are as good analysts as you and I are Chinese scholars. Injustice will pile up on injustice, and they will all continue to be impressed with their own sense of justice. What in the meantime all this will do to psychoanalysis they don't seem to be able to grasp or care. A sad commentary on humans.

I read your statement and colloquy with the board in the stenographic minutes. The pitiful showing of the board stands out even more poignantly when one see it in black and white.

There is nothing that I can do. I did my best, but it irks me to think that the level on which all these things are being worked out is very low indeed.

God bless you.

As ever,

FROM GREGORY ZILBOORG, NEW YORK, JANUARY 23, 1942

Dear Karl:

This is a confidential report meant only for you and for Bob Knight through you, if you deem it advisable. Your and Bob's serenity and loyal objectivity moved me deeply. Hence this letter.

The hearing is over; the Board had before them a truly dirty police-court performance on the part of Levy's lawyer, which even the members of the board did not easily stomach, and another statement by Alexander, who this time came with another lawyer from Chicago. Alexander's second statement was the best self-accusation he could present; he practically canceled a number of important things he had said before and presented a series of new and untruthful statements betraying conspicuously and openly his hostility against me, calling me "an irrational, desperate man" to whom he was "kinder than I should have been."

At any rate it is now over a month that the hearings have been over; the Board met by themselves several times and could not agree.

Three of them consider that I am innocent; that I made no mistake; that I am to be fully cleared. They would not recede from their position; they will present to the Society a minority report. The other seven will present their report. They, I understand, state that I did not exploit the patient, that I showed no bad faith, etc., but that as a result of a countertransference I committed technical errors which were to the detriment of the psychoanalytic movement and that therefore I am to be reprimanded. There is grave doubt whether this majority report will gather the necessary three-fourths vote. But they seem to be adamant. They apparently are willing to overlook completely Levy's and Alexander's unethical procedure and ill will. They apparently also consider that, without Alexander, Levy or the board of directors having examined the patient clinically, they have a right to assume that there is a standard technique for psychotic, nonanalytical cases—without stating what that standard is. A precedent injurious to psychoanalysis, a number of such principles, is thus being established—which is immoral from the human and professional point of view.

Apparently there is a very safe margin of votes to kill (in the Society) the "majority" report, but I wonder what to do. After all, as long as I am a member of the Society I cannot very well accept these precedents and injury done to me. The prejudiced attitude of some of the board is seen, for instance, in the fact that Millet[3] just nominated Levy to the Educational Committee. Blumgart,[4] long before the official hearings began, stated to others, nonmembers of the board, that I should resign and if found innocent be reinstated; he suggested this procedure because "Levy never undertakes anything without being sure of his facts."

There will be a special meeting of the Society which will be announced one week in advance and at which the two reports will be presented. I shall have copies of these reports before the meeting. I am very curious about your and Bob's reactions to the whole thing as it stands now because I don't want to overlook anything which would save psychoanalysis from a big stink. I was injured enough. I cannot be injured more and therefore I, if I am to continue in the profession, am vitally interested that the profession not be infested with inhumaness, stupidity, rancor and political blackmail.

My warmest regards to you.

As always,

TO GREGORY ZILBOORG, NEW YORK, FEBRUARY 7, 1942

Dear Gregory:

I was prodigiously relieved to learn that the hearings were over and that some of the members of the board were intelligent enough to realize that

---

3 John A. P. Millet was professor of psychiatry at Columbia Medical School.

4 Leonard Blumgart, a New York analyst. An analysand of Freud, in 1942 he was president of the New York Psychoanalytic Society.

there was only one thing that they could find and that was that you had made no mistake discoverable or reviewable by them. What I mean by that is simply this. Of course you have made mistakes; so has every other analyst. In the instance of this patient, you may have made a mistake or you may not have made a mistake. If you did make a mistake and someone else sees it and wants to be of help to you and hence points out your mistake and gives advice and counsel in a friendly way—that's one thing. Whether you take such advice or not is another thing, but both things happen in the course of ordinary, decent professional relationships.

But when, on the other hand, a patient feels you have made a mistake and persuades one or two or half a dozen colleagues that you have made a mistake and then one or two of these colleagues pursue the matter by complaining to an organized scientific society about your mistakes and charge you with fraudulent intentions, which is to say criminal intentions, and when this scientific body takes such complaints seriously and listens to them and debates them over a period of months, I think an extremely serious miscarriage of good taste, public policy, scientific principle and common decency has occurred. A number of very bad precedents were set by what occurred in New York, and whatever mistakes you may have made (I do not believe any more that you even made any mistakes but I am putting this subjunctive clause in here because I don't think it matters whether you did or not) it is a resounding shame and disgrace that these alleged mistakes should have been exploited and capitalized upon by colleagues with personal grudges against you. The bringing of a patient to a scientific organization to give evidence against a physician is one of the most dangerous and vicious precedents that I can think of and violates all medical precedents.

For these reasons I am inclined to agree with Bob Knight whose letter to you of February 6 I have seen. I would not be inclined to accept a reprimand for "technical errors." You either had criminal intent or you did not have criminal intent. If they cannot show that you had criminal intent, the whole proceeding falls flat. My inclination is to say that you should demand complete exoneration and the condemnation of a bad precedent of colleagues egging on patients to file charges against other colleagues, etc. It seems to me that our procedure in regard to so-called unethical behavior stipulated in our constitution should be revised and I would welcome a motion for this at the Boston meeting.

I am trying to look at this broadly as president of the [American Psychoanalytic] Association. I would not blame you for feeling very bitterly against Doctor Levy and Doctor Alexander, but my own attitude must be one of as much tolerance as I can muster. There is Biblical authority for believing that those that live by the sword shall die by the sword, and the present system and the methods used by Doctor Alexander and Doctor Levy threaten their own future even more than that of any of the rest of us. It has even occurred to me that Doctor Levy might see the error of what I told him I believed were good intentions, expressed in this way, and he might even draw up an amendment revising our standard procedure to eliminate the difficulties he got himself into because I feel sure that Doctor Levy wishes to be well thought of and wants to be found on the side of progress, fairness, good sense, etc. That he doesn't approve of you and that you don't approve of him is beside the point, or should be. It is unfair for him to say what his unconscious is; consciously, he thought you were doing something bad and that it was his duty to put a stop to it. To save his face he may still think it was bad but I am sure he cannot still believe that the method he chose was a wise one.

Sincerely yours,

FROM GREGORY ZILBOORG, NEW YORK, FEBRUARY 23, 1942

Dear Karl:

This is a purely personal letter. I read and reread, several times, your remarks on McKinney's book.[5] I reread them several times not because they are so recondite that they need to be ruminated but because in all my sophistication I am very naive at times, and I studied your remarks because I wanted to discover the secret of the extraordinary realignment your aggression has taken of late: you are vivid, terse and direct and outspoken; you pack a true and uncushioned wallop—yet, disagreeable as all this might be to the author, you are not offensive, not surly, not "scoldy"; you are objective, factual—killing without anger or fear, and yet just without unctuous hypocrisy of sanctimonious pseudo-altruism. I am sorry these remarks are just mimeographed. They should have been published in some psychological journal for the purpose of starting a discussion of the subject—a frank and practical discussion which of late years has been sorely lacking so that the psychologist is left alone by the clinical psychiatrist and vice-versa. The result of it is that the psychologist mistakes his aloneness for clinico-scientific independence, to which he has no right and which he cannot possess except in bad books—and the psychiatrist, on the other hand, by turning away from the psychologist, imagines him dead or at least innocuous and he merrily rolls along with his psychiatry without a psychology. The psychoanalyst stands in the middle and is considerably thwarted because the psychologist is afraid of him for one reason and the psychiatrist for another, and much energy and time is misspent in attempts at mutual and reciprocal confutations instead of on cooperation and mutual and reciprocal research and instruction. Your idea of organizing a little symposium or private con-

5 Fred McKinney, author of *Psychology of Personal Adjustment: Students' Introduction to Mental Hygiene* (1941).

gress is highly laudable. It might well prove a potent beginning in the direction of bringing true light into this anomalous situation. I wish I were able to sit in on your discussion.

Another matter—this unofficial and private. You will hear or will have heard by now from Gosselin[6] inviting you to be one of the editors of the *Psychoanalytic Quarterly*. We need you, and even without being an editor you have been very friendly and useful to us. Some deadwood on that body is being cleared out. We are now a corporation, you know: (Gosselin, Secretary; Lewin, Vice-President; and I, President). These three are the only members of the corporation and the other editors carry no other responsibilities than editorial. I do hope you will find it possible to accept the invitation.

My love to both of you,

To GREGORY ZILBOORG, NEW YORK, FEBRUARY 27, 1942

Dear Gregory:

I am fascinated by the plans for the volume on *One Hundred Years of American Psychiatry*. . . . It seems to me you have done a superb job of planning.

As for the content, I haven't very much to suggest unless it might be a chapter dealing with the extension of psychiatry into related fields—military, industrial, education, social, etc. I omit legal because you intend to cover that yourself, and perhaps you ought to cover all of these. I do not like the title of chapter 8 very much—I do not like the words "medico-legal" and I do not like the word "problems"; call it "Psychiatry and Law" or something of that kind.

Now about my writing a chapter for the book, of course I am very pleased with such an invitation and consider it a great honor, but I have been giving it quite a little thought, and I will tell you my impressions: I quite agree with you that Kubie would be a good writer, but I don't quite see him writing "The History of Therapy" because I don't believe he knows enough about intramural therapy. To tell you the honest truth, I think my brother Will knows more about intramural hospital therapy (as described by you on page three of your letter) than anybody in the country, and I would suggest that you ask him to write this chapter and ask Kubie to write the "Mental Hygiene" chapter. I don't need to do anything or I might even join my brother Will in writing the therapy chapter.

I will tell you why I don't want to write the "Mental Hygiene" chapter: In the first place, I am afraid I couldn't resist telling exactly how I feel about it; namely, that it was a blundering attempt of Adolf Meyer which was blown up like a bubble and burst like a bubble without beginning to do the things

6 Raymond Gosselin, New York analyst, managing editor of *Psychoanalytic Quarterly*.

it might have done had Salmon[7] or Southard or even Frankwood Williams taken hold of it and kept hold of it. What I am trying to say is that I don't believe I can take a historically objective attitude toward the whole business because I feel in my bones that Adolf Meyer has done much to retard psychiatry and so-called mental hygiene, and yet a third of the members of our Association, if not more, believe that psychiatry and mental hygiene would not have been heard of if it had not been for Adolf. I would feel myself writing against that resistance all the time. I founded the Kansas Mental Hygiene Society and I have worked on the National Committee. As you know, I also founded the American Orthopsychiatric Association, which was a kind of mental hygiene outgrowth. I have been mixed up in the thing for years, and I don't feel good about it, and you know you can't write under those circumstances. Kubie, I believe, could be very much more objective; if I am not mistaken, he is a Hopkins graduate, and he certainly has not been as close to the movement as I have and so shouldn't have as many "complexes" about it.

This is not a very consecutively organized letter, but, you see, I am trying to make several points, and perhaps, in a disconnected way, I have made them, and shall be eager to hear your reaction to my suggestions . . .

Sincerely,

From Gregory Zilboorg, New York, March 11, 1942

Dear Karl:

The storm is seemingly over, perhaps fully over, and I am busy working, trying to do a job and what they call "forget" about it. While not disturbed, I am profoundly affected by all that happened during the past year. Somehow it is not possible for me to rid myself of a sense of being disquieted by the awareness of how predatory man is and how jungle-like the intertwining of personal animosities. There is something degrading and unhealthy in all this aspect of man—yet so inevitable. Yes, very natural, psychologically fundamental and clear—but also so revolting to one's sense of brotherhood and friendship among men.

Take Binger,[8] for instance, very pious. I learn confidentially that he put immense pressure on various people to become a member of the American Psychiatric Association. So great is his drive to circumvent the rules of requirements that he, the pious and "ethical" person, almost demands that

7 Thomas W. Salmon was a New York psychiatrist. He had been Senior Consultant in Neuropsychiatry, AEF, during World War I; he became the first medical director of the National Committee for Mental Hygiene.

8 Carl Binger, a member of the New York Psychoanalytic Society; in 1939 he helped found the journal *Psychosomatic Medicine*. In 1945 he was president and a charter member of the Association for Psychoanalytic and Psychosomatic Medicine.

the Association stamp its approval on his non-existing psychiatric qualifications so that he be enabled to call himself "legitimately" a psychiatrist.[9] Queer—how could he square this with his scientific and human conscience, he who advertises everywhere his strict scientific training? He spells science with a forty-foot capital S and yet wishes a professional organization to help him prostitute it. I understand that Win[10] stood up and told them in no uncertain terms how dirty it all is on Binger's part and that the matter will be brought up before the council next May.

About my "case." I shall do what you think is wise—regardless of my personal feelings, which at best are not a little hyperesthetic [characterized by abnormal activity of the senses], like a poorly granulating cut covered with salt. Levy, I want to leave alone. He is a moral sadist of the first order and I want to forget that he exists. Alexander is a different matter. Regardless of the merits of the case, Alexander committed an immoral act which is now a precedent and which is potentially and actually injurious to psychoanalysis. As I said, the Lord stayed the hand of Abraham, as if to say that even the most demanding superego would not allow the murder of a son. To permit this precedent to stand without comment means to reverse the fundamental principles of psychoanalysis and guide the hand of Abraham in order to cut off Isaac's head more efficiently.

I could (theoretically) write you officially a letter, tell you about it and say that it is wrong that every young analyst, from now on, may have in the back of his head that his analyst may at any time rise and castrate him—years after—years after that analyst certified him as fit to be an analyst. To come out publicly before the profession to prosecute a former analysand, to call me "a desperate, irrational man," to demand openly and through his lawyer (specially imported from Chicago) that I be punished, to say that he, Alexander, has been too kind to me and now repents, to lie also—is awful. I suppose there are many reasons why such countercharges against Alexander before the American might not be advisable. On the other hand, could such a thing be left alone, as if it never happened? I also wish to say that I would be perfectly satisfied and would not say a word and would not prefer any charges if someone got up and submitted a cool, objective resolution without mentioning any names whatsoever—a resolution stating that one of the first principles of psychoanalytic ethics is that an analyst, particularly one who has already certified an analysand as fit to be analyst, is definitely

9 Zilboorg has written at the bottom of the page, "I learn that he applied three times, deferred once and rejected twice. If he is accepted he will officially have been in practice for twenty years and will have yet to be certified by the American Board of N & P [Neurology and Psychiatry] as a full-fledged etc."

10 Winfred Overholser was then superintendent of St. Elizabeths Hospital, Washington, D.C., and secretary-treasurer of the APA; he was president of the APA from 1947 to 1948.

committing an unethical act if he ever testifies against his former analysand—still worse if he initiates proceedings against a former analysand—and that if he does he should be deprived of the right to train younger men. Alexander in his testimony said: "on the basis of my knowledge of Zilboorg's psychology"—as if implying that I always was a crook. And even if he had not said this, how can an analyst "forget" his former patient's unconscious and how can he, under the influence of his hostility, not utilize his former patient's unconscious in the service of his own hostility; there is something unclean and predatory in all this.

I would love to hear from you and have you tell me what the best course to pursue would be.

As ever,

To Gregory Zilboorg, New York, March 18, 1942

Dear Gregory:

. . . In regard to a resolution opposing the testifying of an analyst against a former analysand, my impression is that, in the first place, this is already an unwritten law which most of us would not think of violating; and, in the second place, it is too soon after the New York goings-on to do anything about it as it might be interpreted as having been engineered by you, which would make even some of your friends irritated, feeling that you were pursuing your victory; and, third, we already have enough trouble for this May meeting without adding this to it. The Washington-Baltimore Society members are taking the position that the Horney group is the result of a local New York squabble, as they call it. I don't know just how they will do it, but I am convinced they will make plenty of trouble.

I wish we could have [had] you come out and give us some seminars, but we are too hard up at present to invite you. The boys have all been talking about it and want you, but I guess we will have to postpone it until conditions improve somewhat. We are changing the Southard School to the foster-parent plan[11] in order to cut expenses. I am working hard trying to get my book *[Love Against Hate]* finished in the next month. God knows, I've been working at it long enough to have had it finished before now.

Sincerely,

To Gregory Zilboorg, New York, March 20, 1942

Dear Gregory:

Since you are writing the history of the relations of psychiatry and the law, I think I should give you a little information.

11 This plan was never effected.

I don't have the date at my fingertip, but when the American Psychiatric Association met in Detroit about 1923 or 1924 there was a big stink about the Loeb-Leopold case and a motion was made that a committee be appointed to investigate the relation of psychiatry to the law and make a report to the Association for its guidance in stipulations to psychiatrists in courts of law.

William A. White was president at that time and he wrote me that he wanted me to take the chairmanship of this committee, that this was a very important committee and I was a very young man but that he felt that it needed a lot of energy and thought, and I was to get a committee together and do something effective in this very important direction. I had a fine committee, the membership of which I can give you, and we worked for five years on the thing. We reported first in 1925, then an amended report in 1926, etc., etc. Then I went personally to the American Bar Association meeting for three years, I believe, and persuaded them to appoint a committee to meet with ours in joint sessions. Then I contacted the American Medical Association and got them to appoint a committee. Then all three of us—the American Bar, the American Medical and the American Psychiatric—had committees. I managed the whole thing and got these committees to agree on a joint statement which was finally passed unanimously as the attitude of the American Bar, the American Psychiatric, and the American Medical Association.

While I was engaged in all this I was very enthusiastic about it and did a lot of work and have an enormous file of my activities.

In 1929, Dr. Samuel J. Orton was made president of the Association, and my feeling toward Orton is very much like your feeling toward Dr. David Levy. Doctor Orton abruptly dismissed me as chairman of the committee on which I had worked for five years and had produced what the secretary of the Association described as "an almost monumental achievement." I was tremendously bitter about it at the time and so were many members of the executive committee of the American Psychiatric Association. As I look back on it now, I think Doctor Orton was fully justified; I think it was very appropriate that some other people in the Association should come face to face with the job, but it was very crudely done, I was young and not fully aware of all of the problems in the American Psychiatric, and I was very enthusiastic about carrying the job through a little further, etc., etc.

I have the entire file of this correspondence and was about to throw it away when it occurred to me that you might want it for historical researches. Some of it is rather personal since many members of the Association felt somewhat bitter, but I think I can entrust it to you. The question is: Do you want it? Or shall I keep it here pending such time as you do want it?

Sincerely,

To Smith Ely Jelliffe, Huletts Landing, New York, April 9, 1942

My dear Smith Ely:

Your newsy letter of several months ago has remained long unanswered. I often think of you up there in Washington County watching the recession of winter and the approach of spring over your beautiful lake, surrounded by your books and your sprightly wife. I gather from your letter that you are feeling fairly well and adjusting yourself to the annoying difficulties[12] with characteristic courage and philosophy. That you are hard at work on the parathyroid theme and your autobiography is characteristic of your energy and scientific curiosity.

Our little foundation is getting along quite well—thanks to some miscellaneous gifts of a few thousand dollars. We have in mind the publication of a series of articles on the interrelationship of psychiatry to the various medical specialties; we are financing a little hypnosis research and some psychological studies because we believe that the psychologists have a lot to offer in the speeding up of psychiatric diagnostic studies.

I am sending my new book [Love Against Hate] to the publishers next week. The theme of it is that something has to be done with our aggressions, and perhaps we could find better ways to manage them than has been done in the past. I have suggested some ideas about work, play, parental guidance, etc., in a rather orderly scheme which I think you will like. It is a sort of a sequel to Man Against Himself, a kind of "Man For Himself," as it were. I hope it indicates some development in my own psychology.

The Psychoanalytic Association meets in Boston, as you know, and I hope you can come over. Dave Levy has resigned from the New York Society, whether to join Horney or not I do not know. He got mad at Zilboorg and charged him with some crimes which neither the executive committee nor the society as a whole were convinced of. He made a lot of stink, however. Alexander got into it, very unwisely, I think, and then there are certain ambitious ones and certain dissatisfied ones, belligerent ones and certain querulous ones, etc. My idea for a presidential address was to call attention to some of the external dangers and some of the internal dangers, and stress the need of a little more tolerance, a little more loyalty—loyalty to one another and loyalty to the essential scientific principles. If you have any ideas for these presidential adjurations, I wish you would send them to me. Freud's death seems to have released a lot of hostility and narcissism in some of the brothers, just as he predicted.

Give my love to Bee, and write me little about yourself when you have time.

Sincerely yours,

---

12 Jelliffe suffered from ill health. Specifically, in the 1930's he was afflicted with increasing deafness and an auricular fibrillation. In 1939 he had an operation for cancer of the prostate, and ultimately died of uremia caused by the cancer.

P.S. Will and father ask to be remembered. Father spent some time in Florida this winter and he is very busy now enlarging the spring gardens at his own place and at the sanitarium. He still teaches neurology to the nurses and visits the patients once a week.

To OTTO FENICHEL, LOS ANGELES, APRIL 20, 1942

My dear Doctor Fenichel:

I am in charge of the scientific books reviewed by *The Nation*, a weekly periodical with which you are no doubt familiar, and I have on my hands at the present time Karen Horney's recent book with the amazing title of *Self-Analysis*. I feel so antagonistic to what seems to me to be Horney's outright intellectual dishonesty that my own inclination is to review the book myself forcefully and critically.

It happens, however, that I am president of the American Psychoanalytic Association, and if I say what I think about the book my official position is likely to make it appear that there is some justification in Horney's paranoid charge that she is being persecuted by us and is justified, therefore, in her secessionist movement. She will have some of her cohorts write long letters to *The Nation* pointing out that the president has attacked her in public. Furthermore, I recently reviewed her friend Fromm's book in *The Nation*,[13] and she evidently organized a barrage of letters which were sent to the editor denouncing me as anti-Semitic, antiforeigner, antirefugee, etc. *The Nation* printed the only one of these letters that was printable and I attempted to answer it. I mention this only to indicate why I feel I should not review the book.

On the other hand, I feel that someone with psychoanalytic authority and acumen and intellectual honesty should do so, and I can think of no one better than yourself. I liked very much the forthright and penetrating review you made of her previous book in the *Quarterly*. For this reason, I wish very much that you would review the Horney book for *The Nation*. Remember, you have a very intelligent audience although one not technically oriented in psychoanalysis. I do not think you would have to "pull any punches," if you are familiar with that American expression. You can write about 500 words, a little more if absolutely necessary, but it may get cut somewhat. I'll send you a copy of the book, and *The Nation* will send you a small check.

If this is agreeable to you, please return the enclosed postcard promptly and I will forward the book.

Best wishes.

Sincerely yours,

13 The book was Erich Fromm's *Escape from Freedom* (1941). KAM's review, "Loneliness in the Modern World," *The Nation* (March 14, 1942), criticized Fromm for excessive subjectivity, inaccuracies, and a labored style.

P.S. You might be interested in a review written by Doctor Knight, of our clinic, for our own library review.

To John Whitehorn,[14] Baltimore, June 11, 1942

My dear John:

If I remember correctly, you were telling me how much it disturbed you to hear certain clichés developed in the psychiatric language as representing some rather fixed lines of thought. I ran across an address delivered by me to the American Orthopsychiatric when I was president of that Association in 1928, over fourteen years ago, and because I included some of my ideas on the above point, I thought you would be interested in a few paragraphs:

"Thus far our programs have been marvels of diffuse and yet centralized variety, but it is easy to conceive of an inbreeding of subject matter that will automatically detach us from the interest and concern of many whom we need. Is it picayunish for me to mention the danger of a trade jargon—a specialized vocabulary which, whatever it may convey to the initiates, is apt to be puzzling, irritating, or misleading to those who might or should be interested in our point of view? I submit some examples—

"The phrase 'in the behavior field' presumably means those institutions which concern themselves with an attack on misbehavior of a sort somewhere between felonies and the manifestations of an acute psychosis. Perhaps it should be called the 'misbehavior field,' if field it must be.

"Again—I repeatedly hear the expression: 'In this situation she will adjust all right' or 'is adjusting satisfactorily.' 'Adjust' is a transitive verb and must be followed by an object. We cannot leave it hanging in the air. Granted that we know approximately what is meant, I question strongly the wisdom of coining neologisms.

"Similarly, I find myself overworking words such as 'systematized,' 'relationships,' 'situations,' 'reactions,' 'drives,' etc."

I have changed my mind about some things since 1928 but not about these things and I know I have at least one person in agreement with me.

While I am writing you, let me tell you, quite confidentially, that it is my intention to see that you are nominated by the American Psychiatric Association for the American Board of Certification next year to replace Macfie Campbell, whose term expires. Originally these terms never expired, and I fought a vigorous fight to get through a resolution to prohibit anybody from succeeding himself. You would have been nominated this year except for the fact that it was necessary to have a Westerner, and, in spite of some

14 A psychiatrist affiliated with Johns Hopkins. He was one of the five-member team sent to Europe by the army in 1945.

pressure to the contrary from certain former members of the board, I pushed the nomination of Karl Bowman,[15] who I think is catholic in his attitude and competent and fair. I do not expect you to reply to this; I'm just telling you for your information. I am interested in seeing the board succeed and I know it won't if it doesn't get a little different spirit and a type of mind and spirit which I think you represent and can bring to it.

Sincerely yours,

To Franz Alexander, Chicago, October 20, 1942

Dear Alex:

I was very much impressed in reading *Our Age of Unreason*, and again the excerpts from it which the Lippincott Company sent me, with how much you and I seem to want to say the same thing in our most recent books (surely that is the sincerest compliment). Our purpose is certainly the same, although our approach is quite different.

We both feel that there is too much hate and destructiveness in the world. We both agree that national peace depends upon international war, although I stress the fact in my book that international war depends upon the private wars within the individual, while you stress the political, social and philosophical aspects. You emphasize that "democratic types of education appear to offer the maximum opportunities for peace," and we both try to supply some postgraduate democratic education. I went into a little more detail about the techniques of education in my book, and I omitted the social philosophy which occupies a good deal of your thought.

I still think of you as my teacher, certainly one of the most influential teachers of my life. I regret that we have seemed to get so far apart in our affiliations and interpretations in recent years. As I have told you, I feel that I learned the lesson that you taught me and it seems just as real and true to me today as it did then. I make allowance for growth and development in myself as well as in you (a fact which I do not think you always give me credit for), but *I do not think the truth changes*.

You think this emphasis on social factors is a new aspect of truth which some people—yourself, for example—had not sufficiently considered hereto. Having grown up in the atmosphere of psychiatric social work long before I knew anything about analysis, it has always seemed to me that you were over-pleased at what was, for you, a new discovery. I don't mean to be patronizing about this; I think it is merely a fact that the emphasis upon the social factors was much better known to American psychiatrists than it was to European psychiatrists prior to 1930. I remember how enthusiastic Hor-

15 A psychiatrist at Boston Psychopathic, Bellevue, and finally head of the Langley Porter Clinic in San Francisco. In 1946, he became president of the APA.

ney became when she met a few social workers and learned what they were doing. You must remember we knew all about that social emphasis from daily practical experience, learned at the same time you were learning about the unconscious. It seems to me we have exchanged fields—you have taken over an interest in the sociological side which once interested us and we have become more interested in the unconscious psychology which once preoccupied you. I do not see why we shouldn't both make extensions and improvements, but the greatest danger is that we become intolerant of one another. No, there is a greater danger, and that is that in our enthusiasm either one of us or both of us throw out the baby with the bath. Forgive me if I tell you that this is what I have felt about you to some extent. I certainly could not come to that conclusion from reading your book, however.

Thank you again for sending me a copy of the book and for giving us all something to think about.

Sincerely yours,

From Franz Alexander, Chicago, October 21, 1942

Dear Karl:

I can't tell you how pleased I was to receive your letter which shows me that the emotional tension between us is on its decline. To be frank, I never had any deep resentment. What chagrined me was that I felt so powerless to convey to you those of my ideas which I considered a progress. Lack of personal contact is mostly responsible for this.

At the same time I felt that your complaint was in part justified, that after having conveyed to you during our earlier contacts a certain point of view, I did not keep you, so to say, up-to-date about certain changes and their explanation. I think this is certainly an anomaly between two people, one of whom once in the past taught something to the other. On the other hand, you know the obstacles which make such a continuous contact so difficult. The other thing which bothered me about you was what I considered an emotionally conditioned orthodoxy. Since I had always such a keen interest in the history of things, particularly of science, I had not much tolerance for orthodoxy in this field. We know so little about things that even the greatest genius's findings need constant modifications as time goes on, and this is certainly true for psychoanalysis.

I think there is very much truth in what you write about the sociological aspects of psychiatry. However, a real correlation of sociodynamics with psychodynamics is still a chapter for the future. What you write about interest in unconscious mechanisms also contains a great element of truth. This reality became an ABC for us who so intensively cooperated in working out the primitive logic of the emotions during the 1920s in Vienna and Berlin.

To stay at this phase for me would have meant stagnation. You are right that the American scene gave me new food for thought, both in the biological and in the sociological borderlines.

I could go on rambling this way, but I stop because it appears to me futile to exchange ideas by this type of correspondence. What we need sometime in the near future is a good leisurely talk about all these things.

Warmly as ever,

To OTTO FENICHEL, LOS ANGELES, NOVEMBER 6, 1942

Dear Doctor Fenichel:

We are sorry you can't undertake something for the foundation, as we would like to make you a grant, but I'm glad to hear you are getting out your book on Freud's *Theory of the Neuroses*.

I think you will be interested in my own new book *Love Against Hate*, which, while couched in somewhat popular language, is actually, I think, a faithful adherence to the Freudian principles and represents to some extent an elaboration of his ideas of instinct fusion. I know you don't feel very convinced about the dual-instinct theory, but I think you will like some of the propositions in the book, and you will be getting a copy shortly.

Our own Institute and our staff would be very, very much obliged to you if you would send us your "Theoretical Implications of Didactic Analysis" and I will be glad to make suggestions as to what to do with it . . .

Sincerely yours,

FROM FRANZ ALEXANDER, CHICAGO, NOVEMBER 13, 1942

Dear Karl:

I wish to thank you for the inscribed copy of your new book which I immediately started to read with the greatest interest. I do not wish to write to you any premature reactions. I have only gotten through the chapter "The Frustrations of the Child." I may say, however, that I was delighted to see you deal this time with psychological realities instead of thin abstractions. The following are only a few marginal remarks.

Reading the chapter about the child made me understand some aspects of your analysis much better than ever before. I cannot escape from the impression that, independently of the correctness of your statements, your emphasis is *strongly influenced by your own experience*. I also would have liked to see you speak not of the influence of "civilization" in general, but of the influence of "our civilization." Also, "savage" life is not always the same. There is a difference between "savage" and "savage civilizations." The Marquesan mothers, for example, show in general much greater maternal rejection than mothers of our civilization. If I may speak frankly, you are beginning to grasp the significance of the cultural factors realistically but still do not recognize explicitly the specific nature of the different cultural patterns which are responsible for different types of personality development. What you postulate as universal has only local and temporal validity. This is true also to a very high degree of the role of the mother, which differs from civilization to civilization and also from family to family. The whole tenor of this chapter reflects some New England and Middle Western patterns and certainly not that of a Sicilian family. Accordingly, the average Sicilian's attitude toward women is different from that of a Middle Westerner.

I am sure you will not resent it if I tell you that reading this chapter, I suddenly remembered an old psychoanalytic anecdote. Two psychoanalysts (I first heard this anecdote in which the two analysts were Dr. Hitschman and Dr. Federn)[16] are traveling on a trolley car in Vienna submerged in a vivacious discussion. A young student of the Vienna Institute overhears the following conversation: Dr. H.: "It is the mother who gives the clue to this case." Dr. F.: "No, it is the father." Dr. H.: "The mother!" Dr. F., raising his voice: "The father!" Dr. H.: "Mother!" Dr. F.: "Father!" Dr. H.: "Mother!" Dr. F.: "Father!" The young psychoanalyst at the next station leaves the trolley car and decides to look for another profession!

I also should like to call your attention to Jung's early article "Die Bedeutung des Vaters fur das Schicksal des Einzelnen" which appeared in *Jahrbuch für Psychoanalytische Forschungen* [Yearbook for Psychoanalytic Research], I:155, 1909, and which you probably should have considered in this chapter.

Please do not take these remarks as criticism. I only want to emphasize the concept of relativity and the specificity of the cultural factor. If you wish, I will write you again about your book after I have read the whole. You promised the same, and I am awaiting your reactions to my book.

Sincerely yours,

To Brig. J. R. Rees, London, December 17, 1942

Dear Brigadier Rees:

Your letter of November 2 arrived here about December 10. It was addressed to my brother Will, who has been commissioned a lieutenant colonel and is now in charge of the psychiatry in one of our eight corps areas. A corps area is a military division of the country, and Will's particular area covers territory roughly 700 miles square, which is relatively small, but which is the busiest area in the country because there are so many camps in that section. It is in the southern part of the United States and the climate is warmer which makes camping a little easier, etc. I am not sure, however, that that was the government's reason for locating so many camps there. At

16 Viennese analysts Edward Hitschmann and Paul Federn were members of Freud's earliest circle.

any rate, Will is down there and he's hard at work; he has been there such a short time that I cannot tell you exactly what he is doing, but I have an idea that he goes about the various military hospitals coordinating the psychiatric work.

I was very interested in your brief mention of the work you are doing in England and wish you had said more about it. We were very grateful for your kind words about our *Bulletin*, and I hope you will like the next issue as well as you liked the September issue. We sent the September issue to about 5000 physicians, in addition to those on our regular subscription list. We send the *Bulletin* to all psychiatrists in the service who wish it, free.

You mention the fact that the *Bulletin* has a considerable circulation among the people in the war office and in your clinic. If you will give us a list of persons who should have it and who would appreciate getting it, we will be glad to put at least some of them on our regular circulation list, with our compliments. They are, I shall assume, either psychiatrists, psychologists, social workers, or medical men who do more general work.

I daresay you know pretty well how things are over here; we are all vigorously pushing the war in our respective capacities and if you hear any comments to the contrary effect, discount them. Americans are a great nation for griping, and there is a lot of griping against the president, the government, etc., but no one intends that to be taken entirely seriously. Perhaps I should say that every American considers it his privilege and even his duty to show his independent-mindedness by announcing a lot of ways that things should have been done better, etc. But we are all wholeheartedly back of the prosecution of the war and of closer affiliation with our Allies— the British, the Chinese and the Russians. Of course, some people find fault with the Russians and a good many people ignore the Chinese and I daresay there are some who criticize the British but actually one hears very little of that. The most we hear, among the intellectuals, is criticism of the policy of the British in India, but we recognize that that is a very complicated matter and not as simple as it looks on paper. We also recognize that our own attitude toward the Negroes has not always been exemplary or democratic and, in fact, isn't yet and probably won't be for a long time. I think it is a very good thing for these things to be discussed and I am sorry that there is, as I understand, a censorship on the news between England and the United States in regard to these matters, but I am sure the men who have charge of such things know more about it than I do, and if they think it is wise for the British public not to know how we feel and the American public not to know how the British people feel on some subjects, it probably is, although it wouldn't be my personal way of doing things. There I go being a typical American and voicing a few gripes!

I am sure my brother will be delighted to hear from you, and I will see that your letter reaches him promptly.

Sincerely yours,

To Brig. Gen. Frank T. Hines,[1] Washington, D.C., January 12, 1943

My dear General Hines:

It was very kind of you to see me when I was in Washington and to give me your encouragement in the plan for allocating more medical interns to psychiatric training opportunities.

I have given a good deal of thought to what we were discussing also in regard to psychiatry in the Veterans Bureau. In view of the fact that 34 percent of the discharges from the Army at the present time are by reasons of psychiatric disability, to say nothing of those medical cases in which emotional disturbances are important contributing factors, I feel that the magnitude of the postwar psychiatric problems is difficult to overestimate. I know you are thinking along these lines and I want to indicate that I am interested in them with you, and I am anxious to be of any service that my experience and interest can supply.

We were talking, as you remember, about the relation of the Veterans Bureau psychiatrists to the other psychiatrists of the country, and we were both deploring the existence of some lines of cleavage between them. I made it a point to speak to a number of colleagues prominent in the American Psychiatric Association and they all concurred with me that it had been a matter of regret that so few psychiatrists of the Veterans Bureau were active in our Association. Perhaps our Association is partly at fault in this matter, but if so I am sure we should take steps to remedy it. Frankly (and I have the courage to speak frankly because you were kind enough to say that that is the sort of talk you appreciated), I have heard some considerable criticism of the psychiatric work in the Veterans Bureau and that criticism may stem in part from ignorance and lack of acquaintance on the part of the main body of psychiatrists with what the Veterans Bureau psychiatrists are doing or trying to do.

If it won't seem presumptuous, I would like to mention a couple of ideas that occurred to me for such value as they might have as suggestions in the course of your reflection about these matters: Would there be any way in which the psychiatrists of the Veterans Bureau institutions could invite visitation or inspection or something of the kind either from individuals or from a representative group from the American Psychiatric Association? This might serve as a stepping stone upon which to make our Association more familiar with what the Veterans Bureau psychiatrists are doing, and it might have some indirect advantages to the Veterans Bureau psychiatrists themselves. They undoubtedly have plenty of worries and troubles and some-

---

1 Hines headed the Veterans Bureau from 1923 to 1930; he served as administrator for Veterans' Affairs from 1930–44. He sometimes held views antipathetic to those of American psychiatrists.

times these are helped by the experience of others in a most unexpected way.

The other thing that occurred to me was that if you were inclined to regard it as a worthwhile service our foundation might be able to do something in the direction of planning for some of the postwar problems in military psychiatry. There is certainly a need for earnest counseling and the exchange of experience among psychiatrists in regard to the best treatment methods, and it might be worthwhile to get together a number of the most thoughtful and representative leaders and teachers in our profession for a sort of symposium discussion. Psychiatrists from the Veterans Bureau hospitals could be invited to participate in the discussions. I would like to give this a little more thought, but if the idea interests you at all, I would be glad to suggest further details.

Please pardon me if recording and sending you these ideas seems presumptuous. I discussed the matter after I left you with a number of prominent psychiatrists, in the Army and out, and I went on thinking about it in my own mind as I rode home on the train, and decided I would pass the ideas on to you for what they might be worth because of your very gracious reception of me during my visit in Washington.

Sincerely yours,

To Gerald Wendt,[2] New York, January 14, 1943

Dear Doctor Wendt:

If I am disappointed that your Books department got hold of and lost my new book, I am more than twice compensated by the pleasure in learning that you yourself went after it and now have it.

The whole problem of psychiatric writing is one I have not solved. I wrote *The Human Mind* for doctors but 200,000 of the general public bought it. Several years later I wrote *Man Against Himself*, again primarily for doctors, but the doctors insisted on regarding it as a popular book. Albert Lernard, in the *Washington Post* for December 27, 1942, said that *Man Against Himself* "contained much that to laymen was curious, shocking and implausible, but the empirical data lay piled in the records of the Menninger Clinic."[3] This is true and it bears out my belief that the book should have been read by doctors instead of laymen. Doctors, as scientists, are supposed to report the results of their medical research to doctors, and that is what I tried to do in my books. Unfortunately, the language of psychiatry is not the traditional

2 A physician, Wendt was a contributing editor to *Time* magazine.

3 Albert Lernard reviewed *Love Against Hate* enthusiastically for the *Washington Post.* Although thinking that the Menninger Clinic was in Kansas City, he praised KAM as falling "naturally into the line of great physicians who have contributed in a broad sense to our enlightenment" (Sunday, Dec. 27, 1942, p. 7).

language of doctors, and since doctors have always been concerned with chemistry and anatomy, there is no way to translate psychiatry into their language, so it inevitably comes about that anything a psychiatrist writes is considered popular unless he resorts to the peculiar terminology of one school of psychology, in which case nobody reads him except those who already know what he has to say.

If I were to write a textbook on accepted psychiatric syndromes or review the literature on melancholia, I suppose my contribution would be dull enough to interest the doctors, but what I wanted to do was to gather together in an interesting way the theory and research in modern psychological thought, relate it and clarify it, and add some semioriginal contributions and precious ideas of my own, even at the risk of having my colleagues ignore them.

In *Love Against Hate*, because of the more optimistic and constructive content of the book, I realized that it was likely to be more acceptable to the layman and I resigned myself to the idea that love can never sound scientific. I think this is a reflection on science and not on love.

It may be that the public will have to introduce psychiatry to the doctors and not vice versa. Anyway, it is a problem which has occupied a good deal of my life, and I do not know the answer. A psychiatrist cannot write about psychology without betraying the fact that human beings have volatile emotions, and emotions seem to be considered a suitable subject for literature but not for science.

I have been extremely interested in some of the letters and reviews I have received on *Love Against Hate*. Curiously enough, several letters have spoken of the therapeutic value of the book to the reader. Don't laugh, but one of the chief saleswomen in one of the big bookstores on Fifth Avenue is pushing the book with all her might and main because (she told me directly) it cured her of asthma, which her personal psychoanalysis had not succeeded in doing!

The book wasn't designed for such purposes, but I'm glad if it has worked that way. I am afraid it was more presumptuous—I realize a psychiatrist cannot prescribe for an entire world, but at the same time some of the world phenomena seem to me to come back to observable psychopathology in the individual and in our culture and these are what I have tried to present— diagnostically and therapeutically.

Anything you say about my book will please me, I am sure.

Sincerely yours,

To James Francis Cooke,[4] Philadelphia, January 26, 1943

Dear Mr. Cooke:

I was very pleased to have your kind letter about my book *Love Against*

4 Editor of *Etude*, a music magazine.

Hate. I am looking forward to receiving the copy of your book *Light, More Light,* which I have not had the good fortune to see.

I am familiar with *Etude* magazine, of course, and have been for many years. It is interesting that you should ask me if I had ever thought of music as work and play. I have thought of it a great deal since it is one of my own interests. I would say that when music is engaged in as a profession it is unquestionably "work," since there is an objective to be accomplished, the activity is directly connected with reality considerations, and no doubt in most cases the aggressive motives of the professional musician are more obvious than those of the amateur or dilettante musician. When I postulated (on page 184), however, that the arts must constitute the highest form of play because the creative elements greatly predominate over the aggressive impulses, I not only had in mind the person who plays for pure pleasure but the professional artist as well, because it is certainly true that pleasure in the activity is more regularly conscious in the arts than in any other forms of work. I believe you will agree with me that the activity is more dissociated from the restrictions of reality than most forms of work. In other words, we expect the artist to be less concerned with his own personal success than he is with furthering his art by a creative contribution. It is true, of course, that many artists work under a strong sense of compulsion, and for them art must be almost entirely work. No doubt you can think of some musicians in whom this element of compulsion has been strong. Van Gogh complained of it in painting.

I felt that it was a tribute to art, however, to classify it as more truly play than work. Ideally artists are people for whom their work is play. The moral attitudes which people adopt toward work and play, however, would tend to make an artist feel that it was a slur upon his life work to call it "play"; of course, my idea was a very different one.

Music is a great help to me in resting myself after work. I have had the same experience that you describe, many a time. Several months ago the members of the staff of our clinic decided to prepare a hobby number of the *Menninger Clinic Bulletin,* and I am sending you a copy. I had difficulty in deciding whether I should write about horticulture or music or chess, since all of these are important forms of recreation for me. One of our other staff members wished to take music, and my father chose horticulture so I wrote about chess. You may find some ideas in this number which will apply to your editorial. You have my permission to quote anything you like from this *Bulletin.* I have no right to answer for the publishers of *Love Against Hate,* but I do not believe that they would object if you quoted from that. Mr. Lambert Davis at Harcourt-Brace is my representative.

I wish we had more careful psychological studies of musicians. Perhaps you could do a few sketches from this standpoint.

Sincerely yours,

To Leo Bartemeier, Detroit, February 16, 1943

Dear Bartie:

So you want a good long letter from me, do you? My dear boy, you never should have said that because here it comes! Alice [KAM's secretary] is taking off her sweater and spitting on her hands!

I got back about two hours ago from Chicago, where I spent a damned hectic day yesterday, believe me. I went up there to represent the American Psychiatric Association at the Thirtieth Annual Congress on Medical Education and Licensure, and I heard speeches all day and had interviews with various men in between the speeches. I talked with General Hugh Morgan, General Parran, Colonel Lull, Morris Fishbein, etc., etc. The long and short of it is that the Army and Navy are after doctors hot and heavy. I found that the Procurement and Assignment Board tried to snatch one of our doctors while I was gone. They are going to take over most of the college students and 80% of the medical students. If anybody gets a resident, it will be because the resident is a female or a cripple. I am writing a long report of this for Ruggles;[5] I don't now how much it interests you, but if you like I can send you a copy. I haven't gotten it written yet because I got sidetracked writing this long letter to you.

Well, after I got through with an all-day meeting and many conferences I went up to have dinner with Lionel [Blitzsten]. He and Dorothy out-vied each other in seeing who could talk the fastest and say the most, and all of it was of the same tenor; namely, that Alexander was just as bad as ever and that the Institute had gone to Hell and was being run by Helen Ross,[6] etc. A week or so ago I had received a letter from Tom French[7] to which I had formulated a reply which I didn't send; then I formulated another reply which I did send. I asked Bob Knight to write up his impressions and he sent his letter.

Well, Blitzsten agreed with my objections and with Bob Knight's objections and I did not learn until later that he was actually a member of the committee that formulated the letter. That's the way Lionel is, you know. Anyway, he called up George Mohr and told him that he ought to pay at-

---

5 At this time, Arthur Ruggles was president of the APA.

6 Helen Ross, a child analyst trained in Vienna, was a member of the Chicago Psychoanalytic Institute and later its administrative director. She was co-author, with Bertram D. Lewin, of an exhaustive four-year study for the American Psychoanalytic Association on *Psychoanalytic Education in the United States* (1960).

7 The letter from Thomas French seeks support for amendments to the American Psychoanalytic Association constitution that would lessen the authority of the institutes' education committees and ensure members' freedom to teach. The issue caused frequent flare-ups within the association. The Chicago Psychoanalytic Society was considering withdrawing from the group and had drafted a letter of withdrawal which was being circulated among its members.

tention to Bob Knight's letter (it was much more detailed than mine). He told me there was a meeting that night to which I should go, although he couldn't.

I went to the meeting and it was a pretty sorry spectacle, believe me. In the first place, there were only about eight or nine of them [members of the Chicago Psychoanalytic Society] there, and George Mohr was all excited about the terrible things that were going to happen if the societies did not ratify those amendments, and Alexander was waving his arms and talking about academic freedom and [Therese] Benedek was grunting and yessing all over the place, and Eisler,[8] who was supposed to be presiding, was giving out a lot of cotton-mouthed words that didn't mean anything. I told them the letter was in bad taste, pious, naive, patronizing, holier than thou and everything else. I told them I was glad they wanted to have something done but that the way to do it was to write personal letters to their friends and not send out a society document as if the Chicago Society were the only pure, good, idealistic bunch in the world. They kept saying that if the other societies did not approve of these amendments, the Association was going to disintegrate, and I kept saying, "Why is it going to disintegrate unless the Chicago Society resigns, and why should the Chicago Society threaten to resign just because they can't have their way?" "Wait and see," I told them, "maybe the societies will approve these amendments, but don't try to threaten them into it."

Well, Alexander got up and waved his arms some more and told me he never had threatened to resign. . . . but I kept cheerful and calm, and when I left I think I had them talked out of sending out the silly letter. (I'll tell you what I'll do; I'll ask Alice to send you Tom's [French] letter and, as soon as she can get it done, a copy of the letter I sent and a copy of Bob Knight's letter, and a scratch copy of the letter I didn't send, and then you can return the whole business after you have read it and wept.)

I honestly cannot see what all the shouting is about. George Mohr said we were all pessimistic about the passage of these amendments and if they didn't pass he didn't know what the world was coming to or what the Chicago Society would do. I told him I simply was not interested in threats and handwringing, that you and I were doing the best we could and we were not going to use pressure on anybody, that we were going to send out the stuff and let them vote and then we would record the results, but that there was no reason why they, as individual members of the Chicago Society, could not do anything that they damned pleased, or that they could make a fool of their Society if they wanted to.

I think everyone was in a fairly good humor when I left except Alex, who was still very black in the face. Helen [McLean] was home sick; Tom French was holding a political meeting somewhere for some alderman; Lionel was

8 Edwin R. Eisler was then president of the Chicago Psychoanalytic Society.

teaching his seminar; [Catherine] Bacon was out of town. Honest to God, Bartie, that society is about as weak a bunch of fellows as one can well imagine. . . . If my bunch here in Topeka were as weak as that I would quit and go out and raise pigs. As a matter of fact, I am raising quite a few pigs now and next time you come down I'll give you the best roast pork you've had in many a month. . . .

I think you are right . . . about the Topeka and Detroit Societies having been approved by the International. But now as to the San Francisco Society, I am completely bewildered: In the first place, when we tried to clear our books here and make some refunds to our former members, we learned that May Romm[9] and Joe Haenel[10] refused to resign from our Society and refused to join the San Francisco Society. [Bernard] Kamm, on the other hand, resigned from our Society, not to join the San Francisco Society as he had intended, but to join the Chicago Society. It seems to me that that leaves them pretty short in the way of members. They never did have the quorum that they submitted to us as being the charter members.[11] In other words, they said that they had such and such a membership and we recognized them, and now they do not have such and such a membership, so where are we and where are they? The thing will be in an awful tangle when it comes to voting on these new amendments, so much as I hate to add to your work I think you'd better write to Simmel and get a certified list of their members and then put the whole thing before our lawyer, Mr. Weiss. On the one hand, we certified them and, on the other hand, we certified them on the basis of something that did not come true and the question is whether they actually have a society.

While I was in Chicago last night the secretary read a letter from David Brunswick[12] saying that he had been made an *active* member of the San Francisco Society and therefore wished to resign as an associate member of the Chicago Society. That made the Chicago people mighty mad because, in the first place, Dave Brunswick should have resigned from the Chicago Society first; and, in the second place, what were they doing making a man who is not even a doctor an active member of their society? Of course there is no law against it but there was a kind of a gentleman's agreement against

9 A Beverly Hills psychoanalyst. In 1944, she served as psychiatric advisor on the filming of *Spellbound*.

10 Joachim Haenel and his wife, Irene, were psychoanalysts in Los Angeles who at this time still retained membership in the Topeka Psychoanalytic Society. They practiced short-term psychotherapy as well as more orthodox psychoanalysis. Irene analyzed Jean Lyle in 1939 prior to her marriage to KAM.

11 At the time of this letter, the San Francisco Psychoanalytic Society, which had previously been under the Menninger aegis, had been certified as an independent entity after submitting to the American Psychoanalytic Association a membership list that included analysts who were not actually part of the society.

12 David Brunswick was a lay analyst in Los Angeles; he had been instrumental in persuading Ernst Simmel to settle in Los Angeles.

it, or at least I thought there was. Thereupon the Chicago Society voted unanimously that no nonmedical people should be allowed to become members of any society belonging to the American Psychoanalytic Association hereafter. You will recall that you had submitted this to them for their vote. They deferred action on the rest of those amendments.

I had a long talk with the Bibrings[13] while I was in Boston and just at present I am waiting to hear how they finally decided and also waiting to hear whether the Rockefeller Foundation is going to give us the money [to fund a new position at the Menninger Foundation]. If the Bibrings do not want to come, I have a pretty good fellow lined up in New York by the name of Loewenstein[14] whom Sterba[15] may know; I think he is or was a Pole and then became a German, but for the past 15 years has been living in Paris. He is married to a pretty Hungarian Catholic countess. . . . Loewenstein is a swell fellow and I believe he would be a good teacher. I had a letter the other day from Kubie about him which I am going to enclose but I want you to shoot it right back to me with any comments that may occur to you. I won't answer the letter until I get it back from you.

Lionel was very friendly but I thought rather jittery and somewhat harassed by Dorothy, who is so full of hate for the Institute and Alexander that she cannot talk about anything else. There was no animosity expressed toward you or me, however. I told Lionel he would be in a much more powerful position if he hadn't got tied up with Horney and he gave the usual long speech about how he had done it originally out of friendship without knowing what they were up to and would have resigned if Helene Deutsch hadn't attacked them, but how he had to stay out of loyalty, etc. . . .

Well, Bartie, in the meanwhile, Jean has been working like a Turk on the foundation and we are going to have a meeting Thursday night and put our machinery in good order according to recommendations made by Alan Gregg.[16] I believe you are going to be really proud of the old foundation one of these days. Personally, I am mighty glad that you are a part of it. I want you to be a more active part of it in the near future. I want you to come down here this spring and make us a few talks and give us some advice on

13 Edward and Grete L. Bibring, Vienna-born psychoanalysts then practicing in Boston; Grete Bibring became chief of psychiatry at the Beth Israel Hospital and was one of the first women professors at Harvard Medical School.

14 Rudolph M. Loewenstein, a European analyst who emigrated to New York, where he taught courses at New York Institute and collaborated with Heinz Hartmann and Ernst Kris in papers on ego psychology. KAM is mistaken about the nationality of Loewenstein's wife, the child analyst Elisabeth Geleerd, who was a Dutch refugee.

15 Richard Sterba and his wife, Editha, were Viennese psychoanalysts who settled in Detroit.

16 Director of the Medical Sciences Division of the Rockefeller Foundation in New York City. A distinguished, philosophically minded physician, he was especially interested in psychiatry; although he never had a formal connection with the Menninger Clinic or Foundation, KAM sometimes solicited Gregg's advice.

our research, eat some of our pork and live out at the farm with Jean and me. You can sleep on the davenport. But if Bess would come it would be still nicer; in that case you could both sleep on our bed and we'll sleep on the davenport! You should plan on at least two or three days. . . .

Affectionately,

To Iago Galdston,[17] New York, March 11, 1943

Dear Iago:

Unlike yourself I am a great joiner. This is not alone through some need of my ego for the satisfaction that I am accepted here, there and the other place, but it's because I very firmly believe that only in unity is there any strength in the development of the principles represented by this group or the other. Perhaps that's an ambiguous sentence but what I'm trying to say is that I distrust the old adage about truth being so strong that it springs up and dominates the field in spite of all opposition. I think the truth is weak and shy, especially new truth. It needs the support of being presented, examined, reexamined, tested, extended, and so on. This one can only do if one is in an organization where there are certain principles in common. These principles have to be supported. This requires a certain legal structure. Such a legal structure always involves a certain amount of quarreling and dissension, but on the other hand it does serve to support the development of these ideas.

Perhaps I've already said too much about that, but at any rate I believe in it. I believe that as a psychiatrist outside of any psychiatric organization your contributions are definitely handicapped. I certainly do think that you ought to get into the American Psychiatric Association, and I don't think that you ought to get in there by any fluke or accident. I don't know exactly what would be required but I think that you could find out by making the proper investigations. Address a letter to the secretary and let him refer it to the chairman of the membership committee, etc. Maybe it's true that you need some didactic psychiatric instruction, not because you don't know certain things but because others don't know that you know them. Or maybe it is possible that you don't know them in relation to certain accepted principles which may be right or which may be wrong, but which are nevertheless accepted and which serve as a kind of earmark for these general categories.

I for one would like to see you do this. Of course, Freud himself was never a member of any psychiatric organizations, nor was he ever regarded by the hidebound stupid psychiatrists of Germany as being a psychiatrist. Perhaps he wasn't, but God knows he has contributed more to psychiatry than anybody who has lived in the past 5,000 years, unless it be Jesus.

Sincerely yours,

17 A New York City psychiatrist and psychoanalyst.

To Morris Fishbein, Chicago, March 17, 1943

Dear Morris:

Your editorial in the *Journal of the American Medical Association* for March 6 has stimulated a lot of comment, and I have been the recipient of quite a number of letters which should really have gone to you. The writers seem to think that I know you better than they do and make the absurd assumption that I have some influence with you. I do not delude myself on this point but I am going to write you anyway.

In the first place, why did you so conspicuously omit any reference to psychiatry in describing the work of the medical department of the Army? You know full well that 30 percent of the casualties now arriving from the war zone are psychiatric. You know that psychiatric problems are the biggest problems that the medical department has. You know that the Army has a chief psychiatric consultant in the person of Roy Halloran; . . . Why did you omit Halloran?

You have your ear to the ground better than anybody I know. You know the facts well enough; what are the politics of giving psychiatry the blackout in an article like this? Among those facts is certainly the well-known fact that the medical department of our Army shamefully neglected the knowledge it learned in World War I in regard to the need for psychiatrists. Is some experience or contact of yours in Chicago souring you on psychiatry? I am gravely concerned about this and I can assure you that many other leading psychiatrists feel exactly as I do.

Having given you these hooks to the chin, I want to hand you a bouquet on the last paragraph of the editorial. I agree with you that information about the work of the Army Medical Corps should be made available to us, and I am glad you called for it.

Sincerely yours,

P.S. I think letters to the editor for publication are usually the bunk and that is why I do not send you a formal document. I think you ought to write another editorial in the way of an admission and correction of the omission. You are the one that readers want to get the views of, not Karl Menninger, etc.

From Ruth Mack Brunswick, New York, May 3, 1943

Dear Karl:

Thanks for your letter of April 7th. I was very interested in your exchange of cables with Anna Freud.[18]

---

18 Copies of these cables were not preserved.

Jenny Waelder[19] was here last week and told me that the Bibrings have a great deal to do in Boston. I had thought, like you, that they were professionally very unhappy there, but I am not at all sure that this is now the case. I certainly think that one of them should visit Topeka before making a decision. But I have not been in contact with them for a long time and hesitate to mix in. You certainly have an international staff.

The Chicago Society letter was pretty bad. The ambivalence between Rado and Alexander is an old, old story—I remember it from Berlin—and is not likely to get better with time. But those Hungarians do a lot of fraternizing no matter how ambivalent they are toward each other.

My purpose in writing you today is to ask for any suggestions which you may have in the following matter: Oliver, the middle son of Professor Freud, landed here a few days ago with his wife after an illegal escape from France via Spain to Portugal. . . . They came with nothing but the clothes on their backs and without a cent to their name. They are starved and hungry, but already less so than on their arrival. Oliver is an engineer with great mechanical knowledge and gifts. He is, however, shy and compulsive. Can you suggest any contacts which would help him to get some sort of engineering job? After 1933 he went to Nice where he spent the last ten years as a photographer. His engineering knowledge is said to be very great and very thorough. His wife is really a painter but will have to take a job wherever she can get one. Oliver is a very nice man and very pathetic. So wreck [sic][20] your brains and see what you can think up. We are doing everything that we can.

Please thank Jean for her note on your letter. I am much better, though not very strong. In addition my father has been very ill for the last two months.

It is just beginning to be spring here at last. It's been a long, hard winter.

My affectionate regards to you both—and thanks for all the literature.

To ABRAHAM MYERSON, BOSTON, MAY 5, 1943

Dear Abe:

I just read your review of Alexander's book [*The Age of Unreason*], and I want to tell you I fully agree with you; if anything, you were too kind. For example, it isn't true that the first part of the book is as you say "accurate, comprehensive, etc." One of the men on our staff who is well versed in these fields has found all kinds of inaccuracies in it. Another mistake you

19 Jenny Waelder-Hall was a Viennese child analyst who had emigrated with her husband, Robert Waelder, also a prominent psychoanalyst, whom she later divorced. She settled in Washington, where her Viennese orthodoxy soon came into conflict with the more eclectic position espoused by Harry Stack Sullivan.

20 Dr. Brunswick has added: "Secretary's slip! I dictated 'rack.'"

made was in talking about the sleight-of-hand technique characteristic of orthodox Freudianism. Alexander is not an orthodox Freudian; if he were, he wouldn't do some of these things.

But I agree with you strongly that Alexander does a poor job in his analysis of play. I suggest you read my own analysis in *Love Against Hate*. I think you will like it better. I don't think you are correct in calling it a biological instinct, although I know what you mean. It is one expression of instinct, but I don't think it is "a" instinct, if you get me. As you say yourself, there is a "recuperative response."

I don't agree with you about the inadvisability of giving the psychiatrist more authority in the ultimate councils of the mighty, although I do agree with you that there is a lot about human beings that we will have to learn before we will be as effective as we should be.

I hope to see you in Detroit.

Sincerely yours,

From Ernest Jones, Elsted, Sussex, England, May 13, 1943

Dear Dr. Menninger,

To be frank, I have been a little disappointed by the relatively small contact it has been possible to maintain between British and American psychoanalysts since the war began. This feeling relates particularly, it is true, to the refugee analysts who, after reaching America, seem to have forgotten all about this side of the water and all that we did for them then here. Your warm and friendly letter was therefore doubly welcome, and I reciprocate with the utmost cordiality all the sentiments you express. Naturally the feeling of isolation grows as the years pass and one becomes increasingly hungry for contact with the outside world and for news of it. I get much less news than you might expect, and did not even know that you had been elected president of the American [Psychoanalytic] Association. It is encouraging to hear that they have made such a worthy choice, and I congratulate you also on it.

When I do get news it is apt to be of a tantalizingly elusive nature, and I am afraid that your own letter is not altogether an exception in that respect. What correspondents usually write is: "You have doubtless heard of such and such a difficulty we have had, or such and such an affair, so I need not tell you anything about it." I am always glad to hear any actual *facts*, and now that we resumed correspondence I may ask you to send me some more. What, for instance, was the Zilboorg legal case to which someone made an allusion?

I have been able to follow Karen Horney's evolution through her writings, and it is a fairly typical one. I hope that, like Adler and Jung, she will be forced after a while to give up using the word psychoanalysis; that depends on the pressure brought to bear from the societies. Alexander, with his talk of "Neo-Freudians" and "revision of psycho-analysis," must, I am afraid, have done some little harm also. It is very interesting to notice how many scientific splits and disputes can be traced ultimately to the age-old question of cultural environment versus innate dispositions. It is not surprising that many Americans, owing to their political history, tend to stress the former. Jung, on the other hand, went to the other extreme with his preindividual "collective unconscious"; that is perhaps why he had less success in America than Adler. It would appear that few people are prepared to hold an unprejudiced balance in this question, as Freud so well did. Here in the British Society we have a similar conflict between Melanie Klein, who concentrates on the infant's spontaneous impulses and fantasies, and who in my opinion has thereby contributed very considerably to our analytical knowledge, and Miss Freud and Melitta Schmideberg,[21] who in my opinion lay too much stress on environmental, i.e. parental, influence. For myself I want to go ever deeper, and to me the most interesting problems concern the nodal points at which specific internal and specific external factors click together by pure chance in certain constellations.

I have just reviewed two excellent American books: Zilboorg's *History of Medical Psychology*, which is remarkably admirable until he comes to psychoanalysis, where his objectivity somewhat fails him; and Alexander's *Age of Unreason*, which is much better on the sociological than on the psychological side.

I was glad of the information you gave me about the Rado movement in New York.[22] What a pity Alexander supports him. After all, Hungarians keep close together, though there are doubtless other factors in the common aetiology.

I have inquired about the question you raised concerning the *Journal* index.[23] You will know, by the way, that Mr. Strachey has succeeded me as editor, and I must say he is an admirably conscientious one. It appears that Dr. Bryan,[24] who had made the index for the first ten volumes, has completed one for the second ten. Its publication has been held up not by lack of funds but by the absolute impossibility of getting the requisite paper. I would suggest that you consider the possibility of publishing it in America,

21 Melitta Schmideberg was one of Melanie Klein's three children. She grew up in Budapest and practiced first in New York, later in London. She specialized in borderline personalities.

22 Rado was one of the leaders of a dissenting faction within the New York Psychoanalytic Society. Two years later he was among those who split with the New York Society to found the Association for Psychoanalytic Medicine.

23 KAM had complained that the *Journal of the International Psychoanalytic Society* did not provide an adequate index.

24 Clement A. Douglas Bryan was a psychoanalyst and a senior editor of the *International Journal of Psycho-Analysis*.

in which event you should communicate with Mr. James Strachey, Lord's Wood, Marlow, Bucks. If you decide to proceed with it I hope you will try to procure the same format and style as the previous volume, for the sake of uniformity.

What news can I give you from this side? After my London house was damaged I came to live here, in my country one, and here I am likely to remain. It is a couple of hours from London, but I go there only about once a month. I have enough patients here to keep me busy. The personal circumstances, health, work, etc. of our analytical colleagues are pretty satisfactory. A considerable number are of course doing hospital work with the Forces, and a few are, like myself, working in different parts of the country. This scattering, together with more important factors, has led to the formation of various cliques in the Society, the disputes between whom have gravely hampered our scientific work. Though our Society is probably not so disharmonious as the New York one, it is certainly no longer the unified body I was for many years proud to lead, and its future is very uncertain.

We hear practically nothing from the Continent, nor have I heard for a long time from Dr. Eitingon, who, I learn, has had some heart trouble.

I heard recently from Princess Marie [Bonaparte], who is in S. Africa with her family and is as keen on work as ever.

I should especially like to hear of any analysts who may be crossing the water. Surely they should make contact with us, so that we can welcome them. Will you keep this in mind?

Please give my kindest greetings to Dr. Geleerd, whom I know well. She is a very sincere and friendly person. . . .

You see I have also written to you at length, and it has been a pleasure to do so.

With my most cordial greetings to you and our mutual friends.

Very Sincerely Yours

To Smith Ely Jelliffe, New York, May 17, 1943

My dear Smith Ely:

. . . I am just back from Detroit where we had a very busy, very noisy, very complicated meeting of the American Psychiatric and American Psychoanalytic Associations, and I was relieved of the presidency of the latter after two years. I have come home to try to catch up with the work. One of the first things I want to do is to answer this letter of yours of May 12 in which you were so kind as to congratulate me on *Love Against Hate:* I'm awfully glad you like it. I don't know what you mean by "one of our associates," but whoever it was I am sure he reviewed it to the best of his ability.

You say in this letter you wonder if I have some hard feelings. Good Lord, *no!* I have only the kindliest and most friendly feelings about you, consciously at least. I don't know why you have intimations of that kind. Maybe I was a little disappointed that you did not donate your library to the Menninger Foundation where I think it would have better usage than at its present location, but, after all, if they could afford to pay you money for it, I know you can use the money, and I certainly didn't hold any grudge against you on that account. It is just a matter of being so busy that I haven't written you my usual newsy letters, I guess. But everything is all right between us, so don't give another thought to that.

I have about twenty doctors here now, but it isn't enough. We are being swamped with work. We have waiting lists for both adults and children. I am doing as much teaching as I can of the young doctors and we have quite a nice little research program going. We need more funds for the latter, and I am not a very good money raiser, but one of our doctors is in New York at present trying to find some individuals who want to give $5, $500, or $5000. I don't know whether you have kept up with the developments about our foundation, and in case you haven't I am enclosing a copy of the first annual report, made now nearly a year ago; the foundation has grown since then in personnel, if not in money. One of these days we are going to get the money and we are going to go to town!

Best wishes.

Sincerely,

FROM K. R. EISSLER,[25] CHICAGO, MAY 22, 1943

Dear Dr. Menninger:

I would like to express my appreciation of the excellence of the last meeting in Detroit. Before I left for the meeting, I was somewhat depressed and worried about the future of psychoanalysis, but the impression of that meeting taught me that I was not justified and unwarrantedly pessimistic. Especially the peacefulness and dignity of all discussions were very comforting, and this, I think, was in great part due to your leadership.

I assume that it was due to the strain of your work during the last few months that a suggestion of mine I wrote you escaped your attention. Permit me to repeat it. I believe there is a concrete need for a Central War Record Office. Such an office should be a collecting agency for all reports of psychiatric interest concerning the war, such as letters written by soldiers, diaries, newspaper clippings and informal reports of physicians. It is my

25 Psychoanalyst, and Freud scholar, Eissler received his M.D. degree from the University of Vienna in 1937 and practiced in Chicago and New York City before becoming director of the Freud Archives in Washington, D.C. (1951–1984). He made notable psychoanalytic investigations into delinquency, the dying patient, and creativity in Goethe and Shakespeare. He lives in New York City. KAM has written at the top of this letter: "Very interesting idea! I am for it."

impression that psychiatrists on duty face a wealth of observations on new clinical material as well as on themselves. The latter, I believe, are of greatest importance. Most psychiatrists on duty have no time and leisure to write papers on their impressions and observations. However, if they had an opportunity to send some agency informal reports, this might stimulate them to verbalize their present experiences. In view of the psychiatric literature of the postwar period of 1920 to 1939, it is reasonable to surmise that after World War II war experiences will fall victim to group repressive forces again. Therefore, I think it a duty to rescue as much material as possible as long as the war goes on.

This material could be constructively sifted and edited after the war will be over. I fear that much material has been lost already, and speedy action would be necessary to catch up with historical events. Since Topeka is the geometrical center of the present battlefronts, I think that it would be a good place to found such an agency.

I am very sincerely yours,

To Ives Hendrick, Boston, June 28, 1943

Dear Ives:

I am glad to know that you are getting back into the activities of the Boston Psychoanalytic Society and the American Psychoanalytic Association. . . .

I don't know what it is you want me to tell you about the Chicago Society. I think you know as well as I what the situation is there. Alexander has announced on numerous occasions that he is not Freudian, that he thinks there is much to agree with in the deviations of Horney, Rado, etc. He has repeatedly threatened to resign and he tried to persuade his Society to resign from the American Psychoanalytic Association. Why he does this, I leave to your imagination. It has been a great disappointment to me and one of the major difficulties of my administration. Fortunately, I am no longer president.

Sincerely,

To Morris Fishbein, Chicago, July 21, 1943

Dear Morris:

I am looking at an editorial on page 811 of the *Journal of the American Medical Association* entitled "Psychoanalysis and the Scientific Method."

Will you please tell me what the Hell is the need to find a whipping boy and do this public admonishing and spanking? I can tell from the atrocious, clumsy literary style that it was not written by you because what you write is clear, grammatical and timely. This stupid editorial begins by reference to a man who was not a doctor and quotes him in regard to what the medical profession thinks. This piece of heresy would certainly not be committed by you.

But I return to the question: Why should psychoanalysis be picked on? Why not pick on urology or obstetrics or Christian Science or the Catholics or the Jews. There is nothing constructive about this article, and I think it would be just as easy to get the doctors suspicious of your business or the drug business or the Roman Catholic church or the Jews as it is to get them suspicious of psychoanalysis in this nasty, unscientific, pointless way.

Some of us are working damned hard to get psychoanalysis, psychiatry, and general medicine closer together, and an editorial in your *Journal* of an intelligent type could do a lot of good. A stupid piece of writing like this does harm and makes some of us mad and discouraged.

Sincerely yours,

To Lillian Smith ΛND Paula Snelling,[26] Clayton, Georgia, August 9, 1943

My dear Lillian and Paula:

The spring issue of *The South Today*, which I just finished reading, was another super-fine number. I showed it to my colleague and friend Dr. Robert P. Knight, head of our psychotherapy department and one of the best psychiatrists in the country, and he was so enthusiastic about it that I believe he has written you subscribing.

I am more and more convinced that the greatest postwar problem will be a continuation of what was from the psychological standpoint a prewar problem; namely, the attitude of the majority (or those who believe themselves to be the majority) toward the slightly different-looking person. This means the attitude toward Jews, Negroes, Indians and, I am afraid, even Chinese, magnificent as they are. In this country, it will certainly be the Negro chiefly, although anti-Semitism is increasing in a shocking way up here.

Keep up your brave work. Don't print this letter. If you want something from me, I will write it especially for you.

Sincerely yours,

To Leo and Bess Bartemeier, Helen and Franklin McLean, Vermont, August 16, 1943

Dear Bartie, Bess, Helen, and Frank,

We envy you very much indeed sitting together in the pleasant Vermont

26 In 1943, Lillian Smith was editor of the journal *The South Today*. KAM was strongly moved by her 1944 novel, *Strange Fruit*. Paula Snelling was Smith's long-time companion.

valley looking at the maple trees and the blue hills around you, drinking highballs and eating belated sweet corn. Until yesterday, we should have also envied you the coolness because it has been very hot here, but it turned cool this morning and now what we envy most is the opportunity you are all having to be together in friendly communion, of which there isn't nearly enough in this world. . . .

In regard to the Council on Psychotherapy at the Institute in October concerning which you ask me, Bartie, I think I had better let Helen give you her impressions: In the project of shortening psychotherapy, I think we are all interested. In the project of calling any kind of psychotherapy "brief" or "briefer," I am not at all interested, as I think it is a very unfortunate phrase and really almost in bad taste. Helen thinks I am hopelessly prejudiced against Alex for permitting such undiplomatic and, I really believe, unscientific phrases as brief psychotherapy and briefer psychotherapy to become current. They arouse false hopes in patients and, in many instances, they set up false goals for doctors. In a way, I think the very names are a reflection upon psychoanalysis; it is as if to say that it is too long. Of course, it is too long, but at present we cannot change that and we only play into the resistance of many people when we intimate that it isn't necessary for it to be so long.

I recently saw a patient who is very critical of Dr. Alexander because he said that she could probably be cured in three months. After she had been treated for three months, he told her it would be another three months and she went another three months. Now Dr. Alexander thinks it will take a year or two more, and I think he is right. Naturally, I defend him the best I can, but his enthusiasm about making a treatment brief led him to have false hopes and led his patient to have false hopes and now disappointment and even bitterness replace these hopes. I think it is necessary that all of us steel ourselves against the idea that psychoanalysis can be made brief. On the other hand, that some cases can be treated psychotherapeutically with considerable benefit in relatively short periods has been known to psychiatrists for a hundred years. There, however, I think what we should emphasize is not the briefness. This briefness has been emphasized and held up to us and thrown in our faces by the old-time psychiatrists for years. I have done a great deal of it, and I was doing it long before there were any conferences about it in Chicago or elsewhere, and so were many other psychiatrists in the country, but I don't like to do it because I learned long before I was analyzed and also since then that it is very unreliable and leads to a great many disappointments.

Well, I have talked enough about that, especially when you are on your vacation and not very interested in such technical matters. I am thinking how beautiful it is up there at the home of Helen and Frank and remembering my visit there wistfully. I would like to be physically and mentally as close to all four of you right now as I have been many times in the past, and I am glad that the four of you can be together. Jean joins me in these sentiments.

Sincerely,

To ERNEST JONES, ELSTED, SUSSEX, ENGLAND, AUGUST 19, 1943

My dear Doctor Jones:

I was delighted with your long letter of May 13 and I am glad you were frank in expressing your disappointment. I can assure you that the disappointment is mutual. Wartime seems to be conducive to a feeling of disappointment on the part of everyone, and the feeling that we are being forgotten seems to be shared by the people at home and the people at war, the people in England and the people in America.

You say you have heard little from your American colleagues in recent years about the developments in our country. I must tell you that I, as president of the American Psychoanalytic Association for two years, never heard from you or from any other members of the British Association. This is not a reproach; it is merely to remind you that your feelings are not unique but reciprocal.

You go on to say that your correspondents have not written you very fully as a rule but have assumed that other correspondents have written you more fully. I have no idea, Dr. Jones, with whom you correspond in this country. So far as I know, you have not corresponded with me very much in the past, and I must remind you that there is a general feeling on the part of Americans that the British are, if I may use a frank expression, somewhat "choosy" in their friends, and I have assumed that you had both friends and acquaintances with whom you felt more inclined to correspond than with me.

I fully agree with you that the psychology of the refugee analysts has sometimes been very disappointing. You say that many of them who came by way of England to America seem to have forgotten all you did for them there. I think I could add that they are not here very long until they have forgotten all we have done for them here; this applies to some of them, not to all of them. One cannot help but be a little irritated at this, but it still remains an interesting psychological problem, and I don't know the answer to it.

At the clinic we have had a score of refugees, eight of whom are still with us; most of the others are now in private practice for themselves and are grateful, I believe, and, in fact, grow more grateful as they realize what we have done for them and how difficult they were for us in some respects at the beginning. These are not the refugees that I am disappointed in. A good many of the refugees—I may say the vast majority of them—have settled in

New York and Chicago. I used to feel a little critical of them for this, as did many others, because the ostensible reasons seemed to be because they could hobnob with a lot of other foreigners, pose as superior foreign-trained physicians, make more money than they ever made before in their lives. I don't feel so critical of them now because I think American physicians are partly to blame for this. The states of New York and Illinois, in which New York City and Chicago are located, are among the very few states in the union which haven't taken an exceedingly selfish, mean, exclusive attitude toward the foreigners, refusing them licenses and making it generally difficult for them to practice medicine legally. It is a bad situation, contributed to from both sides.

Much more serious I think is the fact that the private practice of psychoanalysis in this country has been a great temptation to the character of some of the foreign analysts. In the first place, some of them came over with a very authoritative, eloquent attitude as if they were about to instruct the benighted American savages in the highlights of European science. When more refugees came, those who got here first turned their sadistic trends toward the newcomers and played politics with the Americans. Of course, gradually the real assets and liabilities of the individuals became known, and it was next in order for some of them to turn their attention to playing politics with the American public or with the medical profession at large or the social workers or the anthropologists. I should like to refrain from mentioning names or I could make this more specific and perhaps more clear.

What distresses me is a more fundamental problem, and that is the fact that the great lure of making money has destroyed the incentive of so many of the older analysts to do teaching. I could name six of your good friends whom we have recently invited one after the other to accept a position here at our clinic with a guaranteed net salary income of ten thousand a year to do nothing but teach—all of them have declined the offer. All of them express great interest in the opportunity; all of them say it is what they have longed for all their lives; all of them say that the basic principles of psychoanalysis must be upheld by systematic teaching in a place free from political interference, etc., such as this would be. Most of them concede it is the greatest teaching opportunity in the United States at present, even in the world. All of them say that a few years ago they might have considered it, etc. But all of them say that they are so busy, that they have so many contacts, or they have so many obligations, etc. that they cannot come. I really cannot blame them in a way because I realize they have had terrible insecurity in their lives in the past few years and they are rather suspicious of Americans, including ourselves, and when they get settled and begin to get patients who can pay sizable fees so that they can make from fifteen to twenty thousand a year and even more, why should they want to give it up and go back to a job of teaching psychoanalysis? I do not mean to imply that mercenary motives are the only factors involved. The Bibrings, for example, much as we would like to have them, and much as I think they would like to come in some respects, do have an advantage in Massachusetts which they cannot have in Kansas; namely, they can be licensed as physicians.

I am rambling on at too great length in discussing the refugee problem and, even now, I feel that I am not doing it justice. Many of the so-called refugees are among the finest additions to our scientific professional personnel. . . .

To take up some of your questions: The Zilboorg matter which you inquire about would require many pages to explain fully. Zilboorg is one of the most brilliant, one of the most stimulating, and at times one of the most irritating American analysts. He is a very warm personal friend of mine and I find it less difficult to overlook some of his minor faults than do others. He has been particularly irritating to Dr. Franz Alexander, his former analyst, and to Dr. David Levy, who, feeling his own incompetence as an analyst, resigned from the American Psychoanalytic Association some time ago. Before he resigned, however, Dr. Levy and Dr. Alexander felt that they had uncovered some evidence that Dr. Zilboorg had been unethical in his conduct of the analysis of a patient and they preferred charges against him which were heard at great length by the Board of Directors of the New York Society, who, after causing Dr. Zilboorg and themselves a great deal of expense and trouble, recommended to their Society that Dr. Zilboorg be censored publicly. The Society voted not to accept these recommendations and the matter was, therefore, dropped. I think it was a great mistake for Alexander and Levy to have preferred the charges and a great mistake for the matter to have been thrashed out with so much leakage. References of it were in the New York newspapers and of course there was widespread gossip. All of this was based on the sworn declaration of a very sick patient of Dr. Zilboorg's.

In regard to Horney, I think there is very little of importance to say since her dissenting movement has, I believe, completely broken down. I believe she has only a few medical adherents. Of course quite a number of nonmedical persons still believe she is a woman of great sense and breadth. I must say I don't agree with them.

Nor do I agree with you that Alexander's *Age of Unreason* is an excellent book. His historical and philosophical allusions are inaccurate and his psychoanalytic interpretations seem to me to be biased and tendentious.

Dr. Geleerd is still with us. She has recently had some additional analysis. She works mostly with children. I read portions of your letter to the members of the Topeka Society and all of them were delighted to know of your interest in us and to hear news about things in England.

Here at the clinic we are faced with a curious situation: on the one hand, we are very short of doctors and nurses, recreational therapists, occupational therapists, educational therapists, etc., and, on the other hand, we have more patients and prospective patients than we know what to do with. We have to turn away people daily and we have a considerable waiting list for admission to the hospital and to the psychotherapeutic department, which includes the analytic cases.

Sincerely yours,

To Lieut. Col. Malcolm J. Farrell,[27] Washington, D.C., November 19, 1943

Deal Colonel Farrell:

I have hesitated to write you at a time when I knew that your duties were doubled because of the death of your chief, but I am going to assume that you have a routine that will enable you to make some disposition of my suggestions without too much extra work. Or, of course, you may simply shelve them if you think best.

The Winter General Hospital is a 1500- or 2000-bed institution right here in Topeka. The chief psychiatrist is Maj. Forest Anderson, an old friend of mine from Los Angeles who has done child guidance all his life. He is a kindly, pleasant, modest man who had his original training here in Kansas and then took one of those three-year fellowships at Pennsylvania, tried private practice a while and then went to Los Angeles to run a child-guidance clinic at which he was fairly successful.

When he first came here he was obviously bewildered and I think a little frightened by the huge job that was piled on him. He has seven or possibly eight buildings full of patients—adult patients, of course—and originally he had one assistant, a young man from Los Angeles who has been coming out here to the clinic privately once a week for some additional instruction from me on psychoanalysis. Another assistant who recently arrived is, I think, an old state hospital man. Our consultant in this area was Major Pace, who I understand gave them no help whatsoever.

All of that is entirely beside the point and I merely mention it to indicate the background. These fellows have more than enough material and I am sure they are doing the best they can with it. They wanted us to come out and help and wanted to make arrangements for us to do so, but the commanding officer is a "big stuffed shirt" whom most of the men dislike because of his pompous, imperialistic arbitrariness, and while he professes great personal friendship for me and for the clinic he said that no civilian

27 A close friend of WCM. Both men were affiliated with the Office of the Army Surgeon General.

doctors could work in his hospital—so that's that. The Station Hospital at Ft. Riley welcomes us with gratitude and much honor and courtesy whenever we can find time to go down and give a little voluntary help to them, so I know this is not a general order from S.O.S.

What I am leading up to, however, has nothing to do with voluntary assistance to these doctors. It's this. You have, I understand, a very definite shortage of psychiatrists in the Army. You have an increasing number of psychiatric casualties coming back. Some of these you are referring to Veterans Bureau hospitals as fast as you can, but of course the Veterans Bureau hospitals are going to be filled up pretty soon and a lot of these psychiatric cases are going to land in station hospitals or other hospitals directly under the Army Medical Corps supervision. That means you are going to need more psychiatrists or trained men with some knowledge of psychiatry than you can possibly get hold of. You have a school, I believe, formerly at Atlanta and now on Long Island in which you give an excellent one-month course to brush up psychiatrists and others who will do some psychiatric work in military psychiatry. What has occurred to me is the possibility of your establishing at Winter General Hospital a school for medical officers not previously trained in psychiatry who with the aid of an intensive course of lectures and supervised clinical work could learn something abut psychiatric diagnosis and perhaps even the main principles of psychiatric treatment in the course of say six months or even four months. You are sending a lot of people to the Mayo Clinic for lectures in neurology and other subjects, but I understand that they are not permitted to examine or work with the Mayo Clinic patients. Here at the Winter General Hospital you have your own patients so there would not be any difficulty in getting material and your doctors could be working under supervision with these patients. If staff meetings, case conferences, private conferences and general lectures could be conducted by some of the men from our staff, with the assistance of Major Anderson, of course, these men could get a very good survey of psychiatry with some good practical experience which would at the same time be of much profit and help to Major Anderson and Winter General Hospital. Then you could send the men to this Long Island school and give them an intensive month of military psychiatry. These men would then be fairly useful as assistants in psychiatric units; even though they could not be considered to be trained psychiatrists they would in effect have an intensive four months of psychiatric residency followed by some special military psychiatry pointers and then some continued psychiatric experience.

I have plenty to do and I am not eager to take on more work, but something like this would be interesting and I believe valuable to the Army, to the war effort, and I think I could find time to organize a faculty and participate in it myself. I understand that General Hillman[28] is interested in such

28 Brig. Gen. Charles C. Hillman was Chief of Professional Services, Office of the Army Surgeon General, from 1939 to 1944.

a program in general and perhaps you could sound him out on this, and if it looks feasible let me know.

The question of compensation might rear its ugly head and so I hasten to add that I submit the suggestion with no idea of monetary reward. I have been told that the government does not want to accept voluntary help and wants to pay for everything, etc. and if that is the way it is we would not of course turn it down because I have no objection to being a part-time government employee, but I am sure that I could get the faculty compensated through the Menninger Foundation from one of our donors who wants to see psychiatric education pushed. . . .

Another idea. Are you giving some thought to what we are going to do about psychiatry in China and in collaboration with Russia? I think we should be sending psychiatrists to Russia right now to build up good will toward us among the Chinese medical men. I don't see that anybody is thinking about these things and I think it is going to be up to you. You probably haven't got enough to do as it is!

Sincerely yours,

From Leo Bartemeier, Detroit, November 23, 1943

My dear Karl:

First, I want to express my gratitude for the splendid changes you made in my Foreword.[29] I too have some pretty strong resistances against the term "psychosomatic' but it has caught fire everywhere and is apparently more acceptable than the terms psychoanalysis and psychiatry. Isn't it funny how the use of that word, together with the necessities which the war has brought about, has loosened the general resistances to the psychological aspects of medical work? You and I know that these resistances have been undergoing steady loosening as the result of the persistent pressure [from] analysts and psychiatrists during the past. The reports I get from various army camps indicate that the internists and surgeons are accepting the psychosomatic lectures, etc., quite readily. In some camps where psychological theories and techniques are not presented under the heading of psychosomatic medicine, I understand that the attitude is more encouraging than we have known it in civilian life. I only hope that the present flare for psychosomatic medicine does not mean a watering-down of analysis. I have a hunch some of our brother analysts are already changing their type of work. As for brief or briefer psychotherapy, you and I are in complete agreement about that also and let us maintain a firm stand against it.

I am glad that you and Jean are probably going to arrive in New York the morning of the sixteenth. . . .

29 Bartemeier had written the foreword to the *Bulletin of the Menninger Clinic* (January 1944).

I hope that Jean is all over her flu. Please give her my love and tell her I am looking forward to being with her in New York.

Affectionately,

To Robert Knight, Stockbridge, Massachusetts, February 11, 1944

Dr. Knight:

I promised to let you know my general line of approach to the medical students.[1] I began in different ways but, in the main, I made the following points:

1. I was visiting several medical schools talking privately and informally to some of the men because I had reached a point in life where I realized how important it was to get into the right niche. I explained how it was apparently by the merest chance that I got into psychiatry through the suggestion of an older fraternity brother who was visiting me at a time when I thought neurosurgery was the only important field.
2. Then I tell them how many medical men realize only too late that they have to practice psychiatry whether they like it or not and wish they knew more about it so that they could enjoy what they had to do.
3. I stress rather vividly the fact that most of the patients they will see in general practice will not have any of the conditions that the boys have spent four years in medical school studying about. I mention that statistics show that at least one-half of all the patients at the Mayo Clinic and perhaps more than half of the patients of the general practitioner are nonorganic and require treatment concerning which the medical student is totally uninformed.
4. I describe the different reactions of men to this discovery—those who are stimulated to overintensive searches for organic diseases, those who minimize, those who deny the existence of the neuroses, those who get mad like Colonel Patton, those who try the "kiddem along" techniques, etc. This, I find, is particularly effective because they have seen all of these things happen.
5. Then I go into detail about the enormous need for psychiatrists in the armed forces along the lines of the foundation newsletter, and I make the contrast as vivid as possible, and then ask them why the Hell they are thinking in terms of specializing in dermatology, laryngology, etc. I point out that if we had ten times as many psychiatrists we would not have enough and this is true of no other specialty.
6. I take up some of the reasons why they have had doubts about the field and notions that psychiatry consists of the sort of cases they saw in the

1 Knight had asked KAM to describe his technique for persuading medical students to specialize in psychiatry.

state hospital and the idea that most psychiatric cases are incurable, etc. See the items marked on the attached questionnaire.

7. I make two or three dramatic statements; for example, I contradict the idea that organic disease should be eliminated first, a false axiom which many of them are taught and which all psychosomatic medicine argues against now. I point out that surgeons have been on top in the medical profession for fifty years, but psychiatry is there now and will continue to be. I warn them that their professors will not encourage their interest in psychiatry as a rule, and I tell them why. If they say their instructors in psychiatry are pretty dull, etc., I say that I know it and tell them how I would teach psychiatry to medical students, beginning with one of them who is failing in his work after a good record, and show some of the different things that might be happening to him, which I would try to find out about, how I would do it, etc.

I found it was helpful (because most of them are in uniform) to refer to Will, his connection with the clinic and his job and problems, etc., not extensively but enough to give them a feeling that this was something of national knowledge and not a private theory of mine. . . .

Sincerely yours,

To Lillian Smith, Clayton, Georgia, March 14, 1944

Dear Lillian:

I have just finished *Strange Fruit*. You had told me something about the book while it was in the process of being written and I read some of the advance passages in *The South Today*. I was prepared for something extraordinary and I found it.

I don't know just what to say in a few words to convey my feelings. Perhaps I ought to tell you just what thoughts went through my mind and what I did about them. I was so shocked—not by the lynching, not by the sexual goings-on, not by the condescending, patronizing, humiliating attitude of even the most ignorant whites toward even the most intelligent and educated Negroes, but by words and pictures here and there which really do not come home to those of us who are not living under the conditions that prevail in Maxwell.

The words of the minister, for example, when he talked so earnestly with Tracy and told him about "that Negro line"; the words of Tracy to Nonnie when he was drunk; the words of the turpentine foreman to the doctor who recommended typhoid innoculations; and, most of all of course, the words of the doctor to Mr. Harris: "It'd be such a little thing to call us Mister . . . it wouldn't take a penny . . . it oughtn't to shame you much . . . it's things like that that drive us crazy . . . the little things." And "Taking our women

. . . manure, that's all they are to you . . . dung . . . to make something grow green in your life . . . threw her aside like something filthy and stinking.''

The book was pretty tough on me. I have spent a good many years of my life championing the rights of people who are discriminated against—people who are called crazy, nuts and neuros, etc.; not only them but the Chinese, the Japanese-Americans, and especially the Jews of whom I am very fond. When I finished reading your book, I realized I hadn't done a damn thing about the biggest problem of all. I hadn't even thought it through. I don't think I like Negroes particularly, but even in saying that I am ashamed of myself, not because of my feelings but because of my generalizing.

I called up to see if the department stores in Topeka allowed Negro women to use the restrooms and toilets without discrimination. They do. But I learned that no Negro can get a bite of food in a drugstore here or even a soda or ice cream; not a single restaurant or hotel allows them to be served except in private rooms. And then I got to thinking: What have I ever done about it? Well, I have visited a few of them in their homes as their guest. I have invited some of them to come out and visit my wife and myself at our home, but they always protest that we might have company and when I tell them this would not embarrass me, they just smile and say they will come out some time. Have I ever invited any of them to dinner? No. Have I even told any civic group or the ministerial union what a piece of narrow-minded undemocratic prejudice it represents to treat Negroes this way in our town? No. When the swimming pool row was up and it was decided that the high school swimming pool should never be used because no decision could be made as to whether and when the Negro students could use it, what did I say? Nothing publicly.

When my friend, Dr. [Mack L.] Ross, one of the colored doctors here, comes to the medical society dinners and sits off in one corner, I go and get him and invite him to come and sit by me and nobody objects to this at all because everyone likes Dr. Ross. But when my associate Dr. Crank, a Southerner born and reared, gets acquainted with Dr. Ross, what does he do? He invites him to his apartment for a drink, which makes me feel pretty much ashamed of my passivity. Dr. Ross was a great friend of Dr. [George] Washington Carver and Dr. Carver visited him several times here, but Dr. Ross was too shy to invite me over to meet Dr. Carver at his home; he thought I probably wouldn't care to come to dinner with a few Negroes, and he was probably right. I think I would have been squeamish about it—then—much as I admire and marvel at the career and achievements of that modest, quiet, little genius, Washington Carver.

Some rather prominent friends of mine in Chicago often have Negroes for dinner, and I have mentioned this to people at times as an outstanding event, something to exclaim about.

Well, these things show just exactly how narrow-minded I am and how prejudiced. Unlike the Southerners, I haven't any excuse for it. I was not brought up that way. I was taken care of by Negro servants in our home who were treated with great respect by my mother. They ate at the table with me when I was a child. I was telling my mother about your book and my reflections regarding it, and she smiled rather sadly and told me a long story about a Bible class she organized once for the Negro women of Topeka.

Tired from their long days of hard work, these wistful women would trudge down to an ill-lighted basement room in a Negro church and, bearing hard on little stubs of pencils, they would try to follow the outlines and answer the questions. Meanwhile my mother had half a dozen large, flourishing white Bible classes going in the town, and she told the Negro women that their class would simply have to find a better place to meet. Every church in town turned her down. The Y.W.C.A. agreed to let the Negro women meet there if the white classes met there, because by this time they were all rather anxious to get the prestige of my mother's teaching. My mother raised a thousand dollars among her friends and equipped the room with chairs, etc. The class for the Negro women was announced and, gratefully and joyfully, hundreds of them signed up. On the day of the first meeting of the class my mother was obliged to announce that the directors of the Y.W.C.A. had reconsidered their decision and could not permit the Negro women to meet there. Recently the Y.W.C.A. has reversed its policy again, but the Negro women are very cautious, understandably so.

I don't want to sound reproachful in all this, either of myself or my community, but at the same time I do feel reproachful. It is more accurate to say that I feel disturbed to think that, silently and mysteriously, for reasons that I don't at all understand, there is a strange and inconsistent attitude in the world which involves me, however much I may imagine myself freed from it. When I read a book like yours I do not feel condemning in my heart toward those people in Maxwell because I see only an exaggeration of the things that are true in Topeka and in me. They may naively attempt to explain their feelings which I am too old and too sophisticated to attempt to do, and certainly they are too complacent about them, but so have I been. I think I am rather like Mr. Harris in the book. I deplore it, but I go about my business and let someone else try to figure it out.

Well, I can't think of any greater compliment I could pay your book or any other book than to admit that it has stirred up this much thinking and feeling on my part. Being a person more inclined to action than to rumination, it will probably lead to my doing something, and I hope that whatever I do will be thought out enough to be effective. Meanwhile, I want to say something that will get other people to read your book, something you can tell your publishers. If you like, you can tell them this: No thoughtful person can read *Strange Fruit* and ever be the same afterwards. Some books are read for amusement, some for diversion, some for information and some for the necessary purposes of disturbing our complacency. To be complacent about the greatest social problem in America is surely a form of passive suicide. At a time when newspaper headlines would make us think that all of our troubles are in Europe and in the Pacific, this is a book for every American to read and, having read, to act upon.

Sincerely yours,

To Morris Fishbein, Chicago, March 17, 1944

Dear Morris:

I am opposed to the passage of the Wagner-Murray-Dingell Bill[2] and so are many other doctors. But I am afraid you and your friends in Chicago are going to turn the tide in favor of the bill if you don't cut out the dirty work. By dirty work I mean for example this absurd propaganda of the National Physicians Committee. You may not be back of that but you print their stuff in the *Journal*. So I'm writing you. Besides, you have brains; I'm not sure about them.

This is what I mean by dirty work: One of these questions, for example, reads, "Would you still approve if this meant increasing Social Security taxes to 6 percent?" If I read the bill correctly, this 6 percent Social Security tax would cover not only medical and hospital insurance but unemployment insurance, old age pensions, maternity benefits, etc. The Social Security tax for medical care and hospital insurance would only be 1 1/2 percent. To imply it is 6 percent is dirty work and bad tactics, I think.

Are we in such a tight spot that we have to misrepresent and distort the facts? It makes me damned uncomfortable to think that my point of view is being supported by tricky and essentially false representations by my Association [AMA]. Furthermore, why all this excitement? Why all these pamphlets and newsletters I keep receiving in the mail? Two came today, one yesterday, and some last week. Why am I being deluged with this damned stuff? Almost nobody I meet thinks the Wagner-Dingell Bill has the ghost of a chance to pass. . . .

I wish you would put me straight about this because, to tell you the truth, what I hear on all sides is, "I am opposed to the Wagner Bill but I am even more opposed to that doctors' trust you belong to in Chicago" (or if it is a

2 The AMA—both nationally and through many local groups—had organized strong opposition to this bill, which, in its differing versions, would have offered national health insurance to persons with annual incomes of less than $2,000 or $2,500. The proposed bill also encouraged the practice of cooperative medicine and the establishment of health centers for patients whose illness did not require hospitalization. In an editorial, Fishbein called the bill "perhaps the most virulent scheme ever to be conjured out of the mind of man."

doctor speaking), "I am against the Wagner Bill, but I think our American Medical Association representatives in Chicago are selling us down the river and making us look like a bunch of thugs."

I am not a medical politician. I hold no offices and covet none; I cast no votes in the organization. I expect to survive, no matter what happens, but it seems to me you are making a terrible mistake. Just because some of the fellows on the pinkish side say the same thing, it ought not to lead you to condemn some of us who think we are pretty levelheaded and conservative and who try to tell you as plainly as we can that it don't look right, and "it ain't funny, McGee."[3]

Sincerely,

P.S. Have you read *Strange Fruit* by Lillian Smith? I recommend it, four stars. It has nothing to do with the subject of this letter.

FROM JOSEPH MANKIEWICZ,[4] BEVERLY HILLS, JULY 13, 1944

Dear Dr. Karl:

David O. Selznick[5] started production this week on a picture to be called *The House of Dr. Edwards*.[6] Its stars are Ingrid Bergman and Gregory Peck; the director is Alfred Hitchcock. Like every other Selznick production, it will be heavily exploited and there is every reason to believe that it will be an enormously successful film—which means that it will have an audience of many millions of people.

The commercial film's ability to prejudice mass opinion has been too well documented for me to go into it now. The *House of Dr. Edwards* is a murder mystery, played against a background of psychiatrists, psychoanalysis, and a sanitarium very much like your own. Bear in mind as you read this that Alfred Hitchcock is our outstanding specialist in horror films.

The murderer in the story is a psychoanalyst named Murchison. He is the administrative head of "Green Manors, a private institution for mental cases." He murders another psychoanalyst who had been chosen to replace him as head of the institution. It is explained that he did this during a period of "panic" in which he fancied that his job had been stolen from him. In the climactic scene of the story, however, he is quite ready to kill also the young lady psychoanalyst (Ingrid Bergman) who has unmasked him.

---

3 Molly's often repeated line to Fibber McGee on the popular radio show *Fibber McGee and Molly*.

4 An American writer, director, and producer of such famous films as *All About Eve, Cleopatra*, and *Sleuth*.

5 An American film producer, Selznick's credits include *Gone with the Wind, Rebecca*, and, in 1945, *Spellbound*.

6 The picture was released as *Spellbound*. The book on which it was based was *The House of Dr. Edwardes*, by Francis Beeding. The shooting script used the novel's title, but dropped the final "e" in Edwardes.

The opening sequences of the script are devoted to establishing the background and characters. Two patients of the sanitarium are described. The first, referred to as a woman suffering from "sex aberration," flies into a rage at Ingrid Bergman during an analytic hour, throws a book at her, and is forcibly removed.

Later, Miss Bergman walks into the office of another psychoanalyst while a patient is in the middle of an hour. She joins in the analysis, and explains carefully to the patient why his over-whelming feeling of guilt is without basis in reality. This patient later makes an attempt on his own life and that of a guard.

The leading man of the picture is a young medical doctor who is shocked into total amnesia as the result of a trauma received on the Italian war front. As a patient of the doctor who is murdered by Murchison, he becomes obsessed with the belief that it was *he* who murdered the man. It is postulated that in an effort too compensate for this guilt he shows up at the sanitarium in the assumed identity of the man, to carry on in his place. In order to make this believable, it is necessary to assume that none of the doctors at the sanitarium have ever met the man who was expected as their new administrative head.

The psychoanalysts at the sanitarium are almost without exception maladjusted men—and they spend their time twitting each other about their fallibilities. They take turns in making passes at Bergman, whom they constantly tease as being emotionally and sexually frigid. I think I have rung enough gongs—it's time I got down to the purpose of this letter.

The script was written by Ben Hecht. Therefore, it is always glib and, at times, fascinating and witty. I know that Ben is acquainted with Dr. May Romm, and it is my purely personal assumption that he garnered from her, and from some hasty reading, a sufficient number of psychiatric truisms to justify dramaturgically the points he wanted to make. I would be willing to bet that she has not read and certainly not approved the script.

I am convinced that the next period of years will bring psychiatry in general, and psychoanalysis in particular, into great prominence as a most important source of literary, dramatic and motion picture material. The word "Psycho-neurotic" has already become a catchword (and catch-all), and in time will pass even "inferiority complex" in popularity. Remember that while books and plays reach limited audiences, the customers of the cinema are without number. I suggest to you, then, that both the American Psychiatric Association and the American Psychoanalytic Association consider *now* what can be done, in some way, to control—or at least temper—the presentation of their respective sciences that will be sent out to the far corners of the globe on millions of feet of film—and to prevent, if possible, the resultant disrespect and distrust that may be generated in the minds of millions of people.

I do not know whether the American Medical Association has a permanent liaison with the motion picture industry. I do know, however, that no picture is made involving a medical background which is not submitted to an authoritative medical authority; and that a recognized technical adviser is present throughout the shooting of scenes involving therapeutic procedure. The Catholic church, of course, has the problem licked. They have literally thrown the fear of God into the producers and have the final word on anything involving their particular racket.

I do not know how exercised you will become over what I have written you. Perhaps you will not regard an unrestrained Hollywood let loose on psychiatry as nearly so dangerous to public confidence in it as I do. But I assure you that there will be pictures compared to which the idiocies of *Lady in the Dark* will seem like a treatise by David Rapaport.

If you feel like doing anything about *The House of Dr. Edwards*, I suggest that you, yourself, write directly to David O. Selznick. . . .

I see I have rambled on in my usual wordy fashion, but I hope not too incoherently. It goes without saying that I will do anything you ask, and serve in any capacity you indicate. Even if the suggestion is that I mind my own business.

Dr. Fenichel "did not object" to my writing this letter, and agreed that you were the one to write to. Rosa joins me in sending the best of everything to you and to our very good friends at the clinic and in Topeka.

Sincerely,

To David O. Selznick, Beverly Hills, August 7, 1944

My dear Mr. Selznick:

It has come to my attention that you are planning a picture starring Bergman and Peck and directed by Mr. Hitchcock, which has a considerable background of psychoanalysis. As one very much interested in the moving picture industry as a recreational and educational force, I am particularly interested in your projected play because of its bearing on psychoanalysis. Psychoanalysis is coming to play a very important role in the enormous problems of the psychiatric casualties in the present war. My brother and partner, Col. William C. Menninger, Consultant to the Surgeon General, is in charge of all psychiatry in the Army. I, myself, am a past president of the American Psychoanalytic Association.

I have a high respect for your work, as evidenced in the great pictures you have made, and I feel confident that under your guidance only a dignified and scientifically accurate treatment of psychoanalysis would emerge, particularly at this time when the minds of such a large portion of the population are filled with fears and misconceptions about mental illness and should be focused sanely upon the question of adequate treatment for the many thousands of psychiatric casualties pouring into the country.

National journals have cooperated with the armed forces in a very constructive way in telling the people the facts about mental illness and treatment in an effort to calm the exaggerated and often superstitious fears of the families of these patients. But I think the moving pictures could do even more to show people that mental illness is not a disgrace and that there is scientific medical treatment for it which is successful in the great majority of cases. The general public's conception of psychiatry and particularly of psychoanalysis as you know is medieval, being a compound of honor, superstition, violence, sex mania and dual personalities, largely behind bars. These erroneous ideas are changing rapidly, however. Perhaps we psychiatrists and psychoanalysts are partly to blame for these misapprehensions, because we have been too busy treating patients to worry about educating the public. But if there was ever a time to present a true picture of what psychiatry is and does, it is now, in order to avoid many thousands of potentially useful and sensitive men suffering tortures from people's thoughtless cruelty. We psychiatrists are awakening to our responsibility in this matter.

I am sure the American Psychiatric Association and the American Psychoanalytic Association will be very willing to cooperate with the motion picture industry whenever they present psychiatric or psychoanalytic material in films. We are not yet so organized as to furnish technical advisors. I myself would welcome an opportunity of discussing the matter with you or any of your collaborators involved in the preparation of your new film. In this endeavor, it occurs to me that it might be useful if you and anyone you might suggest would come to inspect an institution like we have here and make your own observations on the spot, and discuss every kind of explanation we would be glad to give you. For this purpose I would like to extend a cordial invitation to you to arrange such a visit at any time suitable to you. Needless to say, this offer is entirely for public-spirited reasons and does not imply any compensation or publicity.

Sincerely yours,

To Joseph Mankiewicz, Beverly Hills, August 8, 1944

Dear Joe:

I think the matter you wrote me about some time ago is of the utmost importance and we have had long debates around here as to just what I should say to Mr. Selznick and, after writing the letter over two or three times, finally evolved the enclosed. It may not be quite what you think it should be, but we will see what happens. I wrote it on foundation stationery.

I am sending your original letter and a copy of my letter to the president of the American Psychoanalytic Association [Bartemeier], who is one of my most intimate friends and who will not do anything about it without consulting me. Dr. Knight is secretary of the Association and he feels very strongly something should be done right now. We will wait and see what Selznick says, and I will let you know what Drs. Bartemeier and Knight think.

I think you have done psychoanalysis a great service in having called it to our attention.

Sincerely yours,

FROM DAVID SELZNICK, CULVER CITY, CALIFORNIA, SEPTEMBER 22, 1944

Dear Dr. Menninger:

. . . I have for some time been hopeful that the screen would do its share in giving the American public a greater understanding of psychiatry, including psychoanalysis. I entirely agree with you about the general widespread misconception, fears, superstition, et cetera. As just one example of what I myself have encountered, I learned that there is a widespread impression, for some mysterious reason, that Catholicism and psychoanalysis are incompatible.

It seems to me that the American Psychiatric Association and the American Psychoanalytic Association should have a public relations and publicity division. Interest in the subject is growing to such an extent that I think such a group would have very little difficulty in getting enormous publicity for the great strides forward that have been taken in recent years in the psychiatric field, and the magnificent results that have been achieved both in and out of the armed forces. If a Hollywood division could not be afforded (although I can think of few places potentially more valuable as headquarters for such a publicity branch, and would personally suggest that you have one man in New York and another in Los Angeles) then at least periodic visits conceivably could result in greater use of psychiatric subjects or incidents on the screen. The short-subject field in particular lends itself to such publicity and education; and I should be glad to be helpful in arranging introductions to the proper executives in the short-subject field for whomever your societies designate for such work.

Our studio is a comparatively small one, but we try to make our pictures most carefully, with particular regard to research accuracy (let me thank you for your kind comments about our work) but we have dealt with psychiatry in each of our last three pictures. I should like to suggest that you make it a point to see *Since You Went Away*, which includes a sequence that I personally conceived and wrote in the hope that it would have a value in making the American public aware of the work being done by psychiatrists to rebuild men who have been shaken by their war experiences. Our succeeding production, *I'll Be Seeing You*, deals in its entirety with a case of combat fatigue and war nerves. *I'll Be Seeing You* will be released sometime this winter. Both pictures are considered outstanding in the motion picture industry, have been produced under very high budgets, have commensurate advertising budgets, and possess casts that insure huge audiences.

Our third picture of the season, *Spellbound*, is presently in the process of editing and presumably is the one to which you refer. We have been fortunate in having the direction of Alfred Hitchcock, with whose work you are undoubtedly familiar. As it is a type of mystery and horror play, the subject matter is perhaps one that would occasion cause for nervousness on your part. But we were most careful about everything in connection with the film. Ben Hecht, who possibly knows more about psychiatry than any other writer in Hollywood, wrote the screen play; and everything in the scenario, as well as in the picture itself, has been subjected to the approval of Dr. May Romm, whom I believe you know.

The picture opens with a spoken foreword designed to make the very points that you stress in your letter. This presents an extraordinary opportunity, one not likely soon to be again offered through the media of the motion picture. I am enclosing a copy of this narration in its present form.[7] Changing anything else in the picture would be almost impossible; but we still do have time to consider changes in this narration, if we receive any suggestions that will accomplish our mutual objectives as well as the dramatic necessities of the film. And since I feel that this is the very best spot in the picture to achieve what you are after, I should like to suggest that you examine it and let us have your suggestions, if any, without delay. Hopefully, you will be pleased with it in its present form. The reference to Dr. Edwardes and the book *The Labyrinth of the Guilt Complex* are of course fictitious and are designed to tie the narration into the picture proper, since Dr. Edwardes is the principal character in the piece, and *The Labyrinth of the Guilt Complex* is referred to often in the film as one of his works.

Incidentally, Miss Ingrid Bergman plays the young psychiatrist brilliantly.

I appreciate greatly your kind invitation to visit the Menninger Clinic about which I have heard so much. While this is impossible at the moment, I hope that you will leave the invitation open for a future date as I am sure Mrs. Selznick, who has a deep interest in psychiatry, would find such a visit interesting, as would I.

Sincerely yours,

P.S. Since dictating the above I have heard from Dr. Romm that she is not happy with this proposed introductory narration and is submitting to us for dramatic rewrite an alternative suggested draft.

---

7 The credits for the film include "May E. Romm, M.D., Psychiatric Advisor." The foreword in its final version reads:

"Our story deals with psychoanalysis, the method by which modern science treats the emotional problems of the sane.

"The analyst seeks only to induce the patient to talk about his hidden problems, to open the locked doors of his mind.

"Once the complexes that have been disturbing the patient are uncovered and interpreted, the illness and confusion disappear . . . and the devils of unreason are driven from the human soul."

If you are sufficiently interested to wish to make any comments we will naturally receive these with interest.

In the finished film we will not be able to have a narration of perhaps more than half the length of the one enclosed.

FROM MAY ROMM, BEVERLY HILLS, SEPTEMBER 25, 1944

Dear Karl Menninger:

From various sources, including a letter from Lionel Blitzsten, I gather that there is a considerable amount of confusion about the picture *The House of Dr. Edwards*. Perhaps I can clarify the situation since I am involved in it. Ben Hecht, who is a friend of mine, wrote an original story based on an idea found in the book *The House of Dr. Edwards*. He did this while he was working for Mr. David Selznick, whom I know quite well. The movie script was complete to the expense of somewhere in the neighborhood of a couple of hundred thousand dollars before I as much as knew of its existence. I spent considerable time with Ben Hecht trying to modify or eliminate some of the unscientific viewpoints. It was no easy task, but a great deal was altered on the script for the better. However, it was impossible, according to Mr. Hecht, to eliminate the part, or to alter it, so as not to have the head of this private sanitarium commit murder.

In order to do that, Mr. Hecht would have had to write a new story at a new fee. Both Mr. Hecht and Mr. Selznick are psychiatrically minded and sympathetic toward psychoanalysis, but when it comes to throwing away what to us would be a big fortune, granted to them a small fortune, then resistances set in.

I do not know which script you have seen, whether it was the first or the last, because the last one is definitely "doctored." Naturally the question arises, why should I have had anything to do with a picture which many have interpreted as casting aspersions on psychiatry. Simply because had I not done so it would have been produced in a much more undesirable form than it is now.

To give you an example, I wanted to take out the word psychoanalyst and substitute psychiatrist in regard to the leading feminine character, but it was impossible to accomplish that. For even what I considered improvement, I had to chew carpet.

I, personally, feel that this is not an important picture from the standpoint of giving the public an understanding of the meaning of psychiatry or psychoanalysis. It is just an ordinary murder mystery, the setting of which is in a small, private psychiatric hospital. I happen to know that in several studios, writers are bashing their brains out to bring psychiatry into their stories and the outlook for psychiatry is not too good. But, not having any contact with them, I can only hope that one of these days somebody will produce a picture on psychiatry which will have actual merit and educational value.

Last week I happened to talk to Dr. Raulston, the Dean of the University of Southern California Medical School, to whom I mentioned that you may be here in December. He expressed the wish to have you give a talk to the medical students. Would you perhaps be willing to address our local Society for Neurology and Psychiatry? If you want peace, you may have it. On the other hand, if you have an overwhelming desire to enlighten some of us backwoodsmen, just make your wish known.

Sincerely,

To David Selznick, Culver City, California, October 2, 1944

My dear Mr. Selznick:

I have just received your letter of September 22. To much of your letter I would like to reply at length and will do so in a few days. Since, however, there is some urgency about the introductory material which you enclosed I am replying about that immediately.

At the end of your letter you state that this is too long (with which I should agree) and that Doctor Romm is again revising it. This makes me a little hesitant to go into much detail about correcting the present version, but I should be very happy to see the revised version and to make suggestions if you wish them, of course without any financial or other obligation to you. (I am told that such assurances are desired by the movie people; please forgive me if this seems unnecessary.)

In the present version I think many very unfortunate phrases and terms are used although the main idea is correct. I would strongly advise against the use of the word "insanity." Furthermore, I think you do your gospel an injury by implying that one is either crazy enough to be locked up in a hospital or else perfectly well. The vast majority of patients with mental illnesses are not in mental hospitals—they are walking around on the streets of Hollywood, Topeka and other cities of our country.

From the tone of your letter I would judge that you have forgotten that you consulted me about the picture *Since You Went Away*, and that it was I who suggested that you confer with my colleague, Doctor Romm. I am glad you have found her services useful.

As I said, I shall write you again shortly.

Sincerely yours,

From Leo Bartemeier, Detroit, October 3, 1944

Dear Karl:

I don't understand why this nice letter from May Romm does not entirely satisfy you because I think it represents a frank, honest statement of her effort to modify the script so as to make it as favorable as possible for psychiatry and psychoanalysis. I do not mistrust May Romm and I hope you will express our sincere appreciation to her for her efforts. . . .

Sincerely,

To BELINDA JELLIFFE, NEW YORK, NOVEMBER 28, 1944

Dear Bee:

I just this minute learned of Dr. Jelliffe's serious illness. I don't know whether or not he is in any condition to receive the message but I wish you would tell him that I am thinking about him this afternoon and the great things he has done for American medicine and for psychiatry and for America, and incidentally for me.

I am sure he has been appreciated in other countries even more than many of us in this country realized and I am afraid that sometimes he thought that some of us had forgotten that. Time rushes on and we are apt to forget the older people but tell Dr. Jelliffe that we haven't forgotten him and won't forget him. I often remember the last line in that play about the life of Jesus that made such a success in New York. I remember the mother Mary was so pleased when one of the young Jewish women was going to name her baby Jesus, she said because she would not like to have his name forgotten. Dr. Jelliffe will never be forgotten.

Affectionately,

To RUTH MACK BRUNSWICK, NEW YORK, FEBRUARY 17, 1945

My dear Dr. Ruth:

It's been a long time since I've written you or since I have heard from you. Many things have happened.

Suppose I begin about the first of December. Jean and I went out to California for about five weeks to see if we could enlist some financial support from some of our friends for the Menninger Foundation. Although we got a few thousand dollars we were on the whole very disappointed, as we had hoped to get about a hundred thousand dollars out there. One of our psychoanalytic colleagues who is very proud of making $50,000 or $60,000 a year gave us $10. It is a little bit disheartening to see psychoanalysis used as a method of making lots of money and not the slightest concern for the greater problems implied.

You know how I feel about it. My brother and I decided to give away all of our possessions to the foundation and all of our so-called profits from the practice of medicine and take salaries only for the rest of our lives. I don't want to be in the commercial practice of medicine. It hurts my conscience and makes me feel disagreeable. I'm very happy in the new arrangement and all the rest of us are.

Jean and I came back from California where we worked tremendously hard, by the way, and were here for a couple weeks when I had to go up to Chicago for a meeting of the committee on the reorganization of the American Psychiatric Association. Previous to this I had been in Detroit for three or four days to get some money for the foundation and the effort there was rather more successful than the California trip.

Then of course there was a lot of clinical work and correspondence and six or seven controls per week and all the rest of the things that I am doing here at the clinic, and I have been busy with that up [to] the present moment.

A week ago my mother after only a few hours of illness died. Naturally this has made necessary a number of internal readjustments in me which are still going on. I had a good deal of anxiety and depression the first few days but since then I had rather less than I expected, in fact almost none. Of course consciously I realize that she had lived her years and done a good job and influenced me as much as she could and that I owed her much both for better and for worse, but unconsciously I don't know exactly what her death means. There is a certain kind of freedom which it implies, which is a strange expression to use. Anyway, my last recollections of her are happy ones and in a way I am glad that her poor troubled spirit is resting now.

I am leaving tomorrow for the Mayo Clinic where I shall spend the better part of a month on a research project. They have invited me to come up there to see what I can suggest in regard to some of their "psychosomatic" cases. Please notice the quotation marks around the word because I hate it. In between times I have to dash over to Cleveland and Columbus, Ohio, to make some speeches and once more up to Chicago, but I think I can get in a number of good licks in Rochester and maybe learn something.

I'll enclose the latest issue of *TPR*[1] which may interest you. When you have time I wish you'd write me a note and tell me what you're doing.

Sincerely,

FROM SANDOR RADO, NEW YORK, FEBRUARY 22, 1945

Dear Karl:

I heard about the non-profit reorganization of your establishment, but knew none of the details. This is a fine, far-sighted move—pioneering at its best.

To my mind, it is a responsibility not only of the universities but also of

---

1 *Temperature, Pulse, Respiration,* an in-house periodical of the Menninger Clinic. The first issue appeared in July 1940.

our leading hospitals to offer graduate training in the medical specialties. Following the example of the medical schools, undoubtedly the hospitals too will include psychoanalytic services, internships and training in their work. This development must not be confused by the analysts' reluctance to make the necessary financial adjustments.

For half a century the clinical art of psychoanalysis had to be kept alive without the benefit of clinics and hospitals. Now this historical era comes to a close. With my best regards,

Sincerely yours,

To Donald C. Balfour,[2] Rochester, Minnesota, April 10, 1945

My dear Doctor Balfour:

I shall always consider it to have been one of the high points in my professional life to have spent six weeks with you at the Mayo Clinic. . . . I was glad to be able to give the foundation lecture you had invited me for—a small contribution in return for the privileges I was granted. For the $1000.00 check which the clinic gave me as an honorarium I am also grateful and I wish you would thank the board of governors again for me. As I told you, we are trying to build up an education fund for assisting in the financing of psychiatric education for promising young physicians and this will help it greatly.

May I say something about an impression which I carried away with me? In addition to all those things which impress every visitor to your great institution—the wonderful opportunities for education, new vision and grasp of medicine as a whole—I think I was most impressed by the spirit of humility and modesty which seems to characterize so many of your staff members. I suppose it is merely the consequence of such great experience, the kind of wisdom that comes from seeing so many things and knowing so much; it leads one to realize how much we do not know and do not understand. At any rate I think it is an enviable spirit and one which I hope I have to some extent absorbed and can communicate to those about me here in Topeka. We shall certainly try to continue to emulate the example set us by the Mayo Foundation and Mayo Clinic, not excluding this important lesson. This has been my father's ideal since his visit with Doctor Will and Doctor Charlie [Mayo] many, many years ago. No one is more gratified by the occasion of my stay in Rochester than my father.

In conclusion, let me tell you again how much interested I am in the idea we talked about, namely, that of having a psychiatric education arrangement here for those of your fellows who want to add psychiatry to their

2 Director of the Mayo Foundation.

preparation. I shall await further word from you in regard to working out the details of this.

May I ask you again to thank the officials of the clinic and of the foundation for their courtesies to me which I know were extended in part because of their confidence in the opinion of Dr. Paul O'Leary,[3] a warm personal friendship with whom is one of the additional fruits of my visit.

Sincerely yours

FROM KARL T. COMPTON,[4] WASHINGTON, D.C., APRIL 19, 1945

Dear Dr. Menninger:

In accordance with a request from the Commanding General, transmitted to the Office of Field Service through the New Developments Division, Special Staff, U.S. Army, these offices have arranged for you to proceed under an appointment as a Scientific Consultant to the U.S. Army, and with military orders, to report to the Office of the Chief Surgeon, ETOUSA.

It is understood that with the cooperation of one or more officers assigned from that headquarters you will undertake certain scientific studies in connection with neuro-psychiatric casualties among our own troops and will perform such duties and services in this connection as may be requested by that headquarters. You understand that the primary purpose of this mission is to assemble observational information that may be helpful in the proper diagnosis, treatment and possible prevention of such casualties. It is expected that in the performance of these duties you will be able to visit and discuss the scientific aspects of this problem with officers at battle stations, collecting and clearing stations, field hospitals, evacuation hospitals, and other centers for the handling of NP [neuro-psychiatric] cases, both on the continent and in England. Details of procedure in carrying out this mission have already been carefully outlined to you by the Office of the Surgeon General in this country and we understand that your activities will be greatly aided through your personal contact with the numerous medical officers in the theater of operations whom you already know as colleagues.

By mutual agreement between the Office of Field Service, the Office of the Chief Surgeon ETOUSA and yourself, the duration of your assignment in the theater will be approximately two months. If there should be a military request for a continuation of your services in the theatre beyond that period, we are sure that you will make every effort to arrange your personal commitments in this country so as to permit such extension and this office would be glad to consider authorizing it.

3 A member of the section on dermatology at the Mayo Clinic.

4 Compton, a physicist, was Chief of the Office of Scientific Research and Development of the Office of Field Service of the War Department.

As you know, the OSRD [Office of Scientific Research and Development] maintains offices both in London and in Paris, to assist civilian representatives abroad who are working in direct cooperation with the armed forces. We would suggest that soon after arrival you establish contact with these offices, the addresses of which and key personnel we have already made known to you. The OSRD Liaison Office in Washington has already notified them of your anticipated arrival. Copies of these instructions are being forwarded for their files and you will, of course, be able to explain in greater detail the nature and importance of your mission.

It is expected that you will conform to military regulations and etiquette during your turn as an appointee of the Army. You will find your military associates in the theater and our offices abroad most helpful in guiding you in these matters and in supplementing the brief indoctrination which this office and the New Developments Division were able to supply during the short interval of your preparations for departure.

It is also expected that you will, when it seems appropriate or necessary, transmit to the Office of Field Service, the New Developments Division and the Office of the Surgeon General information concerning your investigations which may be helpful to related programs in this country. You understand, of course, that such information may be forwarded only by permission of the military authorities and through the usual military channels. May I also caution you to observe the pertinent regulations in transmitting classified information.

The Office of Field Service appreciates your willingness to undergo personal inconvenience and sacrifice in order to assist the war effort more directly through this assignment on an urgent problem and wishes you every success in undertaking it.

Sincerely yours,

Paris

To Jeanetta Menninger, Topeka, April 23, 1945

Dear Jean: (And all others interested)

I have just come from lunch in the only place that we Americans may eat in the "Com Z" (Communications Zone) headquarters. It was formerly a hotel. Having studied the circulars given us regarding censorship, I discover that it is permissible to tell you that we are in Paris.

At the moment I am sitting in one of the offices of the Surgeon General of the Theatre, Gen. Hawley,[5] whom we called on this a.m. He and all others

5 Major General Paul R. Hawley, Chief Surgeon in the ETO (European theater of operations), had extended an official invitation to the five participating psychiatrists.

have been most cordial and cooperative. We conversed with Col. Thompson[6] and Col. Parsons[7] until nearly midnight last night about our trip, and this conference continues 1.30 p.m. today. We studied some excellent psychiatric movies.

Earlier in the p.m. (yesterday) we strolled down the Champs Elysées and studied the throngs of promenading Parisians and soldiers (many nationalities but chiefly U.S.) and then crossed the Seine and came back along it. Yesterday was the Patron Saint day of Scouts, and a long parade of Boy *and* Girl Scouts (mixed!) with many detachments here and there attracted crowds. Also a boat race on the Seine, skiffs "manned" by girls, each with a *man* coxswain!

It was bright, sunny, *coolish,* slightly dusty but altogether a charming spring Sunday in Paris. Most conspicuous are the horse chestnut trees along the streets everywhere, all in full bloom (interspersed with platanus orientalis). I see many people carrying bouquets of lilacs, iris and lilies of the valley altho in the parts of Paris we see there are no visible gardens.

Our quarters are excellent, but *very* temporary; by this time tomorrow we may be in another country. The hospital facilities for our soldiers here are excellent.

Dr. Kubie's son was wounded, captured, and then recaptured and we had a most interesting visit with him. We have met members of other commissions, some of them Army, some semi-army civilians like ourselves (but we are treated everywhere exactly like officers). Some of them are just back from inspecting the terrible prison camps which you (and I) read about in the USA papers some days (weeks?) ago and they were really shocked, in spite of all their war experiences. Bins like a potato cellar, four to six bins high, eighteen inches apart, and SIX starving, dying, filthy men on each. Enormous piles of carcasses outside! The Army paper, *Stars and Stripes,* is full of pictures. I'll try to send you one.

The Parisians do not look at us or smile at us or (usually) humor us in our attempts to speak French.

The German prisons are said to be indescribably awful. Lice *in handfuls* inside plaster casts, anti-Hitler German citizens *by the hundreds* in these prisons, typhus, typhoid, TB, etc., rife among them, dirt dripping on and plastered over them, etc., etc. This includes captured Americans! . . .

I am wondering how Karlyle Woods[8] is looking, and the sanitarium grounds

6 Col. Lloyd J. Thompson, Senior Consultant in Neuropsychiatry for the Office of the Chief Surgeon in the ETO.

7 Col. Ernest Parsons escorted and guided the group during the first three weeks of their European stay.

8 A wooded tract about three miles north of Topeka, originally used as a summer retreat and a site for social gatherings of the Menninger Clinic staff. In 1941, Jean and Karl Menninger moved into a house on the property and made it their full-time residence until 1946, when they moved into a home in Topeka.

and how Dad is and where Bob goes and how the clinic is faring. I'll have lots of news for you when I get back but don't be surprised if some days or weeks of silence supervene.

Love to you all.

Paris

Dear Dad:

Your traveling representative is sitting at a little round table across from Dr. Leo Bartemeier in a room in a fine Paris hospital. This hospital was used by the German Luftwaffe and these rooms where we are billetted were the nurses' quarters. They are very nice—2 beds, 2 wardrobes, 2 chairs, and a wash bowl. The toilet is ⅛ mile down the corridor and the bath is 2½ miles further! However, we scarcely have time to use the bath, the table or the chairs. We have been on the go constantly. It is not "secret" that I am (at the moment) in Paris.

We are beautifully looked after by the Surgeon General's office; and I think we can be proud of the excellent medical and hospital services they are maintaining for the troops here. We have visited several of the hospitals. Today we called on the Dean of the U. of Paris medical school (5000 students in peace times, 2000 now, 50% women) and then tramped thru the *huge*, ancient, old Salpetrière and saw the courtyard where Pinel struck off the chains, etc.[9] and also the room where Charcot, etc., demonstrated hypnosis to Freud & others.[10] & I went and sat for a moment in one of the hard, plain, wooden benches where perhaps Freud once sat, and certainly many others. The old place looks like a penitentiary—with many inner buildings & all full of destitute senile females—5000 of them! & various "dispensaries."

In addition we have visited a few Army hospitals and made rounds in one of them. This one where we are billetted (all hotels are taken over for various depts., groups, offices, etc.) is one of the finest, in fact one of the best I ever saw. Frank L. Wright designed it, they say.[11] Too complicated to draw.

9 In the time of Louis XIII, this Paris hospital was an arsenal that manufactured gunpowder from saltpeter. Louis XIV made it a hospital for the poor of Paris. In 1795 it came to specialize in the insane, when Dr. Philippe Pinel (1745–1826), a Parisian psychiatrist and reformer, moved there. On May 23, 1793, he authorized the removal of chains from patients. This reform was widely adopted after publication of Pinel's *Treatise on Mania* (1801), which outlined more liberal methods of organizing asylums and treating the insane.

10 Jean-Martin Charcot (1825–93), a French neurologist, was appointed head of Salpetrière in 1862. Charcot classified a number of hitherto unknown disorders of the nervous system; his clinical descriptions of hysteria and of hypnosis were landmark studies. In 1885, Freud traveled to Paris for several months of intensive study with Charcot.

11 The committee was billeted at the Beaujon Hospital in Clichy, which was serving as

Transportation is a problem. No taxis and the subway is *very* crowded, & complicated. I bought 40¢ worth of tickets the 1st time we rode on it, not realizing we could travel free. All meals are free but we have to go certain places. They send cars for us (jeeps usually) with drivers most of the time but in spite of this we all have sore feet, sore backs from walking so much.

Tonight we tried the Opéra Comique (we wanted grand opera but tonight is the only free time we had & grand opera is "off" tonight. All operas being 6.30 p.m. We stuck it out 1½ hrs. & left—couldn't understand it—music & costumes very pretty. The program was totally incomprehensible—even the English translation which I'll mail you.

Most everything is *very* expensive—women's hats $60 etc., especially with our low rate of exchange. We aren't allowed to buy any food of the French. The reverse lend-lease arrangement is very interesting. There are hundreds of French girls (thousands) & taxi drivers etc. working for the Army (*our* Army) but paid by the French govt. in exchange for our supplies to the French Army. Similarly we get the use of hotels, hospitals, etc. The French hairdos are very strange and striking and I don't like 'em—all look very frizzly, dyed strange colors & put up in front something like this [illustration] (quite high up in front) and *hats* are similarly shaped & very big. And the poor French women are *so* homely anyway.

Col. Parsons is to be our escort & he is pretty influential around here. He had us out to dinner last night with some other psychiatrists. (Of course [the] U.S. Army supplies the food—you *can't* buy any food & neither can he or anyone else.) He also helped us to arrange (obtain) many preparations such as long underwear (wool), helmets, canteens, mess kits, etc. All officers eat at certain designated places—cafeteria-style in most of them.

We all five (Whitehorn, Bartie, Kubie, Romano & I) stick together altho we often laugh at our tendency to go down the street Indian file (some of us having gotten too weary to keep up or too independent to remain behind), or have a big argument about whether rue de la Paix runs into boulevard des Capucines this side or the other side of la place Bambujino, etc.; as you know, Paris is no town of orderly streets or blocks. We would like to visit the Louvre, Luxemburg, etc., but won't have time—that's not our business & we are on the rush right now.

I think about you and the affairs at the clinic and in connection with each of you individually, but I'll have to leave all that to you pro tem. I'll have lots to tell you later.

You would have been pleased this p.m. when the Dean of the U. of Paris asked each of us what university we came from. I was the last one in the

---

the 108th General Hospital. Designed by Jean Walter (not Frank Lloyd Wright) of the American firm Cassan, Plonsey, and Walter, it was finished in 1935 and introduced into France the American-style high-rise hospital.

row—Whitehorn was first. Of course, the dean said he had heard of Johns Hopkins and visited it, etc., etc. And when my turn came I said we had no university, just the Menninger Clinic and he brightened up and said—Oh yes indeed, I know about the Menninger Clinic and its work—and went on about someone of our people he had met in N.Y. Anyway I felt very gratified. We talked to him a long time about psychiatric education. They think we do it better but they put more emphasis on clinical contacts of student with pt *from the first. . . .*

Regen, Germany

To Jeanetta Menninger, Topeka, May 7, 1945

Dear Jean:

I'm in headquarters tent, down near the front. Around me are typists, officers, enlisted men, my colleagues and others—typing, talking, smoking, sitting, standing, looking at the big maps on the board, etc.

Outside the scene is idyllic. We are in the mountains, and our tents (along with others for the officers, including the nurses) are highest on the hill; below about 1000 feet are the hospital tents, and smoke goes up from their chimneys slowly and picturesquely. Beside the hospital flows a mountain stream and many soldiers were fishing (and catching trout!). Beyond the stream is a spruce forest and beyond it the mountain sides go up again [Sketch of locations].

It is a very beautiful scene—so quiet and peaceful—with the big red cross on the green grass of the valley, and on many of the 100-plus tents. Occasionally we hear the nearby antiaircraft guns testing—they were attacked by German aircraft here three days ago—but all seems very peaceful now, the more so because we have just learned that the war is to end in twenty-six hours—tomorrow at midnight. We are wondering where you will be and what [you will be] doing when this theatre of the war ends; we will probably be near the front—can tell you [where] in my next letter. We can't realize we are so far away from you—I wonder what the appropriate way to celebrate peace really is. Prayer I should think. The feeling of "it's over" brings great relief to many millions—but it is so obvious that "it" isn't over—I mean the tragedies and troubles of the world and the people that make it up. So many blind people have put their hands on such different parts of the elephant's anatomy and think they know so much about it—and do—but there are so many *other* aspects. I feel inhibited in writing my impressions but perhaps after I get back to Paris they will be more crystallized.

We have a lot of formal military courtesies to do everywhere. I've seen all sorts of hospitals and medical installations and met many doctors—most of them pretty tired and some of them disgruntled and querulous.

Nuremberg—the ancient city part—1000 years old, plus, is a heap of crumbled rock and dust. Practically all German cities and many villages are the same. Our bombs, British bombs, our artillery, German artillery, and finally hand grenades manage to wreck things indescribably.

As you probably know, each "Army" (1st, 3rd, 7th, etc.) has a rear and a middle and a forward "echelon," and there are many technical names for these, and for the various parts, and the medical installations appropriate to them [Sketch]. *Transportation* is a bigger problem than you can imagine— troops *up,* supplies, equipment up; and prisoners and patients *back,* all along shot-up roads with bridges out, mudholes, etc., etc., etc. Planes fly patients back (to Paris, often) at certain stages (of war and of clinical course). The organization is elaborate and on the whole amazingly efficient. For most of these hospitals there are two to twelve operating rooms, *all* operating on 24-hr. shifts! I mean several shifts—24-hour use.

We stayed in a tent last night, too—near Nuremberg (actually Erlangen) and again exchanged some of our clothes for others. The Colonel is from Omaha and knows Bennett[12] well, so I wrote Bennett and told him about it and showed the letter to the Colonel, who was pleased. He was *so* pleased, too, because WCM had written him after *his* visit here. We are taking names and addresses so we can do so even though they will probably be moved by then.

Now I must go because the C.O. of this hospital wants to receive us officially and "talk" a while—so we will all go and sit and have a drink and maybe have an interesting talk, and maybe yawn and wish we could make our beds (with 6 to 8 blankets on cots) and go to bed. . . .

Lunéville, France

To C. F. MENNINGER, TOPEKA, MAY 11, 1945

Dear Dad:

I don't know just how you people are managing with my letters but I'll address this one to you tonight altho I imagine you see them all and have been tracing my journey on a map.

After the dip into Czechoslovakia and return to *Titling*[13] we headed for Munich and Augsburg, riding on the Autobahn most of the way but detoured for 50 miles a couple of times. You see, the retreating Germans "blew" their bridges, *wonderful* huge bridges some of them were, to delay the pursuing Americans whose engineers had to either make temporary bridges or find detours which used other routes and bridges.

Because so many French people are walking or cycling home toward France, Russians wandering toward Russia, Germans walking or ox-carting loads of

12 A. E. Bennett was a psychoanalyst in private practice in Omaha.
13 Germany, near the 110th Evacuation Hospital.

wood or rutabagas or manure, *and* because so many, many trucks of provisions have to move forward 500 miles every day, *and* so many truckloads of prisoners have to be hauled west, the roads are very busy, and where broken (as often) *very* dusty. They narrow down to one vehicle width thru most of the towns and all these things slow us up.

Last night and the night before we stayed at what was left of a hotel in Augsburg—a rather large city, about one-third destroyed. About 30 miles east Munich, a *very* large city, is 90% destroyed. The extensiveness of this destruction is hard to believe until you see it.

We had a very valuable day at Augsburg with the most competent and most articulate psychiatrist we have met yet—a Boston chap, Ludwig.[14] His parents were born in Germany and we were interested in his reactions, as an American, of mixed feelings—which we all shared. We met one American psychiatrist who was born in the U.S. but lived 17 years in Frankfurt am Main, and then returned to the U.S. (I think this is correct). He said he was *glad* to see Frankfurt in ruins. Some feel that way—that only the most drastic things can stamp it out—but others feel that in a way these old cities belonged not just to Germany but to the world, and we all suffer thru their loss.

Today we came on west thru Wurtemburg, not so prosperous as Bavaria or the northern provinces. Some mountains, and the boys think we came thru the Black Forest (Freudenwald to Bad Peterstall) but I'm not sure they are right. *Most* of Germany seems to be forested; all carefully lumbered according to blocks, and replanted with little ones. Also, there are more mountains than I had any idea. The whole place is a big park—and (now) ruined cities.

We came thru Tubingen (where I noted numerous nurseries) and on to Strasbourg, in Alsace. There was lots of fighting in here. We went almost down to Kolmar where the pocket was. These huge trucks and tanks tear the roads up terribly.

We got here to Lunéville, south of Nancy (new censorship rules permit us to tell where we are), and arrived about 9 p.m. *very* dirty, so we all had a shower and then supper and then chatted with the officers awhile and now the others have all gone to bed except Bart and me. They have 30 doctors and 40 nurses here and 14 patients! Supposed to be an NP hospital but there is some slip-up so that it gets bypassed—patients are mostly flown in by plane from the outlying hospitals to Paris or to the one we go to tomorrow at Sine near Liège (Belgium). We will probably be there several days as it is an NP center.

I feel like saying again and again how grateful I am to you and all of our

14 Alfred O. Ludwig was Chief Psychiatrist for the Seventh Army and later president of the Boston Psychoanalytic Society (1966–68).

people there who are carrying on so faithfully and making it possible for me to have this incomparable experience. I think I'll be able to get much out of it for all of us, but the personal pleasure and opportunities are very great and very conscious with me, and my love to you all, especially our Dad, for encouraging me to go and carrying on while I'm gone.

From Sine we will probably go to Paris, then London.

Love,

FROM WILLIAM C. MENNINGER, WASHINGTON, D.C., MAY 29, 1945

Dear Karl:

Your letter of the 14th arrived here on Saturday, having taken just two weeks to get here. I am wondering if you are in London now and on that chance I am sending a carbon copy of this to you there. Your letters were so enthusiastic and they pleased me very much. I knew it would be awfully worthwhile and a highlight in anyone's life. You are having a chance to cover far more territory and I am sure to see many more men than was possible on my trip.

We were very interested in the possibility that you might be permitted to examine psychiatrically some of the high German war prisoners like Streicher and Goering. I know that Brickner[15] and Stevenson[16] and some others are going to . . . make such a request through the War Department. I don't know whether it has come to anything or not.

In your letter you asked for other possible suggestions. We of course were primarily interested initially in getting some information about psychodynamics, particularly with regard to psychiatric reactions in so-called reasonably normal personalities under abnormal conditions. We are interested not only in the psychodynamics but whether we are treating them right. I wondered whether all the sedation was necessary in the treatment. I wondered what the impression of your group was as to the use of other means, particularly in psychotherapy, possibly hypnotherapy. Mo Kaufman[17] used the latter almost entirely in Okinawa and got splendid results. I thought the 130th as I saw its methods in action in the 312th was not unpsychiatric but could just as well have been carried out by others than psychiatrists. The

15 Richard Brickner, a neurologist, had written *Is Germany Incurable?* (1943), an attempt to fathom Germany's terroristic behavior through the application of psychiatric and neurological principles.

16 George Stevenson, psychiatrist and neurologist, was medical director of the National Committee for Mental Hygiene. During World War II, the committee urged careful examinations of draftees to detect psychological problem cases. They also advocated camp mental health units to deal with maladjustments in the field and proposed training of psychiatrists through a liberalized GI Bill of Rights.

17 M. Ralph Kaufman was a New York analyst who became chief of military psychiatry in the Pacific theater.

frequent and common misuse of terminology distressed me—everybody was a C.P.S. [Constitutional Psychopathic State] who went AWOL or did anything in the way of behavior out of line. I was impressed with the fact that most of the men psychiatrically sick enough to be evacuated got minimal treatment because they were moved from one place to the next. I wondered what the real relationships between the quotas and mental illness were. I hope that your group may get ideas about most of these, if not all of these suggestions, and no doubt you will see lots of other things.

Other thoughts occur to me. Where can we more closely tie psychiatry into internal medicine with regard to psychosomatic problems? What could we do in the way of prophylaxis [for] men who become wounded and then develop anxiety as their wounds heal? What sort of postwar educational plans should be carried out, and could this group of civilians do something to stimulate the planning of it on your return? Now that you are a part of the Army you have all had an opportunity to see things which to me seem awfully important (not that you hadn't seen them before) but have the additional experience to bring pressure to bear on the APA [American Psychiatric Association] in directions we ought to follow. I am thinking specifically about postgraduate postwar education in psychiatry, about the relationships of psychiatry to other branches of medicine, about psychiatry's relationship and methods in medical education, about psychiatry's opportunities to affect the civilian social situation as it does the military situation with ramifications into every branch of activity. I hope you will see from the disciplinary units and have some ideas about the things that psychiatry might contribute to the military offenders. . . .

Affectionately yours,

P.S. Feel at liberty to show this letter to any of the other fellows and by all means give them my warm regards and my appreciation.

London

To Family in Topeka, May 29, 1945

Well, here I am in Merrie England and we all feel better already. Altho it has its interesting features, Paris is tiring and a bit depressing to me. The difficulties of transportation plus of language plus of buying anything (you see our money is devaluated 80% . . . 1 franc equals 2¢ whereas for the Germans 5 francs equals 2¢ Hence prices are *sky* high).

After a hectic evening trying to get back some trousers from the tailor shop after hours (we got our orders to leave about 6 p.m.) . . . I'll spare you the details BUT I got the pants 11:50 p.m. and turned in (all others preceded me). Up at 5.30 a.m. and all staggered around each other into bathroom, shave, gather grips, etc., etc., and off in the car at 6 p.m. to waiting room *in* town. After weighing, signing, etc., etc., etc., we got off in a bus (back over

same route as we had come, only *further* SW) to air field, and at 8.15 a.m.
took off in a 28-passenger 2-motor "bucket seat" plane—seats along the sides.
Slept after we saw the British mainland (40" to cross channel) because clouds
hid everything. We sailed on 30 miles *north* of London and landed at an
airfield near a town I can't locate on the map—Bovingdon (about 30 miles N
of London) and after weighing and signing and customs inspection (formalities, etc.) we get in a bus and ride thru lanes and narrow roads (left side
street of course) where I noticed *many Standard roses* & poppies and other
pretty flowers and on into London.

Again a series of formalities . . . signing in, etc., call on Chief Surgeon
. . . get billets . . . get lunch at big officers' mess . . . and then wait 1 hr. for
a truck (5 phone calls) . . . ending up at the present quaint 5 story residential
hotel. (We are lucky to get a *hotel;* many demands for them now). We've
unpacked, bathed, rearranged things, studied maps, and are soon to meet
Col. Thompson again (who came with us) and have supper and take a walk
or something. Tomorrow Dr. Earl Bond's son, an air force psychiatrist, and
some others are coming in for a conference.

The next two days we'll be on the road again and then back here. Try
sending me some letters at this address (Hotel Bailey, 140 Gloucester St.,
SW 7 - London). However, we will only be here two or three weeks, and
APO 887 is safer I guess.

Already we feel the thrill of being in this great and ancient and historic
and rich city—full of museums and people and legends and history. We
can't do much sightseeing but we'll try to see Westminster, the British Mu-
seum and I want to go to the Kew Gardens. How I wish you were here to
do the former with me and CFM the latter (He'd like all of them, however.)
Weather nice today.

More tomorrow.

All my life I've wanted to come to London!

Near Birmingham, England

To Jeanetta Menninger, Topeka, June 7, 1945

Dear Jeanie:

I'm at a long breakfast table at which numerous colleagues Amer. & Br.
are sitting—finishing their coffee, reading papers, talking or writing. We are
in what *was* a state hosp. for mental disease just out of Birmingham. It is
now a "neurosis center." When we arrived yesterday noon we were given
schedules (mimeographed) just like those *we* prepare there at Topeka. I will
try to get a copy to enclose. It will show you how busy we have been.

Demonstrations, lectures, conferences, stops for tea and then on again
. . . till 11 p.m. last night. (This included a formal dinner . . . at which one
doesn't smoke till after the postprandial ceremony of drinking the King's
health (and then the President's). It isn't nearly as stuffy or stiff as it sounds—

the men are very warm and sociable and do their best to give us an impression of their work. It does impress us, too . . . it is *much* like the Menninger Sanit [arium]. . . .

What they are doing here in group therapy thrills me (all of us) very much and I think I have acquired a number of ideas we might try in Topeka—e.g. the *patients*, not the Med. Director, are writing (and illustrating) the booklet to be given all *entering* patients. They (patients) have a kind of representative council that meets weekly with the MDs and administrators.

The British are *generally* more democratic than we, I think. They use dramatherapy and lots of interesting devices. I'm anxious to tell Greist[18] about it and see how it would work there—as well as in the Sanitarium. Of course this type of therapy is more appealing to us than the shock therapy, etc., used in some (U.S.) hospitals. Their art shop here is remarkable! Good instruction, chiefly. Everything is oriented around the idea of *groups*. New patients join a small group—and the "wards" are groups of groups, and have names and representation, etc. Group loyalties develop as in army units (platoons, regiments, etc) which we have found to be *very* important emotionally.

You don't know how hard it is to *mail* a letter. We can't use British post boxes or POs and have to make a trip to U.S. headquarters and we are now guests of British Army and have no chance to get there.

I'm *very* disappointed not to have heard word from Bob Knight, Bob Worthington, Gill, JRS or anyone.[19] Bill writes us quite often. Of course I've only had one letter from *you* in two weeks.

Yesterday I wired for Bill to get from you and send to me some foundation booklets and *bulletins* because I have many opportunities here to line up staff members, students, etc., and may be able to work out an exchange with Guy's Hospital.[20]

London

To Jeanetta Menninger, Topeka, June 18, 1945

Dear Jeanie:

For 3½ days now we have worried and stewed and conferred and dis-

18 John Howard Greist was chief of psychiatry at the Winter General Hospital in Topeka between 1944 and 1945.

19 Robert Worthington was a psychiatrist on the Menninger Clinic staff from 1941 to 1949; he later joined a psychiatric clinic in Seattle. Merton Gill was a Menninger Clinic staff psychiatrist until 1947 when he graduated from the Topeka Institute for Psychoanalysis. Later, he was on the staff of the Austen Riggs Center and assistant professor of psychiatry at Yale. At present, he is professor of psychiatry at the Abraham Lincoln School of Medicine, University of Illinois. His publications include *Hypnosis and Related States* (1959, with Margaret Brenman) and *Topography and Psychoanalytic Theory* (1963). "JRS" refers to John R. Stone.

20 Guy's Hospital in London, founded in the eighteenth century.

cussed and written and listened and rewritten on this report. The boys realize now that I was right when I told them last week that we couldn't do it
in a week and inasmuch as it must be carefully done, and well done if possible, we are all working hard and trying to do a good job before we start
back, because once in Washington we will *never* get it done, and all will
scatter, etc.

So they have amended their idea about leaving this week and we will
apply for a place as soon as we see the end of the report in sight which, in
my own estimation, will be about in time to get to Washington July 1. Not
sooner, I'm sure.

The boys accepted my idea that the report should be written cooperatively
rather than conjointly (because you can't get 5 prima donnas to write conjointly) so I outlined the whole theme and we assigned one topic to each
one of us and we are all at work on our subject. Then we get together and
read it to the other and take a beating. They insisted that one part be written
conjointly so I proposed that one of us act as the writer, amalgamator of
ideas, etc. and the others explain *their* views to him. Bart appointed me to
do this but I ducked out—I'm writing up the clinical syndromes. It'll be a
quite interesting report I think. . . .

Had to get back yesterday at 6 (after visit to Kew Gardens) to talk medical
education to a chap who has the ear of the Nuffield Foundation and wants
to arrange exchange fellowships for psychiatric training, U.S. and Britain. I
told him we had people who would like to come over for a year but couldn't
spare them NOW. We may get something fixed up. I also intend to see
Anna Freud whom Bartie thinks would like to get out of London. Her nursery is closing up and she is having a big fight here.[21] The Psychoanalytic
Society meets Wed. but I don't think I will go. I think they are stupid not to
have asked us to speak. Balint,[22] the Hungarian, of Manchester, Eng., is
speaking and he is OK but we will be tired from our report, and the psychoanalytic people here are in such a fighting bewildered mood. Our dinner
with the officers of the Society turned into a rather unpleasant session which
is too long to describe and relates not to the members but the one peculiar,
crusty, crabbed guy, [Ernest] Jones. Not he, but many if not most British
take the attitude that England is now entirely dependent on the leadership
of the U.S. One man in the park said, "We're thru, here. We're petered out.
America must lead us and if I was young I'd go there straight off."
Note by Bartie:

21 The "fight" to which KAM refers probably is his perception of the continuing tension
between Anna Freud and her followers and the followers of Melanie Klein, an antagonism
which threatened to create a schism in the British Psychoanalytic Society.

22 Michael Balint, a Budapest-born analyst who settled in England, was author of *Primary Love and Psychoanalytic Technique* (1952), *Problems of Human Pleasure and Behavior* (1957),
and other books.

"We're down to hard work now and Karl is great help in getting it all organized. In fact I think we would never have found a way without his helpful and kindly suggestions."

To the Office of Scientific Research and Development, Washington, D.C., July 14, 1945

Gentlemen:

As a member of the commission on the study of war psychiatry in general and the syndrome of "combat exhaustion" in particular, I left Washington 20 April 1945 and returned 8 July 1945. We made Paris our ETO headquarters, and went from there, by army car and escort, to visit the 9th, 1st, 3rd and 7th Armies, in that order. All were in Germany. We dipped into Czechoslovakia (on VE day) and Austria, traversed much of middle and southern Germany, all of Luxembourg, part of Alsace and Lorraine, and parts of northern France. We spent a week at an Army hospital in Belgium, near Liège. Then we studied some cases in Paris before going to the U.K. where we spent a month. For about one-half of this month we were the guests of the British Government, specifically the medical departments of the Army, the Navy, and the RAF. We visited many British installations and attended numerous conferences, where we were extended every courtesy and given access to all pertinent information and experience relevant to our scientific investigation.

We spent about two weeks formulating our findings, conclusions and recommendations, and then returned to Paris where we made some contacts with Swiss and French psychiatrists and visited French and U.S. Army hospitals and conferred with additional medical (army) personnel with references to their experiences.

The body of our findings and recommendations is represented by a very long report filed elsewhere, which has already been discussed at some length with the psychiatric division of the Surgeon General's office. My own opinion is that the scientific fruitfulness of the trip was of a very satisfactory order. But even more important, in the long run, may have been some of the collateral values of the expedition. One of these was the information gained with reference to the problems of psychiatric education, both for the immediate and for the more distant future. Associated with this is the good effect which I am presumptuous enough to think our visit had on the morale of some very weary and often discouraged young medical officers, especially psychiatrists.

But the most gratifying experience to me, personally, was the rapprochement effected by our contacts with the English, Scottish and French psychiatrists. All of these scientists were very eager to become better acquainted with us and with the scientists of the country which we represent. The thought was frequently expressed that the future peace of the world depended in part upon the cultivation and furthering of Anglo-American understanding and mutual appreciation and dependence. The leadership of America was freely acknowledged in England. Plans for exchanging ideas, scientific reports, students and lecturers were discussed at length.

Finally, I think the experience of seeing at first hand the devastation in Germany, the confusion and anxiety in France, the social ferment in England, to say nothing of the specific problems of the U.S. Army—this experience had an effect upon all of us which cannot but influence our thinking, feeling, talking, planning and working for the critical years immediately ahead.

For the many benefits to myself, personally, and for the incomparable experience that has been afforded me by the assignment, I want to express my deep appreciation and gratitude to the OSRD in general, and to its efficient and helpful representatives—Dr. Lincoln R. Thiesmeyer and Miss Mooney in particular.

Sincerely yours

FROM NORMAN COUSINS,[23] NEW YORK, JULY 27, 1945

Dear Karl:

The *Saturday Review* right now is with child; we expect the new baby to put in its appearance some time next spring.[24] It is a pretty ambitious baby and it may be a lot bigger than its parents while still quite young. Specifically, the plan is for a national weekly addressed to a mass circulation. The project has developed sufficiently to enable us to go into the market for articles.

Something occurred to us this afternoon that we thought we might put up to you. Perhaps the most effective way of dealing with the Bilbos[25] and Rankins[26] is either through ridicule or by way of special examination. We

23 Editor of the *Saturday Review of Literature* from 1940 to 1971 and again from 1973 to 1977.

24 In 1945, at the request of Marshall Field, the *Saturday Review* was engaged in planning for a new general weekly publication to be called *U.S.A.* The project was abandoned in July 1946.

25 Theodore G. Bilbo, a Democrat, served as governor of Mississippi from 1916 to 1920 and from 1928 to 1932. From 1935 to 1947 he was a U.S. Senator. Bilbo was a member of the Ku Klux Klan, a proponent of white supremacy, and an opponent of antilynching legislation. He advocated deportation of blacks to Africa to promote "racial purity" and urged his supporters in Mississippi to use any methods to prevent blacks from voting. He died of cancer in New Orleans in 1947.

26 Congressman John E. Rankin of Mississippi was notable for co-authoring a bill to create the Tennessee Valley Authority, for his leadership in the House in support of rural electrification, and, in 1945, for introducing an amendment of the House Rules establishing the permanent committee on un-American activities. Despite his support for the TVA he was, like Bilbo, deeply reactionary.

wonder whether you will agree that this might well be accomplished through a piece on "A Psychiatrist Looks at Bilbo" (or Rankin), in which you would examine the record of one of these gentlemen for evidences which seem to you to indicate certain clinical conditions?

We realize that the piece is a tough one, especially since it requires a blend of two apparently contradictory ingredients. On the one hand, we must remember that the article would be addressed to a large popular audience, making mandatory, therefore, a simple expository style; on the other hand, it requires, to some extent at least, scientific analysis with some of the trade terms thrown in, which would in effect constitute a psychiatric examination or psychoanalysis in print. Back in 1937, I believe that Joseph Jastrow[27] very effectively and successfully applied the same technique to Hitler and Mussolini, his pieces arousing wide comment.

I repeat that I hope you can do this not only because of the intrinsic interest the article will have, but because it can do a hell of a lot of good. Would 2,500–3,500 words be ample? Our modest fee would be $350, the deadline September 15.

We are collecting Bilbo's speeches and clippings on his career, which we shall send you when we hear that you can do the article.

Sincerely yours,

To Norman Cousins, New York, August 2, 1945

Dear Norman:

I am delighted to learn from your letter of July 27 of your ambitious plans for the *Saturday Review*. At any rate, I am interested. I can see many advantages although I hope nothing happens to weaken or impair the present high qualities of the *Saturday Review*.

The idea of having a psychiatrist look at Bilbo or Rankin pleases me immensely. Of course, every psychiatrist actually does see patients whose symptoms very much resemble the public demonstrations of these two characters. Every psychiatrist sees them every day and I might add that we feel pretty pessimistic about any treatment other than confinement.

It is quite natural for you as a layman to suppose that since we have had this experience all we would have to do is to examine the record of these two gentlemen and then write down the obvious interpretation. What you forget is that a psychiatrist can't do this for publication any more than a neurologist could write up an article on Roosevelt's paralysis or a surgeon could write up a description of the probable illness of Colonel Hobby. It is,

27 Joseph Jastrow was a Polish-born psychologist. From 1888 to 1927 he taught at the University of Wisconsin. He was president of the American Psychological Association in 1900. A prolific author, Jastrow wrote the syndicated column "Keeping Mentally Fit" (1928–32) and was a radio commentator for NBC (1935–38).

you see, strictly unethical. I am aware of the fact that it has been done; I declined an offer of a dollar a word for as many words as I would write about Hitler and then one of my colleagues did the very thing I declined to do.[28]

You are thinking ahead of the great mass of the people to whom it probably never occurs that Bilbo or Rankin might be psychopathic personalities, but you are not thinking quite far enough ahead. I don't think it is a matter of your opinion or my opinion or your intelligent readers' opinions—I don't think it is a matter for summer reading or for that matter for serious reading in a literary journal. I think it is a matter of political science. I think every member of Congress, perhaps even every candidate for membership in Congress, and certainly every member of the State Department and every high ranking officer in the Army and Navy, ought to be subject to some kind of scientific psychiatric scrutiny which will be official. Every soldier in the Army is and most of the officers. If a soldier acted the way Bilbo does don't you suppose he would be sent promptly to the neuropsychiatric department for observation? You see, I take it seriously—this business of scientific personality study—and taking it seriously means doing it thoroughly, carefully and at firsthand. You don't have to get a psychiatrist to see that some of the things that Senator So-and-So does sound crazy, even if you do get a psychiatrist to say that he hasn't proved anything.

What I think you need—and I'm too busy to write it so I'm not asking for a job—is an article on scientific personality study in public service. Let us assume for the moment that there was some official way to describe Senator Bilbo as a psychopathic personality. How would the people of the state of Mississippi who voted for him react to this information? Apparently that is the kind of a man they want to represent them. Hitler was apparently the kind of a man that a considerable number of Germans wanted to represent them. I know a little about the psychology of a few individuals that I have studied over a period of years but I must say that I don't understand the psychology of masses of people. I don't have the slightest idea what makes the average newspaper owner tick. Why, for example, do they consistently back and expect to win the man who consistently loses? In such fields as this certain shrewd politicians are far wiser and have much greater knowledge than do we psychiatrists.

However, we psychiatrists do know enough not to sound off about men whom we haven't examined and thereby I think we avoid some libel suits for ourselves and the kind journal editors who want us to write for them.

Sincerely yours,

---

28 See, for example, Lewis M. Terman, "Hitler's Success Attributed to Personality Factors," *Science News Letter* 37 (June 29, 1940): 410, and E. Bloch, "My Patient, Hitler," *Collier's*, March 15, 1941, p. 11, and March 22, 1941, pp. 69–70.

P.S. I just got back from about a 5,000 mile trip on the Continent. I went over on a special mission for the War Department to study psychiatry in military situations. It will take me a long time to digest or fully understand the many things I saw and experienced. My wife adds her best wishes.

To BRIG. J. R. REES, LONDON, AUGUST 9, 1945

My dear Brigadier Rees:

I haven't any very good excuse for not having written you long before now. I'll give you a brief history of what happened, however. We were stalled for about a week in Paris and we might have been there months if my brother hadn't arranged an SOS telegram through Army channels that brought us home promptly. We had a smooth passage (by air) coming back and were somewhat thrilled to learn that a plane was leaving for America every six minutes. We got put off at the Azores but only for an hour.

We spent a few days in Washington making our official reports verbally and I don't think we did a very good job of it although we had a lot of generals and others from the Medical Department in the audience. We all hastened home then and I got back to such a discouraging pile of correspondence and such a lot of demands for immediate interviews with this staff member and that one, and imperative conferences with this patient and that one—and then there was the necessity for finishing up our written report and the necessity for seeing my family, relatives, etc. and assuring them that I was back safe and sound—and then a few talks to the staff, etc. and so on. Every now and then I try to take a few minutes and drop a line to some of the many friends I made in England, France and Germany, but I haven't made much progress with that. I have had the pictures developed and want to send you a set of them but there again I run into difficulties because the photographers are so busy and so arbitrary, and of course they make mistakes on the number of prints and so do I, and then I get them mixed up and try to sort them to send you some.

Well, just to complicate things I kept my uniform on for several weeks after I got back and worked out at Winter General Hospital, and sometimes I think I have learned more about the problems of Army psychiatry since I have been home than I did while I was in Europe. Of course, actually that's an exaggeration but I do very much enjoy the couple of hours I spend at Winter Hospital each day and they have given me everything I wanted and treated me grand. I am also trying to help Will with his new nomenclature which I think is going to be a great boost to psychiatry. For one thing it's logical and for another thing it's comprehensible and practical. It's based on a slightly new scheme of psychiatric classification which I worked out a year or two ago and which appealed to Will very much. You'll be seeing it I am sure.

Well, let me see. To complicate matters still further, I have quite a peach crop, crabapple crop, plum crop and blackberry crop, but no sugar. We have suddenly gotten as hard up for sugar over here as you are in England so all my plums are lying on the ground except those we eat off the tree. The crabapples are a brilliant color and look very pretty even if not being converted into jelly. We have had a great deal of rain this year and it's been very cool all summer except for the last few days. My place looks like Kew Gardens or something. I wish you could see it now. It's a great deal prettier than when you saw it.

It might interest you to know that I've made a number of talks over here and I always tell the audience that the British made a tremendous hit with me, especially their not complaining and their courtesy and dignity and friendliness. How in the name of goodness the British got the reputation of being cold I can't imagine. You were all so warm and friendly and good-humored and sociable that I keep thinking about it over and over. I imagine that your own cheeriness is typical and also contagious.

I have told Will and Father and Pearl and of course Jean and everyone about the wonderful times we had together and show them the pictures, including the one I made of you and also the sketch I made of the scenery from your front porch—I shall live it over in my memory many times. I wish you would write me and tell me about your new adjustment to civilian life. I felt very badly the day I had to take off my uniform (only a few days ago) and so I know very well how it must feel to one who has done as much for world psychiatry and the British Army and the Allied Forces as you have to give up the Army connections and symbols. However, you'll go on doing big things in civilian life and I hope you'll do some of them with us.

Sincerely,

To Anna Freud, London, October 16, 1945

Dear Anna Freud:

You have probably wondered whatever became of me after that charming visit we had. As you may remember, I was to come out again but your friend[29] took ill and I have often wondered if she made an uneventful recovery. The next day we were ordered to Paris where we remained about a week, expecting to leave any minute or perhaps any month. During this period of uncertainty we met a number of psychiatrists and psychoanalysts in Paris, which was very pleasant. We left on very sudden notice and went

29 Presumably Dorothy Burlingham, who with Anna Freud directed the Hampstead Nursery, providing wartime homes for children whose families had been broken apart by the war. Freud and Burlingham co-authored *War and Children* (1943) and *Infants Without Families* (1944).

by plane to Washington where we gave our reports, and then returned to our homes.

I arrived home to find things very busy. There was a large pile of correspondence waiting for me and a number of patients and staff members had also been waiting for appointments which they considered imperative. In addition, I felt more or less compelled to continue to work with the Army part-time since there is a large military hospital in this city and I had become very much interested in certain problems of military psychiatry.

The sudden termination of the war brought a number of new problems, one of which was a flood of applications from medical officers still in the Army but expecting to be discharged who had decided they wanted to pursue psychiatric training. Many of them also want psychoanalytic training. We have well over 100 of these applications now and more are coming in every day.

To meet this challenging opportunity we decided to formulate something we had long contemplated, namely a formal and systematic school of psychiatry, including, of course, psychoanalytic training for selected students. The enclosed prospectus will give you some idea of the first groping attempts to do this. As you will see, we have already started in a way. Yesterday we had a visitor in the person of a representative of the Surgeon General of the Veterans Administration which is the governmental agency responsible for the postwar care of ex-soldiers, and what seems to be in the air now is the contemplation of a central psychiatric training institution under government auspices, with us as the faculty. This thrills us very much, of course, since it would provide unlimited clinical facilities and a considerable financial support. To have all this done under the aegis of "psychoanalytic psychiatry" thrills us very much also, and I am just thinking how amazed, even if somewhat skeptical, your father might have been.

Of course, it is still on paper as yet, or perhaps I should say not even on paper yet, and in a sense I must ask you to keep it confidential since there is really nothing to announce at present. I am telling you about it because I am still very much in hopes that you will feel tempted to carry out the fantasy I sketched to you of leaving England and coming over to join us. I remember that you felt in talking to me that a three months' visit should precede any final decision to move again, as I remember also that your chief anxiety was the question of whether or not you could be readmitted to England after such a visit. I am wondering if you ever found out about that possibility.

As a matter of fact, the moment I landed on this continent, I went to see friends in the government agencies in regard to the possibility of transportation and a visitor's visa for you. They said it would be difficult but that if we wanted you very much it might be arranged, but of course they couldn't say anything about the question of readmission to England.

If you still feel that you don't want to make the irrevocable plunge I wonder if you could find out about the possibilities of reentry because we are very anxious indeed to have you come for three months or thirty months, or as many months or years as you would like. I have appointed a committee of staff members to work on plans for such a three months' visit and I am sure that they will feel that the sooner you can come the better. I am going to Washington next week and shall take up with the State Department again the question of visas and transportation for you and leave the matter open for confirmation upon hearing affirmatively from you.

There are lots of things I would like to tell you about and many items of news which might interest you. Van Ophuijsen of New York was here yesterday with a patient and gave a little lecture last night and had dinner with me before taking the plane home. . . . My brother has been promoted to be a general, the first psychoanalyst who has ever been a general as well as the first psychiatrist in this country ever to be made a general. Bob Knight is spending most of his time doing didactic analyses. We have far more candidates for training than we can possibly accept. The Southard School is flourishing and we would be very happy if you could see it.

Sincerely yours,